FUNDAMENTALS OF
PHILOSOPHY

FIFTH EDITION

DAVID STEWART

H. GENE BLOCKER

Ohio University

Prentice
Hall

Upper Saddle River, New Jersey 07458

Library of Congress Cataloging-in-Publication Data

Stewart, David,
    Fundamentals of philosophy / David Stewart, H. Gene Blocker.—5th ed.
      p. cm.
    Includes bibliographical references and index.
    ISBN 0-13-030896-X
    1. Philosophy—Introductions.   I. Blocker, H. Gene.
    II. Fundamentals of Philosophy
  BD21.577 2001
  100—dc21   00-044584
                                      CIP

Editorial Director: Charlyce Jones-Owen
Acquisition Editor: Ross Miller
Managing Editor: Jan Stephan
Production Liaison: Fran Russello
Project Manager: Beth Brown, D&G Limited, LLC
Prepress and Manufacturing Buyer: Tricia Kenny
Interior Design: D&G Limited, LLC.
Art Director: Jayne Conte
Cover Designer: Kiwi Design
Director, Image Resource Center: Melinda lee Reo
Manager, Rights & Permissions: Kay Dellosa
Image Specialist: Beth Boyd

This book was set in 10 point New Century Schoolbook by D&G Limited, LLC.
and was printed and bound by RR Donnelley & Sons Company.
The cover was printed by Phoenix Color Corp.

 ©2001 by Prentice-Hall, Inc.
A Division of Pearson Education
Upper Saddle River New Jersey 07458

Printed in the United States of America

10 9 8 7 6 5 4

ISBN 0-13-030896-X

Prentice-Hall International (UK) Limited, *London*
Prentice-Hall of Australia Pty. Limited, *Sydney*
Prentice-Hall Canada, Inc., *Toronto*
Prentice-Hall Hispanoamericana, S.A., *Mexico*
Prentice-Hall of India Private Limited, *New Delhi*
Prentice-Hall of Japan, Inc., *Tokyo*
Pearson Education Asia Pte. Ltd., *Singapore*
Editora Prentice-Hall do Brasil, Ltda., *Rio de Janeiro*

≡ Contents

Preface

From our years of experience in teaching the introductory philosophy course, we have concluded that such a course should do two things: (1) introduce students to the major themes and thinkers in the philosophic tradition and (2) show how the issues they encounter in the great thinkers apply to concerns they encounter in their life experiences. A beginning philosophy course can attempt to do too much and, as a consequence, accomplish too little. However, we think that an introductory philosophy course should contribute to students' general education by helping them develop a conceptual framework and vocabulary for discussing important intellectual and social issues.

Philosophy has something to say when people become upset over a controversial art exhibit or groups complain about art works that critics say degrade a religious or ethnic group. It also has something to say when people are misled by specious arguments and faulty reasoning. It can assist us in understanding that claims to absolute knowledge are not to be taken at face value, and it can guide us through the perplexing issues raised in public policy debates, such as the ongoing tugs of war about the protection of minority groups or life styles. Students probably first begin to think philosophically about matters of ethics and religion, though they may not be fully aware that they are doing philosophy when they encounter such problems in their own thinking. And with the increased awareness of other countries and cultures, students today need to have an understanding of non-Western thought systems.

At the same time, we do not intend this book to be just about philosophy, that is, a second-hand recounting of philosophical positions. We believe that students need to encounter the great thinkers directly. Therefore we offer here the best features of the reader and the expository text. The readings themselves have been selected to represent a wide range of philosophical styles and temperaments—from Kant, Berkeley, Hume, and Descartes to Tolstoy, Mencius, Wittgenstein, and Kenneth Clark. The readings are no mere snippets but are solid chunks of material that form relatively self-contained units, ranging from five to ten pages in length.

The book is divided into forty chapters (arranged under nine topics), and within each part users may select some readings and omit others without loss of pedagogical effectiveness. Since the book contains more material than can be covered in a single academic term, instructors may pick and choose those chapters that best suit their own philosophical dispositions. The book offers a wide array of selections from classic as well as contemporary philosophers so that students can understand philosophy as a living discipline that draws from its past in order to deal with current issues.

The fifth edition has allowed us to make several changes in response to readers' suggestions. The first part dealing with the nature of philosophy has been completely rewritten. Several readings were removed and a new chapter dealing with philosophy's history added, since users felt that students needed an introduction to the history of ideas. New in the section on logic is a selection on critical thinking, and the philosophy of religion section now includes the "Vale of Soul-Making" theodicy by the noted philosopher of religion, John Hick. The more "existential" selection from Tolstoy has been set off in its own separate chapter rather than being included as an introduction to the entire section. The discussion of issues in esthetics now connects modernism with the issues raised by postmodernism (featured in the section on epistemology). Finally, the section on social and political philosophy has been recast by adding one old classic (Mill, *On Liberty*) and two new readings dealing with the relationship between the individual and the state and the rising political reality of minorities within a state who call for independent nation status or demand special treatment just because of their minority status.

It is regrettable that any revision cannot incorporate all the good suggestions made by reviewers, but we hope that enough of them have been made to increase the usefulness of this text. In its production we wish to thank Ross Miller, philosophy editor at Prentice Hall, and assistant editor Katie Janssen, who was a constant source of help and encouragement. We would also like to acknowledge the work of David Bruce and thank him for his proofreading and indexing skills.

D.S.
H.G.B.

What is Philosophy?

PART 1

CHAPTER 1

The Activity of Philosophy

It is difficult to define philosophy with precision, and the attempt to do so forms an interesting and important part of philosophy itself. Even though we should not expect a pat definition, one way to define philosophy is to see what it is that philosophers do.

Sometimes people use the word philosophy to refer in a very general way to a person's overall theory or outlook. For example, you might refer to someone's attitude toward doing business as a "business philosophy" or an individual's general outlook as that person's "philosophy of life." "My philosophy is: honesty is the best policy," a recent advertisement said. Used in this way, the term philosophy is a kind of synonym for outlook or general viewpoint. You will sometimes find philosophers using the term in this general sense, but more is implied by the word than that.

In the minds of others, being philosophical means having a passive attitude, taking life as it comes. For these people, to be philosophical would be to accept things without worrying about them. The ancient Stoics, believing that all things are ultimately rational and orderly, argued for a somewhat similar view, but not all philosophers have adopted a passive attitude that calls for a calm acceptance of the troubles of life.

If you look in the dictionary you will discover that the term philosophy is derived from two Greek words that mean "the love of wisdom." Philosophy, then, has something to do with wisdom, but wisdom is also a term that a lot of people use without knowing exactly what they mean by it. When the ancient Greek thinkers referred to wisdom, they usually meant the knowledge of fundamental principles and laws, an awareness of that which was basic and unchanging, as opposed to those things that are transitory and changing. Ever since then, the term philosophy has taken on something of this meaning and refers to attempts on the part of serious thinkers to get at the basis of things. Not the superficial, trivial details, but the underlying fundamentals. Not how many chemical elements there are, but what matter is in general; not what differentiates Baroque from Romantic music, but what art is in general. Unlike the social scientist who specializes in one small area, such as the initiation rites of a South American tribe, philosophy traditionally looks for principles underlying the whole of art, morality, religion, or the physical universe. Putting these meanings together results in a more satisfactory definition of philosophy—the attempt to provide for oneself an outlook on life based on the discovery of broad, fundamental principles.

Rational Reflection: Thinking Hard

First of all, then, philosophy is different from other subjects in its attempt to discover the most general and fundamental underlying principles. But philosophy is also different in its method, a method that can be described as rational reflection. As one contemporary philosopher put it, philosophy is not much different from simply the act of thinking hard about something. Unlike the sciences, philosophy does not discover new empirical facts, but instead reflects on the facts we are already familiar with, or those given to us by the empirical sciences, to see what they lead to and how they all hang together. You can see the connection with the first point about philosophy—that philosophy tries to discover the most fundamental, underlying principles.

From our knowledge of science and our everyday experience, all of us have a great many ideas and opinions before we begin the study of philosophy, for example, about what the world is like and how we come to know it. We also have some opinions, before our first college course in philosophy, about how we ought to live. But by rationally reflecting on this prereflective understanding of things, in philosophy we try to deepen that understanding to see what it implies, what it all adds up to, in short, to see it all in a larger perspective.

Through rational reflection, philosophy offers a means of coming to an understanding of humankind, the world, and our responsibilities in the world. Some of the earliest philosophers inquired into the nature of reality, or the philosophy of nature. Many of their investigations formed the basis of the natural sciences, but there was always a residue of concern that could not be delved into by the natural sciences. For example, what is reality, ultimately? Is it merely matter in continuous motion? Or is reality ultimately more akin to mind and mental processes? Is nature merely a blind and purposeless scheme, or does it exhibit purpose? These and similar questions form the basis of an inquiry known as *metaphysics*.

> *Philosophy =*
> *philos (love) +*
> *sophia (wisdom)*

Metaphysical questions directly lead into questions concerning knowledge. How do we have knowledge? Is it through the five senses alone? Or must the senses be corrected by reasoning and judgment? Which is more reliable, the senses or reason? These concerns are among those of the theory of knowledge. Closely allied with the theory of knowledge is the study of correct thinking, known as logic. Logic deals with the difference between a valid and an invalid argument, how to spot fallacious reasoning, and how to proceed in reasoning so that the conclusion of an argument is justified by the premises.

Another ongoing concern of philosophy is *ethics*, or the analysis of principles of conduct. What makes an action right or wrong? What is my duty to myself and others? And what principles of action are consistent with my understanding of the nature of human beings? These and other concerns must be looked into before one is in a position to decide about the problems of ethics raised by advances in medicine, so that we are faced with difficult decisions on abortion, euthanasia, and the morality of organ transplants and genetic manipulation. When the questions of ethics are broadened to include an entire society, one is concerned with social and political philosophy and the problems generated by a desire to live in a well-ordered society.

In general, the philosopher is trained to rationally reflect on how the fundamental questions relate to all human activities. Later we will see how these same philosophical methods can be applied to such specific activities as art, history, education, science, and religion.

The Normative Function of Philosophy

So far we have mentioned philosophy's use of the method of rational reflection in its attempt to discover the most general principles underlying everything. Now we add a second characterization. Philosophy differs from other subjects in being normative. By normative we mean that unlike other disciplines philosophy tries to distinguish, in very broad ways, what is from what ought to be. To establish norms, philosophy often appeals to the nature or essence of things. For instance, when a philosopher says that humans are essentially rational, this is not a description of the way people are (since they often act irrationally) but how they ought to be. The philosopher is saying that it is only the rational part of a person that deserves to be called human, because that rational part makes human beings different from animals. And, of course, this normative definition implies normative modes of behavior. That is, some kinds of activities should be encouraged, given this conception of what it means to be human, and other kinds of activities should be discouraged.

The normative function of philosophy also overlaps philosophers' overriding concern with getting to the heart of things, to uncover the general, underlying principles. When we ask in the broadest sense what something is in general we are asking for something like a definition, and definitions are usually normative. If we ask "What is education?" or "What is love?" we are asking for a definition of things as they ideally ought to be, and it is in terms of this ideal concept that we judge the way things actually are. If we define education, for example, as learning to use one's mind in the most creative way, then we can use that concept to criticize "educational" institutions as they actually exist, say our schools, for emphasizing rote memory and repetitive conformity. "Why, this is not education at all," we will say, "but only a parody of it." Similarly, if we define love as a kind of mutual concern and caring between people, then we will criticize those activities that some people call love but do not meet that definition, and we will praise those that do.

Here again, philosophy differs sharply from the natural and social sciences, which deliberately avoid any kind of value judgments. For example, individuals and societies differ widely in what they consider real and unreal. Psychologists and sociologists try to describe the actual belief systems of these individuals and societies as impartially as possible, simply recording different notions of what is real and unreal. The metaphysician, on the other hand, tries to arbitrate these differences and decide what is real and not merely what is believed or said to be real. Similarly in the theory of knowledge. Unlike the psychologist or historian, who describes what people claim to know, the epistemologist (as the philosopher interested in the theory of knowledge is called) tries to find some general basis for distinguishing genuine from bogus knowledge claims. And rather than describe, as a psychologist might, how people do in fact reason, logicians try to find rules for distinguishing correct from incorrect reasoning. And so in ethics: unlike psychologists, who describe moral attitudes and beliefs as they actually exist, the moral philosopher tries to distinguish correct from incorrect moral thinking and behaving.

In general, then, we can characterize the normative function of philosophy as concern for establishing in every major area of philosophy standards or criteria for correct and incorrect ways of thinking and acting: standards for correct decisions about reality, knowledge, morality, beauty, justice, and so on. The search for these normative criteria is no less important a task for philosophy than is its search for general principles. And in accomplishing both tasks, philosophy is guided by reason and logic. The following illustration summarizes the twin functions of philosophy discussed so far.

$$\text{Philosophy} \overline{\qquad} \frac{\text{Rational}}{\text{reflection}} \overline{\qquad} £ \begin{array}{l} \text{General principles} \\ \\ \text{Normative criteria} \end{array}$$

To learn what philosophy is, one must begin looking at the actual work of philosophers as they examine particular issues, and this is what we will do in the following chapters. But in this introductory section we offer some general guidelines to direct your progress through the rest of the book.

≡ The Subject Matter of Philosophy

We have defined philosophy as the use of a rational, reflective method for attempting to get at the most basic underlying principles and to discover normative

The agora, or marketplace, was the setting for the communal life of Athens, including such events as the trial of Socrates. The temple of Hephaestus still overlooks the agora, now a popular archeological site for visitors to Athens. Photo by David Stewart.

criteria. But what is the subject matter of philosophy? In principle, any area of human concern can become the subject of philosophical interest. Unlike, say, accounting, philosophy does not have a narrowly restricted subject matter.

Originally philosophers were interested in everything, and much of what the ancient Greek philosophers concerned themselves with would now be classified as physics, zoology, psychology, anthropology, political science, literary criticism, and mathematics. In addition, the ancient philosophers also were interested in discovering the principles of reasoning, the nature of beauty in art, the principles that regulate human conduct, the standards for distinguishing just from unjust societies, and even the nature of reality itself.

Philosophy, then, can include a number of things. Which of these is the most important depends on whom you happen to ask. If you ask a philosopher who is concerned with the principles that should govern human actions, you might be told that ethics is the heart of philosophy. On the other hand, a philosopher who is fascinated by the nature and function of language might tell you that the most important task of philosophy is linguistic analysis that dispels the ambiguity and confusion that lurk in our ordinary use of words. A political philosopher might insist that the really important task of philosophy is to discover the principles of social justice. We shall come back later to this question of why different philosophers emphasize different aspects of philosophy.

Notice, however, that the state of affairs in philosophy is not so different from what you might find in physics. There are many different areas investigated by physicists. Some are concerned with understanding atomic and subatomic reality. Others direct their attention outward to the exploration of space, and they would insist that astrophysics is the real subject matter of physics. Still another area of physics is physical chemistry, which in turn is quite different from the activity that interests physicists who explore the various theories of the origin of the universe—a concern known as cosmology and an activity that used to occupy a good deal of philosophical attention in the past.

Suppose that you ask a physicist which of these varied concerns is really physics. The answer probably would be that they all are the concern of physics, and that each has its place in the overall activity that we call physics. At different times a particular area of physics might be more popular than the others. There are fads in physics, and the same is true of philosophy.

To put this last point more positively, each generation of thinkers raises its own questions, and these may be in part brought to the surface by other events. An upheaval in political affairs may prompt discussion of basic issues in social and political philosophy. Major triumphs of science will give rise to a serious reexamination of knowledge and reality.

In our own time, for example, advances in medical technology have forced philosophers to deal with a wide range of bioethical issues.

Of the many matters with which philosophers concern themselves, it would be difficult to say that any one is the real task of philosophy, or that any one of the various questions dealt with by philosophers today is the most important. What may be most important to you may not seem to be as important to someone else. What one age considers to be of serious philosophical importance may seem to the next generation to be completely trivial. This, in part, explains why it is so difficult to come up with a single definition of philosophy that all philosophers would accept as completely adequate.

Constructive or Analytical?

As philosophy goes about its task of discovering general principles and normative criteria, always using rational reflection as its method, it seems to be faced with what appear, at first, to be two quite different ways of proceeding. The first we will refer to as the *constructive*, and the second as the *analytical*.

On the whole it does seem that even though philosophy is not primarily a body of doctrine or set of beliefs, most philosophy does attempt to find the answers to the basic and important issues in life. We will refer to this as the constructive task of philosophy. Philosophers in general have believed that philosophy is a systematic, rational way (as opposed to a religiously inspired way) of discovering the ultimate, underlying reality of which the ordinary space-time, physical world is only a manifestation. In its constructive role philosophy directs itself to developing a total world view. For philosophers emphasizing this type of activity, philosophy becomes a kind of superscience. It attempts to answer the most basic, fundamental, important questions of all: What is a person? What is the nature of the world? Why are we here? Some philosophers have even rebelled against the strictly rational and logical way philosophy has traditionally tried to answer these questions and have chosen a more personal and emotional approach. Since we are creatures of emotions and will, any philosophy must include those aspects of the human situation as well as concern for the use of reason.

The view of philosophy as analysis provides a still different approach to the activity of philosophy— one that is not opposed to the constructive role of philosophy but can be seen to serve a supporting function. Take the important question, "What is a human being?" The concept, or idea, of a human being seems to be pretty straightforward, and on one level this question may seem merely silly. Everybody knows what a human being is; so if all that philosophy does is to define a term everyone already knows, then what is the point? It is true that most people can pick out human beings from vegetables and pieces of furniture. But what about a four-month-old fetus in the mother's womb? While the fetus is human in the obvious sense of being of the human genus (as opposed, say, to a bovine or other animal genus), should the fetus be considered a human person? What is at stake here, among other questions, is whether aborting the fetus should be considered an act of murder.

How do we decide such a question? Certainly not by looking at facts, because both the pro-life and pro-choice advocates agree on the facts — that the fetus develops progressively from a fertilized egg to a human infant, that it will die if removed from the mother's womb, that it will probably live if left there. Agreeing on all these facts, we are still left with the question of how to describe an abortion — as an act of murder or simply as removing an unwanted organism from a female body?

We can see how the analysis of one concept quickly leads to the analysis of another one: that of "murder." Although there is a publicly accepted meaning for murder, it is not a precise meaning; the center of the concept may be fixed, but its boundaries are vaguely drawn and hence open to debate. If we take the definition of murder to be "the deliberate act of killing another human person," what do we say about the solider who deliberately kills another soldier in battle? Or the executioner who carries out an execution? The deliberate bombing of civilian noncombatants? The taking of a life in an act of self-defense? Assisting a terminally ill patient to die with self-chosen dignity? As we analyze each of these concepts we are doing philosophy, although at times we may not be clear about the difference between murder and assisted suicide. It is along these fuzzy borders of ordinary concepts that philosophers battle. If, as you followed the preceding discussion, you said to yourself, "of course abortion is murder, but killing in wartime isn't because the two are totally different," then, as a philosopher, you must say how they are different and why the concept "murder" can apply to the former but not the latter.

Philosophy is therefore probably best characterized as a rational examination or critique of the most basic elements of our everyday experience and beliefs. Two consequences follow from this: first, that philosophy cannot teach us anything totally new but can only clarify what we already take for granted, and, second, that philosophy takes nothing for granted. Here we can see how philosophy as analysis and philosophy as constructive are mutually interwoven. Since the world as we are aware of it is at least partly conceptual in nature (a world which includes murder, abortion, violence), the analysis of our concepts of "murder," "abortion," and "violence" entails analysis of our world. And if philosophy seeks in its constructive mode to develop a world view, then the analysis of concepts is essential for that task.

Nothing escapes the light of philosophical criticism, not even the assumptions of philosophers themselves. For this reason there are no absolute starting points in philosophy, and philosophy is continually examining the views of other philosophers and of its own past. This is why any understanding of the nature of philosophy must also include some knowledge of philosophy's history, and that is the topic of the next chapter.

Questions for Discussion

1. In your own words, can you state what philosophy is? What aspects of philosophy do you still find puzzling?

2. Some philosophers have claimed that everybody does philosophy or has a philosophy. Do you think this is true?

3. To clarify in your own mind the normative function of philosophy, give examples of the difference between a descriptive and a normative treatment of a topic such as "honesty" or "fidelity" (or one of your own choosing).

4. What is implied in the definition of philosophy as the "love of wisdom?"

5. Do you think some of the activities of philosophy are more important than others? Explain.

CHAPTER 2

Philosophy's History

Because it is the nature of philosophy to take nothing for granted, philosophers look at philosophy's history as important for understanding both the successes and failures of their predecessors. Although every generation asks its own questions, there is a set of perennial issues that seem to recur: What ought we to do? (ethics); What is reality? (metaphysics); How do we know anything? (epistemology); What is the nature of correct reasoning? (logic); What is art? (esthetics). Some of the answers to these questions given by past philosophers have led to dead ends. Other answers seem only partial and incomplete. Some of the issues even elude the best efforts of past as well as present philosophers to answer fully.

One way to study philosophy is to take a problem and see how it was handled by past philosophers and how it is treated by contemporary ones. This could be called the problems approach to philosophy. Another way to study philosophy is to see how each era defined the important issues and how they responded to them. This is the historical approach. The former is probably the best way for beginning philosophy students to get a grasp of the nature of philosophical reasoning. Accordingly, in the following chapters we will move about rather freely among different problems and examine responses to them from various historical periods and geographical areas. Nonetheless, it is important to have a general overview of how philosophy and its problems developed, beginning in ancient Greece. We should also make clear that the following summary is that of Western philosophy. In a later section of this book we will look at Eastern modes of thought and discuss the philosophically difficult and important question of whether the term "philosophy" should be applied to them or whether that title is better reserved for the Western and European history of certain ideas. For the moment, however, we will bracket this question and look at the initial stirrings of that search which, Aristotle said, begins in wonder.

══ Early Greek Philosophy

Western philosophy appeared in Greece in the sixth century B.C.E. as the first attempt to provide a thoroughly secular and rational explanation of the natural world. People have always tried to explain the world, of course, but they had previously framed their theories in religious, mythological and magical terms, leaning mainly on mystical and magical grounds for support. The first group of philosophers, known as the pre-Socratic Milesians, limited their explanation of the world to natural elements, such as air, water, heat, and condensation, and their mode of justification to analytical reason and logic.

The question which dominated this early period was, what is the basic reality underlying the world, the changeless stuff of which all things are made? This question arises from a pessimistic view of change: Everything is transient, nothing seems permanent. The early philosophers felt there must be some "ageless, deathless" reality underlying the world as we know it—something eternal and unchanging from which everything else is derived. Thales (624–550 B.C.E.) said it was water. Anaximander (611–547 B.C.E.) objected that if everything had to come from one basic stuff, this primary substance would have to be "boundless" or indeterminate in character. Anaximenes (588–524 B.C.E.) responded that everything could be produced from one definite element, which he thought was air, if it could be differentiated into various forms by opposing principles, which he designated as the rarification and condensation of air. Already two important themes of Western philosophy had been struck: the concern with reality as an underlying substratum and the problem of the "one and the many"—how to account for the many different objects in the world of ordinary experience on the basis of one unchanging substance.

The implications of this quest gradually became clear. The basic reality had to be eternal, unchanging, and undifferentiated. This definition of reality has dominated philosophy ever since; and early in its history led to two quite different schools of thought, remnants of which continue up to the present day: the Eleatics Parmenides (c. 495 B.C.E.) and Zeno (c. 490–430 B.C.E.) and the Atomists, Democritus (460–370 B.C.E.) and Leucippus (c. 440 B.C.E.).

The Eleatics (so named after Parmenides' native town, Elea) argued that the one unchanging, eternal reality could not be identified with any of the elements known to ordinary experience, but had to be defined simply as the proper object of logical thought (whatever that turned out to be). That is, the only thing that really answers the criterion for reality is, ironically, what we think. Everyday things like tables and trees are not unchanging and so are not real. What is real is a special kind of object defined in terms of rational thought. When you think logically, you must be thinking about something, and that something is real, though it is not the kind of thing you can see, touch, or locate in space and time.

What was gradually emerging, though it did not become clear until much later, was that area of philosophy known as idealism (nothing exists but what is thought; "to be is to be perceived"), or as rationalism ("whatever is real is rational and whatever is rational is real"). In analyzing the Milesian requirements for the primary substance, Parmenides found that its main element was noncontradiction (that it must not contradict itself). Since noncontradiction is a logical requirement of thought, reality was thus defined as whatever can be consistently thought. If this is not something in the physical world, then there must be some other kind of object specially suited to reason which we think about when we think logically. This is an instance of what might be called the objectification of reason as a principle of reality.

Supporting this early trend toward idealism and rationalism were the Pythagoreans (Pythagoras, 572–497 B.C.E.) who maintained that the basic substance of the world consisted of mathematical entities—numbers, relations, geometrical figures, and so on. This sounds odd, but it is not hard to understand in terms of the objectification of reason. Many of our explanations of things are framed in terms of mathematics. This was especially true of the Pythagoreans, who were the first to develop mathematics as we understand it today as a set of propositions derived logically from primitive axioms in a hypothetical, deductive system. The Pythagoreans also saw that although mathematics dealt with pure abstract entities (numbers, triangles, and so on), it could be used to explain the ordinary world of sense experience. This suggested to them that the underlying reality of the world was mathematical and ideal, a view still popular among scientists and philosophers of science.

The Pythagoreans, for example, discovered that the musical triad (tonic chord) was based on the relation 3:4:6. This applied to all such musical sounds and therefore seemed to be the one underlying principle behind them all. Whether you fill bottles with water or cut bamboo gongs, as long as the ratio is 3 to 4 to 6, the sound produced will be that of the triadic chord. The underlying reality of the chord seems to be the mathematical relation. If the explanation is relational, then the reality must be relational as well. We make a similar assumption today when we speak of the scientist discovering the "laws" of nature, as though there were a rational system of relationships in the world corresponding to the mathematical formula which scientists use in their explanation. Thus, one major development arising out of the Milesian investigation into the one underlying substance of the world was the view that the underlying reality consisted of abstract ideal objects of thought. From the very beginning, the philosopher's concern with the world was rational and conceptual.

The atomists, on the other hand, argued that there were many unchanging, eternal, self-consistent entities of a physical nature which they called "atoms."

There is nothing in reality, they said, but these atoms and empty space, every-thing else is to be explained as different arrangements of atoms. By emphasizing the material elements over their arrangement, the atomists established them-selves as the forerunners of modern materialism. Pythagoras, of course, would argue that the immaterial arrangement of the atoms was more important for ex-plaining why things are as they are, and this was the beginning of a long debate between the Idealists and the Materialists.

The next major philosophical development was that of Plato (427–347 B.C.E.) and his prize student, Aristotle (384–322 B.C.E.), who together established a powerful synthesis of pre-Socratic thought, setting it forth in a clear and com-pelling way which survived almost unchanged for 2000 years. Plato was inspired by the life and doctrines of Socrates (469–399 B.C.E.), one of the most interest-ing figures in western civilization. Socrates never wrote anything, but spent most of his time dialectically annoying the smug, self-satisfied establishment, for which he was tried and sentenced to death. Socrates was interested primarily in moral problems of justice, piety, and so on, and this made a powerful impression on Plato.

Plato combined the Pythagorean and Eleatic conception of reality with the Socratic concern with morality, and explained the multiplicity of the ordinary physical world on the basis of eternal, unchanging, ideal entities. Justice, Plato argued, is an ideal entity, along with the mathematical entities of the Pythagoreans, and these ideal entities are the only genuinely real things in the world. Like the Eleatics and Pythagoreans, Plato noted the discrepancy be-tween our ideas and those things in the world to which those ideas refer. We talk about justice, equality, goodness, and beauty, for example, but it is hard to find anything in the world exactly corresponding to these ideas. No single in-stance of beauty, for example, can be identified with beauty itself because it is only one of many beautiful things and because it is not perfectly beautiful. Therefore, Plato reasoned, when we talk about beauty, we must be talking about something else, some ideal Beauty of which ordinary instances of beauty in the day to day world of sense experience are but dim reflections. Since Plato found such physical objects involved in the same sort of contradictions charged by the Eleatics, Plato made the bold claim that the ideal entities (which he called the Forms) were more real than their ordinary counterparts which we actually en-counter in daily life.

But unlike the Pythagoreans or Eleatics, Plato went on to try to explain the or-dinary world of sense particulars on the basis of the universal Forms. The Eleat-ics held that only the one underlying substratum was real. But what about all the other things in the ordinary physical world? The Eleatics never seriously tried to explain these; they just said that if you apply your logical principle of re-ality (that a thing cannot both be and not be at the same time), you will see that these things are not real. But this is very unsatisfying. If they are not real, then what are they? Plato said we must somehow account for these appearances.

Plato's solution was to blend Eleaticism with Materialism. He concluded that there is a basic material "stuff." It is not completely real, but it is not exactly nothing either. By shaping this stuff, like a potter, into different forms resembling the ideal Forms that make up reality, God creates the ordinary physical world of tables, chairs, trees, animals, and people. These things "participate" or share in reality and more or less resemble it, but they are not identical with it. This is Plato's way of expressing the point made earlier that the world and our experience of it is concept-laden, except that Plato is also objectifying the concepts into the Forms. When we inquire into justice, we are not asking about a particular law, state, or person; we are trying to define the essential characteristic of the real Form, Justice, which all the other things we call "just" more or less resemble. Plato, then, represents a compromise that favors the idealist aspects of pre-Socratic thought.

Aristotle, who is sometimes called the philosopher of common sense, objected to some of Plato's reasoning. He argued that although it is true that reality is conceptual, ideal, one, unchanging, and so on, it is not true that these ideal entities can exist by themselves. The Forms can only exist in particular physical things, and these ordinary objects composed of matter and form are what make up the real world. Still, Aristotle did admit that what is most real about these particular things is their form and that the more form a thing has the more real it is, so his position did not really differ too much from Plato's.

Philosophy in the Middle Ages

One important philosophical accomplishment of the Middle Ages was to wed philosophy to the requirements of the expanding Christian religion. The theological synthesis was achieved by defining God as the most real being (that is, pure Form) in the Platonic-Aristotelian sense and by treating the Greek Forms as ideas in the mind of God. Otherwise, Greek philosophy survived the transition intact, and the debate over the reality of the Forms continued. Realists such as Thomas Aquinas (1225–1274) and Duns Scotus (1270–1308) argued with Aristotle that Forms were real, but only in particular things. Nominalists such as William of Occam (1300–1350) argued with the early Atomists that Forms are only names to which no abstract entity corresponds in reality. The basic realities, Occam argued, are particular things, but in order to talk about specific things, we must introduce general terms and relations into our language. Just because there is a word for something (such as justice), it does not follow that there is a real object corresponding to it (Justice).

With the rise of the New Science toward the end of the Renaissance (late sixteenth and early seventeenth centuries), philosophy took a new turn and the period known as Modern Philosophy began (the seventeenth through the twentieth centuries). If the previous, or Classical era, philosophy is characterized by an overriding concern with the nature of reality (see Chapter 1, "The Activity of Philosophy"), Modern Philosophy was dominated by a concern with knowledge. This was an exciting period in which Europeans felt themselves on the verge of a dramatic new breakthrough in accurate scientific understanding of the world, and they wanted to get off to a good start. The primary goal therefore was to discover the most secure foundation possible for our knowledge of the external world.

Modern Philosophy

René Descartes (1596–1650) was the first major figure of the modern period. Knowledge must be erected on a solid foundation of certainty, he argued; nothing less than complete certainty will do. But although the purpose was to secure our scientific knowledge of the physical world, the logical implications of this initial starting point led ironically toward subjective idealism. It was held that what we are most sure of is our own thoughts, just as it had been held much earlier that what answered the criterion of reality was what can be thought. A person could say, "I may not know how things really stand, but at least I know what I think about them." The gaze outward toward the physical world therefore turned inward toward the self, and Descartes' "I think, therefore I am" became the foundation for all subsequent developments in Modern Philosophy until the early part of this century.

This idealist trend took two forms: the *Continental Rationalists* (including Descartes, Spinoza [1632–1677], and Leibniz [1646–1716]), who stressed the importance of reason in the acquisition of knowledge, and the *British Empiricists* (Hobbes [1588–1679], Locke [1632–1704], Berkeley [1685–1753], and Hume [1711–1776]) who stressed the role of sensation and observation. The rationalists looked primarily to Plato as their source of inspiration, while the empiricists called upon the authority of Aristotle and the atomists. Both groups were in essential agreement that our knowledge of the external world had to be constructed out of subjective certainties, regardless of whether they were derived from our reasoning faculty or our faculty of sensation. The empiricists began, with Hobbes and Locke, on the materialist note that our sensations are caused by the interaction of our bodies with the physical world. But as it gradually became clear to Berkeley and Hume that this was only a supposition of which we could by no means be certain, empiricism moved progressively toward a kind of idealism known as phenomenalism.

Much of the debate between the rationalists and the empiricists centered on the possibility of *a priori* knowledge. Did all knowledge come from sensation, as the empiricists claimed, or did all or some if it come innately from within by pure reason, as the rationalists insisted? The rationalists naturally stressed logical and mathematical knowledge as the basis of knowledge, emphasizing the uncertainties of opinions about the physical world, while the empiricists stressed perceptual knowledge, explaining logical and mathematical certainty nominalistically, as being true simply by definition.

Just as Plato worked out a lasting compromise between competing views of his predecessors, so the eighteenth-century German philosopher Immanuel Kant (1724–1804) came up with an ingenious resolution of rationalism and empiricism that held together for several centuries and is still important today. Borrowing

Plato's distinction of matter and form, Kant held that the materials of our knowledge come from sensation (conceding to the empiricists), while the form of our knowledge comes from reason and the other cognitive faculties (which he interpreted the rationalists to mean). Kant was one of the first to see how concept-laden our everyday experience of the world is. We cannot perceive, much less think, raw sense impressions; we can only assimilate information that has been "programmed" through our own forms of perception and reason. Just as Aristotle had said that neither matter nor form could exist alone, but that things could only exist as a mixture of form in matter, so Kant argued that the objects of our experience can be neither pure sensation (matter) nor pure thought (form), but must always be a combination of the two.

The roots of the old controversy went too deep, however, and during the nineteenth century the old battle lines were gradually redrawn along the English Channel, emerging in a somewhat different form as the split between contemporary Anglo-American "analytic" philosophers and European "phenomenologists" (not to be confused with the phenomenalists).

Twentieth-Century Philosophy

The twentieth century was characterized by a revolution against the past. The dominant mood among philosophers of that century was to denounce all previous philosophy as a colossal mistake and to begin reexamining the nature of philosophy itself and the reconstruction of its foundations. The more positive character of this revolution could be described as a break with the metaphysical dream of discovering the real nature of the world and a new conception of the role of philosophy as the analysis of meaning (though not so new as many of those philosophers thought). For the Analysts, who consisted of Ludwig Wittgenstein (1889–1951), Gilbert Ryle (1900–1976), John L. Austin (1911–1960), and P.F. Strawson (b. 1919) among others, this meant the analysis of words and concepts. For the phenomenologists, such as Edmund Husserl (1859–1938), Jean-Paul Sartre (1905–1980), Maurice Merlearu-Ponty (1908–1961), it was the analysis and meaning of the most general structures of our experience.

In retrospect, the differences between these approaches to philosophy seem less radical, though there has yet to be a reconciliation between the two, yet some contemporary philosophers, such as Thomas Nagel, Richard Rorty, and Paul Ricoeur, seemed comfortable drawing from both traditions. Much of the distinction between these two important philosophical movements resulted from differences in historical background and style rather than in substance. Analytic philosophers prided themselves on their tough-minded rigor. They thrived on logic and avoided discussions of such things as sex, death, and anxiety. The phenomenologists tended to revel in more tender, emotional, relevant issues, which they dealt with in a sometimes literary style. The phenomenologists complained that the analysts were too mechanical, aloof, trivial, and irrelevant. The analysts responded that the phenomenologists were vague, wishy-washy, and too poetical.

What about the future? Perhaps there will yet be reconciliation between philosophy's past and present, British and Continental, Analytic and Phenomenological. What is clear is that as our world shrinks before our eyes, philosophers are beginning to absorb currents of thought outside their own Western tradition from Africa, the Middle East, and especially the Far East. What precise direction this will take depends on the work of philosophers from your own generation.

This book will give you an introduction to philosophy and, we hope, whet your appetite for more. The following chapters offer a more detailed sampling of some of the major issues of lasting philosophical concern, and as we go along, you will doubtlessly raise considerations of your own. It will be up to you to test your positions rationally against the philosophers you are reading. In refining your views, you will at the same time be strengthening your own reflective habits of mind. Remember, in the end, as Socrates tells us, everyone has to be his or her own philosopher. And as we will see in the following selection, for Socrates, philosophy was both a habit of thinking and a way of life.

Questions for Discussion

1. Can you think of reasons why philosophy's history is more important to philosophers than, say, the history of physics is to physicists?

2. Which of the issues raised by the ancient Greek philosophers strikes you as the most "modern?" Why?

3. How does the emphasis apparent in Modern Philosophy reflect the new scientific discoveries of its age?

4. Show how the differences between Analytic and Phenomenological philosophers reflect the distinction discussed in Chapter 1 between philosophy's constructive and analytical roles.

5. Do you think philosophers should ignore their history and start afresh each generation? Why or why not?

CHAPTER 3

Philosophy and the Examined Life

In the foregoing chapter, we referred to both the analytical and the constructive functions of philosophy. In the following chapter, we see the ancient Greek philosopher Socrates describing his own philosophic activity. Although Socrates represents both tasks of philosophy, the following reading shows him giving more attention to philosophy's analytical task. Indeed, Socrates reports that it was actually this function of philosophy that stirred up so much controversy.

Socrates was the first philosopher to use the analytical method of philosophy, and no one since has used it with quite the same persistence as did Socrates in what has come to be called the "Socratic method." Socrates spent most of his life talking philosophy with people on the streets. He would seek out someone in the city of Athens known to be an expert on some subject to learn what he could from this supposed authority. But in the course of Socrates' probing questioning it always turned out that the person did not really know what he was talking about, and under examination his views turned out to be full of contradictions and inconsistencies. This approach did not make Socrates very popular as we shall see.

But Socrates' purpose was really constructive. How is one going to learn the truth? In another Socratic conversation reported by Plato, Socrates relates how as a young man he had high hopes of discovering a fail-safe philosophical method, one which would produce the absolute truth on every subject with complete certainty and conviction. Later, Socrates reports, he became skeptical of this approach. There were simply too many authorities claiming such absolute knowledge, each with different and even contradictory messages! Therefore, Socrates concluded, he must choose a more realistic compromise: consider all existing contenders for truth, subject each to rigorous scrutiny, and tentatively embrace, for the moment at least, whichever turned out to be the strongest.

Let us look again at this function of philosophy. This side of philosophy's task might better be referred to as the development of a nonsense detector. Philosophy is the search for the significant in contrast to the silly. It is concerned with discovering when people are talking nonsense and helping us to keep from wasting our time with meaningless drivel. When we look back at some of the great philosophers of the past, we discover that they spent considerable time pointing out the errors of others. This activity does not especially endear philosophers to their associates, and it also gives rise to the view that philosophy is purely negative. While this function of philosophy might appear to be negative, it does offer a positive service, for if you discover errors that have been made by others, you can perhaps avoid them yourself.

For Socrates philosophy was a total way of life, and something each person must do individually. If you are sick, Socrates once said, you must hire a physician, just as when you are in trouble with the law, you must hire a qualified lawyer, but each person must be his or her own philosopher. This is a point worth stressing. Despite its often seemingly technical nature, philosophy is really the most natural human activity, and there is a sense in which everyone engages in it. That is, we have all decided (whether or not we are consciously aware of it) what our standards of conduct will be, what principles we base our reasoning on, and what importance we attach to our humanness. But not everyone critically examines these views. It is this critical examination that studying philosophy provides. As Socrates, the father of Western philosophy, put it, "The unexamined life is not worth living." As you will see from the following reading, Socrates meant what he said.

The Apology of Socrates

The word *apology* comes from the Greek word for defense, and in the selection that follows, Socrates is literally defending himself in a court of law. The official charges against him were that he taught that people should not believe in the gods and that he was responsible for corrupting the young men of Athens by making them critical of authority.

Socrates was born about 470 B.C.E. and died in 399 B.C.E. Although he is one of the most important figures in the history of Western philosophy, he wrote nothing and established no school. His whole life was spent in questioning his associates and seeking to discover the truth. Why would this apparently harmless activity produce such a reaction, a reaction against Socrates that was so strong that he was on trial for his life? This question has been the subject of much historical conjecture. One theory is that Socrates was too closely identified with the old political regime that had just been deposed. Another theory is that Socrates was simply viewed as a troublemaker and that his accusers did not want to kill him but just wanted to force him to quit stirring everybody up. Probably there is truth in both views. In the reading that follows, it is obvious that Socrates realizes that were he to promise to halt his philosophical pursuits, the charges against him would be dropped. Such a surrender of his principles, however, was impossible for him: "So long as I draw breath and have my faculties, I shall never stop practicing philosophy and exhorting you and elucidating the truth for everyone that I meet."

> **The unexamined life is not worth living.**
>
> **Socrates**

Whatever the real reason for Socrates' trial, the verdict was that Socrates was guilty of crimes against the state, and he was condemned to death. The death scene is reported by Plato in another dialogue, *Phaedo*, which describes the last hours of Socrates with his friends and the administration of hemlock, the poison drunk by Socrates as the method of execution prescribed by law.

Socrates: In Defense of Philosophy

Perhaps some of you may reply: "But, Socrates, what is the trouble with you? What has given rise to these prejudices against you? You must have been doing something out of the ordinary. All these rumors and reports of you would never have arisen if you had not been doing something different from other men. So tell us what it is, that we may not give our verdict arbitrarily." I think that is a fair question, and I will try to explain to you what it is that has raised these prejudices against me and given me this reputation. Listen, then. Some of you, perhaps, will think that I am joking, but I assure you that I will tell you the whole truth. I have gained this reputation, Athenians, simply by reason of a certain wisdom. But by what kind of wisdom? It is by just that wisdom which is perhaps human wisdom. In that, it may be, I am really wise. But the men of whom I was speaking just now must be wise in a wisdom which is greater than human wisdom, or else I cannot describe it, for certainly I know nothing of it myself, and if any man says that I do, he lies and speaks to arouse prejudice against me. Do not interrupt me with shouts, Athenians, even if you think that I am boasting. What I am going to say is not my own statement. I will tell you who says it, and he is worthy of your respect. I will bring the god of Delphi to the witness of my wisdom, if it is wisdom at all, and of its nature. You remember Chaerephon. From youth upwards he was my comrade, and also a partisan of your democracy, sharing your recent exile[1] and returning with you. You remember, too, Chaerephon's character —how impulsive he was in carrying through whatever he took in hand. Once he went to Delphi and ventured to put this question to the oracle—I entreat you

From Plato: *The Apology* in *Euthyphro, Apology and Crito*. Translated by F.J. Church. Library of Liberal Arts. Used by permission of Prentice Hall.

[1]During the totalitarian regime of The Thirty, which remained in power for eight months (404 B.C.E.), five years before the trial—Ed.

Socrates (c. 470–399 B.C.E.): Greek philosopher condemned to death by his fellow Athenians for philosophic activity. Socrates wrote nothing, but we know of his life and work through the writings of his student, Plato. Courtesy of The Library of Congress.

again, my friends, not to interrupt me with your shouts—he asked if there was anyone who was wiser than I. The priestess answered that there was no one. Chaerephon himself is dead, but his brother here will witness to what I say.

Now see why I tell you this. I am going to explain to you how the prejudice against me has arisen. When I heard of the oracle, I began to reflect: What can the god mean by this riddle? I know very well that I am not wise, even in the smallest degree. Then what can he mean by saying that I am the wisest of men? It cannot be that he is speaking falsely, for he is a god and cannot lie. For a long time I was at a loss to understand his meaning. Then, very reluctantly, I turned to investigate it in this manner: I went to a man who was reputed to be wise, thinking that there, if anywhere, I should prove the answer wrong, and meaning to point out to the oracle its mistake, and to say, "You said that I was the wisest of men, but this man is wiser than I am." So I examined the man—I need not tell you his name, he was a politician—but this was the result, Athenians. When I conversed with him, I came to see that, though a great many persons, and most of all he himself, thought that he was wise, yet he was not wise. Then I tried to prove to him that he was not wise, though he fancied that he was. By so doing, I made him indignant, and many of the bystanders. So when I went away, I thought to myself, I am wiser than this man: neither of us knows anything that is really worth knowing, but he thinks that he has knowledge when he has not, while I, having no knowledge, do not think that I have. I seem, at any rate, to be a little wiser than he is on this point: "I do not think that I know what I do not know." Next I went to another man who was reputed to be still wiser than the last, with exactly the same result. And there again I made him, and many other men, indignant.

Then I went on to one man after another, realizing that I was arousing indignation every day, which caused me much pain and anxiety. Still I thought that I must set the god's command above everything. So I had to go to every man who seemed to possess any knowledge, and investigate the meaning of the oracle. Athenians, I must tell you the truth; I swear, this was the result of the investigation which I made at the god's command: I found that the men whose reputation for wisdom stood highest were nearly the most lacking in it, while others who were looked down on as common people were much more intelligent. Now I must describe to you the wanderings which I undertook, like Herculean labors, to prove the oracle irrefutable. After the politicians, I went to the poets, tragic, dithyrambic, and others, thinking that there I should find myself manifestly more ignorant than they. So I took up the poems on which I thought that they had spent most pains, and asked them what they meant, hoping at the same time to learn something from them. I am ashamed to tell you the truth, my friends, but I must say it. Almost any one of the bystanders could have talked about the works of these poets better than the poets themselves. So I soon found that it is not by wisdom that the poets create their works, but by a certain instinctive inspiration, like soothsayers and prophets, who say many fine things, but understand nothing of what they say. The poets seemed to me to be in a similar situation. And at the same time I perceived that, because of their poetry they thought that they were the wisest of men in other matters too, which they were not. So I went away again, thinking that I had the same advantage over the poets that I had over the politicians.

Finally, I went to the artisans, for I knew very well that I possessed no knowledge at all worth speaking of, and I was sure that I should find that they knew many fine things. And in that I was not mistaken. They knew what I did not know, and so far they were wiser than I. But, Athenians, it seemed to me that the skilled artisans had the same failing as the poets. Each of them believed himself to be extremely wise in matters of the greatest importance because he was skillful in his own art, and this presumption of theirs obscured their real wisdom. So I asked myself, on behalf of the oracle, whether I would choose to remain as I was, without either their wisdom or their ignorance, or to possess both, as they did. And I answered to myself and to the oracle that it was better for me to remain as I was.

From this examination, Athenians, has arisen much fierce and bitter indignation, and as a result, a great many prejudices about me. People say that I am "a wise man." For the bystanders always think that I am wise myself in any matter wherein I refute another. But, gentlemen, I believe that the god is really wise, and that by this oracle he meant that human wisdom is worth little or nothing. I do not think that he meant that Socrates was wise. He only made use of my name and took me as an example, as though he would say to men, "He among you is the wisest who, like Socrates, knows that his wisdom is really worth nothing at all." Therefore, I still go about testing and examining every man whom I think wise, whether he be a citizen or a stranger, as the god has commanded me. Whenever I find that he is not wise, I point out to him, on the god's behalf, that he is not wise. I am so busy in this pursuit that I have never had leisure to take any part worth mentioning in public matters or to look after my private affairs. I am in great poverty as the result of my service to the god.

Here at Delphi Socrates was pronounced by the oracle as the wisest man on earth. At the entrance of the sanctuary were the words "know thyself," which embody Socrates' personal quest for truth. Photo by David Stewart.

Besides this, the young men who follow me about, who are the sons of wealthy persons and have the most leisure, take pleasure in hearing men cross-examined. They often imitate me among themselves, then they try their hands at cross-examining other people. And, I imagine, they find plenty of men who think that they know a great deal when in fact they know little or nothing. Then the persons who are cross-examined get angry with me instead of with themselves, and say that Socrates is an abomination and corrupts the young. When they are asked, "Why, what does he do? What does he teach?" they do not know what to say. Not to seem at a loss, they repeat the stock charges against all philosophers, and allege that he investigates things in the air and under the earth, and that he teaches people to disbelieve in the gods, and to make the worse argument appear the stronger. For, I suppose, they would not like to confess the truth, which is that they are shown up as ignorant pretenders to knowledge that they do not possess. So they have been filling your ears with their bitter prejudices for a long time, for they are ambitious, energetic, and numerous, and they speak vigorously and persuasively against me. Relying on this, Meletus, Anytus, and Lycon have attacked me. Meletus is indignant with me on behalf of the poets, Anytus on behalf of the artisans and politicians, and Lycon on behalf of the orators. And so, as I said at the beginning, I shall be surprised if I am able, in the short time allowed me for my defense, to remove from your minds this prejudice which has grown so strong. What I have told you, Athenians, is the truth: I neither conceal nor do I suppress anything, trivial or important. Yet I know that it is just this outspokenness which rouses indignation. But that is only a proof that my words are true, and that the prejudice against me, and the causes of it, are what I have said. And whether you investigate them now or hereafter, you will find that they are so. For this, Athenians, I believe to be the truth. Wherever a man's station is, whether he has chosen it of his own will, or whether he has been placed at it by his commander, there it is his duty to remain and face the danger without thinking of death or of any other things except disgrace.

When the generals whom you chose to command me, Athenians, assigned me to my station during the battles of Potidaea, Amphipolis, and Delium, I remained where they stationed me and ran the risk of death, like other men. It would be very strange conduct on my part if I were to desert my station now from fear of death or of any other thing when the god has commanded me—as I am persuaded that he has done—to spend my life in searching for wisdom, and in examining myself and others. That would indeed be a very strange thing. Then certainly I might with justice be brought to trial for not believing in the gods, for I should be disobeying the oracle, and fearing death and thinking myself wise when I was not wise. For to fear death, my friends, is only to think ourselves wise without really being wise, for it is to think that we know what we do not know. For no one knows whether death may not be the greatest good that can happen to man. But men fear it as if they knew quite well that it was the greatest of evils. And what is this but that shameful ignorance of thinking that we know what we do not know? In this matter, too, my friends, perhaps I am different from the multitude. And if I were to claim to be at all wiser than others, it would be because, not knowing very much about the other world, I do not think I know. But I do know very well that it is evil and disgraceful to do an unjust act, and to disobey my superior, whether man or god. I will never do what I know to be evil, and shrink in fear from what I do not know to be good or evil. Even if you acquit me now, and do not listen to Anytus' argument that, if I am to be acquitted, I ought never to have been brought to trial at all, and that, as it is, you are bound to put me to death because, as he said, if I escape, all your sons will be utterly corrupted by practicing what Socrates teaches. If you were therefore to say to me, "Socrates, this time we will not listen to Anytus. We will let you go, but on the condition that you give up this investigation of yours, and philosophy. If you are found following these pursuits again, you shall die." I say, if you offered to let me go on these terms, I should reply: "Athenians, I hold you in the highest regard and affection, but I will be persuaded by the god rather than you. As long as I have breath and strength I will not give up philosophy and exhorting you and declaring the truth to every one of you whom I meet, saying, as I am accustomed, 'My good friend, you are a citizen of Athens, a city which is very great and very famous for its wisdom and power— are you not ashamed of caring so much for the making of money and for fame and prestige, when you neither think nor care about wisdom and truth and the improvement of your soul?'" If he disputes my words and says that he does care about these things, I shall not at once release him and go away: I shall question him and cross-examine him and test him. If I think that he has not attained excellence, though he says that he has, I shall reproach him for undervaluing the most valuable things, and overvaluing those that are less valuable. This I shall do to everyone whom I meet, young or old, citizen or stranger, but especially to citizens, since they are more closely related to me. This, you must recognize, the god has commanded me to do. And I think that no greater good has ever befallen you in the state than my service to the god. For I spend my whole life in going about and persuading you all to give your first and greatest care to the improvement of your souls, and not till you have done that to think of your bodies or your wealth. And I tell you that wealth does not bring excellence, but that wealth, and every other good thing which men have, whether in public or in private, comes from excellence. If then I corrupt the youth by this teaching, these things must be harmful. But if any man says that I teach anything else, there is nothing in what he says. And therefore, Athenians, I say whether you are persuaded by Anytus or not, whether you acquit me or not, I shall not change my way of life; no, not if I have to die for it many times.

Do not interrupt me, Athenians, with your shouts. Remember the request which I made to you and do not interrupt my words. I think that it will profit you to hear them. I am going to say something more to you, at which you may be inclined to protest, but do not do that. Be sure that if you put me to death, I who am what I have told you that I am, you will do yourselves more harm than me. Meletus and Anytus can do me no harm: that is impossible, for I am sure it is not allowed that a good man be injured by a worse. He may indeed kill me, or drive me into exile, or deprive me of my civil rights. Perhaps, Meletus and others think those things great evil. But I do not think so. I think it is a much greater evil to do what he is doing now and to try to put a man to death unjustly. And now, Athenians, I am not arguing in my own defense at all, as you might expect me to do, but rather in yours in order you may not make a mistake about the gift of the god to you by condemning me. For if you put me to death, you will not easily find another who, if I may use a ludicrous comparison, clings to the state as a sort of gadfly to a horse that is large and well-bred but rather sluggish because of its size, so that it needs to be aroused. It seems to me that the god has attached me like that to the state, for I am constantly alighting upon you at every point to arouse, persuade, and reproach each of you all day long. You will not easily find anything else my friends, to fill my place, and if you are persuaded by me, you will spare my life. You are indignant, as drowsy persons are when they are awakened, and, of course, if you are persuaded by Anytus you could easily kill me with a single blow, and then sleep on undisturbed for the rest of your lives, unless the god in his care for you sends another to arouse you . . .

Questions for Discussion

1. Which parts of the selection from the *Apology* show Socrates' concern with the constructive function of philosophy? The analytical?

2. Socrates claimed that discovering your own ignorance is an important step on the road to knowledge. Do you agree? Why or why not?

3. Can you think of any recent examples of philosophers arousing public hostility? What does this tell you about the current status of philosophy?

4. Do you agree with Socrates when he said, "To be afraid of death is only another form of thinking that one is wise when one is not." What are your reasons?

5. If we accept Socrates' claim that society needs philosophers, what sorts of issues should philosophers be raising today if they are to benefit society?

Suggestions for Further Reading

Blackburn, Simon. *Think: A Compelling Introduction to Philosophy*. Oxford: Oxford University Press, 1999. Discusses the "big" questions of philosophy: knowledge, consciousness, fate, God, truth, goodness, justice.

Honderick, Ted., ed. *The Philosophers: Introducing Great Western Thinkers*. Oxford: Oxford University Press, 1999. Twenty-eight philosophers are covered in articles drawn from the Oxford Companion to Philosophy.

Midgley, Mary. *Utopias, Dolphins and Computers*. New York: Routledge, 1996. Midgley argues for the need for philosophy in the "real world" and applies philosophical reasoning to issues in education, animal rights, feminism, and computers.

Solomon, Robert C. *The Joy of Philosophy*. New York: Oxford University Press, 1999. Solomon discusses the perennial questions of philosophy and shows how philosophy helps us understand who we are.

Thinking About Thinking (Logic)

PART 2

CHAPTER 4

The Life of Reason

Now that we have taken a brief look at what philosophers do, in general, you may be wondering *how* they do it. How do philosophers arrive at their conclusions, and more important, how do they defend or justify those conclusions? Notice that although every discipline must have some means of defending its claims and deciding between conflicting claims, there are different means for different disciplines. An acceptable criterion in one area may not be acceptable in another, and the question can arise, what in general is the best all-around procedure?

In Western culture, an important shift occurred in what was considered acceptable criteria for truth and falsity around the fifth and sixth centuries B.C.E., largely due to the birth of Western philosophy, which began to move away from mythological criteria and toward rationalism. This shift of emphasis has dominated Western culture ever since, not only in the rise of philosophy, but also in science, law, theology, and history. From Socrates on, the dominant mood has been an appeal to reason to settle questions of truth and falsity.

The Appeal to Reason

What do we mean by an "appeal to reason"? First of all, we can say what it is not an appeal to. It is not an appeal to any authority over and above the individual. It is not an appeal to any type of authority, whether it be the authority of the oldest, the most divinely inspired, the most respected, the most powerful person in the community, or the authority of the past. The rational appeal, then, is first of all an appeal to the individual who is considering an issue. If you are wondering whether to accept some doctrine, or how to decide between two competing assertions, you cannot, if the appeal is to reason, turn the matter over to some other more knowledgeable person, that is, to an authority. The appeal is to *your* reason.

At the same time, however, the appeal to reason is not an appeal to whatever you happen to think at any given moment in whatever mood you happen to be. It is also not an appeal to your passions or emotions. It is an appeal to that part of you that can set aside an issue from the heat of the moment and quietly and calmly reflect on a situation before deciding. This gives reason a kind of universality.

The odd thing about the appeal to reason is that although it is an appeal to *your* reason, it is at the same time an appeal to what *any* person would think in a calm and reflective moment. It is an appeal to you *as* a rational person. By abstracting from the particular emotions and self-interests of the individual, the appeal to reason is *universal*, claiming to be correct for everyone who considers the question in this reasonable way. If I ask a group of people how they feel about the current political scene, I would expect widely different answers from the different individuals, but if I ask someone if he or she agrees that $5 + 7 = 12$, I would expect anyone of average intelligence who took the time to reflect on this to agree. Not that everyone actually does agree on principles of reason, but this is what the appeal is to, this is the expectation.

What is a reasonable decision, or a reasonable person? What, in short, is reason? Making an important decision in the heat of the moment is often a big mistake. Why? For one thing, you tend to confuse distinct issues, accepting one thing because you really believe another quite different thing. If a man is accused of brutally murdering a small child in your community, you may at first think that he should be killed immediately, with or without a trial. But later, in a calmer moment and given the time to reflect on the situation, you will probably come to realize that your decision is based on confusing two or more quite distinct issues: whether the death of the child is unfortunate, whether murder is a heinous crime, whether the accused is the murderer, whether accused murderers, including this one, deserve a fair trial, and whether convicted murderers should be sentenced to death. An affirmative answer to one question is not necessarily an affirmative answer to the others. Upon reflection, you will probably decide that although you think murder in general, and more so in the case of a small child, is reprehensible, you also believe that the accused has the right to a fair trial. You also do not *know* whether the accused is guilty or not and are not sure *how* you feel about capital punishment in general.

Another general inadequacy of emotional or snap judgments is that, in making them, people fail to consider all the relevant issues when deciding on a particular question. For members of the jury in the trial of the accused murderer in the example above, a great many issues must be considered, such as the reports of witnesses, the reliability of the witnesses, motives, the law, the past record of the defendant, and so on.

The use of reasoning to make decisions, then, can be characterized as an appeal to considerations that each person must address within his or her own mind, as a reflective person, with concentration on distinguishing the different issues and considering all the relevant points, including the consequences. The most important feature of reasoning, however, is one we have not yet considered: seeing the *connections* and *relations* among all the relevant issues. How do some considerations contradict certain others? How do some of the facts of the case strengthen one conclusion and weaken another? Given a certain set of beliefs or facts, what can be inferred from them? By focusing attention on all the considerations relevant to a particular decision, we become conscious of *why* we are doing something, and this is a crucial part of what it means to be reasonable. A reasonable person is one who asks why, who looks for good reasons for doing or believing something, and who is willing, when asked, to supply reasons why. One thing is true *because* other things are true; some things become reasons why we should believe other things. I do not just think the accused is guilty, for example, but I have reasons *why* I think so, reasons that connect my understanding of all the relevant issues into a single compelling conclusion.

▬ Reason and Philosophy

The study of such connections is the study of *logic*, and logic in conjunction with *reflection* is the primary research tool of philosophy. Science is also based on an appeal to reason, but the scientist, unlike the philosopher, can also appeal to empirical facts. A scientific hypothesis is based on reasoning; if the hypothesis is true, then we will empirically observe a certain result if we carry out a certain experiment based on it. But having offered this argument or piece of reasoning, the scientist must then enter the laboratory, conduct the experiment, and observe the results, and this part of the task involves technical skill and an empirical, factual component not common to philosophy.

The philosopher's reasoning must also be related to the facts of our experience, but in a different way, which we referred to briefly in the first chapter as reflection. The philosopher tries to articulate and sharpen our ordinary beliefs, attitudes, and assumptions about the world, and then tries to see, through the use of reason, what those beliefs presuppose, how they are logically tied together, and what they logically lead to. The philosopher is therefore more concerned with finding a theory that fits the facts and shows their interrelations than with discovering new facts. Since the facts appealed to are all well known, philosophy is not an empirical science, as are physics, botany, geology, or chemistry.

Thus, the philosopher's *primary* tool is reason. Reason is also, as we have indicated, an important part of everyday life, especially in the tradition of Western culture. In the remainder of this chapter, we will look first at the use of reason in everyday life, and then examine the use of reasoning in philosophical investigation.

Since the time of Socrates, we have been encouraged to live our lives according to reason, to be reasonable, or rational. Any passing familiarity with history will reveal that Western civilization has *not*, on the whole, been particularly reasonable, certainly no more than other cultures. Nonetheless, we are urged to adopt the rational life, at least as an ideal. In saying, "The unexamined life is not worth living," Socrates was asserting that a life not in accord with reason is worthless. Why? What exactly is this ideal rational life and what are its advantages?

First of all, let us distinguish the ideal of a rational life from other views with which it is often confused. One position often confused with the ideal of a rational life is the view that since reason is presumably common to all people, reason is therefore the essence of human nature and the most important part of human existence. But this is not the same as the ideal of rational life, which asserts that living by the dictates of reason is the best way to live. It might well be the case that our capacity for human love or sympathy is the most distinctive and ennobling aspect of human nature, and yet it might also be true that a life based on reason is better than one based on emotion.

Another view frequently confused with the rational ideal is the position that the world is inherently rational or that people in particular are basically reasonable. But the rational ideal says nothing about the way things actually are in the world or the way people actually behave. It simply asserts that the best practical guide to belief and action is the principle of reason. Often the appeal to reason is based on the fact that people are *not* fundamentally or usually reasonable, but more frequently are given to irrational outbursts of passion and madness. Certainly, in the light of studies by Darwin, Marx, and Freud, who placed great emphasis on nonrational forces governing human nature, we cannot ignore the importance of nonrational factors in human existence, but it is quite another matter to advocate living one's life and basing decisions upon unconscious and irrational fears.

The Advantages of Reason

Now that we have limited the appeal to reason to the view that the rational course is the best way to decide on important issues, what are the advantages of such a view and why should we adopt it? First of all, the rational ideal helps to resolve and coordinate important nonrational feelings and intuitions. Why not make decisions simply on the basis of our strongest feelings and intuition? Why not do what seems best at the moment? In principle, nothing is intrinsically wrong with this approach. In fact, what we call feeling or intuition is often simply the end product of a rational deliberation of which we are no longer aware.

The decision to terminate a relationship, for example, might seem a sudden spur-of-the-moment thing, but it is in fact the end product of many sober reflections on several different and interrelated considerations over a long period of time—concerning dissimilar interests, conflicting tastes, opposed life goals, and so on. It is not the role of reason to replace this natural decision mechanism. Indeed, for most of our lives, this is the approach we must use. We simply don't have time to consciously deliberate on each and every decision affecting our lives. Think how confusing, chaotic, and generally unworkable it would be if we had to reason out whether to stop at the red light, open the mail now, or start dinner, and so on. It is essential that most of our decisions be made quickly and automatically.

The problem with this method of decision making is simply that it will not work *all* the time. The job of reason is not to replace it, but to complement it, especially when important, long-range decisions have to be made and when our intuitions conflict with one another. Intuition works fine until a conflict arises. You want to go to the concert tonight, but you also want to finish your English assignment on time. Since your feelings are in conflict, it will not help to decide by consulting your feelings. It is their conflict that is causing the problem. What is now required is a more conscious, deliberate, methodical way to calculate all the pros and cons, weighing them carefully and making a decision on that basis. In short, it is a job for reason.

Notice that in resolving conflicts among intuitions and feelings, we are not trying to replace them, but simply to coordinate them—to find a way in which our many wants, desires, and goals can all fit harmoniously together. The more important the decision (involving career, lifestyle, marriage, having children, and so on), the greater the scope of coordination required. This is part of what is meant by the examined life, assigning priorities and working out relationships among goals and objectives.

A second advantage in adopting the rational ideal is that it is a more humane way of dealing with conflicts of opinion among different people. If everyone in the same society holds the same opinions on everything, the search for reasons would probably be unnecessary. In such a world, our beliefs would simply be instincts shared by all and therefore in no need of justification, but this is not the world we actually live in. In the real world, people hold different opinions, and this can lead to conflict and tension. The question we face is how best to *handle* conflicting opinions, and this is a deep and serious dilemma of human social existence. On the one hand, each of us is a distinct and unique individual with different beliefs, attitudes, likes, and dislikes. On the other hand, we are forced to live in a common social world, and this is impossible if conflicts arising out of differences cannot be resolved. Every society must therefore have some way of reconciling differences of opinion on matters that affect more than one person.

Consider some alternatives. One approach is the old standby that "might makes right." Those in positions of authority simply decide what is right and wrong for everyone else (perhaps in terms of what they see as in their own interests as the power elite), and any disputes are settled by conforming to this institutionalized position. This would result in the enforced dogmatism of the ruling elite of the society. In such a society one would have no right to come to one's own conclusions, much less to express them publicly.

A more palatable approach might therefore be to reject *dogmatism* in favor of a kind of total *relativism* of opinion. That is, we could agree to "live and let live," and "to each his own," or "different strokes for different folks." We could adopt the approach that since each person has a right to his or her own view, there should not be any way of arbitrating disagreements. We would avoid conflict by ignoring it. "You go your way; I'll go mine."

The problem with such an approach is that certain conflicts cannot be avoided, such as territorial disputes or, in general, whenever two people want the same thing. What is wrong here is that this approach automatically closes all lines of communication between people. One would think, "I can only communicate with people I happen to agree with; the others are forever outside the realm of communication." Thus, it would be impossible, even as an ideal, for everyone in the society to live in a common, shared world.

Finally, there is the approach that appeals to reason. The appeal to reason fosters communication between people and supports the idea that, despite our differences, we do live in a common world in which it is possible to come to some agreement. When two people argue about their differences, they may seem to be alienating themselves from one another, but in fact they are at least trying to find some common ground on which to reconcile their differences. A genuine dispute presupposes that both parties believe that they live in a common world, that they hold different opinions about a common reality, and that their differences can be resolved by patient appeal to reason. In an argument between two individuals, one person offers reasons for holding a view (rather than dogmatically insisting on it) and the reasons that he or she thinks will lead the other person to look at the matter in a different light. But the other person has an equal right to state his or her reasons and attempt to persuade the first. Their objective is not to *retain* their differences but to find some common ground.

This approach has a twofold advantage: first, by facilitating communication and, second, by supporting the autonomy and dignity of the individual. By avoiding the extremes of dogmatism and of total relativism, the appeal to reason fosters the ideal of an attainable, though difficult-to-reach common world of communication among different individuals without sacrificing the right of the individual to be different. In a reasoned argument, each side has a right to his or her opinion. To be reasonable in this sense means that I must listen to you, try to understand why you think as you do, and try to explain myself to you. This position is based on a realistic assessment of the problem of distinct individuals with different perspectives trying to come to a common view without either falsifying the world or denying the rights of individuals.

As Plato pointed out in *The Republic,* another advantage to grounding your opinions on reason is that these opinions are more stable than those not supported by reason. Opinions unsupported by reasons, Plato says, are like the statues of the ancient sculptor Daedalus, which were said to be so lifelike they would simply walk away in the night. Beliefs that have not been critically examined are more likely to give way to the arguments of others, whereas those that have been thought out in terms of rational arguments can better withstand attacks and not walk away from us in the night.

In addition, the rational ideal of the life of reason is the most likely means of attaining accurate, reliable knowledge about the world. Given our common human condition, with its limitations on our ability to know, as well as our individual biases and prejudices that color all our perceptions, we are more likely to arrive at the truth by letting everyone have his or her say, examining all points of view, and weighing each of these opinions in terms of all the available evidence. That way, we know that we have made our decisions in the light of the best sources of evidence available to us in a frame of mind most conducive to finding the truth, rather than on the basis of prejudice and limited experience. This does not mean that we will always be right, of course, but it does mean that given our limited human understanding and the complexity of the world, we have done the very best we could.

In planning a career, for example, the rational approach would be to weigh carefully all the relevant information about what you really want out of life, what your chances of success are in various fields, what the job prospects in those fields are likely to be in the next five to ten years, and so on. Having made that decision, however, it is always possible that things will turn out differently—that you won't enjoy your chosen career as much as you had thought, that it costs more to attain than you had estimated, or that despite all the economic indicators when you made your decision, no jobs will be available when you graduate and are ready to begin your career. But that is due to the precariousness of even the best knowledge of the future, not to the weakness in your method. It is not a question of selecting a criterion of knowledge that will always and necessarily be right, which is impossible, but in choosing one that has the best overall track record. In the long run, the argument is that if you let every opinion be heard, however crazy it may sound at the time, and if you look at all the evidence as carefully as possible, then you will be more often right than wrong, and you will treat people in a more humane fashion.

Questions for Discussion

1. Why do we need decision procedures in any branch of learning?
2. What advantage does the appeal to reason offer as a decision procedure? Can you think of others? Can you think of any disadvantages?
3. What does it mean to "be reasonable?"
4. Do you think reason is in conflict with feeling?
5. "Love is all you need." Comment.

CHAPTER 5

Argument Forms

Almost any human activity can be improved by working at it. If you do not play tennis as well as you would like to, you can take lessons from a tennis pro and learn how to improve your game. The same is true of golf, swimming, or almost any other sport. There is nothing strange about this state of affairs; we naturally assume that working with someone who has made a study of a particular activity will improve our performance of this activity.

Some activities are so natural, however, that it might strike a novice as unnecessary to seek expert advice to improve one's ability in an activity. Take running, for example. What could be more natural than running? Yet if you want to excel at this activity, make the Olympic team, and perhaps win the gold, you will have to be coached by someone who has studied the fine points of this form of physical activity. And you might be surprised to learn that improving your running demands that you familiarize yourself with matters of physiology, nutrition, and a host of other subjects that you might never associate with running.

Thinking About Thinking

All this is leading up to a consideration of *thinking*. What could be more natural than thinking? We all do it. Thinking does not even seem to require any special training. Or does it? We all know people who do not seem to be able to respond to logical analysis and arguments. "Listen to reason," we say. By an appeal like this, we are asking someone to accept logical arguments offered to support a point of view that we are recommending. And it is probably evident to you that some people are better at problem solving than others and seem to be naturally more logical in their thinking. Since reasoning is so important in philosophy, we need to give some special attention to the methods and techniques for distinguishing correct from incorrect reasoning. Even though reasoning and argumentation are activities we all engage in every day, because of its special importance in philosophy, philosophers have over the years refined the principles of correct reasoning into the discipline known as *logic.* By reflecting on our ordinary, intuitive sense of what are good and bad arguments and trying to state *why* they are good or bad, philosophers have sharpened and made more explicit the principles underlying sound reasoning.

Perhaps it will clarify the goal of logic as a philosophical activity if we can see the difference between the ways psychology and philosophy deal with thinking. Psychology is concerned with describing how the human mind actually functions and the various factors that seem to enter into the process of decision making. We could say then that psychology's interest in thinking is *descriptive.* Philosophy, in contrast, seeks to distinguish between correct and incorrect ways of thinking. Its concern is *prescriptive,* a function of philosophy we discussed in Part I as the search for *normative* criteria. In this unit, we will look at some of the important distinctions made in logic and will examine a few of the major argument forms found in philosophical literature.

Some Basic Terms

The first term you need to familiarize yourself with is the notion of an argument. An argument, in the philosophical sense, has little to do with agreements or disagreements among people. An argument results when a group of statements, called *premises*, is said to lead to another statement referred to as the *conclusion*. The relationship between premises and a conclusion can be described in various ways, but in general we can say that the premises support the truth of the conclusion, ideally (in deductive arguments) *entailing* or *necessitating* the conclusion, but at least (in inductive arguments) showing the conclusion *most likely* to be true.

One aim of philosophical logic is to examine the strengths and weaknesses of arguments by examining the correctness of their logical form. Why this is a valuable approach will become clearer as we examine some of the more usual argument forms. Arguments can take many forms and a detailed study of logic enables one to analyze the major forms of arguments. However, since this chapter is only an introduction to logic, and not even a short course on the topic, we will mention only a few argument forms in order to illustrate the kind of philosophical distinctions that one must master in order to tell the difference between correct and incorrect reasoning.

Consider an example taken from everyday life. What if I argue that whenever it rains, the streets get wet, and that since the streets are in fact wet, then it must have rained. How good is my argument? Does it necessarily follow that it rained last night just because the streets are wet and are always wet after a rain? Not necessarily. It might have snowed during the night and then melted because of the salt on the road. Or the street sweepers may have been out during the night sprinkling down the roads. Or a water main may have broken, and so on. Obviously, the reasons do not support the conclusion. They are not reasons that ought to persuade us to accept the conclusion, but now if we concentrate on *why* this argument is a poor one, we may be able to extract a useful principle or rule. Our argument looks like this:

> *If it rains, then the streets get wet.*
> *The streets got wet.*
> *Therefore, it must have rained.*

Can you see the pattern in this argument? Only two basic statements are used here; let's call them *P* and *Q*, arranged in the following way:

> *If P, then Q*
> *Q*
> *Therefore, P*

The problem with this argument is that the first statement (If *P*, then *Q*) does not claim that *P* is the *only* way to get *Q*; it just says that it is *one* way. That is why the fact that *Q* occurs doesn't necessarily mean that *P* occurs. But now we see why *any* argument of this form is a bad one, and this can now be used as a principle of logic. Whenever we find an argument of this form, we know that it is not a good argument.

Notice what we have done. By reflecting on our common-sense understanding of good reasoning, we have extracted an explicit principle of logic. By continuing this process, philosophers have, since Aristotle in the fourth century B.C.E., developed an elaborate system of logic. Since it is closely related to our ordinary sense of reasoning in everyday life, logic can be used, not only by philosophers, but by all of us to improve our rational thinking ability.

Truth and Validity

One of the first things philosophers discovered about arguments when they began to examine the processes of logical thought is that arguments can go wrong and lead us to errors in two different ways. The first way is when the statements in the argument are false. The second way is when the relationship between the premises and conclusion is such that the conclusion is not entailed by the premises. When the conclusion does not follow from the premises, we say that the argument is *invalid*. When we can show that the premises do lead to the conclusion, we say that the argument is *valid*. As logicians use the term, only *arguments* can be valid or invalid. The *statements* in an argument are either true or false, but are never valid or invalid. To illustrate this distinction, let's look at some more examples.

Suppose you are walking across the college green to your class and someone hands you a pamphlet that contains an argument designed to persuade you that abortion is wrong because it is murder. Consider the following argument:

> *Abortion is the destruction of a human fetus and the destruction of a fetus is the taking of a human life. So if the taking of a human life is murder, then so is abortion.*

You read the argument over, but for some reason you don't want to accept the conclusion that abortion is murder. Yet the reasoning seems to make sense. How can you respond to the argument?

Or suppose you are sitting in your room quietly studying on a Saturday afternoon when a man selling religious literature knocks on the door. You get into a discussion about the existence of God and your guest tries to persuade you that God exists. You ask the person why you should believe that God exists and he responds that God exists because the Bible says so, and the Bible is true because it is the word of God. You agree with his conclusion, yet something seems to be wrong with his reasoning. Something just doesn't seem to follow.

In the first argument mentioned, the author has presented a *valid* argument. Simply stated, this means that he has employed good reasoning. Yet this does not mean that the conclusion is necessarily true. It may be the case that although the author of the argument is using good reasoning, the conclusion is false. How can this be the case? *An argument can be valid, yet contain false propositions, as in the following example:*

> *All spiders have six legs.*
> *All six-legged creatures have wings.*
> *Therefore, all spiders have wings.*

Clearly, all spiders do not have wings. The argument is valid, however, because *if* the premises were true, the conclusion *would* follow. So, we can add to our definition of validity the following condition. *A valid argument is one in which, if the premises are true, the conclusion must be true.*

So, let us reconsider the argument concerning abortion. The argument is valid in that *if* the premises are true, the conclusion is true. *If* it is really true that taking a human life is murder, and that the destruction of a human fetus *is* the taking of a human life, and that abortion *is* the destruction of a human fetus, then the conclusion is inescapable that abortion is murder. If these premises are true, then the conclusion could not possibly be false. The conclusion cannot be false if the premises are true because the conclusion is already implicitly contained in the premises. To accept the premises in a valid argument but deny the conclusion is self-contradictory. So, if you argue that the conclusion *is* false, that abortion is *not* murder, you would not want to say that the author used bad reasoning. You would instead demonstrate that one of the premises is false, probably the premise that asserts that the destruction of a fetus is the taking of a human life. If this premise can be shown to be false, then we are not forced to accept the conclusion.

What about the second argument concerning the existence of God? Here you most likely sense some fault in the reasoning employed. This is an example of an invalid argument. Although the conclusion may in fact be true, the reasoning used to support the argument is faulty. It is an example of what is sometimes called a *circular argument*. It assumes the truth of what it attempts to prove. In fact, all the propositions in the argument *may* be true; God exists, the Bible is true, and so on, yet these statements have not been arranged to form a valid argument.

Let us summarize. If the conclusion of an argument is justified by the premises (that is, if the conclusion follows from the premises), the argument is *valid*. If the premises do not justify the conclusion, the argument is *invalid*. Validity or invalidity is only attributed to arguments, never to the statements in an argument.

Now let us turn to the matter of truth and falsity. The statements in an argument can be either true or false. How to determine whether they are true or false is another matter, one that is not the concern of logic. The reason for this surprising attitude of logicians toward truth and falsity is that logicians are concerned solely with the form of an argument, not with its content. And the reason logicians can ignore the question of the truth or falsity of the statements in an argument is that *an argument can be valid even though one or more of its premises is false*. Conversely, an argument can be *invalid* even though all its statements are true. Nor is it silly to argue about things that are false, since this is the best way to work out the consequences of untried possibilities. What would happen if I jumped from the fifth floor window? I would get hurt. I haven't really jumped and I haven't gotten hurt, and this is because my reasoning was correct that I *would* get hurt if I *were* to jump. Or, to consider another example, if I were a lawyer, I would be wealthy. In fact, I am neither, but this kind of reasoning might persuade me to *become* a lawyer.

Discovering the distinction between truth and validity was a major step forward in the study of human thought. As far as we know, Aristotle was the first Western thinker to make the distinction explicit, and it may well have been his most important contribution to the development of logic. It is surprising, though, how many people two thousand years after Aristotle's time still have trouble with the distinction.

Maybe the following chart will help. Since we can talk about an argument in terms of the truth or falsity of its premises and the validity or invalidity of its inferences, any argument has four possibilities:

Premises	*Argument*	
False	Invalid	
True	Invalid	
False	Valid	
True	Valid	Argument is *sound*.

What we want, of course, are arguments that are valid and whose premises are true. Logicians refer to such arguments as *sound*. Unsound arguments may be either invalid or valid arguments that contain false premises.

▤ Argument Forms

It is not always easy to tell whether an argument is valid or invalid. This is especially the case when we are attempting to analyze arguments written in a natural language such as English. To help in analyzing the structure of an argument, logicians have found a powerful tool in the use of algebraic notation for logical analysis, a method that has gained widespread support among logicians since it was introduced into logic in the early years of the twentieth century. To see why the use of symbolism is such an aid to logical analysis, notice how difficult it would be to add the following numbers: four thousand six hundred and sixty-seven plus two thousand eight hundred and twenty-nine. Try to work the problem without using numerical notation. Then notice how easy the problem becomes when you use numerical symbols:

$$4,667$$
$$+2,829$$

We introduced the notion of an argument form in our discussion of the distinction between truth and validity earlier in this section. Now let us take a closer look at some of the more common argument forms, using to a limited degree the algebraic notation that has become such an important tool in logical analysis. Since this is only an introduction to logical analysis, we will simplify this notation. For illustrative purposes, we will consider the following argument, which has two premises that are claimed to provide support for a conclusion:

Premises   { If I owned a hotel in Hawaii, I would be wealthy.
                 { I own a hotel in Hawaii.
Conclusion   { Therefore, I am wealthy.

Of course, most of the arguments we are puzzled about are not this simple, but it is better to take a simple example first in order to be sure that we understand the distinctions that must be made before going on to more complicated arguments. To see better the logical form of this argument, we can use symbolic notation by letting P represent the statement that refers to hotel ownership in Hawaii, and Q stand for the quality of being wealthy. (For the sake of logical analysis you can suppress all the tenses and moods of the statements.) The arrow $\rightarrow$ indicates that the relationship between P and Q is an "if-then" type of relationship. $P \rightarrow Q$ symbolizes the first statement in the argument. The symbol $\therefore$ means "therefore."

$$P \rightarrow Q$$
$$\underline{\begin{array}{c} P \end{array}}$$
$$\therefore Q$$

But is this a *valid* form of argument? Remember what the term *validity* means. It means that if the premises are true, the conclusion must also be true (and cannot possibly be false). This indicates how we can determine whether this argument form is valid or not. Is it possible in an argument of that form for the premises to be true and the conclusion to be false? If it is really true that whoever owns a Hawaiian hotel is wealthy and that I actually own one, is there anything that could prevent me from being wealthy? No, given these premises, I would have to be wealthy. This is therefore a valid argument form.

Four Standard Argument Forms

The key to assessing the validity of deductive arguments is the fact that their validity depends entirely on their form, not on the truth of the statements in the argument. The form of the argument just given is very simple, yet the same form is found in many different arguments, some of which are much more complicated. Because they recur frequently in arguments, the more common argument forms have been given standardized names (some of which go back to the Middle Ages). The argument form just cited is known as *modus ponens* (the affirming mode). Let's examine it a little more closely.

Modus Ponens

We can discover the *modus ponens* (hereafter referred to as MP) form in many different arguments. Having identified it as a *valid* argument form, we have a quick and easy way of testing other arguments for their validity. The test is simple. If the argument displays that pattern (or has that form), it is valid. Since this is not the *only* valid form, however, the fact that an argument does *not* display the MP form does not prove that it is invalid, since it might display some other valid argument form. So, if we find the following argument in our reading, we see that it has the same form of MP, and so is valid:

> Whenever the leading business indicators show a decline for two successive months, we are in a recession. Since they have declined during the past two months, we can conclude that we are now in a recession.

Argument forms will not always be as easy to spot as this, however, and the reader must often rephrase and restructure the sentences (preserving their original meaning, of course) to see if they fit this pattern. So, for example, an earlier example of MP might have read:

I wouldn't take the car out today, not with those worn, slick tires of yours on those wet streets. Didn't you hear the weather man last night?

Here the first premise (If it rains, the streets will be wet) is merely assumed and left unstated. It is so well known and obviously true that it does not *need* to be stated. Also, the conclusion is stated first, not last, and other material that is not relevant to the argument (about the weather man) is present. Nonetheless, the passage does display the MP form, though in a disguised and submerged fashion. Another argument displaying MP in a disguised way might be the following:

I think he slipped off the road. It had been raining that night.
Look, I told you not to come if it rained. You know how impossible those roads become when it rains.

Sometimes people think they are reasoning by MP when they really are not. MP could be described as *affirming the antecedent* (in $P \rightarrow Q$, P is the antecedent, Q the consequent). If one *affirms the consequent,* however, a faulty form of argument results. Look again at the argument we considered earlier:

If it rains the streets will be wet, and the streets are wet.
So, it must have rained.

What is the argument form here?

$$P \rightarrow Q$$
$$\underline{Q}$$
$$\therefore P$$

This differs from MP in that the second premise is Q, not P, and the conclusion is P, not Q. But now ask yourself whether the conclusion *has got* to be true, assuming that the premises are true. Suppose it is true that whenever it rains, the streets get wet. And assume further that the streets are in fact wet. Does that *prove* that it rained? Of course not. As noted before, the street cleaner may have washed down the streets, or a water main may have burst, and so on, without its having rained at all.

If it is possible for the conclusion to be false when the premises are true, however, then (by definition of validity) the argument is invalid. This indicates an important way of showing an argument to be invalid by constructing an *obviously* invalid *counterexample* of the same form (one in which the premises are obviously true and the conclusion is obviously false). If an argument form is valid, then it will be impossible to find *any* arguments of that same form with true premises and a false conclusion. So, when you find such an argument, you know that that argument form is invalid. In this case, we can easily find such counter instances.

> If I took a trip to Europe, I would be broke. I am broke. Therefore I took a trip to Europe.

From what we have said about argument forms, if *this* argument is invalid, then so is every other one that has this same pattern. Whenever you find an argument of this form (overt or disguised),

$$P \rightarrow Q$$
$$\underline{Q}$$
$$\therefore P$$

you know it is invalid, because it commits the mistake of *affirming the consequent.*

Modus Tollens

Another common valid argument form is *modus tollens* (MT), which is an inference resulting from *denying the consequent.* Let us go back to the same argument terms just mentioned:

> *If it rains, then the streets get wet.*
> *The streets didn't get wet.*
> *Therefore, it hasn't rained.*

Can you see the pattern in this argument? Using *P* and *Q* for the two terms of the argument, and a hyphen before a letter to mean negation, we can see that it has the following form:

$$P \rightarrow Q$$
$$\underline{-Q}$$
$$\therefore -P$$

The contrast between the valid forms of MT and MP and their invalid forms will be apparent in the following diagram.

Valid Form (MP)	*Invalid Form (Affirming the Consequent)*
$P \rightarrow Q$ P $\therefore Q$	$P \rightarrow Q$ Q $\therefore P$
If I owned a hotel, I would be rich. I own a hotel. Therefore, I am rich.	If I owned a hotel, I would be rich. I am rich. Therefore, I own a hotel.

Valid Form (MT)	*Invalid Form (Denying the Antecedent)*
$P \rightarrow Q$ $-Q$ $\therefore -P$	$P \rightarrow Q$ $-P$ $\therefore -Q$
If I owned a hotel, I would be rich. I am not rich. Therefore, I don't own a hotel.	If I owned a hotel, I would be rich. I don't own a hotel. Therefore, I am not rich.

It may not at first be obvious why the invalid forms given above are fallacious, but think of it this way. Suppose that you do not own a hotel but are rich for other reasons (you own a gold mine). All the premises in the invalid forms would be true, yet the conclusion would be false. Remember that in a valid deductive argument *if the premises are true, the conclusion must be true also.* Since the premises in the interpretation suggested would be true but the conclusion false, the argument is shown to be invalid.

A useful way of spotting invalid arguments, which we used before in our example of taking a trip to Europe, is to think up a counterexample *having the same form* but whose premises are true and whose conclusion is false. An example of an argument that is invalid because it denies the antecedent is the following:

If this is a psychology textbook, it will be used in college classrooms.
This is not a psychology textbook.
So, it won't be used in college classrooms.

Even though this is a *philosophy* textbook, it will nevertheless be used in college classrooms.

≡ Hypothetical Syllogism

Another often-used argument form consists of a string of if-then statements. Look at the following argument, for example.

If I get an A on the midterm, I will ace the course. Furthermore, if I ace the course, I will graduate with a 4.0 grade point average. So, it seems that if I get an A on the midterm, I will graduate with a 4.0.

Does the argument seem valid? It can be symbolized as follows:

$$P \rightarrow Q$$
$$Q \rightarrow R$$
$$\therefore P \rightarrow R$$

This valid argument form is called the *hypothetical syllogism* (HS). It is an argument form commonly used in tracing a causal chain of consequences (like the domino theory). A *syllogism* is a deductive argument with two premises and a conclusion. The example above contains hypothetical (sometimes called *conditional*) statements and is therefore referred to as a hypothetical syllogism.

Disjunctive Syllogism

Another common argument form involves the use of statements involving an either/or choice, symbolized by v as in P v Q, which means "either P or Q, or both." (The sense of "or" here is inclusive, meaning either or both.) Consider the following argument:

Either Macbeth or his wife is mad. Since Lady Macbeth obviously is not mad, Macbeth must be mad.

We can symbolize the argument form as follows:

$$P \text{ v } Q$$
$$-Q$$
$$\therefore P$$

Statements of the either-or kind are called *disjunctive statements,* and this argument form is called the *disjunctive syllogism* (DS). Denying either term of a disjunction (that is, denying either P or Q) allows one to affirm the other disjunct, but an invalid form of this argument exists as well.

Either Macbeth or his wife is mad. Lady Macbeth is obviously mad, so Macbeth is not mad.

$$P \text{ v } Q$$
$$Q$$
$$\therefore -P$$

▬▬ Summary of Valid Argument Forms

We have examined four valid argument forms. These are not the only valid argument forms but are ones used a great deal in philosophical arguments. Using symbolic notation, we can state them as follows:

$$1.\ \text{MP:} \quad \begin{array}{l} P \rightarrow Q \\ \underline{P} \\ \therefore Q \end{array} \qquad 2.\ \text{MT:} \quad \begin{array}{l} P \rightarrow Q \\ \underline{-Q} \\ \therefore -P \end{array}$$

$$3.\ \text{HS:} \quad \begin{array}{l} P \rightarrow Q \\ \underline{Q \rightarrow R} \\ \therefore P \rightarrow R \end{array} \qquad 4.\ \text{DS:} \quad \begin{array}{l} P \text{ v } Q \\ \underline{-P} \\ \therefore Q \end{array} \quad \text{or} \quad \begin{array}{l} P \text{ v } Q \\ \underline{-Q} \\ \therefore P \end{array}$$

What one often finds in philosophical and other kinds of argumentation is a combination of several of these basic valid argument forms. Consider the following argument, for example:

Every society is governed by its own set of norms of behavior (N). But if so (that is, if N), then behavior in accord with those norms will be consistently rewarded while deviant behavior will be persistently punished (B). It follows from this (that is, from B) that a sharp class division will be created in every society composed of those preferred individuals more willing and able to follow the norms and those rejected and despised individuals who are unwilling or incapable of adhering to the norms of that society (C). Therefore, class divisions are a necessary and unavoidable part of every society.

The structure of the argument is immediately apparent if we symbolize it in the manner introduced in the preceding section:

$$\begin{array}{l} 1.\ N \\ 2.\ N \rightarrow B \\ \underline{3.\ B \rightarrow C} \\ \therefore C \end{array}$$

Here we find several argument forms combined into a single complex argument. Steps 2 and 3 lead to the conclusion N → C by HS, and this conclusion, along with step 1, leads to C, the conclusion of the argument, by MP. So we really have two arguments in one:

$$\begin{array}{ll} N \rightarrow B \\ \underline{B \rightarrow C} & \text{HS} \\ \therefore N \rightarrow C \end{array}$$

and

$$N \rightarrow C$$
$$\underline{N} \qquad \text{MP}$$
$$\therefore C$$

Alternatively, we could analyze the argument as a combination of several MPs, with steps 1 and 2 leading to B, and B, along with step 3, leading to C. According to this restructuring of the argument the two component arguments are

$$N \rightarrow B$$
$$\underline{N} \qquad \text{MP}$$
$$\therefore B$$

and

$$B \rightarrow C$$
$$\underline{B} \qquad \text{MP}$$
$$\therefore C$$

Now, imagine a counterargument to the one above:

Yes, if every society is governed by its own set of norms, then of course behavior will be rewarded and punished accordingly. And if that is true, then it will indeed follow that two distinct classes will emerge. But if we look at the facts we see that this (C) does not occur. Therefore, it is not the case that every society is governed by its own set of norms.

Here our argument is composed either of an HS and an MT in one interpretation or in another interpretation of two MTs. The counterargument, which can be symbolized as follows:

$$N \rightarrow B$$
$$B \rightarrow C$$
$$\underline{-C}$$
$$\therefore -N$$

can be symbolized as either

$$N \rightarrow B$$
$$\underline{B \rightarrow C} \quad \text{HS}$$
$$\therefore N \rightarrow C$$

and

$$N \to C$$
$$\underline{-C} \qquad \text{MT}$$
$$\therefore -N$$

or

$$B \to C$$
$$\underline{-C} \qquad \text{MT}$$
$$\therefore -B$$

and

$$N \to B$$
$$\underline{-B} \qquad \text{MT}$$
$$\therefore -N$$

Other combinations include mixtures of MT, HS, and MP with DS. Almost any grouping of these basic argument forms can be found in both philosophical literature and other writings. You might enjoy trying your hand at analyzing one of these other possibilities.

$$P \to Q$$
$$Q \to R$$
$$P \text{ v } S$$
$$\underline{-S}$$
$$\therefore R$$

Questions for Discussion

1. What is an argument?
2. What is the difference between something being true, valid, and sound?
3. Determine the validity or invalidity of the following examples by identifying the underlying basic argument form.*

   (a) "Since tests proved that it took at least 2.3 seconds to operate the bolt on Oswald's rifle, Oswald obviously could not have fired three times—hitting Kennedy twice and Connally once—in 5.6 seconds or less." *(Time Magazine)*

---

*Many of the examples used in this chapter are taken from Irving M. Copi, *Introduction to Logic*

(b) "Barry Goldwater to the contrary notwithstanding, extremism in defense of liberty, or virtue, or whatever is *always* a vice because extremism is but another name for fanaticism which is a vice by definition." (Irving Kristol, "The Environmental Crusade" in *The Wall Street Journal*)

(c) "I have already said that he must have gone to King's Pyland or to Capleton. He is not at King's Pyland; therefore, he is at Capleton." (A. Conan Doyle, *Silver Blaze*)

(d) "If then, it is agreed that things are either the result of coincidence or for an end, and these cannot be the result of coincidence or spontaneity, it follows that they must be for an end." (Aristotle, *Physics*)

(e) "Either wealth is an evil or wealth is a good, but wealth is not an evil; therefore, wealth is a good." (Sextus Empiricus, *Against the Logicians*)

(f) "Since then to fight against neighbors is an evil, and to fight against the Thebans is to fight against neighbors, it is clear that to fight against the Thebans is an evil." (Aristotle, *Prior Analytics*)

(g) "Also, what is simple cannot be separated from itself. The soul is simple; therefore, it cannot be separated from itself." (Duns Scotus, *Oxford Commentary on the Sentences of Peter Lombard*)

CHAPTER 6

Inductive Arguments and Scientific Reasoning

Arguments vary greatly in their relative strengths. Some arguments are so strong that the conclusion could not possibly be false if the premises themselves are all true. These are known as *deductive* arguments, and they *prove* the conclusion conclusively. A valid deductive argument is one in which, if the premises are true, the conclusion *must* be true.

Deductive arguments, however, have a major drawback. You probably have already spotted it: You cannot get any more out of the conclusion than is present in the premises, and when we want to enlarge our knowledge of the world, especially when we engage in empirical investigation, as natural scientists do, deductive arguments are not sufficient because we want to go beyond the premises we begin with. In the vast majority of arguments, one finds in the natural sciences and in such social sciences as psychology, geography, history, linguistics, and anthropology that the reasons lend weight to the conclusion without demonstrating conclusively the truth of these conclusions. These arguments are called *inductive* arguments, a type of reasoning that has been a source of great perplexity to philosophers. An inductive argument is one in which the premises, if true, make the conclusion *probable,* or *likely* to be true, and therefore make it reasonable to accept the conclusion.

Inductive arguments are, however, neither valid nor invalid, since they do not prove or fail to prove their conclusion absolutely. In assessing the merits of an argument, we must be sure first of all what kind of argument it is, and not, like the man who entered his cat in a dog show, judge inductive arguments by deductive standards. A good inductive argument is one whose premises, if true, establish the conclusion as being more likely to be true than its competitors, and, for the moment at least, the most reasonable one to accept.

Inductive arguments vary among themselves according to *how* strong the reasons offered are, that is, according to how probable the conclusion has been shown to be. In a murder trial, for example, the mere fact that the suspect owns a gun of the same caliber as that which killed the victim adds very little weight to the conclusion that the suspect is the murderer. The prosecutor's case would be greatly strengthened if it could be shown that the bullet that killed the victim was fired from the suspect's own gun. This too would hardly be convincing without additional evidence, such as that the suspect had a motive for killing the deceased, had threatened the victim, was seen by eyewitnesses in the vicinity of the murder immediately before and after the fatal shots were fired, and so forth. In spite of the accumulation of evidence, the argument against the suspect still is not conclusive, since it is possible for all this to be true, even though the victim was shot by someone who was trying to frame the suspect.

To summarize, it is the nature of induction that the conclusion of an inductive argument is never *absolutely* proved; we accept it with some degree of probability. We cannot speak of inductive arguments as being either valid or invalid, only better or worse. We also do not have the precise tests for determining the soundness of an inductive argument that we have for deductive arguments. The following chart gives a summary of some of the differences between the two types of reasoning.

Inductive and Deductive Arguments

Deductive	*Inductive*
Every mammal has a heart. All horses are mammals. ∴ Every horse has a heart.	Every horse that has ever been observed has had a heart. ∴ Every horse has a heart.
1. If all the premises are true in a valid argument the conclusion must be true.	1. If all the premises are true in a good inductive argument, the conclusion is probably true.
2. All of the information or factual content in the conclusion was already contained, at least implicitly, in the premises.	2. The conclusion contains information not present, even implicitly, in the premises.
3. Deductive arguments are either valid or invalid.	3. Inductive arguments are either better or worse.
4. Premises, taken together with negation of the conclusion, imply a contradiction.	4. Premises taken together with the negation of the conclusion do not imply a contradiction.

Induction and Scientific Reasoning

At some point in school, we may have been told that scientific theories are generated by a process of *inductive* generalizations from particular instances. "This swan is white, that one is white, and so on; therefore, all swans are white." Without some specific problem to be solved or question to be answered, however, inductive generalizations are aimless. Many observable similarities among objects in the world could stimulate generalizations, but most of them are not of great importance. Stones, for example, generally lie on the ground, while peaches are found higher up in trees, with insects somewhere in between, but so what? Only some special concern would make such generalizations worth noting. Theorizing must be directed, and it is the question or problem that provides this direction.

Inductive generalization alone, assuming we use it, would be hopelessly weak as a form of reasoning. Suppose I notice that all the animals on my farm are white (a white dog, a white horse, several white sheep, and so on). Would I be justified in concluding that all animals are white? Of course not. Even the generalization that all swans are white has been disproved by the discovery of a group of black swans in Australia. The weakness of this form of reasoning is that it always argues from the fact that some *A* is *B* to the conclusion that all *A* is *B*, which is obviously invalid (that is, it is always possible for the premises to be true and the conclusion to be false). The inductive method is useful only when it is supplemented by a great deal more implied information. If we already know, for example, that the color of birds' eggs is specific to a particular species of bird, then from the fact that some mallard eggs are green, we can infer that all mallard eggs are green. Because we already accept the theory about birds' eggs in general, we do not need more green mallard eggs to support our argument.

The appeal to empirical facts is important in the formulation of scientific theories, of course. The question is, *how* is it important? Empirical facts are not simply collected like birds' eggs; they are used to test hypotheses that have been formulated to solve a particular question, and this process involves a certain amount of deductive reasoning. Suppose we notice that two widely separated groups of people, *A* and *C*, speak a similar language. This is puzzling; we would expect that the more remote the groups are in space and time, the greater the language differences between them. How can we explain this problematic phenomenon? We begin with a problem, some fact that needs explaining. We must then formulate one or more possible solutions or hypotheses. Since there is always more than one possible explanation for anything, this requires a certain amount of imagination. We certainly cannot hope to answer our question by just staring at all the facts. Investigations, whether scientific or not, require a creative effort. Perhaps *A* and *C* were originally one people driven apart in some remote period of history by an invasion of an alien group, *B*, which now separates them. In formulating this hypothesis, we treat our problematic fact as the *conclusion* of a deductive argument for which we construct a *hypothetical premise.* We are asking what is essentially a hypothetical question: "What must have happened to account for the facts as we know them? What supposition can we come up with that would logically imply that *A* and *C* speak a similar language?"

Sometimes the scientist constructs higher order hypotheses to account, not for specific events, as in our present example, but for other *hypotheses.* Here the scientist's approach resembles even more closely the philosophical task of the dialectic outlined by Plato in *The Republic*. The value of these higher order hypotheses and the test of their credibility lie in their ability to account for (that is, to logically imply) other hypotheses, bringing many separate hypotheses under one large umbrella. Part of Newton's success was his ability to infer from his general laws almost all the important hypotheses of his predecessors, Kepler and Galileo. The acceptance of Einstein's general theory of relativity was due in large part to Einstein's success in embracing in his theory not only the work of Newton, which it then replaced as a higher order theory, but also the widely divergent theories of his contemporaries concerning electromagnetism, radiation, and subatomic particles.

Usually, however, the hypothesis is formulated to account for (or imply) some more specific event that needs to be explained, such as a supposition, that, if true, would explain the fact, in our example, that A and C speak similar languages. Our hypothetical reasoning, then, is

If A and C were driven apart by B,
Then A and C would speak a similar language today (which they do).

But we do not know that B drove them apart. This is merely assumed as a possible solution. How can we determine if this is indeed the correct answer? What right have we to assume that this provides a better answer than some other possibility? It is at this point that empirical testing becomes important. We must now try to infer from our hypothesis some new, empirically observable phenomenon, which we can then proceed to test. We stake the truth of our hypothesis, in other words, on a prediction that can be empirically decided one way or the other. In the earlier stages of our reasoning, in formulating our hypothesis, we argued dialectically "upward" from conclusion to premise (from the fact that A and C are apart due to the hypothetical cause, B). To test our hypothesis, we reason "downward" from premise to conclusion, that is, from our hypothesis to some new empirically observable event. We reason, for example, that if A and C had been separated by the warlike activities of B (that is, if our hypothesis is true), then A and C would still be telling similar stories about the cruel B people, and B would still be telling a different story about the brave exploits of their ancestors scattering their enemies when B first came to the land. Having staked our claim to observable facts, we can proceed to test our hypothesis. We record the stories of A, B, and C, and if they are not as predicted, we have falsified our hypothesis and have to start all over again. But if things turn out as we predicted, we have confirmed and supported our hypothesis though we have not yet proved it. Our test procedure is based on the reasoning that

If P, then Q and
Q.
Therefore, P.

Setting up our argument in this form, we have:

If A and C were originally one people, then they will have similar mythologies.
They do have similar mythologies.
Therefore, they were originally one people.

However, upon close scrutiny, we find that this is not a valid argument. It is in fact a form of the fallacy discussed earlier of *affirming the consequent,* a bogus form of *modus ponens* (MP). Ironically, we can support and strengthen scientific hypotheses, but we can never conclusively *prove* them to be true. Thus, we find it is easier to falsify a theory than to prove it, since a valid argument can, however, be formulated to prove the falsity of a theory.

If P, then Q and
Not Q.
Therefore, not P.

This is the kind of valid argument form we identified earlier as *modus tollens* (MT).

Informal Reasoning

There is nothing mysterious about this form of reasoning. It is precisely what we do every day in solving problems that crop up in the normal course of events. Suppose that toward the end of the semester you decide to pay a visit to a college friend and find that he is not in. Where could he be? You hypothesize: Perhaps his exams are over and he has gone home for the semester break. But how can you be sure? Well, if he has gone home his car will be gone, which you can check. If the car is not in the garage, you can be reasonably sure he has gone away for the week. If you find the car in the garage, however, you must begin thinking of an alternative hypothesis. Maybe he is at Mary's, which you can test by going there to see for yourself.

Your form of reasoning is precisely that of the scientist. You began with a puzzling fact (John is not in). You constructed an hypothesis (he has gone home for the break), which if true would account for the unexplained fact. From this hypothesis you inferred a new testable consequence (that his garage would be empty), which you went on to check. From all this you concluded that he has probably gone home for the break.

Other Inductive Arguments

Correctly predicting something previously unknown is very persuasive, though it is not a complete proof. Instead of looking at induction as "going from the particular to the general," it is probably better to think of induction as all those forms of argument whose premises support but do not necessarily prove the conclusions. You might think that since inductive arguments are not valid, they are mistaken or *fallacious*. In many instances, however, they lend support or weight to a conclusion and are a legitimate source of evidence. The only mistake would be in pretending that inductive arguments are deductive.

Does it follow, for example, that because most drivers under 25 are insurance risks, that *you* are an insurance risk simply because you are under 25? The conclusion does not logically or necessarily follow from the premises, but the insurance company is correct in supposing that their statistical information about drivers lends some weight to the claim that, other things being equal, you are probably not as safe a driver as your mother. If you dispute this claim, you can only do so by another argument of the same form. You may say, "But look, I have never had an accident, have no police record, and do not take drugs or alcohol in excess." This might carry some weight. You are assuming that since most people who have had no accidents, who do not have a police record, and so on are less accident-prone, that you are a safe driver. But this no more follows from the premises than the original argument by your would-be insurance company. (Don't worry, your argument is better since it includes a more complete profile of yourself.)

Another kind of inductive argument frequently used by philosophers is the *argument from analogy*. This argument, as the name implies, is based on an analogy drawn between the relation of A and B to that of C and X, where A, B, and C are known quantities and X is unknown. This type of reasoning rests on the claim that if two things resemble each other in one respect, they are likely to resemble each other in some other respect, which the argument seeks to establish. One argument for the existence of God, for example, goes like this. The world is as well organized as a clock; since a clock could only have been made by a skilled craftsman, the world must have been created by a Divine Craftsman. The argument exploits the analogy that the world is to the Divine Craftsman what the clock is to the clock maker. We are using our knowledge of three of the terms (clocks, clock makers, and the natural world) to infer something about the fourth (God), which is in question. The argument rests on the similarity of the "products" (the clock and the world) and is only as strong as the degree of similarity between the clock and the world. Is the world like a clock? How similar are they? Not very, according to some philosophers. In *Dialogues Concerning Natural Religion,* the eighteenth-century Scottish philosopher David Hume argued that the world was as much like a plant (which is not "manufactured") as like a clock, from which he concluded that the grounds for supposing that the world was created by an intelligent agent were no greater than the grounds for supposing it just grew like a weed.

Inductive generalization, we said earlier, is only useful when it is supplemented by a great deal more implied background information. If we already know that the color of birds' eggs is the same for all members of a species, then we can infer from the fact that these 10 mallard eggs are pale green that all mallard eggs are pale green without looking at them all. Still, even with all this additional information the argument is far from conclusive. How do we know that there is a distinct kind of egg for each species of bird? This is itself based on the empirical generalization that the members of a species share many properties in common. Of course, members of a species don't share all properties in common (some dogs are black, and others are white, yet they all belong to the same species), so how do we know which properties are shared and which may not be shared? All our argument about mallard eggs shows is that it is likely that other mallard eggs will also be pale green.

The form of the argument in our example is *hypothetical*. *If* it is true that animals belong to a species and if it is true that members of a species share common properties, and *if* it is true that one of these common properties is the color of their eggs (when they have eggs), and *if* it is true that some mallard eggs are pale green, *then* it is probably true that all mallard eggs will be pale green. But *is* all this true? For the moment, it seems to be empirically supported, but new information some time in the future may overturn these empirical observations.

This type of reasoning is also *analogical*. We are reasoning that because mallards share many other common features, they will therefore share *this* common feature. That is, because all mallard ducklings look alike, and all adult females look alike and all males look alike, and all have the same feeding and migratory habits, they will therefore all have the same colored eggs.

Behind this argument lie the more general analogical assumptions mentioned earlier, that because the animals within a species share certain common features of coloration, mating habits, and color of eggs, the members of *this* species (mallard) will also all have the same colored eggs.

Much of our everyday reasoning about things is analogical in this sense.

I infer that a new movie featuring my favorite star will be good because other movies featuring this person were good. I believe that my new automobile will be reliable because this brand of automobile has proved reliable in the past. In other words I am arguing that because this new film is like other films in *some* respects (starring Redford, for example) that it will be like the others in this *new* respect (in being good). The deeper assumption underlying this argument is of the same form, except more general. Because actors are generally consistent in their capacity to produce good films (and that auto manufacturers are generally consistent in the way they make cars), new films by the same actor can be expected to share many properties with old ones (and that new cars by this company will share many properties of the old models). Without this more general background information, analogical reasoning can obviously go astray.

Inductive generalizations are not then the major function of scientific reasoning, and even where they do occur, they are not based on the simplistic rule that because some things have a certain property, all of them do. In assessing this type of reasoning, we must take into account how broad the sample is and in how many respects the items being compared resemble one another. If we have seen only one film featuring a favorite actor, we have little basis on which to make a prediction about the actor's new film, and our prediction will be strengthened if the new film also shares with the other films the same costars, director, and so on. The other important criterion is the *relevance* of the factors being compared, and this can only be assessed in terms of the general background information presupposed in all such reasoning. Is it really true that, generally speaking, film stars and auto manufacturers are consistent? If not, then it is irrelevant to argue that this new automobile will be reliable because the older models were.

Causal Arguments

A great deal of inductive, scientific reasoning concerns causality. Often we want to know what causes what. Here is a disease: What causes it? Obviously, if we knew the cause, we could more easily work on a cure by blocking or stopping the cause. Before 1920, many people living in the tropics died of malaria. What caused it? Since people from North America and Europe did not get malaria until they began living in the tropics, and since they almost all got malaria once they moved to the tropics, the cause seemed to have something to do with living in a hot, moist climate. At first, malaria was thought to be caused by hot, damp, stagnant air in low-lying areas, and the cure was to move to a higher, more breezy, drier location.

The first question is whether there is any connection between incidences of malaria and living in a region of warm, moist, stagnant air. Suppose we looked at early European missionaries living in West Africa, comparing those who settled along the low-lying, forested coast with those who lived at higher elevations further inland. Is there any significant difference in the incidence of malaria? Perhaps some people with malaria did improve once they moved to a higher elevation, but maybe they would have survived in any case without moving to the mountains. Only by careful, empirical, statistical data can we tell what real difference a higher and drier climate makes.

In the late nineteenth century, a serious epidemic of anthrax broke out among cattle in France. Pasteur had heard about a French veterinarian who had cured hundreds of cows by employing an unusual treatment he had developed on his own in which he raised the sick cow's body temperature by vigorous rubbing and then making cuts in the skin into which was poured turpentine and hot vinegar. Of course, the poor cow bellowed in pain, but in many cases the cows fully recovered. The question for Pasteur, however, was whether the rate of recovery was any better for the cows receiving this painful and unusual treatment than for cows who received no treatment. Like many diseases, not all cows afflicted with anthrax died. Some of the infected animals died and some lived. Pasteur carried out an experiment in which half a certain number of cows infected with anthrax were given the veterinarian's treatment, and half were left untreated. The results of the two groups turned out to be the same! Half of each group lived and half died. The conclusion was obvious. The cows who recovered after receiving the treatment were not cured by it but would have gotten better in any case. The treatment did nothing to benefit the cows.

Naturally, Pasteur's discovery was a great shock. Many intelligent people had reasoned wrongly and badly, engaging in what is known as the fallacy of "false cause." Just because one thing precedes another does not prove the first is the cause of the second. Bertrand Russell tells the story of the rooster who got up early each morning before sunrise, hopped up on a fence post, and began crowing until the sun came up. This went on day after day until the rooster came to feel his crowing *caused* the sun to rise. The sad end of the story comes with the farmer's wife who wrung the rooster's neck, cooked him for Sunday supper, and the sun continued to rise as before.

In the case of malaria, on the other hand, it turns out that it did make a difference whether one lived in a low, wet area versus an area that was higher and drier. The incidence of malaria tended to be much greater in the lower, wetter locations. So, unlike the case of the phony cure for the sick cows, there was a statistical correlation, but it is still not obvious that this explains what *causes* malaria. Despite this correlation, it is not clear that malaria is caused by moist, stagnant air. Although it helped to move to the mountains, people still got and died from malaria in the higher and drier elevations. So, despite the correlation, the cause of malaria had not been discovered. But what exactly are we looking for? What exactly do we mean by causality? It is not at all clear what is meant by causality. Is it supposed to be a necessary condition or a sufficient condition, or both a necessary and a sufficient condition? Or is causality perhaps something far weaker, that is, just one of many contributing conditions?

The scientist Eijkman fed chickens white, polished rice, and they all developed polyneuritis and died. He then fed another group of chickens unpolished rice, and none of them contracted the disease. Finally, he fed a third group of infected chickens the discarded outer husks of rice from polished rice, and these chickens all quickly recovered. Here the evidence is overwhelming that the lack of the outer rice covering causes polyneuritis. Without it, the chickens all get the disease and die. With it, they do not get the disease, and indeed sick chickens recover from it if given the outer rice parts. Clearly, then, the lack of the brown outer part of the rice is both a necessary and sufficient condition for polyneuritis, and this is causality in the strongest, most obvious sense. But not all cases of causal linkage are so clear. Does smoking cause cancer? Some people who smoke all their lives live into their nineties; others who never smoke die of lung cancer. Yet we feel there is some connection between smoking and cancer. What is it exactly? Statistically, a correlation exists between heavy smokers and those who die of lung cancer: a higher percentage of smokers get lung cancer than nonsmokers. Does this prove that smoking is a cause of cancer?

Suppose, in the earlier example, we found, as it was discovered before 1920, that people who lived in swampy, tropical areas contracted malaria more frequently on average than those living in higher, drier tropical locations. Does this prove that breathing moist, warm air causes or even contributes to malaria? No, we now know that malaria is caused by a microbe that enters the bloodstream through the bite of a mosquito. So, what is the connection between warm, moist stagnant air and malaria? Only the indirect connection that mosquitoes thrive in such conditions. If we could get rid of the mosquitoes or prevent them from biting us, there would be no danger of malaria, even in warm, moist areas of stagnant, slow-moving air. So, the fact that there are statistical correlations does not prove by itself causal connections.

Questions for Discussion

1. What is the difference between an inductive argument and a deductive argument?

2. Is all scientific reasoning inductive generalization from particulars? If not, what else is it?

3. How does hypothesis formulation and testing resemble MT?

4. Assess the strengths and weaknesses of the following arguments:

    (a) "In attempting to understand the elements out of which mental phenomena are compounded, it is of the greatest importance to remember that from the protozoa to man there is nowhere a very wide gap either in structure or in behavior. From this fact, it is a highly probable inference that there is also nowhere a very wide mental gap." (Bertrand Russell, *The Analysis of Mind*)

    (b) "And indeed since the planets are seen at varying distances from the earth, the center of the earth is surely not the center of their orbits." (Nicolaus Copernicus, "On the Revolutions of the Heavenly Spheres")

    (c) "Suppose someone tells me that he has had a tooth extracted without an anesthetic, and I express my sympathy, and suppose that I am then asked, 'How do you know that it hurt him?' I might reasonably reply, 'Well, I know that it would hurt me. I have been to the dentist and know how painful it is to have a tooth filled without an anesthetic, let alone taken out. And he has the same sort of nervous system as I have. I infer therefore that in these conditions he felt considerable pain, just as I should myself." (A. J. Ayer)

    (d) "Since Venus rotates so slowly, we might be tempted to conclude that Venus, like Mercury, keeps one face always toward the Sun. If this hypothesis were correct, we should expect that the dark side would be exceedingly cold. Pettit and Nicholson have measured the temperature of the dark side of Venus. They find that the temperature is not low . . . The planet must rotate fairly often to keep the dark side from cooling excessively." (Fred L. Whipple, *Earth, Moon and Planets*)

CHAPTER 7

Strategies for Philosophical Arguments

The valid argument forms we have been considering, taken singly or in some combination, can be used as strategies for constructing arguments in any area of discourse. Since reasoning is the *primary* tool of philosophers, however, such argument strategies are especially prominent in philosophical writing. Here are a few examples of argument strategies based on a single basic valid argument form.

It seems that mercy cannot be attributed to God. For mercy is a kind of sorrow, as Damascene says. But there is no sorrow in God; and therefore there is no mercy in him. (Thomas Aquinas, *Summa Theologica*)

M: Mercy is attributed to God.
S: Sorrow is attributed to God.

$$\frac{\begin{array}{l} M \to S \\ -S \end{array}}{\therefore \; -M} \qquad \text{MT}$$

Intense heat is nothing else but a particular kind of painful sensation, and pain cannot exist but in a perceiving being. It follows that no intense heat can really exist in an unperceiving corporeal substance. (George Berkeley, *Three Dialogues Between Hylas and Philonous*)

H: Something is heat.
S: Something is sensation.
P: Something cannot exist in an unperceiving being.

$$H \rightarrow S$$
$$\underline{S \rightarrow P} \quad HS$$
$$\therefore H \rightarrow P$$

Our ideas reach no farther than our experience. We have no experience of divine attributes and operations. I need not conclude my syllogism. You can draw the inference yourself. (David Hume, *Dialogues Concerning Natural Religion*)

E: We do not experience divine attributes.
I: We do not have ideas of divine attributes.

$$E \rightarrow I$$
$$\underline{E} \qquad MP$$
$$\therefore I$$

If then, it is agreed that things are either the result of coincidence or for an end, and these cannot be the result of coincidence or spontaneity, it follows that they must be for an end. (Aristotle, *Physics*)

C: Things are the result of coincidence.
E: Things are for an end.

$$C \text{ v } E$$
$$\underline{-C} \qquad DS$$
$$\therefore E$$

Here are several arguments that display more than one basic valid argument form.

Whensoever a man transfers his right, or renounces it, it is either in consideration of some right reciprocally transferred to himself, or for some other good he hopes for thereby. For it is a voluntary act: and of the voluntary acts of every man, the object is some good to himself. And therefore there be some rights, which no man can be understood by any words, or other signs, to have abandoned or transferred. As first a man cannot lay down the right of resisting them, that assault him by force, to take away his life, because he cannot be understood to aim thereby at any good to himself. (Hobbes, *The Leviathan*)

T: A person transfers or abandons his right.
V: A person acts voluntarily.
G: A person aims at some good for himself.
R: A person abandons his right to protect himself.

$$T \rightarrow V$$
$$V \rightarrow G \quad \text{HS}$$
$$\therefore T \rightarrow G$$

$$R \rightarrow T$$
$$T \rightarrow G \quad \text{HS}$$
$$\therefore R \rightarrow G$$

$$R \rightarrow G$$
$$-G \qquad \text{MT}$$
$$\therefore -R$$

And no man can be a rhapsode who does not understand the meaning of the poet. For the rhapsode ought to interpret the mind of the poet to his hearers, but how can he interpret him well unless he knows what he means? (Plato, *Ion*)

R: A person is a true rhapsode.
I: A person interprets the poet.
M: A person knows what the poet means.

$$R \rightarrow I$$
$$I \rightarrow M \quad \text{HS}$$
$$\therefore R \rightarrow M$$

$$R \rightarrow M$$
$$-M \qquad \text{MT}$$
$$\therefore -R$$

Here are some more examples of the use of modus tollens (MT). See if you can formulate each one as an MT.

I do know that this pencil exists, but I could not know this if Hume's principles were true. Therefore, Hume's principles, one or both of them, are false. (G.E. Moore, *Some Main Problems of Philosophy*)

If number were an idea, then arithmetic would be psychology. But arithmetic is no more psychology than, say, astronomy is. Astronomy is concerned not with ideas of the planets, but with the planets themselves and by the same token the objects of arithmetic are not ideas either. (Gottlob Frege, *The Foundations of Arithmetic*)

If error were something positive, God would be its cause, and by Him it would continually be procreated (by Prop. 12). But this is absurd (by Prop. 13). Therefore error is nothing positive. (Baruch Spinoza, *The Principles of Philosophy Demonstrated by the Method of Geometry*)

Necessary and Sufficient Conditions

In addition to constructing arguments that utilize basic valid argument forms, another important philosophical activity with which the reader will want to be familiar is the attempt to provide definitions or "analyses" of important philosophical concepts by specifying what are known as "necessary and sufficient conditions." This can be readily understood in terms of our discussion of conditional statements $(P \rightarrow Q)$ and their role in MP and MT.

What a conditional statement $(P \rightarrow Q)$ says is that P is a sufficient but not a necessary condition for Q and that Q is necessary but not sufficient for P. What do we mean here by *necessary* and *sufficient*? P is sufficient for Q if P is all that is required for Q to occur. Thus, raining is all that is required to get the streets wet. But P is not *necessary* for Q, meaning that P is not the only way for Q to occur. Although raining is sufficient for getting the streets wet, they could be gotten wet in other ways, without it having rained. This is all that MP really says. It states that since P is sufficient for Q (that is, P is all that is required to show Q) and P actually occurred, that is all we need in order to know that Q also occurred. MP, in other words, goes through because P is a sufficient condition for Q. And, by the same token, the fallacy of affirming the consequent is based on the idea that Q is *not* a sufficient condition for P. Just because the streets are wet is not enough to enable us to know that it rained, since there are other ways the streets could have gotten wet.

On the other hand, Q is a necessary but not a sufficient condition for P, meaning that although it is possible for the streets to be wet without it having rained, it is not possible for it to rain without the streets getting wet. A necessary condition of it raining therefore is that the streets get wet. This is simply what the conditional $(P \rightarrow Q)$ states. So if Q is absolutely necessary for P to occur, then we know that without Q, P cannot occur. And this is really what MT asserts. If Q is necessary to P $(P \rightarrow Q)$, then P cannot occur without Q. Hence, $-Q \rightarrow -P$. By the same token, the fallacy of denying the antecedent is based on the fact that P is not necessary for Q. Does it have to rain in order for the streets to get wet? No. So, the mere fact that it did not rain does not guarantee the conclusion that the streets are not wet.

A frequent method of philosophical analysis of an important concept is to try to state its necessary and sufficient conditions. Take the concept *knowledge,* for example. Many philosophers believe that if we can state the necessary and sufficient conditions for knowing something, we will have succeeded in adequately explaining what knowledge is. Plato offers an example of such an attempt in *Theaetetus.* One necessary condition for knowing something is believing it (you cannot know something without believing it), but that is obviously not sufficient. Why not? The answer to this question will indicate to us another necessary condition. The reason believing is not sufficient for knowledge is that you could believe something that was not true. Thus, truth is a second necessary condition for knowledge. You cannot know something unless you believe it *and* it is true. But is *this* sufficient? Could a person believe something that was true and yet not know it, and if so, why not? (Again, the answer will give us a third condition.) What if a person believed that an earthquake would occur in southern California on March 14 and, sure enough, it does. It looks as though he *knew* it would occur. But what if we ask him why, and he replies that he made this discovery by consulting tea leaves. Now what would we say? Did he know there would be an earthquake or not? And if not, *why* not? Many of us would say he did *not know* there would be an earthquake because he did not have any good reasons for believing it. Thus, we have a third necessary condition to add to the other two. In order to know something, a person must believe something that is true and have good reasons for so believing. But is this at last sufficient? Plato and many contemporary philosophers have thought so, though others disagree. But if so, then by adding to our list of necessary conditions until the entire list is also sufficient, we have succeeded in adequately explaining what knowledge is.

Indirect Proofs

Philosophers have traditionally spent a great deal of effort trying to find flaws in the arguments of others. This is not as negative as it may sound, for discovering errors is one step toward finding the truth. Socrates claimed over and over that until we know our view is wrong, we are not in a position to seek the truth. Consequently, much of Socrates' philosophical life was spent criticizing the views of his contemporaries, especially those who claimed to be authorities in some particular area. He would ask if they knew the answer to some pressing question (What is justice? What is religious piety? What is knowledge?). His friends would answer as best they could. Socrates would then examine each view to see what it logically implied, and if it entailed something patently false, absurd, or self-contradictory. Then the person would have to admit that his original position was untenable. The basic form of this strategy, known as indirect proof, resembles MT, where the original position being criticized is P and the absurd consequence is Q.

$$P \to Q$$
$$-Q$$
$$\therefore -P$$

Indirect proofs are one of the most common forms of philosophical reasoning, though some people who use such methods do not even realize that they are doing it. In addition to understanding indirect proofs as a form of MT, you can think of them also in the following way. Suppose your opponent in a philosophical argument holds a position you think is silly. To convince your friend of this, you do the following:

1. Accept provisionally your opponent's view.
2. Show how, on your opponent's premises, an absurdity results.
3. Conclude that, since your opponent's view leads to absurdity, his or her view must be mistaken, and your view, which is the *opposite, is* therefore correct.

In the history of philosophy, indirect proofs were used quite successfully by the ancient Greek philosopher Zeno, who is credited with developing this method of proof. Zeno was a disciple of Parmenides, who held the view that nothing could change. Things appear to change, but Parmenides held that they didn't *really* change and that change itself was an illusion. To defend his teacher's point of view, Zeno took his opponents' viewpoint and showed how the assumption that things do change leads to startling and, he thought, absurd consequences.

We can diagram an indirect proof as follows:

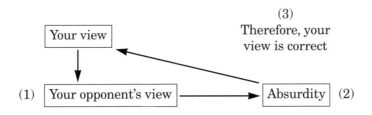

Zeno argued, on the basis of commonly accepted notions of space, that it was impossible for a man to run across the equivalent of a football field! His argument went something like this. Let's say a football player receives a kickoff in his end zone and decides to run it out. Before he can reach the opposite goal line, he must cross the 50-yard line, and before he can do that he must cross the 25, and before that the 12, the 6, and so on to infinity according to the common notion that space is infinitely divisible. So, no matter how hard he runs, he will never make it, though he is very good and has a clear field ahead. The point of this argument is not to prove that a man *cannot* run the length of a football field. This would be absurd. We all know that he can. The point is that our ordinary viewpoint seems to imply an absurd conclusion. There must, then, be something wrong with the ordinary concept, some unclarity that, until tested, was not known to exist. In this case, Zeno's argument showed that our ordinary concepts are contradictory. Once we see it, it is obvious, but it took Zeno's shock tactics to make this clear.

▬▬▬ Dialectical Reasoning

After Socrates' death, Plato developed Socrates' critical approach into a more structured philosophical method known as *dialectic.* Dialectic is basically an attempt to discover the truth about something using critical reasoning to work your way through a series of partial truths, discarding the ones that cannot stand the test of scrutiny, until you reach the insight you seek. In the process of dialectical arguments, as Plato understood it, one begins with a partial and perhaps even inaccurate understanding. Through a process of examination and critical inquiry, the inadequacies of this beginning point are seen, and a new attempt is made to formulate a newly discovered insight—a whole series, in other words, of *indirect proofs,* gradually approximating to an acceptable position.

Crucial to the process of dialectical reasoning, Plato thought, was the willingness to subject each idea to the test of rigorous examination and debate. Consequently, Plato, like Socrates, thought that a philosophical inquiry took place best in a dialogue in which two or more persons debate the strength of proposed definitions or ideas. We might diagram the dialectical process in the following way.

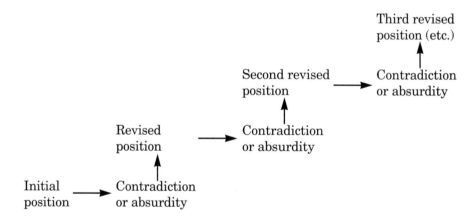

In Plato's *Phaedo,* the character representing Socrates describes his hypothetical method of doing philosophy by criticizing other people's views.

> This was the method I adopted: I first assumed some principle which I judged to be the strongest, and then I affirmed as true whatever seemed to agree with this ... and that which disagreed I regarded as untrue. (Plato, *Phaedo*)

This is the Socratic method of the early Platonic dialogues in which Socrates examines some common belief by "knowledgeable" people to see what its logical implications are. Usually, these consequences reveal some inconsistency and thus the unacceptability of the original belief. Thus, the form of the procedure is hypothetical. "Suppose P is true. If so, then Q, but if Q, then R, but R is clearly unacceptable, so we cannot accept P after all." This is an example of an indirect proof, assuming the truth of a premise in order to show, by its absurd consequences, its falseness.

In *The Republic,* Socrates asks, "What is justice?" To this, Cephalus, a respected and honorable merchant, replies that justice is speaking the truth and paying your debts. Socrates' response is to see where such a view leads, that is, to determine whether its consequences are acceptable or not.

> Suppose that a friend when in his right mind has deposited arms with me and he asks for them when he is not in his right mind. Ought I to give them back to him? No one would say that . . . I should be right in doing so, any more than they would say that I ought always to speak the truth to one who is in his condition. (Plato, *The Republic*)

So, Cephalus' definition is unacceptable and another definition is proposed that also founders on inconsistencies, and so on through much of the first part of the dialogue. This negative form of argument, called indirect proof, can be seen as a form of MT:

$$P \rightarrow Q$$
$$\underline{-Q}$$
$$\therefore -P$$

This is a common form of argument in everyday life: "If the senator were a wise legislator, then our state would have benefited during his 12 years in office, but in all important respects, the fortunes of our state have declined these past 12 years. Therefore, I conclude that the senator has not been a wise legislator."

The Dilemma

Finally, a popular argument among philosophers is the *dilemma*. Formally, it looks like this:

$$P \text{ v } R$$
$$P \rightarrow Q$$
$$\underline{R \rightarrow S}$$
$$\therefore Q \text{ v } S$$

Your opponent is forced to accept one of two possibilities (P or R), each of which leads to unacceptable consequences (Q or S). Either you have stolen some money or you have made a bookkeeping error, but in either case, you are unfit to be a bookkeeper. Either you knew your subordinates were breaking the law, or you did not, but either way you fell down on the job. This painful choice is picturesquely described as 'being impaled on the horns of a dilemma." The following is an example of a dilemma from a lecture by William James.

> The dilemma of this determinism is one whose left horn is pessimism and whose right horn is subjectivism. In other words, if determinism is to escape pessimism, it must leave off looking at the goods and ills of life in a simple objective way, and regard them as materials, indifferent in themselves, for the production of consciousness, scientific and ethical in us. (William James, "The Dilemma of Determinism")

In the preceding example, the dilemma is explicitly labeled as such. Other dilemmas may not be indicated as clearly as these examples but are present nonetheless, as in the case of the following two passages from Plato:

> A man cannot enquire either about that which he knows, or about that which he does not know. For if he knows, he has no need to enquire, and if not, he cannot, for he does not know the very subject about which he is to enquire. (Plato, *Meno*)

> And what a life should I lead, at my age, wandering from city to city, ever changing my place of exile, and always being driven out! For I am quite sure that wherever I go, there, as here, the young men will flock to me, and if I drive them away, their elders will drive me out at their request, and if I let them come, their fathers and friends will drive me out for their sakes. (Plato, *Apology*)

Once you develop the ability to recognize dilemmas, you will find them in more places than you might expect.

The argument strategies given in this unit are only a few of the types found in philosophical analysis and argumentation. They are fairly common, however, and you will discover these as well as other examples used in the course of the readings in this book.

▬▬ Definitions

From Plato to the contemporary philosopher John Rawls, much work in philosophy has been concerned with successfully defining important words, such as justice, art, religion, and knowledge, just to mention four. Why is this such a problem? Why not just look up the word in the dictionary? In Part 1, "What Is Philosophy?," we talked about how philosophy is reflective of commonsense, intuitive, everyday prephilosophical notions, yet philosophical theories of justice, art, religion, and knowledge are more than mere statements of what people already think. These ordinary intuitive, prephilosophical notions are generally vague, unclear, even contradictory. Partly this is because these words of a natural language (English, French, Chinese, German) have a long history of slowly evolving and changing meanings.

Art, for example, originally meant anything humanly made, as in the word *artifact,* and was synonymous with a skillful craft, a kind of technological application of knowledge to some desired end. Later the word came to mean only the fine arts, and so a division was created between the making of poetry, music, sculpture, and the making of beer kegs, harnesses, and candles. Still later, *art* became associated with important ideas of brilliant individuals who were able to express those ideas in works of fine art. Finally, *art* came to be associated with the view that these ideas expressed in art had to be highly original, innovative, inventive, creative, and not just well done or beautiful.

In the gradual evolution of language, the older meanings do not drop out of sight altogether. They merely get covered over with newer meanings, the result being that all these different meanings coexist together, but in a volatile, unstable mix. By reflecting on such ambiguities, confusions, and unclarities, philosophers want not only to call attention to these problems, but to fix them, and that often means proposing more consistent definitions that, although they are in line with ordinary intuitive notions, make these ordinary notions more consistent by emphasizing certain features of the ordinary notion and deemphasizing others. For example, *art* might be defined in terms of innovative ideas expressed by the artist and thereby down-playing the skill required to create artwork. If the philosopher is successful in getting us to accept this new definition, it will have the effect of altering our ideas and our approach to what is being defined. In the preceding case, by defining art in terms of innovative ideas (rather than the skillful creation of the artwork), we are more likely to include "ready-mades" as art than we were before. As an example, Marcel Duchamp displayed an ordinary hat rack as a work of art.

Because philosophy is reflective, such definitions stand or fall by their capability to correspond to ordinary usage. If the newly proposed definition is too far from ordinary usage, critics will challenge the new definition by calling attention to precisely where it deviates from common sense. In the preceding example, the critic will argue that a machine-made object cannot be a work of art because a work of art must be made by someone because that is the part of the meaning of the word *art* left out of the new definition. Of course, the philosopher proposing the new definition can reply that, in a sense, Duchamp did "make" the ready-made object. That is, by displaying it as a work of art, he modified the object in a significant way. In the new definition of art, attention shifts from the word *art* to the word *making.*

Another commonly used word is a term political theorists often speak about: *human rights.* But what exactly are rights? Until we have a clear sense (or definition) of what rights are, it will be impossible to answer related questions. For example, do human beings really have unalienable, God-given human rights? Do animals have rights? Do future generations of humans have rights? Do a thousand acres of wetlands have rights? If we define rights, as some philosophers do, as interests, then it will be easy to argue that landscapes or environments do not have rights since, being inanimate, they can have no interests. Do animals, however, have interests? That depends on whether a creature has to be *aware* of interests in order to have them. Now the philosophical debate can shift to what it means to "have an interest." If having an interest requires *wanting* something, then that would seem to exclude the wetlands but might include animals. At least a case could be made that animals do want certain things, and so have interests in this sense; therefore, animals indeed do have rights.

Another important term in philosophical discussion since Plato's time is *justice*. In general, philosophers agree that the word *justice* has something to do with equality; equals should be treated equally. But this does not tell us what are equals and what are not. Some philosophers define justice as equal goods for equal talent, with the unequal distribution of goods based on unequal merit or talent (that is, some people deserve more than others because they are smarter or work harder). Other philosophers, in contrast, define justice as an equal distribution of goods: the total goods divided equally among the people. If you want to argue for an unequal distribution (that is, there is no injustice in a physician earning more money than a server at a fast-food restaurant), then you will want to define justice in terms of what people deserve. If justice is defined as what people deserve, however, that will raise additional questions about what it means to say a person deserves something. Do you deserve the benefits you receive by having wealthy or influential parents (or were you just lucky)? Do you deserve the benefits you receive by being smart or physically attractive (or, again, were you just lucky)? Do you deserve the benefits you receive from working harder than anyone else (or were you just lucky to be born with good genes that enable you to work hard)? If no one deserves the fruits of any of these advantages, then perhaps justice is best defined as dividing the pie into equal shares, the same for everyone, since no one really deserves any more than any other person. If you favor justice as unequal shares, you will want to define justice in terms of desert and define desert as innate talents. If you favor justice as equal shares, you will want to challenge the idea of desert and argue that no one *deserves* anything, so therefore no one deserves more than anyone else.

Philosophical Analysis

Closely related to a definition is the effort by philosophers to analyze the meanings of a word in order to verify some of these meanings while discarding others. Again, consider the word *art* that estheticians, or philosophers of art, try to define in order to provide a theory of art. An early twentieth-century philosopher, R. G. Collingwood, distinguishes between art as technology and art proper. Collingwood is well aware that the word *art* has shifted considerably over the centuries and, as we indicated earlier, that the old meanings hang on as new meanings become attached to the old ones. Collingwood knows that this creates problems in our understanding of art.

In the past, *art* could refer to the skillful means of accomplishing an intended task, as in the phrase *medical arts*. Universities contain colleges of arts and sciences, and here *arts* does not include fine arts (such as painting, sculpture, and dance), but the application of knowledge to accomplish certain goals. In this sense, although medicine is based on science, it is nonetheless an art and not a science. As Collingwood is aware, this sense of *art* has tended to become dissociated with the notion of the fine arts, but he is nonetheless worried that some of the old ideas of art as technology linger on in a disguised way that confuses our contemporary notions of fine art. Specifically, he worries that because of the old notion of art as technology, many people continue to think of the fine arts as designed to accomplish specific tasks, such as to induce a quasi-religious, mystical state, to make us happy, or to make us feel patriotic. This is precisely the sort of idea about art that Collingwood strongly opposes. So his philosophical method differentiates these meanings of art as sharply as possible, allowing him to argue for the relevance of some of these meanings and against others.

Similarly, a philosopher who favors the definition of punishment as retribution (an eye for an eye and a tooth for a tooth) will want to differentiate sharply the idea of retribution from the associated notion of vengeance, since retribution will tend to be rejected if it is associated in people's minds with the spiteful, negative connotations of revenge. On the other hand, a philosopher favoring the notion of punishment as a deterrent will want to identify retribution with getting even because that is what works. What good does it do to coddle criminals if they persist in their criminality? Prison should be unpleasant so criminals will *want* to avoid going there. Still other philosophers may admit that the word *punishment* does connote the notion of taking revenge, getting even, but argue that this is a primitive, savage notion that we should avoid while moving on toward more progressive concepts such as rehabilitation.

As in the preceding example, a philosophical analysis can refer to dividing a complex issue into more manageable parts. Consider the question of abortion. One of the reasons this issue is so hard to deal with is that it contains so many different issues. There is the religious issue, which sees the fetus as having an immortal soul and therefore being fully a person. This makes abortion an act of murder. There is also the legal issue of how to enforce the law now that abortion is legal in certain circumstances. There is the issue of free speech, in terms of which pro-life advocates argue that they should be free to protest at abortion clinics. There is the question of civil disobedience when protesters block clinic doors and try to prevent others from entering them. There is also the issue of a woman's right to use her own body as she chooses, which includes the right not to use her body to carry a fetus that she does not want to carry to full term. There is also the political issue argued by the pro-choice advocates that the state has no right to restrict a woman's decision even when what she decides to do might be morally wrong.

Those who favor abortion may want to separate these issues so that they can focus attention on the political issue to the exclusion of other issues. Yes, they may say, abortion may be morally wrong; it may also be contrary to your most deeply held religious convictions. Nonetheless, we live in a pluralistic democracy in which no one has the right to impose moral or religious belief on others. So we reluctantly have to allow people to decide for themselves, even though we know they will often decide to do the wrong thing. Pro-life advocates will not want to separate the moral and religious questions from the political issues. They will argue that whereas, generally speaking, we have to live and let live, this principle reaches a limit where the murder of innocent children is concerned. Here, they say, we have to impose restrictions on the behavior of our fellow citizens.

The Discovery of Fallacies

Another important philosophical strategy in criticizing others' arguments is to spot within the argument common mistakes in reasoning, traditionally known as fallacies. In ordinary language, the word *fallacy* has a number of different meanings. For our purposes, however, we will use the term to refer to a common error in reasoning. The term is used most often to refer to an error in reasoning that is not immediately obvious. In other words, we attach the term *fallacy* to an argument that at first glance may seem convincing but upon closer scrutiny turns out not to be so.

In the previous chapter, "Inductive Arguments and Scientific Reasoning," we saw some of the common fallacies in deductive arguments. In this section, we shall be concerned with informal fallacies, or fallacies that pertain to inductive arguments. It is important to be on the lookout for these fallacies, as they occur in daily life. Sometimes an author will purposely employ a fallacy, as in the case of advertising, but often an author is unaware of employing fallacious reasoning.

In this unit, we will familiarize ourselves with some of the more widespread fallacies. By becoming familiar with certain fallacious arguments, you will then be better equipped to read more critically and not be misled by these types of arguments.

Argumentum ad Baculum

This fallacy is an appeal to force as the basis for accepting or rejecting a point of view. It is committed whenever a proposition is said to be true because those in positions of power say it is. It occurs not only in its blatant forms when someone makes "an offer you can't refuse," but also in more subtle instances, such as the following statement from a letter to a congressman: "May I remind you, Congressman, that your vote against the pro-life bill is unacceptable and that 80 percent of the voters in your district are Roman Catholics."

Ad Hominem Attack

The *ad hominem* fallacy is committed when an author attempts to refute another author's position by attacking the person rather than the argument. In other words, rather than attempting to disprove an author's argument, you attack the author. Suppose you are reading an article that argues in favor of reverse discrimination for blacks, and you say that the position is wrong because it was written by a black person and that a black person would naturally favor reverse discrimination. You would be attacking the author rather than the argument.

Argument from Ignorance

This fallacy is committed whenever it is argued that a proposition is true because it has not been proved false, or a certain proposition is false because it has not been proved true. This fallacy often occurs in situations in which there exists little evidence either for or against a position. So, if you argue that there is no life after death because it has not been proved that there is, or that there must be flying saucers since they have never been disproved, you are guilty of this fallacy.

Appeal to Pity

This occurs when a writer makes an appeal to pity in order to get a position accepted. This fallacy often occurs in law courts when a defense attorney will plead for the acquittal of the defendant by appealing to the pity of the jurors. An attorney might argue that the jury should not convict a certain woman of shoplifting because she is unmarried, out of work, and has six children. This has nothing to do with her guilt or innocence but is employed for the purpose of arousing pity in the jurors.

Appeal to Authority

The appeal to authority is a little more tricky. It occurs when an author appeals to the testimony of an authority in matters *outside that authority's realm of specialization.* Often such an appeal can strengthen an argument if it is an appeal for testimony within the authority's province of specialization. So, it is often a matter of degree. If a tennis star endorses a particular tennis shoe, this is all well and good, but if the tennis star endorses a certain sports car, the appeal becomes fallacious. After all, what does a professional basketball player know about breakfast cereals? What does a movie star know about long distance telephone companies?

Hasty Generalization

This occurs when an author cites an example that is not typical in order to make a general point covering all cases. Often it is argued that marijuana should be legal because in some cases it is valuable in treating illnesses. If you were to say that because your father is an alcoholic, alcohol is evil, you would be making a hasty generalization.

Argumentum ad Populum

A favorite device of the propagandist and the advertiser, the *argumentum ad populum* occurs when one attempts to win popular assent to a conclusion by arousing enthusiasm in the masses or appealing to emotional issues of patriotism, motherhood, or decency, rather than by appealing to facts. "Are we going to let these newfangled notions make us forget the virtues of honesty, hard work, fair play, and basic decency—values which made our country great?"

Begging the Question

This fallacy, which we came across earlier, occurs whenever a person *assumes* what the argument is trying to *prove*. For example, "To allow complete, unfettered freedom of speech is advantageous to the interests of the state. For it is clearly helpful to the community to have each individual freely express his or her own point of view." Begging the question is one of the most frequently committed fallacies.

Complex Question

This is the familiar double or loaded question, such as "Have you stopped beating your wife?" Here the stated question presupposes an affirmative answer to an unasked question. More serious forms occur in propaganda techniques that *presume,* rather than *win,* our assent to some highly controversial issue, as in the following example. "Why are privately controlled industries so much more efficient than government-run operations like the post office?"

Equivocation

This fallacy occurs whenever an argument turns on a crucial shift in the meaning of a significant word or phrase. A famous example is attributed by G.E. Moore to John Stuart Mill's argument for ethical utilitarianism, in which Mill argues that the only proof possible that something is desirable is that people actually desire it. The argument turns on a crucial ambiguity in the meaning of the word *de-*

sirable. On the one hand, *desirable* means "capable of being desired," and in *that* sense the fact that people do actually desire something is ample evidence that it is desirable. But, on the other hand, when we say in an ethical context that something is desirable, we mean that it *ought* to be desired or *deserves* to be desired, not just that it *can* be desired. In *that* sense, it does *not* follow that something is desirable just because people actually desire it. Is it desirable, for example, that a recovering alcoholic have a double martini for lunch?

Red Herring

This is the fallacy of sidetracking the argument from the issue under consideration to a completely different issue. Usually, this occurs when the central question at issue is problematic or doubtful and the red herring issue is one readily agreed to by all sides. By confusing the central issue with the red herring issue, the illusion is created that our assent to the red herring issue is really assent to the controversial central issue. Consider this example: "More money should be budgeted for the library. Look at the value books have brought to people's lives for hundreds of years: sheer reading pleasure, intellectual stimulation, helpful advice, information storage, to mention only a few." We all agree that books are a good thing, but that is not what is being debated—namely, whether more money should be set aside for the library.

Straw Man

This is the fallacy of substituting for your opponent's position a simplistic caricature. By defeating the caricature (the straw man), the fallacious impression is created that you have defeated your opponent's position. For example, "The Democratic party doesn't trust the hard-working American citizen to know best how to spend their own money," or "The Republican party is willing to jeopardize social security to give the wealthy a tax break." Neither political party would accept the position attributed to it.

Questions for Discussion

1. What is the difference between a necessary condition and a sufficient condition?
2. The following arguments are examples of MT, MP, disjunctive syllogism, and dilemma. Analyze and correctly classify them.
   (a) "No names come in contradictory pairs, but all predictables come in contradictory pairs. Therefore, no name is a predictable." (Peter Geach, *Reference and Generality*)
   (b) "The argument under the present head may be put into a very concise form. Either the mode in which the federal government is to be

constructed will render it sufficiently dependent on the people, or it will not. On the first supposition, it will be restrained by that dependence from forming schemes obnoxious to their constituents. On the other supposition, it will not possess the confidence of the people, and its schemes of usurpation will be easily defeated by the state governments, who will be supported by the people." (James Madison, *The Federalist Papers*)

(c) "Man tends to increase at a greater rate than his means of subsistence; consequently he is occasionally subject to a severe struggle for existence." (Charles Darwin, *The Descent of Man*)

(d) "According to Aristotle, none of the products of Nature are due to chance. His proof is this: That which is due to chance does not reappear constantly nor frequently, but all products of Nature reappear either constantly or at least frequently." (Moses Maimonides, *The Guide for the Perplexed*)

(e) "We seem unable to clear ourselves from the old dilemma. If you predicate what is different, you ascribe to the subject what it is *not;* and if you predicate what is *not* different, you say nothing at all." (F. H. Bradley, *Appearance and Reality*)

(f) "Logic is a matter of profound human importance precisely because it is empirically founded and experimentally applied." (John Dewey, *Reconstruction in Philosophy*)

(g) "The after-image is not in physical space. The brain process is. So the after-image is not a brain process." (J. J. C. Smart, "Sensations and Brain Processes," in *Philosophical Review,* 1959)

(h) "If a mental state is to be identical with a physical state, the two must share all properties in common. But there is one property, spatial localizability, that is not so shared. Hence, mental events and states are different from physical ones." (Jaegwon Kim, "On the Psycho-Physical Identity Theory," in *American Philosophical Quarterly,* 1966)

(i) "The law does not expressly permit suicide, and what it does not expressly permit it forbids." (Aristotle, *Nicomachean Ethics*)

(j) "Since morals therefore have an influence on the actions and affections, it follows that they cannot be derived from reason, and that because reason alone, as we have already proved, can never have any such influence." (David Hume, *A Treatise of Human Nature*)

(k) "If error were something positive, God would be its cause, and by Him it would continually be procreated. But this is absurd. Therefore, error is nothing positive." (Baruch Spinoza, *The Principles of Philosophy Demonstrated by the Method of Geometry*)

(l) "Either wealth is an evil or wealth is a good, but wealth is not an evil. Therefore, wealth is a good." (Sextus Empiricus, *Against the Logicians*)

(m) "We possess some immaterial knowledge. No sense knowledge, however, can be immaterial; therefore, and so on." (Duns Scotus, *Oxford Commentary on the Sentences of Peter Lombard*)

(n) "If each man had a definite set of rules of conduct by which he regulated his life he would be no better than a machine. But there are no such rules, so men cannot be machines." (A. M. Turing, "Computing Machinery and Intelligence," *Mind,* 1950)

(o) "We define a metaphysical sentence as a sentence which purports to express a genuine proposition, but does, in fact, express neither a tautology nor an empirical hypothesis. And as tautologies and empirical hypotheses form the entire class of significant propositions, we are justified in concluding that all metaphysical assertions are nonsensical." (A. J. Ayer, *Language, Truth and Logic*)

(p) "I am an Idealist, since I believe that all that exists is spiritual." (John McTaggart, *Philosophical Studies*)

(q) "There is no case in which a thing is found to be the efficient cause of itself; for in such a case, it would be prior to itself, which is impossible." (Thomas Aquinas, *Summa Theologicae*)

(r) "The soul through all her being is immortal, for that which is ever in motion is immortal." (Plato, *Phaedrus*)

Thomas A. Shipka: Are You a Critical Thinker?

Most people that I encounter assume that they reason well, that they are "critical thinkers." Is this assumption justified? Take the following test of critical thinking skills which I developed for my students and award yourself a mark as high as 5 or as low as 1 on each item.

- I am a successful problemsolver.
- I am an informed and responsible decision-maker. I gather as many relevant facts as time constraints permit and I anticipate the likely consequences of each option before I make a decision.
- I strive for informed beliefs, that is, beliefs based on compelling evidence and strong arguments.
- I use language with precision and clarity.
- My beliefs are coherent; that is, some of my beliefs do not contradict others.

*Thomas A. Shipka is professor and chair of
the Department of Philosophy and Religious
Studies at Youngstown State University.*

- I can explain and defend my beliefs capably.
- I am a good listener.
- I am objective and even-handed in my assessments. I do not exaggerate the benefits or harms of a belief, an argument, a person, an organization, a life style, a movement, a product or a service.
- I know that my perceptions can be distorted by my expectations, beliefs, biases and state of mind.
- I know that my memory is selective and constructive, and seldom provides a literal report of past events.
- I appreciate the important role of skepticism in my life, refusing to embrace a claim, however satisfying or intriguing, until I find reasonable grounds for it.
- I am open-minded and flexible. I am willing to consider a different perspective on an issue than the one that I am used to taking, and I am willing to hear or read an elaboration and defense of a claim which strikes me initially as weird or far-fetched.
- I am sensitive to my own fallibility, that is, my proneness as a human being to make mistakes. I have the courage to acknowledge the possibility that a long-cherished belief of mine may be mistaken.
- I successfully detect bias, propaganda, special pleading, code words and exaggeration in what I hear and read.
- I am aware that many television programs, films and publications deviate from the historical record and contradict well-established scientific laws and theories.
- I strive to stay intellectually alive. I regularly read books, newspapers, magazines and other publications. I balance my reading so that I expose myself to a variety of views and perspectives. I participate regularly in serious, civil conversations about significant issues in the news.
- I understand and detect common fallacies in reasoning, including begging the question (assuming what one is supposed to prove); equivocation

(using the same word in different senses); the appeal to ignorance (assuming the correctness of a claim because it has not been disproved); stereotyping and hasty generalization (jumping to a conclusion based upon one or few observations); *post hoc ergo propter hoc* (assuming that because one event preceded another the former caused the latter); *ad hominem* (disqualifying an argument because of its presenter and not its merit); the appeal to authority (sanctioning a claim based solely on its advocate or supporter); and the slippery slope (assuming that a modest change will necessarily trigger dire consequences).

- I strive to avoid the use of such fallacies in my own reasoning.
- TOTAL

The highest score possible is 90. How did you do? Now if you are especially bold and brave, you might invite another person to evaluate your critical thinking skills on this test and then compare the two scores. Remember, good thinking, like good health, is a lifelong challenge.

Suggestions for Further Reading

Chaffee, John. *Thinking Critically.* Houghton Mifflin, 6th ed., 2000. A good, readable introduction to critical thinking.

Glymer, Clark. *Philosophy of Science.* Boulder: Westview Press, 1990. An introduction to issues in scientific reasoning.

Schick, Theodore, Jr., and Lewis Vaughn. *How to Think About Weird Things.* 2nd ed. Mountain View, CA: Mayfield, 1998. An impressive introduction to critical thinking through a discussion of paranormal claims.

Shermer, Michael. *Why People Believe Weird Things: Pseudoscience, Superstition, and Other Confusions of Our Time.* W. H. Freeman & Co., 1998. Considers the range of beliefs and the errors in logic used to support them.

Waller, Bruce H. *Critical Thinking: Consider the Verdict,* 3rd ed. Upper Saddle River, NJ: Prentice Hall, 1997. An introduction to strategies for critical thinking.

What is Real? (Metaphysics)

PART 3

CHAPTER 8

Introduction to Metaphysics

Metaphysics is an area of philosophy that tries to answer this question:
What is reality? Just as moral philosophy attempts to discover general criteria
for what is morally good, and how that differs from other good things, such as
music or art, and just as epistemology (or the theory of knowledge) tries to determine what is knowledge and how that differs from mere opinion, so metaphysics seeks to discover general normative criteria for what is real and how that
differs from what may seem to be real but actually is not.

Appearance and Reality

The distinction between appearance and reality is already familiar to us, of
course, through common sense and ordinary language. That is, we know what
someone means who says that the building *appeared* to be structurally sound, but
really was severely damaged by termites. What philosophers try to do is *explain*
this difference, that is, to say *why* something is said to be real, or what *counts* as
reality; in short, to state clearly the standards or criteria for what is real.

Metaphysics is by far the most ancient branch of philosophy, beginning with
the pre-Socratic Milesian philosopher-scientists (sixth century B.C.E.), who
speculated on the "ageless, deathless" substance underlying the changing tem-
poral world. Some thought this was water, others air, and still others felt there
had to be more than one basic ingredient in order to account for the enormous variety of things in the world. For many centuries this occupied the central place in
philosophy. Originally called First Philosophy, metaphysics was thought to be the
necessary starting point, or foundation, for all the other areas of philosophy. Before one could reasonably decide in moral philosophy, for example, if values are

relative or absolute, one must first decide whether values are the kind of thing that can exist independently of human perception. If so, then values could indeed be absolute, but if not, then all values would be relative to an individual's or a society's point of view. Similarly, before one could reasonably speculate on the fate of the soul after death, one would first have to determine if there *is* a soul. In this sense metaphysics was seen as the most fundamental part of philosophy, presupposed by all the rest.

Despite its profound, occult, and mysterious sound, the word *metaphysics* resulted from a misunderstanding by an editor. Aristotle wrote a series of books dealing with nature which he called the *Physics* (from the Greek word *physis,* "nature"). An even more fundamental inquiry, he thought, was the nature of ultimate reality. Aristotle called this inquiry "first philosophy." But when his editor, several decades after Aristotle's death, was sorting through his works and giving them titles, he came to the batch of writings that followed the *Physics* (most of which, incidentally, were probably Aristotle's students' lecture notes). The editor did not know what to call them, so he invented a word—"After Physics" *(meta* meaning "after," and *physica* meaning "physics"). So the exalted inquiry into the nature of reality forever after has been known as metaphysics—and all due to an editorial mistake.

In the modern period (beginning with Descartes in the seventeenth century), philosophers became increasingly suspicious of the overly ambitious and even pretentious nature of metaphysics. Discovering the ultimate nature of reality, they thought, may simply lie beyond the limits of mortal man. Today the question of metaphysics is being reexamined anew, and many philosophers are returning to metaphysics as an indispensable part of the total task of philosophy.

Metaphysics, then, attempts to determine the difference between appearance and reality. "But," you may say, "why should this be a problem for philosophy? Is it not obvious what is real and what is not? Reality is what one can touch, see, feel, smell, taste, and hear." Notice first that this is itself a definition or theory of reality. It establishes as the criterion for what is real what can be discovered by the five senses, a theory of knowledge that is known in philosophy as *empiricism.* Empirical knowledge is the kind of knowledge that comes from the senses, and if you think that is the only source of knowledge then you are an empiricist and your point of view is called empiricism.

Criteria for Reality

To become philosophically respectable, the empirical view must be subjected to critical scrutiny to determine if it is as obvious as it first sounds. The view that reality is what can be known by the five senses implies two things which we must consider very carefully—first that things which are not empirically detectable cannot be real, and second that whatever is empirically experienced is real. Can we really accept either of these? If not, then we must reject or severely modify our metaphysical view. Let us consider the first problem.

1. The laws of gravity
2. The desk you are sitting on
3. The Fourteenth Amendment to the U.S. Constitution
4. Your love of your parents
5. God
6. Your thoughts at this moment
7. The meaning of the words on this page
8. Justice
9. Hamlet

The list could go on, but stop for a moment and ask yourself which of these items are known by the five senses. Probably only the second. But do you want to conclude that all the others are not real? Which ones *do* you think are real? Probably you will exclude Hamlet. You might also exclude justice if you are a cynic, and God if you are an atheist. But if you consider these and others, such as the laws of nature, the meaning of words, civil laws, thoughts, or Jove, to be real, then you are conceding that some non-empirical things can be real and are thus rejecting empiricism, at least in the simple and extreme form which we are now considering. (You might be tempted to modify your empiricism to include a sixth inner sense by which you realize love, or God. But then you have severely weakened your original position by postulating something very difficult to prove—a sixth sense.)

Now look at the second problem mentioned above: Is everything empirical real? Your senses tell you that there is space behind a mirror, and that objects lose their color in the dark. Sometimes people quite sincerely report having seen little green men emerging from flying saucers. But do we believe any of this really happens? If not, *why* not? Well, for one thing, little green spacemen are very unexpected and unusual, and for another they were not observed by more than one individual at the same time. The space behind the mirror conflicts with our firm belief that there is a solid brick wall just behind the mirror. But now we are introducing other sets of criteria for what is real, which may conflict with the empirical criteria:

1. Observable to more than one individual (intersubjectively verifiable)
2. Fits in with normal expectations (consistent with our other beliefs)

And these criteria are just as plausible intuitively as the empiricist criterion. Suppose you think you hear someone at the door, so you ask me if I heard anything. If I say no, you will assume it was just your imagination (you were hearing things). But if I say yes, then you will get up to see who is there. If you believe in the laws of biology and the general rules governing common sense, then you will tend to discount a walking, talking tree even though you "saw it with your own eyes."

But since there are other plausible criteria for reality which may conflict with the empiricist criterion, it is clearly not obvious that reality is limited to what we can see and touch. Nor can we simply conclude that there are several criteria for what is real, since the criteria may conflict—one telling us that so-and-so is real and others saying it is not. In order to come up with a dependable and usable criterion we must reconcile these differences and establish some sort of priority among them—and this calls for philosophical reflection. The problem with common sense or intuitively "obvious" criteria is that they often turn out, upon examination, to be inconsistent. We may find that each of these criteria is intuitively obvious, but since they conflict our intuitions are of no use to us in deciding what is real.

We have now mentioned several plausible standards for reality, and we can easily think of others. Which is more real, the Cheshire cat or its smile, that is, an object or its properties? If you think the object is more real, *why* do you think so? Probably you are thinking that it is more permanent and independent. The properties can change (the cat begins to frown), but the object remains the same. The smile cannot exist without the cat (except in Lewis Carroll), but the cat does quite well without the smile. In this sense one might conclude that the chemical elements which make up the physical world are more real than the objects which they comprise. The wood is converted into paper and the paper finally burned, but the particles of carbon, which existed all along, linger on in the air. One could then go a step further and conclude that since the chemical elements are made out of still simpler elements (atoms and molecules), these entities are more real than the chemical elements of which they are a part. One might even conclude that the mathematical principles governing these atomic and chemical compositions are still more real, since even if there were no such chemicals, the mathematical principles would remain in force. Instead of saying that what is most real is what we know through the *senses,* this view asserts that what is most real is what we know through the *intellect*, a view that gives rise to a theory of knowledge known as rationalism.

The Mind and Reality

Closely related to the notion of reality as independent of other *things* is the idea that what is real must be independent of the *mind*. Imagine that instead of completing your philosophy assignment, you are now lying on the beach in Florida. Of course, you are not really there, but *why* not, in what sense are you not? It is simply in your imagination. This pleasant fantasy exists only so long as you are thinking of it; as soon as your mind returns to the philosophy assignment, the fantasy dissolves. It is in this sense we feel that we cannot control reality simply by thinking about it. You cannot change your philosophy assignment by imagining it is not there, nor can you complete it simply by *thinking* you have. Reality, in this sense, stubbornly opposes our minds; we must conform our thinking to it if we are to have an accurate and reliable picture of the world. In short, reality is not dependent on our minds.

We have now mentioned five criteria for what is real:

1. Empirically observable
2. Intersubjectively verifiable
3. Consistent with other beliefs
4. Permanent and independent of other objects
5. Mind-independent

Assuming we could reconcile differences in the criteria for what is real, our second task as metaphysicians would be to *use* that standard to determine what sorts of things in the world actually meet those standards, that is, to find out what *is* real by the criteria established. So, for example, if our standard of reality is what can be seen and touched, then we will conclude that physical objects are real while atoms and molecules, thoughts, laws, and rules are not. Or if we decide on permanence and independence from other entities as our criteria, then physical objects will be less real than atoms, which will, in turn, be less real than physical and mathematical laws. Pushing this line of argument to its logical conclusion, Baruch Spinoza (1632-1677) argued that only God was fully real since God alone existed completely independent and unchanging, whereas all other things depended at least on God for their existence. In a similar way, idealist metaphysicians have carried empiricism from its commonsensical position that physical objects are real because we can see and touch them, to the opposite extreme conclusion that since we are most immediately aware of our own sensations, rather than physical objects, which we simply infer from the sensations, our sensations are therefore more real than physical objects.

Although the philosophical pursuit of metaphysics is a specialized and often highly technical discipline, metaphysics is really only an extension of a fundamental and necessary drive in every human being to know what is real. One of the most important tasks each of us faces in our lives is sorting out the differences between appearance and reality, the phony and the genuine, the mask and the substance. In fact, everyone distinguishes appearance from reality, though not usually in a very systematic way. Most of us simply rely on the appearance-reality distinction which we were taught by our parents and teachers at an early age—Santa Claus and the Wicked Weasel are not real, but Alaska, Eskimos, and blue whales are. In your childhood games you are not really a doctor, or a fireman, or a mother, but you really did break some of your mother's fine china playing house, for which you must be punished. Throughout our formative years we are taught to distinguish fiction from fact, film and dramatic representation from reality. Consider the role of expressions like "this is only make believe," "it is only a movie," "it is just a play; they are only acting." Similarly, most of us learn fairly early the difference between telling a joke and telling a lie. If you are being chased by an angry tree, but at the last moment find yourself lying in your own bed at home, you realize (and at an early age are taught) that the tree monster was "not real" but was "only a dream."

As we grow older we may begin to modify what we have been taught is real and unreal, selecting our own personal views about reality in the light of our experiences and beliefs. We may begin to think the Devil is real, though our parents told us this was not so, or we may begin to think that the American Dream, which we were taught is real, is only a fiction. It is very important for each person to decide what is real and learn how to balance reality against fantasies, dreams, hopes, and wishes—which are also important, but only if clearly distinguished from reality. A key factor in assessing mental and emotional health is the ability to distinguish reality from fantasy and wishful thinking. Much of our *public* debate is also concerned with distinguishing what is real from what is not. What really happened in Dallas on November 22, 1963, when John F. Kennedy was fatally shot?

Candid Camera, an old TV series, was based on our ordinary sense of reality and appearance. Highly unusual things happen to people and the audience gets to see how people respond to bizarre situations. In one episode an unattended hot-dog stand talks to customers, taking their orders, asking whether they prefer mustard or sauerkraut, challenging customers who tried to shortchange this clever vending machine. Some of the passersby accepted this situation as though nothing was wrong. But others were clearly startled. Suppose it happened to you, what would you think or do? Would you suspect that some trick was being played on you and start looking under or inside for hidden microphones? Or would you think you were dreaming, hallucinating, or simply gone crazy? If you were to respond in any of these ways, you would clearly demonstrate that you do not think that what appears before you is real. "It just *couldn't* be real." Why not? "It's impossible! Mechanical things can't talk." Why not? We know how they are made; we also know something about the relation of speech to intelligence and intelligence to life. In other words, the talking hot dog stand just doesn't fit with a great many other things which we believe strongly to be real and on which many other beliefs rest.

This example reveals a lot about the metaphysician's search for reality, and we can learn from it if we reflect on it philosophically. What we ordinarily call reality is only a small part of the totality of our experience. We experience things in daydreams, fantasies, playacting, wishing, planning, and imagination, but these are usually discounted as unreal. Why? Because they do not fit with our decided opinions about reality—opinions which do for the most part fit snugly together into a total pattern we call reality. But notice, in the example, that as soon as you feel that what you experienced is not real, you immediately feel the need to explain what it *is.* If the hot dog stand did not really speak to you, then what did happen? How did the sound of a man's voice emanate from the stand? *Something* happened, a voice certainly came from the cart, there is no denying that. The question is how to account for this unreal thing in terms of what you can accept as real. Thus, a very big part of the metaphysician's task is to explain that part of our experience which we call unreal in terms of what we call real. Electronic sound equipment inside the hot dog stand linked to a microphone inside the cafe across the street could really occur, and if so would explain what we are experiencing—a hot dog stand which appears to be talking is really only a man across the street talking to us through a microphone. It was not really a talking hot dog stand, it only seemed to be. Now we feel a sense of relief. At first that mass of ordinary beliefs about the world seemed threatened; maybe we have been mistaken about the links between speaking, intelligence, and life, on which so much of the rest of our thinking is based. But now we have dissipated that threat and explained the bizarre phenomenon in terms of the ordinary.

Looking at it this way, the task of the metaphysician is to select from all the things we experience those which fit together into a coherent package, and call this *reality*. Those things which do not fit are called *appearance*. Then the metaphysician tries to explain the group known as appearance on the basis of the group known as reality.

It is important for us to understand the difference between saying that something is not real and saying that it does not exist at all. When materialist philosophers, whose views we shall examine later, claim that minds are not real, they do not mean that there are no thoughts, wishes, or intelligence. They simply mean that thoughts, wishes, intelligence, and the like are by-products of and can be explained in terms of physical matter, in this case the human body and particularly the brain and nervous system. Similarly, when idealist philosophers, whose views we will also look at in more detail, say that material substance is unreal, they do not mean that there are no rocks, trees, or mountains. They simply mean that rocks, trees, and mountains exist only because of and as parts of thinking minds. There are rocks and trees, but they only exist in the mind. A famous story is told of Dr. Samuel Johnson; this well-known eighteenth-century British critic, when hearing of George Berkeley's idealist metaphysical system, went out and kicked a stone and remarked, "Thus I refute Berkeley." But Johnson failed to understand the nature of a metaphysical claim. Berkeley did not deny that stones exist, nor did he deny that they hurt one's toe when kicked; he simply explained all this in terms of minds and their sensations. There was a visual sensation of the stone, then the desire to kick it, then the kinesthetic sensation of kicking it, then the sharp pain from having done so—all sensations! Calling something real or unreal is therefore a way of classifying it. Calling something unreal is putting it in a category of things considered less basic, less important in the scheme of things. If you explain minds on the basis of bodily functions, as the materialists do, then you are elevating matter and playing down mind; if you explain material bodies on the basis of mental phenomenon, as the idealists do, then you are elevating mind and playing down matter.

The Tasks of Metaphysics

What is the point of all this elaborate sorting, classifying of things into different systems? Why do we, as well as metaphysicians, break up the world into these two compartments, reality and appearance, explaining the latter in terms of the former? Basically it is the only way yet devised to make sense of an often contrary and confusing world. There are so many things we experience, many of which are jumbled, contradictory, and confusing, that we try to simplify, reducing this incoherent mass to some more systematic order. But we can only do this by selecting some kinds of experience as more basic and explaining other kinds in terms of those more fundamental. And those which finally prove most useful in explaining the others are considered more real.

Simplicity, comprehensibility, comprehensiveness, and consistency within our view of the world are therefore crucial in our determination of what is real and what is not. And this is true both in everyday life and in the history of metaphysics. But, as with other areas of philosophy, although metaphysics arises out of everyday life and common sense, it often goes beyond common sense in its search for perfection. In our everyday attempts to understand the world in terms of appearance and reality we try to make things comprehensible by simplifying, reducing the mass of things we call appearance to a relatively fewer number of things we call reality. But the metaphysician carries this process much further, trying to find the fewest possible elements of reality which will suffice to explain all the rest. Thus, most metaphysical accounts attempt to reduce the wealth of experience to one or two or at most three basic elements. It is this tendency to reduce the many items of experience to one or two basic underlying realities which has led to the charge (which we will examine shortly) that metaphysics is *reductionist,* always claiming that the whole of reality is "nothing but" this or that.

Philosophical accounts of reality also differ from those of the ordinary person in that, whereas ordinary persons tend to select as reality the same sorts of everyday items of experience as those which they designate appearance, the philosophical metaphysician tends to call reality elements which lie beyond ordinary experience. And this too requires some explanation.

At first it might seem that the most obvious way to explain things metaphysically would be to select as "reality" a common element from everyday experience and to use this to explain everything else. But, paradoxically, it turns out that the most comprehensible, comprehensive, and simple metaphysical systems tend to explain the things we can experience in terms of things which we cannot experience in daily life. Let us try to see why this is so. Suppose we said, with the first metaphysician, Thales, that everything is water. That is, we are claiming that everything we experience can be divided up into two categories—water, which we call "reality," and everything else, which we call "appearance," and we then set out to try to explain everything else (appearance) in terms of water (reality). Clouds, for example, or blocks of ice do not look like water, but they can be explained in terms of water—when water evaporates it becomes clouds, and when water freezes it becomes ice. We might, then, try to go a step further and say that all those things which *depend* on water and which we already know are largely *composed* of water are also really nothing but water. But even if we were successful and could make a plausible, convincing case for such examples, what could we say about rocks or fire? How can these things, which intuitively seem the opposite of water, be explained in terms of water? The problem is that water is already understood in daily life to have certain properties that can be experienced, namely, wetness, transparency, and so on, and it is difficult to see how these properties can ever account for their opposites. It was for this reason that Thales' successor, Anaximander, proposed that the basic reality out of which everything was to be explained could not be any known element but something completely different. And most metaphysicians thereafter have agreed with Anaximander. If you set out trying to explain everything in terms of one or two basic elements, this element or elements must be different from the usual sorts of things we experience in everyday life.

Metaphysics and Everyday Experience

As it turns out, the simplest, most comprehensible, comprehensive, and consistent of all views often involve explaining the things we can experience in terms of things we cannot directly experience. To illustrate this point, consider a problem that Greek philosophers faced over two thousand years ago. How is it that children grow by eating bread, cheese, milk, and so on? The food they eat does not simply accumulate and expand their bodies; the added weight is in flesh, and blood, and bones, not in meat and grain. Somehow the food gets converted into flesh and bone, but how? Various answers were proposed, but the most interesting was the atomic hypothesis. The atomists reasoned that if food and flesh and bones were all made of the same particles, then it would be easy to explain how the food becomes flesh and bone. But, of course, this is contrary to direct empirical observation. No matter how small you break up the piece of bread you cannot find any tiny flesh or bone fragments in it. So, they reasoned, these ultimate particles must be very small—so small you cannot see them. And the atomic theory also proved useful in explaining many other things—for example, how rings gradually wear away without having their visible parts fall out. But this is very curious. In order to explain observable phenomena (the fact that children grow by eating food), the atomists had to postulate unobservable entities (the atoms). And so it is with most metaphysical theories. It is very hard to explain, as the early Greek philosophers tried to do, everything on the basis of water, air, or any other common, observable element. How can water be changed into things like fire or dust, which seem completely unlike water as we know it? Thus, the tendency is to look for some unobservable substance *underlying* observable substances, which has no well-defined empirical character of its own that might conflict with the character of things we want to explain. Both the idealist and the materialist metaphysical theories are similarly based on unobservable entities— mind and matter. Of course, we can see things *made* of matter, such as a book or a chair, but we cannot see the underlying matter itself. And although we can experience within our own minds thoughts, ideas, plans, desires, and fantasies, we cannot observe or experience the mind itself which is having these thoughts, ideas, and desires.

It is this tendency to explain the observable in terms of the unobservable that has given metaphysics a bad name in the minds of more down-to-earth, empirically minded philosophers. How do we know that these unobservable entities exist if we cannot directly see or touch them? And if we do not know for sure that they exist, why bother speculating about them? And how can we decide between competing metaphysical theories if each appeals to a different unobservable principle? If you say the table is made of atoms and I say it is made of tiny gremlins, who can say which of us is correct, since neither the atoms nor the tiny gremlins can be observed? Of course, the effects of each can be observed, but what if these effects are just the same? You say that it is the atoms that give the table its shape, color, texture, and so on, and I reply that it is the tiny gremlins that give it its shape, color, texture, and so on. On the level of what is directly observable, there appears absolutely no difference between the two theories. And if that is the case, many philosophers will conclude that there is no real debate between the two, that it is a phony, idle speculation, simply a waste of time.

We have seen that the metaphysician's motive in postulating unobservable entities is not simply to dream up fanciful things which no one can prove or disprove, but to explain the observable world in the simplest, most comprehensible, comprehensive, and consistent way possible. Still, the critics have a point. There is little agreement among metaphysicians. The reason is that there is more than one way to explain anything. This is not to say that any theory is as good as any other. There are certain tests which any good metaphysical theory will have to pass—it must be simple, consistent, comprehensible, and comprehensive (that is, it must explain everything that needs explaining). But even so, there will still be many adequate metaphysical theories which pass these tests. And since there seem to be no other independent tests for choosing among adequate metaphysical schemes, there seems little we can do to reduce the disagreement among metaphysicians. Every good science should have built within it a procedure for deciding which among competing theories are the best and discarding the rest, but there does not seem to be any such decision procedure for metaphysics, and so it has been attacked as a sham science.

Everyone has dreams, for example, but how can we explain them? One metaphysical theory is that dreams are unreal and exist "only in the mind."

But other theories are possible which are initially just as plausible. What if we said that there was both a physical reality and a mental reality and that dreams were real examples of mental reality? What if we went a step further and said that dreams connect us with a spiritual realm which is more real than the physical world? In our dreams, we might say, the ancestors or spirits speak to us and carry us off to faraway places in a higher, spirit world. How comprehensible, consistent, and comprehensive is this theory in terms of the rest of our waking experience? That is, can other things be explained in terms of it? Sure. Why do accidents occur, where do people go when they die, why do some people suddenly go crazy, why do some people occasionally go into a trance, dancing or speaking in strange ways which they later do not remember? We now have a simple, consistent, comprehensible, and comprehensive explanation for all this—in terms of spiritual forces acting inside material objects. And there are many other ways of metaphysically explaining dreams. See if you can think of a few.

The Value of Metaphysics

What is the value of metaphysical speculation if there is no way to prove or disprove metaphysical theories? Even if metaphysics fails as a *science* of reality in the strictest sense, it still provides a much needed and perhaps even necessary tool for organizing our experience into a comprehensible, intelligible, and meaningful whole. And this is the sense in which contemporary philosophers are returning to metaphysics with renewed interest, although this interpretation of metaphysics was first articulated by Immanuel Kant in the eighteenth century. In Kant's view, we look at metaphysics not so much as a science of the underlying reality of the world, but as a set of guiding assumptions or hypotheses which the mind requires to make sense of the world. Kant called this interpretation of metaphysics a *second* Copernican revolution, because of its radical shift of attention from metaphysics as a description of the world to metaphysics as a description of how human beings must think if they are to make sense of the world at all.

As an example, do you think you could have a coherent view of the world if you did not group your various experiences into relatively stable entities which you could name and place in groups of like kinds (dogs, tables, trees)? Suppose for example that instead of regarding the top view of the desk, the side view, the view of the desk from a distance, at twilight, and so on, as parts of one identical object, you saw each as a separate entity. Now consider further what would happen if you regarded each change affecting an entity not simply as a modification of that entity, but as a transformation into a different entity. You would not be the same person you were yesterday since you have lost an ounce, or grown a few sprigs of hair, or gotten a bruise or a tan. Indeed, each second, each millisecond, you would be something different until finally there would be nothing left of you at all. In such a world, what would you call things, how would you recognize them, how could you talk about them? Obviously, the entire enterprise of organizing the world into meaningful units by which we can communicate with other people would come to a halt. Could you even *think* if there were no things to think about? So, to think or talk, we must treat our various perceptions as belonging to identifiable entities which are relatively unchanging over time. We must think of the world as made up of physical objects even if it is not! The value of metaphysics, therefore, according to this view lies in giving us a comprehensible view of the world. Ironically, those who continue to conduct metaphysics in the old positive and constructive sense of actually discovering the most basic structure of the universe are mainly the scientists, rather than the philosophers.

In the following chapters we will look more closely at several specific metaphysical points of view. For now we are concerned with arriving at as clear an idea as possible concerning the basic nature of metaphysics. And already we can see that there are at least two basic types or ideas of metaphysics. First, the more ambitious task of a kind of science of reality, or, since reality is, as we have just noted, usually something which cannot be experienced, we might call this type of metaphysics a science of the supersensible. Just as physics is a science of sensible reality, so, in this view, metaphysics is a science of supersensible reality, those things which cannot be seen. The second type of metaphysics is the more modest task of describing the most basic principles of the world as we experience it. In either case it would be unfair, as already indicated, to charge the metaphysical with constructing "castles of air" for the sheer sport of it. In every case, we have said, the metaphysician is trying to make sense of the world of ordinary experience. The difference, then, has to do with the degree to which the metaphysician is prepared to depart from ordinary experience in order to find those principles which he or she thinks are needed to make sense of the ordinary world of our sense experience. Metaphysicians of the first sort are prepared to speculate fairly widely and to depart fairly radically from ordinary experience, whereas those of the second sort are more pedestrian and stick closer to the confines of common sense.

Questions for Discussion

1. Can you think of an instance in your own experience where you at first thought something was real and later decided that it was not? What criteria did you use to make that decision?

2. Review how Kant redefined our understanding of the nature of metaphysics. How does metaphysics in this sense relate to metaphysics in the older sense of an "inquiry into ultimate reality?"

3. Several large bookstore chains have sections of books labeled "Metaphysics." What sort of books would you find there? Why are these books called metaphysical?

4. Look at the list of items given earlier in this chapter as candidates for reality. Which of them do you think should be excluded from the list as unreal? Why? What other realities might you add to the list?

5. Can you give specific reasons why the study of metaphysics is beneficial?

CHAPTER 9

Materialism

Now that we have completed a brief overview of metaphysics as a whole, let us take a closer look at two competing metaphysical theories: idealism and materialism. These theories are opposites and are usually found in competition with each other. Idealism is the view that only mind and its ideas and thoughts are real, and that matter is an unfounded illusion. Materialists, on the other hand, believe that only matter and its physical properties are real, while mind, thoughts, and the like are simply manifestations of matter. The idealist tries to explain physical matter as a by-product of mind; the materialist tries to explain mind as a by-product of matter.

Materialism and Idealism

As we have indicated, materialism is an ancient philosophical view. The first philosophers, the Milesians in ancient Greece, looked at the world primarily from a materialist outlook, seeking always to find the underlying material substratum of the universe, whether water, air, or some combination of such elements. We have mentioned the emergence in Greek philosophy of atomism, which is primarily a materialist theory. Idealism, on the other hand, is a distinctly modern philosophical outlook. The roots of modern idealism can be traced to René Descartes, although Descartes was not himself an idealist. We shall examine Descartes' views in more detail in Part 4, on epistemology (or theory of knowledge), but for now we shall look briefly at Descartes' famous dictum, *cogito ergo sum*, "I think, therefore I am."

Descartes vowed to believe nothing of which he could not be absolutely certain, and so he sought those things which were beyond doubt. Everything,

Descartes reasoned, could be doubted except the fact that he was thinking. If I think I am thinking, how could I be wrong? Even if I were mistaken, I would still be mistakenly *thinking*. More important for later philosophers was Descartes' argument that we are far more certain that we are *thinking* that something exists than we are certain that that thing exists. If I believe that my car is in the garage, I may be proved wrong (I forgot I had left it in the driveway). But even so, it is certainly true that I *thought* my car was in the garage. If I say "The car is in the garage," I am more likely to be proved wrong than if I say "I *think* my car is in the garage." This is why, in ordinary speech, we will generally retreat to "I think so" whenever we are uncertain, as a kind of guarantee against being contradicted. The conclusion seems to be that those things we actually know most immediately, directly, and with the greatest assurance are not physical objects and facts as we might suppose at first, but our own thoughts and ideas. When we make statements about physical objects, we always go beyond what we actually see before us, interpreting, judging, evaluating what we see, and it is in this leap that error can occur.

In a murder trial, for example, the witness for the prosecution claims to have seen the accused, Jones, running from the victim's house immediately after hearing the gunshot and the victim's screams for help. But now the defense attorney, during cross-examination, will ask how the witness can be sure it was Jones. "What did you actually see?" the lawyer will ask. "Well," the witness responds, now taking a more cautious stance, "I saw someone running out of the house, and the person I saw was certainly dressed like Jones." "But are you positive?" the defense will press. "Isn't it just possible that it was not Jones at all but someone else masquerading as Jones?" "Well, it's possible, I suppose," the witness will be forced to admit. When we make claims about objects in the physical world we are claiming that our idea of that object corresponds with the object itself. But since the object and the idea of it can conflict, no matter how careful we are, there is always a gap between the two into which error can creep. We can never be certain about those objective entities to which our thoughts and ideas are directed. But if we limit our claims just to the ideas themselves, then there is no way for them to fail to correspond to some physical object and thus no way for them to be mistaken. So if I say "It looked like Jones," or "I thought it was Jones," I make no claim whatever about whether it was actually Jones or not. I simply report what my thoughts were like at that moment and about that I can apparently never be mistaken. This is the essential step in all idealists' arguments that mind alone is real. The only thing we know for sure, argue the idealists, is our own thoughts and ideas. These ideas may correspond to some nonmental object, or they may not, but we cannot know for sure. So why not stick to what you know rather than speculate on what you do not know?

At first it may seem sheer madness to try to deny the physical reality of the world. If I am not thinking of you, do you cease to exist? Every metaphysical theory aims for comprehensiveness, and so idealism tries to avoid the appearance of contradicting the plain facts of everyday life. Of course, physical objects exist, replies the idealist, but their existence consists in their being perceived. As Berkeley put it, *esse* is *percipi*, "to be is to be perceived." But common sense seems to insist that physical objects exist even when they are not being perceived. Does not the desk exist later at night when everyone is asleep? Yes, reply the idealists, but only in the sense that the desk would be perceived if anyone were there to look at it. Berkeley adds that, even so, God is always there to keep an eye on things, so that physical objects constantly exist because they are constantly being perceived by God.

Here we find the greatest contrast between idealism and materialism. In our ordinary experience we are not normally aware of any conflict between the empiricist criterion and the mind-independent criterion. We see tables and chairs, and they exist independently of our seeing or thinking of them. But there is an implicit conflict which emerges very clearly in the idealist-materialist debate. For if the idealist's argument is correct, the empiricist criterion reduces to a mind-dependent criterion, which obviously contradicts the mind-independent criterion. If reality is what we know through sense experience, and what we know through sense experience are simply sensations which are mind-dependent, then reality is mind-dependent. So if we stress the empiricist criterion of reality, that what is real is what is directly perceptible, then it looks like the idealists are right and the materialists are wrong. But if we insist on the mind-independent criterion, then the idealists are clearly mistaken from the start and the materialists emerge triumphant.

Materialism and Science

Materialism is the metaphysical system supporting and supported by both common sense and science. Whatever speculative problems arise in trying to prove there is a physical world outside my mind, there are few beliefs more stubbornly held by the vast majority of people. And because natural scientists concentrate their attentions on the physical aspect of the world, and because they have been so enormously successful in their theorizing, it seems plausible to suppose that scientists are on the right metaphysical track. If we are successful in constructing simple, comprehensive, and comprehensible theories based solely on matter, then is materialism clearly not the best metaphysical theory for today?

But is it completely comprehensive? Just as idealism has trouble explaining the existence of an unperceived physical world, so materialism has great difficulty in explaining the mind and its activities. Does it really make sense to say that thoughts are simply electrochemical events in the brain? Thoughts seem so nonphysical. You do not gain weight by learning more, nor can you diet by trying to forget. The size of our skull or brain seems to pose no limitations on what we can think about. It just does not seem to make any sense to ask how big, heavy, smooth, or solid your ideas are. Physicists do not have to worry about this problem, since as physicists they do not claim that *everything* can be explained physically (and in fact many physicists believe that some things can be explained only on religious grounds). It is only the *philosophical* metaphysician who makes this larger claim and thereby takes on the larger problem of explaining the mental in terms of the physical.

Dualism and the Mind-Body Problem

Many philosophers of the modern period, including Descartes, avoid both the problem of idealism in explaining matter and the problem of materialism in explaining mind by combining both in what is known as dualism. Descartes believed that the human body is a physical object inside which is a mental substance of a quite different sort. But dualism faces very serious problems of its own, particularly in trying to explain the obvious interaction between mind and body within ordinary human experience. When physical injury causes mental anguish, the body seems to be acting on the mind. And when we decide to get up and walk out of a boring movie, the mind seems clearly to be acting on the body. As we have seen, the metaphysician's task is not to invent or deny the way things normally appear, but to account for and explain the appearances in terms of a theory of reality. Even if there is no real mind-body interaction, why does it seem that way? If mind and body are two completely different kinds of things, how *can* they interact on one another? This is known in philosophy as the mind-body problem.

In the modern period, following Descartes, materialism and idealism have flourished primarily to avoid this problem. Each can claim to have removed the mind-body problem simply by denying one of the two items which make up the duality. So the materialist says, "There is no problem in explaining how mind and body can interact since there is no such thing as mind," and the idealist responds that idealism resolves the mind-body problem by eliminating matter. Modern idealist theories more often arise, however, as a reaction to some of the negative implications of materialism. As the American philosopher William James noted, philosophical theories are differentiated not only by logical arguments and conclusions, they are also distinguished by more subtle factors of temperament and lifestyle. So, materialism is more the philosophy of what James called the "tough-minded" and idealism of the "tender-minded." Materialism tends to endorse a deterministic and mechanistic world view which appears to threaten both religious and humanistic values. The materialist tends to believe that everything that happens in the universe, including human behavior, is the product of strict causal laws governing the movement of material bodies. Thus when I decided to get up and walk out of the boring movie, it seemed to me that I first made up my mind and then moved my body. It appears, on a common-sense level, that the decision was mine. I was not forced to leave. I could have stayed had I wanted to. I left only because I decided to. But most materialists argue that this is only an illusion, that in reality your body moved because it was acted on by other physical forces, such as nerve impulses, which in turn were the inevitable product of other physical causes, so that you really had nothing to do with it at all. In fact, despite the appearances to the contrary, you actually had no choice in the matter whatsoever; you could not have done anything but get up and leave. Of course, the materialist would admit that the fact that you wanted to leave influenced your action, but this desire was itself caused by other factors, and these by still other factors, such as your biological makeup, your early training, and so on, factors over which you had absolutely no control. But if this is so, then people are not free, and if they are not free, then they are not responsible for their actions, and if not, then they cannot reasonably be criticized, blamed, praised, or otherwise held accountable for their actions. All of this is devastating to our view of human beings as autonomous agents in control of their lives, responsible for their actions and accountable for them; for if materialism is true then so is determinism, but if determinism is true then our entire moral and ethical framework is nothing but a pretense. Thus, arguing by hypothetical syllogism, introduced in Chapter 5, if materialism is true, then morality is a sham. Materialism is therefore often seen as the enemy of morality.

Materialism and Religious Belief

Materialism is also perceived as a threat to religious belief. If the world is nothing but a giant machine, then there is no place in such a system for God, or the immortal Soul, or of any possibility of God's working out his plan in the universe, or of our freely accepting God's plan for humankind. This is not to say that a materialist cannot have a moral theory or be a moral person, or even be a religious person in a certain sense, and have religious beliefs. Indeed, some materialists have been deeply religious men (e.g., Gassendi). Nonetheless, the main thrust of materialism is often perceived, with some justification, to be antithetical to some of the most basic tenets of morality and religion. As we look at materialism more closely in this chapter we will consider some of these responses to the apparently negative side of materialism.

The idealist also finds materialism strangely alien to our most immediate and direct experience of the world. The irony is that while materialism seems at first glance to correspond closely to ordinary commonsense beliefs, which the idealist appears to flatly contradict, in some ways quite the opposite is true. The idealist's theory is based on those things most immediately familiar to each of us, our thoughts, feelings, ideas, beliefs, and our own experience in *thinking* those thoughts, and *feeling* those feelings, and *sensing* those sensations. The materialist's theory, on the other hand, is generally based on things such as atoms, molecules, light waves, photons, alpha particles, and so on, which play no part in anyone's direct experience of the world. These things may help to *explain* what we experience, but they are not themselves directly experienced, as the mental phenomena on which the idealist bases his theory surely are. Thus, materialist philosophers usually distinguish between primary and secondary qualities of objects. Primary qualities are those properties of objects, such as hardness, weight, and solidity, which really are in the object as they appear to us in perception. Secondary qualities are those properties of objects, such as colors, tastes, and odors, which are not at all in the object as they appear to us in perception. In fact, these qualities arise only *in* perception. The apple is not really red; it simply has the kind of primary qualities which can cause the sensation of red in the perceptions of men and animals. Here again, materialism diverges sharply from common sense. Where materialism *is* closer to commonsense beliefs is in the assumption of an unperceived physical reality, which idealism denies.

Materialism has often been perceived by its opponents as a threat to religious and humanistic values and as alienating us from our direct experience of the world. This negative perception of materialism and the desire to counteract it has provided the main springboard for the development of modern idealism. The great strength of materialism, on the other hand, is its alliance with science. Scientists appear to have explained almost everything in materialistic terms, everything in fact but the essence of life and thought, and even here they claim to be getting closer and closer. Why cling to the archaic view that there exists something forever out of reach of a materialist explanation, say the materialists; it is simply a matter of time before everything will be explained in purely physical terms. Thus materialists see themselves as visionaries optimistically anticipating the future, and they see idealists as reactionaries anxiously clinging to an antiquated past. The materialist's advice to the idealist is to "get with it."

More recent scientific developments, especially in relativity and quantum theory, have softened the clash between idealists and materialists. Today when scientists speak of matter, it is less palpably hard, solid, and unchanging, and the deterministic model of the world has given way to one governed more by chance and statistical probability. Still, the debate is far from over. And we must now examine that debate for ourselves.

Ancient Materialism: Atomism

The most persistent form of materialism is known as atomism. This is the metaphysical view that reality consists of nothing but atoms and empty space. Atoms are defined as the smallest units of matter which cannot themselves be further divided or destroyed. Like Plato's Ideas, they are therefore eternal and unchanging. They can move about through the empty space, and, by joining and breaking apart from other atoms, they are responsible for all the physical objects and their properties which we find in everyday experience. When the atoms are joined together and densely packed they create the appearance of things like tables and chairs, hard and solid objects. When they are more loosely packed, the conglomerate appears to us as a liquid, and when further dispersed, they are perceived by us as gases. As atoms are constantly being emitted from objects, their interaction with our bodies, especially our sense organs, produce what we perceive as sense qualities, smells, colors, sounds, etc.

Atomism is one of the earliest philosophical and scientific theories, appearing first among the presocratic Greeks, Leucippus and Democritus, but so little remains of their writings that we know little of the details of this early form of atomism. Atomism next appears among the philosophers who followed Plato and Aristotle, especially in the work of Epicurus and his Roman follower, Lucretius. Epicurus (born 342 B.C.E.) is best known as a hedonist from whom the familiar term *epicureanism* derives. But as often happens, different branches of philosophy are closely interwoven in a particular philosophical system, with especially close links between metaphysical, epistemological, moral, and religious positions. It is easy to see how this might occur. In general, materialism will be conducive to the view that all knowledge comes from sense experience. For a materialist, a human being is nothing more than a complex material machine. Therefore, his explanation of knowledge will tend to be in terms of our bodily interaction with the physical world, that is, sense experience in which my body physically interacts with physical stimuli bombarding me from surrounding physical objects, air vibrations striking the ear, light waves hitting the eye, and so on. Similarly, with its stress on the body, materialists will tend to emphasize physical pleasure as the good life when they discuss ethics and morality. And in addressing religious concerns, the materialist will tend to deny the existence of immaterial human souls or gods.

And so it is with Epicurus. Knowledge comes from sense impressions, the "images," "effluences," or "idols" he speaks of; good is to be understood in terms of pleasure (though here it must be said that Epicurus was no voluptuary and was very refined in his own tastes). Unlike Plato and Aristotle, who started schools dedicated to the discovery and dissemination of pure knowledge for its own sake, much like our modern day universities, Epicurus' school, which lasted long after his death, was primarily concerned with establishing a personally satisfying way of life for the individual, a kind of substitute for religion.

Materialism and Freedom

Although Epicurus follows the usual trend of materialists regarding the good life and how we come to know things, he departs in some very interesting ways from the usual pattern when it comes to the implications of materialism for religion and for the question of human freedom. In general, as we have seen, materialism will tend to have negative conclusions regarding religion. Since God, gods, and the human soul are usually considered immaterial objects, the materialist cannot accept them as such, and since the existence of God, gods, and the soul are usually thought to be of comfort to human beings, this materialist conclusion is generally a pessimistic one. But Epicurus and his follower, Lucretius, argue that the denial of an immaterial soul which outlives the body in some nonmaterial afterlife is *good* news rather than bad, since, according to them, the greatest cause of human suffering is our fear of the terrors of life after death, like our own "hellfire and damnation." Interestingly, Epicurus and Lucretius do not deny the existence of gods or the soul but only their immateriality. We have a soul, they say, but it is a material object made up of atoms, as are the gods. Nor should we worry very much about the gods even during our lifetimes, according to the Atomists, since the course of natural events is largely controlled by natural, material forces over which the gods are virtually powerless.

Finally, unlike most materialists who are strict determinists, Epicurus and Lucretius argue for an element of human freedom, choice, spontaneity, and accident in the world generally. This is introduced in the following reading, from a letter Epicurus wrote to Herodotus, in the curious discussion of the occasional "swerving" of the atoms. Generally all an atomist thinks he needs to explain everything in the world is physical atoms moving in straight lines through empty space. Everything else that happens in our world is explained in terms of the collisions of atoms which result in their joining together and breaking apart again. Since the atoms are described as moving in a completely mechanical fashion, like billiard balls on a pool table, everything that happens is caused by previous events; that ball moved because it was hit by this one which in turn was struck by a cue stick, and so on, in a completely deterministic fashion which rules out the possibility of choice or freedom of action. Everything I do is caused by the previous motions of atoms going back millions of years, and there is nothing I can now do about it. I may *imagine* I am free to close this book and turn on the TV if I choose, and I may think that if I decide not to watch TV that I nonetheless *could* have done so had I chosen to. But this is merely an illusion.

Epicurus is unusual in trying to reconcile materialistic atomism with human freedom. He also needs the "swerve" to explain how the collisions between the atoms get started. He postulates that at first the atoms are raining down in straight parallel lines and never colliding with one another. But then, he says, there are occasional, spontaneous, unexplainable "swervings" which cause collisions, which, in turn, cause others, and so on. This is obviously a very weak explanation, and indicates more than anything else problems within Epicurus' system. As often happens in any philosophical system, there are things which the philosopher wants to say which can't be said or are difficult to say within the system, and then he is tempted to introduce additional ad hoc elements which do nothing but allow him to say those things but don't really fit in with the rest of the system. So, in this case, in a materialistic, mechanistic account, there is really no place for such spontaneous movement. To the extent that such things do occur, they indicate the *inadequacy* of a materialistic account of the world.

The Greek Atomists believed that circular motion of the atoms was what gave rise to a cosmos, a theory for which the Whirlpool Galaxy would have given support had they been able to see it. Courtesy of Hansen Planetarium Publications, Salt Lake City, Utah.

Materialism and Mental Phenomena

Another obvious problem for Epicurus, as for most materialists, is how to explain mental phenomena, especially how we come to have ideas of things and to think about them and describe them linguistically. Sensations, ideas, the meanings of words—these are the things which it is difficult for a materialist to explain. Epicurus holds that tiny, thin images or likenesses of objects are constantly being emitted by those objects, and perception occurs when some of these happen to enter the eye. But there are many problems with such a view. First, there is no evidence that such images *are* thrown off by objects. Certainly we cannot *see* them as they are being emitted. To account for this, Epicurus postulates that the images move very fast just as the reason given why we can't *see* atoms is that they are very small, but this seems very ad hoc. Secondly, if they are made of atoms, which they must be, how do they penetrate the eye, which is also made of atoms? We would expect some resistance, some collisions. To explain away this discrepancy, Epicurus argues that the images are so finely textured they can penetrate solid objects, which again sounds like an ad hoc explanation. Finally, even if the images or "idols" did enter the eye, how do we *see* them? When a photograph is put in front of a fence post, does perception take place? A picture of an object is not the same as *seeing* that picture, and it would seem to be just as difficult to explain how the picture is seen as to explain how the object is seen (which the picture has been introduced to explain!).

In other ways, however, Epicurus seems very modern and convincing, anticipating recent views. He describes error, much like Descartes and others nearly two thousand years later, as going beyond what is actually given in sensation (I see a person in a crowd but mistakenly judge that she is my friend). He distinguished between what later became known as primary and secondary qualities. Primary qualities are those properties of objects which exist in the objects as we perceive them (the materialistic properties of the hardness and weight of the atoms themselves). Secondary qualities are those properties of things which do not exist in objects as we suppose them to be (red is not a property of physical objects as it seems to be, but arises only in the mind, having been caused by other, primary properties of objects).

Finally, Epicurus anticipates the modern mind-body problem when he remarks that it is nonsense to talk about an incorporeal soul without sensations. Epicurus is not merely claiming that immaterial souls do not exist; he is saying, much like the contemporary philosopher, Antony Flew, that it makes no sense to even imagine an immaterial soul. Why? According to Epicurus (and Flew), the only way we can really think of our minds or souls is in terms of their interaction with our bodies (feeling cold, receiving sensations of color, sound, and so on). An immaterial soul, which, by definition, can have no contact or interaction with a body, is therefore inconceivable.

Epicurus (341–270 B.C.E.) Born on the island of Samos, Epicurus founded a philosophical community in Athens that was open to all and stressed the atomistic physics of Democritus. The belief that all reality was matter led him to conclude that pleasure is the goal of life. This hedonistic view was tempered by rational evaluation of pleasures and led to the conclusion that intellectual pleasures are superior to physical ones. Epicureans held that the soul has no independent reality apart from the body and does not survive its death. Courtesy of Bettmann Archive.

Epicurus: First Principle of Materialism

Now . . . we must consider the phenomena that cannot be perceived by the senses. The first principle is that nothing can be created from the nonexistent; for otherwise any thing would be formed from any thing without the need of seed. If all that disappears were destroyed into the nonexistent, all matter would be destroyed, since that into which it would be dissolved has no existence. Truly this universe has always been such as it now is, and so it shall always be; for there is nothing into which it can change, and there is nothing outside the universe that can enter into it and bring about a change.

Moreover, the universe consists of material bodies and void. That the bodies exist is made clear to all by sensation itself, on which reason must base its judgment in regard to what is imperceptible, as I have said above. If that which we call "void" and "space" and "the untouchable" did not exist, the particles of matter would have no place in which to exist or through which to move, as it is clear they do move.

In addition to these two, there is nothing that we can grasp in the mind, either through concepts or through analogy with concepts, that has real existence and is not referred to merely as a property or an accident of material things or of the void.

Of material things, some are compounds, others are the simple particles from which the compounds are formed. The particles are indivisible and unchangeable, as is necessary if all is not to be dissolved to nothing, but something strong is to remain after the dissolution of the compounds, something solid, which cannot be destroyed in any way. Therefore, it is necessary that the first beginnings be indivisible particles of matter.

Moreover, the universe as a whole is infinite, for whatever is limited has an outermost edge to limit it, and such an edge is defined by something beyond. Since the universe does not have an edge, it has no limit; and since it lacks a limit, it is infinite and unbounded. Moreover, the universe is infinite both in the number of its atoms and in the extent of its void. If, on the one hand, the void were infinite and matter finite, the atoms would not remain anywhere but would be carried away and scattered through the infinite void, since there would be no atoms from without to support them and hold them together by striking them. If, on the other hand, the void were finite, there would not be room in it for an infinite number of atoms.

In addition, the indivisible solid particles of matter, from which composite bodies are formed and into which such bodies are dissolved, exist in so many different shapes that the mind cannot grasp their number; for it would not be possible for visible objects to exhibit such great variation in form and quality if they were made by repeated use of atoms of conceivable variety. The number of atoms of each shape is infinite, but the number of varieties cannot be infinite, only inconceivably great.

The atoms move without interruption through all time. Some of them fall in a straight line, some swerve from their courses, and others move back and forth

From: Epicurus, "Letter to Herodotus in *Letters, Principal Doctrines and Vatican Sayings.* Translated by Russel M. Geer. The Library of Liberal Arts. Used by permission of Prentice Hall.

as the result of collisions. These last make up the objects that our senses recognize. Some of those that move in this way after collisions separate far from each other; the others maintain a vibrating motion, either closely entangled with each other or confined by other atoms that have become entangled. There are two reasons for this continued vibration. The nature of the void that separates each of the atoms from the next permits it, for the void is not able to offer any resistance; and the elasticity that is characteristic of the atoms causes them to rebound after each collision. The degree of entanglement of the atoms determines the extent of the recoil from the collisions. These motions had no beginning, for the atoms and the void have always existed.

If all these things are remembered, a statement as brief as this provides a sufficient outline for our understanding of the nature of that which exists.

Finally, the number of worlds, some like ours and some unlike, is also infinite. For the atoms are infinite in number, as has been shown above, and they move through the greatest distances. The atoms suited for the creation and maintenance of a world have not been used up in the formation of a single world or of a limited number of them, whether like our world or different from it. There is nothing therefore that will stand in the way of there being an infinite number of worlds.

Moreover, there are images of the same shape as the solid bodies from which they come but in thinness far surpassing anything that the senses can perceive. It is not impossible that emanations of this sort are formed in the air that surrounds a body, that there are thin, hollow films, and that the particles composing them retain as they flow from the solid object the same position and relative order that they had while on its surface. Such images we call "idols."

Nothing in nature as we see it prevents our believing that the idols are of a texture unsurpassed in fineness. For this reason, their velocity is also unsurpassed, since they always find a proper passage, and since moreover their course is retarded by few if any collisions, while a body made up of an inconceivably large number of atoms suffers many collisions as soon as it begins to move.

Moreover, there is nothing to prevent our believing that the creation of idols is as swift as thought. They flow from the surfaces of a body in a constant stream, but this is not made evident by any decrease in the size of the body since other atoms are flooding in. For a long time the idols keep their atoms in the same relative position and order that they occupied on the surface of the solid, although sometimes they combine in the air . . .

We must suppose that we see or think of the outer form of a thing when something comes to us from its surface . . .

When, by the purposeful use of our mind or of our organs or sense, we receive a mental picture of the shape of an object or of its concomitant qualities, this picture is true, since it is created by the continuous impact of the idols or by an impression left by one of them. Whatever is false and erroneous is due to what opinion adds (to an image that is waiting) to be confirmed, or at least not to be contradicted, by further evidence of the senses, and which then fails to be so confirmed (or is contradicted). The mental pictures that we receive in the images that either come to our minds in sleep or are formed by the purposeful use of the mind or of the other instruments of judgment would not have such similarity to those things that exist and that we call true if there were not some such material effluence actually coming to us from the objects, and the errors would not occur if we did not permit in ourselves some other activity similar (to the purposeful

Here in the colonnaded porch, or stoa, in Athens, the Epicureans argued with the Stoics about the nature of reality. The Stoics took their name from the fact that they frequented the stoa, which has been reconstructed in Athens using some ancient materials. Photo by David Stewart.

apprehension of mental images) but yet different. From this other activity error results if its conclusions are not confirmed by further evidence or are contradicted, but truth if they are so confirmed or are not contradicted . . .

Moreover, we hear when a kind of stream is carried *to* our ears from a person who speaks or from an object that makes a sound or noise or in any way whatever arouses in us the sense of hearing . . .

We must also suppose that, like sounds, smells could not produce any sensation if there were not carried from the object certain particles of a nature proper to stir the organ of this sense. Some of these are disorderly and unpleasant; some are gentle and agreeable.

We must suppose that the atoms possess none of the qualities of visible things except shape, mass, and size, and whatever is a necessary concomitant of shape. For every quality changes, but the atoms do not change in any way, since in the dissolution of composite things something hard and indestructible must survive that will make changes possible; not changes into nothingness and from nothingness, but changes brought about by alterations in the positions of some atoms and by the addition or removal of some. It is necessary that the particles that alter their positions and come and go be indestructible, not sharing in the nature of the visible things that are changed, but having their own peculiar shapes and masses, for this much must be unalterable. Even among sensible things, we see that those that are altered by the loss of matter on all sides still retain shape, but the other qualities do not survive in the changing object, as shape survives, but are removed from the whole body. These properties that remain are enough to cause the differences in composite things, since it is necessary that something survive and be not utterly destroyed.

Next, we cannot suppose that in a finite body the parts, no matter how small, are infinite in number. Therefore, not only must we exclude infinite division into smaller and smaller parts lest we make everything weak, and in our conception of the parts that compose a whole be compelled to make them less and less, finally reducing real things to nothingness, but also in dealing with finite things we must not accept as possible an infinite progression to parts each smaller than the last. For if once you say that in a finite thing there are parts infinite in number even if of the least possible size, you cannot think how this can be. For how can a thing containing infinite parts be finite in size? It is clear that the infinite parts are each of some size, and however small they may be, the whole must be infinite in magnitude . . .

Moreover, it is necessary that the atoms possess equal velocity whenever they are moving through the void and nothing collides with them. For heavy bodies will not be carried more quickly than small, light ones when nothing at all opposes them, nor do the small bodies, because they all find suitable passages, excel the large ones, provided the latter are not obstructed. This is equally true of the atoms' motions upwards or to the side because of collisions and of their downward motion because of their own weight. The atom will traverse space with the speed of thought as long as the motion caused in either of these ways maintains itself, that is, until the atom is deflected either by some external force or by its own weight which counteracts the force of the earlier collision. Moreover, since the motion through the void takes place without any interference from colliding particles, any conceivable distance is completed in an inconceivably brief time. For it is the occurrence or nonoccurrence of collisions that gives the appearance of slow or rapid motion . . .

Next, referring to the sensations and the feelings as the most certain foundation for belief, we must see that, in general terms, the soul is a finely divided, material thing, scattered through the whole aggregation of atoms that make up the body, most similar to breath with a certain admixture of heat, in some ways resembling the one, in some ways the other. But there is also a part of the soul that goes beyond even these two in fineness, and for this reason it is more ready to share in the feelings of the body. All this is made evident to us by the powers of the soul, that is, by its feelings, its rapidity of action, its rational faculties, and its possession of those things whose loss brings death to us.

Next, we must conclude that the primary cause of sensation in the soul, yet it would not have acquired sensation if it had not been in some way enclosed by the rest of the body. But the rest of the body, having given the soul the proper setting for experiencing sensation, has itself also gained from the soul a certain share in this capacity. Yet it does not fully share with the soul, and for this reason when the soul departs, the body no longer experiences sensation . . . For this reason, sensation is never lost while the soul remains, even though other parts of the body have been destroyed. Indeed, even if a portion of the soul is lost with the loss in whole or in part of that portion of the body that enclosed it, if any part at all of the soul survives, it will still experience sensation . . . However, if the whole body is destroyed, the soul is scattered and no longer enjoys the same powers and motions, and as a result, it no longer possesses sensation. Whenever that in which the soul has existed is no longer able to confine and hold it in, we cannot think of the soul as still enjoying sensation, since it would no longer be within its proper system and would no longer have the use of the appropriate motions.

Moreover, we must clearly observe this also, that the word "incorporeal" in its common use is applied only to that which we can think of as existing by itself. Now there is no incorporeal thing that we can think of as existing by itself except the void. The void can neither act nor be acted upon; it only gives to corporeal things a space through which to move. Therefore, those who say that the soul is incorporeal are talking nonsense; for in that case the soul would be unable to act or be acted upon, and we clearly see that the soul is capable of both . . .

In the next place, shapes, colors, sizes, mass, and all other things that are spoken of as belonging to a body must be thought of as properties either of bodies in general or of bodies that are perceptible and are recognized by our perception of these properties. These properties are not to be regarded as having existence by themselves, for we cannot think of them apart from things of which they are properties, nor are they wholly without existence. They are not some kind of immaterial thing attached to the body, not are they parts of the body, but from all of them together the body as a whole receives its permanent character . . .

In addition to what we have said, it is necessary to believe that the worlds and every limited complex that has a continuous similarity to the visible world have been formed from the infinite, each of them, greater and smaller, separating out from its own whirling mass. We must suppose also that these will all be dissolved again, some more quickly and some more slowly, some afflicted by one calamity and others by another.

One must not suppose that because of necessity worlds in a single pattern (were created, or in every possible pattern . . . Moreover, we may believe that in all the worlds there are animals, plants, and the other things we see; for no one can show that the seeds from which grow animals, plants, and the other things we see might or might not have been included in one particular world and that in another kind of world this was impossible.

Moreover, we may assume that by the conditions that surround them, men were taught or forced by instinct to do many things of many kinds, but reason later elaborated on what had been begun by instinct and introduced new inventions. In some fields, great progress was made, in others, less; and in some times and ages reason had more success in freeing men from their fears of the powers above than in others.

So too we may suppose that in the beginning words did not receive meaning by design. The natural characters of men who underwent different experiences and received different impressions according to their tribes, caused them to emit air from their lips formed in harmony with each of the experiences and impressions, the men of each tribe different in their own separate ways as the tribes differed because of their differing environments. But later in each race, by common agreement, men assigned particular meanings to particular sounds so that what they said to each other might be less ambiguous and the meaning be more quickly made clear. When men who had known them introduced certain things not previously seen, they assigned names to them, sometimes being forced instinctively to utter the word, but someone making their meaning clear by logically selecting the sound in accordance with the general usage.

Now as to celestial phenomena, we must believe that these motions, periods, eclipses, risings, settings, and the like do not take place because there is some divinity in charge of them, who so arranges them in order and will maintain them in that order, and who at the same time enjoys both perfect happiness and immortality; for activity and anxiety, anger and kindness are not in harmony with blessedness, but are found along with weakness, fear, and dependence on one's neighbors. We must also avoid the belief that masses of concentrated fire have attained a state of divine blessedness and undertaken these motions of their own free will. In all the terms with which we set forth our conceptions of such blessedness, we must preserve due reverence lest from irreverent words there grow opinions that deny this majesty. If we fail, this contradiction will cause the greatest confusion in our souls. Therefore we must believe that, at the time of the first formation of these bodies at the creation of the world, the law of their motions was fully ordained . . .

In addition to these general matters, we must observe this also, that there are three things that account for the major disturbances in men's minds. First, they assume that the celestial bodies are blessed and eternal yet have impulses, actions, and purposes quite inconsistent with divinity. Next, they anticipate and foresee eternal suffering as depicted in the myths, or even fear the very lack of consciousness that comes with death as if this could be of concern to them. Finally they suffer all this, not as a result of reasonable conjecture, but through some sort of unreasoning imagination; and since in imagination they set no limit to suffering, they are beset by turmoil as great as if there were a reasonable basis for their dread, or even greater. But it is peace of mind to have the essential principles of the whole system of belief. We must therefore turn our minds to immediate feelings and sensations—in matters of general concern to the common feelings and to every immediate evidence from each of the means of judgment. If we heed these, we shall rightly track down the sources of disturbance and fear, and when we have learned the causes of celestial phenomena and of the other occasional happenings, we shall be free from what other men most dread.

Materialism and the New Science

After the Greek and Roman period, materialism did not reappear again until its incorporation in the rise of modern science in the sixteenth century. The conception of atomism during this period of the "new science" was virtually the same as it was for the ancient philosopher-scientists, with this important exception: What the Greeks and Romans had merely speculated about, the modern physicists, Galileo, Kepler, and others, tried to support with hard, empirical evidence.

Crucial to materialistic atomism during its renaissance in the sixteenth and seventeenth centuries was its apparent clash with Christianity, and it was to soften that clash that Pierre Gassendi (1592–1655), a contemporary of Descartes, devoted much of his writing. After the fall of the Roman Empire in the fourth century C.E., philosophy was almost forgotten in Europe until it was reintroduced through Muslim Arabic translations of Plato, Aristotle, and other Greek and Roman writers uncovered during the Muslim conquest of much of the Mideastern world. At first the church was unsure whether to accept such pagan learning,

especially as it appeared to contradict certain parts of holy scriptures contained in the Bible. Most Greek and Roman philosophers held, for example, that the physical world had not been created from scratch at some point in time, but that creation had rather been a matter of ordering and rearranging preexistent physical material. And this directly contradicted the biblical account of God's creation of the world from nothing. The Muslims finally decided that it was unwise to try to mix religion with the newly discovered Greek and Roman philosophy and science and so rejected it in the end. But the Christians worked out a different formula by which those parts of ancient, preChristian learning which contradicted church teaching could be rejected while those parts which did not directly contradict Christian doctrine could be retained.

In general terms, this accommodation of Greek philosophy-science with Christianity had been worked out by the end of the thirteenth century. But the rise of modern science raised some of the same issues all over again, and Gassendi was one of those who tried to continue the reconciliation of Greek thought with Judeo-Christian traditions. As we will see in the section on the Philosophy of Religion (Part 6), this reconciliation is an ongoing affair, continuing up to the present day.

≡ Reconciling Materialism and Religion

Insofar as ancient materialists, like Epicurus, held that the atoms were eternal, they must be refuted and corrected in the light of more recent biblical knowledge. But in correcting their limited insights, Gassendi argued that we do not have to reject everything they had to say about atoms. All we need to add is that in creating the world from nothing, God created the atoms. We must also correct the Greek view that atoms move by themselves, since this too seems to detract from

---

God and Materialism

There is nothing to prevent us from defending the opinion which decides that the matter of the world and all the things contained in it is made up of atoms, provided that we repudiate whatever falsehood is mixed in with it. Therefore, in order to recommend the theory, we declare first that the idea that atoms are eternal and uncreated is to be rejected and also the idea that they are infinite in number and occur in any sort of shape; once this is done, it can be admitted that atoms are the primary form of matter, which God created.

Next we declare that the idea that atoms have impetus, or the power to move themselves inherent in their nature, is to be rejected. It may then be admitted that atoms are mobile and active from the power of moving and acting which God instilled in them at their very creation, and which functions with his assent, for he compels all things just as he conserves all things.

Pierre Gassendi

God's active role in the creation. So, we must also add that material bodies such as atoms have no inherent principle of motion; they are essentially lifeless and can only be made to move by the agency of some immaterial soul or spirit, such as God. Thus, in creating the world, God not only creates the atoms, He also sets them in motion. But thereafter the future history of each atom is determined naturalistically, simply by the physical principles involved in its speed, mass, angle of collision, shape, and so on, just as we found in Epicurus. Once God has created the atoms and set them in motion, God can then sit back and relax and let the rest take care of itself automatically. This is a position known later as Deism, but, as you can see, its reconciliation with Christianity preserves only a part of religious thinking. In Deism the existence of God and his creation of the world is preserved, but lost is the biblical account of God's ongoing concern to intervene in the world. God would not be very important in a Deist's day-to-day life. You would not pray to God or ask for anything, since, having created the world, God has no ongoing concern with the world.

Gassendi's attempt to reconcile materialism with Christian faith is interesting, since materialism has historically been used to undercut the claims of those who believe in an immaterial God. One could argue that Gassendi was not really a materialist, since he believed that at least one immaterial soul or spirit (God) exists. Perhaps he should be classified more as a dualist. But Gassendi claimed to be a materialist and argued that this metaphysical position was not opposed to the Christian faith. Gassendi was also a French Catholic priest who never renounced his Christian commitments.

Today we may feel that neither materialism nor idealism leads inevitably to belief in God. This is due in part to the fact that we no longer think of matter as little bits of *"stuff"* floating through the void, the view of materialism shared by Epicurus and by Gassendi. Our own views of physical reality have been shaped by the breakthroughs in physics in our own century that force on us the realization that matter can be transformed into energy and that the constituent parts of atoms are units of energy. Once again we see that scientific knowledge does not answer questions of ultimate reality and why such questions are fundamentally not physical, but metaphysical ones.

Questions for Discussion

1. The ancient materialists agreed that materialism removes the fear of death. For if *all* consciousness ceases when the body ceases to function, then there is nothing to fear *after* death. Do you agree that a materialistic view makes death less fearsome? Why or why not?

2. Does the view that the mind is nothing but a highly complex mechanism operating according to mechanical law pose any threat to the independence and rationality of thought? Explain.

3. Do you think that a materialistic metaphysics is supported or threatened by contemporary views of natural science? Give reasons to support your answer.

4. Some materialists claim that if our knowledge were unlimited, all future events could be predicted. What evidence is there for this view? Against it?

5. Do you find materialism to be a convincing viewpoint? Why or why not?

CHAPTER 10

Idealism

We have just seen various responses to the pessimistic consequences of materialism, especially for moral, humanistic, and religious values. For Bishop George Berkeley the only way round these difficulties of materialism was to reject it completely in favor of its opposite, idealism.

Berkeley's Subjective Idealism

There are two kinds of idealism in the modern period, subjective idealism and absolute idealism. Subjective idealism, represented in the readings by George Berkeley, is the view that only minds and their thoughts and feelings are real. Absolute idealism developed out of subjective idealism in the nineteenth century, especially from the philosophy of Hegel, expanding the mental substance of Berkeley to include the whole world, and unifying the individual minds of subjective idealism into a single all-encompassing world soul or mind. Where the subjective idealist sees the world as a collection of minds and their ideas, the absolute idealist sees everything in the world as a part of one all-embracing universal mind.

George Berkeley was an Irish clergyman who tried to undo the dangers he perceived in the growing scientific materialism of his day, a materialism first articulated in Britain by Thomas Hobbes and later popularized in the scientific theories of Sir Isaac Newton. Berkeley's main argument is that all we know immediately are our own ideas, and since we have no direct experience of any underlying material substrate, there is no reason to believe such a thing actually exists. The only reason for introducing the fiction of an unperceived underlying matter, Berkeley

GEORGE BERKELEY (1685–1753): Irish philosopher and Anglican Bishop of Cloyne. Believing that accepting the existence of matter led to atheism, Berkeley argued for his idealistic metaphysics principally in two works: A Treatise Concerning the Principles of Human Knowledge *and* Three Dialogues Between Hylas and Philonous. Courtesy of the Library of Congress.

thought, was to provide some unifying foundation for the many different properties of physical objects. As we saw earlier in our discussion of Kant and the Copernican revolution, it seems useful, if not absolutely necessary, to group the redness, tartness, roundness, shininess of an object such as a tomato into a single composite entity, the tomato. But what holds these different properties together? The materialist's answer is that they all inhere in a material "stuff" or substrate. But Berkeley argues that this is unnecessary, since a better alternative is available. *I* see the redness, *I* taste the tartness, *I* feel the roundness, hence these sensations are brought together and integrated within my *mind.* As John Locke, an English philosopher, had argued a generation earlier, the mind itself associates or combines the "simple" ideas of redness, tartness, and so on into the "complex" idea of a tomato. Since Berkeley analyzes the perception of any property as the sensing of sensations, he finds the idea of properties (i.e., sensations) inhering in an unperceived, unperceiving material substance not only unverifiable, but downright contradictory. If properties, such as redness, are sensations, then it makes no more sense to say that there are sensations which are not being perceived than it would to speak of pains which are not felt by anyone.

In Chapter 7 we described briefly the process of philosophical analysis of key concepts in terms of necessary and sufficient conditions. One of Berkeley's major problems is that he confuses the necessary conditions for knowledge with its sufficient conditions.

According to Berkeley's analysis, seeing an object such as a tomato *is the same* as having sensations of a certain sort. But if we allow him to make this identification, then we do indeed seem to be committed to idealism. It would seem to follow that if all our knowledge and perception of the world is no more than having sensations (which are by definition mind-dependent), then everything in the world which we know and perceive is mind-dependent. And so we arrive at idealism. Let us take a closer look at Berkeley's argument.

The reading from Berkeley begins with the statement: "The objects of human knowledge . . . are . . . ideas." What kinds of things can we know and perceive? Common sense would answer: physical objects, people, mathematical laws, and so on. But Berkeley says we can know *only* ideas. Why? Berkeley's answer is that when we see a tomato, which is a physical object, we are only having sensations of redness, roundness, and so forth. Since sensations are ideas which exist only in the mind, then it follows that what we see is only an idea existing, as ideas must, in the mind. But there is an obvious problem here. While it may be true that in seeing a tomato we have certain sensations and indeed that without these sensations we could not see the tomato, it does not follow from this that seeing a tomato *is the same thing* as having sensations. Having sensations is a *necessary* condition for our knowledge of the world, but it is not a *sufficient* condition. If *seeing an object* and *having sensations* are not identical, then it does not follow that what I see (the objects of perception) are only ideas as Berkeley says.

Additional Problems in Berkeley's view

Berkeley faces two further problems in his metaphysical scheme: (1) the problem we would expect any idealist to have to confront: namely how to account for our ordinary belief in physical objects, and (2) the more unexpected and surprising problem of how to account for our knowledge of our own minds. No philosopher wants to appear to directly contradict common sense, and Berkeley tries hard to show that there is nothing in the commonsense view of physical objects which is denied by him. When the man on the street says that there is a tomato, does he mean anything more than that he sees it, tastes it (or could taste and feel it)? Berkeley thinks not, but his critics have always insisted that there *is* something more to the commonsense belief which Berkeley denies. But what is this missing ingredient? Perhaps it is what Samuel Johnson was getting at when he kicked the stone—the stubborn, if inarticulate, belief that there is an unperceived, unperceiving physical reality which exists completely independently of anyone's mind. Surely, we feel, objects exist when they are not being perceived. As we have already indicated, Berkeley handles this difficulty by recourse to the ever-watchful mind of God.

The relation in Berkeley's philosophy between the mind of God and the reality of the physical world is well put in the following limerick, attributed to Ronald Knox.

> There was a young man who said, God
> Must think it exceedingly odd
>   If he finds that this tree
>   Continues to be
> When there's no one about in the
> Quad.

REPLY

Dear Sir:
　　Your astonishment's odd:
I am always about in the Quad.
　　And that's why the tree
　　Will continue to be,
Since observed by

　　　　　　　　Yours
　　　　　　　　faithfully,
　　　　　　　　GOD.

Although Berkeley is an idealist he also has great difficulty explaining how we know our own minds. All we know, he says, are ideas, but the underlying mental substance which *has* these ideas cannot be directly experienced, and so cannot itself be an idea. Thus, it should follow that we cannot know the underlying mental substance of the mind. This is precisely the kind of argument Berkeley uses against the belief in *material* substance. As David Hume later said of Berkeley, the argument works equally well against mental substance as it does against physical substance (so Hume's metaphysical system consists solely of ideas with no underlying substance of any kind!). Berkeley tries to get around this difficulty by arguing that while we do not have an *idea* of mind, we do have a "notion" of it. He must have felt a little sheepish when he said that.

Idealistic philosophy was no mere eighteenth-century intellectual curiosity; it reigned virtually supreme in European universities until the beginning of the twentieth century, when it was replaced by a philosophy less concerned with traditional metaphysical questions than with the analytical skills philosophy could bring to bear on the problems that arose out of the work of natural science.

George Berkeley, Three Dialogues Between Hylas and Philonous
In Opposition to Skeptics and Atheists

The First Dialogue

Hyl.　　You were represented in last night's conversation as one who maintained the most extravagant opinion that ever entered into the mind of man, to wit, that there is no such thing as *material substance* in the world.

Phil.　　That there is no such thing as what philosophers call "material substance," I am seriously persuaded, but if I were made to see anything absurd or skeptical in this, I should then have the same reason to renounce this that I imagine I have now to reject the contrary opinion.

Hyl. What! can anything be more fantastical, more repugnant to common sense or a more manifest piece of skepticism than to believe there is no such thing as matter?

Phil. Softly, good Hylas. What if it should prove that you, who hold there is, are, by virtue of that opinion, a greater skeptic and maintain more paradoxes and repugnancies to common sense than I who believe no such thing?

Hyl. You may as soon persuade me the part is greater than the whole, as that, in order to avoid absurdity and skepticism, I should ever be obliged to give up my opinion in this point.

Phil. Well, then, are you content to admit that opinion for true which, upon examination, shall appear most agreeable to common sense and remote from skepticism?

Hyl. With all my heart. Since you are for raising disputes about the plainest things in nature, I am content for once to hear what you have to say.

Phil. Pray Hylas? What do you mean by a "skeptic? . . . "

Hyl. I mean what all men mean, one that doubts of everything . . . but I should have added: or who denies the reality and truth of things.

Phil. What things? Do you mean the principles and theorems of sciences? But these you know are universal intellectual notions, and consequently independent of matter; the denial therefore of this does not imply the denying them.

Hyl. I grant it. But are there no other things? What think you of distrusting the senses, of denying the real existence of sensible things, or pretending to know nothing of them. Is not this sufficient to denominate a man a skeptic?

Phil. Shall we therefore examine which of us it is that denies the reality of sensible things or professes the greatest ignorance of them, since, if I take you rightly, he is to be esteemed the greatest skeptic?

Hyl. That is what I desire.

Phil. What mean you by "sensible things?"

Hyl. Those things which are perceived by the senses. Can you imagine that I mean anything else?

Phil. Pardon me, Hylas, if I am desirous clearly to apprehend your notions, since this may much shorten our inquiry. Suffer me then to ask you this further question. Are those things only perceived by the senses which are perceived immediately? Or may those things properly be said to be "sensible" which are perceived mediately, or not without the intervention of others?

Hyl. I do not sufficiently understand you.

Phil. In reading a book, what I immediately perceive are the letters, but mediately, or by means of these, are suggested to my mind the notions of God, virtue, truth, etc. Now, that the letters are truly sensible things, or perceived by sense, there is no doubt, but I would know whether you take the things suggested by them to be so too.

Hyl.   No, certainly, it was absurd to think God or virtue sensible things, though they may be signified and suggested to the mind by sensible marks with which they have an arbitrary connection.

Phil.   It seems then, that by "sensible things" you mean those only which can be perceived immediately by sense.

Hyl.   Right.

Phil.   Does it not follow from this that, though I see one part of the sky red, and another blue, and that my reason does thence evidently conclude there must be some cause of that diversity of colors, yet that cause cannot be said to be a sensible thing or perceived by the sense of seeing?

Hyl.   It does.

Phil.   In like manner, though I hear a variety of sounds, yet I cannot be said to hear the causes of those sounds.

Hyl.   You cannot.

Phil.   And when by my touch I perceive a thing to be hot and heavy, I cannot say, with any truth or propriety, that I feel the cause of its heat or weight.

Hyl.   To prevent any more questions of this kind, I tell you once for all that by "sensible things" I mean those only which are perceived by sense, and that in truth the senses perceive nothing which they do not perceive immediately, for they make no inferences: The deducing therefore of causes or occasions from effects and appearances, which alone are perceived by sense, entirely relates to reason.

Phil.   This point then is agreed between us—that sensible things are those only which are immediately perceived by sense. You will further inform me whether we immediately perceive by sight anything besides light and colors and figures; or by hearing, anything but sounds; by the palate anything besides tastes; by the smell, besides odors; or by the touch more than tangible qualities.

Hyl.   We do not.

Phil.   It seems, therefore, that if you take away all sensible qualities, there remains nothing sensible?

Hyl.   I grant it.

Phil.   Sensible things therefore are nothing else but so many sensible qualities or combinations of sensible qualities?

Hyl.   Nothing else.

Phil.   Heat is then a sensible thing?

Hyl.   Certainly.

Phil.   Does the reality of sensible things consist in being perceived, or is it something distinct from their being perceived, and that bears no relation to the mind?

Hyl.   To exist is one thing, and to be perceived is another.

Phil.   I speak with regard to sensible things only, and of these I ask, whether by their real existence you mean a subsistence exterior to the mind and distinct from their being perceived?

Hyl.   I mean a real absolute being, distinct from and without any relation to their being perceived.

Phil.   Heat therefore, if it be allowed a real being, must exist without the mind?

Hyl.   It must.

Phil.   Tell me, Hylas, is this real existence equally compatible to *all* degrees of heat, which we perceive, or is there any reason why we should attribute it to some and deny it to others? And if there be, pray let me know that reason.

Hyl.   Whatever degree of heat we perceive by sense, we may be sure the same exists in the object that occasions it.

Phil.   What! the greatest as well as the least?

Hyl.   I tell you, the reason is plainly the same in respect of both: they are both perceived by sense; nay, the greater degree of heat is more sensibly perceived; and consequently, if there is any difference, we are more certain of its real existence than we can be of the reality of a lesser degree.

Phil.   But is not the most vehement and intense degree of heat a very great pain?

Hyl.   No one can deny it.

Phil.   And is any unperceiving thing capable of pain or pleasure?

Hyl.   No, certainly.

Phil.   Is your material substance a senseless being or a being endowed with sense and perception?

Hyl.   It is senseless, without doubt.

Phil.   It cannot, therefore, be the subject of pain?

Hyl.   By no means.

Phil.   Nor, consequently, of the greatest heat perceived by sense, since you acknowledge this to be no small pain?

Hyl.   I grant it.

Phil.   What shall we say then of your external object: is it a material substance, or no?

Hyl.   It is a material substance with the sensible qualities inhering in it.

Phil.   How then can a great heat exist in it, since you own it cannot in a material substance? I desire you would clear this point.

Hyl.   Hold Philonous, I fear I was out in yielding intense heat to be a pain. It should seem rather that pain is something distinct from heat, and the consequence or effect of it.

Phil.   Upon putting your hand near the fire, do you perceive one simple uniform sensation or two distinct sensations?

Hyl.   But one simple sensation.

Phil.   Is not the heat immediately perceived?

Hyl.   It is.

Phil.   And the pain?

Hyl.   True.

Phil.   Seeing therefore they are both immediately perceived at the same time and the fire affects you duly with one simple or uncompounded idea it follows that this same simple idea is both the intense heat immediately perceived and the pain; and, consequently, that the intense heat immediately perceived is nothing distinct from a particular sort of pain.

Hyl.   It seems so.

Phil.   Again try in your thoughts, Hylas, if you can conceive a vehement sensation to be without pain or pleasure.

Hyl.   I cannot.

Phil.   Or can you frame to yourself an idea of sensible pain or pleasure, in general, abstracted from every particular idea of heat, cold, tastes, smells, etc.?

Hyl.   I do not find that I can.

Phil.   Does it not therefore follow that sensible pain is nothing distinct from those sensations or ideas—in an intense degree?

Hyl.   It is undeniable and, to speak the truth, I begin to suspect a very great heat cannot exist but in a mind perceiving it . . . .

Phil.   Suppose now one of your hands hot, and the other cold, and that they are both at once put into the same vessel of water, in an intermediate state. Will not the water seem cold to one hand, and warm to the other?

Hyl.   It will.

Phil.   Ought we not therefore, by your principles, to conclude it is really both cold and warm at the same time, that is, according to your own concession, to believe an absurdity?

Hyl.   I confess it seems so.

Phil.   Consequently, the principles themselves are false, since you have granted that no true principle leads to an absurdity.

Hyl.   But, after all, can anything be more absurd than to say, "there is no heat in the fire?"

Phil.   To make the point still clearer, tell me whether, in two cases exactly alike, we ought not to make the same judgment?

Hyl.   We ought.

Phil.   When a pin pricks your finger, does it not rend and divide the fibers of your flesh?

Hyl.   It does.

Phil.   And when a coal burns your finger, does it any more?

Hyl.   It does not.

Phil.   Since, therefore, you neither judge the sensation itself occasioned by the pin, nor anything like it to be in the pin, you should not, conformably to what you have now granted, judge the sensation occasioned by the fire, or anything like it, to be in the fire.

Hyl.   Well, since it must be so, I am content to yield this point and acknowledge that heat and cold are only sensations existing in our minds. But there still remain qualities enough to secure the reality of external things.

Phil.   But what will you say, Hylas, if it shall appear that the case is the same with regard to all other sensible qualities, and that they can no more be supposed to exist without the mind than heat and cold?

Hyl.   Then, indeed, you will have done something to the purpose, but that is what I despair of seeing proved.

Phil.   Let us examine them in order. What think you of tastes—do they exist without the mind, or no?

Hyl.   Can any man in his senses doubt whether sugar is sweet, or wormwood bitter?

Phil.   Inform me, Hylas. Is a sweet taste a particular kind of pleasure or pleasant sensation, or is it not?

Hyl.   It is.

Phil.   And is not bitterness some kind of uneasiness or pain?

Hyl.   I grant it.

Phil.   If, therefore, sugar and wormwood are unthinking corporeal substances existing without the mind, how can sweetness and bitterness, that is, pleasure and pain, agree to them? . . .

    May we not therefore conclude of smells, as of the other forementioned qualities, that they cannot exist in any but a perceiving substance or mind?

Hyl.   I think so.

Phil.   Then as to sounds, what must we think of them, are they accidents really inherent in external bodies or not?

Hyl.   That they inhere not in the sonorous bodies is plain from hence because a bell struck in the exhausted receiver of an air pump [i.e., a vacuum] sends forth no sound. The air, therefore, must be thought the subject of sound.

Phil.   What reason is there for that, Hylas?

Hyl.   Because, when any motion is raised in the air, we perceive a sound greater or lesser in proportion to the air's motion, but without some motion in the air we never hear any sound at all.

Phil.   And granting that we never hear a sound but when some motion is produced in the air yet I do not see how you can infer from thence that the sound itself is in the air.

Hyl.   It is this very motion in the external air that produces in the mind the sensation of sound. For, striking on the drum of the ear, it causes a vibration which by the auditory nerves being communicated to the brain, the soul is thereupon affected with the sensation called "sound."

Phil.   What! Is sound then a sensation?

Hyl.   I tell you, as perceived by us it is a particular sensation in the mind.

Phil.   And can any sensation exist without the mind?

Hyl.   No, certainly.

Phil.   How then can sound, being a sensation, exist in the air if by the air you mean a senseless substance existing without the mind? . . .

Hyl.   To deal ingenuously, I do not like it. And, after the concessions already made, I had as well grant that sounds, too, have no real being without the mind.

Phil.   And I hope you will make no difficulty to acknowledge the same of colors.

Hyl.   Pardon me, the case of colors is very different. Can anything be plainer than that we see them on the objects?

Phil.   The objects you speak of are, I suppose, corporeal substances existing without the mind?

Hyl.   They are.

Phil.   And have true and real colors inhering in them?

Hyl.   Each visible object has that color which we see in it.

Phil.   How is there anything visible but what we perceive by sight?

Hyl.   There is not.

Phil.   What! Are then the beautiful red and purple we see on yonder clouds really in them? Or do you imagine they have in themselves any other form than that of a dark mist or vapor?

Hyl.   I must own, Philonous, those colors are not really in the clouds as they seem to be at this distance. They are only apparent colors.

Phil.   "Apparent" call you them? How shall we distinguish these apparent colors from real?

Hyl.   Very easily. Those are to be thought apparent which, appearing only at a distance, vanish upon a nearer approach.

Phil.   And those, I suppose, are to be thought real which are discovered by the most near and exact survey.

Hyl.   Right.

Phil.   Is the nearest and exactest survey made by the help of a microscope or by the naked eye?

Hyl.   By a microscope, doubtless.

Phil.   But a microscope often discovers colors in an object different from those perceived by the unassisted sight. And in case we had microscopes magnifying to any assigned degree it is certain that no object whatsoever viewed through them would appear in the same color? which it exhibits to the naked eye.

Hyl.   I confess there is something in what you say.

Phil.   Besides, it is not only possible but manifest that there actually are animals whose eyes are by nature framed to perceive those things which by reason of their minuteness escape our sight. What think you of those inconceivably small animals perceived by glasses? Must we suppose they are all stark blind? Or, in case they see, can it be imagined their sight has not the same use in preserving their bodies from injuries which appears in that of all other animals? And if it has, is it not evident they must see particles less than their own bodies, which will present them with a far different view in each object from that which strikes our senses? Even our own eyes do not always represent objects to us after the same manner. In the jaundice everyone knows that all things seem yellow. Is it not therefore highly probable those animals in whose eyes we discern a very different texture from that of ours, and whose bodies abound with different humors, do not see the same colors in every object that we do? From all which should it not seem to follow that all colors are equally apparent, and that none of those which we perceive are really inherent in any outward object?

Hyl.   It should.

Phil.   The point will be past all doubt if you consider that, in case colors were real properties or affections inherent in external bodies, they could admit of no alteration without some change wrought in the very bodies themselves, but is it not evident from what has been said that, upon the use of microscopes, upon a change happening in the humors of the eye, or a variation of distance, without any manner of real alteration in the thing itself, the colors of any object are either changed or totally disappear? Nay, all other circumstances remaining the same, change but the situation of some objects and they shall present different colors to the eye. The same thing happens upon viewing an object in various degrees of light. And what is more known than that the same bodies appear differently colored by candlelight from what they do in the open day? Add to these the experiment of a prism which, separating the heterogeneous rays of light, alters the color of any object and will cause the whitest to appear of a deep blue or red to the naked eye. And now tell me whether you are still of opinion that every body has its true real color inhering in it, and if you think it has, I would fain know further from you what certain distance and position of the object, what peculiar texture and formation of the eye, what degree or kind of light is necessary for ascertaining that true color and distinguishing it from apparent ones . . . .

Hyl.   I frankly own, Philonous, that it is in vain to stand out any longer. Colors, sounds, tastes, in a word, all those termed "secondary qualities," have certainly no existence without the mind. But by this acknowledgment I must not be supposed to derogate anything from the reality of matter or external objects; seeing it is no more than several philosophers maintain, who nevertheless are the farthest imaginable from denying matter. For the clearer understanding of this you must know sensible qualities are by philosophers divided into *primary* and *secondary*. The former are extension, figure, solidity, gravity, motion, and rest. And these they hold exist really in bodies. The latter are those above enumerated, or, briefly, all sensible qualities besides the primary, which they assert are only so many sensations or ideas existing nowhere but in the mind. But all this, I doubt not, you are already apprised of. For my part I have been a long time sensible there was such an opinion current among philosophers, but was never thoroughly convinced of its truth 'til now.

Phil.   You are still then of opinion that *extension* and *figure* are inherent in external unthinking substances?

Hyl.   I am.

Phil.   But what if the same arguments which are brought against secondary qualities will hold good against these also?

Hyl.   Why then I shall be obliged to think they too exist only in the mind. . . .

Phil.   Is it not the very same reasoning to conclude there is no extension or figure in an object because to one eye it shall seem little, smooth, and round, when at the same time it appears to the other great, uneven, and angular?

Hyl.   The very same. But does this latter fact ever happen?

Phil.   You may at any time make the experiment by looking with one eye bare, and with the other through a microscope.

Hyl.   I know not how to maintain it, and yet I am loath to give up *extension;* I see so many odd consequences following upon such a concession.

Phil.   Then as for *solidity* either you do not mean any sensible quality by that word, and so it is beside our inquiry, or if you do, it must be either hardness or resistance. But both the one and the other are plainly relative to our senses: it being evident that what seems hard to one animal may appear soft to another who has greater force and firmness of limbs. Nor is it less plain that the resistance I feel is not in the body.

Hyl.   I own the very sensation of resistance, which is all you immediately perceive, is not in the *body,* but the cause of that sensation is.

Phil.   But the causes of our sensations are not things immediately perceived, and therefore not sensible. This point I thought had been already determined. . . .

Hyl.   I acknowledge, Philonous, that, upon a fair observation of what passes in my mind, I can discover nothing else but that I am a thinking being affected with variety of sensations, neither is it possible to conceive how a sensation should exist in an unperceiving substance. But then, on the other hand, when I look on sensible things in a different view, considering them as so many modes and qualities, I find it necessary to suppose a material *substratum,* without which they cannot be conceived to exist.

Phil.   "Material substratum" call you it? Pray, by which of your senses came you acquainted with that being?

Hyl.   It is not itself sensible; its modes and qualities only being perceived by the senses.

Phil.   I presume then it was by reflection and reason you obtained the idea of it?

Hyl.   I do not pretend to any proper positive idea of it. However, I conclude it exists because qualities cannot be conceived to exist without a support....

To speak the truth, Philonous, I think there are two kinds of objects: the one perceived immediately which are likewise called "ideas;" the other are real things or external objects, perceived by the mediation of ideas which are their images and representations. Now I own ideas do not exist without the mind, but the latter sort of objects do. I am sorry I did not think of this distinction sooner; it would probably have cut short your discourse.

Phil.   Are those external objects perceived by sense or by some other faculty?

Hyl.   They are perceived by sense.

Phil.   How! Is there anything perceived by sense which is not immediately perceived?

Hyl.   Yes, Philonous, in some sort there is. For example, when I look on a picture or statue of Julius Caesar, I may be said, after a manner, to perceive him (though not immediately) by my senses.

Phil.   It seems then you will have our ideas, which alone are immediately perceived, to be pictures of external things: and that these also are perceived by sense in as much they have a conformity or resemblance to our ideas?

Hyl.   That is my meaning.

Phil.   And in the same way that Julius Caesar, in himself invisible, is nevertheless perceived by sight, real things, in themselves imperceptible, are perceived by sense.

Hyl.   In the very same.

Phil.   Tell me, Hylas, when you behold the picture of Julius Caesar, do you see with your eyes any more than some colors and figures, with a certain symmetry and composition of the whole?

Hyl.   Nothing else.

Phil.   And would not a man who had never known anything of Julius Caesar see as much?

Hyl.   He would.

Phil.   Consequently, he has his sight and the use of it in as perfect a degree as you?

Hyl.   I agree with you.

Phil.   Whence comes it then that your thoughts are directed to the Roman emperor, and his are not? This cannot proceed from the sensations or ideas of sense by you then perceived, since you acknowledge you have no advantage over him in that respect. It should seem therefore to proceed from reason and memory, should it not?

Hyl.   It should.

Phil.   Consequently, it will not follow from that instance that anything is perceived by sense which is not immediately perceived. Though I grant we may, in one acceptation, be said to perceive sensible things mediately by sense—that is, when, from a frequently perceived connection, the immediate perception of ideas by one sense suggests to the mind others, perhaps belonging to another sense, which are wont to be connected with them. For instance, when I hear a coach drive along the streets, immediately I perceive only the sound; but from the experience I have had that such a sound is connected with a coach, I am said to hear the coach. It is nevertheless evident that, in truth and strictness, nothing can be *heard* but *sound,* and the coach is not then properly perceived by sense, but suggested from experience. So likewise when we are said to see a red-hot bar of iron; the solidity and heat of the iron are not the objects of sight, but suggested to the imagination by the color and figure which are properly perceived by that sense. In short, those things alone are actually and strictly perceived by any sense which would have been perceived in case that same sense had then been first conferred on us. As for other things, it is plain they are only suggested to the mind by experience grounded on former perceptions. But, to return to your comparison of Caesar's picture, it is plain, if you keep to that, you must hold the real things or archetypes of our ideas are not perceived by sense, but by some internal faculty of the soul, as reason or memory. I would, therefore, fain know what arguments you can draw from reason for the existence of what you call "real things" or "material objects," or whether you remember to have seen them formerly as they are in themselves, or if you have heard or read of anyone that did.

Hyl.   I see, Philonous, you are disposed to raillery, but that will never convince me.

Phil.   My aim is only to learn from you the way to come at the knowledge of *material beings.* Whatever we perceive is perceived either immediately or mediately—by sense, or by reason and reflection. But, as you have excluded sense, pray show me what reason you have to believe their existence, or what *medium* you can possibly make use of to prove it, either to mine or your own understanding.

Hyl.   To deal ingenuously, Philonous, now I consider the point, I do not find I can give you any good reason for it. But this much seems pretty plain, that it is at least possible such things may really exist. And as long as there is no absurdity in supposing them, I am resolved to believe as I did, till you bring good reasons to the contrary.

Phil.   What! Is it come to this, that you only believe the existence of material objects, and that your belief is founded barely on the possibility of its being true? Then you will have me bring reasons against it, though another would think it reasonable the proof should lie on him who holds the affirmative.

 . . . How then is it possible that things perpetually fleeting and variable as our ideas should be copies or images of anything fixed and constant? Or, in other words, since all sensible qualities, as size, figure, color, etc., that is, our ideas, are continually changing upon every alteration in the distance, medium, or instruments of sensation—how can any determinate material objects be properly represented or painted forth by several distinct things each of which is so different from and unlike the rest? Or, if you say it resembles some one only of our ideas, how shall we be able to distinguish the true copy from all the false ones?

Hyl.   I profess, Philonous, I am at a loss. I know not what to say to this.

Phil.   But neither is this all. Which are material objects in themselves—perceptible or imperceptible?

Hyl.   Properly and immediately nothing can be perceived but ideas. All material things, therefore, are in themselves insensible and to be perceived only by their ideas.

Phil.   Ideas then are sensible, and their archetypes or originals insensible?

Hyl.   Right.

Phil.   But how can that which is sensible be like that which is insensible? Can a real thing, in itself *invisible,* be like a *color,* or a real thing which is not *audible* be like a *sound?* In a word, can anything be like a sensation or idea, but another sensation or idea?

Hyl.   I must own, I think not. . . .

Questions for Discussion

1. When asked how to refute Berkeley, Samuel Johnson kicked a stone and said, "I refute him thus." Was this really a refutation of Berkeley? Why or why not?

2. Make sure you understand the difference between Berkeley's idealism and Epicurus' materialism. Assuming that you had to choose one of these metaphysical views, which would you select? Why?

3. How would *you* criticize Berkeley's assertion that all we know are ideas? Give reasons for your answer.

4. Crucial for Berkeley's argument is to collapse the distinction between primary and secondary qualities. Do you find his arguments on this point convincing? Why or why not?

5. Do you think Berkeley's idealistic metaphysics is supported or threatened by contemporary findings in natural science? Give reasons to support your answer.

CHAPTER 11

The Mind-Body Problem

Both materialism and idealism are extreme metaphysical positions; each tries to reduce the complexity and plurality of the world to a single kind of reality. Perhaps as you were reading through the preceding selections you were convinced first by the arguments of Epicurus and Gassendi that materialism was the only plausible metaphysical position, only to be dissuaded by the equally compelling arguments of George Berkeley. How are we to decide which view is the correct one?

Most contemporary philosophers would tell you that neither materialism nor idealism by itself is an adequate metaphysical theory. Both have strong points, but each has its fatal flaws, and no issue makes this more apparent than the mind-body problem. To be more specific, you are a reality that is both mind and body, and when we are speaking of the mind-body problem we are not talking about a highly abstract, purely theoretical issue but rather about concrete individuals, real persons. Our ordinary ways of speaking certainly refer to two different kinds of reality; we speak of our mind as though it were a reality as real as our body, and we speak of our body as a part of the visible world in which we live.

Metaphysical Dualism

This is the position known as *dualism, dual* meaning that there are *two* things, both mind *and* matter. The best known dualist in the modern period (from the sixteenth century onward) is Descartes (see Chapter 15). Strictly speaking, Descartes held that there were *three* realities, or "substances" as he called them, one uncreated reality (God) and two created realities (mind and matter). Yet, at least in his account of the natural or "created" world, Descartes held a dualistic position. For Descartes these two realities are completely different from each other; matter is defined by its spatial extension, and mind by its ability to think. Minds cannot be spatially located or described, and material objects cannot think, nor can minds be broken up or divided, as can physical objects. Thus, the two are not only different, they are totally different *kinds* of things.

The ancient Greek philosopher Plato argues for a human being in which the soul is sharply distinguished from the body, the soul belonging to the eternal, intelligible, unchanging realm of ideas, and the body, a part of the changing, confusing, and contradictory world of physical appearances. Like Descartes, Plato also sees the human being as the temporary joining together of two completely different sorts of things. The soul, Plato says, is like a bird in the cage of the body waiting to be released.

The advantage of dualism, then, is that it allows us to express philosophically some of the facts of everyday experience which seem difficult to express from either the materialist or the idealist positions, and is therefore in many ways much closer to common sense and ordinary experience and a better articulation of the facts of our experience. The problem with dualism, however, is to see and to say precisely how the two *are* joined together. How can two such fundamentally different sorts of things be joined together? It just doesn't seem possible. Of course, we know that minds and bodies do affect each other because we experience this in our own cases a hundred times each day. I want to answer a question in class so I raise my arm; here apparently my mind is directing and controlling my body. And when I try to finish my term paper with a severe case of flu, I know perfectly well how my body affects my mind. Of course mind and body interact, but how *can* they if they are as different from each other as we have said? To raise my arm,

---

I must begin by observing the great difference between mind and body. Body is of its nature always divisible; mind is wholly indivisible. When I consider the mind—that is, myself insofar as I am merely a conscious being—I can distinguish no parts within myself and understand myself to be a single and complete thing. Although the whole mind seems to be united to the whole body, yet when a foot or an arm or any other part of the body is cut off I am not aware that any subtraction has been made from the mind. Nor can the faculties of will, feeling, understanding and so on be called its parts, for it is one and the same mind that wills, feels, and understands. On the other hand, I cannot think of any corporeal or extended object without being readily able to divide it in thought and therefore conceiving of it as divisible. This would be enough to show me the total difference between mind and body, even if I did not sufficiently know this already.

René Descartes
Meditations on First Philosophy

I have to move certain bones, and in order to do that I have to contract certain muscles, and in order to do that, I have to transfer certain chemical-electrical energy to the muscle. But how is a completely immaterial mind, which cannot even be located in space, going to accomplish that? Similarly, how are the fever and muscle stiffness of flu able to causally interact with a nonphysical, nonspatial mental thing I call my mind?

The Problem of Interaction

The problem of interaction is the famous "mind-body problem." It is the problem of how mind and body can interact if they are such different sorts of things. And this is an excellent example of a philosophical problem. A philosophical problem occurs when we want to hold—and there are good reasons to hold—two apparently contradictory positions. We want to say—and we have good reason to say—that there are both minds and physical objects which are fundamentally different from each other, and we also want to say that they can act on one another. The problem is how both these statements can be true at the same time. If mind and body are so different, then they cannot interact, and if they interact then they cannot be so different from each other. To solve a philosophical problem is to figure out a way around such difficulties. Perhaps minds and bodies do not really interact, they only seem to. This is the position known as *parallelism*. Mental events go on in one realm and physical events go on in another, but the two realms never connect. Of course, there are problems with this position, too, but at least it might solve the mind-body problem. Or we might say that the problem is due to a faulty and confused conception of causality which makes it seem so difficult for different kinds of things to interact on each other, and so we might try to formulate a more refined interaction theory with a different causal concept to solve the mind-body problem.

The Identity Thesis

One way to solve the mind-body problem is by accepting one of the two nondualistic theories we started off with—materialism or idealism. A current form of materialism is known as the "identity thesis," which holds that words like *mind* and *body* refer to the same "identical," material entity. How would accepting a monistic theory "solve" the mind-body problem?

The materialist's answer would be that anything you say about the mind is really about the body, since the body is material, and matter is the only reality. The idealist would insist, to the contrary, that statements made about the body are

RICHARD TAYLOR (B. 1919): *American philosopher who has taught at the University of Rochester and other American universities. Among his books are* Good and Evil *and* Freedom, Anarchy and the Law.

really statements about minds and ideas, since that is the only reality. If you want to have it both ways and say that there are minds and bodies, then you are a dualist and are stuck with all the problems that have plagued that position. In the reading that follows, Richard Taylor, a contemporary American philosopher, explains what some of these problems are. And he goes on to sort out some of the more prevalent theories that have been developed to get around the difficulties raised by a dualistic point of view: parallelism, occasionalism, interactionalism, preestablished harmony, and so forth.

We can use our knowledge of logic from Part 2 to analyze Taylor's arguments against materialism. Taylor points to a central difficulty of the materialist's position as the following: If mind and body are identical, then whatever we say about the one we must also be able to say about the other. For example, if we say that "my mind has a wish" then we must also say that "my body has a wish," which sounds odd. Or if we say, "I am religious," this also means "my body is religious," which makes no sense at all. We can readily see that we have here an "indirect argument" based on *modus tollens* (MT). Remember that the MT argument form has the following structure.

$$P \rightarrow Q$$
$$\underline{-Q}$$
$$\therefore -P$$

Taylor's argument against materialism (an argument that a dualist would accept) can be cast into the MT form:

If mind and body are identical (P), then it follows to say "I am religious" also means that "my body is religious" (Q).

It is absurd to say that "I am religious" means that "my body is religious" (−Q).

Therefore, it cannot be the case that my mind and body are identical (−P).

Taylor at this stage is not taking either the materialist or the dualist position; he is simply presenting the problem faced by the materialist, a problem he poses as a dilemma: The identity of mind and body implies that mental attributes must also apply to the body. But this forces the materialist into the dilemma of either (1) accepting absurd consequences or (2) abandoning materialism in favor of dualism.

What does Taylor think of the dualist option? Not much. The difficulty with dualism is that it leads to the awful problem of indicating how mind and body, if different, are nonetheless related. Each theory proposed for answering the mind-body problem, Taylor argues, is so bizarre as to lead many philosophers to abandon dualism altogether. Taylor's attack on dualism is, of course, a modified form of indirect argument, this time one proposed by the materialist against the dualist. If dualism is true, the materialist argues, then we are forced to accept one of the several strange and ridiculous theories for showing how mind and body are connected. That being the case, dualism ought to be rejected.

Taylor is an exceptionally clear writer, and little in the way of additional comment or discussion here is called for.

Richard Taylor: Materialism and Personal Identity

Materialism

I know that I have a body, and that this is a material thing, though a somewhat unusual and highly complicated one. There would, in fact, be no other reason for calling it my body, except to affirm that it is entirely material, for nothing that is not matter could possibly be a part of my body. Now if my having a body consists simply in the identity of myself with my body, then it follows that I *am* body, and nothing more. Nor would the affirmation of the identity of myself with my body be at all inconsistent with saying that I have a body, for we often express the relationship of identity in just this way. Thus, one might correctly say of a table that

Richard Taylor, *Metaphysics,* 4th ed. 1992. pp. 11–15. Reprinted by permission of Prentice-Hall, Inc., it *has* four legs and a top, or of a bicycle that it *has* two wheels, a frame, a seat, and handlebars. In such cases, no one would suppose that the table or the bicycle is one thing, and its parts or "body" another, the two being somehow mysteriously connected. The table or the bicycle just *is* its parts, suitably related. So likewise, I might just *be* the totality of my bodily parts, suitably related and all functioning together in the manner expressed by saying that I am a living body, or a living, material animal organism.

This materialistic conception of a person has the great advantage of simplicity. We do know that there are bodies, that there are living animal bodies, and that some of these are in common speech denominated men. A person is, then, on this view, nothing mysterious or metaphysical, at least as regards the *kind* of thing he is.

A consequence of this simplicity is that we need not speculate upon the relationship between one's body and his mind or ask how the two are connected, or how one can act upon the other, all such questions being rendered senseless within the framework of this view, which in the first place denies that we are dealing with two things. The death of the animal organism—which is, of course, an empirical fact and not subject to speculation—will, moreover, be equivalent to the destruction of the person, consisting simply in the cessation of those functions which together constitute being alive. Hence, the fate of a person is simply, on this view, the fate of his body, which is ultimately a return to the dust whence he sprang. This alleged identity of oneself with his body accounts, moreover, for the solicitude every man has for his body, and for its health and well-being. If a person is identical with his body, then any threat to the latter is a threat to himself, and he must view the destruction of it as the destruction of himself. And such, in fact, does seem to be the attitude of all men, whatever may be their philosophical or religious opinions.

Such a conception has nevertheless always presented enormous difficulties, and these have seemed so grave to most philosophers that almost any theory, however absurd when examined closely, has at one time or another seemed to them preferable to materialism. Indeed, the difficulties of materialism are so grave that, for some persons, they need only to be mentioned to render the theory unworthy of discussion.

The Meaning of "Identity"

By "identity" the materialist must mean a strict and total identity of himself and his body, nothing less. Now to say of anything, X, and anything, Y, that X and Y are identical, or that they are really one and the same thing, one must be willing to assert of X anything whatever that he asserts of Y, and vice versa. This is simply a consequence of their identity, for if there is anything whatever that can be truly asserted of any object X, but cannot be truly asserted of some object Y, then it logically follows that X and Y are two different things, and not the same thing . . .

The question can now be asked, then, whether there is anything true of me that is not true of my body, and vice versa . . . It might, for instance, be true of me at a certain time that I am morally blameworthy or praiseworthy. Can we then say that my body or some part of it, such as my brain, is in exactly the same sense blameworthy or praiseworthy? Can moral predicates be applied without gross incongruity to any physical object at all? Or suppose I have some profound wish or desire, or some thought—the desire, say, to be in some foreign land at a given moment or thoughts of the Homeric gods. It seems at least odd to assert that my body or some part of it, wishes that it were elsewhere, or has thoughts of the gods. How, indeed, can any purely physical state of any purely physical object ever be a state that is for something, or of something, in the way that my desires and thoughts are such? And how, in particular, could a purely physical state be in this sense *for* or of something that is not real? Or again, suppose that I am religious, and can truly say that I love God and neighbor, for instance. Can I without absurdity say that my body or some part of it, such as my foot or brain, is religious, and loves God and neighbor? Or can one suppose that my being religious, or having such love, consists simply in my body's being in a certain state, or behaving in a certain way? If I claim the identity of myself with my body, I must say all these odd things; that is, I must be willing to assert of my body or some part of it, everything I assert of myself. There is perhaps no logical absurdity or clear falsity in speaking thus of one's corporeal frame, but such assertions as these are at least strange, and it can be questioned whether, as applied to the body, they are even still meaningful.

The disparity between bodily and personal predicates becomes even more apparent, however, if we consider epistemological predicates, involved in statements about belief and knowledge. Thus, if I believe something, for instance, that today is February 31—then I am in a certain state; the state, namely, of having a certain belief which is in this case necessarily a false one. Now how can a physical state of any physical object be identical with that? And how, in particular, can anything be a *false* physical state of an object? The physical states of things, it would seem, just *are,* and one cannot even think of anything that could ever distinguish one such state from another as being either true or false. A physiologist might give a complete physical description of a brain and nervous system at a particular time, but he could never distinguish some of those states as true and others as false, nor would he have any idea what to look for if he were asked to do this. At least, so it would certainly seem.

Platonic Dualism

It is this sort of reflection that has always led metaphysicians and theologians to distinguish radically between the mind or soul of a man and his body, ascribing properties to the mind that are utterly different in kind from those exhibited by the body; properties which, it is supposed, could not be possessed by any body, just because of its nature as a physical object.

The simplest and most radical of such views *identifies* the person or self with a soul or mind, and declares its relationship to the body to be the almost accidental one of mere occupancy, possession, or use. Thus Plato, and many mystical philosophers before and after him, thought of the body as a veritable prison of the soul, a gross thing of clay from which the soul one day gladly escapes, to live its own independent and untrammeled existence, much as a bird flees its cage or a snake sheds its skin. A person, thus conceived, is a nonmaterial substance—a *spirit,* in the strictest sense—related to an animal body as possessor to thing possessed, tenant to abode, or user to thing used. A person *has* a body only in the sense that he, perhaps temporarily, occupies, owns, or uses a body, being something quite distinct from it and having, perhaps, a destiny quite different from the melancholy one that is known sooner or later to overtake the corporeal frame.

This dualism of mind and body has been, and always is, firmly received by millions of unthinking men, partly because it is congenial to the religious framework in which their everyday metaphysical opinions are formed, and partly, no doubt, because every man wishes to think of himself as something more than just one more item of matter in the world. Wise philosophers, too, speak easily of the attributes of the mind as distinct from those of the body, thereby sundering the two once and for all. Some form of dualism seems in fact indicated by the metaphysical, moral, and epistemological difficulties of materialism which are, it must be confessed, formidable indeed.

But whatever difficulties such simple dualism may resolve, it appears to raise others equally grave. For one thing, it is not nearly as simple as it seems. Whatever a partisan of such a view might say of the simplicity of the mind or soul, a *man* is nonetheless, on this view, *two* quite disparate things, a mind and a body, having almost nothing in common and only the flimsiest connection with each other. This difficulty, once it is acutely felt, is usually minimized by conceiving of a man in his true self as nothing but a mind, and representing his body as something ancillary to this true self, something that is not really any part of him at all but only one among the many physical objects that he happens to possess, use, or what not, much as he possesses and uses various other things in life. His body does, to be sure, occupy a pre-eminent place among such things, for it is something without which he would be quite helpless, but this renders it no more a part or whole of this true self or person than any other of the world's physical things.

Possession, however, is essentially a social concept, and sometimes a strictly legal one. Something counts as one of my possessions by virtue of my title to it, and this is something conferred by men, in accordance with conventions and laws fabricated by men themselves. Thus does a field or a building count as one of my possessions. But a certain animal body, which I identify as mine, is not mine in any sense such as this. My dominion over my body arises from no human conventions or laws, and is not alterable by them. The body of a slave, though it may be owned by another man in the fullest sense of ownership that is reflected in the idea of possession, is nevertheless the slave's body in a metaphysical sense in which it could not possibly be the body of his master. . . .

The ideas of occupancy or use do not express the relation of mind and body any better. *Occupancy,* for instance, is a physical concept; one thing occupies another by being in or upon it. But the mind, on this view, is no physical thing, and no sense can be attached to its resting within or upon any body; the conception is simply ridiculous. Nor does one simply *use* his body the way he uses implements and tools. One does, to be sure, sometimes use his limbs and other parts, over which he has voluntary control, in somewhat the manner in which he uses tools but many of one's bodily parts, including some that are vital, the very existence of which may be unknown to him, are not within his control at all. They are nonetheless parts of his body. Artificial devices, too, like hearing aids, spectacles, and the like, do not in the least become parts of one's body merely by being used, even in the case of a man who can barely do without them. They are merely things worn or used. Nor can one say that one's body is that physical being in the world upon which one absolutely depends for his continuing life, for there are many such things. One depends on the sun, for instance, and the air he breathes and without these would perish as certainly as if deprived of his heart, yet no one regards the sun or the air around him as any part of his body.

A man does not, then, *have* a body in the way in which he has anything else at all, and any comparison of the body to a material possession or instrument is about as misleading as likening it to a chamber in which one is more or less temporarily closeted. The connection between oneself and one's body is far more intimate and metaphysical than anything else we can think of. One's body is at least a part of himself, and is so regarded by every man. Yet it is not merely a part, as the arm is part of the body, and we are so far without any hint of how the mind and the body are connected.

A Counter-Argument for the Identity Thesis

Before leaving this topic, we will briefly examine the counter-argument for the identity thesis, represented by the work of such contemporary philosophers as J.J.C. Smart. While the argument of Taylor and others does indeed show that at *least* there must be two different *languages,* Smart argues that that is also the *most* that it shows. The fact that we *speak* in two different ways does not prove that there are two different *things* being referred to. Smart uses an example which had already been made famous fifty years earlier by the German philosopher, Gottlob Frege, concerning the "morning star" and the "evening star." The evening star has been known for thousands of years as the first star to appear in the evening; and the morning star as the last highly visible star to become invisible in the morning. Astronomers discovered in the nineteenth century that the morning star and the evening star were in fact the same, identical "star," namely, the planet Venus. Here, then, is a clear example of one and the same object being described in two different ways, with very different meanings. The expression "evening star" obviously *means* something different from the expression "morning star;" "evening star" means "the first star to appear in the evening" (that's why it's called the evening star) and "morning star" is defined to mean "the last star to disappear from view in the morning" (hence called the morning star). But this does not prove there must be two different *things* to which these words refer. Another well-known example often used in this regard concerns Sir Walter Scott, the author of the Waverley novels. Imagine a student taking freshman English who didn't know that the author of the Waverley novels was in fact Scott. The words *Sir Walter* Scott will mean *something* to this person. She may understand these words to refer to a man who lived and wrote in Scotland during the nineteenth century, who was knighted by the British monarchy, and perhaps even that this is the man who wrote *Ivanhoe*. Such a person will also understand some of the meaning of the expression "the author of the Waverley novels," namely, that this word refers to a person who wrote several novels which are called the Waverley novels. But when we ask the student, perhaps in the English III final exam, "Who is the author of Waverley?", she may think it was Tennyson. Thus, she is in very much the same position as the majority of people in the nineteenth century who knew what the words "morning star" and "evening star" meant but mistakenly believed they referred to two different things. And just as these individuals later learned that these two expressions with their two different meanings referred to the same thing, so the poor freshman student will discover when she picks up her exam that "Sir Walter Scott" and "the author of Waverley" are in fact one and the same person.

But suppose we agree with Smart that the fact that mental concepts and physical concepts have fundamentally different meanings, even amounting to two quite different languages, does not prove that these different meanings or languages refer to two different objects. Two different concepts with quite different meanings can refer to one and the same identical object. Even if we agree with Smart, does it follow that only matter exists? Not at all. As we have seen many times in this book, to refute your opponent's argument does not prove your position to be the correct one. If Smart's argument is sound, it shows only that Taylor and others are wrong in arguing that the fact that we speak and think differently about minds and bodies proves that minds and bodies are distinct entities. Even if Smart is correct, it is still possible that mind and bodies *are* distinct, though not for the reasons Taylor offers. And even if dualism is defeated, it doesn't follow that all is *matter*. It is just as plausible that what we call matter is an aspect of an underlying mind as it is to conclude, as Smart would want us to, that what we call mind is just an aspect of an underlying matter, as the materialists would have us think. It is also possible that mind and matter are aspects of a third reality underlying both, a dual-aspect position held by the seventeenth-century philosopher Spinoza, by the early twentieth-century philosopher Husserl, and by the contemporary philosopher P. F. Strawson. Nonetheless, the "identity thesis" is a topic of ongoing debate among philosophers today.

A Defense of Dualism

The identity thesis is really just a modern, somewhat more sophisticated version of materialism, which holds that minds are really identical with our physical bodies. Taylor offered one of the most persuasive arguments against the identity of mind and body, namely that what we *mean* by mental words and concepts is fundamentally different and cannot be reduced to what we *mean* by physical-object words and concepts.

Dualism in Our Language

Whether minds and bodies are identical or not, we certainly cannot *talk* or *think* about them in the same way. At the very least there are two quite different languages, the mental language we use to describe minds (she is clever, intelligent, sulky, stubborn, moody) and a different language we use to describe physical objects (it is too heavy, too large, too hard). Of course, we can describe human beings in *either* way, but this is precisely because human beings have both minds and bodies.

In any metaphysical system in which many different things are explained in terms of one of several fundamental underlying realities, there is always the attempt to explain one thing, which is understood in its own way and has its own meaning, in terms of some other thing which is understood in a very different way and has its quite distinct meaning. When the atomist, for example, tries to explain a table in terms of atoms, a table *means* something quite different from atoms. A dining room table we see and understand as a piece of furniture, something humanly made which serves a certain human use, in this case, "to eat off of" and which is sold in furniture shops, usually made of wood, and so on. None of this conception of what we *mean* by "dining room table" is contained in what we mean by the word "atom." By "atom" we mean "the smallest indivisible unit of matter." The idealist encounters similar problems when trying to account for the same dining room table in terms of ideas and sensations in someone's mind. The meaning of "idea" is quite different from the meaning of "table" and so it is just as surprising to hear Berkeley proposing that tables are nothing but ideas as it is to hear Epicurus proclaiming that the same table is nothing but a collection of atoms.

Nonetheless, there is an important difference, which the dualist urges, between these attempts to explain one thing in terms of another, and the identity theorist's attempt to explain mind in purely physical terms. In the other cases, although we are initially shocked and surprised by the translation of "table" into either atoms or ideas, we can, after a while, begin to see how the one could be explained in terms of the other. That is, we can, after some time, begin to see how you get from the one to the other. All the individual trees of a forest look like one solid object from an airplane. Perhaps if we were very small the table would appear to us as a collection of distinct, individual objects. We may not *agree* with atomism, but at least we can see how the explanation works, we can see how it might be true. Idealism is a similar case. People have dreams and in those dreams objects seem to be fully real; they can be touched, tasted, heard, and yet when we awaken we realize that it was all in our minds. Might it not be possible that this is what occurs in our waking life? Again, we may not *accept* idealism, but at least we can understand how the physical world can be explained in terms of ideas and sensations. In this sense to explain A in terms of B we must be able to see how A could be experienced as B. But, the dualist insists, this is precisely what we cannot do when we try to explain life or mind in terms of inanimate matter. We begin with lifeless matter and end up with a living, thinking person. Can you see how the one will become the other? Sometimes we look at a friend's baby picture and cannot see how he got to be the person he or she is today. But his brothers and sisters have no problem because they saw all the intervening steps. If we cannot understand the intervening steps, that is, cannot see how matter could become mind, then, according to this sense of explanation, the one cannot be explained in terms of the other, and so we must retain both.

The Importance at the Debate

Having examined the mind-body problem and the lengthy dispute which that problem has generated, you may well wonder what difference it makes who eventually wins the debate. There are problems if you distinguish mind and body, and there are problems if you identify the two. In the end, really, who cares?

One obviously important ramification of the mind-body problem will be its outcome for the question of life after death. Clearly, if the mind is inseparable from the body, the immortality of the mind, or soul, is inconceivable and impossible. Only if mind and body are separable could life after death be possible.

This obviously acts as a powerful support for dualism. Otherwise, some form of a nondualistic, or monistic, theory might seem to have a clear edge. Apart from the question of immortality, looking, that is, just at the ability of different theories of mind to account for our everyday experience, we might very well feel more comfortable with the identity thesis, whether materialistically eliminating mind or idealistically eliminating matter, or perhaps some form of the dual-aspect theory in which both mind and body appear to us as different aspects, each with a different language and set of meanings, of some third underlying entity. Such a monistic theory could at once solve the problems of dualistic interaction and also handle the double-meaning difficulties which Taylor raises against monistic theories. But this solution would be bought at the price of the possibility of the immortality of the soul.

Questions for Discussion

1. In what ways is the identity thesis a problem for the materialist? Does it also present problems for an idealist? Explain.

2. Taylor claims that a person does not "*have* a body in the way in which he has anything else at all." Do you agree? Why or why not?

3. What, in your view, is the most serious problem associated with metaphysical dualism?

4. How do you think a person's view of the mind-body problem would affect that individual's practice of medicine? of psychotherapy?

5. Think of other areas of human activity in which people's attitudes would be affected by what they believe about the mind-body question. Here are two to start with: the penal system; our response to substance abuse. Discuss these and add to the list.

CHAPTER 12

Metaphysics and Language

The discussion of the mind-body problem in the previous chapter showed how central the analysis of our use of language is to our exploration of certain metaphysical issues. Part of the difficulty we encounter in metaphysical questions may simply be due to the way we use, or perhaps misuse, language. As George Berkeley noted, many philosophical problems are entirely of our own making.

> Upon the whole, I am inclined to think that the far greater part, if not all, of those difficulties which have hitherto amused philosophers, and blocked up the way to knowledge, are entirely owing to ourselves. We have raised a dust, and then complain we cannot see. (George Berkeley, Introduction, *Principles of Human Knowledge*)

We also hear Berkeley's attitude echoed in such English philosophers as G.E. Moore (1873-1958), who challenged the idealist philosophy then dominant in English universities by what came to be called his common sense philosophy.

Against the idealists, Moore asked whether anyone could honestly believe that nothing existed unless some mind were experiencing it. Suppose you have entered a train, Moore asks; do you ever, even for a moment, doubt that the wheels of the train are there underneath you resting firmly on the tracks? Similarly, against those skeptics, following Descartes, who raised doubts about the existence of the external world, Moore would simply ask whether anyone has ever really had such doubts. Do you remember Hans Christian Andersen's story of the emperor's clothes? The difference between the boy and the rest of the townspeople was not that he had better eyesight or was more intelligent than they but only that the boy was more honest in admitting what he actually could see and could not see. Again the force of Moore's common sense attack was to caution us against overexplaining things before we have simply described them. Do not get your feet too far off the ground.

The idealists were not the only ones guilty of such linguistic confusions. In his *Enquiry Concerning Human Understanding* Hume offers a devastating argument against real cause-effect relationships. You see wood being put into the fire and then you see the wood catch fire and burn, but you cannot observe any causality, you cannot actually see any causal necessity or relation. So really there is no good reason to expect that the next piece of wood you throw into the fire will also burn. There is only the mental habit you have formed based on past experience. Immediately following this famous passage, Hume remarks that despite all his fine arguments against causality, as soon as he leaves his study and goes down to the local pub for a glass of wine and a game of backgammon, all his doubts disappear. Moore's point is that Hume has put the cart before the horse. Hume should have stuck with what were surely the most obvious of all his experiences, his everyday experience of causal relations, and made this the basic, pivotal point of his philosophy, not the result of some tortured argument which might or might not be sound.

What are you really most sure about, Moore would like to ask Descartes: that you are sitting in your robe with a pen in your hand and paper in front of you, or that you are essentially a thinking substance? Surely nothing can be more obvious than the former. This is where any account of reality must begin. Start with obvious everyday assurances and go on from there, not with something far less obvious to everyday experience.

This emphasis on the ordinary way we experience reality and the way we use ordinary language to describe it was to dominate English-American philosophy for a good part of the twentieth century. Starting with Ludwig Wittgenstein in the 1930s, the concern of much philosophy in Britain and the United States was with the nature and function of language. Much like Moore's common sense philosophy, the ordinary language philosophers argued that in order to avoid being misled by language when we deal with such perennial philosophical topics as metaphysics, we must begin with a thorough knowledge of how ordinary language actually works. As Wittgenstein put it, think of language as a tool for doing many different things. Think for a moment of all the things you can use words to do beside communicating information, though that is certainly one such use of language. "Shut the door." "Can you lend me ten dollars until Monday?" "This is the third time this week you have been late for work." In these sentences information is certainly conveyed (the door is open and I desire it to be closed, I have a cash-flow problem, you have in fact been late for work three times this week). But the primary use or purpose of uttering these words is not to convey such information but to request, or order, beg, warn, or threaten, and our list could go on and on. We use words to insult, flatter, forgive, punish, get ourselves married ("I do"), and so on.

In everyday life language works as well and creates relatively few confusions because all these different uses of language are governed by socially agreed-upon

conventions. If I am your superior (the king, the boss, the sergeant) I can, according to conventional usage, order you to do certain things (but not anything and everything). But if not, I can only make a polite request, which you are free to refuse. If I borrow ten dollars from you, conventional usage implies that I have thereby obligated myself to repay you. Breaking any of these conventions results in odd, puzzling situations, as when an army private says to his commanding officer, "I order you to shine my shoes," or having borrowed ten dollars from you, I later express surprise that you expect to be repaid. "By borrowing this money it became mine; if you wanted to get it back, why did you give it to me in the first place?"

The problem with the philosophical use of language, according to the analytic, ordinary language philosophers, is that it is not governed by conventional language. It is, as Wittgenstein said, language "on a holiday." Philosophers use words but relax or ignore their well-established, conventional usages. This leads to philosophically puzzling metaphysical theories that table and chairs and other physical objects are not "really there," or that they exist only "in a perceiving mind." The words *real* and *in a mind* are expressions of ordinary English; they are not technical terms coined by philosophers. As such they have well-established usage. What we mainly see are physical objects which are also the paradigm cases of things which are "real" and not in a mind.

According to ordinary language philosophers, many metaphysical problems would never arise if philosophers had not ignored the ordinary boundaries established by the everyday use of language. For example, if we use the word *see* in the ordinary way, as ordinary people use it, we will never be inclined to say that all we can see are sense data and that we never see tables and chairs and other physical objects. Seeing things like tables and chairs are paradigm cases of seeing in terms of which we have learned to use the word in the first place. In the view of the ordinary language philosophers, some philosophical problems were not to be solved so much as dissolved. There is no need to solve the "problem" of freedom versus determinism because there is no problem to start with.

What does it mean in ordinary language to say that I am not free to go to the movies tonight? It means that some concrete, external force or situation prevents me from doing what I want to do, namely, to go to the movies. This might be lack of money, a previous engagement which I feel honor bound to keep, that I am in jail, or tied to a tree. In that sense I am free to do some things, though not all, and therefore it is wrong to suppose that I am never free. In particular, it makes absolutely no sense whatever to say, as many philosophers have said, that I am not free to go to the movies because my desire and decision to go were caused by other factors outside my control. This is completely irrelevant in ordinary language to the question whether I am free or not. All that matters is whether I have it within my power to do what I want and have decided to do. Does it inhibit my freedom that I do not have it in my power to want something else? Not at all, in plain language. This is the only kind of freedom that really interests anyone, whether you have or do not have the ability or wherewithal to do what you want to do. Once we remove any external impediment, then you are free in the one sense that is legitimate in plain language terms.

One can object that ordinary language philosophy restricts us to merely describing the status quo, merely restating what we already know and believe. It does not allow us to explain the underlying causes, or to provide some overarching pattern that will give us a more comprehensible picture of the whole. That, however, is what the ordinary language philosophers say is precisely the disease of which they are trying to cure you. You obviously need more therapy sessions.

Language philosophy did not put metaphysical inquiry out of business, but it did change its concerns. Even before the ordinary language philosophers came on the scene, Immanuel Kant (who died in 1804) shifted the topic of metaphysics away from the study of ultimate reality to an analysis of the function and scope of human reason. It is important to recognize, Kant argued, that the human mind can ask questions it is not empowered to answer. When we try to answer such questions we fall into error and illusion. Better then to put our efforts into understanding the concepts most basic to human thinking. In a similar spirit, ordinary language philosophers, in addition to devoting considerable attention to understanding the scope and function of language itself, also dealt with the clarification of basic concepts, especially those that could clarify scientific investigations.

The following selection, taken from Ludwig Wittgenstein's book *Philosophical Investigations,* is written in an abbreviated, aphoristic style that is often difficult to understand. But the selection does introduce his view of the nature of language and the tasks of philosophy. Central to Wittgenstein's analysis of language is the notion of a "language-game," his way of stating that speaking a language is to engage in an activity. Just as we engage in many different activities, we also have different language-games to describe them. Some of these language-games share similarities with others, which Wittgenstein calls "family resemblances." When we inappropriately switch the usage of language from one game to another, we get ourselves into perplexity. The task of philosophy is to help us avoid such perplexities and, when they occur, to dispel them.

Ludwig Wittgenstein: Philosophical Investigations

23. But how many kinds of sentence are there? Say assertion, question, and command?—There are countless kinds: countless different kinds of uses of what we call "symbols," "words," "sentences." And this multiplicity is not something fixed, given once for all; but new types of language, new language games, as we may say, come into existence, and others become obsolete and get forgotten. (We can get a *rough picture* of this from the changes in mathematics.)

Here the term "language-game" is meant to bring into prominence the fact that the *speaking* of language is part of an activity, or of a form of life.

Review the multiplicity of language games in the following examples and in others:

> Giving orders, and obeying them—
> Describing the appearance of an object, or giving its measurements—
> Constructing an object from a description (a drawing)—
> Reporting an event—
> Speculating about an event—
> Forming and testing a hypothesis—
> Presenting the results of an experiment in tables and diagrams—
> Making up a story and reading it—
> Play-acting—
> Singing catches—
> Guessing riddles—
> Making a joke; telling it—
> Solving a problem in practical arithmetic—

Ludwig Wittgenstein *Philosophical Investigations,* 3rd ed., trans. G.E.M. Anscombe. New York: The Macmillan Co. 1968. By permission of Prentice Hall, Upper Saddle River, NJ.

Translating from one language into another—

Asking, thanking, cursing, greeting, praying . . . .

65.   Here we come up against the great question that lies behind all these considerations.—For someone might object against me: "You take the easy way out! You talk about all sort of language-games, but have nowhere said what the essence of a language-game, and hence of language, is: what is common to all these activities, and that makes them into language or parts of language So you let yourself off the very part of the investigation that once gave you yourself most headache, the part about the *general form of propositions* and of language.

And this is true—Instead of producing something common to all that we call language, I am saying that these phenomena have no one thing in common which makes us use the same word for all,—but that they are *related* to one another in many different ways. And it is because of this relationship, or these relationships, that we call them all "language." I will try to explain this.

66.   Consider for example the proceedings that we call "games." I mean board-games, card-games, ball-games, Olympic games, and so on. What is common to them all?—Don't say: "There *must* be something common, or they would not be called 'games'" but *look and see* whether there is anything common to all.—For if you look at them you will not see something that is common to *all,* but similarities, relationships, and a whole series of them at that. To repeat: don't think, but look . . .

And the result of this examination is: we see a complicated network of similarities overlapping and criss-crossing: sometimes overall similarities, sometimes similarities of detail.

67.   I can think of no better expression to characterize these similarities than "family resemblances"; for the various resemblances between members of a family: build, features, colour of eyes, gait, temperament, etc., etc., overlap and criss-cross in the same way—And I shall say: "games" form a family . . . .

116.   When philosophers use a word—"knowledge," "being," "object," "I," "proposition," "name"—and try to grasp the *essence* of the thing, one must always ask oneself: is the word ever actually used in this way in the language-game which is its original home?—

What *we* do is to bring words back from their metaphysical to their everyday use . . . .

118.   Where does our investigation get its importance from, since it seems only to destroy everything interesting, that is, all that is great and important? (As it were all the buildings, leaving behind only bits of stone and rubble.) What we are destroying is nothing but houses of cards and we are clearing up the ground of language on which they stand.

119.   The results of philosophy are the uncovering of one or another piece of plain nonsense and of bumps that the understanding has got by running its head up against the limits of language. These bumps make us see the value of the discovery.

122.   A main source of our failure to understand is that we do not *command a clear view* of the use of our words—Our grammar is lacking in this sort of perspicuity. A perspicuous representation produces just that understanding which consists in 'seeing connections.' Hence the importance of finding and inventing *intermediate cases* . . . .

123.   A philosophical problem has the form: "I don't know my way about."

124.   Philosophy may in no way interfere with the actual use of language; it can in the end only describe it.
    For it cannot give it any foundation either.
    It leaves everything as it is. . . .

133.   It is not our aim to refine or complete the system of rules for the use of our words in unheard-of ways.
    For the clarity that we are aiming at is indeed *complete* clarity. But this simply means that the philosophical problems should *completely* disappear.

Questions for Discussion

1. What effect do you think the successes of science had on the changing attitudes of philosophers toward the role of philosophy?
2. What do you think Wittgenstein meant by saying that philosophy "leaves everything as it is?" Do you agree with him? Why, or why not?
3. Expand on Wittgenstein's list of the different language games. In case you think that Wittgenstein's list in the reading is already complete, you should know that the English philosopher J. L. Austin thought there were *hundreds* of such different usages.
4. If the ordinary language philosophers are right, does that mean we should no longer study the works of Plato, Epicurus, Berkeley, and Descartes? Give reasons for your answer.
5. Which of the traditional metaphysical questions covered in this section of the book are aided by applying Wittgenstein's insights? If none of them, why not?

Suggestions for Further Reading

Aune, Bruce. *Metaphysics: The Elements.* Minneapolis: University of Minnesota Press, 1985. Clearly written for university students, a development of Professor Aune's metaphysical speculations over many years.

Chisolm, Roderick M. *On Metaphysics.* Minneapolis: University of Minnesota Press, 1989. A brief, clearly written overview by an outstanding American philosopher.

Gracia, Jorge J. E. *Metaphysics and Its Task. The Search for the Categorical Foundation of Knowledge.* Albany: State University of New York Press, 1999. Offers a systematic survey of the discipline and how it has survived the attacks of its critics.

Hamlyn, D. V. *Metaphysics.* Cambridge: Cambridge University Press, 1984. A defense of metaphysics interpreted in an Aristotelian form of what Hamlyn calls "ontology."

Körner, Stephan. *Metaphysics: Its Structure and Function.* Cambridge: Cambridge University Press, 1984. A defense of metaphysics on Kantian grounds as necessary to most fields of thought.

Sprague, Elmer. *Metaphysical Thinking.* New York: Oxford University Press, 1978. Clear, short general introduction to metaphysics.

How Do We Know? (Epistemology)

PART 4

CHAPTER 13

Introduction to Epistemology

The *theory of knowledge,* or, as it is sometimes called, *epistemology,* is a branch of philosophy which investigates the nature, scope, and quality of human knowledge. What is knowledge? How extensive is it? How good is it? Just as metaphysics tries to discover what is real and how reality differs from appearance, so the theory of knowledge tries to discover what knowledge is and how it differs from mere opinion. That is, epistemology tries to establish normative criteria for what is to count as knowledge. Epistemology is obviously an important topic, since knowledge is so important in human life. Human beings are capable of holding and expressing a wide range of opinions on a variety of topics. But although we may be said to possess genuine knowledge in some of these cases, there are many others in which we do *not* know, but only *think* we know. And the most obvious difference between the two clearly indicates why knowledge is so important.

Knowledge, Opinion, and Belief

When you know something you not only have an opinion, but that opinion is true; that is, it coincides with reality. When you merely believe something but do not know it, then it is possible that what you believe is not true, but only exists in your mind. This means that when we think something is the case but do not know it we are more liable to be mistaken. And herein lies the practical importance of knowledge. The whole point of a great deal of our thinking is to correctly adjust our beliefs to the way things actually are in the world. It is essential to our very survival that we be able to do so at least most of the time. Apart from daydreaming, storytelling, and the like, the function of human thinking is to align thought and behavior with reality. For these reasons it is clear why knowledge is preferable to mere opinion. The very word *knowledge* has an honorific quality, connoting a positive value. Knowledge is, in short, a much more reliable guide to action than mere belief or opinion.

Now we see the significance of the philosopher's question, "What is the difference between knowledge and mere opinion?" Since knowledge is so important and desirable in human affairs, it would be very good if we had a reliable way of picking it out from the larger class of beliefs.

This is going to be a difficult thing to do, however, as we will see. Let us examine the problem to see what solving it involves. At first glance it seems fair to say that although everything we know is also believed, not everything we believe is known. Why, what is the difference?

As we saw in Part 2 in discussing the traditional analysis of knowledge in terms of necessary and sufficient conditions, it seems intuitively clear that where we believe something which we do not know, that belief could be false, whereas when we truly know something it could not be false. Here we see the intimate connection between problems of knowledge and considerations of truth and falsity. Can a person believe something which is false? Sure. But can a person *know* something that is false? Here we come back to the honorific or complimentary character of the word *knowledge.* When you say that someone knows something, you are paying that person a compliment, that what the person believes is true. But what if we later discover that what we said this person knew turned out to be false after all? We would retract our claim that we were dealing with knowledge and substitute the more evaluatively neutral claim that the person merely believed or thought it was true.

But now we can begin to see why the theory of knowledge is so difficult. To discover the difference between knowledge and belief we must differentiate between those beliefs which are true and those which might not be. But how can we do that? Everything I believe I believe to be true. Otherwise I would not believe it! To believe something implies that the person holds the belief to be true. In my own case it would seem very difficult indeed to sort my true from my false (or possibly false) beliefs. Of course we can draw the distinction quite easily in judging what other people think. It is easy for me to say that my friend believes things which are not true. But if I turn that around now and ask whether I know or merely believe that my friend's opinion is not true, I am right back where I started. I can distinguish knowledge from belief in others, but surprisingly not in my own case. We will return to the problem of truth in a moment. But first let us look at some other seemingly obvious differences between knowledge and belief which might serve as a criterion for distinguishing them.

Knowledge and Certainty

Part of the complimentary flavor of the word *knowledge* lies in the fact that those who know something have a right to a certain confidence in their belief as a true and reliable guide to action. Knowledge implies being sure, being certain. Would you say you knew something if you were not sure about it? "I know he will be here, but I am not sure." This sounds odd. On the other hand, there is no problem saying you believe something but are not sure. "I think so, but I'm not sure." Might not this provide us with the criterion we are seeking? Descartes thought so, making this the cornerstone of his entire philosophy. But there are problems with this, too. If I merely believe something I will have some hesitancy, some doubt about it, and if I claim to know something I will feel much more certain and confident about it. But will this criterion always and necessarily work? Do people always know what they feel confident about? No. People we judge to be fanatics are precisely those we feel have maximum feelings of certitude and minimum information. I can, of course, always tell how certain I feel about a given opinion, but that will do me little good in my theory of knowledge unless that feeling of certainty is firmly linked with genuine knowledge of the truth, which, unfortunately, is not the case. We shall return to the relationship of knowledge and certainty in a moment, but first let us examine one final possible criterion for distinguishing knowledge from belief.

Part of our greater confidence in the truth of what we claim to know arises from the fact that we have better *reasons* for believing our information to be true. We examined this position briefly in the chapter on reasoning. Sometimes we deny that a person knows something even though it turns out to be true, simply because the person's reasons for believing it were not good enough. In other words, part of our compliment in saying that someone knows something is that the person has good grounds for confidence in its truth. And this criterion, though perhaps not perfect, as we shall see, does provide a better practical guide than either truth or certainty. The other criteria do not really tell us what to do; this one does. The human dilemma as regards knowledge is that we cannot easily distinguish in our own case what is true from what we merely think is true, and we cannot place too much confidence simply in our own feelings of certainty. But what we *can* do is to get ourselves into the best possible position to know—weighing all the evidence, examining all the arguments, pro and con. The result of this is not necessarily or absolutely the truth, but what is most probable and therefore the likeliest to be true. And this, short of our becoming gods, may be all that humans are capable of.

Epistemology and Psychology

Perhaps the goals and concerns of epistemology will be clearer if we contrast them with the goals and concerns of psychology. Both epistemology and psychology are concerned with human consciousness, and it might at first appear that epistemology is only trying to do what psychology is in a position to do better. But there is a fundamental difference between the two approaches. Psychology is an attempt to *describe* the way the human mind actually operates; epistemology

seeks to establish normative criteria for how we *ought* to think. In its more ex-
perimental mode, psychology centers its attention on the physiological aspects of
the knowing process on the brain, stimulus-response mechanisms, the nervous
system, and so forth. As a descriptive enterprise, it is not the purpose of psychology to delve into the intricacies of separating opinion from knowledge and belief
from opinion. Whereas the epistemologist is concerned with standards of accept-
ability in terms of which to judge beliefs, the psychologist is mainly interested in
understanding the *how* of human thinking.

In short, epistemology is concerned with discovering a sure guide to truth. But
what *is* truth? This is an old question, the question Pilate asked Jesus. When we
look at the kinds of answers given by philosophers, they all gravitate toward
three principal theories: (1) the correspondence theory of truth, (2) the coherence
theory, and (3) the pragmatic test of truth. Generally speaking, we can say that
most empiricists accept a correspondence theory of truth and most rationalists
accept a coherence theory. The difference between them is basically this: The correspondence theory holds that our thoughts are true if they *correspond* to reality. This theory works best if you hold to a theory of knowledge (such as the
British empiricists did) that thoughts and ideas are copies of physical objects me-
diated by the senses. The correspondence theory works pretty well as long as you
are dealing with physical objects, less well when dealing with nonphysical objects
—moods, emotions, hopes, ambitions, fears, moral truths, arithmetic, and so on.
The coherence theory, in contrast to the correspondence theory, holds that we are
entitled to accept the truth of a statement if it is *coherent* with our other accepted items of belief and knowledge. For example, astronomers believed in the existence of the planet Pluto before they were able to see it with telescopes; they
predicted its existence from the behavior of the other planets whose orbits were
skewed as they would be if there existed a ninth planet. Moreover, there was
nothing about believing in the existence of another planet that in any way
threatened existing views about the solar system. Adding another planet is coherent with our established beliefs, and it causes the minimum of alteration in
these beliefs.

Suppose, though, we do not have empirical evidence for the truth of a new
claim, but it is coherent with our other established beliefs. How do we determine
whether to accept or reject it? Here the *pragmatic test* is suggested by some
philosophers as a way of judging hypotheses proposed to us for acceptance. If
given two hypotheses, and no other way of determining the truth or falsity of
them, ask yourself what the practical difference would be if you accepted one and
rejected the other. If you have no other basis on which to decide, make your choice
on the basis of this practical difference. If there is no practical difference between
them, then no matter of truth is really at stake. A difference that makes no difference is really no difference at all.

Philosophers who argue for each of these views of truth are usually pretty one-
sided in their defense of their view. A defender of a correspondence theory of
truth will want you to believe that all matters of truth must be so decided. The

defender of a coherence theory will similarly try to convince you that the coherence test is the only satisfactory way of resolving doubt. In practice, we probably use all three methods of judging the truth of claims presented to us. We accept some claims because there is a correspondence with empirical data. Others we adopt because they fit in well with our other well-established views. Still other matters must be decided by appealing to the practical difference resulting from our acceptance or rejection of the truth claim or item presented to us for belief.

Epistemology is also important in philosophy because it serves as a bridge to other philosophical issues. If we are concerned with knowing reality, we must also take up the question of what is real (metaphysics). A consideration of how we should judge statements as to their truth value leads us directly into a consideration of principles of reasoning (logic). And when we attempt to relate matters of belief and knowledge to choices of action, we are led immediately into a discussion of principles that should guide our actions (ethics).

Sources of Knowledge

Having looked at the area of epistemology in general, we shall now examine in detail one very important problem in epistemology, the source of our knowledge. Is knowledge based entirely on reason, or must it be grounded in direct sense experience of the world, or some combination of the two? In the readings we will look at an example of the first (rationalism), an example of the second (empiricism), and one attempt to reconcile or combine the two.

Perhaps the best way to approach our question is to return to the discussion in the previous paragraphs about certainty. The ideal kind of knowledge we are all after is knowledge that tells us something about the real world and that is absolutely certain. But is such ideal knowledge possible? Empirical knowledge seems in principle to fall short of this ideal. All of our claims to know something about the objective physical world are liable to error, no matter how careful we are. It is always possible to be mistaken (as we shall see from the Descartes reading). But what *can* we know with complete certainty? Perhaps only that I exist, and some mathematical, logical, self-evident truths. Can we build the whole of knowledge on this meager basis? At first some philosophers in the modern period, such as Descartes, thought we could. But it finally dawned on other philosophers, such as Hume, that this was an impossible dream. The cost of saying something about the real world is to be liable to error. And the price of absolute certainty is not to say anything about the real world. Let us look at this. How is error possible? Error enters, we may say, in the gap between thought and reality, between what we *think* things are like and what they really are. The only way to avoid the gap *completely* is not to make claims about the world at all.

But what sort of knowledge is it that makes no claim at all about the world? Historically, there have been two proposals, one that appealed to the *rationalists* and one that became the foundation for the *empiricists* (though the roots of both, as we shall see, are to be found in the rationalist, Descartes). In the first sort of case, imagine a weather reporter who becomes so frustrated at being mistaken night after night, saying it will snow when it does not and that it will not snow when it does, that in desperation the reporter finally announces that "tomorrow either it will snow or it will not." This statement avoids all possibility of being proved wrong, but what have we learned about the weather? Nothing. This is an example of a statement which is "analytically" true, that is, true by definition. Another example is, "All bachelors are unmarried." This statement is analytically true simply because "unmarried" is part of the definition of "bachelor" (a bachelor is "an unmarried man"). By tracing out the logical implications embedded in concepts like this, elaborate systems of logic and mathematics can be constructed, and on this model rationalist philosophers, such as Descartes, Spinoza, and Leibniz, hoped to erect the structure of knowledge on a solid and secure foundation of complete certainty.

The other kind of certainty, which appealed to empiricist philosophers, but which is also purchased at the price of not saying anything about the external world, consists of purely introspective claims about how things appear to us. If I say that I see a pool of water in the road ahead, I may be proved wrong (if it turns out to be a mirage, for example), but if I say that it *looks* like a pool of water, there is nothing that can prove me *wrong—whatever* it is, it does *look* to me like a pool of water. And it was on this basis that the empiricists proposed to erect the foundations of all knowledge.

Both the empiricist account and the rationalist account are based on certainty and each avoids error by restricting itself to a special kind of knowledge which does not claim any sort of correspondence to an external reality—the rationalists by limiting claims to the relation of words to ideas, and the empiricists by restricting themselves to claims about the quality of internal sensations. Since they do not *claim* any correspondence with an external reality, there is no possibility of a *failed* correspondence, and hence no possibility of error. Nor is there, however, any possibility of knowledge of informational content. The choice seems to be as follows: If you want to say something about the world, you will have to give up the quest for absolute certainty, and if you want complete certainty, you must give up the idea of talking about the world. In either case, the long-sought goal of certain knowledge about the actual world seems to be an illusion.

Before turning to selections from the philosophers themselves, a final word about a commitment shared by almost all philosophers concerned with epistemology: Philosophers are generally a breed of folks who think that knowledge is possible. At various points in the history of philosophy, persons have appeared who argued that knowledge is not possible. In ancient Greece, Gorgias, a contemporary of Plato, claimed that there is no such thing as reality and if there were we could never have knowledge of it, and even if we could know about it we could not communicate this knowledge! This is perhaps the most extreme form of *skepticism—denial* of the possibility of knowledge—in the history of philosophy. Plato rejected skepticism, as have most of the other principal figures in the history of philosophy, for skepticism is not only a philosophical dead end, it is also internally inconsistent. Skepticism is a dead end for the reason that, if we accept skeptical conclusions, there is no knowledge and therefore no epistemology. But a more serious objection to skepticism is that it contradicts itself. If you say, à la Gorgias, that there is no knowledge, do you *know* this to be true? How can you *know* that you cannot *know*? See the problem? A similar difficulty confronts the person who says, "There is no truth." (Is *that* statement true?) If your epistemological reasoning leads you to skepticism, you can either assume that you made a mistake somewhere in your reasoning and start all over again (which is what Descartes did) or you can simply accept your skeptical conclusions, give up philosophy, and go about your other business (which is what Hume did).

We will examine selections from the writings of both these philosophers, but first we will examine a much older theory of knowledge—that of Plato.

Questions for Discussion

1. If you had to characterize your own epistemological views, would you say you accept a correspondence, coherence, or pragmatic theory? Why?

2. In your own words, characterize the difference between *knowledge, belief* and *opinion.*

3. From your own experience give an example of how your thinking about a particular issue moved from error to truth. What considerations supported this change? Can you formulate them precisely?

4. What is appealing about giving the senses a primary role in knowledge? What are the limitations of this approach?

5. What is appealing about giving reason a primary role in knowledge? What are the strengths and weaknesses of this approach?

CHAPTER 14

Appearance and Reality

Like most of the philosophical issues we are considering, the first attempts to deal with the issue of knowledge, at least in Western thought, occurred in ancient Greece. This again points up one of the reasons the Greeks were so important: They formulated many of the questions that have dominated Western thought, even though they were not able to give satisfactory answers. Questions of knowledge and reality were at the heart of Plato's philosophical concerns. It is difficult to separate Plato's metaphysics from his epistemology, since in *The Republic* he defines levels of knowledge in terms of levels of reality, and vice versa.

Plato's Theory of Knowledge

The distinction between appearance and reality was an essential ingredient in Plato's theory of knowledge. But this distinction was elaborated in a way that tied in with Plato's view of reality, his political theories, his ethical viewpoint, indeed, the whole of his philosophy. We can see in Plato's work perhaps as clearly as in the work of any other philosopher the intimate connection between epistemology and metaphysics.

But before looking at some specifics of Plato's view, consider the following questions.

1. Would you agree that Einstein discovered rather than invented the theory of relativity?
2. If all the people who understand the theory of relativity were to die suddenly, would the theory still be true in some important sense?
3. Were the principles of relativity true before Einstein formulated them?

4. In general, does it seem to be the case that something that is eternal would be more real than something that has only a limited existence?

5. Does it make sense to you to say that a dream world (such as you experience in sleep) is not as real as the world you inhabit while awake?

6. Does the fact that we can achieve greater certainty when we are dealing with mathematical proofs (such as in geometry) than when we base our knowledge on sense experience suggest that knowledge gained through reasoning alone is truer than knowledge gained through the senses?

We could extend the list more, but we will stop here. If you answered yes to all these questions, then you are an incipient Platonist.

Degrees of Knowing

First, think about the simplest kind of knowledge. Suppose you are in a dimly lit room and you see shadows moving (though you are not sure what they are shadows of). You could say that you think you see somebody, but you are not sure. Missing from this situation is an important ingredient for sight, namely light. All you can see are images, shadows, dim shapes. Then turn on the light or open the shades and let the sun shine in, and the shapes take on new dimensions. When they were only shadows, dim images, you could say you imagined that you saw a person, whereas it was really a coat hanging on the hall tree. When you are dealing with images, you cannot say that you have knowledge; you are unsure, confused, because you are only imagining things.

In this example, when we let the sunlight stream into the room, the images become visible things. Remember this example. It will come up again.

Now consider physical objects themselves. Once they are properly lighted, we can be more certain of our knowledge since we are now dealing with physical things. But we still are not absolutely certain of our knowledge claims. In Part 2 we talked about one such difficulty posed to claims based on sense experience when we saw how hard it is to draw a conclusion from generalized data. Suppose that you are an ornithologist and have observed that every swan you have seen is white. Can you say that you therefore know that all swans are white? No, because it is possible that there is a species of swan with different coloration. You are simply limited by your powers of observation to partial knowledge. In the attempt by physical scientists to measure the position of a subatomic particle, the possibility of knowing other things about it is destroyed by the very act of observation.

But when we deal with mathematical proofs, suddenly the state of our knowledge changes. We may not be able to measure a triangle perfectly to determine whether its angles equal 180°, but we can demonstrate by a mathematical proof that this is so. One of the first things you learned in high school geometry is that there are no perfect triangles in the world, no absolutely straight lines, or spheres that are perfectly round. All these are mathematical ideals, entities that we can think about and use in our reasoning to deduce other characteristics of geometrical figures. Does this mean that knowledge gained by reason alone through deduction is more certain than knowledge gained by sense experience? It would seem so. And it would also seem that the objects we know by mathematical deduction (perfect triangles, straight lines, absolutely round spheres, and so forth) simply cannot exist in the world of the senses, yet we can know of these objects through the mind alone. Again to go back to an example from physics, we can speak of a perfect vacuum, but this does not exist in the realm of our experience. So what are we to conclude? Certainly not that these objects—the perfect triangle, a vacuum, a straight line—are imaginary. Remember that things we imagine are *less* certain, not more certain. What are we to conclude if not that we have moved to a higher level of knowledge?

The interesting thing about mathematics is that it is a kind of bridge between the world of thought and the world of the senses, between the visible and the intelligible world. You may recall that when you studied geometry, the classroom was filled with all kinds of differently shaped objects—pyramids, spheres, cubes. They were there not to serve as the object of study but to jog your mind as you puzzled out a geometrical proof. The physical, visible object was a bridge between the physical world and the world of pure thought.

Finally, we come to a class of objects of knowledge that seem even more basic to thought than mathematical objects. Consider such basic ideas as equality, difference, sameness, unity, diversity. Abstractions? In a sense, yes. But if you think about them, they seem to be presupposed in every act of knowing. Unless, in some sense, you already recognized the meaning of difference, you could not perceive two objects and make the judgment about them that they are different. You can conclude that they are an instance of difference, but you would not derive that notion from a mere inspection of them. Plato called such objects of knowledge *Forms,* or in Greek *Ideas* (which means "forms"). The most important epistemological task is to discover these most basic ideas, without which an understanding of knowledge would be impossible.

Equally important for the well-being of humans is knowledge of the Forms that should govern human society—justice, piety, excellence, virtue. All of these Forms are essential to our knowledge of our place in the world, yet none of them exists as an object in the world to be known by the senses. They are known rather by reason itself, and the pursuit of these Forms is the highest activity of reason.

The Great Chain of Being

Plato's argument for degrees of knowledge is presented in the following selections from *The Republic.* What should be obvious to you now is that corresponding to each of the degrees of knowing is a level of reality. All that is real can be classified on an ascending scale, from that which has minimal existence to that which has greater reality.

Plato thought there were Forms, or Ideas, for abstract entities. But what about constructed objects such as this treasury of Athens at Delphi? Questions such as these pushed Plato's theory of Forms to its limits. Photo by David Stewart.

We tend not to think of the world in this way, but why not? Perhaps it is because the epistemological texture of our world is not as rich as Plato's. We tend to think in only two categories: something is either real or unreal. But is this the case? Is it not plausible to distinguish between the reality of dreams and the objects of which dream images are only pale shadows? If I dream of my car, surely we would want to say that the dream image of the car is not as real and is not known as clearly by me as is the car itself. And as for the engineering principles that are embodied in the car; are they less real than the car? Surely not, since without them the car could never have been constructed. So instead of the two-dimensional world in which many of us live, Plato offers us a multistoried reality to which each level offers us a degree of knowing.

Plato describes these levels of knowing in one of the passages in the reading that follows. He refers there to the "divided line." That may not strike you as what Plato intended it to be—a musical analogy. The Pythagoreans (named after their leader Pythagoras, who also gave his name to the famous geometrical theorem) discovered that the principles of music lie in mathematical ratios. In fact, we owe a great deal of our current musical terminology to them: we speak of fourths, fifths, thirds, and so on—mathematical ratios to express musical tones.

If we take a musical instrument with a single string, a monochord, and tune it to A 440 and then stop it with our finger exactly halfway between its two ends, the tone we get is an octave above A 440. The analogy Plato therefore suggests to us is a twofold division between appearance and reality, with reality a term reserved for the higher level.

For each of the degrees of knowing, and its corresponding degree of reality, Plato used a specific term. The divided-line illustration with the Greek terms Plato used and their usual English translations are given in the following diagram, which accompanies Professor Cornford's translation of *The Republic*.

Appropriate to each level of reality is a type of knowledge and a means of knowing. The senses guide us through the world of appearance, but reason takes us beyond appearance into the realm of the Forms: pure Ideas unalloyed with the uncertainty of the world of appearances.

Better at this point to let Plato speak for himself. But first a word about *The Republic* and how it is structured. *The Republic* is a far-ranging treatise touching on virtually every area of Plato's philosophy. It can also be read as a work on the ideal political organization for human society, as a utopia. It is presented as a dialogue between Socrates and Glaucon, one of Plato's older brothers, though he is here portrayed as a young man. The literary form of the dialogue was a favorite of Plato's, but here the conversations are recalled by Socrates, so what we really have is a reminiscence of a dialogue.

We break in on the conversation (or on Socrates' recollections of the conversation) when he and Glaucon begin to talk about education for the rulers of the

	Objects		**States of Mind**
	The Good		
			Intelligence *(noesis)* or
Intelligible World	Forms	D	knowledge *(episteme)*
	Mathematical objects	C	Thinking *(dianoia)*
World of Appearances	Visible things	B	Belief *(pistis)*
	Images	A	Imagining *(eikasia)*

ideal state. Socrates is making a case for the view that education of the rulers (here called Guardians) should be a philosophical education. In short, the rulers should be philosophers, because philosophers are not interested in transitory things that might corrupt them but rather have their concerns directed toward the eternal principles of things and the organization of human society on the ideal model of perfect justice and the ideal state. In the process of describing why kings should be philosophers, Socrates also tells us a great deal about Plato's theory of knowledge. The conversation recorded here never took place, but Plato uses Socrates—his teacher—and his brother as the dramatic personae of this engaging philosophical work. Some of the views presented may have been those Socrates taught Plato, but we should consider them mainly as Plato's own.

Plato: The Visible and the Invisible

Conceive, then, that there are these two powers I speak of; the Good reigning over the domain of all that is intelligible, the Sun over the visible world for the heaven as I might call it; only you would think I was showing off my skill in etymology. At any rate you have these two orders of things clearly before your mind: the visible and the intelligible?

I have.

Now take a line divided into two unequal parts, one to represent the visible order, the other the intelligible, and divide each part again in the same proportion, symbolizing degrees of comparative clearness or obscurity. Then (A) one of the two sections in the visible world will stand for images. By images I mean first shadows, and then reflections in water or in close grained, polished surfaces, and everything of that kind, if you understand.

Yes, I understand.

Let the second section (B) stand for the actual things of which the first are likenesses, the living creatures about us and all the works of nature or of human hands.

So be it.

Will you also take the proportion in which the visible World has been divided as corresponding to degrees of reality and truth, so that the likeness shall stand to the original in the same ratio as the sphere of appearances and belief to the sphere of knowledge?

Certainly.

Reprinted from *The Republic of Plato*, translated by F. M. Cornford (1941). By permission of Oxford University Press. From books 6 and 7.

Now consider how we are to divide the part which stands for the intelligible world. There are two sections. In the first (C) the mind uses as images those actual things which themselves had images in the visible world, and it is compelled to pursue its inquiry by starting from assumptions and traveling, not up to a principle, but down to a conclusion. In the second (D) the mind moves in the other direction, from an assumption up towards a principle which is not hypothetical, and it makes no use of the images employed in the other section, but only of Forms, and conducts its inquiry solely by their means.

I don't quite understand what you mean.

Then we will try again; what I have just said will help you to understand. (C) You know, of course, how students of subjects like geometry and arithmetic begin by postulating odd and even numbers, or the various figures and the three kinds of angles and other such data in each subject. These data they take as known, and, having adopted them as assumptions, they do not feel called upon to give any account of them to themselves or to anyone else, but treat them as self-evident. Then, starting from these assumptions, they go on until they arrive, by a series of consistent steps, at all the conclusions they set out to investigate.

Yes, I know that.

You also know how they make use of visible figures and discourse about them, though what they really have in mind is the originals of which these figures are images: they are not reasoning, for instance, about this particular square and diagonal which they have drawn, but about *the* Square and *the* Diagonal and so in all cases. The diagrams they draw and the models they make are actual things,

PLATO (428/7–348/7 B.C.E.) Born in Athens, Plato became a student of Socrates and is mentioned in the Apology *as being present at his trial. After the death of Socrates, Plato traveled outside of Greece but returned eventually to Athens where he founded the Academy in 388 or 387 B.C.E. In many ways the first university, the Academy provided study in philosophy, mathematics, and the physical sciences. Courtesy of The Bettmann Archive.*

which may have their shadows or images in water, but now they serve in their turn as images, while the student is seeking to behold those realities which only thought can apprehend.

True.

This, then, is the class of things that I spoke of as intelligible, but with two qualifications: first that the mind, in studying them, is compelled to employ assumptions and because it cannot rise above these, does not travel upwards to a first principle; and second, that it uses as images those actual things which have images of their own in the section below them and which, in comparison with those shadows and reflections, are reputed to be more palpable and valued accordingly.

I understand: you mean the subject-matter of geometry and of the kindred arts.

(D) Then by the second section of the intelligible world you may understand me to mean all that unaided reasoning apprehends by the power of dialectic, when it treats its assumptions, not as first principles, but as *hypotheses* in the literal sense, things 'laid down' like a flight of steps up which it may mount all the way to something that is not hypothetical, the first principle of all; and having grasped this, may turn back and, holding on to the consequences which depend upon it, descend at last to a conclusion, never making use of any sensible object, but only of Forms, moving through Forms from one to another, and ending with Forms.

I understand, he said, though not perfectly, for the procedure you describe sounds like an enormous undertaking. But I see that you mean to distinguish the field of intelligible reality studied by dialectic as having a greater certainty and truth than the subject-matter of the 'arts,' as they are called, which treat their assumptions as first principles. The students of these arts are, it is true, compelled to exercise thought in contemplating objects which the senses cannot perceive, but because they start from assumptions without going back to a first principle, you do not regard them as gaining true understanding about those objects, although the objects themselves, when connected with a first principle, are intelligible. And I think you would call the state of mind of the students of geometry and other such arts, not intelligence, but thinking, arts being something between intelligence and mere acceptance of appearances.

You have understood me quite well enough, I replied. And now you may take, as corresponding to the four sections, these four states of mind: *intelligence* for the highest, *thinking* for the second, *belief* for the third, and for the last *imagining*. These you may arrange as the terms in a proportion, assigning to each a degree of clearness and certainty corresponding to the measure in which their objects possess truth and reality.

I understand and agree with you. I will arrange them as you say.

Knowledge Is Knowledge of Forms

Before going further, we should reflect a bit more on the Forms, or Ideas. Consider the Form of justice. What is justice? An important and difficult question, one that Plato considers in many of his dialogues since Plato's theory of reality is intertwined with his theory of knowledge. Unless we know what justice is, how will we ever be able to manifest it in human affairs? Unless we understand such basic principles, we can never achieve them, even in a partial and limited way, in our state. The same thing holds for such Ideas as excellence or virtue, piety, and so on. Many colleges state on their letterheads that they are committed to excellence in education, but what is it that is named by excellence? Before claiming they are committed to it, should not the leaders of such colleges at least know what it is they are talking about? Plato would have thought so.

Are there also Forms, or Ideas, of particular things—beds, chairs, tables, horses? Plato does not offer a completely satisfactory answer to this question, at least in the works still available to us. However, it is clear that for Plato knowledge is, in some important sense, knowledge of the Forms of the particular things we know. For example, if you are in a laboratory dissecting a frog, you are not interested in that particular frog, you want rather to understand the nature of frogness—that reality which every frog insofar as it is a frog and not something else possesses. So, in some sense, frogness transcends any particular frog. The expert zoologist is the one who knows the general principles of animate objects, not the particulars of individual animals. It remained for Plato's student Aristotle to develop this aspect of Plato's theory of knowledge more fully.

The Allegory of the Cave

In the allegory of the cave (from the following selection) we get Plato's view of the difference between those who claim knowledge but only know the particular things of sense experience and those whose knowledge is of universal principles. The situation he describes is of a group of prisoners sitting in an underground cavern looking at shadows on the wall made by persons holding up cut-out figures of objects in front of a fire. The prisoners have never seen anything but the images; for them, that is reality. But one of the prisoners is freed from his chains and makes his way up a long and tortuous ascent to the outside world. There his vision is blinded by the sun, but as his eyes adjust themselves, he sees real objects, the realities of which he has heretofore experienced only in the images he has seen. Think how stunned he must be to suddenly grasp the difference between appearance and reality, between images and real things. He then returns to the cave to deliver the truth to his fellow prisoners. But they do not want to hear that what they think is reality is only a dim shadow of the real. So they kill the messenger and are content to remain in ignorance.

This allegory has several levels of meaning. At one level Plato uses it to explain why the citizens of Athens executed his teacher Socrates. Socrates was accused of corrupting the youth by leading them to question authority and the accepted explanations for things; he was a troubling influence. It also offers Plato's account of the human situation. People are happy in their ignorance. They resent those who force them to recognize that they are ignorant. That is why

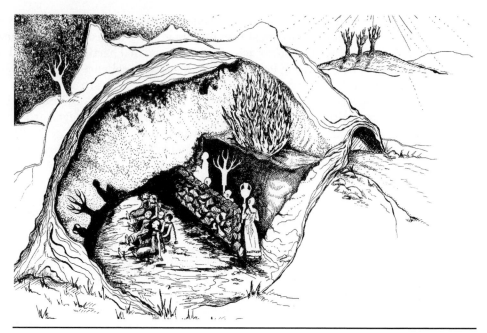

In the allegory of the cave, Plato likened individuals unenlightened by philosophy to persons chained in a cave who think that images cast on a wall are reality. Drawing copyright 1987 by Candice Blocker.

philosophers are viewed with suspicion and distrust. We are comfortable with our prejudices and do not want them disturbed.

At another level, the allegory characterizes Plato's view of philosophy. Philosophy is a time-consuming and difficult way of life (comparable to the long and difficult ascent from the cave). How do we know the Forms? It is not easy, but it is possible, and Plato describes the proper preparation for the pursuit of such knowledge. Young people should not begin the study of philosophy because their interests are distracted by other things. Only in middle age, and after a rigorous study of mathematics, should one be allowed to pursue the disciplines of philosophy. The method whereby one seeks knowledge of the Forms is the dialectic (discussed in some detail in Part 2). To discover the nature of justice, for example, one has to begin with whatever provisional and partial understanding of justice one has. But through careful questioning that exposes the limitations of this provisional view, one can then proceed to a better definition. Again, one examines this definition and exposes its inadequacies. This process, repeated again and again, leads us ever closer to the truth we seek.

At still another level, the allegory states Plato's view of knowledge and reality. The Forms or general principles of things are the proper objects of knowledge.

And philosophers are not like other persons, for they have their gaze firmly fixed on the unchanging Forms, on the eternally true principles of things, not the changing and transient world of experience. For this reason, Plato thought a society's rulers should be philosophically trained, for they would seek the good of society and would not be misled by a search for fame, fortune, or wealth.

Next, said I, here is a parable to illustrate the degrees to which our nature may be enlightened or unenlightened. Imagine the condition of men living in a sort of cavernous chamber underground, with an entrance open to the light and a long passage all down the cave. Here they have been from childhood, chained by the leg and also by the neck, so that they cannot move and can see only what is in front of them, because the chains will not let them turn their heads. At some distance higher up is the light of a fire burning behind them: and between the prisoners and the fire is a track with a parapet built along it, like the screen at a puppet-show, which hides the performers while they show their puppets over the top.

I see, said he.

Now behind this parapet imagine persons carrying along various artificial objects, including figures of men and animals in wood or stone or other materials, which project above the parapet. Naturally, some of these persons will be talking, others silent.

It is a strange picture, he said, and a strange sort of prisoners.

Like ourselves, I replied, for in the first place prisoners so confined would have seen nothing of themselves or of one another, except the shadows thrown by the firelight on the wall of the Cave facing them, would they?

Not if all their lives they had been prevented from moving their heads.

And they would have seen as little of the objects carried past.

Of course.

Now, if they could talk to one another, would they not suppose that their words referred only to those passing shadows which they saw?

Necessarily.

And suppose their prison had an echo from the wall facing them? When one of the people crossing behind them spoke, they could only suppose that the sound came from the shadow passing before their eyes.

No doubt.

In every way, then, such prisoners would recognize as reality nothing but the shadows of those artificial objects.

Inevitably.

Now consider what would happen if their release from the chains and the healing of their unwisdom should come about in this way. Suppose one of them set free and forced suddenly to stand up, turn his head, and walk with eyes lifted to the light; all these movements would be painful, and he would be too dazzled to make out the objects whose shadows he had been used to seeing. What do you think he would say, if someone told him that what he had formerly seen was meaningless illusion, but now, being somewhat nearer to reality and turned towards more real objects, he was getting a truer view? Suppose further that he were shown the various objects being carried by and were made to say, in reply to questions, what each of them was. Would he not be perplexed and believe the objects now shown him to be not so real as what he formerly saw?

Yes, not nearly so real.

And if he were forced to look at the fire-light itself, would not his eyes ache, so that he would try to escape and turn back to the things which he could see distinctly, convinced that they really were clearer than these other objects now being shown to him?

Yes.

And suppose someone were to drag him away forcibly up the steep and rugged ascent and not let him go until he had hauled him out into the sunlight, would he not suffer pain and vexation at such treatment, and, when he had come out into the light, find his eyes so full of its radiance that he could not see a single one of the things that he was not told were real?

Certainly he would not see them all at once.

He would need, then, to grow accustomed before he could see things in that upper world. At first, it would be easiest to make out shadows, and then the images of men and things reflected in water, and later on the things themselves. After that, it would be easier to watch the heavenly bodies and the sky itself by night, looking at the light of the moon and stars rather than the Sun and the Sun's light in the daytime.

Yes, surely.

Last of all, he would begin to draw the conclusion that it is the Sun that produces the seasons and the course of the year and controls everything in the visible world, and moreover is in a way the cause of all that he and his companions used to see.

Clearly he would come at last to that conclusion.

No doubt.

And now he would begin to draw the conclusion that it is the Sun that produces the seasons and the course of the year and controls everything in the visible world, and moreover is in a way the cause of all that he and his companions used to see.

Clearly he would come at last to that conclusion.

Then if he called to mind his fellow prisoners and what passed for wisdom in his former dwelling-place, he would surely think himself happy in the change and be sorry for them. They may have had a practice of honouring and commending one another, with prizes for the man who had the keenest eye for the passing shadows and the best memory for the order in which they followed or accompanied one another, so that he could make a good guess as to which was going to come next. Would our released prisoner be likely to covet those prizes or to envy the men exalted to honour and power in the Cave? Would he not feel like Homer's Achilles, that he would far sooner 'be on earth as a hired servant in the house of a landless man' or endure anything rather than go back to his old beliefs and live in the old way?

Yes, he would prefer any fate to such a life.

Now imagine what would happen if he went down again to take his former seat in the Cave. Coming suddenly out of the sunlight, his eyes would be filled with darkness. He might be required once more to deliver his opinion on those shadows, in competition with the prisoners who had never been released, while his eyesight was still dim and unsteady, and it might take some time to become used to the darkness. They would laugh at him and say that he had gone up only to come back with his sight ruined; it was worth no one's while even to attempt to ascent. If they could lay hands on the man who was trying to set them free and lead them up, they would kill him.

Yes, they would.

Every feature in this parable, my dear Glaucon, is meant to fit our earlier analysis. The prison dwelling corresponds to the region revealed to us through the sense of sight, and the fire-light within it to the power of the Sun. The ascent to see the things in the upper world you may take as standing for the upward journey of the soul into the region of the intelligible; then you will be in possession of what I surmise, since that is what you wish to be told. Heaven knows whether it is true, but this, at any rate, is how it appears to me. In the world of knowledge, the last thing to be perceived and only with great difficulty is the essential Form of Goodness. Once it is perceived, the conclusion must follow that, for all things, this is the cause of whatever is right and good; in the visible world it gives birth to light and to the lord of light, while it is itself sovereign in the intelligible world and the parent of intelligence and truth. Without having had a vision of this Form no one can act with wisdom, either in his own life or in matters of state.

So far as I can understand, I share your belief.

Then you may also agree that it is no wonder if those who have reached this height are reluctant to manage the affairs of men. Their souls long to spend all their time in that upper world—naturally enough, if here once more our parable holds true . . .

That is a fair statement.

If this is true, then, we must conclude that education is not what it is said to be by some, who profess to put knowledge into a soul which does not possess it, as if they could put sight into blind eyes. On the contrary, our own account signifies that the soul of every man does possess the power of learning the truth and the organ to see it with; and that, just as one might have to turn the whole body round in order that the eye should see light instead of darkness, so the entire soul must be turned away from this changing world, until its eye can bear to contemplate reality and that supreme splendour which we have called Good. Hence there may well be an art whose aim would be to effect this very thing, the conversion of the soul, in the readiest way, not to put to power of sight into the soul's eye which already has it, but to ensure that, instead of looking in the wrong direction, it is turned the way it ought to be.

Yes, it may well be so.

It looks, then as though wisdom were different from those ordinary virtues, as they are called, which are not far removed from bodily qualities, in that they can be produced by habitation and exercise in a soul which has not possessed them from the first. Wisdom, it seems, is certainly a virtue of some diviner faculty, which never loses its power, though its use for good or harm depends on the direction towards which it is turned. You must have noticed in dishonest men with a reputation for sagacity the shrewd glance of a narrow intelligence piercing the objects to which it is directed. There is nothing wrong with their power of vision, but it has been forced into the service of evil, so that the keener its sight, the more harm it works.

Quite true.

And yet if the growth of a nature like this had been pruned from earliest childhood, cleared of those clinging overgrowths which come of gluttony and all luxurious pleasure and, like leaden weights charged with affinity to this mortal world, hang upon the soul, bending its vision downwards; if freed from these, the soul were turned round towards true reality, then this same power in these very men would see the truth as keenly as the objects it is turned to now.

Yes, very likely.

Is it not also likely, or indeed certain after what has been said, that a state can never be properly governed either by the uneducated who know nothing of truth or by men who are allowed to spend all their days in the pursuit of culture? . . .

Quite true.

It is for us, then, as founders of a commonwealth, to bring compulsion to bear on the noblest natures. They must be made to climb the ascent to the vision of Goodness, which we called the highest object of knowledge, and, when they have looked upon it long enough, they must not be allowed, as they now are, to remain on the heights, refusing to come down again to the prisoners or to take any part in their labours and rewards, however much or little these may be worth.

The Form of the Good

Running throughout the passages cited here are reference to the Form of the Good. The Good looms large in Plato's theory of knowledge, but he never really tells us what the Good is. The closest he comes to a definition is a simile: The Good is to knowing as the sun is to seeing. When Plato speaks of the Good, it is always with the greatest awe. Knowledge of the Good is the highest kind of knowledge, a kind of enlightenment of which it is said that only a few fortunate seekers achieve. It is easy to see how the Christian philosophers of the Middle Ages equated the Good with God. For them, the power of reason comes from God. Each of us exhibits in our own reasoning ability a reflection of the rationality that permeates the whole created order. The Greek term *logos* can mean both "word" and "reason." Such texts as John 1:1 "In the beginning was the word . . ." gave added impetus to this interpretation.

After Plato's death, some of his followers emphasized this side of his philosophy to the exclusion of the dialectical and logical aspects of this thought.

They sought the Good for its own sake in a kind of mystical experience. This philosophical tradition culminated in the neo-Platonists represented by the thinker Plotinus. Other followers of Plato devoted themselves to the mathematical and analytical side of Plato's work. Among these was his most famous student, Aristotle, who took some of the basic Platonic views and reshaped them into works of considerable power and endurance. We will examine some of Aristotle's writings on ethics in Part 5.

Questions for Discussion

1. Show how the allegory of the cave illustrates both Plato's theory of knowledge and his view of the importance of philosophy.

2. What considerations can be advanced in support of Plato's theory of Forms? Against it? On which side do you find yourself? Give reasons for your answer.

3. Why do you think we find it difficult to accept the view that there are degrees of knowing corresponding to degrees of reality?

4. Do you agree that mathematics is a bridge between the sensible and the intelligible realms of knowledge? Why or why not?

5. Read again Plato's discussion of the Good. What do you think the Good is? Be prepared to defend your answer.

CHAPTER 15

The Quest for Certainty

The need to achieve certainty was the principal philosophic concern of René Descartes. During the seventeenth century, one could find philosophers arguing for a certain point of view, convinced of their correctness, even though one could also find other philosophers arguing for the exact opposite view. In contrast to the skeptical disrepute into which philosophy had fallen, mathematics seemed to be a model of elegance and certainty. The proofs of mathematicians could be checked by other mathematicians, and universal agreement could be claimed for their conclusions. No similar state of affairs could be claimed for philosophy. Confusion seemed to reign everywhere, with philosophers divided over all manner of issues, not the least of which was the proper method philosophy ought to pursue in its quest for knowledge. It seemed to Descartes that perhaps by imitating the methods of mathematics, philosophy could be reconstituted on better foundations and so find the certainty that had thus far proved to be so elusive.

Search for a Method

Descartes was not the first philosopher to be enticed by the rigors of mathematics as a model for philosophical inquiry. In ancient Greece Plato had even prescribed a stiff program of mathematical studies as preparation for students who wished to engage in philosophical inquiry. After Descartes, the Dutch philosopher Benedict Spinoza and the German Wilhelm Leibniz had likewise attempted to mathematize philosophy. In the twentieth century, Edmund Husserl and Bertrand Russell were attracted to mathematics as a possible model for certain kinds of philosophical inquiry. But Descartes was the first philosopher in modern

RENÉ DESCARTES (1596–1650): French philosopher and mathematician, regarded by many as the thinker who signaled the end of medieval philosophy and the rise of modern philosophical themes. His two most famous philosophical works are Discourse on Method *and* Meditations on First Philosophy. *Courtesy of the Library of Congress.*

times to approach the epistemological problem with the methods of mathematical inquiry.

What is the mathematical method? Think of geometry as a model. There you begin with axioms. To these are added postulates, and on the basis of those first principles of the system you are able to derive theorems for all the things you wish to prove. Notice that in a deductive system like mathematics the certainty of the conclusions depends on the certainty of the initial assumptions, which is the reason that geometry begins with axioms that are claimed to be, in some sense, self-evident. Axioms like "the shortest distance between two points is a straight line" cannot really be proved; without something that is given as self-evident, as too plain to be doubted, there could be no deductive science like geometry. What we need in philosophy, Descartes thought, was a similar self-evident axiom on which to build—or better, rebuild—the whole of philosophy. Such an axiomatic beginning point would have to be self-evident at least in the sense of being beyond the possibility of skeptical doubt.

Is such a self-evident point of departure possible? Descartes found the search for the elusive point of departure all-important, especially so in view of the skeptical attacks of the enemies of philosophy. In what was a brilliant insight into the nature of the problem, Descartes decided to use skepticism as a means of overturning skepticism. Like the enemies of philosophy, Descartes would doubt; in fact he would out-doubt the skeptics by doubting everything he had ever believed until (he hoped) he arrived at something that could not be doubted.

Montaigne on Skepticism

Let us leave aside that infinite confusion of opinions that is seen among the philosophers themselves, and that perpetual and universal debate over the knowledge of things. For this is a very true presupposition: that men are in agreement about nothing. I mean even the most gifted and ablest scholars, not even that the sky is over our head. For those who doubt everything also doubt that, and those who deny that we can understand anything say that we have not understood that the sky is over our head, and these two views are incomparably the strongest in number.

Besides this infinite diversity and division, it is easy to see by the confusion that our judgment gives to our own selves, and the uncertainty that each man feels within himself that it has a very insecure seat. How diversely we judge things! How many times we change our notions! What I hold today and what I believe; I hold and believe it with all my belief; all my tools and all my springs of action grip this opinion and sponsor it for me in every way they can. I could not embrace or preserve any truth with more strength than this one. I belong to it entirely, I belong to it truly. But has it not happened to me, not once, but a hundred times, a thousand times, and every day, to have embraced with these same instruments, in this same condition, something else that I have since judged false?

Michel de Montaigne
from *Apology for Raimond Sebond*

Grounds for Doubt

Descartes describes the process whereby he discovered the grounds for certainty in a series of essays entitled *Meditations*. In the following selection from the first meditation, Descartes explores every conceivable basis for doubt. When reading this selection, it is important to understand that Descartes had to explore all the grounds for doubt in order to overcome doubt. The American thinker C. S. Peirce argued that Descartes' method was illegitimate, since he did not really doubt all the things he mentions. But this criticism misses the point: Descartes was using methodic doubt as a way of overcoming doubt. Whether he really doubted in his heart all the things he mentions is irrelevant. He could not accept anything for certain unless he had dispelled all basis for doubt. So what we encounter in his first meditation and the opening pages of the second meditation is a list of all plausible reasons for doubting the testimony of our senses.

The first ground for doubt is the common experience of being deceived by the senses. We all know about persons who suffer from delusions—the insane, persons on drugs. There are other instances in which the senses mislead us: mirages, delirium tremens, delusions stemming from fever. And there are those who are so deranged that they have established their own private reality. Certainly for these people, what they think is reality seems real to them, and so our individual confidence in what we claim to know is no guarantee of anything.

A second ground for doubt is that, while sleeping, we dream of all sorts of situations that do not correspond to the reality of our waking life. While dreaming, the dreamworld is real, it is only upon waking that we can tell the difference between the waking world and the dreamworld. How can we be sure that we are not, at this very moment, dreaming—that you are not really reading this book but only dreaming that you are reading it? It is an interesting question, one that Descartes considered sufficient to give us pause in uncritically trusting our senses. The important issue is how we can know when we are dreaming and when we are awake. Again, our individual feelings of confidence in what we claim to know are insufficient as a guide to certainty.

A third reason for doubting our senses may seem to you at first more farfetched than the first two. But, again, it is a plausible reason to be suspicious of our senses. Those who believe in God usually do not think that God intervenes in the knowing process so as to deceive us. But suppose that instead of the good God of Judeo-Christian belief, for example, there existed a malevolent deity, or even a very powerful demon, who delighted in deceiving us. Such a being—not unlike the wicked witches of fairy tales—might deceive us just for fun. Yet how can we be sure that this is not already happening to us, that what we take for certainty is merely a delusion forced upon us by an evil demon?

At this point we will let Descartes speak for himself as he describes the beginning of this search that he refers to as the "arduous" quest for certainty.

René Descartes: Meditations

First Meditation Concerning Things That Can Be Doubted

There is no novelty to me in the reflection that, from my earliest years, I have accepted many false opinions as true; and that what I have concluded from such badly assured premises could not but be highly doubtful and uncertain. From the time that I first recognized this fact, I have realized that if I wished to have any firm and constant knowledge in the sciences, I would have to undertake, once and for all, to set aside all the opinions which I had previously accepted among my beliefs and start again from the very beginning . . . .

I will therefore make a serious and unimpeded effort to destroy generally all my former opinions. In order to do this, however, it will not be necessary to show

From René Descartes, *Meditations*, translated by Laurence J. Lafleur. Copyright 1951 by Macmillan Publishing Company, copyright renewed 1979. Library of Liberal Arts. Used by permission of Prentice Hall.

that they are all false, a task which I might never be able to complete, because, since reason already convinces me that I should abstain from the belief in things which are not entirely certain and indubitable no less carefully than from the belief in those which appear to me to be manifestly false, it will be enough to make me reject them all if I can find in each some ground for doubt. And for that it will not be necessary for me to examine each one in particular, which would be an infinite labor, but since the destruction of the foundation necessarily involves the collapse of all the rest of the edifice, I shall first attack the principles upon which all my former opinions were founded.

Everything which I have thus far accepted as entirely true (and assured) bas been acquired from the senses or by means of the senses. But I have learned by experience that these senses sometimes mislead me and it is prudent never to trust wholly those things which have once deceived us.

But it is possible that, even though the senses occasionally deceive us about things which are barely perceptible and very far away, there are many other things which we cannot reasonably doubt, even though we know them through the senses—as, for example, that I am here, seated by the fire, wearing a (winter) dressing gown, holding this paper in my hands, and other things of this nature. And how could I deny that these hands and this body are mine, unless I am to compare myself with certain lunatics whose brain is so troubled and befogged by the black vapors of the bile that they continually affirm that they are kings while they are paupers, that they are clothed in [gold and] purple while they are naked; or imagine (that their head is made of clay, or) that they are gourds, or that their body is glass? [But this is ridiculous;] such men are fools, and I would be no less insane than they if I followed their example.

Nevertheless, I must remember that I am a man, and that consequently l am accustomed to sleep and in my dreams to imagine the same things that lunatics imagine when awake, or sometimes things which are even less plausible. How many times has it occurred that (the quiet of) the night made me dream (of my usual habits:) that I was here, clothed (in a dressing gown), and sitting by the fire, although I was in fact lying undressed in bed! It seems apparent to me now, that I am not looking at this paper with my eyes closed, that this head that I shake is not drugged with sleep, that it is with design and deliberate intent that I stretch out this hand and perceive it. What happens in sleep seems not at all as clear and as distinct as all this. But I am speaking as though I never recall having been misled, while asleep, by similar illusions! When I consider these matters carefully, I realize so clearly that there are no conclusive indications by which waking life can be distinguished from sleep that I am quite astonished, and my bewilderment is such that it is almost able to convince me that I am sleeping.

So let us suppose now that we are asleep and that all these details, such as opening the eyes, shaking the head, extending the hands, and similar things, are merely illusions and let us think that perhaps our hands and our whole body are not such as we see them. Nevertheless, . . . even if these types of things—namely, [a body,] eyes, head, hands, and other similar things—could be imaginary, nevertheless, we are bound to confess that there are some other still more simple and universal concepts which are true [and existent], from the mixture of which, neither more nor less than in the case of the mixture of real colors, all these images of things are formed in our minds, whether they are true [and real] or imaginary [and fantastic].

Of this class of entities is corporeal nature in general and its extension, including the shape of extended things, their quantity, or size and number, and also the place where they are, the time that measures their duration, and so forth. That is why we will perhaps not be reasoning badly if we conclude that physics, astronomy, medicine, and all the other sciences which follow from the consideration of composite entities are very dubious [and uncertain], whereas arithmetic, geometry, and the other sciences of this nature, which treat only of very simple and general things without concerning themselves as to whether they occur in nature or not, contain some element of certainty and sureness. For whether I am awake or whether I am asleep, two and three together will always make the number five, and the square will never have more than four sides; and it does not seem possible that truths [(so clear and) so apparent can ever be suspected of any falsity [or uncertainty].

Nevertheless, I have long held the belief that there is a God who can do anything, by whom I have been created and made what I am. But how can I be sure but that he has brought it to pass that there is no earth, no sky, no extended bodies, no shape, no size, no place, and that nevertheless I have the impressions of all these things [and cannot imagine that things might be other than] as I now see them? And furthermore, just as I sometimes judge that others are mistaken about those things which they think they know best, how can I be sure but that [God has brought it about that] I am always mistaken when I add two and three or count the sides of a square, or when I judge of something else even easier, if I can imagine anything easier than that?

I am at last constrained to admit that there is nothing in what I formerly believed to be true which I cannot somehow doubt, and this not for lack of thought and attention, but for weighty and well-considered reasons. Thus I find that, in the future, I should [withhold and suspend my judgment from these matters, and] guard myself no less carefully from believing them than I should from believing what is manifestly false if I wish to find any certain and assured knowledge [in the sciences].

I will therefore suppose that, not [a true] God, (who is very good and I who) is the supreme source of truth, but a certain evil spirit, not less clever and deceitful than powerful, has bent all his efforts to deceiving me. I will suppose that the sky, the air, the earth, colors, shapes, sounds and all other objective things [that we see] are nothing but illusions and dreams that he has used to trick my credulity. I will consider myself as having no hands, no eyes, no flesh, no blood, nor any senses, yet falsely believing that I have all these things. I will remain resolutely attached to this hypothesis; and if I cannot attain the knowledge of any truth by this method, at any rate [it is in my power to suspend my judgment. That is why] I shall take great care not to accept any falsity among my beliefs and shall prepare my mind so well for all the ruses of this great deceiver that, however powerful and artful he may be, he will never be able to mislead me in anything.

Cogito Ergo Sum

If we are to achieve certainty, we must be able to establish something that cannot be doubted. It next occurs to Descartes that the act of doubting itself shows us the way. Doubting is a form of mental activity, a type of thinking. Even if we are confused about what we are, where we are, or the nature of the world that surrounds us, we cannot doubt that we are a thinking, feeling, willing, doubting being. All these forms of mental activity are undoubtable. Even if we are deceived in dreams, by mental disorders, or even by a powerful but evil demon, the one thing of which I can never be deceived is that there is an I, an ego that is being deceived. That I think (in the broadest sense of the term) is a certainty of which I cannot be in error. From the fact that I think I can conclude that I exist. Here is the undoubtable, axiomatic truth: cogito ergo sum, I think, therefore I am. Nothing can cause us to deny the truth of this, and *it is true every time we think it.*

Notice that in the process of attempting to discover an undoubtable truth on which he could base his rebuilding of philosophy, Descartes never appealed to the senses. The senses too often deceive us. Descartes' standard for proof was rational and deductive. Only if we can discover an argument through the power of reason alone do we have a basis for accepting anything. So far this approach led Descartes to a first truth—*cogito ergo sum*—which, while perhaps certain, is also empty. All we can know at this point in our investigation is the existence of the thinking self. We do not know if there exists anything else to think about, since we have already discarded the testimony of the senses as unreliable.

Second Meditation of the Nature of the Human Mind, and That It Is More Easily Known Than the Body

Yesterday's Meditation has filled my mind with so many doubts that it is no longer in my power to forget them. Nor do I yet see how I will be able to resolve them; I feel as though I were suddenly thrown into deep water, being so disconcerted that I can neither plant my feet on the bottom nor swim on the surface. I shall nevertheless make every effort to conform precisely to the plan commenced yesterday and put aside every belief in which I could imagine the least doubt, just as though I knew that it was absolutely false. And I shall continue in this manner until I have found something certain, or at least, if I can do nothing else, until I have learned with certainty that there is nothing certain in this world. Archimedes, to move the earth from its orbit and place it in a new position, demanded nothing more than a fixed and immovable fulcrum; in a similar manner I shall have the right to entertain high hopes if I am fortunate enough to find a single truth which is certain and indubitable.

I suppose, accordingly, that everything that I see is false; I convince myself that nothing has ever existed of all that my deceitful memory recalls to me. I think that I have no senses, and I believe that body, shape, extension, motion, and location are merely inventions of my mind. What then could still be thought true? Perhaps nothing else, unless it is that there is nothing certain in the world.

But how do I know that there is not some entity, of a different nature from what I have just judged uncertain, of which there cannot be the least doubt? Is there not some God or some other power who gives me those thoughts? But I need not think this to be true, for possibly I am able to produce them myself. Then, at the very least, am I not an entity myself? But I have already denied that I had any senses or any body. However, at this point I hesitate, for what follows from that? Am I so dependent upon the body and the senses that I could not exist without them? I have just convinced myself that nothing whatsoever existed in the world, that there was no sky, no earth, no minds, and no bodies, have I not thereby convinced myself that I did not exist? Not at all; without doubt I existed if I was convinced [or even if I thought anything]. Even though there may be a deceiver of some sort, very powerful and very tricky, who bends all his efforts to keep me perpetually deceived, there can be no slightest doubt that I exist, since he deceives me, and let him deceive me as much as he will, he can never make me be nothing as long as I think that I am something. Thus, after having thought well on this matter, and after examining all things with care, I must finally conclude and maintain that this proposition: *I am, I exist,* is necessarily true every time that I pronounce it or conceive it in my mind.

But I do not yet know sufficiently clearly what I am, I who am sure that I exist. So I must henceforth take very great care that I do not incautiously mistake some other thing for myself, and so make an error even in that knowledge which I maintain to be more certain and more evident than all other knowledge [that I previously had]. That is why I shall now consider once more what I thought myself to be before I began these last deliberations. Of my former opinions I shall reject all that are rendered even slightly doubtful by the arguments that I have just now offered, so that there will remain just that part alone which is entirely certain and indubitable.

What then have I previously believed myself to be? Clearly, I believed that I was a man. But what is a man? . . .

I shall rather pause here to consider the ideas which previously arose naturally and of themselves in my mind whenever I considered what I was. I thought of myself first as having a face, hands, arms, and all this mechanism composed of (bone and flesh and members), just as it appears in a corpse, and which I designated by the name of "body." In addition, I thought of the fact that I consumed nourishment, that I walked, that I perceived and thought, and I ascribed all these actions to the soul . . . .

But I, what am I, on the basis of the present hypothesis that there is a certain spirit who is extremely powerful and, if I may dare to say so, malicious [and tricky], and who uses all his abilities and efforts in order to deceive me? Can I be sure that I possess the smallest fraction of all those characteristics which I have just now said belonged to the nature of body? I pause to consider this attentively. I pass and repass in review in my mind each one of all these things—it is not necessary to pause to take the time to list them—and I do not find any one of them which I can pronounce to be part of me. Is it characteristic of me to consume nourishment and to walk? But if it is true that I do not have a body, these also are nothing but figments of the imagination. To perceive? But once more, I cannot perceive without the body, except in the sense that I have thought I perceived various things during sleep, which I recognized upon waking not to have been really perceived. To think? Here I find the answer. Thought is an attribute that belongs to me; it alone is inseparable from my nature.

I am, I exist—that is certain, but for how long do I exist? For as long as I think, for it might perhaps happen, if I totally ceased thinking, that I would at the same time completely cease to be. I am now admitting nothing except what is necessarily true. I am therefore, to speak precisely, only a thinking being, that is to say, a mind, an understanding, or a reasoning being, which are terms whose meaning was previously unknown to me.

I am something real and really existing, but what thing am I? I have already given the answer: a thing which thinks . . . A thinking being. What is a thinking being? It is a being which doubts, which understands, [which conceives,] which affirms, which denies, which wills, which rejects, which imagines also, and which perceives. It is certainly not a trivial matter if all these things belong to my nature. But why should they not belong to it? Am I not that same person who now doubts almost everything, who nevertheless understands [and conceives] certain things, who [is sure of and] affirms the truth of this one thing alone, who denies all the others, who wills and desires to know more about them, who rejects error, who imagines many things, sometimes even against my will, and who also perceives many things, as though the medium of (the senses) [or [the organs of the body]? Is there anything in all that which is not just as true as it is certain that I am and that I exist, even though I were always asleep and though the one who created me directed all his efforts to deluding me? And is there any one of these attributes which can be distinguished from my thinking or which can be said to be separable from my nature? For it is so obvious that it is I who doubt, understand, and desire, that nothing could be added to make it more evident. And I am also certainly the same one who imagines, for once more, even though it could happen that the things I imagine are not true, nevertheless this power of imagining cannot fail to be real and it is part of my thinking. Finally I am the same being which perceives—that is, which observes certain objects as though by means of the sense organs, because I do really see light, hear noises, feel heat. Will it be said that these appearances are false and that I am sleeping? [Let it he so yet at the very least] it is certain that it seems to me that I see light, hear noises, and feel heat. This much cannot be false, and it is this, properly considered, which in my nature is called perceiving and that, again speaking precisely, is nothing else but thinking.

The Role of the Senses

Descartes' next move, however, is to show that we can accept the senses as avenues for knowledge of the world, provided that we are able to judge their testimony by the standards of rational insight. The following reading picks up a section in the second Meditation where Descartes is examining the relative power of the senses and of reason. He shows that a piece of beeswax freshly taken from the honeycomb has a completely different set of characteristics before we bring it near the fire and after we bring it near the fire. If we had only the data supplied by the senses to go on, we might conclude that we are dealing with two objects—one solid, hard, of a certain shape, the other soft, pliable, and having a completely different shape. Yet we know that it is the same piece of wax. How? Not through the senses, but through the power of reason. Descartes concludes, in good rationalistic fashion, that physical objects "are not known insofar as they are seen or touched, but only insofar as they are understood by thinking." The real source of genuine knowledge, then, is not the senses but reason.

Let us examine Descartes' argument. When we first look at the wax, it has certain sense qualities: It is sweet, has an aromatic odor, is amber in color, hard, and cold. After it is brought near the fire, however, all these sense qualities change: It is no longer sweet but has lost its odor, color, and so on. None of this is very surprising. But look at the conclusion Descartes draws from these ordinary facts— that we do not know material objects by means of our senses! How does he arrive at this conclusion? We can clarify Descartes' reasoning if we construct his argument as an indirect argument utilizing *modus tollens* (MT). Descartes wants to *dis*prove the popular idea that we know about physical objects by means of our five senses. Suppose this is true, Descartes reasons; what follows from it? If we know the wax by means of its sense qualities, then it would be a different object whenever its sense qualities changed. Since that is not true, it follows, by indirect argument, that we do not know the wax by means of the senses. Let P be "I know the wax by its sense qualities" and Q be "It is a different object whenever its sense qualities change," and we have the following MT argument:

$$P \to Q$$
$$\frac{-Q}{\therefore -P}$$

How, then, *do* we know the wax, if not by the senses? Perhaps, Descartes suggests, it is by means of our imagination. We know that the wax is flexible and movable, not by sense experience, but, let us suppose, by imagining it having different shapes. But that cannot be right, either, Descartes argues. If it were, we would have to imagine the wax having an infinite number of shapes, which is impossible. This, then, is another indirect argument of the MT form in which P is "I know the wax is flexible and movable by imagining all the different shapes it can take," and Q is "I imagine the infinite shapes the wax can take."

$$P \to Q$$
$$\frac{-Q}{\therefore -P}$$

If it is not by means of either sense or imagination, then how is it we know the wax, which we surely do? By a process of elimination, there is no answer left but to say that we know the wax by the understanding. Here Descartes uses the disjunctive syllogism argument form (DS): We know the wax either by imagination (I) or by understanding (U); we do not know it by imagination (as Descartes thinks he has just shown); therefore, we must know it by understanding.

$$
\begin{array}{r}
I \lor U \\
-I \\
\hline
\therefore U
\end{array}
$$

Similarly, when we say that we "see" men in hats and cloaks walking in the streets below, we cannot actually see that they are men; all we actually see are hats and cloaks, and these could be covering robots, not men. We do not really see men but only intellectually judge that this is what they are. Ordinarily, of course, we do not worry about such remote, even farfetched, possibilities of error. But sometimes, as in a court of law, in a murder case, for example, we do try to draw the same sort of distinction Descartes does between what we actually see and what we intellectually judge to be the case. We turn now to the remainder of the second meditation in which Descartes explores these issues.

The Wax Example

Let us now consider the commonest things, which are commonly believed to be the most distinctly known and the easiest of all to know, namely, the bodies which we touch and see. I do not intend to speak of bodies in general, for general notions are usually somewhat more confused; let us rather consider one body in particular. Let us take, for example, this bit of wax which has just been taken from the hive. It has not yet completely lost the sweetness of the honey it contained; it still retains something of the odor of the flowers from which it was collected; its color, shape, and size are apparent; it is hard and cold, it can easily be touched; and, if you knock on it, it will give out some sound. Thus everything which can make a body distinctly known are found in this example.

But now while I am talking, I bring it close to the fire. What remains of the taste evaporates; the odor vanishes; its color changes; its shape is lost; its size increases; it becomes liquid; it grows hot; one can hardly touch it; and although it is knocked upon, it will give out no sound. Does the same wax remain after this change? We must admit that it does; no one denies it, no one judges otherwise. What is it then in this bit of wax that we recognize with so much distinctness? Certainly it cannot be anything that I observed by means of the senses, since everything in the field of taste, smell, sight, touch and hearing are changed, and since the same wax nevertheless remains.

The truth of the matter perhaps, as I now suspect, is that this wax was neither that sweetness of honey, nor that pleasant odor of flowers, nor that whiteness, nor that shape, nor that sound, but only a body which a little while ago appeared to my senses under these forms and which now makes itself felt under others. But what is it, to speak precisely, that I imagine when I conceive it in this fashion? Let us consider it attentively and, rejecting everything that does not belong to the wax, see what remains. Certainly nothing is left but something extended, flexible, and movable. But what is meant by flexible and movable? Does it consist in my picturing that this wax, being round, is capable of becoming square and of passing from the square into a triangular shape? Certainly not; it is not that, since I conceive it capable of undergoing an infinity of similar changes, and I could not compass this infinity in my imagination. Consequently this conception that I have of the wax is not achieved by the faculty of imagination.

Now what is this extension? Is it not also unknown? For it becomes greater in the melting wax, still greater when it is completely melted, and much greater again when the heat increases still more. And I would not conceive clearly and truthfully what wax was, if I did not think that even this bit of wax is capable of receiving more variations in extension than I have ever imagined. We must therefore agree that I cannot even conceive what this bit of wax is by means of the imagination, and that there is nothing but my understanding alone which does conceive it. I say this bit of wax in particular, for as to wax in general, it is still more evident. But what is this bit of wax which cannot be comprehended except by the understanding, or by the mind? Certainly it is the same as the one that I see, that I touch, that I imagine; and finally it is the same as I always believed it to be from the beginning. But what is here important to notice is that perception, or the action by which we perceive, is not a vision, a touch, nor an imagination, and has never been that, even though it formerly appeared so, but is solely an inspection by the mind, which can be imperfect and confused as it was formerly, or clear and distinct as it is at present, as I attend more or less to the things which are in it and of which it is composed.

Now I am truly astonished when I consider how weak my mind is and how apt I am to fall into error. For even though I consider all this in my mind without speaking, still words impede me, and I am nearly deceived by the terms of ordinary language. For we say that we see the same wax if it is present and not that we judge that it is the same from the fact that it has the same color or shape. Thus I might be tempted to conclude that one knows the wax by means of eyesight, and not uniquely by the perception of the mind so I may by chance look out of a window and notice some men passing in the street, at the sight of whom I do not fail to say that I see men, just as I say that I see wax. Nevertheless what do I see from this window except hats and cloaks which might cover ghosts, or automata which move only by springs? But I judge that they are men, and thus I comprehend, solely by the faculty of judgment which resides in my mind, that which I believed I saw with my eyes.

A person who attempts to improve his understanding beyond the ordinary ought to be ashamed to go out of his way to criticize the forms of speech used by ordinary men. I prefer to pass over this matter and to consider whether I understood what wax was more evidently and more perfectly when I first noticed it and when I thought I knew it by means of the external senses, or at the very least by common sense, as it is called, or the imaginative faculty, or whether I conceive it better at present, after having more carefully examined what it is and how it can be known. Certainly it would be ridiculous to doubt the superiority of the latter method of knowing. For what was there in that first perception which was distinct and evident? What was there which might not occur similarly to the senses of the lowest of the animals? But when I distinguished the real wax from its superficial appearances, and when, just as though I had removed its garments, I consider it all naked; it is certain that although there might still be some error in my judgment, I could not conceive it in this fashion without a human mind.

And now what shall I say of the mind, that is to say, of myself? For so far I do not admit in myself anything other than the mind. Can it be that I, who seem to perceive this bit of wax so clearly and distinctly, do not know my own self not only with much more truth and certainty, but also much more distinctly and evidently? For if I judge that the wax exists because I see it, certainly it follows much more evidently that I exist myself because I see it. For it might happen that what I see is not really wax; it might also happen that I do not even possess eyes to see anything, but it could not happen that, when I see, or what amounts to the same thing, when I think I see, I who think am not something. For a similar reason, if I judge that the wax exists because I touch it, the same conclusion follows once more, namely, that I am. And if I hold to this judgment because my imagination, or whatever other entity it might be, persuades me of it, I will still reach the same conclusion. And what I have said here about the wax can be applied to all other things which are external to me.

Furthermore, if the idea or knowledge of the wax seems clearer and more distinct to me after I have investigated it, not only by sight or touch, but also in many other ways, with how much more evidence, distinctness and clarity must it be admitted that I now know myself, since all the reasons which help me to know and conceive the nature of the wax, or of any other body whatsoever, serve much better to show the nature of my mind! And we also find so many other things in the mind itself which can contribute to the clarification of its nature, that those which depend on the body, such as the ones I have just mentioned, hardly deserve to be taken into account.

And at last here I am, having insensibly returned to where I wished to be, for since it is at present manifest to me that even bodies are not properly known by the senses nor by the faculty of imagination, but by the understanding alone; and since they are not known in so far as they are seen or touched, but only in so far as they are understood by thinking, I see clearly that there is nothing easier for me to understand than my mind. But since it is almost impossible to rid oneself so soon of an opinion of long standing, it would be wise to stop a while at this point, in order that, by the length of my meditation, I may impress this new knowledge more deeply upon my memory.

Questions for Discussion

1. In your own words, state what you find to be the philosophical problem raised by Descartes' example of the piece of wax.

2. Do you think that philosophy can and should be modeled after the methods of mathematics? Why, or why not?

3. Descartes felt that the most important question for philosophy at the outset was the basis for certainty. Do you agree? Give reasons for your answer.

4. Explain the meaning of *cogito ergo sum* in the context of Descartes' philosophy.

5. Explain what Descartes meant by the following statement: "It is at present manifest to me that even bodies are not properly known by the senses nor by the faculty of imagination, but by the understanding alone." Do you think his argument to support this statement is sound? Why or why not?

CHAPTER 16

Trust Your Senses

What could be more obvious than the view that the senses are the only dependable source of knowledge? "Seeing is believing," we say. If you cannot trust your own sense experience, what can you trust?

Such sentiments were readily acceptable to David Hume, the eighteenth-century thinker who was a librarian by profession and a philosopher by obsession. Hume, like many other thinkers of the eighteenth century, was concerned with human knowledge more than with any other philosophical problem. Hume's major contribution to the growing literature of the eighteenth century dealing with epistemology was entitled *An Enquiry Concerning Human Understanding*. Hume had earlier written a book dealing with similar topics under the title *A Treatise of Human Nature*. Like the first book of many authors, the *Treatise* did not sell well; Hume described it as having fallen "stillborn from the press." So he rewrote the arguments of the book, simplifying them in places, and reissued his work under the new title *An Enquiry Concerning Human Understanding*, a book he described as the *Treatise* "shorn of its nobler parts." Because the presentation of the second work is clearer, it is from the *Enquiry* that the selections from Hume in this chapter are taken.

Search for Simplicity

Insofar as there is a national temperament in philosophy, Hume represents a very British attitude toward philosophical investigation. English philosophers have almost always been concerned with cutting through obfuscation and getting to the heart of issues. They tend to reject complicated lines of dialectical reasoning, the sort of thing one finds in German philosophers, aiming instead for clarity of expression and simplicity of analysis. English philosophers are also generally empirical, logical, and concerned with common sense. John Locke, whom we shall meet again in the chapter on social and political philosophy, laid the foundations for the kind of empirical philosophy Hume continued by analyzing knowledge in terms of what Locke referred to as a *historical plain* method. It was *historical* in that he examined the history of knowledge, beginning with its origins and showing how knowledge developed in ways ever more complex; it was plain in the sense that Locke rejected the "scholastic disputations" of continental philosophers and preferred to emphasize common sense in his analysis.

Locke argued that there is nothing in the mind that was not previously in the senses; the senses are the only means we have of knowing anything. He found an innate idea now and then (such as the idea of God, implanted in our understanding by the creator), but everything else is presented to us through the senses. Locke thought that the senses gave us a sort of "alphabet" of knowledge. Just as we take twenty-six simple letters and combine them in units of ever increasing complexity—words, sentences, arguments—so in learning, we begin with simple impressions, which are then combined into units of increasing complexity. We can recall to mind past sensations through the power of memory, and we can combine sensations and the ideas resulting from them in fanciful ways through the power of the imagination—winged horses, centaurs, and things like that. All this was pretty much accepted by Hume. His contribution to the philosophic tradition, however, was in pushing these principles to their conclusion, which produced some very startling consequences, consequences which show that empiricism by itself tends to lead to skepticism.

"All the objects of human reason," Hume claims, "may naturally be divided into two kinds . . . 'relations of ideas' and 'matters of fact.'" Relations of ideas refers to that kind of knowledge which is purely *a priori* and is known not by appealing to the senses but by examining the logical relations among the ideas. Mathematics provides the clearest examples of this kind of knowledge: Mathematics is not about the world (though aspects of mathematics are applicable to the world); it is about the relations among numbers (if we are dealing with arithmetic) or among geometrical figures (in the case of geometry) or relations among other formulas in the mathematical system. Matters of fact, by contrast, deal directly with the observable world and are known through the senses.

Here is another way to think about the difference between these two kinds of knowledge: The negation of a mathematical truth leads to a contradiction, whereas the negation of what Hume calls a matter of fact does not. Consider the two statements:

1. $2 + 5 = 7$
2. The grass is green.

The negation of statement 1 ("It is not the case that $2 + 5 = 7$") is false because it contradicts the meaning of the terms in the statement. The negation of

John Locke on Knowledge

All ideas come from sensation or reflection. Let us then suppose the mind to be, as we say, white paper void of all characters, without any ideas; how comes it to be finished? Whence comes it by that vast store, which the busy and boundless fancy of man has painted on it with an almost endless variety? Whence has it all the materials of reason and knowledge? To this I answer in one word, from EXPERIENCE; in that all our knowledge is founded, and from that it ultimately derives itself. Our observation, employed either about external sensible objects, or about the internal operations of our minds, perceived and reflected on by ourselves, is that which supplies our understandings with all the materials of thinking. These two are the fountains of knowledge, from whence all the ideas we have, or can naturally have, do spring.

The objects of sensation one source of ideas. *First, our senses, conversant about particular sensible objects, do convey into the mind several distinct perceptions of things, according to those various ways wherein those objects do affect thence; and thus we come by those ideas we have of yellow, white, heat, cold, soft, hard, bitter, sweet, and all those which we call sensible qualities, which when I say the senses convey into the mind, I mean, they from external objects convey into the mind what produces there those perceptions. This great source of most of the ideas we have, depending wholly upon our senses, and derived by them to the understanding, I call SENSATION.*

The operations of our minds the other source of them. *Secondly, the other fountain, from which experience furnisheth the understanding with ideas, is the perception of the operation of our own minds within us, as it is employed about the ideas it has got, which operations, when the soul comes to reflect on and consider do furnish the understanding with another set of ideas which could not be had from things without: and such are perception, thinking, doubting, believing, reasoning, knowing, willing, and all the different actings of our own minds, which we being conscious of, and observing in ourselves, do from these receive into our understanding as distinct ideas, as we do from bodies affecting our senses . . . But as I call the other Sensation, so I call this REFLECTION, the ideas it affords being such only as the mind gets by reflecting on its own operations within itself.*

JOHN LOCKE
An Essay Concerning Human Understanding, Book II, Chapter 1

statement 1 could never be true; the negation of statement 2, however, might or might not be true, depending on what the data from the senses provide us. The only way we can determine the truth or falsity of matters of fact is to appeal to our senses.

Cause and Effect

But here is another problem: What about things we do not *personally* experience? If we cannot appeal to our present sense impressions, or summon past impressions from our memory, how do we extend our knowledge of things?

Hume's answer to this is to point out that the principle of cause and effect is the link that ties our present experience of the world to other possible experiences of the world both past and future. We assume that grass we have never seen is green because whatever makes grass green operates uniformly all around the world all the time. When we see the sun rising in the east in the morning, we assume that there is some kind of causal relationship that makes this matter of fact not only true for us at the present moment when we are experiencing it but also true in the future. How do we know that the future will resemble the past? Or that the past resembled the present? We know that tomorrow $2 + 5 = 7$ will be true, for its truth is independent of the senses and is based on the meaning of the terms themselves. But what about matters of fact which seem to depend upon our being able to prove that things are related causally?

This line of questioning only leads us closer to the crucial issue: How can we prove the principle of cause and effect? We derive it from experience—that is, we ordinarily think about things in terms of this principle—but how can we prove that it is true? Hume's answer may be disappointing to you, for he says that we cannot prove the principle. Being unable to prove it, however, does not mean that we discard it; it does mean that the basic principle operative in human understanding cannot be demonstrated to be true. As an empiricist Hume is unable to prove that causality exists because we never *experience* a necessary connection (causal link) between discrete events. We only can experience event B following event A, which eventually leads us to associate them in our thinking in terms of a causal relationship. What is the reason for this? Hume answers that it is *custom* or *habit*. By a constant conjunction of event A and event B we come to anticipate B whenever we experience A. But this does not prove there is any necessary causal connection between the two, as the rooster in a story by Bertrand Russell discovered who thought his crowing caused the sun to rise each morning until the farmer's wife wrung his neck one morning in preparation for Sunday dinner. Can you see how startling this is? A dedicated empiricist, for whom sense experience is the basis of all knowledge, discovers that we cannot offer empirical proof for the most basic of principles required for knowledge. Empiricism has thus proved that there is no proof for empiricism.

Hume may not have liked his skeptical conclusion; there is evidence that he did not. But he did accept it. He also accepted the corollary to his reasonings

about cause and effect, which is that we cannot be certain about much of anything. Certainty, that elusive epistemological goal, seems to be beyond our grasp. That is the conclusion of the matter.

David Hume: Skeptical Doubts Concerning the Operations of the Understanding

All the objects of human reason or inquiry may naturally be divided into two kinds to wit, "Relations of Ideas," and "Matters of Fact." Of the first kind are the sciences of Geometry, Algebra, and Arithmetic, and, in short every affirmation which is either intuitively or demonstratively certain. That the square of the hypotenuse is equal to the square of the two sides is a proposition which expresses a relation between these figures. That three times five is equal to the half of thirty expresses a relation between these numbers. Propositions of this kind are discoverable by the mere operation of thought, without dependence on what is anywhere existent in the universe. Though there never were a circle or a trian-

From David Hume, *An Enquiry Concerning Human Understanding,* selections from Sections IV and V.

gle in nature, the truths demonstrated by Euclid would forever retain their certainty and evidence.

Matters of fact, which are the second objects of human reason, are not ascertained in the same manner, nor is our evidence of their truth, however great, of a like nature with the foregoing. The contrary of every matter of fact is still possible, because it can never imply a contradiction and is conceived by the mind with the same facility and distinctness as if ever so conformable to reality. That the sun will not rise tomorrow is no less intelligible a proposition and implies no more contradiction than the affirmation *that it will rise*. We should in vain, therefore, attempt to demonstrate its falsehood. Were it demonstratively false, it would imply a contradiction and could never be distinctly conceived by the mind.

It may, therefore, be a subject worthy of curiosity to inquire what is the nature of that evidence which assures us of any real existence and matter of fact beyond the present testimony of our senses or the records of our memory. This part of philosophy, it is observable, had been little cultivated either by the ancients or moderns, and, therefore, our doubts and errors in the prosecution of so important an inquiry may be the more excusable while we march through such difficult paths without any guide or direction. They may even prove useful by exciting curiosity and destroying that implicit faith and security which is the bane of all reasoning and free injury. The discovery of defects in the common philosophy, if any such there be, will not, I presume, be a discouragement, but rather an incitement, as is usual, to attempt something more full and satisfactory than has yet been proposed to the public.

All reasonings concerning matter of fact seem to be founded on the relation of cause and effect. By means of that relation alone we can go beyond the evidence of our memory and senses. If you were to ask a man why he believes any matter of fact which is absent, for instance, that his friend is in the country or in France, he would give you a reason, and this reason would be some other fact: as a letter received from him or the knowledge of his former resolutions and promises. A man finding a watch or any other machine in a desert island would conclude that there had once been men in that island. All our reasonings concerning fact are of the same nature. And here it is constantly supposed that there is a connection between the present fact and that, which is inferred from it. Were there nothing to bind them together, the inference would be entirely precarious. The hearing of an articulate voice and rational discourse in the dark assures us of the presence of some person. Why? Because these are the effects of the human make and fabric, and closely connected with it. If we anatomize all the other reasonings of this nature, we shall find that they are founded on the relation of cause and effect.

===============

Suppose a person, though endowed with the strongest faculties of reason and reflection, to be brought on a sudden into this world; he would, indeed, immediately observe a continual succession of objects and one event following another, but he would not be able to discover anything further. He would not at first, by any reasoning, be able to reach the idea of cause and effect, since the particular powers by which all natural operations are performed never appear to the senses, nor is it reasonable to conclude, merely because one event in one instance precedes another, that therefore the one is the cause, the other the effect. The conjunction may be arbitrary and casual. There may be no reason to infer the existence of one from the appearance of the other: and, in a word, such a person without more experience could never employ his conjecture or reasoning concerning any matter of fact or be assured of anything beyond what was immediately present to his memory or senses.

Suppose again that he has acquired more experience and has lived so long in the world as to have observed similar objects or events to be constantly conjoined together—what is the consequence of this experience? He immediately infers the existence of one object from the appearance of the other, yet he has not, by all his experience, acquired any idea or knowledge of the secret power by which the one object produces the other, nor is it by any process of reasoning he is engaged to draw this inference, but still he finds himself determined to draw it, and though he should be convinced that his understanding has no part in the operation, he would nevertheless continue in the same course of thinking. There is some other principle which determines him to form such a conclusion.

This principle is *custom* or *habit*. For wherever the repetition of any particular act or operation produces a propensity to renew the same act or operation without being impelled by any reasoning or process of the understanding, we always say that this propensity is the effect of custom. By employing that word we pretend not to have given the ultimate reason of such a propensity. We only point out a principle of human nature which is universally acknowledged, and which is well known by its effects. Perhaps we can push our inquiries no further or pretend to give the cause of this cause, but must rest contented with it as the ultimate principle which we can assign of all our conclusions from experience. It is sufficient satisfaction that we can go so far without repining at the narrowness of our faculties, because they will carry us no further. And it is certain we here advance a very intelligible proposition at least, if not a true one, when we assert that after the constant conjunction of two objects, heat and flame, for instance, weight and solidity, we are determined by custom alone to expect the one from the appearance of the other. This hypothesis seems even the only one which explains the difficulty why we draw from a thousand instances an inference which we are not able to draw from one instance that is in no respect different from them. Reason is incapable of any such variation. The conclusions which it draws from considering one circle are the same which it would form upon surveying all the circles in the universe. But no man, having seen only one body move after being impelled by another, could infer that every other body will move after a like impulse. All inferences from experience, therefore, are effects of custom, not of reasoning.

Custom, then, is the great guide of human life. It is that principle alone which renders our experience useful to us and makes us expect, for the future, a similar train of events with those which have appeared in the past. Without the influence of custom we should be entirely ignorant of every matter of fact beyond what is immediately present to the memory and senses. We should never know how to adjust means to ends or to employ our natural powers in the production of any effect. There would be an end at once of all action as well as of the chief part of speculation.

What, then, is the conclusion of the whole matter? A simple one, though, it must be confessed, pretty remote from the common theories of philosophy. All belief of matter of fact or real existence is derived merely from some object present to the memory or senses and a customary conjunction between that and some other object; or, in other words, having found, in many instances, that any two kinds of objects, flame and heat, snow and cold, have always been conjoined together: if flame or snow be presented anew to the senses, the mind is carried by custom to expect heat or cold, and to believe that such a quality does exist and will discover itself upon a nearer approach. This belief is the necessary result of placing the mind in such circumstances. It is an operation of the soul, when we are so situated, as unavoidable as to feel the passion of love, when we receive benefits, or hatred, when we meet with injuries. All these operations are a species of natural instincts, which no reasoning or process of the thought and understanding is able either to produce or to prevent. At this point it would be very allowable for us to stop our philosophical researches. In most questions we can never make a single step further, and in all questions we must terminate here at last, after our most restless and curious inquiries. But still our curiosity will be pardonable, perhaps commendable, if it carry us on to still further researches and make us examine more accurately the nature of this belief and of the customary conjunction whence it is derived. By this means we may meet with some explications and analogies that will give satisfaction, at least to such as love the abstract sciences, and can be entertained with speculations which, however accurate, may still retain a degree of doubt and uncertainty As to readers of a different taste, the remaining part of this Section is not calculated for them, and the following inquiries may well be understood, though it be neglected.

Questions for Discussion

1. Both Hume and Descartes see mathematics as an important kind of knowledge. But are their respective views about mathematics the same or different? Explain.

2. Explain in your own words the distinction Hume makes between "matters of fact" and "relations of ideas." Do you agree that these are different objects of knowledge? Are there others? Why or why not?

3. Explain why cause and effect pose such a problem for Hume. Do you think causality would offer similar difficulties for any empiricist? Give reasons for your answer.

4. Would it be correct to say that Hume did not believe in cause and effect? If so, why? If not, why not?

5. Do you see any way for an empiricist like Hume to avoid skepticism?

CHAPTER 17

A Compromise

Who is right in this epistemological debate: the empiricists, with their emphasis on the senses as the exclusive source of our knowledge of the world, or the rationalists, who insist on reason alone as the final arbiter of truth? As is often the case in philosophical quarrels, many philosophers settled on an answer that was at neither extreme of this polarity by finding a middle ground between the one-sided claims of the antagonists in this debate. The philosopher who did the most to bring rationalism and empiricism together in a workable harmony was Immanuel Kant.

Kant, who was familiar with the philosophy of Locke, Berkeley, and Hume, was steeped in a form of rationalistic philosophy stemming from Descartes but was more immediately influenced by the German philosopher Leibniz. The form of rationalistic philosophy that dominated German universities in the eighteenth century was even more confident in the power of reason to discover the ultimate truth about reality than was Cartesian thought, and was optimistic about its power to discover the complete, and certain, truth about the nature of God, the nature and destiny of the human soul, and the world as a totality. Questions like whether the world has a beginning in time or is eternal, inquiries into the nature of the soul—whether it is an indissoluble unity (Leibniz's view) or a collection of discrete soul substances—and arguments over the attributes of God were commonplace. Each side in every such philosophical debate was absolutely convinced that its arguments were inviolate and its conclusions unassailable. Though all sides to the controversies invoked reason as authority, none of them could lay out standards that were so universally clear and agreed to that everyone would recognize that a solution had been found to a philosophical argument.

Meanwhile, on the other side of the English Channel, empiricists were laying siege to reason's authority by following empirical assumptions to their own, often bitter, conclusions. Hume, as we have seen, was willing to accept these conclu-

IMMANUEL KANT (1724–1804): German philosopher important for his "critical philosophy," an attempt to reconcile continental rationalism and British empiricism. His most famous works include Critique of Pure Reason, Foundations of the Metaphysics of Morals, *and* Critique of Judgment. *Courtesy of the Library of Congress.*

sions, even though they ended in skepticism. Though the empiricists began with opposite assumptions about the source of knowledge, they were driven to conclusions that placed our ability to know in as much jeopardy as did the intricate arguments of the rationalists. Are we to face only the Scylla of dogmatism (Kant's term for rationalism) or the Charybdis of skepticism (Kant's equally unflattering term for empiricism)? Like the rock and whirlpool of Greek mythology, skepticism and rationalism appeared to Kant to pose twin threats to philosophy's fragile ship. Both skepticism and dogmatism give philosophy a bad name, since they present philosophy as engaging only in idle controversies that produce nothing and reach no lasting conclusions. In contrast, the efforts of natural science and mathematics are productive and generate new insights into reality. Can philosophy hope for as much? Kant thought the answer to this was yes, if philosophy examines its own foundations and generates a firm basis for its future work.

The area of philosophical investigation that had been called into question by the wrangles of empiricists and rationalists was metaphysics. "Time was," Kant observed, "when metaphysics was entitled the queen of all the sciences . . . Now, however, the changed fashion of the time brings her only scorn; a matron outcast and forsaken. . . ." Metaphysics' queenly rule has been challenged by dual threats, Kant goes on to say. "Her government under the administration of the dogmatists was at first despotic. But inasmuch as the legislation still bore traces of the ancient barbarism, her empire gradually through intestine wars gave way to complete anarchy, and the skeptics, a species of nomads, despising all settled modes of life, broke up from time to time all civil society."

Kant freely admitted that reading the work of David Hume was the stimulus that roused him from his "dogmatic slumber," as he put it. Hume's attack on the principle of cause and effect as unfounded in reason but due rather to custom or habit was a claim that, if allowed to stand, would undercut the legitimacy of natural science for a start, and could eventually destroy confidence in reason's ability to do anything. A side effect would be to cast further doubt on the legitimacy of philosophy as a tool of analysis. It was with these and similar problems in view that Kant wrote his massive *Critique of Pure Reason*, from which the selections that follow are taken. Before turning to the analysis and arguments offered in the selection, a word about reading Kant is in order. Kant is not easy to read, but you may get some comfort from knowing that one of his friends returned a copy of the *Critique* to him with the comment that he feared reading it completely would drive him mad. One of the reasons Kant is sometimes difficult to understand is simply that he is dealing with difficult topics. In addition, Kant, in his effort to push philosophical analysis beyond the position it had achieved in his day, introduced much new terminology, some of which is now familiar to us because it has entered the standard philosophical vocabulary, though other terms of his still strike modern readers as opaque. Even though Kant may be difficult, he occupies an extremely important place in the history of philosophy, for many of the concerns philosophers have addressed themselves to during the past two hundred years were first articulated by Kant.

Knowledge and Experience

The empiricists had shown a proper concern with understanding the origin of knowledge, but they were guilty of several unexamined assumptions about the knowing process. The first of these assumptions was that the mind of the knower is purely passive, a receptacle for impressions (Hume's term) or sensations (Locke's term). John Locke had explicitly described the knowing mind as a blank tablet, a *tabula rasa* on which the senses write, or as an empty cabinet filled with ideas which are but copies of sensations. The second unexamined assumption was that the mind is incapable of generating anything out of its own internal operations necessary for the knowing process. Empiricists assumed that somehow —though they never really explained it—sense impressions, after being turned into ideas, get associated with each other into composites of ever increasing complexity. Kant challenged both of these assumptions. Even though "there can be no doubt that all our knowledge begins with experience," Kant observed, "it does not follow that it all arises out of experience." The empiricists were right in thinking that all our knowledge is based on our experience of the world; they were wrong in assuming that the mind has a purely passive role and contributes nothing to the knowing process. Kant likened his epistemological view to the Copernican revolution in astronomy. Prior to the time of Copernicus it was believed that the Earth was the center of the universe and that the heavenly bodies revolved around it. Now we know that the sun is the center of our solar system, and the Earth one of the planets orbiting it. Similarly, prior to Kant's time the empiricists thought that ideas were only copies of objects perceived by the senses. Kant's "revolution" reversed prevailing epistemological theories by presenting the view that we know things as objects only because the mind itself contributes important organizing principles which make knowledge of objects possible. The emphasis has shifted from the mind as passive to its playing an active role in shaping the "world" that can be known.

But this is getting ahead of ourselves. Think for a moment about what makes natural science so successful. As we pointed out in Part 2, real insights into nature have not come about merely as the result of collecting a lot of sense impressions, else natural science would have developed long before it did—human beings, after all, have been having perceptual experiences of the world as long as there have been human beings in the world. Natural science really got going, at least according to Kant's description of the scientific process, when human beings began to impose a structure upon their scientific investigation. Discovery of the secrets of nature occurs only when we know what sorts of questions to pose, and the right sort of questions arise when we approach our investigation of nature in terms of a plan of investigation (such as a scientific hypothesis). In a comparable way, if we are to know about *knowing* we have to approach the knowing process with a plan of attack, and Kant's proposed plan of attack was to question the prevailing assumption about the passivity of the mind and see if assuming that the mind plays an active role in the knowing process gets us any further.

A Priori and A Posteriori Knowledge

Armed with his new hypothesis, Kant plunged into the difficult question of investigating the knowing process. Here he discovers that there are two sorts of knowledge: knowledge completely independent of the senses (*a priori* knowledge) and knowledge wholly empirical (*a posteriori* knowledge). In defining *a priori* knowledge, Kant stresses its utter and complete independence from experience. The best example of completely *a priori* knowledge, Kant thinks, is found in mathematics, for in mathematics the concepts used are not derived from experience in any way but are generated entirely by the human mind. Sometimes Kant refers to that which is *a priori* as "pure," meaning by that term simply that it has no admixture of the senses.

A posteriori knowledge, or empirical knowledge as Kant usually calls it, is derived from our sense experience. Examples of this kind of knowledge are easy to give: "The temperature of the air is 70° F." "The sky is blue." "The lawn needs mowing." There is really nothing much new in the distinction between *a priori* and *a posteriori* knowledge; it is similar to Hume's distinction between "matters of fact" and "relations of ideas." But Kant takes this distinction one step further in relating it to the distinction between analytic and synthetic judgments.

▆▆▆ Analytic and Synthetic Judgments

By the term *judgment* Kant means a statement in which there is a subject term and a predicate term and which is either true or false (today, judgments are referred to generally as *propositions*). Consider the following list of statements.

1. The temperature of the water is 70° F.
2. The grass is green.
3. All bachelors are males.
4. All physical bodies take up space.
5. All physical bodies are heavy.
6. Water freezes at 0° C.

Not all these statements are of the same type. In some the predicate term extends your knowledge; it adds something that is not contained already in the subject. In other statements the predicate does not add anything not already contained in the subject. Kant calls the former kind of statement synthetic, the latter analytic. As Hume also noted, since the predicate of an analytic statement adds nothing new to the subject term, an analytic judgment is true by definition and, if denied, leads (unlike a synthetic statement) to a contradiction.

Here is the distinction again:

Synthetic—Predicate adds something and is not contained in the subject.

Analytic—Predicate adds nothing and is contained in the subject.

Now go back over the list of statements and determine for yourself which are synthetic and which are analytic. If your answer was that statements 1, 2, 5, and 6 are synthetic, and statements 3 and 4 are analytic, you got it right. If your answer was not correct, here is another way to approach the distinction.

Think about how you would determine the truth or falsity of each of the statements 1 through 6. If the truth value is determined through the senses alone, the statement is synthetic; if independently of the senses, the statement is analytic. Consider, for example, that you do not have to do any kind of empirical survey to discover that the statement "All bachelors are males" is true; its truth is a function of the meaning of the term bachelor. The quality or predicate of being male is *contained* in the concept of bachelor. Kant's example, "All bodies are extended," is an equivalent for statement 4. *Extended* (taking up space) is contained in the concept *body*. Kant claims that the concept of body contains the concept *extended* but not the concept *heavy*. Sentence 5 is therefore synthetic.

For the most part we can say that a posteriori statements are synthetic and that a priori statements are analytic. And it is clear that a statement cannot be both a posteriori and analytic, since a posteriori refers to that which is derived from the senses, and analytic means that which is independent of the senses—a manifest contradiction. There is, however, one class of judgment left—judgments that are both synthetic and a priori. Are there any such judgments or concepts? At first, it might seem that there could not be, for how could we extend our knowledge of anything apart from experience? Kant answers that not only are there concepts which are both synthetic and a priori (we find many of them in natural science and mathematics, Kant argues), but that they are the important ingredient in knowledge that the empiricists overlooked. Synthetic a priori knowledge would be that ideal knowledge discussed earlier which has proved so elusive to philosophers—knowledge both certain *and* informative.

We shall not go into all the proofs Kant offers for these synthetic a priori concepts (it took him over 500 pages to work that all out). Kant refers to the most important synthetic a priori concepts involved in the process of achieving knowledge as categories and he was convinced that there were just twelve such concepts. The most important one in the light of Hume's attack was the principle of causality. Hume was correct in thinking that causality is not a principle we can derive from experience, but he was wrong in thinking that there is no legitimacy to this concept. Kant argues that causality was one of the *categories* (i.e., a synthetic a priori concept) that we bring to experience and which makes experience possible. In an extended and detailed argument, Kant argues that without such categories as cause and effect, substance, and others, there would be no way of transforming sensous intuition (Kant's term for sensations) into judgments which can be dignified by the term knowledge. Can we even imagine a world without causality? In such a world there would be no consistency, no predictability, no basis for expectation. Hence we would never know what to expect, and life would be a nightmare of chaos and anxiety. If you squeezed a tube of toothpaste it could as easily explode, fly away, or scream at you as it could produce toothpaste.

Were Kant writing today, he might find metaphors for his description of the knowing process in computer technology. We talk a great deal today about data processing. The empiricists had ignored the *process*; all they were concerned about was the input data. The rationalists had ignored the input data; all they were concerned about was the process. Kant brought both together. We need the data supplied by the senses if we are to have knowledge, but these data need to be processed by the concepts (such as cause and effect) that the mind supplies out of its own operations. Both sensing and thinking are important. Without either, knowledge is impossible. "Thoughts without content are empty, intuitions without concepts are blind."

Kant and Philosophy Today

You would be hard pressed to find a philosopher today who would be willing to accept the label "Kantian" without some kind of qualification. Nonetheless, Kant has continued to exert a mighty impact on philosophy

Some philosophers have attempted to explore the full ramifications of saying that all knowledge is limited to statements that are either empirical or analytic.

Concern for analysis of judgments (or propositions) has led other philosophers into a detailed analysis of the nature and function of language. Philosophers of science, with their concern for the logic of scientific discovery, continue another of the concerns expressed by Kant.

If contemporary philosophy has not followed Kant exactly in working on the same problems he worked on, it has nonetheless continued something of the Kantian style in philosophy. Nobody has much enthusiasm for the one-sidedness of either empiricism or rationalism. And while philosophers today might dispute whether Kant's categories (just twelve of them) are the sole principles operative in the knowing process, there would be general agreement that the mind does contribute important conceptual schema that are essential for knowledge. And in the Kantian fashion, most philosophers would draw a clear line between what we can claim to be knowledge and what we may accept (as Kant did) on grounds of faith. Today philosophers may disagree with Kant on many points, but no one can ignore him. By and large, contemporary philosophers, whatever their disagreements with Kant might be, would tend to accept his understanding of the role of metaphysics. In Kant's time, as in the days of Greek philosophy, the term *metaphysics* referred to the inquiry concerning the nature of ultimate reality. Kant's Copernican revolution, however, resulted in the internalization of these questions and showed that questions of metaphysics and epistemology are interrelated. Additionally, Kant concludes that we cannot adequately answer questions about ultimate reality, though we will continue to ask them. What we can do—and this is the proper task of metaphysics, he argues—is examine the basic principles and rules operative in human knowledge. And what is perhaps clearer to contemporary philosophers than it was to Kant is that the attempt to engage in metaphysical analysis in the new sense also raises many of the questions of metaphysics in the old sense. Questions about causality, substance, possible worlds, the existence of God, and the nature of the self have not disappeared from philosophy, but in the aftermath of Kant's work we may be more cautious in claiming what we can know about such issues.

Immanuel Kant: Two Sources of Knowledge

When Galileo caused balls, the weights of which he had himself previously determined, to roll down an inclined plane, when Torricelli made the air carry a weight which he had calculated beforehand to be equal to that of a definite volume of water, or in more recent times when Stahl changed metals into oxides, and oxides back into metal, by withdrawing something and then restoring it, a

From Immanuel Kant, *Critique of Pure Reason*, trans. Norman Kemp Smith (New York: St. Martin's Press, 1933), pp. 20–21, 41–43, 48–51, 92–93.

light broke upon all students of nature. They learned that reason has insight only into that which it produces after a plan of its own, and that it must not allow itself to be kept, as it were, in nature's leading-strings, but must itself show the way with principles of judgment based upon fixed laws, constraining nature to give answer to questions of reason's own determining. Accidental observations, made in obedience to no previously thought-out plan, can never be made to yield a necessary law, which alone reason is concerned to discover. Reason, holding in one hand its principles, according to which alone concordant appearances can be admitted as equivalent to laws, and in the other hand the experiment which it has devised in conformity with these principles, must approach nature in order to be taught by it. It must not, however, do so in the character of a pupil who listens to everything that the teacher chooses to say, but of an appointed judge who compels the witnesses to answer questions which he has himself formulated. Even physics, therefore, owes the beneficent revolution in its point of view entirely to the happy thought, that while reason must seek in nature, not fictitiously ascribe to it, whatever as not being knowable through reason's own resources has to be learnt, if learnt at all, only from nature, it must adopt as its guide, in so seeking, that which it has itself put into nature. It is thus that the study of nature has entered on the secure path of a science, after having for many centuries been nothing but a process of merely random groping.

The Distinction Between Pure and Empirical Knowledge

There can be no doubt that *all* our knowledge begins with experience. For how should our faculty of knowledge be awakened into action did not objects affecting our senses partly of themselves produce representations, partly arouse the activity of our understanding to compare these representations, and, by combining or separating them, work up the raw material of the sensible impressions into that knowledge of objects which is entitled experience? In the order of time, therefore, we have no knowledge antecedent to experience, and with experience all our knowledge begins.

But though all our knowledge begins with experience, it does not follow that it all arises out of experience. For it may well be that even our empirical knowledge is made up of what we receive through impressions and of what our own faculty of knowledge (sensible impressions serving merely as the occasion) supplies from itself. If our faculty of knowledge makes any such addition, it may be that we are not in a position to distinguish it from the raw material, until with long practice of attention we have become skilled in separating it.

This, then, is a question which at least calls for closer examination, and does not allow of any off-hand answer:—whether there is any knowledge that is thus independent of experience and even of all impressions of the senses. Such knowledge is entitled *a priori,* and distinguished from the empirical, which has its sources *a posteriori,* that is, inexperience.

The expression "*a priori*" does not, however, indicate with sufficient precision the full meaning of our question. For it has been customary to say, even of much knowledge that is derived from empirical sources, that we have it or are capable of having it *a priori,* meaning thereby that we do not derive it immediately from experience, but from a universal rule—a rule which is itself, however, borrowed by us from experience. Thus we would say of a man who undermined the foundations of his house that he might have known *a priori* that it would fall, that is, that he need not have waited for the experience of its actual falling. But still he could not know this completely *a priori.* For he had first to learn through experience that bodies are heavy, and therefore fall when their supports are withdrawn.

In what follows, therefore, we shall understand by *a priori* knowledge, not knowledge independent of this or that experience, but knowledge absolutely independent of all experience. Opposed to it is empirical knowledge, which is knowledge possible only *a posteriori,* that is, through experience. *A priori* modes of knowledge are entitled pure when there is no admixture of anything empirical. Thus, for instance, the proposition, every alteration has its cause, while an a priori proposition, is not a pure proposition because alteration is a concept which can be derived only from experience.

The Distinction Between Analytic and Synthetic Judgments

In all judgments in which the relation of a subject to the predicate is thought (I take into consideration affirmative judgments only, the subsequent application to negative judgments being easily made), this relation is possible in two different ways. Either the predicate B belongs to the subject A as something which is (covertly) contained in this concept A, or B lies outside the concept A, although it does indeed stand in connection with it. In the one case I entitle the judgment analytic, in the other . . . synthetic. Analytic judgments (affirmative) are therefore those in which the connection of the predicate with the subject is thought through identity; those in which this connection is thought without identity should be entitled synthetic. The former, as adding nothing through the predicate to the concept of the subject, but merely breaking it up into those constituent concepts that have all along been thought in it, although confusedly, can also be entitled explicative. The latter, on the other hand, add to the concept of the subject a predicate which has not been in any wise thought in it, and which no analysis could possibly extract from it, and they may therefore be entitled ampliative. If I say, for instance, "All bodies are extended," this is an analytic judgment. For I do not require to go beyond the concept which I connect with "body" in order to find extension as bound up with it. To meet with this predicate, I have merely to analyze the concept, that is, to become conscious to myself of the manifold which I always think in that concept. The judgment is therefore analytic. But when I say, "All bodies are heavy," the predicate is something quite different from anything that I think in the mere concept of body in general, and the addition of such a predicate therefore yields a synthetic judgment.

Judgments of experience, as such, are one and all synthetic. For it would be absurd to found an analytic judgment on experience. Since, in framing the judgment, I must not go outside my concept, there is no need to appeal to the testimony of experience in its support. That a body is extended is a proposition that holds *a priori* and is not empirical. For, before appealing to experience, I have already in the concept of body all the conditions required for my judgment. I have only to extract from it, in accordance with the principle of contradiction, the required predicate, and in so doing can at the same time become conscious of the necessity of the judgment—and that is what experience could never have taught me. On the other hand, though I do not include in the concept of a body in general the predicate "weight," none the less this concept indicates an object of experience through one of its parts, and I can add to that part other parts of this same experience, as in this way belonging together with the concept. From the start I can apprehend the concept of body analytically through the characters of extension, impenetrability, figure, etc., all of which are thought in the concept. Now, however, looking back on the experience from which I have derived this concept of body, and finding weight to be invariably connected with the above characters, I attach it as a predicate to the concept, and in doing so I attach it synthetically, and am therefore extending my knowledge. The possibility of the synthesis of the predicate "weight" with the concept of "body" thus rests upon experience. While the one concept is not contained in the other, they yet belong to one another, though only contingently, as parts of a whole, namely, of an experience which is itself a synthetic combination of intuitions.

But in *a priori* synthetic judgments this help is entirely lacking: I do not here have the advantage of looking around in the field of experience. Upon what, then, am I to rely, when I seek to go beyond the concept A, and to know that another concept B is connected with it? Through what is the synthesis made possible? Let us take the proposition, "Everything which happens has its cause." In the concept of "something which happens," I do indeed think an existence which is preceded by a time, etc., and from this concept analytic judgments may be obtained. But the concept of a "cause" lies entirely outside the other concept, and signifies something different from "that which happens," and is not therefore in any way contained in this latter representation. How come I then to predicate of that which happens something quite different, and to apprehend that the concept of cause, though not contained in it, yet belongs, and indeed necessarily belongs, to it? . . . It cannot be experience, because the suggested principle has connected the second representation with the first, not only with greater universality, but also with the character of necessity, and therefore completely a priori and on the basis of mere concepts. Upon such synthetic, that is, ampliative principles, all our *a priori* speculative knowledge must ultimately rest; analytic judgments are very important, and indeed necessary, but only for obtaining that clearness in the concepts which is requisite for such a sure and wide synthesis as will lead to a genuinely new addition to all previous knowledge.

Logic in General

Our knowledge springs from two fundamental sources of the mind; the first is the capacity of receiving representations (receptivity for impressions), the second is the power of knowing an object through these representations (spontaneity in the production of concepts). Through the first an object is given to us, through the second the object is thought in relation to that given representation (which is a mere determination of the mind). Intuition and concepts constitute, therefore, the elements of all our knowledge, so that neither concepts without an intuition in some way corresponding to them, nor intuition without concepts, can yield knowledge. Both may be either pure or empirical. When they contain sensation (which presupposes the actual presence of the object), they are empirical. When there is no mingling of sensation with the representation, they are pure. Sensation may be entitled the material of sensible knowledge. Pure intuition, therefore, contains only the form under which something is intuited; the pure concept only the form of the thought of an object in general. Pure intuitions or pure concepts alone are possible a priori, empirical intuitions and empirical concepts only a posteriori.

If the receptivity of our mind, its power of receiving representations in so far as it is in any wise affected, is to be entitled sensibility, then the mind's power of producing representations from itself the spontaneity of knowledge should be called the understanding. Our nature is so constituted that our intuition can never be other than sensible; that is, it contains only the mode in which we are affected by objects. The faculty, on the other hand which enables us to think the object of sensible intuition is the understanding. To neither of these powers may a preference be given over the other. Without sensibility no object would be given to us, without understanding no object would be thought. Thoughts without content are empty, intuitions without concepts are blind.

Questions for Discussion

1. Explain what is revolutionary about Kant's "Copernican revolution."
2. What are the similarities, if any, between Kant's analytic and synthetic judgments and Hume's "matters of fact" and "relations of ideas"? Explain.
3. Give some examples of propositions that are analytic and *a priori* other than those cited in the text.
4. Do you think there are synthetic *a priori* judgments? Why or why not? (Note: Kant thought one could find such judgments in mathematics; do you agree?)
5. Explain what Kant meant by the statement, "Thoughts without content are empty, intuitions without concepts are blind."

CHAPTER 18

The Challenges of Postmodernism

One of the things that makes philosophy interesting, and often frustrating, is that issues which seem to be settled do not disappear permanently. They often return in different forms and with renewed force. This is true of such issues in epistemology as relativism and skepticism about the possibilities of knowledge. These issues have again burst upon the philosophic scene under the name postmodernism.

Postmodernism refers not to a single point of view but to a series of related challenges to modern philosophy. As the label implies, such approaches see themselves as being so radical that they will eventually undermine and completely replace "modern" philosophy, that is, philosophy since Descartes (and indeed modernist thought of all sorts).

What is postmodernism? It is a term more and more frequently used but seldom explicitly defined, defended, or discussed. It is often mentioned as something highly controversial that has displaced or is about to displace many long-standing traditions in the modern tradition of philosophy, especially aesthetics and art and literary criticism, and yet it is still not very well understood. This is due in part to the fact that the theoretical underpinning of postmodernism has not arisen from within familiar British and American philosophical traditions but from a variety of very different Continental European traditions with which American and British philosophers are not very familiar. The main elements in the pedigree of postmodernism, include French semiotics (Saussure), French structuralists (Levi-Strauss), German phenomenologists (especially Heidegger), French deconstructionists (Derrida and the American followers of Derrida, the Yale group, de Man, J. Hillis Miller, Bloom), hermeneutics (Gadamer and Habermas), Foucault and his followers, Marxists such as Althusser, Freudians such as Lacan. Much of this tradition is very alien to American and British traditions. To understand de Man, for instance, one would have to know something of Derrida and Heidegger, but in order to appreciate the work of these writers, one would have to know something of Husserl and phenomenology (in the case of Heidegger) and the structuralist tradition of Saussure and Levi-Strauss (in the case of Derrida). Without such a background and preparation, virtually every sentence of de Man, for example, is incomprehensible. Naturally, there has been great resistance to this invasion of alien ideas by those working in the mainstreams of the Anglo-American philosophical tradition. Not only are the postmodernist ideas themselves highly controversial, they are also written in an alien and incomprehensible style.

Without going into a detailed analysis of these difficult and complex theories, let us simply try to explain how all this is being transmitted to the Anglo-American "modernist" philosophical tradition. Whatever its historical origins in French and German traditions, postmodernism is penetrating the domain of Anglo-American philosophy as a series of extremely radical challenges to most of the assumptions, indeed to the very foundations of traditional, "modernist" philosophical thinking. Especially in Derrida and deconstruction, postmodernism challenges the fundamental epistemological assumption of modern philosophy and science, the possibility of discovering the truth about anything. Postmodernists claim that any attempt to verify the truth of a claim by its correspondence with reality is an impossible illusion.

This is not, of course, an entirely new idea. We have seen that at the beginnings of Western philosophy, Plato was also doing battle with skepticism. And throughout its history, philosophers have always been aware of the gap between theory and reality. Skeptics and idealists in different ways have despaired of ever achieving a correct correspondence of thought to some external reality; since the way we describe the world affects the way we experience the world, it is hard to see how we can ever get outside language to see if our language correctly matches the reality we think it describes. Carried to its logical conclusion, such thoroughgoing skepticism about the possibility of objective knowledge leads to radical subjectivism and relativism, the position that any opinion is as good as any other. The challenge to "truth" also undermines, as we will see shortly, the traditional philosophical idea of an independent reality that theories and interpretations seek to describe.

▬ A New Period of Skepticism

Despite a long philosophical tradition of analyzing the problems posed by skepticism, idealism, subjectivism, and relativism, the main tradition of philosophy has always rejected complete skepticism and has always sought ways of overcoming or at least modifying it. In the history of philosophy these positions almost always appear as challenges to be answered; they seldom represent major philosophical traditions. The position adopted by postmodernism is far more radical and controversial in the sense that it rejects completely the attempt of the mainstream Western intellectual tradition to overcome complete subjectivity and relativity and all that would logically entail. If a theory cannot be judged by its faithful correspondence to reality, then no statement can be any more true or false than any other, and therefore no one can be any more correct or incorrect in their descriptions than anyone else; everyone's opinion is as good as anyone else's. The main criterion, therefore, becomes how you, as an individual, feel about it. Again we see here a return to the position taken by Gorgias and the other Sophists with whom Plato argued.

Traditionally, most philosophers have found such a consequence unacceptable and have sought ways around it. Postmodernism is radical and controversial in that it joyfully embraces such radical skeptical subjectivism and relativism and tries to help the rest of us come to terms with this "brave new world." For such reasons, postmodernism has gained little acceptance among philosophers, though it has made major inroads into literary and art criticism and even into social theory. Whether postmodernism represents a major turning point in philosophy or simply one more in a long series of periodical skeptical, "critical" phases in the history of philosophy remains to be seen, though if past history is any judge it is probably the latter.

Let us look for a moment at just what this radical claim means for traditional philosophical assumptions. The only reason it makes sense to speak of one real object or event about which there have been many different theories or interpretations over the years is the assumption, which postmodernism denies, that these interpretations are "about," that is, more or less true or accurate descriptions of, that real object or event. It is because of this modernist assumption that we imagine we are comparing an interpretation to the reality, to see how accurate or inaccurate it is. Since, on this traditional, modern philosophical assumption, there are many more or less accurate interpretations describing the same object, we assume that there is a single reality that all these interpretations are interpretations of and at which they all aim. Imagine many people shooting at the same target; to speak of some shots as "close" and others as "way off" presupposes they are all directed at a single bull's-eye. But if language fails completely to describe an external reality, then there is really no longer any point in talking about an object apart from particular interpretations, or "readings," of it. In the target analogy, if shots going up, down, north, south, east, and west were all said to be equally accurate, we would begin to wonder whether there was a target at all.

The myth of an independent external reality is one that postmodernism tries to expose by "deconstructing" language, that is, by showing first the gap between word and object, language and reality, and then by showing that the so-called reality is simply created by the language itself. Deconstruction shows how language has constructed what we call "reality"; it then deconstructs these linguistic constructions. What this basically accomplishes, when successful, is to expose as myths linguistic descriptions masquerading as reality—the myth of truth as the correspondence of idea to reality, the myth of universal cross-cultural objectivity and rationality, the myth of neutral, value-free scientific investigation, and so on. As the Zen Buddhists say (borrowing from much earlier Taoist philosophers), "When you point to the moon, don't mistake the finger for the moon." The things we refer to are not real, objective parts of reality; they are just ways of speaking which have caught on and have become popular and then "internalized" so that we wrongly assume they accurately describe and reveal an independent reality.

As Derrida and other deconstructionists put it, what is deconstructed are traditional Western value-laden dichotomies ("binaries")—presence/absence, nature/ culture, male/female, central/marginal, in which, in each case, the first of the pair is preferred and ranks above the second. Such value-laden, hierarchical binaries, according to deconstructionists, provide the foundations for our Western intellectual tradition. In order to settle disputes, we must have standards on which we all agree for distinguishing true from false, correct from incorrect, real from illusory, and in order to do that we must be able, in the final analysis, to appeal to something that is beyond dispute. This is what dichotomous "binaries" provide. Without such binaries, there can be no foundation.

For Derrida, "presence" (and its binary opposite, "absence") is the root idea in Western culture that knowledge begins by just seeing just the object "right in front of us," and then comparing "representations" (i.e., interpretations) of the object to the object actually "present" to us. If I say it's green and you say it's red, we simply look at the object and see that it is in fact red, so you are right and I am wrong. Without presence, there can be no representation, and without representation there can be no stability of meaning, that is, no way to decide on the one correct meaning, or interpretation, and therefore no way to determine intersubjectively the final and complete truth about anything, once and for all.

Of course, there are many visible aspects of an object, so we must also distinguish those which are central (color, shape, for example) from those which are of only "marginal" importance (such as aesthetic properties). And without priority or preference for "centrality," what has traditionally been considered marginal is just as important as what has traditionally been considered central, since there really is no difference between what is "central" and what is "marginal." Where previously the evaluatively laden binaries constrained and limited thought and language to a supposed presence (that is, objective truth to which thought and language had to conform), the rejection of presence frees thought and language to "play," as Derrida calls it, with the "reading" or interpretation of the "text," that is, to interpret the object or event freely without being restricted by considerations of correctness or truth.

▬ The Role of Interpretation

There are other voices among contemporary French philosophers that disagree with the relativising tendencies of deconstruction. One of the more important of these is Paul Ricoeur, a philosopher who has taught at universities both in

France and in the United States. Ricoeur's work is broadly in the phenomeno-logical tradition, and he has occupied himself with the problems of developing a comprehensive interpretation theory, or hermeneutics. Unlike the postmoderns, who argue for the relativity of all interpretations of a text, Ricoeur has devoted considerable effort to an analysis of how various kinds of texts are to be read. Religious myths concerning the origins and end of evil are to be understood with a different frame of reference than the dreams of a person undergoing psycho-analysis, and the meanings of narrative texts inhabit a different world of dis-course than do the metaphorical functions of poetic language. The notion of a text can even encompass nonwritten realities, such as human action (we speak even in ordinary language of "reading" someone by their actions).

Drawing heavily on both English and American philosophers, Ricoeur shows that interpretation is a dialectic between the reader and the text. It is not the goal of the reader to reconstruct a meaning that stands behind the text, the in-tentions of the author or the meaning the text had for its original audience, but rather to allow the text to open up new levels of meaning and self-under-standing. While the interests of the reader of the text are important, they are only one pole in the relation between the reader and the text. The text itself has a unity that provides the reader an opportunity for greater self-under-standing. This approach is vastly different than that of postmodernism, which more or less concludes that the text itself does not really constrain the inter-pretations placed on it or allow some interpretations to be more correct than others.

But if no one theory or interpretation is any better than any other, as the post-moderns claim, how is it that in fact some theories and interpretations have suc-ceeded historically while others have failed? Postmodernism says this is due to political forces. There are no truer or better interpretations, only stronger inter-pretations, that is, those which are more persuasive at a particular time and for a particular audience. But what is persuasive is rhetorically powerful for one par-ticular social group at the expense of another. The traditional creation of an offi-cial list of accepted theories is therefore just an advertising sales pitch aimed at elevating one social group into power (aristocratic white European males), and holding other social groups (the lower classes, women, non-Europeans) down. But once we realize that this is the case, then there is a revolutionary side to post-modernism which encourages all the left-out, "marginalized" groups to demand their full share of center stage. Distinctions of scientific and popular, major and minor, good and bad, established and alternative; all are swept away.

Most philosophers would use the same arguments against this view that Plato used against the Sophists. If all theories become important only because they are politically more powerful or acceptable, then if postmodernism becomes accept-ed it is only because it too has become politically acceptable and powerful. But then it could be attacked as putting the views it rejects on the margins and thus becoming guilty of the very things it condemns in the views it attacks. In other words, postmodernism undercuts its own foundations.

For many philosophers today, postmodernism is therefore both disturbing and attractive. On the one hand, it means cutting ourselves adrift from solid and stable boundary markers of what is right and wrong, good and bad, correct and incorrect, true and false, real and illusory and sailing off into the unknown without benefit of map or compass. But it also means an emphasis on the legitimacy of the individual's "reading," or interpretation of an object or event, however it may deviate from the opinion of the experts, and to the "liberation" of marginalized thought of women, minorities, and disenfranchised groups, such as Native Americans, African Americans, Hispanics, and homeless street people.

A Search for Common Ground

Most philosophers probably find themselves somewhere between these extremes. The problem for most philosophers, therefore, is not whether to accept or reject postmodernism, but how to find the right blend or balance between modernism and postmodernism. As often happens when new movements challenge older, established positions, confrontational battle lines are drawn up, with differences between the established tradition and the new challenger exaggerated and each pictured to the other as an extreme, simplistic caricature. Each side ceases to listen to the other and simply ridicules its strawman caricature. As in any intense intellectual debate, there are those who embrace extreme positions as the best way of differentiating their position from "the opposition" as sharply as possible, and this, too, contributes to a sense of an irreconcilable gulf between the two positions, resulting in an uncomfortable either/or dichotomy.

But in fact differences between modernism and postmodernism are not irreconcilable. When we look closely at the "moderns" we can see many anticipations of "postmodern" thought, and when we look closely at the work of the postmoderns we can see that much of their work continues to follow, in a modified form, certain traditional elements of modern philosophical analysis. Indeed, in many ways, the very labels "modern" and "postmodern" are exaggerated and pretentious. As with all historical labels, there is no precise time when modernism comes to a complete halt and is suddenly replaced by postmodernism. These are journalistic labels; the reality is one of gradual change. Kierkegaard, who lived in the early and middle nineteenth century, and Nietzsche, who died around the turn of the twentieth century, are often cited as postmoderns, while many university philosophy departments remain today predominantly modernist in emphasis.

Thus, we can distinguish a radical version of postmodernism, which is deeply antithetical to modern philosophy, from a more modest, less extreme version of postmodernism that is not absolutely incompatible with modernist assumptions and toward which a modern philosophy has been evolving for years and toward which it may continue to evolve in light of postmodernist criticisms. Between the less extreme versions of modernism and postmodernism the possibility of reconciliation surely exists.

How so? We can deny with postmodernism any absolutely privileged foundation (in fact or in reality) without abandoning the relative use of such concepts. For example, we ordinarily distinguish between facts and interpretations of those facts. Suppose someone of a postmodern bent convinces us that anything that we can point to as a fact is also an interpretation. But even if we agree with that, it would not mean that we could not continue to speak, in one context, about "facts" which are given various "interpretations," knowing full well that in another context, those same facts might be interpretations, and vice versa. At first the fact is that Jones committed suicide by jumping out a fifteenth story window, and we look for an interpretation of that fact (why did he do it?), but later that fact may be called into question by new evidence suggesting that Jones was actually murdered, and now Jones's suicide is no longer a fact but an interpretation (which may later be rejected entirely). So, in our relative use of the term, a fact might simply be what is relatively undisputed by a certain group of people at a particular time. If Jones's suicide is undisputed, then it is a fact. If it is disputed, it is an "interpretation," but it cannot be both in the same context.

Or, suppose we agreed that it is impossible for any human being to be completely, absolutely objective; it would not necessarily follow that there was no longer any useful distinction between being objective and being biased (the distinction, for example, between history and propaganda). There could still be a relative distinction between what is considered biased and objective in a given society at a given time in a specified context. In discussions of history we can distinguish and try to eliminate those biases we are aware of at a particular time (for example, today we may recognize male bias, and Euro-bias), and nonetheless recognize that we are probably still victims of biases which we are not currently aware of. Later, if and when we become aware of these biases, we work to eliminate them, and so on, step by step—at any given stage, defining objectivity as eliminating those biases which we are aware of, allowing the possibility of other biases we are not aware of at that time. At any given stage (and we live in only one stage at a time) some things can be meaningfully said to be objective relative to others which are seen to be biased. Propaganda would therefore differ from history, not in that the one is subjectively biased while the other is completely objective, but in that propaganda is deliberately biased while history tries and intends to be objective though it cannot avoid some unconscious biases.

Again, this shows the importance of the study of the history of philosophy. Against the skeptics of his day, Plato argued for a dialectical conception of our pursuit of truth. This means that our current view must be subjected to intense philosophical examination, leading us to modify it and form a new view. That modified view, in turn, is also subjected to intense criticism, leading us to modify it, and so on.

Or, suppose we agreed that human beings could never know reality as it is in itself, that all so-called knowledge of reality involves a subjective point of view.

That does not destroy the utility of the reality/appearance distinction, which, again, can be useful in making a recognized distinction between what is relatively more stable and agreed upon among this group of people at this time and context and what is more open to question and debate. Suppose you and I disagree about who that person is standing there in the corner. I say it is Mary, and you say it is Taiwo. Once we go over to speak to her we discover that you were right and I was wrong. At least relative to this particular situation, we can distinguish reality from appearance, truth from falsity, though not absolutely in a way that makes us immune from error, or removes entirely the subjective human situation we all find ourselves in all of the time. Later, it may turn out, for example, that it really wasn't Taiwo, either, but her sister, Tanya, whom we both wrongly assumed was Taiwo. But now in this new context we can still distinguish reality from appearance, truth from falsity. So long as the same thing cannot be both true and false, real and apparent in the same context, we can distinguish the true from the false, the real from the apparent in any given context.

Thus, we could continue to talk sensibly about the same object or event existing over time, about which interpretations have varied over the centuries, even though we recognize that we have no knowledge of that object or event over and above these interpretations of it. Despite the facts of conventionality and subjectivity, it is very useful as a heuristic device to be able to refer different interpretations to a single, autonomous object. And once we become more sophisticated about what we are doing, there is no longer the danger about which postmodernists are concerned.

In this relative sense the assumptions of modernism are not incompatible with postmodernism. There is a relative sense in which we can speak of foundations, objectivity, truth, rationality, and so on, though in a modified form. While it is probably true that there are no morally or politically neutral judgments or assertions, nonetheless we can and should distinguish judgments which are primarily, overtly moral or political and those which are only marginally, unconsciously, peripherally so. Consider for example, the judgment made of a work of art. While it is true that the standards by which any kind of art is judged are conventional and can therefore change, it is also true that until that change occurs art works can be judged by those standards. And while it is true that the standards by which art is judged are conventional and therefore are socially relative, it is also true that within a given culture or society certain standards do operate and can be used to communicate relatively objective judgments within a community of shared values.

More generally, the fact that standards are conventional does not negate but reinforces the objectivity of criteria of correctness. It is purely conventional that in English we distinguish between trees and shrubs, but once we have accepted that convention and so long as it remains in force (and such things do not typically change very quickly), then it is objectively true (for all those who speak English) that an oak is a tree and false to say that it is a shrub. Similarly with colors. It is completely arbitrary and therefore conventional how we divide the color spectrum into distinct segments and which color labels (red, orange, and so on) we assign to each segment, but once that is agreed upon then it is correct to call indigo blue and false to call it red.

Our response to postmodernism should be, first, to try to understand it, and not to run away from it, pretend it does not exist, claim it is incomprehensible, or dismiss it as outrageous madness. Second, we should try to distinguish the more radical claims, some of which are outrageous, from its more sensible claims. Then, while we may argue against the more extreme claims with which we disagree, we can begin the task of reconciling the more moderate claims with the more sophisticated and progressive elements of the modernist tradition. This will mean modifying modernism in light of postmodernist criticism, but not throwing it out entirely. In general, we must modify modernism by acknowledging a larger measure of subjectivity, conventionality, and politics in our attitudes and judgments about things. That is not a rejection of modern philosophy, but a sophistication of it.

When we finally work through all this to make an assessment of postmodernism, we see some major similarities to the mainstream tradition of modern philosophy, as well as some major differences. The similarities lie in the postmodernist rejection of absolutes—the alleged discovery that it is a fundamental illusion, deeply embedded in our Western intellectual outlook, to think that there are, or that we can ever discover, an absolutely secure and certain foundation for knowledge, reality (the thing in itself as it is in itself), objective truth (free of all human bias), brute fact, a presuppositionless beginning, an objective standard of assessment (whether in epistemology, ethics, or aesthetics). But this is also an important part of the modern philosophical tradition (though not universally accepted by all) from Locke's rejection of innate ideas, to Kant's rejection of knowledge of the thing in itself, to the twentieth-century rejection of an absolute empiricist foundation for knowledge.

The major differences between postmodernism and the tradition of modern philosophy have mainly to do with differences in the responses we make to this rejection of absolutes. The postmodern response is to go from one extreme position to the opposite extreme. The attitude of postmodernism seems to be that "if God is dead, everything is possible." Much of the language of postmodernism is a language of extremes. If there are no absolutes, then in place of knowledge and the rational search for intersubjective, objective truth we are now free to "play" or, in Derrida's expression, to "trope." There are no external standards or even internal standards of personal or cultural consistency and coherence to restrict us. We are therefore free to go with what seems at the moment compelling to us and we are guided in our articulations by only the desire to persuade, to gain a receptive following.

Within the modern philosophic tradition, by contrast, there has been the attempt to recover regulative, relative, pragmatic standards which take the place of (and more or less do the job of) the old absolutes. Even if there is no knowledge of the thing in itself as it is in itself, we can learn more and more about things as they appear to us; even if our knowledge is biased by our interests, we can still learn what an object is like relative to our interests (interests which we more or less share with others for a longer or shorter period of time). Even if our knowledge, beliefs, and meanings are based on changing social conventions, these conventions change slowly enough to allow us to establish acceptable and workable rules operating within a given time span. Even if there is no indubitable empirical given (sense-data), we can still continue to assess our theories in the light of our experience of the world; even if there is no certainty, there can be higher and higher probabilities. Even if analytic statements are true relative to social conventions, there can still be at any given time a very high degree of social agreement on conventions over a long period of time; even if there are no essences, there are family resemblances; even if there are no brute facts, there are relatively more socially acceptable beliefs in any given situation which function as and can be regarded as the facts relative to that context. And even if we cannot know ultimate reality (the thing in itself as it is in itself), we can know aspects of reality and we can continue to talk meaningfully about the regulative ideal of improving our understanding.

Questions for Discussion

1. From your own experience, can you think of any theories, groups or intellectual positions that are "marginalized?" If so, on what basis do you think they are so treated?

2. A question for your own thought and analysis: Why do you think postmodernism has had such an appeal for art and literary critics?

3. Can we claim to have knowledge even if we do not claim to know something absolutely? Explain.

4. To what do you attribute the appeal of a skeptical attitude toward knowledge?

5. What do you think are the best arguments in support of postmodernism? Against it?

Suggestions for Further Reading

Chisholm, Roderick M. *The Foundations of Knowledge*. Minneapolis: University of Minnesota Press, 1982. Clearly written, short overview from Chishoim's modified phenomenological perspective.

McGrew, Timothy. *The Foundations of Knowledge*. Lanham, MD: Littlefield Adams, 1995. Defends foundationalism against a host of recent critics.

Pappas, George S. and Marshall Swain, eds. *Essays on Knowledge and Justification*. Ithaca: Cornell University Press, 1978. Essays by leading contemporary analytic epistemologists.

What Ought We to Do? (Ethics)

PART 5

CHAPTER 19

Introduction to Ethical Reasoning

Ethics, sometimes called moral philosophy, is that area of philosophy which investigates the principles governing human actions in terms of their goodness, badness, rightness, and wrongness. It is concerned with discovering the principles that should govern human conduct and with the investigation of normative issues involving value judgments. In addition to the normative questions, that is, the examination of specific moral problems, recent philosophy, especially during the past thirty years, has been concerned also with moral theory, which does not attempt to deal with specific ethical problems as such but with ethical discourse itself, with what we *mean* when we use ethical terms (such as *right, wrong, good, bad, duty, obligation,* and so on), and how ethical terms should be used. Moral theory has the same relation to ethical decision-making that the study of grammar has to the ability to speak a language. A person can speak a language without ever having studied its grammar, and a person can also make ethical decisions without ever having studied moral theory. But just as our ability to function in a language is often aided by a study of grammar, so does an inquiry into theoretical concerns aid us in clarifying our ethical choices.

Theory and Normative Ethics

In recent years some philosophers have seemed so concerned with theory that the normative questions tended to drop out of sight, but these kinds of excessive interests in theory are not as prevalent today as they once were. Philosophers are now turning more and more to the analysis of normative ethical issues. In fact, some of the most intensive work being done in ethics today involves philosophers in the thorny issues raised by new medical technologies, such issues as the morality of organ transplants, genetic manipulation, DNA research, euthanasia (mercy killing), and even such basic issues as how to define death. The latter is crucial in organ transplantation. If you are awaiting an organ from a donor, the donor must be dead, but not *too* dead; the heart, for example, should still be beating. Thus, a difficult question is raised, "Is the donor dead or not?" Other pressing normative issues involve the allocation of scarce resources, the morality of war (are some wars more just than others?), issues raised by new technologies, nuclear power, nuclear weapons testing, the right to privacy in an age of computers. On and on the list of normative questions goes. There is certainly plenty of work for moral philosophers to do.

Ethics is an important branch of philosophy because it directs our attention not only to human morality but to values in general. Moral philosophy raises questions such as the following: Are there standards that ought to govern all human behavior? If so, how can we know what they are? Even if we know there are such ethical standards, why should we follow them, especially when they seem not to be in our own self-interest? In general, what makes something good or bad? Is there any common property, for example, that not only makes a chocolate cake good but that also makes a lawnmower good? Or is goodness just a feeling people have of liking or wanting something? What makes an action right or wrong? Does the same thing that makes lying wrong make failure to help a friend wrong? Or are rightness and wrongness just arbitrary social conventions? Perhaps the two most important questions in moral philosophy are what is the best way for a person to live and whether this "good life" should be a morally good life or simply a more self-centered life of pleasure and fun.

This last question brings out an important ambiguity in the word *good* which serves to differentiate two main areas within ethics. Aristotle long ago pointed out that when we talk about something being good or bad we usually mean whether it satisfies the purpose or function for which it was made. A lawnmower is good if it cuts the grass evenly, quietly and efficiently, because that is what it is supposed to do. A good pencil, on the other hand, is one that writes evenly, and without a mess. The properties that make a thing good or bad vary with each kind of item according to its particular purpose or function, though all are alike in being good for the same general functional reason, that each does what it was meant to do. Thus, if I ask in general, what makes a grink a good grink, there is no answer forthcoming (except the general answer "if it does what it is supposed to do") until we know what a grink *is* and thereby what its function is.

Notice that while one thing may be good for the sake of some particular end, that end may itself be a means to some further end, and so on and so on. So, for example, the nail is useful in building a house, and the house is useful in providing shelter. By pursuing this line of reasoning we soon arrive at the most general aims or purposes or needs of human life and thus to a theory about what good *in general* is. This means/end analysis of good is called *teleological,* from the Greek word *telos,* meaning end or purpose.

Does the means-end chain go on forever or does it come to rest, and if so where? What, for example, is the shelter which the house provides good for? Health and comfort. OK, but what are these good for? Here we seem to arrive at the end of the road. These and other things are ultimately good for our happiness and well-being, and here the chain definitely comes to an end. If we ask what happiness is good for, the question makes no sense. In this sense, then, happiness is the ultimate or most general or final good. Thus the kind of approach to ethics which emphasizes the purposeful or utility sense of good usually leads to the conclusion that good is ultimately or finally happiness or pleasure.

This position, that the ultimate good is pleasure, is known as *hedonism*, from the Greek word for pleasure. Anything is good according to this theory, if it contributes to human happiness, or pleasure. And here it is customary and useful to distinguish two kinds of hedonism. If the pleasure is for the agent alone, it is egoistic hedonism, but if the pleasure is for the largest number of people possible, then it is known as utilitarianism, the greatest pleasure for the greatest number of people. If cheating in general causes more unhappiness than happiness, then it is bad, but if it creates more pleasure or happiness all round, then it is good. Not all teleological theories are hedonistic, but only those which specify pleasure as the ultimate end, or purpose, of action. If we suppose the ultimate end or purpose of any action is power, or wealth, our theory is teleological but not hedonistic. A theory is teleological if it assesses the worth of an action by the consequences it achieves.

Human and Functional Goodness

This kind of analysis works fairly well for manufactured articles, but what about natural things, and, more important, what about persons? Looked at in this way, what makes a tree a good tree and what makes a person a good person? In the case of natural objects we might consider extending to them, by analogy, the same teleological attitudes we have toward manufactured objects. Although we did not make the tree, we can regard it as an object which can similarly serve our needs and purposes, such as shade, decoration, wood for the fireplace, wood for the new barn, and so on. So a good tree would be one which was either broad and leafy, attractive to look at, slow and even burning, durable yet easily workable. Perhaps we have no right to bend natural objects to our own purposes—if whales are good for their oil, are we justified in using all the remaining whales to meet this need?

Assuming we can justify this treatment of the natural world simply as an object of human use, what can we say about the goodness and badness of people based on this analogy? We know what makes a lawnmower a good one because we know what its purpose is, and we know *that* because we (collectively) made it. But, on this analysis, a good person would be one who served the purpose for which he or she was "made." But is there such a purpose, and if so, can we know what it is? The answers to these questions may be affirmative, but they are not obviously or clearly so.

Perhaps the human purpose or function is as Plato and Aristotle thought, to do what people do best or uniquely. Human purpose on this view would be to fulfill human nature or potential. That might include thinking rationally and creating art, and these activities do sound like good ones for people. But people are also uniquely capable of brutal warfare. Which of these activities are part of our true potential and which are perversions of that potential?

Despite these problems, this approach to ethics (applying the functional analysis of manufactured goods to the analysis of human goodness) does lead to the ethical position known as self-realization, which is the view that human goodness is fulfilling as much of our human potential as possible, a view associated with the philosophy of Aristotle, which we have a chance to examine more closely in the readings for this section, and the psychological theories of Abraham Maslow. A good life, according to this view, is one which taps to the fullest the inherent capacities of each person. This view would prescribe, for example, that, other things being equal, a person would make a grave mistake to reject whole dimensions of human experience—avoiding, for example, all creative endeavor, all leadership capability, all responsibility, all caring for others, and so on. It would also insist that any attempt to restrain the full development of such capacities by outside control (such as slavery or class, race, or sex restrictions) would necessarily be wrong.

Teleological and Deontological Views

Nonetheless, there is something unsatisfactory about looking at human goodness in the same way we look at toothpick goodness. This point can be brought out most forcefully perhaps by considering the ambiguity in the word *good* when applied to human beings. Consider Jones, for example, who is a professional murderer. Is Jones good? Well, in one sense, yes, though certainly not in another sense. Jones is a good professional, does the job of killing well, never makes mistakes and kills the wrong person, makes the kill cleanly, inconspicuously, and never leaves clues which might incriminate Jones's employer. But in another sense we surely feel that Jones is a very bad person and is doing what is bad. But why? Is it because it fails to serve some purpose or does not have a function? No, it seems to be bad for a fundamentally different sort of reason. It is intrinsically bad; it is simply not right. Would it be wrong to deceive another person even if that person never found out, while at the same time, it helped you in some way? If you feel (at least partly) that if no one was hurt it was all right, then you are using the teleological (and utilitarian) criterion. But if you feel (at least partly) that it would be wrong even if no one was hurt (and in fact even if some were benefited by it), then you are applying a different criterion.

An ethical view, such as Kant's, which emphasizes the motives of an action, is called a deontological ethics (from the Greek word for obligation). This is also known, more simply, as the *ethics of duty*.

The ethics of duty, usually associated with the philosophy of Immanuel Kant, presents a striking contrast with teleological ethics, but especially with self-centered, "egoist" varieties of teleological ethics. Some, though not all, teleological positions in ethics are egoist, examining each action from the standpoint of how much benefit or utility it will bring to the agent. What will I get out of it? Something is good if it is good *for me*. But this is the opposite point of view of the ethics of duty. When most persons think of someone doing "the morally right thing," they normally have in mind a person who acts either out of concern for others or as a matter of principle, whether it is to the *agent's* personal benefit or not. Acting from a sense of duty, however, may be contrary to our most immediate interests—I can improve my grades by cheating, avoid embarrassment by lying, strengthen my financial situation by stealing, and so on. Even though acting from duty may demand a sacrifice of self-interest, the two are not always or necessarily incompatible—my self-interest may happen to coincide with what I consider it my duty to do.

The ethics of duty is usually associated with the position that principles of ethics are universal, absolute, and invariable, applying to everyone and in all circumstances. If something is right for one person then it is right for everyone in that situation. This accords with many of our common-sense assumptions about morality. I am apt to be angry when I hear that some people do not pay their taxes whereas I have to. And most of us feel a sense of injustice when we hear that a poor black man was sentenced to twenty years imprisonment for the same crime for which an upper-middle-class white person was given a six-month suspended sentence. Why *shouldn't* the same rule apply in all cases? If there are good, that is, morally relevant, reasons, then we allow for exceptions, although these exceptions themselves simply form a new *universal rule: "Everyone* earning more than $——, and *no one* earning less than that, must pay federal income tax." In the absence of any good reason, we face a conflict of duty and self-interest.

Utilitarian ethical theories are in agreement with the ethics of duty in rejecting the self-interested standpoint of *egoism,* inasmuch as they aim at the greatest happiness of the greatest number of people. And although utilitarians, unlike those who believe in the ethics of duty, might justify lying, stealing, breaking promises, etc., if this creates more happiness, the utilitarian, nonetheless, does believe in the universality of moral standards in the sense that everyone must, in all circumstances, do what produces the most happiness for the largest number of people. But there are other ways in which the ethics of duty sharply differs from utilitarianism.

The most important difference between the ethics of duty and utilitarianism concerns our treatment of people. According to the ethics of duty, a person can never be treated as a means to an end, however worthy that end. If something is wrong, then it is wrong in all circumstances, for every person, regardless of the consequences. This is what we mean when we say that persons have "certain inalienable rights." A right is something a person has *regardless,* and something which others have an absolute obligation to honor and protect. For example, we feel that every person has the right to be free. This is not a gift or a privilege that one must earn, but an inherent untouchable prerogative which every person has simply because one is a human being. It cannot be bought or traded and it cannot be legitimately taken away from that person for any reason whatever.

Imagine a situation in which the happiness of the greatest number of people could be increased by instituting slavery. This is not so difficult to imagine. Some people are less upset about the removal of their freedom than others (though no one is particularly happy about it). What if we selected as slaves those who seemed to value their freedom the least and, say, we selected only a small proportion of our society for this subservient role, and further that we indoctrinated this minority to believe that it was natural and right for them to be slaves, perhaps even drugging them to feel less pain. Finally, we would give them those menial but essential jobs which everyone else in the society was delighted not to have to do. Now, if we measure the total amount (or the average amount) of expected happiness in our society before and after our new program of slavery and found that people were on the whole happier *after,* would we be morally obligated to institute the new slavery program? No, of course not, our moral intuitions tell us. But it is hard to see how the utilitarian could avoid saying that we should, since this would be the best thing to do under the circumstances. The ethics of duty, on the other hand, is more in line with our own intuitions in rejecting this position. In principle it is always wrong to enslave another, whatever the consequences (even if that person *wants* to be enslaved).

As we shall see in the readings, there are problems with the ethics of duty as well. Difficulties with the Kantian ethics of duty arise when you try to apply it to a concrete situation. Moral situations in real life generally involve not one but several conflicting moral principles, each of which we have a duty to perform! By insisting on the absoluteness of every moral duty, the Kantian position is not very helpful in guiding us in making those painful decisions as to which moral principles to obey and which ones to break.

Another way to look at the philosophical enterprise of moral philosophy is to consider it as an attempt to discover the most basic reasons people actually have for thinking we ought or ought not to do something. Starting with particular cases and working our way to the more general, we can construct a kind of tree diagram. Should I copy from my neighbor on an exam, for example? No, why not? Because that is cheating. But what is wrong with cheating? It breaks a tacit agreement with the class and the teacher. What is wrong with breaking an agreement? This seems to be one of the things at the top of the tree which is fundamentally wrong. Start back at the bottom of the tree. Why should I brush my teeth? Because if I do not, I will get cavities. What is wrong with that? I may

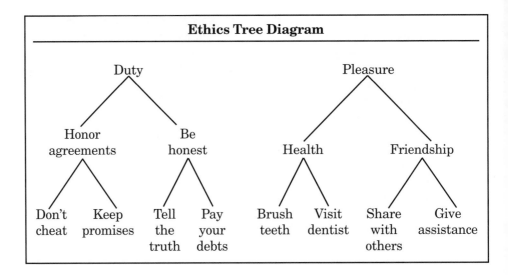

eventually have to have teeth pulled. What is wrong with that? It is painful and uncomfortable. What is wrong with that? Top of the tree again. But now we have two contenders for the top of the tree (the ultimate good) and these are precisely the two we found before (pleasure and duty). Can we find some still higher reason which will include the other two? Most philosophers have thought not, and so, again, there are these two fundamentally different approaches to ethics.

In the following chapters we will examine three approaches to moral thinking: *self-realization,* which takes happiness as the goal of life (Aristotle), the *teleological ethics* of utilitarianism (John Stuart Mill), and finally, the *ethics of duty* (Immanuel Kant). But first we will need to look at a more cynical view of morality—the view expressed by the formula "might makes right" and that is sometimes expressed as a twisted "golden" rule: "those with the gold make the rules." This view is referred to as *egoism,* since it places all the emphasis on the individual agent with no thought for anybody else. Could we build a human society on such a basis? If all people acted only in their own self-interest, what would life be like in such a situation? These are the questions explored in the next chapter, which features the writings of Thomas Hobbes.

Questions for Discussion

1. In your own words, explain the difference between an ethics of duty (deontological ethics) and an ethics driven by concern for consequences (teleological ethics).

2. This is anticipating the discussion of future chapters, but can you think of reasons a teleological approach to ethics *by itself* might be inadequate?

3. Similarly, can you think of acts (other than those cited in the text) that might conceivably be justifiable on utilitarian grounds but which we would judge to be wrong for other reasons?

4. Do you agree that happiness is an intrinsic good? Explain your answer.

5. Think about your own ethical decision making. Would you characterize yourself as following one of the views discussed more than others? If so, which one or ones seem to dominate your own moral deliberations?

CHAPTER 20

The Need for Morality

Why should we be moral? Why not just pursue our own interests and let everybody else do the same? A moment's reflection shows how impossible this would be. Part of the difficulty of life is that there are clashes of self-interest. What is in my best interest may not be in yours. The goals you set for yourself may be in direct conflict with those of your neighbors. And what happens to your self-interest and your personal goals when those of your neighbors conflict with yours and they are stronger than you are? The obvious answer to this question is that the stronger person or group in a society will always prevail, and if you do not happen to be in that group, then you cannot follow your own self-interest.

There have been individuals, though not philosophers, who have argued that justice is simply what the strongest and most powerful in a society say it is. This cynical view toward the foundations of morality asserts that morality is only the name we give to the interests of the strongest and most powerful in society.

Morality and Might

Let's take this view as far as we can and see if it will stand up under scrutiny. We will assume that morality simply is what the most powerful in society want. One practical problem with this view is whether persons holding this view will always have the power to get their way. And if we mean by "morality" what the strongest want, then there is one morality for the strong and another morality for the weak. It will be in the self-interest of the stronger to do what they like and to force others to do likewise. It will be in the interest of the weaker, on the other hand, to suppress their selfish desires and to do what they are told to do. This can be understood as a kind of enlightened self-interest. If I am a peasant, it is not in my self-interest to pay the king sixty percent of my annual harvest, but it is even less in my self-interest to have my head removed, which is the penalty for refusal to pay the annual tax. Looked at in this way, doing the right thing (that is, following self-interest) is simply to do what the strong and powerful believe is in their self-interest and what they command us to do. Might makes right.

The alternative to this form of servitude on the part of the weak is to band together to prevent such tyrannical action by mutual consent. This is the type of compromise Glaucon discussed with Socrates in Plato's work entitled *The Republic* and which we will discuss more fully in Part 8, Social and Political Philosophy, in terms of the social contract. According to Glaucon, acting in a moral way is a kind of compromise between the best of all situations, in which the strong do what they like, take what they want, and always get their way, and the worst of all situations, in which the weaklings must serve the interests of the stronger. Since most of us are afraid that we may not be one of the few lucky strong ones, we decide to agree to submit to certain rules and principles restricting the tyranny of one person over the rights of others.

What is odd about such a view is that it makes ordinary morality sound bad, that is, undesirable, or at best the lesser of two evils. It also devalues such morality as being the result of weakness and fear of those who are stronger. It is, as Nietzsche put it, a "slave morality." It has the extremely odd consequence that the best thing is to be able to do the wrong thing, while the worst thing is to have to do what is right.

The claim that "might makes right" is therefore ambiguous and can mean one of several quite different things, which are often confused. It can mean that the powerful have the power to make it seem as though what they do is right, in the

---

What people say is that to do wrong is, in itself, a desirable thing; on the other hand, it is not at all desirable to suffer wrong, and the harm to the sufferer outweighs the advantage to the doer. Consequently, when we have had a taste of both, those who have not the power to seize the advantage and escape the harm decide that they would be better off if they made a compact neither to do wrong nor to suffer it. Hence they began to make laws and covenants with one another, and whatever the law prescribed they called lawful and right. That is what right or justice is and how it came into existence; it stands half-way between the best things of all—to do wrong with impunity—and the worst, which is to suffer wrong without the power to retaliate. So justice is accepted as a compromise, and valued, not as good in itself, but for lack of power to do wrong; no man worthy of the name, who had that power would ever enter into such a compact with anyone; he would be mad if he did that.

Glaucon
The Republic

sense that unsuccessful rebels are called murderers and terrorists, whereas the successful ones are hailed as liberators and freedom fighters. It can also mean that the powerful have a *right* to get their way, that they have a moral duty to lead and the weak a moral duty to follow. Finally, it can mean that it is better (that is, more in one's interest) to be powerful than to do the conventionally right thing (that nice guys come in last and that people are nice only because they lack strength). We will examine each of these views in turn.

The first view—that morality is nothing but what the strongest in society say it is—is an example of an incorrect use of language known as *reductionism*. When trying to explain anything one is always in the position of describing one thing in terms of another. But when this goes so far that the terms in which one describes the thing are actually the opposites of what one is portraying, the results are perplexing and confusing. Other examples of reductionism include the view that so-called knowledge is really nothing but conceited opinion, that so-called reality is nothing but socially biased appearance, that God is nothing but our adolescent fear of our fathers, and in Marxism the view that justice and tolerance are nothing but the attempt of the ruling class to remain in power. In each case what was thought to be a standard or norm is reduced to its opposite.

Here is another way to think about the problems of reductionism. Suppose you show me a red ball, and I say, "That isn't red, it's gray." You would probably think I was color blind. If I were color blind, I would have a visual impairment such that I am unable to recognize colors that the majority of the population can see. But suppose I am not color blind, that I can perfectly well see that the ball is red, but I defend myself by saying, "I know that most people call that color red, but I prefer to call it gray." Then something very different is going on. I am refusing to

---

So entirely astray are you in your ideas about the just and unjust as not even to know that justice and the just are in reality another's good, that is to say, the interest of the ruler and stronger . . . The just is always a loser in comparison with the unjust. First of all, in private contracts: wherever the unjust is the partner of the just you will find that, when the partnership is dissolved, the unjust man has always more and the just less. Secondly, in their dealings with the State, when there is an income tax, the just man will pay more and the unjust less on the same amount of income . . . But all this is reversed in the case of the unjust man . . . My meaning will be most clearly seen if we turn to that highest form of injustice in which the criminal is the happiest of men, and the sufferers or those who refuse to do injustice are the most miserable—that is to say tyranny, which by fraud and force takes away the property of others . . .

Thrasymachus
The Republic

recognize the common meaning attached to words. We know perfectly well what the term *gray* means and what the term *red* means. To say that red means gray is to misuse language. Similarly, we have different words for moral behavior and immoral behavior. To say that what we call immoral behavior is really moral behavior is also to misuse language. The words we use for those who impose their wills on others are tyrant, dictator, oppressor, despot. To claim that such persons are really moral leaders is to sound like Humpty Dumpty in Lewis Carroll's *Alice's Adventures in Wonderland*, who said, "When I use a word, it means just what I choose it to mean—neither more nor less." It is precisely a view like this that Thrasymachus held, though it did not stand up very well against Socrates' attacks. In Thrasymachus' account, justice is defined as the strong crushing the weak for their own gain. But this is precisely what we mean in ordinary speech by injustice. Now justice, properly understood, means what we used to call injustice, and injustice means acting according to what we know as justice. Or, knowledge is redefined to mean what we used to understand by opinion, and vice versa. Even if such a position were true, it is hard to say it or even think it with any measure of consistency and clarity.

Nietzsche's New Morality

Friedrich Nietzsche was a philosopher who held the second position, that in a new and different sense of right, the strong person who refuses to do the conventionally moral thing and who acts by ordinary standards immorally is in fact the moral person. And Nietzsche also faces up to the fact that his view requires us to rethink the way we use our moral vocabulary.

For Nietzsche, the powerful have a natural right to rule. His is not the cynical view that everything we call right is in fact dictated by the stronger, for Nietzsche was well aware of the fact that the weaker can band together to restrict the powerful and, more than this, that they have the ability to label their weakness "moral right." Once the weaklings have joined together to restrict the bully and the tyrant, then to make sure that everyone follows the new guidelines, they try to make it seem as though this is the morally right way to behave, and people who patiently await their turn, respect the rights of others, help those in need are not just helping themselves in an enlightened self-interested way but are good people. Indeed, what most of us think of as the highest moral principles of Judeo-Christian and liberal thought is branded by Nietzsche as "slave morality," which unjustly robs the powerful of their natural right to rule.

But there are several things in Nietzsche's claim that are not at all clear. First, what exactly is meant by powerful? Imagine two societies about to go to war against each other. The first is ruled by what Nietzsche calls a slave morality. That is, it is governed by laws, and citizens cooperate and work together for mutually agreed upon goals. In the second a few strong individuals try to grab everything for themselves at the expense of everyone else, devoting considerable

FRIEDRICH NIETZSCHE (1844–1900): German philosopher and social historian. Nietzsche was appointed to a professorship of Greek literature and philosophy at Basel when he was only 24. His numerous works include Thus Spoke Zarathustra, The Genealogy of Morals, *and* The Will to Power. *Courtesy of The Bettmann Archive.*

energies to warring against each other and putting down frequent revolts from the miserable underdogs who secretly despise them. Which society would you bet on? Social cooperation is not a weakness but a strength for a society. It is not even a weakness for an individual.

If human beings are by nature social beings, as Aristotle held, then the uncooperative, antagonistic, selfish individual may simply be a deformed and sick individual incapable of living up to full human potential. Even on Nietzsche's own account, there is undoubted strength in the slave's morality. Nietzsche acknowledged, and indeed this is what made him so angry, that by banding together the weak can overpower the strong. But then who is really the stronger? In a democracy where the rule of law operates, the average citizen has enormous power over tyrannical individuals. If might makes right, what right does the person who is in some other sense stronger have to rule over the rest of us? Also, in what sense are we using stronger—physically stronger, possessing aristocratic virtues, more intelligent, more creative, better able to survive, possessing survival value as an individual or as a species, or as a society? Nietzsche does not really clarify these various ways of interpreting the meaning of the term *strong*. He does, however, face up to the problems his view causes in our moral vocabulary. He proposes what he calls the transvaluation of values; that is, he wants to change the use of the terms *good* and *bad*. The slave morality—kindness, beneficence, mutual cooperation—is henceforth to be called bad. The morality of the masters—absolute self-reliance, arrogance, self-will—is to be called good.

In a tour through the many finer and coarser moralities which have hitherto prevailed or still prevail on the earth, I found certain traits recurring regularly together, and connected with one another, until, finally two primary types revealed themselves to me, and a radical distinction was brought to light. There is master morality and slave-morality; I would at once add, however, that in all higher and mixed civilizations, there are also attempts at the reconciliation of the two moralities, but one finds still oftener the confusion and mutual misunderstanding of them, indeed, sometimes their close juxtaposition— even in the same man, within one soul. The distinctions of moral values have either originated in a ruling caste, pleasantly conscious of being different from the ruled—or among the ruled class, the slaves and dependents of all sorts. In the first case, when it is the rulers who determine the conception "good," it is the exalted, proud disposition which is regarded as the distinguishing feature, and that which determines the order of rank. The noble type of man separates from himself the beings in whom the opposite of this exalted, proud disposition displays itself: he despises them. Let it at once be noted that in this first kind of morality the antithesis "good" and "bad" means practically the same as "noble" and "despicable." . . . A morality of the ruling class, however, is more especially foreign and irritating to present-day taste in the sternness of its principle that one has duties only to one's equals, that one may act towards beings of a lower rank, towards all that is foreign, just as seems good to one, or "as the heart desires," and in any case "beyond good and evil."

Friedrich Nietzsche
Beyond Good and Evil

Morality and Self-Interest

The third view—that it is more in one's self-interest to be powerful than to do the conventionally right thing—at first sounds very convincing. But in the reading that follows, the philosopher Thomas Hobbes (1588-1679) probes the limits of this view. Who would not want to be rich and powerful, so powerful that you could do anything you want, go anywhere you choose, and in fact be a complete law unto yourself? The answer: everybody. And there is the rub. To seek your own complete self-interest would be great if everyone else in the world agreed to let you do that. But if it is desirable for you to seek your own unrestrained self-interest, then it is also desirable for everyone else to do likewise. Soon everybody is competing with everybody else for more of the desirable things of life, but who wants to live in a society like this? Such a situation would be, in the words of Thomas Hobbes, a state of war, and life in such a state would be, again to quote

Hobbes, "solitary, poor, nasty, brutish, and short." Such a state of affairs exists in the aftermath of civil unrest, natural disasters, and warfare. Looters, plunderers, murderers, and others taking advantage of the plight of the weak and dispossessed make life in such a situation a living nightmare. Only by the restoration of civil order can people resume their normal affairs.

This is precisely the defense Hobbes gives for the development of civil society. In the state of war that would result from each person's seeking individual self-interest, no one would truly be able to seek self-interest. Even the rich and powerful for the moment are subject to attacks from others. What Hobbes argues is that we are able to pursue our true self-interest only in a society ruled by law, a society resulting from a kind of social compact among members of a society in which they individually agree to give up certain rights in exchange for protections resulting from common laws accepted by all. How do we know what these laws are? Hobbes says that we have the natural ability to discover such laws through the use of reason. He calls these natural laws, and among them are the right of entering into contracts, the duty of keeping promises, the recognition that disputes should be submitted to arbitrators and that punishments should be aimed at changing behavior, not exacting revenge.

Hobbes is one of a group of philosophers who are important for their contribution to the modern ideas of the state. Against the prevailing view that kings ruled by divine right, Hobbes argued that states come into being as a result of a common decision by the governed to surrender some of their power to a sovereign in order to provide greater peace and security to all. Known as the *social contract* theory, this view of the state was further developed by such subsequent philosophers as John Locke and J. J. Rousseau. In the process of arguing for his point of view, Hobbes describes what a society without laws, rules, and standards of morality would be like. He concludes that only within a framework of moral laws are individuals truly able to pursue their own self-interest. But is it really true that all people by nature seek their own good? That is the premise on which Hobbes bases his argument. As you read through this selection, ask yourself if that premise is true.

Thomas Hobbes: Leviathan

Nature hath made men so equal, in the faculties of the body and mind, as that, though there be found one man sometimes manifestly stronger in body or of quicker mind than another, yet when all is reckoned together, the difference between man and man is not so considerable, as that one man can thereupon claim to himself any benefit, to which another may not pretend as well as he. For as to the strength of body, the weakest has strength enough to kill the strongest, either by secret machination, or by confederacy with others that are in the same danger with himself.

Reprinted from Thomas Hobbes' *Leviathan,* Chapters 13–15.

And as to the faculties of the mind setting aside the arts grounded upon words, and especially that skill of proceeding upon general and infallible rules, called science, which very few have, and but in few things, as being not a native faculty, born with us, nor attained, as prudence, while we look after somewhat else find yet a greater equality amongst men, than that of strength. For prudence is but experience which equal time equally bestows on all men, in those things they equally apply themselves unto. That which may perhaps make such equality incredible, is but a vain conceit of one's own wisdom, which almost all men think they have in a greater degree than the vulgar, that is, than all men but themselves, and a few others, whom by fame, or for concurring with themselves, they approve. For such is the nature of men, that howsoever they may acknowledge many others to be more witty, or more eloquent, or more learned, yet they will hardly believe there be many so wise as themselves, for they see their own wit at hand, and other men's at a distance. But this proves rather that men are in that point equal, than unequal. For there is not ordinarily a greater sign of the equal distribution of anything, than that every man is contented with his share.

From this equality of ability, ariseth equality of hope in the attaining of our ends. And therefore if any two men desire the same thing, which nevertheless they cannot both enjoy, they become enemies, and in the way to their end, which is principally their own conservation, and sometimes their delectation only, endeavor to destroy, or subdue one another. And from hence it comes to pass that where an invader hath no more to fear than another man's single power; if one plant, sow, build, or possess a convenient seat, others may probably be expected to come prepared with forces united, to dispossess and deprive him, not only of the fruit of his labor, but also of his life or liberty. And the invader again is in the like danger of another.

And from this diffidence of one another, there is no way for any man to secure himself so reasonable as anticipation; that is, by force or wiles to master the persons of all men he can, so long, till he see no other power great enough to endanger him: and this is no more than his own conservation required, and is generally allowed. Also because there be some, that taking pleasure in contemplating their own power in the acts of conquest, which they pursue farther than their security requires; if others, that otherwise would be glad to be at ease within modest bounds, should not by invasion increase their power, they would not be able, long time, by standing only on their defense, to subsist. And by consequence, such augmentation of dominion over men being necessary to a man's conservation, it ought to be allowed him.

Again, men have no pleasure, but on the contrary a great deal of grief in keeping company, where there is no power able to overawe them all. For every man looketh that his companion should value him at the same rate he sets upon himself, and upon all signs of contempt, or undervaluing, naturally endeavors, as far as he dares (which amongst them that have no common power to keep them in quiet, is far enough to make them destroy each other), to extort a greater value from his contemners by damage, and from others by the example.

So that in the nature of man, we find three principal causes of quarrel. First, competition; second, diffidence; thirdly, glory.

The first maketh men invade for gain; the second, for safety; and the third, for reputation. The first use violence to make themselves masters of other men's persons, wives, children, and cattle; the second, to defend them; the third, for trifles, as a word, a smile, a different opinion, and any other sign of undervalue, either direct in their persons, or by reflection in their kindred, their friends, their nation, their profession, or their name.

Hereby it is manifest that during the time men live without a common power to keep them all in awe, they are in that condition which is called war, and such a war as is of every man against every man. For *war* consisteth not in battle only, or the act of fighting, but in a tract of time wherein the will to contend by battle is sufficiently known, and therefore the notion of *time* is to be considered in the nature of war, as it is in the nature of weather. For as the nature of foul weather lieth not in a shower or two of rain, but in an inclination thereto of many days together, so the nature of war consisteth not in actual fighting, but in the known disposition thereto, during all the time there is no assurance to the contrary. All other time is *peace*.

Whatsoever therefore is consequent to a time of war, where every man is enemy to every man, the same is consequent to the time, wherein men live without other security than what their own strength and their own invention shall furnish them withal. In such condition there is no place for industry, because the fruit thereof is uncertain: and consequently no culture of the earth, no navigation, nor use of the commodious that may be imported by sea, no commodious building, no instruments of moving, and removing, such things as require much force, no knowledge of the face of the earth, no account of time, no arts, no letters, no society, and which is worst of all, continual fear, and danger of violent death, and the life of man, solitary, poor, nasty, brutish, and short.

It may seem strange to some man that has not well weighed these things that nature should thus dissociate, and render men apt to invade and destroy one another and he may therefore, not trusting to this inference made from the passions, desire perhaps to have the same confirmed by experience. Let him therefore consider with himself, when taking a journey he arms himself and seeks to go well accompanied; when going to sleep he locks his doors; when even in his house he locks his chests; and this when he knows there be laws and public officers, armed, to revenge all injuries shall be done him; what opinion he has of his fellow-subjects, when he rides armed; of his fellow citizens, when he locks his doors; and of his children, and servants, when he locks his chests. Does he not there as much accuse mankind by his actions, as I do by my words? But neither of us accuse man's nature of it. The desires, and other passions of man, are in themselves no sin. No more are the actions that proceed from those passions, till they know a law that forbids them: which till laws be made they cannot know, nor can any law be made, till they have agreed upon the person that shall make it.

It may peradventure be thought, there was never such a time nor condition of war as this, and I believe it was never generally so, over all the world but there are many places where they live so now. For the savage people in many places of America except the government of small families, the concord whereof dependeth on natural lust, have no government at all, and live at this day in that brutish manner, as I said before. Howsoever it may be perceived what manner of life there would be, where there were no common power to fear, by the manner of life which men that have formerly lived under a peaceful government, use to degenerate into in a civil war.

But though there had never been any time wherein particular men were in a condition of war one against another, yet in all times, kings, and persons of sovereign authority, because of their independency, are in continual jealousies, and in the state and posture of gladiators, having weapons pointing and their eyes fixed on one another, that is, their forts, garrisons:, and guns upon the frontiers of their kingdoms, and continual spies upon their neighbors, which is a posture of war. But because they uphold thereby the industry of their subjects, there does not follow from it that misery which accompanies the liberty of particular men.

To this war of every man against every man, this also is consequent: that nothing can be unjust. The notions of right and wrong, justice and injustice, have there no place. Where there is no common power there is no law; where no law, no injustice. Force and fraud are in war the two cardinal virtues. Justice and injustice are none of the faculties neither of the body nor mind. If they were, they might be in a man that were alone in the world, as well as his senses and passions. They are qualities. that relate to men in society, not in solitude. It is consequent also to the same condition, that there be no propriety, no dominion, no *mine* and *thine* distinct, but only that to be every man's, that he can get; and for so long, as he can keep it. And thus much for the ill condition which man by mere nature is actually placed in, though with a possibility to come out of it, consisting partly in the passions, partly in his reason.

The passions that incline men to peace are fear of death, desire of such things as are necessary to commodious living, and a hope by their industry to obtain them. And reason suggesteth convenient articles of peace, upon which men may be drawn to agreement. These articles are they which otherwise are called the Laws of Nature whereof I shall speak more particularly in the two following chapters.

The right of nature, which writers commonly call *jus naturale,* is the liberty each man hath to use his own power, as he will himself, for the preservation of his own nature, that is to say, of his own life, and consequently, of doing anything, which in his own judgment and reason, he shall conceive to be the aptest means thereunto.

By *liberty,* is understood, according to the proper signification of the word, the absence of external impediments: which impediments, may oft take away part of a man's power to do what he would, but cannot hinder him from using the power left him, according as his judgment and reason shall dictate to him.

A law *of nature, lex naturalis,* is a precept or general rule, found out by reason, by which a man is forbidden to do that which is destructive of his life, or taketh away the means of preserving the same, and to omit that by which he thinketh it may be best preserved. For though they that speak of this subject, use to confound *jus* and *lex, right* and *law,* yet they ought to be distinguished: because *right* consisteth in liberty to do or to forbear, whereas *law* determineth and bindeth one of them, so that law, and right differ as much as obligation and liberty, which in one and the same matter are inconsistent.

And because the condition of man, as hath been declared in the precedent chapter, is a condition of war of everyone against everyone in which case everyone is governed by his own reason, and there is nothing he can make use of that may not be a help unto him in preserving his life against his enemies: it followeth, that in such a condition every man has a right to everything; even to one another's body. And therefore, as long as this natural right of every man to everything endureth, there can be no security to any man, how strong or wise soever he be, of living out the time which nature ordinarily alloweth men to live. And consequently it is a precept, or general rule of reason, *that every man ought to endeavor peace, as far as he has hope of obtaining it, and when he cannot obtain it, that he may seek and use all helps and advantages of war.* The first branch of which rule containeth the first and fundamental law of nature, which is, *to seek*

The alternative to the state of nature described by Thomas Hobbes was a commonwealth brought into being by a compact among those governed, under which they surrendered some of their individual rights to a central governing authority, the Leviathan, that provides security for all. Courtesy of the Bettman Archive.

peace and follow it. The second, the sum of the right of nature; which is, *by all means we can, to defend ourselves.*

From this fundamental law of nature, by which men are commanded to endeavor peace, is derived this second law: *that a man be willing, when others are so too, as far forth as for peace and defense of himself he shall think it necessary, to lay down this right to all things, and be contented with so much liberty against other men, as he would allow other men against himself.* For as long as every man holdeth this right, of doing anything he liketh, so long are all men in the condition of war. But if other men will not lay down their right, as well as he, then there is no reason for anyone to divest himself of his for that were to expose himself to prey, which no man is bound to, rather than to dispose himself to peace. This is that law of the Gospel: *whatsoever you require that others should do to you, that do ye to them . . .*

To *lay down* a man's *right* to anything, is to *divest* himself of the *liberty,* of hindering another of the benefit of his own right to the same. For he that renounceth or passeth away his right, giveth not to any other man a right which he had not before, because there is nothing to which every man had not right by nature: but only standeth out of his way, that he may enjoy his own original right, without hindrance from him, not without hindrance from another. So that the effect which redoundeth to one man, by another man's defect of right, is but so much diminution of impediments to the use of his own right original.

Right is laid aside, either by simply renouncing it, or by transferring it to another. By *simply renouncing,* when he cares not to whom the benefit thereof redoundeth. By *transferring,* when he intendeth the benefit thereof to some certain person or persons. And when a man hath in either manner abandoned or granted away his right; then is he said to be *obliged,* or bound, not to hinder those to whom such right is granted or abandoned, from the benefit of it, and that he *ought,* and it is his *duty,* not to make void that voluntary act of his own, and that such hindrance is *injustice,* and *injury,* as being *sine jure,* the right being before renounced, or transferred. So that injury, or injustice in the controversies of the world, is somewhat like to that, which in the disputations of scholars is called *absurdity.* For as it is there called an absurdity to contradict what one maintained in the beginning; so in the world, it is called injustice, and injury, voluntarily to undo that which from the beginning he had voluntarily done. The way by which a man either simply renounceth, or transferreth his right, is a declaration, or signification, by some voluntary and sufficient sign or signs, that he doth so renounce or transfer, or hath so renounced or transferred the same, to him that accepteth it. And these signs are either words only, or actions only, or, as it happeneth most often, both words and actions. And the same are the *bonds,* by which men are bound and obliged—bonds that have their strength, not from their own nature, for nothing is more easily broken than a man's word, but from fear of some evil consequence upon the rupture.

Whensoever a man transferreth his right, or renounceth it, it is either in consideration of some right reciprocally transferred to himself, or for some other good he hopeth for thereby. For it is a voluntary act, and of the voluntary acts of every man, the object is some *good to himself.* And therefore there be some rights which no man can be understood by any words, or other signs, to have abandoned or transferred. As first a man cannot lay down the right of resisting them that assault him by force, to take away his life, because he cannot be understood to aim thereby, at any good to himself. The same may be said of wounds, and chains, and imprisonment: both because there is no benefit consequent to such patience, as there is to the patience of suffering another to be wounded or imprisoned, as also because a man cannot tell, when he seeth men proceed against him by violence, whether they intend his death or not. And lastly the motive, an end for which this renouncing and transferring of right is introduced, is nothing else but the security of a man's person, in his life, and in the means of so preserving life as not to be weary of it. And therefore if a man by words, or other signs, seem to despoil himself of the end for which those signs were intended, he is not to be understood as if he meant it, or that it was his will, but that he was ignorant of how such words and actions were to be interpreted.

The mutual transferring of right, is that which men call *contract.* . . .

From that law of nature by which we are obliged to transfer to another such rights as, being retained, hinder the peace of mankind, there followeth a third, which is this, *that men perform their covenants made:* without which, covenants are in vain, and but empty words, and the right of all men to all things remaining, we are still in the condition of war.

And in this law of nature, consisteth the fountain and original of *justice*. For where no covenant hath preceded, there hath no right been transferred, and every man has right to everything; and consequently, no action can be unjust. But when a covenant is made, then to break it is *unjust* and the definition of *injustice is* no other than *the not performance* of *covenant*. And whatsoever is not unjust, is *just*.

But because covenants of mutual trust, where there is a fear of not performance on either part, as hath been said in the former chapter, are invalid, though the original of justice be the making of covenants, yet injustice actually there can be none, till the cause of such fear be taken away, which while men are in the natural condition of war, cannot be done. Therefore before the names of just and unjust can have place, there must be some coercive power, to compel men equally to the performance of their covenants, by the terror of some punishment greater than the benefit they expect by the breach of their covenant, and to make good that propriety which by mutual contract men acquire, in recompense of the universal right they abandon: and such power there is none before the erection of a commonwealth. And this is also to be gathered out of the ordinary definition of justice in the schools, for they say, that justice *is the constant will of giving to every man his own*. And therefore where there is no *own* that *isn't* propriety, there is no injustice; and where is no coercive power erected, that is, where there is no commonwealth, there is no propriety; all men having right to all things: therefore where there is no commonwealth there nothing is unjust. So that the nature of justice consisteth in keeping of valid covenants, but the validity of covenants begins not but with the constitution of a civil power sufficient to compel men to keep them and then it is also that propriety begins. . . .

As justice dependeth on antecedent covenant, so does *gratitude* depend on antecedent grace—that is to say, antecedent free gift—and is the fourth law of nature, which may be conceived in this form, *that a man which receiveth benefit from another of mere grace, endeavor that he, which giveth it, have no reasonable cause to repent him of his good will.* For no man giveth but with intention of good to himself, because gift is voluntary; and of all voluntary acts, the object is to every man his own good; of which if men see they shall be frustrated, there will be no beginning of benevolence or trust, nor consequently of mutual help, nor of reconciliation of one man to another; and therefore they are to remain still in the condition of *war,* which is contrary to the first and fundamental law of nature, which commandeth men to *seek peace.* The breach of this law is called *ingratitude* and hath the same relation to grace that injustice hath to obligation by covenant.

A fifth law of nature is *complaisance,* that is to say, *that every man strive to accommodate himself to the rest.* For the understanding whereof, we may consider that there is in men's aptness to society, a diversity of nature, rising from their diversity of affections, not unlike to that we see in stones brought together for building of an edifice. For as that stone which, by the asperity and irregularity of figure, takes more room from others than itself fills, and for the hardness cannot be easily made plain, and thereby hindereth the building, is by the builders cast away, as unprofitable and troublesome: so also, a man that by asperity of nature will strive to retain those things which to himself are superfluous and to others necessary and for the stubbornness of his passions cannot be corrected, is to be left, or cast out of society, as cumbers me thereunto. For seeing every man, not only by right but also by necessity of nature, is supposed to endeavor all he can to obtain that which is necessary for his conservation; he that shall oppose himself against it, for things superfluous, is guilty of the war that thereupon is to follow, and therefore doth that which is contrary to the fundamental law of nature, which commandeth to seek peace. The observers of this law may be called *sociable;* the Latins call them *commodi,* the contrary stubborn, insociable, froward, intractable.

A sixth law of nature is this, *that upon caution of the future time, a man ought to pardon the offenses past of them that repenting, desire it.* For *pardon* is nothing but granting of peace, which though granted to them that persevere in their hostility, be not peace, but fear, yet not granted to them that give caution of the future time, is sign of an aversion to peace, and therefore contrary to the law of nature.

A seventh is, *that in revenges*—that is, retribution of evil for evil—*men look not at the greatness of the evil past, but the greatness of the good to follow.* Whereby we are forbidden to inflict punishment with any other design than for correction of the offender or direction of others. For this law is consequent to the next before it, that commandeth pardon upon security of the future time. Besides, revenge without respect to the example, and profit to come, is a triumph or glorying in the hurt of another, tending to no end; for the end is always somewhat to come, and glorying to no end is vain-glory and contrary to reason, and to hurt without reason tendeth to the introduction of war, which is against the law of nature, and is commonly styled by the name of *cruelty.*

And because all signs of hatred or contempt provoke to fight, insomuch as most men choose rather to hazard their life than not to be revenged, we may in the eighth place, for a law of nature, set down this precept, *that no man by deed, word, countenance, or gesture, declare hatred or contempt of another.* The breach of which law is commonly called *contumely.*

The question who is the better man, has no place in the condition of mere nature, where, as has been shown before, all men are equal. The inequality that now is, has been introduced by the laws civil. I know that Aristotle in the first book of his *Politics,* for a foundation of his doctrine, maketh men by nature, some more worthy to command, meaning the wiser sort, such as he thought himself to be for his philosophy, others to serve, meaning those that had strong bodies, but were not philosophers as he: as if master and servant were not introduced by consent of men, but by difference of wit, which is not only against reason, but also against experience. For there are very few so foolish, that had not rather govern themselves than he governed by others, nor when the wise in their own conceit contend by force with them who distrust their own wisdom, do they always, or often, or almost at any time, get the victory. If nature therefore have made men equal, that equality is to be acknowledged, or if nature have made men unequal: yet because men that think themselves equal, will not enter into conditions of peace, but upon equal terms, such equality must be admitted. And therefore for the ninth law of nature, I put this, *that every man acknowledge another for his equal by nature.* The breach of this precept is *pride.*

On this law dependeth another, *that at the entrance into conditions of peace, no man require to reserve to himself any right which he is not content should he reserved to everyone of the rest.* As it is necessary for all men that seek peace, to lay down certain rights of nature, that is to say, not to have liberty to do all they list; so is it necessary for man's life, to retain some as right to govern their own bodies; enjoy air, water, motion ways to go from place to place; and all things else without which a man cannot live, or not live well if in this case, at the making of

peace, men require for themselves, that which they would not have to be granted to others, they do contrary to the precedent law, that commandeth the acknowledgment of natural equality, and therefore also against the law of nature.
The observers of this law, are those we call *modest,* and the breakers *arrogant*
men. . . .

Also if a man be trusted to judge between man and man, it is a precept of the
law of nature, *that he deal equally between them.* For without that, the controversies of men cannot be determined but by war. He therefore that is partial in
judgment, doth what in him lies, to deter men from the use of judges and arbitrators, and consequently against the fundamental law of nature, is the cause
of war.

The observance of this law, from the equal distribution to each man of that
which in reason belongeth to him, is called *equity,* and, as I have said before, distributive justice. . . .

And from this followeth another law, *that such things as cannot be divided, be
enjoyed in common, if it can be, and if the quantity of the thing permit, without
stint, otherwise proportionably to the number of them that have right.* For otherwise the distribution is unequal, and contrary to equity.

But some things there be that can neither be divided, nor enjoyed in common.
Then the law of nature which prescribeth equity, requireth *that the entire right
or else making the use alternate, the first possession, be determined by lot.* For
equal distribution is of the law of nature and other means of equal distribution
cannot be imagined. . . .

And therefore those things which cannot be enjoyed in common, nor divided
ought to be adjudged to the first possession, and in some cases to the first born
as acquired by lot.

It is also a law of nature, *that all men that mediate peace, be allowed safe conduct.* For the law that commandeth peace, as the *end,* commandeth intercession,
as the *means,* and to intercession the means is safe conduct.

And because, though men be never so willing to observe these laws, there may
nevertheless arise questions concerning a man's action; first, whether it were
done, or not done secondly, if done, whether against the law or not against the law
the former where it is called a question of *fact,* the latter a question of *right:* therefore unless the parties to the question covenant mutually to stand to the sentence
of another, they are as far from peace as ever. This other to whose sentence they
submit is called an *arbitrator.* And therefore it is of the law of nature, *that they
that are at controversy submit their right to the judgment of an arbitrator.*

And seeing every man is presumed to do all things in order to his own benefit, no man is a fit arbitrator in his own cause; and if he were never so fit, yet equity allowing to each party equal benefit, if one be admitted to be judge, the other
is to be admitted also; and so the controversy, that is, the cause of war remains,
against the law of nature.

For the same reason no man in any cause ought to be received for arbitrator,
to whom greater profit or honor or pleasure apparently ariseth out of the victory
of one party than of the other: for he hath taken, though an unavoidable bribe,
yet a bribe; and no man can be obliged to trust him. And thus also the controversy
and the condition of war remaineth contrary to the law of nature.

And in a controversy of fact, the judge being to give more credit to one than to
the other, if there be no other arguments must give credit to a third, or to a third

and fourth, or more: for else the question is undecided, and left to force, contrary to the law of nature.

These are the laws of nature, dictating peace, for a means of the conservation of men in multitudes; and which not only concern the doctrine of taste, smell, hearing, touch, and sight; but also of what is conformable or disagreeable to reason in the actions of common life. Nay, the same man, in divers times, differs from himself; and one time praiseth, that is, calleth good, what another time he dispraiseth, and calleth evil: from whence arise disputes, controversies; and at last war. And therefore so long as man is in the condition of mere nature, which is a condition of war, his private appetite is the measure of good and evil: and consequently all men agree on this that peace is good, and therefore also the way, of means of peace, which as I have shewed before, are justice, gratitude, modesty, equity, mercy and the rest of the laws of nature, are good; that is to say, *moral virtues* and their contrary *vices,* evil. Now the sciences of virtue and vice is moral philosophy; and therefore the true doctrine of the laws of nature, is the true moral philosophy. But the writers of moral philosophy, though they acknowledge the same virtues and vices; yet not seeing wherein consisted their goodness, nor that they come to be praised as the means of peaceable, sociable, comfortable living, place them in a mediocrity of passions: as if not the cause, but the degree of daring, made fortitude or not the cause, but the quantity of a gift, made liberality.

These dictates of reason men used to call by the name of laws, but improperly: for they are but conclusions, or theorems, concerning what conduceth to the conservation and defense of themselves; whereas law, properly is the word of him that by right hath command over others. But yet if we consider the same theorems as delivered in the word of God, that by right commandeth all things, then are they properly called laws. . . .

Questions for Discussion

1. Hobbes assumes that people basically seek their own self-interest. Do you agree with this claim? What evidence is there to support it? What evidence is there against it?

2. Given Hobbes' point of view, what economic system would he favor? Why?

3. Hobbes claims that apart from a structure of laws, there is no justice or injustice. How does this view follow from his basic assumptions?

4. The notion of laws that are known by reason, that is, by the "law of nature" or *lex naturalis,* is at the heart of Hobbes' view of the state. Can you think of additional laws that Hobbes might list were he living in our own times?

5. Given what you know about Hobbes' views, do you think he would favor the death penalty? Why or why not?

CHAPTER 21

The Morality of Self-Realization

Assuming that we now agree that a moral point of view is necessary, which moral theory should we choose? In the next three chapters we will look at these three theories: Aristotle's self-realization theory, Mill's utilitarian theory, and Kant's ethics of duty.

The whole discussion of morality presupposes that we want to be moral, though we may not be sure what moral standards to follow, how we can know them, assuming they do exist, and how to decide between competing sets of moral principles. But all this is against the background of the assumption that I want to be a moral person. But, really, why *should* I be moral, especially as this often restricts my ability to get what I want?

We have just seen how Hobbes answered this question. His answer was, in effect, that one should be moral because being moral is being reasonable, and one cannot meaningfully question the value of being reasonable. That is, it makes no sense to ask, "Why be reasonable?" Why not? To ask "Why" is to ask for a reason. Thus, asking any question presupposes one wants the reason. Thus, the one question one cannot meaningfully ask is "Why should I want reasons, why should I be reasonable?" This would be as senseless as asking, "Is it reasonable to be reasonable? Give me a reason why I should value reasons?" The question presupposes a positive answer. If you didn't value reasons you wouldn't ask for the reason. Asking for the reason shows you want and therefore value reasons.

Morality and Happiness

The Greek philosophers Plato and Aristotle offered a different answer: In the end, the moral person is happier than the immoral person. And this is because living according to moral standards is an important part of human nature, and the key to happiness, they held, is living according to one's human nature. In order to be happy one must consider what it is to be a human being, what our human nature is. And according to Plato and Aristotle, it is not within a human being's nature to be gluttonous, aggressive, and power hungry.

Plato goes further than Aristotle in this respect, arguing that the moral person *is* the reasonable person and that people do wrong only out of ignorance. All persons aim at their own good, and if they fail, it is only through faulty understanding of what is really good for one and how to achieve it. For Plato, the hardened criminal is a fool who mistakenly thinks a life of crime will bring happiness. If criminals were more intelligent, they would realize that a life of crime is a life of fear, insecurity, social alienation, and isolation and therefore not only immoral but an intellectual mistake. Morality, for Plato, *is reason*.

Aristotle does not go as far as Plato. Aristotle also recognizes the important role played in morality by habit and training. People become moral human beings, Aristotle argues, not just by calculating what is truly in their long-term best interests, but through practice and training which develops good lifelong habits and a permanent disposition to do the right thing. Criminals, similarly, are not only stupid, they are also unfortunate in having formed some bad habits through poor moral training in youth. Nonetheless, Aristotle also holds the criminal responsible for getting into those bad habits in the first place.

How far does Aristotle's answer to the question "Why should I be moral?" differ from that of egoism? Certainly Aristotle agrees that the enlightened egoist will conform to most moral behavior where that involves restraining one's passionate impulses of the moment for long-term greater gain. But there are also important differences, because what is in everyone's self-interest, generally speaking, other things being equal, may not always be in *my* self-interest here and now, in this particular situation. Suppose that I find a foolproof way to steal some money from the community without getting caught. I can, on the one hand, agree that it is in general in our collective self-interest to outlaw stealing, and I am glad to live in a relatively law-abiding community. But I can also believe that it is in my immediate self-interest, nonetheless, to steal this money. Generally, those who break moral rules succeed best in societies where these rules are generally obeyed.

Morality and Human Nature

The root of this Greek way of thinking lies in its teleological perspective. Nothing is good or bad apart from the performance of its particular function which is defined by its nature. Everything is good or bad according to its kind. What makes a screwdriver good, its peculiar virtue, is not the same as what makes a piece of chalk good. To know what makes a piece of chalk good (its virtue), we have to know what it is (its nature), and that is defined in terms of its function. A piece of chalk is a device for writing on a chalkboard. Notice how we have defined its nature by specifying its purpose or function (for the purpose of writing). Thus a piece of chalk which writes evenly, cleanly, clearly, is a good one, and one which is either too hard or too soft to get the job done is a bad one. That is, it is good if it fulfills its functions and bad if it does not.

Already we can anticipate a problem with the outlook of Plato and Aristotle. If we could convince egoists that they will be happier by being moral, we might convince them to be moral. But now it begins to look as though Plato and Aristotle are defining happiness, not as that psychological state of mind associated with pleasure and good times, but simply as each thing fulfilling its function, or purpose, and being true to its nature. Suppose the egoist replies, "Even if my human nature is to be moral, why shouldn't I act immorally, contrary to my human nature? Let all the other wimps be true to their human nature; that will just make it easier for me to get the better of them. Plato and Aristotle say I will be unhappy if I act immorally, but since this turns out to mean no more than that I will not live up to my human nature, I think I can easily forego that, especially since as an immoral egoist I will be much happier in the ordinary sense of having more fun." Perhaps "successful" is a better translation than "happiness" of the Greek word *eudaimonia,* though in English "successful" often refers to economic success, which is far too narrow a definition of *eudaimonia.*

Earlier in Part 5 we saw another problem in applying the teleological model beyond the range of humanly made articles whose purpose and function is clear because we human beings have made them for specific purposes. In the case of natural objects, such as trees, lakes, and more so in the case of human beings, it is less clearly applicable because it is less clear what the purpose and function of a tree, lake, or human being are.

One way to try and answer this question is to ask what is special, distinctive, and peculiar to human beings. What can humans do that no other creature or object in the universe can do? Looked at in this way the answer most philosophers have given over the centuries is the distinctive human capacity for reason. Unlike animals, human beings can reflect, calculate, weigh pros and cons, ask why, formulate explanations, put off short-term enjoyment for long-term satisfaction. Thus, for both Plato and Aristotle, to allow passion, power, or pleasure to dominate one's life is to fail to live up to one's full potential as a human being. This means, for the Greek philosophers, to be deformed and unhappy. To be ruled by reason, to allow reason its rightful place to control our lives, our passions, and desires, to help us find that balance between extremes, which has come to be called the "golden mean," is to be fully human, virtuous, mentally healthy, and happy, all at once.

▤ Morality and Rationality

There are problems with this approach which come back to the difficulty in determining what is human nature. There are many things which human beings uniquely do, and not all of these are as high-sounding and conducive to morality as reason—for example, our potential to murder, engage in warfare, as well as some other morally neutral capacities, such as laughter, wonder, tool making, and so on. Nor is it clear that reason alone will always lead to morality. In its long history, philosophers have used the word *reason* to cover many wonderful and beautiful human capacities. One of the most interesting we will see shortly is Kant's quite different alignment of morality with reason. Insofar as morality is understood as the commitment to *universal* standards, applicable equally to everyone, a moral person must essentially be a rational and logically consistent person.

But in the most obvious sense of the ability to think things through and act in a complex manner, weighing pros and cons, there is no obvious sense in which the immoralist/egoist cannot claim to be equally reasonable. Indeed, the egoist's complaint is precisely that the moral person is a fool, that the smart money is on the egoist. And this seems to be true of what we have called the sophisticated, enlightened egoist—pretending to be a good citizen, caring friend, loyal partner, honest client, but only to get ahead in business and politics.

For Aristotle, reason is aligned with morality in another sense: Reason is a necessary ingredient in any moral action, in that an irrational person, even with the best of intentions, can do the wrong thing. Suppose we consider generosity, courage, and modesty to be important human virtues. Does it follow that the ideally generous person is one who gives whatever money possessed at the time to anyone who asks for it? What will this person's family and creditors think? Is this person virtuous or just plain stupid? Similarly, do we admire as the ideally courageous individual one who fights back whatever the odds? Is the person who singlehandedly attacks a crazed mob brave or foolhardy? Obviously, a virtuous person must exercise common sense and judgment in carrying out moral principles. The blind pursuit of moral rules with no regard for context, balancing competing rules, timing, and a concern for matters of degree, is just that—blind.

Thus, for Aristotle, the moral virtues, being temperate, courageous, and so on, require reason in helping us strike the right balance required by virtuous conduct. All the Greek philosophers stressed balance and order as key ingredients in the good life, but for Aristotle this is especially important in his famous discussion of the "golden mean."

Virtue, Aristotle argues in the reading that follows, is always a balance between extremes, that bravery is avoiding both the extreme of running whenever danger appears and the opposite extreme of rushing headlong into every dangerous situation. The brave person is one who knows when to resist, when to retreat, and when to remain silent, depending on the situation. As he says, Aristotle does not mean by the "golden mean" always to strike the precise halfway point between extremes, but rather to be guided by reason and common sense in finding the right balance appropriate to the situation at hand.

There is one last sense in which Aristotle extols reason and its alliance with morality, and this is the view which he shares with Plato that the ideal life for a human being is a life of intellectual pursuits. It is good for human beings to use their minds, not only for the sake of something else, but because this is good in itself, the self-sufficient perfection of the most unique aspect of human nature—our capacity for rational reflection.

Intellectual and Moral Virtues

The values of such a life of reason Aristotle calls the "intellectual virtues," in contrast to the "moral virtues" associated with the "golden mean." In the moral virtues reason is useful for the further end of practical action, whereas the intellectual virtues represent the intrinsic value of the life of reason for its own sake.

You might think that Aristotle has exaggerated the value of rational activity for its own sake because he is a philosopher, but we will surely agree with Aristotle that the failure to develop one's mind is one of the greatest tragedies which can befall a person. Thus, for Aristotle, reason is a necessary ingredient in any *moral* virtue, but it is also the key to what he calls the *intellectual* virtue of a life dedicated to reasoning for its own sake. As Aristotle rightly points out, things are means to ends which in turn are means to other ends, which turn out to be the means to still other things, and so on. Either this process goes on forever or it comes to rest with an end for the sake of which everything else is done but which is not the means to anything else. From a teleological point of view, and certainly for Aristotle, this is the *highest* good, being completely self-sufficient. And what could this be, Aristotle asks, but the life of reason, that is, the intellectual life of rational contemplation?

This would be a good place to review the four senses in which reason has been praised by philosophers for its role in morality.

1. Reason is required to reject short-term impulses in favor of greater long-term benefits. In this sense, reason is respected by everyone, including the enlightened egoist.
2. Reason is an essential ingredient in recognizing the need for and in consistently following general rules of conduct equally applicable to everyone in any situation.

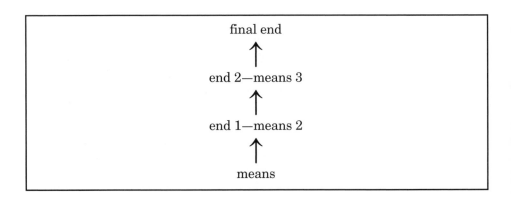

3. Reason is necessary in sensibly applying moral principles to concrete practical situations in everyday life.
4. The life of rational contemplation and intellectual pursuits is an intrinsically good activity for human beings because of human nature.

The Social Dimensions of Morality

Before turning to the selection from Aristotle's most famous discussion of ethics in the book named after his father, the *Nicomachean Ethics,* we should consider another attempt to answer the question, "Why be moral?" This answer is different from that of Aristotle or Plato but is nonetheless like theirs in trying to answer that question from a consideration of human nature. This is the view that it is an important part of human nature to be social. Human beings must live in social groupings, whether as small as the extended family or as large as a modern nation state, or the clan, a tribal arrangement somewhere in between. Human infants cannot survive without considerable attention from adults for at least ten years, and to survive and, more so, advance beyond the most primitive human beginnings seems to require an enormous amount of social cooperation.

But look at what such cooperation involves. Each of us is different; we are competitive, and out of this, tensions arise in any society. So it is an effort for us to try and get along and engage in the minimal cooperation that enables us to survive. But we also enjoy one another's company, shunning loneliness, wanting love,

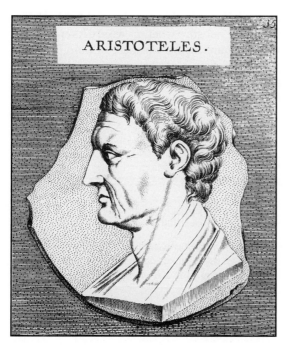

ARISTOTELES.

ARISTOTLE (384–322 B.C.E.): Greek philosopher born in Stagira in Thrace (leading to references to him as the Stagerite). Aristotle's father, Nicomachus, was a court physician to the King of Macedon and sent Aristotle to Athens, where he became associated with Plato and a member of the Academy for over 20 years. After Plato's death, Aristotle accepted the position as tutor to Alexander, son of Philip II of Macedon; Alexander is now better known to us as Alexander the Great. Returning to Athens around 335, Aristotle founded his own school called the Lyceum, whose members carried on their philosophical discussion while walking, giving rise to the label the peripatetics. Courtesy of the Library of Congress.

friends, companionship, to be surrounded by family, and so on. Are human beings by nature lonely egoists who must learn sociability, or are they by nature social creatures whose loneliness and isolation is a deformity and perversion of human nature? Is it true, as Hobbes and others have argued, that human beings are first and foremost isolated individuals who then try to initiate social cooperation as the only rational means for survival? Or is it also, and more true, that people are, by nature, drawn together socially? If the latter, then it is part of human nature to be concerned for our neighbor, to desire cooperation, to shun hostility and aggression, at least within one's most immediate social circle. And if that is so, then the morality which depends on a level of social cooperation, and the inhibition of the most blatant forms of egoism, is not contrary to human nature but an outgrowth of it and a "natural" way for human beings to behave.

Happiness and Pleasure

One of the most interesting and valuable parts of the *Nicomachean Ethics,* selections from which you are about to read, is Aristotle's account of happiness and how it differs from pleasure. At first the two might seem to be the same, or very similar, and John Stuart Mill, whose work we will read later on in this section, certainly argued that they were the same. But think about it: Are they really the same? For one thing, Aristotle points out, happiness characterizes a much longer time span than does pleasure. And, finally, happiness but not pleasure involves our believing both before and after one has achieved one's goals that they are consistent with and fulfill our best image of ourselves, that I am doing well what I really ought to be doing. It is for these reasons that we sometimes are not sure whether we are happy or not, though we can more easily tell whether we are feeling pleasure or pain. To know you are experiencing pleasure requires that you introspect a sensation; to know you are happy requires a cognitive judgment about who you are, what you most want, and whether you are doing what best suits you, all of which may be difficult to know. It is in these senses that Aristotle is able to say that happiness is the goal of life, and also that pleasure is *not* the most significant part of a happy life.

Nicomachean Ethics

Every art of applied science and every systematic investigation, and similarly every action and choice, seem to aim at some good, the good, therefore, has been well defined as that at which all things aim. But it is clear that there is a differ-

Reprinted from *Nicomachean Ethics,* translated by Martin Ostwald. Library of Liberal Arts. Used by permission of Prentice Hall.

ence in the ends at which they aim: in some cases the activity is the end, in others the end is some product beyond the activity. In cases where the end lies beyond the action the product is naturally superior to the activity.

Since there are many activities, arts and sciences, the number of ends is correspondingly large; of medicine, the end is health, of shipbuilding, a vessel, of strategy, victory, and of household management, wealth. In many instances several such pursuits are grouped together under a single capacity: the art of bridle-making, for example, and everything else pertaining to the equipment of a horse are grouped together under horsemanship; horsemanship in turn, along with every other military action, is grouped together under strategy; and other pursuits are grouped together under other capacities. In all these cases the ends of the master sciences are preferable to the ends of the subordinate sciences, since the latter are pursued for the sake of the former. This is true whether the ends of the actions lie in the activities themselves or, as is the case in the disciplines just mentioned, in something beyond the activities.

Now, if there exists an end in the realm of action which we desire for its own sake, an end which determines all our other desires; if, in other words, we do not make all our choices for the sake of something else for in this way the process will go on infinitely so that our desire would be futile and pointless—then obviously this end will be the good, that is, the highest good. Will not the knowledge of this good, consequently, be very important to our lives? Would it not better equip us, like archers who have a target to aim at, to hit the proper mark? If so, we must try to comprehend in outline at least what this good is and to which branch of knowledge or to which capacity it belongs.

This good, one should think, belongs to the most sovereign and most comprehensive master science, and politics clearly fits this description. For it determines which sciences ought to exist in states, what kind of sciences each group of citizens must learn, and what degree of proficiency each must attain. We observe further that the most honored capacities, such as strategy, household management, and oratory, are contained in politics. Since this science uses the rest of the sciences, and since, moreover, it legislates what people are to do and what they are not to do, its end seems to embrace the ends of the other sciences. Thus it follows that the end of politics is the good for man. For even if the good is the same for the individual and the state, the good of the state clearly is the greater and more perfect thing to attain and to safeguard. The attainment of the good for one man alone is, to be sure, a source of satisfaction, yet to secure it for a nation and for states is nobler and more divine. In short, these are the aims of our investigation, which is in a sense an investigation of social and political matters.

Our discussion will be adequate if it achieves clarity within the limits of the subject matter. For precision cannot be expected in the treatment of all subjects alike, any more than it can be expected in all manufactured articles. Problems of what is noble and just, which politics examines, present so much variety and irregularity that some people believe that they exist only by convention and not by nature. The problem of the good, too, presents a similar kind of irregularity, because in many cases good things bring harmful results. There are instances of men ruined by wealth, and others by courage. Therefore, in a discussion of such subjects, which has to start from a basis of this kind, we must be satisfied to indicate the truth with a rough and general sketch: when the subject and the basis of a discussion consist of matters that hold good only as a general rule, but not always, the conclusions reached must be of the same order. The various points that are made must be received in the same spirit. For a well-schooled man is one who searches for that degree of precision in each kind of study which the nature of the subject at hand admits: it is obviously just as foolish to accept arguments of probability from a mathematician as to demand strict demonstrations from an orator.

Each man can judge competently the things he knows, and of these he is a good judge. Accordingly, a good judge in each particular field is one who has been trained in it, and a good judge in general, a man who has received an all-round schooling. For that reason, a young man is not equipped to be a student of politics, for he has no experience in the actions which life demands of him, and these actions form the basis and subject matter of the discussion. Moreover, since he follows his emotions his study will be pointless and unprofitable, for the end of this kind of study is not knowledge but action. Whether he is young in years or immature in character makes no difference, for his deficiency is not a matter of time but of living and of pursuing all his interests under the influence of his emotions. Knowledge brings no benefit to this kind of person, just as it brings none to the morally weak. But those who regulate their desires and actions by a rational principle will greatly benefit from a knowledge of this subject. So much by way of a preface about the student, the limitations which have to be accepted, and the objective before us.

To resume the discussion: since all knowledge and every choice is directed toward some good, let us discuss what is in our view the aim of politics, i.e., the highest good attainable by action. As far as its name is concerned, most people would probably agree: for both the common run of people and cultivated men call it happiness, and understand by "being happy" the same as "living well" and "doing well." But when it comes to defining what happiness is, they disagree, and the account given by the common run differs from that of the philosophers. The former say it is some clear and obvious good, such as pleasure, wealth, or honor; some say it is one thing and others another, and often the very same person identifies it with different things at different times: when he is sick, he thinks it is health, and when he is poor he says it is wealth; and when people are conscious of their own ignorance, they admire those who talk above their heads in accents of greatness. Some thinkers used to believe that there exists over and above these many goods another good, good in itself and by itself, which also is the cause of good in all these things. An examination of all the different opinions would perhaps be a little pointless, and it is sufficient to concentrate on those which are most in evidence or which seem to make some sort of sense. . . .

Let us return again to our investigation into the nature of the good which we are seeking. It is evidently something different in different actions and in each art: it is one thing in medicine, another in strategy, and another again in each of the other arts. What, then, is the good of each? Is it not that for the sake of which everything else is done? That means it is health in the case of medicine, victory in the case of strategy, a house in the case of building, a different thing in the case of different arts, and in all actions and choices it is the end. For it is for the sake of the end that all else is done. Thus, if there is some one end for all that we do, this would be the good attainable by action; if there are several ends, they will be the goods attainable by action.

Our argument has gradually progressed to the same point at which we were before, and we must try to clarify it still further. Since there are evidently several ends, and since we choose some of these e.g., wealth, flutes, and instruments generally—as a means to something else, it is obvious that not all ends are final. The highest good, on the other hand, must be something final. Thus, if there is only one final end, this will be the good we are seeking; if there are several, it will be the most final and perfect of them. We call that which is pursued as an end in itself more final than an end which is pursued for the sake of something else, and what is never chosen as a means to something else we call more final than that which is chosen both as an end in itself and as a means to something else. What is always chosen as an end in itself and never as a means to something else is called final in an unqualified sense. This description seems to apply to happiness above all else: for we always choose happiness as an end in itself and never for the sake of something else. Honor, pleasure, intelligence, and all virtue we choose partly for themselves—for we would choose each of them even if no further advantage would accrue from them—but we also choose them partly for the sake of happiness, because we assume that it is through them that we will be happy. On the other hand, no one chooses happiness for the sake of honor, pleasure, and the like, nor as a means to anything at all.

We arrive at the same conclusion if we approach the question from the standpoint of self-sufficiency. For the final and perfect good seems to be self-sufficient. However, we define something as self-sufficient not by reference to the *"self"* alone. We do not mean a man who lives his life in isolation, but a man who also lives with parents, children, a wife, and friends and fellow citizens generally, since man is by nature a social and political being. But some limit must be set to these relationships; for if they are extended to include ancestors, descendants, and friends of friends, they will go on to infinity. However, this point must be reserved for investigation later. For the present we define as "self-sufficient" that which taken by itself makes life something desirable and deficient in nothing. It is happiness, in our opinion, which fits this description. Moreover, happiness is of all things the one most desirable, and it is not counted as one good thing among many others. But if it were counted as one among many others, it is obvious that the addition of even the least of the goods would make it more desirable, for the addition would produce an extra amount of good, and the greater amount of good is always more desirable than the lesser. We see then that happiness is something final and self-sufficient and the end of our actions.

To call happiness the highest good is perhaps a little trite, and a clearer account of what it is, is still required. Perhaps this is best done by first ascertaining the proper function of man. For just as the goodness and performance of a flute player, a sculptor, or any kind of expert, and generally of anyone who fulfills some function or performs some action, are thought to reside in his proper function, so the goodness and performance of man would seem to reside in whatever is his proper function. Is it then possible that while a carpenter and a shoemaker have their own proper functions and spheres of action, man as man has none, but was left by nature a good-for-nothing without a function? Should we not assume that just as the eye, the hand, the foot, and in general each part of the body clearly has its own proper function, so man too has some function over and above the functions of his parts? What can this function possibly be? Simply living? He shares that even with plants, but we are now looking for something peculiar to man. Accordingly, the life of nutrition and growth must be excluded. Next in line there is a life of sense perception. But this, too, man has in common with the horse, the ox, and every animal. There remains then an active life of the rational element. The rational element has two parts: one is rational in that it obeys the rule of reason, the other in that it possesses and conceives rational rules. Since the expression "life of the rational element" also can be used in two senses, we must make it clear that we mean a life determined by the activity, as opposed to the mere possession, of the rational element. For the activity it seems, has a greater claim to be the function of man.

The proper function of man, then, consists in an activity of the soul in conformity with a rational principle or, at least, not without it. In speaking of the proper function of a given individual we mean that it is the same in kind as the function of an individual who sets high standards for himself: the proper function of a harpist, for example, is the same as the function of a harpist who has set high standards for himself. The same applies to any and every group of individuals: the full attainment of excellence must be added to the mere function. In other words, the function of the harpist is to play the harp; the function of the harpist who has high standards is to play it well. On these assumptions, if we take the proper function of man to be a certain kind of life, and if this kind of life is an activity of the soul and consists in actions performed in conjunction with the rational element, and if a man of high standards is he who performs these actions well and properly, and if a function is well performed when it is performed in accordance with the excellence appropriate to it; we reach the conclusion that the good of man is an activity of the soul in conformity with excellence or virtue, and if there are several virtues, in conformity with the best and most complete.

But we must add "in a complete life." For one swallow does not make a spring, nor does one sunny day; similarly, one day or a short time does not make a man blessed and happy. . . .

Virtue, as we have seen, consists of two kinds, intellectual virtue and moral virtue. Intellectual virtue or excellence owes its origin and development chiefly to teaching, and for that reason requires experience and time. Moral virtue, on the other hand, is formed by habit, *ethos,* and its name, *ethike,* is therefore derived, by a slight variation, from *ethos.* This shows, too, that none of the moral virtues is implanted in us by nature, for nothing which exists by nature can be changed by habit. For example, it is impossible for a stone, which has a natural downward movement, to become habituated to moving upward, even if one should try ten thousand times to inculcate the habit by throwing it in the air, nor can fire be made to move downward, nor can the direction of any nature-given tendency be changed by habituation. Thus, the virtues are implanted in us neither by nature nor contrary to nature: we are by nature equipped with the ability to receive them, and habit brings this ability to completion and fulfillment.

Further, of all the qualities with which we are endowed by nature, we are provided with the capacity first, and display the activity afterward. That this is true is shown by the senses: it is not by frequent seeing or frequent hearing that we acquired our senses, but on the contrary we first possess and then use them; we do not acquire them by use. The virtues, on the other hand, we acquire by first having put them into action, and the same is also true of the arts. For the things which we have to learn before we can do them we learn by doing: men become builders by building houses, and harpists by playing the harp. Similarly, we become just by the practice of just actions, self-controlled by exercising self-control, and courageous by performing acts of courage. . . .

It is not sufficient, however, merely to define virtue in general terms as a characteristic: we must also specify what kind of characteristic it is. It must, then, be remarked that every virtue or excellence (1) renders good the thing itself of which it is the excellence, and (2) causes it to perform its function well. For example, the excellence of the eye makes both the eye and its function good, for good sight is due to the excellence of the eye. Likewise, the excellence of a horse makes it both good as a horse and good at running, at carrying its rider, and at facing the enemy. Now, if this is true of all things, the virtue or excellence of man, too, will be a characteristic which makes him a good man, and which causes him to perform his own function well. To some extent we have already stated how this will be true; the rest will become clear if we study what the nature of virtue is.

Of every continuous entity that is divisible into parts it is possible to take the larger, the smaller, or an equal part, and these parts may be larger, smaller, or equal either in relation to the entity itself, or in relation to us. The "equal" part is something median between excess and deficiency. By the median of an entity I understand a point equidistant from both extremes, and this point is one and the same for everybody. By the median relative to us I understand is an amount neither too large nor too small, and this is neither one nor the same for everybody. To take an example: if ten is many and two is few, six is taken as the median in relation to the entity, for it exceeds and is exceeded by the same amount, and is thus the median in terms of arithmetical proportion. But the median relative to us cannot be determined in this manner: if ten pounds of food is much for a man to eat and two pounds little, it does not follow that the trainer will prescribe six pounds, for this may in turn be much or little for him to eat; it may be little for Milo and much for someone who has just begun to take up athletics. The same applies to running and wrestling. This we see that an expert in any field avoids excess and deficiency, but seeks the median and chooses it not the median of the object but the median relative to us.

We may thus conclude that virtue or excellence is a characteristic involving choice, and that it consists in observing the mean relative to us, a mean which is defined by a rational principle, such as a man of practical wisdom would use to determine it. It is the mean by reference to two vices: the one of excess and the other of deficiency. It is, moreover, a mean because some vices exceed and others fall short of what is required in emotion and in action, whereas virtue finds and chooses the median. Hence, in respect of its essence and the definition of its essential nature virtue is a mean, but in regard to goodness and excellence it is an extreme.

Not every action nor every emotion admits of a mean. There are some actions and emotions whose very names connote baseness, e.g., spite, shamelessness, envy, and among actions, adultery, theft, and murder. These and similar emotions and actions imply by their very names that they are bad; it is not their excess nor their deficiency which is called bad. It is, therefore, impossible ever to do right in performing them: to perform them is always to do wrong. In cases of this sort, let us say adultery, rightness and wrongness do not depend on committing it with the right woman and the right time and in the right manner, but the mere fact of committing such action at all is to do wrong. It would be just as absurd to suppose that there is a mean, an excess, and a deficiency in an unjust or a downwardly or a self-indulgent act. For if there were, we would have a mean of excess and a mean of deficiency, and an excess of excess and a deficiency of deficiency.

Just as there cannot be an excess and a deficiency of self-control and courage because the intermediate is, in a sense, an extreme—so there cannot be a mean, excess, and deficiency in their respective opposites: their opposites are wrong regardless of how they are performed, for, in general, there is no such thing as the mean of an excess or a deficiency, or the excess and deficiency of a mean.

However, this general statement is not enough; we must also show that it fits particular instances. For in a discussion of moral actions, although general statements have a wider range of application, statements on particular points have more truth in them: actions are concerned with particulars and our statements must harmonize with them. Let us now take particular virtues and vices from the following examples.

In feelings of fear and confidence courage is the mean. As for the excess, there is no name that describes a man who exceeds in fearlessness—many virtues and vices have no name: but a man who exceeds in confidence is reckless and a man who exceeds in fear and is deficient in confidence is cowardly.

In regard to pleasures and pains—not all of them and to a lesser degree in the case of pains—the mean is self control and the excess self indulgence. Men deficient in regard to pleasure are not often found, and there is therefore no name for them, but let us call them "insensitive."

In giving and taking money, the mean is generosity; the excess and deficiency are extravagance and stinginess. In the vices excess and deficiency work in opposite ways: an extravagant man exceeds in spending and is deficient in taking, while a stingy man exceeds in taking and is deficient in spending. For our present purposes, we may rest content with an outline and a summary, but we shall later define these qualities more precisely.

There are also some other dispositions in regard to money: magnificence is a mean (for there is a difference between a magnificent and a generous man in that the former operates on a large scale, the latter on a small); gaudiness and vulgarity are excesses, and niggardliness deficiency. These vices differ from the vices opposed to generosity. But we shall postpone until later a discussion of the way in which they differ.

As regards honor and dishonor, the mean is high-mindedness, the excess is what we might call vanity and the deficiency small-mindedness. The same relation which, as we said, exists between magnificence and generosity, the one being distinguished from the other in that it operates on a small scale, exists also between high-mindedness and another virtue: as the former deals with great, so the latter deals with small honors. For it is possible to desire honor as one should or more than one should or less than one should: a man who exceeds in his desires is called ambitious, a man who is deficient unambitious, but there is no name to describe the man in the middle. There are likewise no names for the corresponding dispositions except for the dispositions of an ambitious man which is called ambition. As a result, the men who occupy the extremes lay claim to the middle position. We ourselves, in fact, sometimes call the middle person ambitious and sometimes unambitious; sometimes we praise an ambitious and at other times an unambitious man. The reason why we do that will be discussed in the sequel; for the present, let us discuss the rest of the virtues and vices along the lines we have indicated.

In regard to anger also there exists an excess, a deficiency and a mean. Although there really are no names for them, we might call the mean gentleness, since we call a man who occupies the middle position gentle. Of the extremes, let the man who exceeds be called short-tempered and his vice a short temper, and the deficient man apathetic and his vice apathy. . . .

Questions for Discussion

1. What do you think is the relationship between morality and happiness? Are moral persons always happy? Should they be? Why or why not?
2. How would an egoist respond to Aristotle's analysis of human nature?
3. Do you agree that there is a difference between happiness and pleasure? If so, what is this difference? If not, why not?
4. What is the implication of Aristotle's observation that ethical investigations are inexact for ethics as a philosophical inquiry?
5. Aristotle said, "For one swallow does not make a spring, nor does one sunny day." What does this statement reveal about his ethical theory?

CHAPTER 22

Morality Depends on the Consequences

Unlike many ethical theories that have remained merely theoretical systems which are never given the acid test of real-world application, the ethical view known as utilitarianism was originated as a plan for political action. The founder of the utilitarian movement was Jeremy Bentham (1748-1832), whose book *Principles of Morals and Legislation* was put forward as a guide for legislators as they considered legislation affecting welfare. The utilitarians were an extremely influential group in Great Britain and were responsible for many social reforms of the nineteenth century. Bentham was a close friend of James Mill, whose son John Stuart Mill emerged as one of the utilitarians' most eloquent spokesman. It is therefore from Mill's description of the principles of utilitarianism that the following reading is taken.

John Stuart Mill's statement of basic principle of utilitarianism is worth quoting in full:

> The creed which accepts as the foundation of morals, Utility, or the Greatest Happiness Principle, holds that actions are right in proportion as they tend to promote happiness, wrong as they tend to produce the reverse of happiness. By happiness is intended pleasure and the absence of pain; by unhappiness, pain and the absence of pleasure.

That seems straightforward enough, with the added advantage of appearing to be a fairly simple basis for morality. Since the good aimed at by utilitarianism is pleasure or happiness, utilitarianism is a variety of hedonism. For Bentham, pleasure and pain were the twin standards for determining the rightness or wrongness of an action, and Bentham discovered what every other serious hedonist has known—that in order to maximize one's pleasure it is necessary to consider what has come to be known as a hedonistic calculus. In other words, you have to be able to measure the degree and preferability of one pleasure over another. Bentham actually worked out several standards for this hedonistic calculus, but all of the standards seem to be quantitative, with virtually no emphasis on quality. "Pushpin is as good as poetry," if it produces as much pleasure, he said. (Pushpin was a simple child's game.) The following doggerel verse, which appeared in the second edition of Bentham's book, sums up nicely, he thought, the main tenets of his version of utilitarianism.

> *Intense, long, certain, speedy, fruitful, pure—*
> Such marks in *pleasures* and *pains* endure.
> Such pleasures seek, if *private* be thy end;
> If it be *public,* wide let them *extend.*
> Such *pains* avoid, whichever be thy view;
> If pains *must* come, let them *extend* to few.

How nice to be able to sum up one's philosophy in a few lines of verse!

Bentham's version of what has come to be called hedonistic utilitarianism (though he did not call it that) seemed to bring forth criticism from all sides, but the criticism that hit hardest was that Bentham's emphasis on the sheer quantity of pleasure seemed to rule out of calculation such "higher" pleasures as the enjoyment of philosophical reasoning, good music, esthetic experience in general, and other intellectual pleasures. Is pushpin *really* as good as poetry even if it is just as much fun? Is it better to have a gallon of muscatel rather than a quart of Dom Perignon? Is a bodily pleasure really preferable to an intellectual satisfaction? And is not the pursuit of knowledge really the most important task of all regardless of whether it produces pleasure or not? In short, should we not introduce some sort of *qualitative* distinction into utilitarianism? John Stuart Mill thought so, and he broke with Bentham's interpretation of utilitarianism by suggesting that our hedonistic calculus should have qualitative as well as quantitative standards. Mill's response to this issue got him involved in other difficulties, as we shall see, but at least it appeared to be an improvement over the somewhat narrow focus offered by Bentham. In one of Mill's more famous quotations, he made his emphasis on qualitative distinctions unmistakably clear.

> It is better to be a human being dissatisfied than a pig satisfied; better to be Socrates dissatisfied than a fool satisfied. And if the fool, or the pig, is of a different opinion, it is because they know only their side of the question.

John Stuart Mill and Ideal Utilitarianism

John Stuart Mill (1806–1873), who was destined to become one of the most influential English philosophers of the nineteenth century, was something of a child prodigy. Educated principally by his father at home, young John began the study of Greek at the age of three and Latin at the age of eight.

Bentham's Hedonistic Calculus

To a person considered by **himself,** *the value of a pleasure or pain considered by itself, will be greater or less according to the four following circumstances:*

(1) *Its* **intensity.**

(2) *Its* **duration.**

(3) *Its* **certainty** *or* **uncertainty.**

(4) *Its* **propinquity** *or* **remoteness.**

These are the circumstances which are to be considered in estimating a pleasure or a pain considered each of them by itself. But when the value of any pleasure or pain is considered for the purpose of estimating the tendency of any act *by which it is produced, there are two other circumstances to be taken into the account. These are:*

(5) *Its* **fecundity,** *or the chance it has of being followed by sensations of the same kind: that is, pleasures, if it be a pleasure; pains, if it be a pain.*

(6) *Its* **purity,** *or the chance it has of* not *being followed by sensations of the opposite kind: that is, pains, if it be a pleasure; pleasures, if it be a pain.*

These two last, however, are in strictness scarcely to be deemed properties of the pleasure or the pain itself; they are not, therefore, in strictness to be taken into the account of the value of that pleasure or that pain. They are in strictness to be deemed properties only of the act, or other event, by which such pleasure or pain has been produced; accordingly are only to be taken into the account of the tendency of such act or such event.

The six criteria above apply to an individual's calculation of pleasure. If deliberation concerns the welfare of a group, a seventh criterion must be added—the extent of the pleasure, that is, the number of persons affected. After listing the value of each pain and pleasure, Bentham then says: "Sum up all the values of the *pleasures* on one side, and those of all the pains on the other. The balance, if it be on the side of pleasure, will give the good tendency of the act . . . if on the side of pain, the *bad* tendency of it."

In addition to his work on utilitarianism, John Stuart Mill wrote works entitled *On the Subjection of Women* (which he was against), *On Liberty* (which he was for), as well as works on logic and economics. The form of utilitarianism that recognizes qualitative distinctions and not just the quantitative measure of pleasure has come to be referred to as *ideal utilitarianism,* although the term came to be applied to utilitarianism after Mill's time. Nonetheless, Mill's brand of utilitarianism could certainly be classed as ideal utilitarianism, for he introduced the notion of a qualitative measure of pleasure. But here he got himself into a difficult problem. How are we to tell which of two pleasures is the qualitatively better one? How, for example, are we to distinguish Dom Perignon as being qualitatively superior to muscatel? Poetry to pushpin? Mozart to Mick Jagger? Studying philosophy to working crossword puzzles? Mill's answer seems straightforward enough: Ask the person who has experienced *both* pleasures, for such a person is in a position to tell which of the two is best. Here is how Mill puts it: "Of two pleasures, if there be one to which all or almost all who have experienced of both give a decided preference, irrespective of any feeling of moral obligation to prefer it, that is the more desirable pleasure."

The Introduction of Qualitative Distinctions

Of course, Mill thinks that the person who has experienced two (or more) forms of entertainment will naturally prefer the "higher" of the pleasures, but is this necessarily so? Everyone has read and seen some of Shakespeare's plays, but if there is a choice some evening between watching *King Lear* and a detective show on TV, which is our impartial judge more likely to choose?

And even if Mill's impartial judge did consistently prefer the better pleasures, this would still have some very strange, and possibly contradictory, consequences for this theory. We started out saying that the pleasures of the individual are the good at which our actions should aim. But when we distinguish some pleasures as qualitatively superior to others, we introduce the notion of an expert, another person who, because of wide experience, is able to tell us that what we *thought* makes us happy is not really a very good pleasure. Remember that, as a moral theory, utilitarianism tells us what we *ought* to do. And the principle of utilitarianism is that we ought to do that which produces the greatest pleasure. But *now* we are told that somebody else is a better judge of what makes us happy than we are. Such a conclusion seems to contradict the very spirit of utilitarianism, and it is certainly far removed from Jeremy Bentham's original proposal.

And what can Mill mean by *better* when he says "better to be Socrates dissatisfied than a fool satisfied"? *Better* means *more good* and therefore, according to utilitarianism, *more pleasurable.* But then the test of a better pleasure is one that is more pleasurable and we are thrown back on Bentham's purely quantitative measure. And if *better* means anything else, then we seem to have abandoned the utilitarian theory altogether. This is an example of a *dilemma,* which we discussed in Part 2.

$$P \lor R$$
$$P \to Q$$
$$\underline{R \to S}$$
$$\therefore \overline{Q \lor S}$$

P: Better *means more pleasure.*
R: Better *means something else.*
Q: *Mill's quality of pleasure reduces to Bentham's quantity of pleasure.*
S: *Mill has abandoned utilitarianism.*

It seems difficult, in other words, to see how a utilitarian can sensibly and consistently discuss qualitative differences between higher and lower pleasures.

How do you suppose Aristotle would try to account for this intuitive difference? Why is it better to be a dissatisfied human being than a satisfied pig? Surely Aristotle would say it is because we are human beings and every creature must be true to its nature. But Mill cannot take this line of argument without giving up or seriously modifying his utilitarian stance. (Also recall the distinction Aristotle makes between pleasure and happiness, which Mill seems to equate.) Suppose I offered you a pill which would give you the same feeling of pleasure as accomplishing your most sought after goal—whether to write the great American novel, climb a mountain, travel around the world, or become President of the United States—but without deceiving you into believing that this had really occurred. Would you substitute the pill for the actual accomplishment? Why or why not?

▬▬ Rule and Act Utilitarianism

We have already looked at the *utility principle,* or *greatest happiness principle,* as Mill called it. When we say that those actions are right which tend to produce the most pleasure, we next have to ask, whose pleasure? Mill consistently denied that the pleasure or happiness to be sought was *only* that of the person acting—it should include the greatest number possible. Hence the greatest happiness principle was reworded to include *the greatest happiness of the greatest number.* To look after the welfare of the greatest number of people each time you act is a heavy responsibility. Every act would have to be tested by the greatest happiness principle to determine whether it would produce, on balance, a greater amount of happiness than unhappiness. Utilitarians since Mill's time have distinguished between the view just described, which they call *act utilitarianism,* and *rule utilitarianism.* Again, these are not distinctions that were made during Mill's day, but they seem to be demanded by subsequent interpretations of utilitarianism. Act utilitarianism is the view that we assess the rightness or wrongness of *each act* by its tendency to promote the greatest happiness for the greatest number.

Rule utilitarianism says that we use the greatest happiness principle not to regulate each act but to arrive at general rules which, if kept throughout society, will enhance the general welfare and increase the total amount of happiness. Here is how the distinction works. Suppose that you are an act utilitarian and are tempted to tell a lie. If telling the lie does not seem to decrease the pleasure of others but increases your pleasure, then on act utilitarian principles it would seem to be all right to lie. A rule utilitarian, however, would argue that the rule "tell the truth," if made a general rule of society, contributes to the general happiness and increases the sum total of happiness for everyone. Rule utilitarianism, therefore, would say that lying is wrong because of the rule that was generated on utilitarian principles.

Further Difficulties of Utilitarianism

Utilitarianism, as a moral theory that bases the morality of actions on their consequences, is still alive. However, contemporary defenders recognize that there are several basic difficulties with the original formulation of the utilitarian view, which they must come to terms with if they are to have a viable form of utilitarian ethics. Here are three of the principal ones.

Fairness and Minority Rights

If all we have is the greatest happiness principle ("the greatest happiness for the greatest number"), we would be perfectly justified on utilitarian principles in depriving a minority of basic rights so long as our action contributed to the general welfare. As was mentioned in the first part of this chapter, utilitarianism does not seem to have a strong argument against such extreme denials of basic rights as would result from imposing slavery on a small segment of the population. John Stuart Mill argued strongly in his book *On Liberty* against any kind of infringement of the rights of minorities, and his basic argument was based on the claim that a society will be more peaceful and therefore happier if maximum liberty is extended to all members of society, and a more harmonious society will promote the general welfare and happiness. In general, we probably would want to agree with Mill's principle. But suppose it could be demonstrated that society would be threatened unless it imprisoned a certain minority (say, all those of Japanese ancestry), and it would even be useful to society if Japanese-Americans were forced to sell their property at prices below market value. It is difficult to see how a utilitarian, on utilitarian grounds alone, could object to such a proposal. (During World War II, the United States imprisoned citizens and resident aliens of Japanese ancestry for more or less the grounds just given.) Most of us would probably want to say that the infringement of the rights of a minority, even if it could be justified on utilitarian principles, is morally wrong; clearly, then, we need another principle in addition to the greatest happiness principle, such as a fairness principle, or a principle that points out that some actions are wrong no matter how much happiness may result from them.

The Problem of Conflicting Rules

Even a brief exposure to ethical philosophy makes clear that the really difficult problem in ethics is not the generation of rules to govern conduct but the determination of what to do when our various rules conflict with one another. Rule utilitarianism would be no exception to this, and when the rules generated by utilitarian principles clash, we need some way to rank our rules in order of priority, or perhaps we need another rule that tells us how to choose one rule in preference to another. Such rules as "Do not kill" and "You ought to protect your homeland from invasion" can obviously clash, and when they do utilitarianism does not seem, by itself, to be able to tell you how to choose between them. The addition of rules that regulate the application of other rules is one way of resolving difficulties arising from the clash of rules, and most contemporary forms of utilitarianism offer some sort of ranking system for placing moral rules in a hierarchy of priorities.

Proof for Utilitarianism

Finally, a difficulty in all forms of utilitarianism is the matter of proving that utilitarianism is true. In the conclusion of the following selection from Mill, he takes up the issue of proof. "The only proof capable of being given that an object is visible," he says, "is that people actually see it. The only proof that a sound is audible, is that people hear it: and . . . the sole evidence it is possible to produce that anything is desirable is that people do actually desire it." That sounds okay. Right? Perhaps, but like the introduction by Mill of qualitative distinctions into the hedonistic calculus, Mill's sense of proof produces some very odd consequences.

As we pointed out in Part 2, Mill's proof, according to G.E. Moore, commits the fallacy of equivocation. When we say something is visible, we mean it is *capable* of being seen. By analogy, then, Mill is arguing that "desirable" means *capable* of being desired, and in *that* sense an adequate proof that something is capable of being desired is that people actually do desire it. But is that what "desirable" means in a moral context? If I say that in bicycle-touring a ten-speed bicycle is desirable, do I mean that such a thing is *capable* of being desired, or do I mean that it is what one *ought* to desire? Surely the latter. If Mill means that something is desirable in this second sense, then Mill is indeed guilty of equivocation. In so doing, he collapses the important distinction between the factual descriptions of psychology and the normative prescriptions of moral philosophy.

JOHN STUART MILL (1806-1873): English philosopher, economist, and social critic and one of the leaders in the social movement known as Utilitarianism. Mill was a staunch advocate of individual liberty and women's equality. Among his books are System of Logic *(two volumes),* Principles of Political Economy *(two volumes), and* Utilitarianism. *Courtesy of the Library of Congress.*

Remember that ethics, and Mill would have agreed with this, is *prescriptive:* It tells us how we *ought* to *behave.* And the principle of utilitarianism is that we ought to act in accordance with the greatest happiness principle. As Mill follows this line of argument to its logical conclusion, a most startling thing happens. We can perhaps best indicate this by listing the various steps in Mill's argument:

1. People ought to do what produces the greatest happiness for the greatest number (the *utility* or *greatest happiness* principle).
2. We can discover what produces happiness by examining what people in fact do to bring happiness.
3. Therefore, people ought to do what they in fact do.

But where is the sense of moral obligation? If we *ought* to do what we *do,* then moral philosophy offers only a dazzling glimpse of the obvious.

In spite of its internal difficulties, utilitarianism had a profound effect on English social life in the nineteenth century and continues to offer an appealing framework in which to discuss moral problems. The various attempts to patch up the internal difficulties of the theory and the ongoing debate that centers on utilitarian principles shows that there is still a great deal of vitality in the following views expressed by Mill.

John Stuart Mill: Utilitarianism

The creed which accepts as the foundation of morals *utility,* or the *greatest happiness principle,* holds that actions are right in proportion as they tend to promote happiness, wrong as they tend to produce the reverse of happiness. By "happiness" is intended pleasure, and the absence of pain; by "unhappiness," pain, and the privation of pleasure. To give a clear view of the moral standard set up by the theory, much more requires to be said; in particular, what things it includes in the ideas of pain and pleasure; and to what extent this is left an open question. But these supplementary explanations do not affect the theory of life on which this theory of morality is grounded—namely, that pleasure, and freedom from pain, are the only things desirable as ends; and that all desirable things (which are as numerous in the utilitarian as in any other scheme) are desirable either for the pleasure inherent in themselves, or as means to the promotion of pleasure and the prevention of pain.

Now such a theory of life excites in many minds, and among them in some of the most estimable in feeling and purpose, inveterate dislike. To suppose that life has (as they express it) no higher end than pleasure—no better and nobler object of desire and pursuit—they designate as utterly mean and groveling, as a doctrine worthy only of swine, to whom the followers of Epicurus were, at a very early period, contemptuously likened, and modern holders of the doctrine are occasionally made the subject of equally polite comparisons by its German, French, and English assailants.

When thus attacked, the Epicureans have always answered that it is not they but their accusers who represent human nature in a degrading light, since the accusation supposes human beings to be capable of no pleasures except those of which swine are capable. If this supposition were true, the charge could not be gainsaid, but would then be no longer an imputation, for if the sources of pleasure were precisely the same to human beings and to swine, the rule of life which is good enough for the one would be good enough for the other. The comparison of the Epicurean life to that of beasts is felt as degrading, precisely because a beast's pleasures do not satisfy a human being's conception of happiness. Human beings have faculties more elevated than the animal appetites, and when once made conscious of them, do not regard anything as happiness which does not include their gratification. I do not, indeed, consider the Epicureans to have been by any means faultless in drawing out their scheme of consequences from the utilitarian principle. To do this in any sufficient manner, many Stoic, as well as Christian, elements require to be included. But there is no known Epicurean theory of life which does not assign to the pleasures of the intellect, of the feelings and imagination, and of the moral sentiments, a much higher value as pleasures than to those of mere sensation. It must be admitted, howéver, that utilitarian writers in

From John Stuart Mill, *Utilitarianism.* Selections are from Chapters 2, 3, and 4.

general have placed the superiority of mental over bodily pleasures chiefly in the greater permanency, safety, uncostliness, etc., of the former—that is, in their circumstantial advantages rather than in their intrinsic nature. And on all these points utilitarians have fully proved their case; but they might have taken the other, and, as it may be called, higher ground, with entire consistency. It is quite compatible with the principle of utility to recognize the fact, that some *kinds* of pleasure are more desirable and more valuable than others. It would be absurd that while, in estimating all other things, quality is considered as well as quantity, the estimation of pleasures should be supposed to depend on quantity alone.

If I am asked what I mean by difference of quality in pleasures, or what makes one pleasure more valuable than another merely as a pleasure, except its being greater in amount, there is but one possible answer. Of two pleasures, if there be one to which all or almost all who have experience of both give a decided preference, irrespective of any feeling of moral obligation to prefer it, that is the more desirable pleasure. If one of the two is, by those who are competently acquainted with both, placed so far above the other that they prefer it, even though knowing it to be attended with a greater amount of discontent, and would not resign it for any quantity of the other pleasure which their nature is capable of, we are justified in ascribing to the preferred enjoyment a superiority in quality, so far out-weighing quantity as to render it, in comparison, of small account.

Now it is an unquestionable fact that those who are equally acquainted with, and equally capable of appreciating and enjoying, both, do give a most marked preference to the manner of existence which employs their higher faculties. Few human creatures would consent to be changed into any of the lower animals, for a promise of the fullest allowance of a beast's pleasures; no intelligent human being would consent to be a fool, no instructed person would be an ignoramus, no person of feeling and conscience would be selfish and base, even though they should be persuaded that the fool, the dunce, or the rascal is better satisfied with his lot than they are with theirs. They would not resign what they possess more than he for the most complete satisfaction of all the desires which they have in common with him. If they ever fancy they would, it is only in cases of unhappiness so extreme, that to escape from it they would exchange their lot for almost any other, however undesirable in their own eyes. A being of higher faculties requires more to make him happy, is capable probably of more acute suffering, and certainly accessible to it at more points, than one of an inferior type, but in spite of these liabilities, he can never really wish to sink into what he feels to be a lower grade of existence. We may give what explanation we please of this unwillingness: we may attribute it to pride, a name which is given indiscriminately to some of the most and to some of the least estimable feelings of which mankind are capable; we may refer it to the love of liberty and personal independence, an appeal to which was with the Stoics one of the most effective means for the inculcation of it; to the love of power, or to the love of excitement, both of which do really enter into and contribute to it: but its most appropriate appellation is a sense of dignity, which all human beings possess in one form or other, and in some, though by no means in exact, proportion to their higher facilities, and which is so essential a part of the happiness of those in whom it is strong, that nothing which conflicts with it could be, otherwise than momentarily, an object of desire to them. Whoever supposes that this preference takes place at a sacrifice of happiness—that the superior being, in anything like equal circumstances, is not happier than the inferior—confounds the two very different ideas, of *happiness* and *content*. It is indisputable that the being whose capacities of enjoyment are low, has the greatest chance of having them fully satisfied; and a highly endowed being will always feel that any happiness which he can look for, as the world is constituted, is imperfect. But he can learn to bear its imperfections, if they are at all bearable, and they will not make him envy the being who is indeed unconscious of the imperfections, but only because he feels not at all the good which those imperfections qualify. It is better to be a human being dissatisfied than a pig satisfied; better to be Socrates dissatisfied than a fool satisfied. And if the fool, or the pig, are of a different opinion, it is because they only know their own side of the question. The other party to the comparison knows both sides.

According to the 'greatest happiness principle,' as above explained, the ultimate end, with reference to and for the sake of which all other things are desirable (whether we are considering our own good or that of other people), is an existence exempt as far as possible from pain, and as rich as possible in enjoyments, both in point of quantity and quality; the test of quality, and the rule for measuring it against quantity, being the preference felt by those who in their opportunities of experience, to which must be added their habits of self-consciousness and self-observation, are best furnished with the means of comparison. This, being, according to the utilitarian opinion, the end of human action, is necessarily also the standard of morality; which may accordingly be defined, the rules and precepts for human conduct, by the observance of which an existence such as has been described might be, to the greatest extent possible, secured to all mankind; and not to them only but, so far as the nature of things admits, to the whole sentient creation. . . .

Of What Sort of Proof the Principle of Utility Is Susceptible

It has already been remarked that questions of ultimate ends do not admit of proof, in the ordinary acceptation of the term. To be incapable of proof by reasoning is common to all first principles: to the first premises of our knowledge as well as to those of our conduct. But the former, being matters of fact, may be the subject of a direct appeal to the faculties which judge of fact—namely, our senses, and our internal consciousness. Can an appeal be made to the same faculties on questions of practical ends? Or by what other faculty is cognizance taken of them?

Questions about ends are, in other words, questions what things are desirable. The utilitarian doctrine is that happiness is desirable, and the only thing desirable, as an end; all other things being only desirable as means to that end. What ought to be required of this doctrine—what conditions is it requisite that the doctrine should fulfil—to make good its claim to be believed?

The only proof capable of being given that an object is visible, is that people actually see it. The only proof that a sound is audible, is that people hear it: and so of the other sources of our experience. In like manner, I apprehend, the sole evidence it is possible to produce that anything is desirable, is that people do actually desire it. If the end which the utilitarian doctrine proposes to itself were not, in theory and in practice, acknowledged to be an end, nothing could ever convince any person that it was so. No reason can be given why the general happiness is desirable except that each person, so far as he believes it to be attainable, desires his own happiness. This, however, being a fact, we have not only the proof which the case admits of, but all of which it is possible to require, that happiness is a good: that each person's happiness is a good to that person, and the general happiness, therefore, a good to the aggregate of all persons. Happiness has made out its title as *one* of the ends of conduct, and consequently one of the criteria of morality.

But it has not, by this alone, proved itself to be the sole criterion. To do that, it would seem, by the same rule, necessary to show, not only that people desire happiness, but that they never desire anything else. Now it is palpable that they do desire things which, in common language, are decidedly distinguished from happiness. They desire, for example, virtue, and the absence of vice, no less really than pleasure and the absence of pain. The desire of virtue is not as universal, but it is as authentic a fact, as the desire of happiness. And hence the opponents of the utilitarian standard deem that they have a right to infer that there are other ends of human action besides happiness, and that happiness is not the standard of approbation and disapprobation.

But does the utilitarian doctrine deny that people desire virtue, or maintain that virtue is not a thing to be desired? The very reverse. It maintains not only that virtue is to be desired, but that it is to be desired disinterestedly, for itself. Whatever may be the opinion of utilitarian moralists as to the original conditions by which virtue is made virtue; however they may believe (as they do) that actions and dispositions are only virtuous because they promote another end than virtue: yet this being granted, and it having been decided, from considerations of this description, what *is* virtuous, they not only place virtue at the very head of the things which are good as means to the ultimate end, but they also recognize as a psychological fact the possibility of its being, to the individual, a good in itself, without looking to any end beyond it; and hold that the mind is not in a right state, not in a state conformable to utility, not in the state most conducive to the general happiness, unless it does love virtue in this manner—as a thing desirable in itself, even although, in the individual instance, it should not produce those other desirable consequences which it tends to produce, and on account of which it is held to be virtue. This opinion is not, in the smallest degree, a departure from the happiness principle. The ingredients of happiness are very various, and each of them is desirable in itself, and not merely when considered as swelling an aggregate. The principle of utility does not mean that any given pleasure, as music, for instance, or any given exemption from pain, as for example health, is to be looked upon as means to a collective something termed happiness and to be desired on that account. They are desired and desirable in and for themselves; besides being means, they are a part of the end. Virtue, according to the utilitarian doctrine, is not naturally and originally part of the end, but it is capable of becoming so; and in those who love it disinterestedly it has become so, and is desired and cherished, not as a means to happiness, but as a part of their happiness.

Questions for Discussion

1. Do you think the utility principle would be a useful guide for the Congress of the United States to follow in passing legislation? Why or why not?

2. Do you think that a hedonistic calculus is possible? Why or why not?

3. Do you agree with Mill that some pleasures are qualitatively superior to others? Or do you agree with Bentham that "pushpin is as good as poetry"? Give reasons for your answer.

4. Explain in your own words the difference between act utilitarianism and rule utilitarianism. Which do you think is preferable? Why?

5. After looking at the pros and cons of utilitarianism, would you consider yourself a utilitarian or not? Explain.

CHAPTER 23

Morality Depends on Motives

There are at least two major problems with making the morality of an action depend on its consequences: (1) We are not always in a position to predict correctly the consequences of our actions, and (2) a utilitarian standard of morality would allow for moral worth to be accorded for actions done for the worst possible reasons. Immanuel Kant was the great champion of the moral theory which bases the moral worth of an action on the motives of the acting agent, not the consequences, and there are obvious ways in which our ordinary moral intuitions show that Kant was right.

Consider, for example, an act that has negative moral consequences: hitting and killing someone with a moving automobile. If we judged the morality of that action by the effects, we would have to say that legally and morally the driver of the automobile was guilty of murder. But if we place the emphasis on the motives of the driver, whether or not the driver intended to kill the pedestrian is of vital importance. Our assessment of the moral significance of the act would vary greatly depending on whether the driver was the professional murderer mentioned in the first part of this section, or an ordinary citizen whose right front tire just happened to blow out as the car turned a curve, causing the vehicle to swerve into the pedestrian. In the former case, we would accuse the driver of first-degree murder; in the latter case, assuming that there were no acts of negligence on the part of the driver, we would probably assess no moral blame at all.

In the case of some positive action to which we would want to accord moral worth, we likewise would miss an important aspect of the action were we to ignore the motives. Let us suppose a large gift of money is given to a charity, and we find out that the donor actually saved on income taxes by making the gift and that the giver was not really interested in the charity at all. In contrast, a smaller gift from a person genuinely concerned about relieving human misery would seem to us to have more moral significance than a large gift given out of reasons of self-interest. A morality based solely on consequences would have difficulty making such distinctions as these, whereas Kant thought that morality can only be understood properly if we do emphasize the motives.

The Good Will

As was mentioned in the introductory section, there are many things we would want to call good, but Kant insisted that there is only one good that is good without qualification. Let us see what he means. Many goods can be used for harmful and immoral purposes. Intelligence is a good thing, but when possessed by a crook, intelligence makes the criminal's actions more threatening. Wealth is a good, but in the hands of an evil person can be used to threaten and destroy. No matter what the good is that we are thinking of, unless it is coupled with goodness of intention, it can become the source of great evil. There is only one thing, Kant says, that is good without qualification, and that is the *good will*. Morality resides only in the goodness of intention or motive. By the good will, however, Kant does not mean just a kind of wishful thinking. If you see someone starving and say, "I hope you find something to eat," you are not acting out of a good will. A truly good will is the intention to act coupled with all the powers at your disposal. If you do not act on your motive, how can you say that your motive was good? But if in attempting to act on your good intention you are thwarted and prevented from carrying through on your intention, you nonetheless could be said to have acted morally.

Acting from Duty

The truly moral act, moral in Kant's sense, is an action carried out from a sense of duty. But what is duty? Kant said that duty is the recognition that you are under a moral obligation, an obligation to do what is right. We might say, in good Kantian fashion, that duty is acting out of respect for the moral law. But here are two additional terms that demand clarification: *moral* and *law*. Let us take the notion of law first.

Usually we think of a moral action as one done out of principle rather than out of self-interested expedience of the moment. In that sense moral acts are generally thought of as those which follow a general rule or law. But there are laws imposed on us by others, and there are laws imposed on us by ourselves (if the notion of law seems too formidable, think instead of the notion of rule). Now we cannot be moral if we are acting in accordance with a law or rule imposed on us by someone else. Again, Kant's view is compatible with our moral intuitions. The moral significance of someone's action seems to vanish if we discover that the person was *forced* to act in a certain way by an external law or threat. We would want to agree with Kant that you cannot force people to be moral. If they act in accordance with a law, but it is not a rule that they have accepted freely, the moral significance of their actions seems to disappear. The kind of action based on laws imposed on us Kant refers to as *heteronomy*. The truly moral action is one that is, in contrast, *autonomous*, a word which literally means "self-legislated." In short, we are acting morally when we act in accordance with laws or rules that we freely accept and impose on ourselves.

So far, we can see that a moral action must be based on a self-imposed principle that we freely accept as a law or rule for action. But how are we to discover such rules? Kant's suggestion is that we first ask ourselves what *maxim* (or principle) is the basis for our action. That is, any time we are thinking of doing something, try to state the principle. His example is of a person promising to repay money when the individual knows that repayment will be impossible. The *maxim* or *principle* here would seem to be, "When in distress, I can falsely promise with no intention to keep my promises." Kant then suggests, once we have discovered what our maxim is, that we should ask ourselves whether we could make our maxim a rule for everybody, a universal law. If we can, then our action is moral; if we cannot, then our action is immoral. In the case of falsely promising to repay borrowed money, if everyone acted on our maxim, soon the possibility of anyone's borrowing money would disappear, since it would not be possible to accept anyone's promises to repay. If, when we universalize our maxim, it is seen to contradict itself (that is, I can falsely promise to repay money only because most people *keep* their promises), then the action is immoral.

Let us summarize. Kant is suggesting a two-stage process of self-analysis: First, you discover what your maxim or principle of acting is. Second, you ask yourself whether your maxim could become a universal law. If the answer is no, then the action is immoral.

Hypothetical and Categorical Imperatives

Kant called the principle of morality the *categorical* imperative. Where this term came from can be shown by contrasting it with *hypothetical* imperatives. Both terms come from the study of logic in Kant's day. A hypothetical statement was one with the form "If . . . then." The words that follow the *if* are the conditions that must be fulfilled in order to bring about the consequences. "If (you want to make good grades) then you should study." "If (you want to have friends) then be friendly." The word *imperative* means "command," so a hypothetical imperative is an "if then" sort of command which is based on the acceptance of a set of conditions (the conditions that follow the term *if*).

From Kant's point of view, utilitarianism would be based on hypothetical imperatives: "If you want to do the greatest good for the greatest number, then . . . ." But for reasons we have already looked at, Kant did not think morality could be based on an assessment of consequences. The kind of command Kant thought proper for morality was the *categorical* imperative.

A categorical imperative is unconditioned (it is not "iffy"), and it alone is the principle of moral duty. A categorical command would say, "Tell the truth regardless of the consequences."

Kant's usual formulation of the categorical imperative is to "Act on that maxim that you can will to be a universal law." This is the two-step process referred to previously. He also said that the categorical imperative is a rule freely imposed on us by ourselves; hence, it is autonomous. And a third way he characterized the categorical imperative was with reference to the goal of action. Every action is aimed at some end (though the *calculation* of consequences forms no part of morality). If we could discover something that is always a moral end, we could perhaps better see what the categorical imperative is. The final moral end of an action cannot be our own happiness, for if happiness were the goal of life, then the robber baron would be the most moral of persons. There is one thing, and one thing only, Kant thought, that is the proper end of actions, and that is to treat humanity, whether your own or that of another person, always as an end in itself. We should never use another person merely as a means but should treat everyone as worthy of respect and dignity.

Though Kant claimed there was one and only one categorical imperative, he did suggest three dimensions to it:

1. An action is moral if and only if the maxim on which it is based can be universalized.
2. An action is moral if and only if it is carried out based on a freely imposed rule (autonomy).
3. An action is moral if and only if it treats persons as ends in themselves.

As was mentioned previous, there is much in Kant's view that seems to agree with our ordinary moral intuitions. But there are, nonetheless, problems that arise when we attempt to apply Kantian principles. Are we, for example, always able to know what principles we are acting on? And if we do, are the consequences of an action never important in our moral deliberations? Could we tell a lie in order to save a life? Kant would say no, but we might think that telling a falsehood is preferable to seeing life lost. And it is not as easy to apply the abstract principle of the categorical imperative as Kant seems to suggest. Our moral decisions, particularly the difficult ones, rarely come to us in a neat and tidy choice between an obvious good and an obvious evil; rather, real-life moral problems are a confusing combination of mixed goods and ambiguous evils.

In spite of its limitations, Kantian ethics does provide a needed correction to the calculative ethics of utilitarianism. Some acts are wrong in themselves regardless of the beneficial consequences. But on the other hand, the consequences are sometimes important and should not be ignored in our moral deliberations, as Kant would have us do.

Immanuel Kant: Foundations of the Metaphysics of Morals

Nothing in the world—indeed nothing even beyond the world—can possibly be conceived which could be called good without qualification except a *good will*. Intelligence, wit, judgment, and the other talents of the mind, however they may be named, or courage, resoluteness, and perseverance as qualities of temperament, are doubtless in many respects good and desirable. But they can become extremely bad and harmful if the will, which is to make use of these gifts of nature and which in its special constitution is called character, is not good. It is the same with the gifts of fortune. Power, riches, honor, even health, general well-being, and the contentment with one's condition which is called happiness, make for pride and even arrogance if there is not a good will to correct their influence on the mind and on its principles of actions as to make it universally conformable to its end. It need hardly be mentioned that the sight of a being adorned with no feature of a pure and good will, yet enjoying uninterrupted prosperity can never give pleasure to a rational impartial observer. Thus the good will seems to constitute the indispensable condition even of worthiness to be happy.

Some qualities seem to be conducive to this good will and can facilitate its action, but, in spite of that, they have no intrinsic unconditional worth. They rather presuppose a good will, which limits the high esteem which one otherwise rightly has for them and prevents their being held to be absolutely good. Moderation in emotions and passions, self-control, and calm deliberation not only are good in many respects but even seem to constitute a part of the inner worth of the person. But however unconditionally they were esteemed by the ancients, they are far from being good without qualification. For without the principle of a good will they can become extremely bad, and the coolness of a villain makes him not only far more dangerous but also more directly abominable in our eyes than he would have seemed without it.

The good will is not good because of what it effects or accomplishes or because of its adequacy to achieve some proposed end; it is good only because of its willing, i.e., it is good of itself. And, regarded for itself, it is to be esteemed incomparably higher than anything which could be brought about by it in favor of any inclination or even of the sum total of all inclinations. Even if it should happen that, by a particularly unfortunate fate or by the niggardly provision of a stepmotherly nature, this will should be wholly lacking in power to accomplish its purpose, and if even the greatest effort should not avail it to achieve anything of its end, and if there remained only the good will (not as a mere wish but as the summoning of all the means of our power), it would sparkle like a jewel in its own right, as something that had its full worth in itself. Usefulness or fruitlessness can neither diminish nor augment this worth. Its usefulness would be only its setting, as it were, so as to enable us to handle it more conveniently in commerce or to attract the attention of those who are not yet connoisseurs, but not to recommend it to those who are experts or to determine its worth.

<hr/>

[Thus the first proposition of morality is that to have moral worth an action must be done from duty.] The second proposition is: An action performed from duty does not have its moral worth in the purpose which is to be achieved through it but in the maxim by which it is determined. Its moral value, therefore, does not depend on the realization of the object of the action but merely on the principle of volition by which the action is done, without any regard to the objects of the faculty of desire. From the preceding discussion it is clear that the purposes we may have for our actions and their effects as ends and incentives of the will cannot give the actions any unconditional and moral worth. Wherein, then, can this worth lie, if it is not in the will in relation to its hoped-for effect? It can lie nowhere else than in the principle of the will, irrespective of the ends which can be realized by such action. For the will stands, as it were, at the crossroads halfway between its *a priori* principle which is formal and its *a posteriori* incentive which is material. Since it must be determined by something, if it is done from duty it must be determined by the formal principle of volition as such since every material principle has been withdrawn from it.

The third principle as a consequence of the two preceding, I would express as follows: Duty is the necessity of an action executed from respect for law. I can certainly have an inclination to the object as an effect of the proposed action, but I can never have respect for it precisely because it is a mere effect and not an activity of a will. Similarly, I can have no respect for any inclination whatsoever, whether my own or that of another; in the former case I can at most approve of it and in the latter I can even love it, i.e., see it as favorable to my own advantage. But that which is connected with my will merely as ground and not as consequence, that which does not serve my inclination but overpowers it or at least excludes it from being considered in making a choice—in a word, law itself—can be an object of respect and thus a command. Now as an act from duty wholly excludes the influence of inclination and therewith every object of the will, nothing remains which can determine the will objectively except the law, and nothing subjectively except pure respect for this practical law. This subjective element is the maxim[1] that I ought to follow such a law even if it thwarts all my inclinations.

---

[1] A maxim is the subjective principle of volition. The objective principle (i.e., that which would serve all rational beings also subjectively as a practical principle if reason had full power over the faculty of desire) is the practical law.

Thus the moral worth of an action does not lie in the effect which is expected from it or in any principle of action which has to borrow its motive from this expected effect. For all these effects (agreeableness of my own condition, indeed even the promotion of the happiness of others) could be brought about through other causes and would not require the will of a rational being, while the rights and unconditional good can be found only in such a will. Therefore, the preeminent good can consist only in the conception of the law in itself (which can be present only in a rational being, so far as this conception and not the hoped for effect is the determining ground of the will. This preeminent good which we call moral, is already present in the person who acts according to this conception, and we do not have to look for it first in the result.[2]

But what kind of a law can that be, the conception of which must determine the will without reference to the expected result? Under this condition alone the will can be called absolutely good without qualification. Since I have robbed the will of all impulses which could come to it from obedience to any law, nothing remains to serve as a principle of the will except universal conformity of its action to law as such. That is, I should never act in such a way that I could not also will that my maxim should be a universal law. Mere conformity to law as such (without assuming any particular law applicable to certain actions) serves as the principle of the will, and it must serve as such a principle if duty is not to be a vain delusion and chimerical concept. The common reason of mankind in its practical judgments is in perfect agreement with this and has this principle constantly in view.

Let the question, for example, be: May I, when in distress, make a promise with the intention not to keep it? I easily distinguish the two meanings which the question can have, viz., whether it is prudent to make a false promise, or whether it conforms to my duty. Undoubtedly the former can often be the case, though I do see clearly that it is not sufficient mercy to escape from the present difficulty by this expedient, but that I must consider whether inconveniences much greater

---

[2] It might be objected that I seek to take refuge in an obscure feeling behind the word "respect," instead of clearly resolving the question with a concept of reason. But though respect is a feeling, it is not one received through any [outer] influence but is self-wrought by a rational concept; thus it differs specifically from all feelings of the former kind which may be referred to as inclination or fear. What I recognize directly as a law for myself I recognize with respect, which means merely the consciousness of the submission of my will to a law without the intervention of other influences on my mind. The direct determination of the will by the law and the consciousness of this determination is respect; thus respect can be regarded as the effect of the law on the subject and not as the cause of the law. Respect is properly the conception of a worth which thwarts my self-love. Thus it is regarded as an object neither of inclination nor of fear, though it has something analogous to both. The only object of respect is the law, and indeed only the law which we impose on ourselves and yet recognize as necessary in itself. As a law, we are subject to it without consulting self-love as imposed on us by ourselves, it is a consequence of our will. In the former respect it is analogous to fear and in the latter to inclination. All respect for a person is only respect for the law (of righteousness, etc.) of which the person provides an example. Because we see the improvement of our talents as a duty, we think of a person of talents as the example of a law, as it were (the law that we should by practice become like him in his talents), and that constitutes our respect. All so-called moral interest consists solely in respect for the law.

than the present one may not later spring from this lie. Even with all my supposed cunning, the consequences cannot be so easily foreseen. Loss of credit might be far more disadvantageous than the misfortune I now seek to avoid, and it is hard to tell whether it might not be more prudent to act according to a universal maxim and to make it a habit not to promise anything without intending to fulfill it. But it is soon clear to me that such a maxim is based only on an apprehensive concern with consequences.

To be truthful from duty, however, is an entirely different thing from being truthful out of fear of disadvantageous consequences, for in the former case the concept of the action itself contains a law for me, while in the later I must first look about to see what results for me may be connected with it. For to deviate from the principle of duty is certainly bad, but to be unfaithful to my maxim of prudence can sometimes be very advantageous to me, though it is certainly safer to abide by it. The shortest but most infallible way to find the answer to the question as to whether a deceitful promise is consistent with duty is to ask myself: Would I be content that my maxim (of extricating myself from difficulty by a false promise) should hold as a universal law for myself as well as for others? And could I say to myself that everyone may make a false promise when he is in a difficulty from which he otherwise cannot escape? I immediately see that I could will the lie but not a universal law to lie. For with such a law there would be no promises at all, inasmuch as it would be futile to make a pretense of my intention in regard to future actions to those who would not believe this pretense or—if they overhastily did so—who would pay me back in my own coin. Thus my maxim would necessarily destroy itself as soon as it was made a universal law.

I do not, therefore, need any penetrating acuteness in order to discern what I have to do in order that my volition may be morally good. Inexperienced in the course of the world, incapable of being prepared for all its contingencies, I ask myself only: Can I will that my maxim become a universal law? If not, it must be rejected, not because of any disadvantage accruing to myself or even to others, but because it cannot enter as a principle into a possible universal legislation, and reason extorts from me an immediate respect for such legislation. I do not as yet discern on what it is grounded (a question the philosopher may investigate), but I at least understand that it is an estimation of the worth which far outweighs all the worth of whatever is recommended by the inclinations, and that the necessity of my actions from pure respect for the practical law constitutes duty. To duty every other motive must give place, because duty is the condition of a will good in itself whose worth transcends everything.

———————

All imperatives command either hypothetically or categorically. The former present the practical necessity of a possible action as a means to achieving something else which one desires (or which one may possibly desire). The categorical imperative would be one which presented an action as of itself objectively necessary, without regard to any other end.

Since every practical law presents a possible action as good and thus as necessary for a subject practically determinable by reason, all imperatives are formulas of the determination of action which is necessary by the principle of a will which is in any way good. If the action is good only as a means to something else, the imperative is hypothetical, but if it is thought of as good in itself, and hence as necessary in a will which of itself conforms to reason as the principle of this will, the imperative is categorical.

There is one end, however, which we may presuppose as actual in all rational beings so far as imperatives apply to them, i.e., so far as they are dependent beings; there is one purpose not only which they *can* have but which we can presuppose that they all *do* have by a necessity of nature. This purpose is happiness. The hypothetical imperative which represents the practical necessity of action as means to the promotion of happiness is an assertorical imperative. We may not expound it as merely necessary to an uncertain and a merely possible purpose, but as necessary to a purpose which we can *a priori* and with assurance assume for everyone because it belongs to his essence. Skill in the choice of means to one's own highest welfare can be called prudence in the narrowest sense. Thus the imperative which refers to the choice of means to one's own happiness, i.e., the precept of prudence, is still only hypothetical; the action is not absolutely commanded but commanded only as a means to another end.

Finally, there is one imperative which directly commands a certain conduct without making its condition some purpose to be reached by it. This imperative is categorical. It concerns not the material of the action and its intended result but the form and the principle from which it results. What is essentially good in it consists in the intention, the result being what it may. This imperative may be called the imperative of morality.

Questions for Discussion

1. In the ongoing quarrel between those who say the morality of an action depends on motives and those who say it depends on consequences, which side do you find yourself on? Why?

2. Do you agree with Kant that a moral imperative must be *categorical*? Give reasons for your answer.

3. Do you accept Kant's claim that the only thing that is good without qualification is good will? Be prepared to defend your answer.

4. Do you think that the categorical imperative is similar to the "golden rule" of Jesus? Explain.

5. What do you consider to be the major strong points of Kant's ethical view? Its major weakness?

Suggestions for Further Reading

Blackburn, Simon. *Ruling Passions: A Theory of Practical Reasoning*. Oxford: Clarendon Press, 1998. Shows how a consideration of human nature is important for ethics.

Gilligan, Carol. *In a Different Voice: Psychological Theory and Women's Development*. Cambridge, MA: Harvard University Press, 1993. Offers perspectives on the role of gender in moral issues and in their expression.

Levin, David Michael. *The Philosopher's Gaze*. Berkeley: University of California Press, 1999. Using the language of phenomenology the author explores moral character and the pathologies of the current age.

MacIntyre, Alasdair. *After Virtue: A Study in Moral Theory*. Notre Dame: University of Notre Dame Press, 2nd ed., 1984. Argues that ethics requires membership in a moral community.

Scanlon, T. M. *What We Owe to Each Other*. Cambridge, MA: The Belnap Press of Harvard University Press, 1998. Shows the considerations involved in moral reasoning and why we should give priority to moral judgments.

Philosophy of Religion

PART 6

CHAPTER 24

Introduction to Philosophy of Religion

Consider the following range of activities: A Wednesday night prayer meeting. A group of students studying astral projection. A Hindu holy man sitting motionless in meditation all day. A faith healer calling on a crippled lady to throw down her crutches and walk toward him. Jews praying at the Wailing Wall in Jerusalem. A temple in which food is offered to ancestors. An altar in the forest of Guatemala on which a hen is offered to ward off evil spirits. A Mass celebrated in St. Patrick's Cathedral. A Japanese samurai focusing on his oneness with the Buddha as he lops off the head of his opponent.

What makes all these diverse activities *religious?* Or to pose the question differently, what definition of religion would be adequate to encompass such a wide range of human activities? The list above is only partial; it could be extended for pages just in describing religious *activities.* If we were to include a description of religious *beliefs* and attitudes stemming from these beliefs, the task of describing the phenomenon known as religion would seem formidable indeed.

The question "What *is* religion?" is the kind of question that philosophy of religion considers. In addition to its own proper subject matter, philosophy also is an activity that seeks to understand the basic principles and presuppositions inherent in various *other* activities and disciplines, which gives us philosophies *of* (philosophy *of* science, *of* education, *of* art, *of* law, and even such new areas of inquiry as philosophy of sport). In all these inquiries, the task of philosophy is to analyze and clarify, not necessarily to engage in the activity itself. Of course, there are many ways to analyze and clarify something without being philosophical. And that is certainly true of the study of religion. Religion is such an enormously rich and varied phenomenon that the study of religion is correspondingly diverse. One can engage in a scholarly study of ancient texts and the histories of religions, perhaps coupled with archeological examination of ancient religious centers. Anthropologists study the religious practices of primitive peoples in order to learn more about the meaning and function of religion in different cultural contexts. Adherents to a particular religion develop theological statements designed to unify a body of doctrine and beliefs. Other writers show the relevance of religious doctrines to contemporary issues.

Philosophical Issues in Religion

How does the *philosophy* of religion differ from these approaches? As you might expect from our examination of other kinds of philosophical inquiry, philosophy of religion is concerned with clarifying such basic religious ideas as the concept of God, trying to remove alleged inconsistencies in religious belief, probing the grounds of religious knowledge, examining the problems of religious language, as well as looking at the question of the nature of religion. It may at times be difficult to separate the philosophical study of religion clearly from other approaches, but maybe a few brief examples will show better the kinds of questions with which philosophy of religion is concerned.

First, what do we mean by the word *God*? What are the most basic attributes in our concept of God? God is said to be good, all-powerful, all-knowing, loving, the creator, and a transcendent spirit. But it is not always clear what some of these attributes mean, nor is it obvious that they are consistent with one another. What do we mean, for example, when we say that God is all-powerful? Can God do *anything?* Can God make a square circle, or make something so heavy God can't lift it? Can God break a promise or tell a lie? If not, does it follow that God is *not* all-powerful, after all? As philosophers, we might begin by trying to spell out more precisely what we mean by saying that God "can do anything." We might specify as the seventeenth-century German philosopher Leibniz did, that God can do anything *possible* to which we might want to add, anything possible which God *chooses* to do. That will remove the problem of the square circle and the stone too heavy to lift, but what about God's ability to tell a lie or break a promise? God does not want to do these things, but what if God wanted to? Can God want to do something evil? What, in other words, is the relationship between God's goodness and power? Is God good by choice, or does God choose good because God is by nature good? There are problems with either approach. If God is good because of choice, then we seem to be asserting that God is capable of evil, and this contradicts our religious assumptions that a completely good being *could* not do anything bad. But if we opt for the second approach, that God chooses good things because God *is* good, then we seem to be saying that God does not really freely *choose* good. But being good seems to presuppose choosing to do good. Can God be good if God does not freely choose to do good, and can God freely choose good if God is incapable of evil?

If you were able to follow all the twists and turns of this analysis of attributes of God, you can see how quickly philosophy of religion gets into very complicated issues, issues that occupy the best philosophical minds of every generation.

Perhaps you will conclude that there really is no ultimate contradiction between God's goodness and omnipotence, since God's nature is such that God is wholly good, so if God is true to his nature, God will never choose evil. But just when you think you have that question nailed down, you will discover that it raises another issue; in this case, the difficulty of reconciling God's goodness with omnipotence points us directly to the problem of evil.

The problem of evil has been stated in many ways, but perhaps the following is the simplest and most direct: How can there be evil in the world if God is both good and all-powerful? If God is good and all-powerful, then God would want to and be able to and therefore succeed in preventing evil. These three propositions —God is good, God is all-powerful, evil exists—appear then to be logically inconsistent. Any two of them can be true so long as the third is false, but they cannot all three be true at once. God may be good and want to prevent evil, but not all-powerful and so unable to prevent it. Or God might be able to prevent evil but not want to (that is, be all-powerful but not good). It is even possible that God is both good and all-powerful, and there *really* is no evil in the world (despite some pretty convincing appearances to the contrary). Philosophically, how might we try to reconcile this internal contradiction, that is, how can we analyze these three propositions so that they are no longer in conflict? We might say, with Leibniz, that God does not choose between good and evil but only among the best of all *possible* worlds. We might imagine God considering which of the two following possibilities to bring into creation. On the one hand there could be a world in which evil did not and could not exist. But this would have to be a world in which human beings were compelled to do good and could not choose to do evil. This would have the consequence that people could not freely choose good and so in that sense, as we saw above, could not truly be good of their own free will. On the other hand, there could be a world in which people were free to choose between good and evil, but in that case they would have to be free to choose evil and so the possibility of evil in the world would exist. Faced with these two alternatives, God chooses the better of the two, although neither is perfect. God can only choose the lesser of two evils. Why can God not choose a world where people are free and evil cannot exist? It's because that is impossible, and not even God can make the impossible happen. Does that imply that God is not all-powerful? This takes us back to the problem we considered earlier in analyzing the concept of God.

The consideration of these two questions in the philosophy of religion—the nature of God and the problem of evil—shows how intertwined such separate questions can be. Our consideration of the nature of God leads immediately to problems associated with the nature of religious language. We have been discussing philosophical investigations about the nature of God in plain English. But is this appropriate? Can we legitimately use ordinary language in talking about a reality (God) that is totally beyond human comprehension?

On the one hand, if God is said to lie beyond all limitations of our finite understanding, then God cannot be caught in the web of our human words and concepts. On the other hand, we do describe God in ways similar to ways we describe other things in our world. We say that God is good, knowing, loving, a father, and so on, but if these words are used in their ordinary sense, then such a use of language would seem to erase the *difference* between God and human beings. On the other hand, if we emphasize the fact that God is *totally* different from us, how can we say *anything* about God? One way out of this difficulty—and the way argued for by St. Thomas Aquinas in the thirteenth century—is to suggest that we use language analogously when we speak of God. God is not literally a father but is *like* a father; God's goodness is, when compared to the magnitude of his being, *like* the goodness we attribute to human beings in comparison to our beings.

But suppose that we cannot eliminate all of the logical puzzles from our consideration of the attributes of God. What if we are unable to solve the problem of evil, or come up with a completely adequate view of the nature of religious language? A great deal of effort has been spent in the philosophy of religion trying to construct logical proofs for the existence of God. Yet these too are full of difficulties and unresolved controversies. Are we nonetheless justified in *believing* in God or adopting a religious attitude even when we don't have rational proof? The relation between faith and reason is another of the perennial topics dealt with by the philosophy of religion. Some writers, such as St. Thomas Aquinas, have argued that what we can know about God by reason and what we can know about God through sacred scripture constitute two parallel paths toward knowledge of God. Other philosophers, such as Søren Kierkegaard, have insisted to the contrary that faith is not based on reason at all but is a "leap" beyond rationality in a move that acknowledges utter dependence on a power greater than ourselves. A consideration of the relation between faith and reason also points us toward another question relating to the source of our religious knowledge. Do we learn about the religious life from authority figures, from scripture, from religious experience, or are we completely dependent on reasoning and arguments? On the other hand, are arguments—such as those for the existence of God—really compelling without faith?

Since philosophy of religion is only one topic in this book, we shall have to give our attention to one main question rather than consider the wide range of issues that characterize the philosophical analysis of religion. The question that we shall look at in some detail is the definition of religion itself.

Some Attempts at Definition

At first our task seems easy. Look at all the things we call religions, and figure out what they all have in common. If we can come up with a list of characteristics that apply to every religion, but do not apply to anything else, then we have successfully defined "religion" in terms of a set of necessary and sufficient conditions. Definition in terms of necessary and sufficient conditions, as we saw in Chapter 8 on philosophical reasoning, is the standard model for a precise definition. But when we look at all the things called religion, it begins to appear more difficult to locate even a single feature they all have in common, particularly if we are seeking some feature that is not shared by things which fall outside the scope of religion.

Consider something as apparently basic to religion as belief in God. Though many religions—perhaps even most—include belief in some kind of divine being or beings, this is not true of all religions. Two major world religions, Buddhism and Confucianism, do not embrace the concept of God. Some religions are exclusively concerned with developing powers to ward off evil spirits. Others are devoted principally to developing certain kinds of physical powers through mastery of spiritual laws. Other religions are committed mainly to ancestor worship. On the other hand, there are persons who might admit to belief in God or in divine beings of some kind but who nonetheless do not engage in any activity or hold any other beliefs that could be legitimately called religious. If we cannot find a defining characteristic of religion in something as apparently basic as belief in God, then we can see the difficulty in discovering any characteristic common to all religions.

One alternative is to group religions into families determined by features they have in common but do not share with other religions. This approach would give us a family of monotheistic religions, another family of polytheistic religions, and another of pantheistic religions, depending on whether a religion espoused belief in one god, many gods, or held the view that *everything* is God. Within each family we could separate out additional families of common characteristics: religions that have priesthoods versus those that do not, religions with sacred scriptures, religions that believe in immortality, religions that have a high ethical content, and so on. This kind of descriptive enterprise is interesting and useful to those who want to understand religion as a cultural or historical phenomenon, but it fails as a philosophical analysis because it does not, by itself, lead to an understanding of the nature of religion.

Intrinsic and Extrinsic Criteria

If we cannot find a defining characteristic of religion, we might try discovering what *function* religion serves. Here we seem to be on firmer ground, for defining religion in terms of its function rather than something inherent in its practice at least allows us to examine features that will enable us to see religion as a whole. When we look at the various proposed *functional* definitions of religion, we find that they fall into two broad categories. In the first category are those attempts to explain religion in terms of *extrinsic criteria;* in the second are those attempts which try to explain religion in its own terms. The first kind of definition attempts to explain what religion is by explaining how it is related to things other than religion, through things extrinsic to religion, as though religion had no intrinsic character of its own. The second kind of definition attempts to explain the function of religion in terms something having value and importance in and of itself.

We might want to say that attempts to provide extrinsic definitions of religion are reductive put-downs; that is, they insist that religion is "nothing but" a fear of the unknown, or an attempt to provide consolation in the face of life's uncertainties, or "nothing but" a device used by the ruling classes to keep the laboring classes in line. The extrinsic definitions of religion would not be accepted by the followers of religions so described. Believers in a religion would prefer intrinsic definitions that emphasize religion as the search for God, or the holy, or the infinite, or however they understand the nature of their religious commitments. They would also claim that a religious commitment makes life more meaningful than a nonreligious view of things. To be sure, it would be difficult to imagine anyone being committed to an activity unless that activity had some meaning and purpose, and religion is no exception. Unless the followers of a religion feel that it contributes in some sense to the meaning of their lives, they would cease to devote themselves to it with the intensity demanded by a religious concern. In the next chapter we will examine one thinker's expression of the centrality of religious faith for a meaningful life.

Questions for Discussion

1. Try your own hand at defining religion. Based on your experience, how would you describe it?

2. Given what you know about philosophy at this point, how would a study called *philosophy* of religion differ from the study of a particular religious tradition?

3. Who do you think is in a better position to understand a particular religion—a believer who accepts the claims of that religion or a nonbeliever who has some distance from that religion?

4. What are some of the reasons people are religious? What are some of the barriers to religious belief?

5. From your own analysis and experience, what do you think are the most important issues in the study of religion?

CHAPTER 25

Religion and Life's Meaning

The question of the relation between religion and life can be formulated in many different ways. Some religions, such as Christianity and Islam, find that the present life can only be fully understood as preparation for a future life. This means, among other things, that there can be no comprehension of the significance of life on earth without this added belief in human destiny. There is a strong sense that this present life is not the life we were meant to have, but only a preparation for life in the fullest sense.

At the opposite pole is Confucianism with its total absence of any belief either in God or a future life. The primary concern of Confucianism is with the correct ordering of this present life with its emphasis on the well-organized society, filial piety, and respect for ancestors. Still another view is that shared by Hinduism and Buddhism, which consider release from human life on earth as their goal. Trapped in a cycle of birth, death, and rebirth, human beings seek *moksha,* or release, from this cycle through piety and inner illumination. Salvation is considered not a future life, as in Christianity and Islam, but Nirvana, a state in which there is the total loss of individual identity.

What are we really asking when we inquire into life's meaning? To explore this issue is such a huge task that we cannot examine all the varieties of answers given to the question. Indeed, some philosophers have even suggested that the question of life's meaning is either so vast or so vague as to be unanswerable. Whatever else it might entail, the question involves attention to such additional issues as these: Who, or what, am I? Why am I here? What am I to do? These questions form the basis for an attempt to make rational sense out of life. We might say that this cluster of concerns raises the issue of the significance of life itself. Some philosophers have concluded that no one single thing gives life meaning, no big fact that makes life purposeful. What we can have, they conclude, is a collection of activities, beliefs, and relationships that provide many small meanings that together give life purpose and significance.

The Absurdist Response

Others are not so sure. They ask what life would be like without any overall meaning at all. This attitude has found expression in the literature of the absurd, which focuses on the meaninglessness of life and the vacuity of human existence. Represented by the novels and short stories of Franz Kafka and the plays of Samuel Beckett, the absurdists present a vision of life devoid of any significance and purpose. Perhaps the paradigm for this point of view is contained in Beckett's play *Waiting for Godot,* whose entire action centers on two vagrants who are waiting for a Mr. Godot (God?) who never arrives. This vision of things seems to imply that life is a kind of cosmic joke in which the major participants wait vainly for an understanding of the significance of this situation. There is no answer to the question of meaning, so human life goes on without it. The absurdists present a stark picture of human existence in which no meaning and purpose seems to be available.

The philosophers of the mid-twentieth century classified as *existentialists* reject such a gloomy conclusion, though they agree that the question of the meaning of human existence is a central one for philosophy. This would not be the first time nor the first issue on which philosophers have disagreed with literary figures. Philosophers, whose business is meaning, by and large reject the meaninglessness of life portrayed by absurdist literature and find significance even in a world without a God to provide a single, overarching meaning. The nineteenth-century philosopher Friedrich Nietzsche expressed this philosophical attitude well when he said that "any meaning is better than no meaning." He found the possibility of meaningful life in the creation of noble values, great artistic achievements, and, in general, the elevation of human creativity in all its forms. Another nineteenth-century philosopher who is also cited as a precursor of existential philosophy, Søren Kierkegaard, gave a different answer. For him, life's meaning comes only through faith in God. Since God cannot be known by reason, a meaningful life requires a personal commitment, a *leap* of faith, as he put it. These twin responses to the question of life's meaning were continued in the existentialist philosophy of the twentieth century. Gabriel Marcel and Nikolai Berdyaev, among others, continued the themes of Kierkegaard by responding to the question from the context of the traditions of the Judeo-Christian religion. Others, such as Jean-Paul Sartre and Albert Camus, worked out the meaning of human existence in a completely nontheistic context, although the intensity with which they devote themselves to the question of meaning can be perhaps thought of as "religious" in Paul Tillich's sense of faith as "ultimate concern."

≡ Tolstoy's Response

What makes Tolstoy's response so interesting is that he considered both alternatives—theistic and nontheistic—to the question of life's meaning. He found the question itself overwhelming: "One can only live while one is intoxicated with life," he said. "As soon as one is sober it is impossible not to see that it is all a mere fraud and a stupid fraud! That is precisely what it is: there is nothing either amusing or witty about it, it is simply cruel and stupid." Tolstoy gravitated to this gloomy conclusion as a result of the realization that life is not only difficult and hard, but ends in utter defeat—death. How can we possibly have any delight in an enterprise that is ultimately doomed to disaster? Tolstoy desperately wanted an answer, and he searched—in vain, as he discovered—in science and philosophy for it. As he analyzed possible responses to life's meaninglessness, he discovered four common responses given to the question. The first was simply ignorance, a refusal of people to face up to the absurdity of life. The second kind of response was epicureanism, Tolstoy's term for seeking the maximum of pleasures in life. (Epicureanism was an ancient Greek hedonistic ethical system.) The third way was strength and energy—the noblest response, Tolstoy thought—and culminated in suicide: "a rope round one's neck, water, a knife to stick into one's heart, or the trains on the railways." Finally there is the fourth way, that of weakness, which involves recognizing the absurdity of life yet doing nothing about it. This is the class of people in which Tolstoy found himself.

LEO TOLSTOY (1828–1910): Born into the Russian aristocracy, Count Leo Nikolaevich Tolstoy was trained in law and oriental languages but did not take a university degree. He renounced his fortune and position and sought the meaning of life in a return to a simple Christian lifestyle. Tolstoy was one of the great Russian novelists of the nineteenth century, the author of War and Peace *and* Anna Karenina. Courtesy of the Library of Congress.

Tolstoy, the distinguished author of *War and Peace* and *Anna Karenina* is an exceptionally powerful writer, and in the selection that follows from "A Confession" one can sense the anxiety and dread experienced by Tolstoy as he grappled with the question of life's meaning. There was, it turned out, a fifth response to life finally discovered by Tolstoy, and that was the response of faith in God. The road to faith as Tolstoy experienced it was neither quick nor easy, but it provided the solace he needed. "I should long ago have killed myself," he says, "had I not had a dim hope of finding Him. I live, really live, only when I feel Him and seek Him."

One of the obstacles standing in the way of assessing statements of religious experience such as that offered by Tolstoy is the difficulty of understanding what he is talking about if you have never had a similar experience. The sense of the presence of God is an intensely private experience, more like falling in love than providing the proof of a geometrical theorem or demonstrating a chemical reaction in a laboratory.

A second difficulty experienced by many people who are drawn to faith in God is that while they can believe in God, they have trouble accepting the practice of religion as it goes on in the churches. This was Tolstoy's concern, for he found much in the Russian Orthodox Church that disturbed him. Like Marx, Tolstoy saw that religious *institutions* can be used to manipulate the poor and oppressed. And he was appalled by the fact that the gospel's message of peace and love had been largely ignored by the churches. Rather than preach nonviolence, the clergy stressed the patriotic duty to serve the czar by destroying the enemies of mother Russia. Rather than accepting the simple life and giving all their goods to the poor, the churches had become repositories of great wealth and privilege. Tolstoy's response was to seek a simple life of piety and faith, while remaining one of his generation's severest critics of the churches. It is ironic that during his lifetime Tolstoy's religious writings were suppressed by the Russian Orthodox Church, and after his death his religious writings were suppressed by the political authorities. The following selection is taken from the short work entitled 'A Confession," which describes not only Tolstoy's religious pilgrimage but also his difficulties accepting the practices of the established church.

Leo Tolstoy: A Confession

There is an Eastern fable, told long ago, of a traveller overtaken on a plain by an enraged beast. Escaping from the beast he gets into a dry well, but sees at the bottom of the well a dragon that has opened its jaws to swallow him. And the unfortunate man, not daring to climb out lest he should be destroyed by the enraged

Abridged from *A Confession and the Gospel in Brief* by Leo Tolstoy translated by Aylmer Maude (1921).

beast, and not daring to leap to the bottom of the well lest he should be eaten by the dragon, seizes a twig growing in a crack in the well and clings to it. His hands are growing weaker and he feels he will soon have to resign himself to the destruction that awaits him above or below, but still he clings on. Then he sees that two mice, a black and a white one, go regularly round and round the stem of the twig to which he is clinging and gnaw at it. And soon the twig itself will snap and he will fall into the dragon's jaws. The traveller sees this and knows that he will inevitably perish; but while still hanging he looks around, sees some drops of honey on the leaves of the twig, reaches them with his tongue and licks them. So I too clung to the twig of life, knowing that the dragon of death was inevitably awaiting me, ready to tear me pieces; and I could not understand why I had fallen into such torment. I tried to lick the honey which formerly consoled me, but the honey no longer gave me pleasure, and the white and black mice of day and night gnawed at the branch by which I hung. I saw the dragon clearly and the honey no longer tasted sweet. I only saw the unescapable dragon and the mice, and I could not tear my gaze from them. And this is not a fable but the real unanswerable truth intelligible to all.

The deception of the joys of life which formerly allayed my terror of the dragon now no longer deceived me. No matter how often I may be told, 'You cannot understand the meaning of life so do not think about it, but live,' I can no longer do it: I have already done it too long. I cannot now help seeing day and night going round and bringing me to death. That is all I see, for that alone is true. All else is false.

The two drops of honey which diverted my eyes from the cruel truth longer than the rest: my love of family, and of writing—art as I called it—were no longer sweet to me.

'Family' . . . said I to myself. But my family—wife and children—are also human. They are placed just as I am: they must either live in a lie or see the terrible truth. Why should they live? Why should I love them, guard them, bring them up, or watch them? That they may come to the despair that I feel, or else be stupid? Loving them, I cannot hide the truth from them: each step in knowledge leads them to the truth. And the truth is death.

'Art, poetry?' . . . Under the influence of success and the praise of men, I had long assured myself that this was a thing one could do though death was drawing near—death which destroys all things, including my work and its remembrance; but soon I saw that too was a fraud. It was plain to me that art is an adornment of life, an allurement to life. But life had lost its attraction for me, so how could I attract others? As long as I was not living my own life but was borne on the waves of some other life—as long as I believed that life had a meaning, though one I could not express—the reflection of life in poetry and art of all kinds afforded me pleasure: it was pleasant to look at life in the mirror of art. But when I began to seek the meaning of life and felt the necessity of living my own life, that mirror became for me unnecessary, superfluous, ridiculous, or painful. I could no longer soothe myself with what I now saw in the mirror, namely, that my position was stupid and desperate. It was all very well to enjoy the sight when in the depth of my soul I believed that my life had a meaning. Then the play of lights—comic, tragic, touching, beautiful, and terrible—in life amused me. But when I knew life to be meaningless and terrible, the play in the mirror could no longer amuse me. No sweetness of honey could be sweet to me when I saw the dragon and saw the mice gnawing away my support.

Nor was that all. Had I simply understood that life had no meaning I could have borne it quietly, knowing that that was my lot. But I could not satisfy myself with that. Had I been like a man living in a wood from which he knows there is no exit, I could have lived; but I was like one lost in a wood who, horrified at having lost his way, rushes about wishing to find the road. He knows that each step he takes confuses him more and more, but still he cannot help rushing about.

It was indeed terrible. And to rid myself of the terror I wished to kill myself. I experienced terror at what awaited me—knew that that terror was even worse than the position I was in, but still I could not patiently await the end. However convincing the argument might be that in any case some vessel in my heart would give way, or something would burst and all would be over, I could not patiently await that end. The horror of darkness was too great, and I wished to free myself from it as quickly as possible by a noose or bullet. That was the feeling which drew me most strongly towards suicide.

━━━━━━━━━

Not finding an explanation in science I began to seek for it in life, hoping to find it among the people around me. And I began to observe how the people around me—people like myself—lived, and what their attitude was to this question which had brought me to despair.

And this is what I found among people who were in the same position as myself as regards education and manner of life.

I found that for people of my circle there were four ways out of the terrible position in which we are all placed.

The first was that of ignorance. It consists in not knowing, not understanding, that life is an evil and an absurdity. People of this sort—chiefly women, or very young or very dull people—have not yet understood that question of life which presented itself to Schopenhauer, Solomon, and Buddha. They see neither the dragon that awaits them nor the mice gnawing the shrub by which they are hanging, and they lick the drops of honey. But they lick those drops of honey only for a while: something will turn their attention to the dragon and the mice, and there will be an end to their licking. From them I had nothing to learn—one cannot cease to know what one does know.

The second way out is epicureanism. It consists, while knowing the hopelessness of life, in making use meanwhile of the advantages one has, disregarding the dragon and the mice, and licking the honey in the best way, especially if there is much of it within reach. Solomon expresses this way out thus when I commended mirth, because a man hath no better thing under the sun, than to eat, and to drink, and to be merry: and that this should accompany him in his labour the days of his life, which God giveth him under the sun.

'Therefore eat thy bread with joy and drink thy wine with a merry heart . . . . Live joyfully with the wife whom thou lovest all the days of the life of thy vanity . . . for this is thy portion in life and in thy labours which thou takest under the sun. . . . Whatsoever thy hand findeth to do, do it with thy might, for there is no work, nor device, nor knowledge, nor wisdom, in the grave, whither thou goest.'

That is the way in which the majority of people of our circle make life possible for themselves. Their circumstances furnish them with more of welfare than of hardship, and their moral dullness makes it possible for them to forget that the advantage of their position is accidental, and that not everyone can have a thousand wives and palaces like Solomon, that for everyone who has a thousand wives there are a thousand without a wife, and that for each palace there are a thousand people who have to build it in the sweat of their brows; and that the accident that has today made me a Solomon may tomorrow make me a Solomon's slave. The dullness of these people's imagination enables them to forget the things that gave Buddha no peace—the inevitability of sickness, old age, and death, which to-day or to-morrow will destroy all these pleasures.

So think and feel the majority of people of our day and our manner of life. The fact that some of these people declare the dullness of their thoughts and imaginations to be a philosophy, which they call Positive, does not remove them, in my opinion, from the ranks of those who, to avoid seeing the question, lick the honey. I could not imitate these people; not having their dullness of imagination I could not artificially produce it in myself. I could not tear my eyes from the mice and the dragon, as no vital man can after he has once seen them.

The third escape is that of strength and energy. It consists of destroying life, when one has understood that it is an evil and an absurdity. A few exceptionally strong and consistent people act so. Having understood the stupidity of the joke that has been played on them, and having understood that it is better to be dead than to be alive, and that it is best of all not to exist, they act accordingly and promptly end this stupid joke since there are means: a rope round one's neck, water, a knife to stick into one's heart, or the trains on the railways; and the number of those of our circle who act in this way becomes greater and greater, and for the most part they act so at the best time of their life, when the strength of their mind is in full bloom and few habits degrading to the mind have as yet been acquired.

I saw that this was the worthiest way to escape and I wished to adopt it.

The fourth way out is that of weakness. It consists of seeing the truth of the situation and yet clinging to life, knowing in advance that nothing can come of it. People of this kind know that death is better than life, but not having the strength to act rationally—to end the deception quickly and kill themselves—they seem to wait for something. This is the escape of weakness, for if I know what is best and it is within my power; why not yield to what is best? . . . I found myself in that category.

———————

During that time this is what happened to me. During that whole year when I was asking myself almost every moment whether I should not end matters with a noose or a bullet—all that time, together with the course of thought and observation about which I have spoken, my heart was oppressed with a painful feeling, which I can only describe as a search for God.

I say that that search for God was not reasoning, but a feeling, because that search proceeded not from the course of my thoughts—it was even directly contrary to them—but proceeded from the heart. It was a feeling of fear, orphanage, isolation in a strange land, and a hope of help from someone.

Though I was quite convinced of the impossibility of proving the existence of a Deity (Kant had shown, and I quite understood him, that it could not be proved), I yet sought for God, hoped that I should find Him, and from old habit addressed prayers to that which I sought but had not found. I went over in my mind the arguments of Kant and Schopenhauer showing the impossibility of proving the existence of a God, and I began to verify those arguments and to refute them. Cause, said I to myself, is not a category of thought such as are Time and Space. If I exist, there must be some cause for it, and a cause of causes. And that first cause of all is what men have called 'God.' And I paused on that thought, and tried with all my being to recognize the presence of that cause. And as soon as I acknowledged that there is a force in whose power I am, I at once felt that I could live. But I asked myself: What is that cause, that force? How am I to think of it? What are my relations to that which I call 'God'? And only the familiar replies occurred to me: 'He is the Creator and Preserver.' This reply did not satisfy me, and I felt I was losing within me what I needed for my life. I became terrified and began to pray to Him whom I sought, that He should help me. But the more I prayed the more apparent it became to me that He did not hear me, and that there was no one to whom to address myself. And with despair in my heart that there is no God at all, I said: 'Lord, have mercy, save me! Lord, teach me!' But no one had mercy on me, and I felt that my life was coming to a standstill.

But again and again, from various sides, I returned to the same conclusion that I could not have come into the world without any cause or reason or meaning; I could not be such a fledgling fallen from its nest as I felt myself to be. Or, granting that I be such, lying on my back crying in the high grass, even then I cry because I know that a mother has borne me within her, has hatched me, warmed me, fed me, and loved me. Where is she—that mother? If I have been deserted, who has deserted me? I cannot hide from myself that someone bore me, loving me. Who was that someone? Again 'God'? He knows and sees my searching, my despair, and my struggle.

'He exists,' said I to myself. And I had only for an instant to admit that, and at once life rose within me, and I felt the possibility and joy of being. But again, from the admission of the existence of a God I went on to seek my relation with Him; and again I imagined *that* God—our Creator in Three Persons who sent His Son, the Saviour—and again *that* God, detached from the world and from me, melted like a block of ice, melted before my eyes, and again nothing remained, and again the spring of life dried up within me, and I despaired and felt that I had nothing to do but to kill myself. And the worst of all was, that I felt I could not do it.

Not twice or three times, but tens and hundreds of times, I reached those conditions, first of joy and animation, and then of despair and consciousness of the impossibility of living.

I remember that it was in early spring: I was alone in the wood listening to its sounds. I listened and thought ever of the same thing, as I had constantly done during those last three years. I was again seeking God.

'Very well, there is no God,' said I to myself; 'there is no one who is not my imagination but a reality like my whole life. He does not exist, and no miracles can prove His existence, because the miracles would be my imagination, besides being irrational.

'But my *perception* of God, of Him whom I seek,' I asked myself, 'where has that perception come from?' And again at this thought the glad waves of life rose within me. All that was around me came to life and received a meaning. But my joy did not last long. My mind continued its work.

'The conception of God is not God,' said I to myself. 'The conception is what takes place within me. The conception of God is something I can evoke or can refrain from evoking in myself. That is not what I seek. I seek that without which there can be no life.' And again all around me and within me began to die, and again I wished to kill myself.

But then I turned my gaze upon myself, on what went on within me, and I remembered all those cessations of life and reanimations that recurred within me hundreds of times. I remembered that I only lived at those times when I believed in God. As it was before, so it was now; I need only be aware of God to live; I need only to forget Him, or disbelieve Him, and I died.

What is this animation and dying? I do not live when I lose belief in the existence of God. I should long ago have killed myself had I not had a dim hope of finding Him. I live, really live, only when I feel Him and seek Him. 'What more do you seek?' exclaimed a voice within me. 'This is He. He is that without which one cannot live. To know God and to live is one and the same thing. God is life.'

'Live seeking God, and then you will not live without God.' And more than ever before, all within me and around me lit up, and the light did not again abandon me.

And I was saved from suicide. When and how this change occurred I could not say. As imperceptibly and gradually the force of life in me had been destroyed and I had reached the impossibility of living, a cessation of life and the necessity of suicide, so imperceptibly and gradually did that force of life return to me. And strange to say the strength of life which returned to me was not new, but quite old—the same that had borne me along in my earliest days.

I quite returned to what belonged to my earliest childhood and youth. I returned to the belief in that Will which produced me and desires something of me. I returned to the belief that the chief and only aim of my life is to be better, i.e. to live in accord with that Will. And I returned to the belief that I can find the expression of that Will in what humanity, in the distant past hidden from me, has produced for its guidance: that is to say, I returned to a belief in God, in moral perfection, and in a tradition transmitting the meaning of life. There was only this difference, that then all this was accepted unconsciously, while now I knew that without it I could not live.

Questions for Discussion

1. What question, or problem, does religion answer, according to Tolstoy? Do you agree with Tolstoy that religion is the *only* answer to this question? Give reasons for your answer.

2. Although Tolstoy found faith in God to be the source of the meaning he sought, he was not attracted to the kind of religion offered by the churches. Was this a contradiction in his views? Why or why not?

3. Tolstoy said that he considered, and rejected, the possibility that life simply has no meaning. What were his reasons for such a conclusion? Do you agree with them?

4. Explain, in your own words, the four ways Tolstoy thinks people try to come to terms with the question of life's meaning. Do you think there are others? Which one have *you* chosen?

CHAPTER 26

Arguments for God's Existence: The Ontological Argument

Are psychological grounds for belief in God—that is, our need for God—a sufficient basis for belief? Tolstoy asserted that, in his own search for meaning and significance in life, it was only after he had found God that life became meaningful. But is the human need for God due, as Tolstoy put it, to the inevitable emptiness that we feel apart from God? Or is it a creation occasioned by our weakness when faced with life's trials and tribulations? To answer this question we must go beyond the human need for God to rational grounds for knowledge claims about God. But can we claim to have knowledge of God? If so, how? If not, why not? Is such knowledge the result of reason and inference, of argument and analysis? Or does it come from some direct experience of the divine presence? The latter claim is made by the *mystics,* those who say they have had an experience of God. Usually mystics claim such experiences to be extremely private, and they are unable to describe this experience. Such experiences, they claim, are *ineffable,* beyond explanation and understanding. Mystical experience, indeed, religious experience in general, is itself a fascinating topic in the philosophy of religion, as well as a topic of interest to the psychology of religion. The American philosopher William James produced one of the classics dealing with this topic in his monumental work *Varieties of Religious Experience.* Rather than examine the nature, scope, and veracity of religious experience as evidence for the existence of God, we will turn instead to the arguments that have been advanced for God's existence.

Reason and Religion

Two things commend our attention to arguments for God's existence rather than to evidence for God's existence from religious experience. The first is that arguments are public; they can be examined by anyone and tested by the standards of logic, in contrast to religious experience, which tends to be private and perhaps even unexplainable. The second advantage offered by arguments for God's existence is that the religious heritage of the West has always given an important place to reason. In the Christian thought of the Middle Ages, reason and divine revelation (that is, holy scripture) were considered twin paths to the truth. According to this twofold truth view, there could be no contradiction between reason and revelation since truth was truth, no matter whether one arrived at it through reason unaided by revelation or from sacred scripture. If there appeared to be a conflict, it was due either to the faultiness of one's reasoning or error in one's interpretation of scripture.

It is therefore to a Christian thinker of the Middle Ages that we first turn for an argument for God's existence. It is an argument that continues to fascinate theologians and philosophers even though it was formulated nine hundred years ago. A vast contemporary literature has arisen dealing with the argument; even those thinkers who find the argument unconvincing still are fascinated by it. The argument is called the *ontological argument,* and its first proponent was St. Anselm.

The Ontological Argument

The term *ontological* comes from the Greek word for *being;* an ontological analysis is simply an analysis of the nature or being of something. Sometimes ontological analysis is virtually a synonym for what we have referred to as metaphysical analysis in Part 3. We could carry out an ontological analysis of anything—a chair, a table, a human being, a triangle, a painting. As part of our analysis we would attempt to define the object, to understand its nature and to

ANSELM OF CANTERBURY (1033–1109): A French monk who became one of the first major thinkers of the Middle Ages to defend rational analysis of theological doctrines. Born of a noble family, Anselm studied at the Benedictine Abbey at Le Bec and subsequently became a Benedictine. In 1093 he became the Archbishop of Canterbury. Courtesy of Topham Picture Source.

be able to list all its qualities or attributes. Another task of ontological analysis would be to distinguish between something that is merely imagined and something that is real. Remember that determining the difference between appearance and reality was one of the tasks of metaphysics.

Let us consider a painting as the object of our ontological analysis. Before the artist paints it, the painting is merely imagined. It does not exist until the painter commits it to canvas. Then the painting is both in the artist's understanding and exists as an object for others to examine. Would you say that the painting that has been painted by the painter is, in some sense, greater than the painting only imagined by the painter? If so, you would probably want to say that it is greater because the real painting is both as the artist imagined it *and* available as a reality to be examined by others. It certainly would seem strange to say that the imagined painting was greater than the real painting. We might say that the conception of the painter was greater than the painter's ability to draw, but that is only a comment about the painter's ability, not about the difference between appearance and reality. The real painting is *ontologically* greater than the imagined painting.

Armed with this commonsense distinction, Anselm proceeds to construct an argument for God's existence based on an analysis of the concept of God, or we could say on an ontological analysis of the concept of God.

What do we mean when we use the term *God?* Most Jews and Christians have meant a being that is greatest in power, in knowledge, in goodness, and in reality; in short, God is conceived as the most perfect being. This is a view of God that accords with the faith commitments of most believers, so Anselm uses it in his ontological analysis. God, according to Anselm's definition, is "that being than which none greater can be conceived." God is not only the greatest being, God is the greatest *conceivable* being.

Now, suppose someone says that such a being exists only in one's understanding. This is flatly contradictory, according to Anselm. For a being that existed *both* in the understanding *and* in reality would be greater than a being that existed in the understanding alone (remember the difference between the imagined and the real painting?). Therefore, a person who says that God exists only in the understanding is a fool ("The fool says in his heart, 'There is no God,'" Psalms 14:1). Anselm's argument is that to say that one has a conception of a nonexisting God would be as foolish as to say that one has a conception of a four-sided triangle, a round square, or a conception of water that is really fire.

Before looking at Anselm's argument, consider a word or two about who he was. Anselm was an eleventh century archbishop (of Canterbury, England). He lived at a time when Christianity provided the total intellectual and cultural milieu of Europe. But in addition to Christian influences, the intellectual heritage of Europe was Greek as well. And in Greek philosophy, reason held a prominent place. The Christian philosophers of the Middle Ages, as has already been mentioned, sought to meld faith and reason by showing that one could by reason discover what one also believed by faith. Anselm was a believer, but he sought a single argument for God's existence that would not depend upon sacred scripture or upon the faith commitments of the believer. When he discovered such an argument, he formulated it in a small document he entitled *Proslogion,* that is, a "dialogue." The form of the *Proslogion* is a meditation, an almost prayerlike statement to God of the argument and Anselm's thankfulness for being allowed to discover it. Before commenting further on the argument, we will look at Chapters II, III, and IV of the *Proslogion.*

St. Anselm Proslogion

Chapter II

And so, Lord, do thou, who dost give understanding to faith, give me, so far as thou knowest it to be profitable, to understand that thou art as we believe; and that thou art that which we believe. And, indeed, we believe that thou art a being than which nothing greater can be conceived. Or is there no such nature, since the fool hath said in his heart, there is no God? (Psalms xiv. i) But, at any rate, this very fool, when he hears of this being of which I speak—a being than which nothing greater can be conceived—understands what he hears, and what he understands is in his understanding; although he does not understand it to exist.

For it is one thing for an object to be in the understanding, and another to understand that the object exists. When a painter first conceives of what he will afterwards perform, he has it in his understanding, but he does not yet understand it to be, because he has not yet performed it. But after he has made the painting, he both has it in his understanding, and he understands that it exists, because he has made it.

Hence even the fool is convinced that something exists in the understanding at least, than which nothing greater can be conceived. For, when he hears of this, he understands it. And whatever is understood, exists in the understanding. And assuredly that, than which nothing greater can be conceived, cannot exist in the understanding alone. For, suppose it exists in the understanding alone: then it can be conceived to exist in reality, which is greater.

Therefore, if that than which nothing greater can be conceived, exists in the understanding alone, the very being, than which nothing greater can be conceived, is one than which a greater can be conceived. But obviously this is impossible. Hence there is no doubt that there exists a being than which nothing greater can be conceived, and it exists both in the understanding and in reality.

Reprinted from *St. Anselm: Basic Writings,* trans. by S. N. Deane, by permission of the Open Court Publishing Company, LaSalle, Illinois. Second Edition Copyright © by The Open Court Publishing Co. 1962.

Chapter III

And it assuredly exists so truly, that it cannot be conceived not to exist. For, it is possible to conceive of a being which cannot be conceived not to exist; and this is greater than one which can be conceived not to exist. Hence, if that, than which nothing greater can be conceived, can be conceived not to exist, it is not that, than which nothing greater can be conceived. But this is an irreconcilable contradiction. There is, then, so truly a being than which nothing greater can be conceived to exist, that it cannot even be conceived not to exist; and this being thou art, O Lord, our God.

So truly, therefore, dost thou exist, O Lord, my God, that thou canst not be conceived not to exist; and rightly. For if a mind could conceive of a being better than thee, the creature would rise above the Creator: and this is most absurd. And, indeed, whatever else there is, except thee alone, can be conceived not to exist. To thee alone, therefore, it belongs to exist more truly than all other beings, and hence in a higher degree than all others. For, whatever else exists does not exist so truly, and hence in a less degree it belongs to it to exist. Why, then, has the fool said in his heart, there is no God (Psalms xiv. 1), since it is so evident, to a rational mind, that thou dost exist in the highest degree of all? Why, except that he is dull and a fool.

Chapter IV

But how has the fool said in his heart what he could not conceive; or how is it that he could not conceive what he said in his heart, since it is the same to say in the heart, and to conceive.

But, if really, nay, since really he both conceived, because he said in his heart; and did not say in his heart, because he could not conceive; there is more than one way in which a thing is said in the heart or conceived. For, in one sense, an object is conceived when the word signifying it is conceived; and in another, when the very entity, which the object is, is understood.

In the former sense, then, God can be conceived not to exist; but in the latter not at all. For no one who understands what fire and water are can conceive fire to be water, in accordance with the nature of the facts themselves, although this is possible according to the words. So, then, no one who understands what God is can conceive that God does not exist; although he says these words in his heart, either without any, or with some foreign, signification. For, God is that than which a greater cannot be conceived. And he who thoroughly understands this, assuredly understands that this being so truly exists, that not even in concept can it be non-existent. Therefore, he who understands that God so exists cannot conceive that he does not exist.

I thank thee, gracious Lord, I thank thee; because what I formerly believed by thy bounty, I now so understand by thine illumination, that if I were unwilling to believe that thou dost exist, I should not be able not to understand this to be true.

The Ontological Argument In Recent Thought

Although first formulated in the eleventh century, the ontological argument continues to fascinate philosophers. In the seventeenth century, Descartes advanced an argument remarkably like that of Anselm, although there is no evidence that Descartes knew of Anselm's argument. In the eighteenth century Kant attacked the ontological argument as an example of the fallacious reasoning that the human mind falls into when it attempts to soar beyond its proper boundaries.

In the formulations of the ontological argument by both Descartes and Anselm, the assumption is made that existence is a perfection. To put this another way, both philosophers assume that existence is a quality that adds something to the concept of a thing. An existing triangle or painting is greater than the mere idea of a triangle or painting, since the real triangle and the real painting have an additional quality—existence—and hence are more perfect than the mere concept of them. Without the assumption that existence is a quality that can be predicated of a thing, neither Anselm's argument nor Descartes' formulation of the ontological argument is satisfactory, for they both argue that the most perfect being, or the being than which nothing greater can be conceived, would have to possess existence as one of the qualities or perfections that are part of the idea of God.

The assumption that existence is a perfection or quality was examined thoroughly by Immanuel Kant. We have already seen in the section on metaphysics something of the distinction Kant makes between *analytic* and *synthetic* statements, and this distinction is important to his criticism of the ontological argument. One aspect of his critique was to attempt to clarify the ambiguity that surrounds the use of the term *is,* or its other tense forms (*are, was,* etc.) when it is used as a synonym for *exists.* The forms of the verb *to be* function in different ways. Notice the ways they function in the following three sentences:

1. Bachelors are.
2. Bachelors are males.
3. Bachelors are deplorable.

Statement 1 is a claim that there are things in the world called bachelors, and we can substitute for the statement "bachelors are" the synonymous statement "bachelors exist." Statement 2 offers what Kant called an "identical proposition," that is, the predicate "males" is contained in the subject "bachelors."

There are several interesting things about statement 2. First, we can tell whether the statement is true or false simply by examining the meaning of the term *bachelors.* In a purely *a priori* fashion we can determine quite apart from sense experience, that the statement is true, assuming that we know the meaning of the English language and the term *bachelor.* Kant called this type of statement *analytic,* and a second interesting thing about analytic statements is that we cannot deny the predicate without contradicting ourselves. It would be an obvious contradiction to say that bachelors are not males, since the very meaning of the term *bachelor* implies maleness. We can, however, deny the predicate "males" without contradiction if we also deny the subject, that is, if we deny that there are things in the universe to which the name *bachelor* properly belongs. This may sound very strange when we are dealing with things such as bachelors, which we all agree exist. But suppose we are talking about unicorns. We can state that "unicorns are one-horned creatures," and this statement would be analytically true. However, we can deny that there are unicorns, and in so doing we are denying the subject (unicorn) with its predicates (one-horned). The very meaning of unicorn implies creatures with one horn; a two-horned unicorn would be as contradictory as a four-sided triangle.

Statement 3 is different from statement 2 in that it adds a predicate (deplorable) to the subject (bachelors). There is nothing in the concept of bachelor that leads us to say *a priori* that bachelors are deplorable. This statement may be true, or it may be false, and there is no way to determine which merely by examining the meaning of the terms, as we could do with statement 2. The only way to determine whether statement 3 is true or false is to appeal to experience—ours or that of someone else. In other words, statements like statement 3 can only be verified *a posteriori*. Kant called such statements *synthetic,* since the predicate adds something to the subject *(synthetic* literally means "putting together"). We take a predicate, or quality, and add it to a subject, and a synthetic statement results. In synthetic statements the predicate is what Kant called a *real* predicate, since it predicates something of the subject not contained in the idea of the subject itself. Unlike the predicates of analytic statements (which are not *real* predicates in Kant's sense), we can deny the predicates of synthetic statements without contradiction. It is not contradictory to say "Bachelors are not deplorable," for whether or not bachelors are deplorable can be discovered only by an appeal to our experience of bachelors.

In both statements 2 and 3, the term *are* functions only as a copula; it links the predicates with the subject. In neither case does it add anything to the subject. In statement 1, however, it appears that *are* does add something to the subject, namely, existence. But, according to Kant, when we use one of the forms of the verb *to be* to mean "exists," it does not serve as a predicate, since existence is not a real predicate. This is the basis for Kant's rejection of the ontological argument. To say that something exists in no way changes or adds to the concept of the thing (remember that Kant claims that existence is not a *real* predicate). What is the difference between an existing triangle and the mere concept of a triangle? Kant's reply is that *there is no real difference.* Both the existing triangle and the idea of a triangle contain the same predicates: three sides, three angles, and so on.

But surely, we might want to say, an existing triangle is different in some sense from the mere idea of a triangle. Any difference we might want to attribute to the existing triangle, however, has nothing to do with the nature of triangularity. About all we can say is that when we state that a triangle exists, we are making a claim that there are objects in reality to which we can correctly give the name *triangle* with all the predicates that inhere in this idea. In short, we are claiming that there is an instance of "triangle," the idea of which we can explore purely *a priori.* Whether or not something exists, though, is not a matter of *a priori* investigation but rather requires an appeal to the senses and hence is *a posteriori.*

Kant admits that it is possible to make analytically true statements about God. Such statements would include "God is all-powerful," "God is eternal," "God is infinite." All these statements derive their predicates from an analysis of the concept of God. What we cannot claim is that "existence" is one of the predicates that belongs to the idea of God, since existence is not a predicate. Hence the ontological argument is fallacious.

Existence Is Not a Quality

Kant's objections to the ontological argument may sound difficult, but the charges he makes against the argument amount principally to two:

1. Existence is not a perfection (or a quality or predicate) that can be added to a concept to change the concept in any way.
2. All existence statements are synthetic.

Most philosophers today would agree with Kant that existence is not a perfection. We do not speak of "existence," even in ordinary language, as something that changes the concept or idea of a thing. For example, if you were describing your ideal automobile, you could list all its qualities, among which would be that it has a turbo-charged engine, four-on-the floor, removable top, red paint, and so forth. No matter how exhaustive you might make this list of qualities, you would not include the statement, "and oh yes, it exists." There is nothing illogical about making such a statement, it just is not the way we ordinarily use language. But if existence is not a quality, what is it? To say that something exists is to claim that there is something in reality (in space and time and open to verification by experience) to which our concept refers. And how do we know the existence of something? Kant's answer is that the way we discover the existence of anything is by empirical verification. That is, our senses (or the senses of someone else) tell us whether or not a thing exists. That is what Kant means when he says that all existence claims are synthetic. We take a concept and add to it the claim that there is in fact something that can be experienced corresponding to our concept.

Therefore, Kant's claim that existence is not a predicate and that all existence statements are synthetic is another way of saying that all we can legitimately term "knowledge" must be derived from what we can experience with our senses. This, of course, would include what others have experienced and have related to us. But in general, Kant argues that unless a thing can be experienced, it cannot be known. This point brings us full circle—back to the question of religious experience with which we began Part 6. We seem to be as far from having a logical argument for God's existence as ever.

As we saw in the discussion of Kant in the section on metaphysics, the human mind is capable of asking a great many questions it cannot answer. The human mind being what it is, we want knowledge about things we cannot experience through the senses. We want to know about God. We want to know about the human soul, whether it is an indivisible unity, or whether it is composed of parts, or just if there is a human soul independent of the body. In addition, we want to ask questions about the universe: Did the world have a beginning in time, or is it eternal? While all these questions are interesting and arise in human consciousness inevitably, they cannot possibly be answered—at least if we accept Kant's view. As has already been pointed out during our discussion of metaphysics, Kant devotes considerable attention to showing that when philosophers attempt to answer such questions, they fall helplessly into confusion and phony reasoning. If Kant is right, then the ontological argument is only an enticing temptation to faulty reasoning.

Kant was not an atheist. He believed in God, and he believed that faith was philosophically defensible. But he insisted that we cannot *prove* that there is a God or claim to *know* that God exists. His attack on the ontological argument undercuts its attempt to provide a basis in knowledge for what we also believe by faith. Kant was arguing that there is no way we can go from the mere thought of something to the claim that it exists. To demonstrate existence requires that we be able to appeal to sense experience. But the ontological argument attempts precisely to argue for God's existence completely *a priori* and without any appeal to sense experience whatsoever.

The Ontological Argument's Ongoing Relevance

Does this mean that the ontological argument is entirely discredited and that in studying it we are merely exhuming a few bones of a philosophic carcass one thousand years old? Far from it. In spite of Kant's (and others') objections, the ontological argument is still debated by respectable philosophers. In fact, thinkers have consumed an astonishing amount of scholarly paper and ink in recent years in examining further the issues raised by Anselm. To conclude our examination of the ontological argument, we will briefly note two of these.

The objection that we cannot go from the mere thought of something to the existence of that thing is a fairly obvious rejoinder to the ontological argument. You may have thought of this objection yourself as you were reading through the argument. It is obvious that we can think of many things that have no real existence. The world of fiction and mythology is filled with them. Even on a more ordinary level, you can think of the perfect house you would like to build, or the most perfect painting you hope to paint, or whatever. In all these cases, you have no illusion that merely thinking about a thing proves that it exists or even that it will exist sometime in the future.

This obvious objection to the ontological argument was made to Anselm by a brother monk, Gaunilo, who wrote a treatise entitled "On Behalf of the Fool." Here Gaunilo attempted to show that the ontological argument was faulty, and his objection took the form of a counterexample. Think of the most perfect islands which, because they are situated in a remote part of the ocean, have not been discovered. They are islands of inestimable wealth; in fact, they are greater than all the countries now inhabited. And since they are the most perfect islands, and actually existing islands are more perfect than merely imaginary islands, these islands must exist. Guanilo did not think this argument was valid, but he argued that it was exactly like the ontological argument. Consequently, the ontological argument is invalid also.

In responding to Gaunilo, Anselm reiterated a form of the ontological argument he previously presented in Chapter III. (You might at this point go back and reread Chapters II and III of the Anselm selection.) Many philosophers have noticed that the form of the ontological argument in Chapter III is different from the form of the argument in Chapter II. It is not evident that Anselm was aware of the difference or that he had presented two different forms of the ontological argument.

The difference between these two forms of the argument centers on the kind of existence attributed to God. In his first argument (in Chapter II) Anselm merely speaks of the existence of a being than which nothing greater can be conceived. In his second argument (in Chapter III), Anselm speaks of God as existing *necessarily,* although he does not use those exact words. Here is how Anselm puts it:

> And it assuredly exists so truly, that it cannot be conceived not to exist. For it is possible to conceive of a being which cannot be conceived not to exist, and this is greater than one which can be conceived not to exist.

Contingent and Necessary Existence

The distinction between the two kinds of existence discussed previously is currently stated as the difference between *contingent existence* and *necessary existence.* That which exists contingently depends on something else for its existence. The notion of contingency has figured prominently in arguments for God's existence, and more will be said about it in the next chapter, which deals with cosmological arguments for God's existence.

Basic to a contingent being's existence is the possibility of its nonexistence. A tree, for example, is a contingent being. It depends upon soil or its equivalent, carbon dioxide, water, and light. Deprive it of any of these, and it will die. A tree is only one example. It seems, however, that everything in nature is contingent and dependent upon something else. A necessary being, in contrast, is not dependent upon anything else for its existence. And it is precisely the thought of God as a *necessary* being that Anselm proposes in his second form of the ontological argument.

The British philosopher Norman Malcolm has written extensively in defense of the ontological argument. He bases his defense on the claim that Anselm's formulation of the argument in terms of necessary existence avoids the usual criticisms. Malcolm agrees that contingent existence is not a perfection but argues that necessary existence is a perfection. That is, a necessary being is more perfect than a contingent being. Part of what is implied by the notion of a necessary being is a being whose nonexistence is logically impossible. Hence when opponents of the ontological argument say that all it proves is that "If God exists, then God exists necessarily," they are contradicting themselves. For the "if" of the above statement implies the possibility that God does not exist, but a necessary being cannot not exist.

We can summarize the differences between the two kinds of existence in the following way:

Contingent Existence	Necessary Existence
Nonexistence is possible	Nonexistence is impossible
Dependent	Independent
Not a quality or perfection	Is a perfection

Even if we accept the claim that necessary existence is a quality or perfection that is immune to Kant's attack on the ontological argument, what about Kant's claim that all existence statements are synthetic and must be proved by an appeal to sense experience? Malcolm responds by reminding us that in geometry we accept the proof that there is an infinite set of prime numbers. *In some sense,* then, we would want to say that an infinite set of prime numbers *exists,* although they do not exist in the same sense that tables, stones, and trees exist. And we can prove the theorem that there is an infinite set of prime numbers by the use of reason alone without any appeal to the senses, just as we can argue for the existence of God without appealing to experience.

Whereas Kant's attack on the ontological argument pointed out the ambiguity of the word *is,* Malcolm's defense of the argument turns on the ambiguity of the word *exists.* There may be many different senses in which things can exist, and in one of these senses one could say that the ontological argument proves that God exists. But in what sense? Do entities that exist in this sense exist in a greater degree? If so, what is this degree? And how can we be sure that we are not just playing verbal games?

There is another line of attack frequently made against the ontological argument, and it too has its origins in Kant's distinction between analytic and synthetic statements. One of the features of analytic statements is that their truth can be determined completely *a priori,* and such true statements are *necessarily true.* The truth of such statements cannot be disproved by experience because the truth (or falsity) of analytic statements is a function of the terms in the statement. Some philosophers have argued that, although we can perfectly well understand what it means to speak of a statement as being necessarily true, it makes no sense to speak of a *being* as necessarily existing. In other words, necessity is a property not of beings but of statements. Failure to see this leads us to think that we can go from making necessarily true statements about God to the conclusion that God necessarily exists.

We can summarize the usual attacks on the ontological argument as follows:

1. Existence is not a perfection or quality that adds to the concept of a thing.
2. All claims about existence are synthetic and are derived only from sense experience.
3. Necessity is a property of statements, not of beings.

Even though the ontological argument still has its defenders, there are many philosophers who have found other kinds of arguments for God's existence more attractive. We will consider some of these in the next chapter.

Questions for Discussion

1. A common objection to the ontological argument is that the fact that we can think of something is not proof that it exists. What would be Anselm's response to this objection?
2. Do you agree with Kant's claim that existence is not a predicate? Why or why not?
3. Is there a difference between viewing God as the *supreme being* and the *greatest conceivable being?* Give reasons for your answer.
4. The ontological argument has had a continuing attraction for philosophers since its inception in the eleventh century. To what do you attribute philosophers' fascination with it?
5. Do you find the ontological argument convincing? Why or why not?

CHAPTER 27

Arguments for God's Existence: The Cosmological Arguments

The trouble many people have with the ontological argument is that it seems to be spinning proofs out of thin air. It is abstract, removed from the reality of everyday life, and seems to be nothing other than a philosopher's trick. Since the ontological argument is an attempt to prove God's existence completely *a priori* and absolutely separate from any knowledge we have through the senses, it turns on definitions and distinctions that we have to accept before feeling the force of the argument. But there is another way. Jews and Christians have always believed that the world is the result of God's creative activity. If that is the case, then is there not some feature of the world that points to God as its creator? Those who think the answer to this question is yes are proponents of cosmological arguments for God's existence.

Nature: A Cosmos, Not a Chaos

The Greeks were the first Western thinkers to label nature a *cosmos,* an ordered system rather than a random chaos. The term *cosmos* itself comes from a Greek word that means to order or structure (note that "cosmetics" are another means of bringing order out of chaos). Some of the ancient Greek philosophers thought that the transition from chaos to order was due to something like chance; as particles of matter moved through the void, they eventually began to move in a spiral motion—like the spiral nebulae, had the Greeks been able to see them. From this motion there arose greater and greater order until eventually the world and all life on it arose. Other Greeks rejected sheer chance as the source of the world's order, arguing instead that the cause of the world is something more like mind or reason than anything else we can imagine it to be. This principle of ultimate order they referred to as God, though they did not conceive God in the same manner as did Jews and, later, as did Christians. For them, it was because all reality is permeated with rationality that we can search for and find rational explanations for nature's behavior.

On the side of chance were such Greek philosophers as Democritus, Leucippus, and the Epicurean philosophers. On the side of reason and God were such philosophers as Plato, Aristotle, and the Stoics. The debate over whether the world order has a rational cause or is due merely to chance combination of eternal bits of matter is older than the debate over God's existence. But as Christianity moved outward from its Palestinian origins to the world permeated by Greek philosophy and culture, it turned to categories of Greek philosophy to express the basic tenets of Christian doctrine. One area in which Greek thought had a direct impact was the construction of arguments for God's existence.

In neither the Jewish nor Christian Bibles is there any argument for God's existence. For the biblical writers, proving God's existence would be as pointless as trying to prove the existence of the air we breathe. The "fool" of Psalms 14:1 ("The fool has said in his heart, 'There is no God'") is the practical, not theoretical, atheist. The fool lives life as though there is no God, knowing full well that God exists. The religious problem reflected in Old Testament narratives is not atheism but polytheism, not the denial of God but the worship of too many gods. Likewise, in the New Testament, the reality of God is unquestioned due to the conviction that in Jesus of Nazareth the eternal God became flesh and dwelt among human beings. In its earliest missionary endeavors, Christians directed their preaching to Jews who accepted the reality of God. It was only later when Christian missionaries confronted a variety of naturalistic philosophies that they felt the need to argue philosophically for the existence of God. But even then, the task was not considered too formidable, for the basic structure of the arguments was already present in the writings of the Greek philosophers.

For the first thousand years of the existence of the faith, Christian writers found the most useful philosophical framework within the philosophy of Plato. Indeed, the ontological argument is highly compatible with the Platonic view of reality, about which more will be said later. Most of the works of Aristotle, in contrast, had been lost to Western scholars, and what was known of his philosophy was through the work of such Arabic commentators as Avicenna and Averoës. In the thirteenth century, Plato was considered to be the Christian philosopher; Aristotle was the pagan philosopher. In such a climate of opinion, Thomas Aquinas nonetheless found in Aristotle a better set of categories for communicating the Christian faith to the world. He was so successful in his use of Aristotelian thought that Thomistic thought became the official doctrinal framework of the Roman Catholic Church for centuries. Thomas' was no small achievement: He single-handedly transformed the perceptions of Aristotle as a pagan philosopher into the perceptions of him as *the* Christian philosopher. Frequently, Thomas refers to Aristotle simply as *the philosopher.*

Thomas Aquinas (1225–1274):
Born in Aquino in Italy, Thomas
studied at the University of Naples and
subsequently became a Dominican
monk. He entered the Dominican
College in Paris and later became a teacher
there. In the days of handwritten books, his
writings were voluminous, numbering over
twenty-five volumes in modern editions.
During his time, Aristotle's philosophy was
associated with Islam, due to Arabic scholars'
extensive use of his work. Thomas' most
astounding intellectual feat was to adapt the
philosophy of Aristotle as a vehicle for the
expression of Christian theology. His major
philosophical works are Summa Theologica
and Summa Contra Gentiles. *Courtesy of The*
Bettmann Archive.

The Disputed Question

The form adopted by Thomas in his presentation of the arguments for God's existence is known as the *disputed question*. It was a traditional pedagogical device
in the Middle Ages. In this exercise, a student was expected to give objections to
the thesis being presented, then present arguments for the thesis, and finally
give answers to the initial objections. It was his announcement of a willingness
to debate, in disputed fashion form, ninety-five theses that led Martin Luther to
nail his proclamation to the door of the parish church.

The arguments for God's existence that Thomas offered are found in two
places: his huge *Summa Theologica,* and his *Summa Contra Gentiles.* The first
was a handbook of Christian theology for theologians, offering arguments for
most points of doctrine. The latter was a handbook for missionaries to the pagan
world and offered arguments for the conversion of those who would not accept
the dictates of scripture. The arguments presented here are from the *Summa*
Theologica. Though a "handbook," it comprises over a dozen volumes, even in
modern editions.

An approach to religious questions of the form presented here by Thomas' arguments are often called *natural theology*. One way of defining natural theology
is to see it as a way of using what we know about nature to discover truths about
God. Can we legitimately infer from certain aspects of the natural order that the
most satisfactory explanation for these features of nature is that God exists?

Thomas clearly thinks the answer to that question is yes. Whereas the ontological argument is an argument completely *a priori,* the various cosmological arguments presented here are *a posteriori,* based on knowledge we first gain from the senses.

Before turning to the arguments proper, Thomas considers two objections (again, using standard disputed question format). The first objection to any argument for God is the presence of evil in the world. If there exists an all-powerful, all-good God, then there should not be evil in the world. But there is evil in the world. Therefore God does not exist. You will recognize this as a standard *modus tollens* argument. The second objection to arguments for the existence of God is that we can account for the world on its own without appealing to God as its cause. Therefore, any need for God to explain the world is superfluous. Thomas will return to these objections at the end of his proofs.

In order to give you the full flavor of the disputed-question format, and to allow you to encounter the arguments undisturbed by additional commentary, we will present the text from Thomas first and then follow it with our own exposition.

St. Thomas Aquinas: The Five Ways

Whether God Exists?

We proceed thus to the Third Article:

Objection 1. It seems that God does not exist; because if one of two contraries be infinite the other would be altogether destroyed. But the name God means that He is infinite goodness. If, therefore, God existed, there would be no evil discoverable; but there is evil in the world. Therefore God does not exist.

Objection 2. Further it is superfluous to suppose that what can be accounted for by a few principles has been produced by many. But it seems that everything we see in the world can be accounted for by other principles, supposing God did not exist. For all natural things can be reduced to one principle, which is nature; and all voluntary things can be reduced to one principle, which is human reason, or will. Therefore there is no need to suppose God's existence.

From Thomas Aquinas, *Summa Theologica,* Question 2, Article 3, in *Introduction to Saint Thomas Aquinas,* edited by Anton C. Pegis. New York: The Modern Library, 1948. Used by permission.

On the contrary, it is said in the person of God: *I am Who am* (Exodus 3:14) . . . .

The Existence of God can be proved in five ways.

The first and more manifest way is the argument from motion. It is certain and evident to our senses, that in the world some things are in motion. Now whatever is moved is moved by another, for nothing can be moved except it is in potentiality to that towards which it is moved; whereas a thing moves inasmuch as it is in act. For motion is nothing else than the reduction of something from potentiality to actuality. But nothing can be reduced from potentially to actuality, except by something in a state of actuality. Thus that which is actually hot, as fire, makes wood, which is potentially hot, to be actually hot, and thereby moves and changes it. Now it is not possible that the same thing should be at once in actuality and potentially in the same respect, but only in different respects. For what is actually hot cannot simultaneously be potentially hot; but it is simultaneously potentially cold. It is therefore impossible that in the same respect and in the same way a thing should be both mover and moved, *i.e.,* that it should move itself. Therefore, whatever is moved must be moved by another. If that by which it is moved be itself moved, then this also must needs be moved by another, and that by another again. But this cannot go on to infinity, because then there would be no first mover, and, consequently, no other mover, seeing that subsequent movers move only inasmuch as they are moved by the first mover; as the staff moves only because it is moved by the hand. Therefore it is necessary to arrive at a first mover, moved by no other; and this everyone understands to be God.

The second way is from the nature of efficient cause. In the world of sensible things we find there is an order of efficient causes. There is no case known (neither is it, indeed, possible) in which a thing is found to be the efficient cause of itself; for so it would be prior to itself, which is impossible. Now in efficient causes it is not possible to go on to infinity, because in all efficient causes following in order, the first is the cause of the immediate cause, and the intermediate is the cause of the ultimate cause, whether the intermediate cause be several, or one only. Now to take away the cause is to take away the effect. Therefore, if there be no first cause among efficient causes, there will be no ultimate, nor any intermediate, cause. But if in efficient causes it is possible to go on to infinity, there will be no first efficient cause, neither will there be an ultimate effect, nor any intermediate efficient causes; all of which is plainly false. Therefore it is necessary to admit a first efficient cause, to which everyone gives the name of God.

The third way is taken from possibility and necessity, and runs thus. We find in nature things that are possible to be and not to be, since they are found to be generated, and to be corrupted, and consequently, it is possible for them to be and not to be. But it is impossible for these always to exist, for that which can not-be at some time is not. Therefore, if everything can not-be, then at one time there was nothing in existence. Now if this were true, even now there would be nothing in existence, because that which does not exist begins to exist only through something already existing. Therefore, if at one time nothing was in existence, it would have been impossible for anything to have begun to exist; and thus even now nothing would be in existence—which is absurd. Therefore, not all beings are merely possible, but there must exist something the existence of which is necessary. But every necessary thing either has its necessity caused by another, or not. Now it is impossible to go on to infinity in necessary things which have their ne-

cessity caused by another, as has been already proved in regard to efficient causes. Therefore we cannot but admit the existence of some being having of itself its
own necessity, and not receiving it from another, but rather causing in others
their necessity. This all men speak of as God.

The fourth way is taken from the gradation to be found in things. Among beings there are some more and some less good, true, noble, and the like. But *more*
and *less* are predicated of different things according as they resemble in their different ways something which is the maximum, as a thing is said to be hotter according as it more nearly resembles that which is hottest; so that there is
something which is truest, something best, something noblest and, consequently, something which is most being, for those things that are greatest in truth are
greatest in being . . . . Now the maximum in any genus is the cause of all in that
genus, as fire, which is the maximum of heat, is the cause of all hot things . . .
Therefore there must also be something which is to all beings the cause of their
being, goodness, and every other perfection; and this we call God.

The fifth way is taken from the governance of the world. We see that things
which lack knowledge, such as natural bodies, act for an end, and this is evident
from their acting always, or nearly always, in the same way, so as to obtain the
best result. Hence it is plain that they achieve their end, not fortuitously but de-
signedly. Now whatever lacks knowledge cannot move towards an end, unless it
be directed by some being endowed with knowledge and intelligence; as the
arrow is directed by the archer. Therefore, some intelligent being exists by whom
all natural things are directed to their end; and this being we call God.

Reply Objection 1. As Augustine says: Since God is the highest good, He would
not allow any evil to exist in His works, unless His omnipotence and goodness
were such as to bring good men even out of evil. This is part of the infinite goodness of God, that He should allow evil to exist, and out of it produce good.

Reply Objection 2. Since nature works for a determinate end under the direction of a higher agent, whatever is done by nature must be traced back to God as
to its first cause. So likewise whatever is done voluntarily must be traced back to
some higher cause other than human reason and will, since these can change and
fail; for all things that are changeable and capable of defect must be traced back
to an immovable and self-necessary first principle, as has been shown.

First Argument From Change

The ancient Greeks were fascinated by change, for it seemed to them an intricate
puzzle. If something changed from A to B, it was *not-B* during the time it was A
(else it would not be changing). But for A to become B, it first had to cease being
A. But if it ceased to be A, how would it ever become B?

Let's restate this using "acorn" for A and "oak" for B. When an acorn becomes
an oak, it first ceases to be an acorn. But if while an acorn it is not yet an oak,
how, then, does it ever become an oak? If it were already an oak, it would not be

an acorn and would, in fact, not have changed at all. Aristotle dealt with these puzzles by distinguishing between two modes of being.

The acorn is *actually* an acorn but is *potentially* an oak. When it ceases to be an acorn and becomes an oak, it changes from its actual state to its potential state. It is now an oak. But an oak has other potentialities. It can become lumber that is used to make a house. So we can say that the oak is actually an oak but potentially a house. It actually becomes a house when someone acts on it to bring forth its potentialities.

We can generalize by saying that change is the movement from a thing's potentiality to its actuality. In the argument, the translator used the term *motion* to mean the same as *change,* since Aristotle defined *change* as movement from potentiality to actuality. In our experience, how do we account for something's potentiality? The answer is that it comes from some prior actuality. We get acorns from oaks. Aristotle, perhaps inadvertently, supplied the answer to the question "Which comes first, the chicken or the egg?" The chicken, of course; that is the prior actuality.

Thomas' second argument (which is really Aristotle's argument) is that all change presupposes some cause of that change. Nothing changes itself. Iron, in his example, is potentially hot but becomes actually hot when some source of change acts upon it. Since, in our experience, everything that changes is changed by something else, and nothing is its own source of change, we come to a choice. Either the series of changes is infinite and has no cause, or else there is at least one reality that is unchanged and is the source of change. The latter fits in better with our experience of the world and makes more sense to us. There must therefore be a first source of change which itself does not depend upon any prior actuality, and this is what we mean by God.

Most modern interpreters of the argument do not understand this argument to be pointing to an infinite series of changes and sources of changes stretching backward in time to a primordial big bang. They see it rather as a statement of the way the world is at every moment. Thomas is arguing that if the observable fact of change is to make sense to us, there must be some ultimate source for change outside the system of changes itself. And this is God.

The Argument from Causality

If you followed carefully the argument from change, you will recognize in Thomas' second argument—the argument from causality—the same basic structure. There is a certain fact about the world. We can account for this fact either by referring to God as its source, or we can assume that there is no satisfactory explanation. The fact to be explained: cause and effect.

Before looking at the argument in detail, we need to clarify Thomas' terminology. Again borrowing from Aristotle, Thomas used terms for causality that have pretty much dropped out of our philosophical vocabulary. When we say that

X causes Y, we mean a relationship such that *X* precedes *Y* in time and that *Y* is dependent upon *X.* Aristotle called this kind of causality the *efficient cause.* But Aristotle also used the term *cause* to refer to other than efficient causality. For example, *Y* may be related to *Z* as a future goal it will achieve. Aristotle referred to this kind of causality as the *final* cause. We can illustrate these two kinds of causality using the acorn-oak example cited previously. The efficient cause of the acorn is an oak tree. The final cause of the acorn is the oak tree the acorn will become. But these two causes do not exhaust the causal analysis we could perform. An acorn is an acorn because it is composed of a certain kind of matter; let's call this *acorn stuff.* Aristotle would refer to acorn stuff as the *material cause.* But there is more to an acorn than just being made of certain kinds of matter. There is also its form or structure that makes it an acorn and not a walnut. This structural differentiation Aristotle referred to as the *formal cause.*

Let's use another example. You are asked to write a paper for class. You are the efficient cause of your paper. The grade you hope for, or the knowledge you want to attain, is the final cause of the paper. The content is the material cause, and the structure you impose upon the words is the formal cause of the paper. Two different students may have the same material and final causes but not the same formal cause. Or at least they had better not if they want to avoid charges of plagiarism.

Now, among this set of causes, the efficient cause is the fact about the world that needs to be explained. Our experience of the world tells us that nothing causes itself, at least nothing within our experience is its own cause. Everything seems to depend upon something else as its cause. That cause, in turn, depends upon another cause, and so on. How far does this series of causes extend? Is it an endless chain of causes and effects? Or is there a first cause, something that is not caused by anything else? How do we choose between these two possibilities?

Thomas, of course, chooses the uncaused cause. His argument is as follows (and it is an argument of the *reductio ad absurdum* form). Suppose we assume that there is no first cause. Then we would have to conclude that all other causes in the series are intermediate. But if we deny the first cause, then there is no effect, that is, nothing to be the intermediate causes. But this is absurd. Therefore there must be a first cause. And that is what we mean by God.

We might depart from Thomas' form of the argument slightly but still be within its spirit by pointing out the following argument. Since the argument is *a posteriori,* based on our experience of the world, we can note that it would be unsatisfying from a logical point of view to deny that every effect has a cause. Suppose your television set quits working. You immediately assume something caused it to quit—some part failed, the TV station went off the air, the electricity was cut off. *Something* caused the TV set to quit. But let's suppose your roommate has a particularly stubborn frame of mind. She argues (having had a philosophy class) that there is no proof that every effect has a cause; maybe your TV set failed for no reason at all. "But," you say, "things do not happen for no reason at all. You must mean that you don't know the reason the set doesn't work."

"Not at all," she replies. "I meant exactly what I said. You are foolish to seek the cause of your TV set's failure, for there isn't any cause."

"That's not a logical explanation," you say. "Things *always* have a cause. I don't have to take a philosophy course to know *that.*"

Who is right in this philosophical debate? In a sense, both are. Can we prove that every effect has a cause? Probably not. No one has yet come up with a proof. But we do assume that every effect has a cause. Without this assumption the world just would not make sense to us. Is this assumption a psychological fact about our makeup? Or is it an insight into the way the world is? We really do not know. And, worse, we cannot know. If we assume that the series of causes and effects is infinite, that there is no first cause, then we have accepted a principle that leads to the view that the world cannot be understood logically. The retort to this is to say, as Bertrand Russell said, that when we find causes, we are satisfied. But when we look for them, sometimes we find them, sometimes we do not. The argument for the existence of God does not present us with an irrefutable proof. For consider this counterargument: Even though every member of a series of objects has a certain characteristic, the set as a whole may not share that same characteristic. Every human being has a mother; but this fact does not lead to the conclusion that the human race has a mother.

Again as in the case of the first argument, most modern interpreters do not understand the chain of causes and effects to be one stretching back in time. Rather, they interpret it as claiming that at every moment of time there is a series of dependencies such that all aspects of nature are caused, in the sense of being dependent upon something else. Either we accept the view that there is no ultimate cause of this series or the view that the series of causes is endless. But does the latter alternative make sense? Thomas gives us reasons in his third proof of thinking that it does not.

The Argument from Possibility and Necessity

Critical for understanding the third argument is the notion of *contingency.* A contingent being is a dependent being. The opposite of a contingent being is a necessary being. We saw in our discussion of the ontological argument that many thinkers have trouble with the notion of a necessary *being.* Statements can be necessary (that is, analytically true), but what does it mean to say that a being is necessary?

One reason we have trouble conceptualizing the notion of a necessary being is that we never encounter such a being in experience. Nothing in the world is necessary; everything is contingent, dependent upon something else. The relation between an effect and its efficient cause is a relationship of dependency. If X causes Y, then Y is dependent upon X. In a sense, the notion of contingency makes explicit at least one aspect of the relationship between cause and effect.

But the third argument is not just a restatement of the second argument. Thomas makes an interesting new argument. It turns on the notion of contingency. A contingent being is not only dependent, it is also merely *possible*. To say that something is merely possible is to say that it could exist, or it could not exist. But a merely possible being has no necessity for its existence. Even though it exists now, among its possibilities is the possibility of not existing.

If the universe is infinitely old, all possibilities would have been realized. Remember that among the possibilities of a merely contingent being is that of nonexistence. In an infinite past, all possibilities would have occurred, among which is the possibility of nonexistence. Therefore, one possibility is that nothing would exist if all beings are merely contingent. But something does exist; therefore not all beings are contingent. There must be one being that is necessary. And this is what we mean by God.

By this point it is clear what God's characteristics are. God is the unchanged source of change, the uncaused cause, the necessary being. To be necessary is to be radically nondependent. The term *aseity* is used to refer to this characteristic whereby God does not depend on anything else. The third argument, therefore, brings us back to the notion of God as a necessary being, and we have already seen the objections that have been lodged against the notion of a necessary *being*.

Thomas, however, gives us two additional arguments, neither of which depends upon this notion of a necessary being.

The Argument from Gradations of Being

Just as we describe degrees of heat and cold, good, true, more and less according to some standard, so also there must be a being by which all things *are*. Think of the argument in this way: We could make a catalog of existing things arranged in the order of their degree of reality. At the bottom of the list would be nonbeing or nothingness. Next in order of reality would be dreams and mental images. They have some reality but are not as real as the people who have them. Perhaps next in our catalog we would list fictional persons: Hamlet, Santa Claus, Mr. Pickwick. Next we would perhaps want to list physical objects. Then persons. Perhaps next would be principles that outlast any human being's knowledge of them —the principles of physics, mathematics, mechanics, and so on. We could discuss and argue about the proper order of our list, but however we constructed it, we could in principle arrange it so that we are going from those things with less being to those with more being or reality. If we are to construct such a list, there must be a first member of it, some being which is ultimate in reality in terms of which we judge all lesser things to be less real. That being we call God.

The fourth argument may be more difficult for us to understand than the others because we are not used to structuring the world in terms of a hierarchy of reality. Our natural tendency is to divide things into real and unreal. One can argue for a view presupposed by the fourth argument, but the problem with the argument is that one first has to be convinced that there are gradations of beings before the argument has any force. The argument does, however, point out one of the important ways of thinking about God. The argument assumes that being is a perfection; things with more being are more perfect than things with less being. If we equate existence with being, then we are back to one of the arguable points on which the ontological argument turns.

In Thomistic thought, again following Aristotle, anything that *is* must possess certain qualities common to all other beings. Sometimes these were called perfections; other times they were called *transcendental* perfections, transcendental because they are found in all realities. The list of transcendental perfections varied, but it usually contained the following: truth, goodness, beauty, and being. To say that these are perfections implies that they are positive attributes. Their opposites have no real existence. Evil is not a reality; it is rather the absence of goodness. Ugliness likewise is the absence of beauty. Nonbeing is the lack of being. Falsehood is the absence of truth. God, according to this view, is the highest instance of all these transcendental perfections. God is Truth, Beauty, Goodness, Being. Not only is God the highest instance of all these perfections, they come together in God in perfect unity. One definition of God would be the *unity of all transcendental perfections.*

Today one does not often encounter an argument for God's existence structured like Thomas' fourth argument. This is largely due to the changed way we view reality. It is no longer in fashion to construct what Arthur Lovejoy called the "great chain of being." So the fourth argument carries very little weight these days. But the fifth argument is probably the most popular argument ever constructed for the existence of God, and today it is as widely supported as ever.

The Argument from Design

The last of Thomas' arguments is based on the observance of order and apparent purpose in the world. We observe natural processes that appear to be working toward an end. The purpose of nature seems to be to sustain life. The purpose of life seems to be to give rise to thought. What is more reasonable, to believe that the apparent design in the world is due to chance, or to accept the view that design is the result of the activity of a designer? Even if one does not accept the interpretation that nature exhibits purposes, there is still the incredible complexity of the world to be explained. The fifth argument directs us to God as the most adequate explanation for such complexity.

Although the theory of evolution was unknown in Thomas' day, an evolutionary view would not, by itself, undercut the argument. Indeed, a supporter of the argument could use evolution as a proof rather than a disproof of the existence of God, seeing evolution simply as the means of divine creation. The nineteenth-

WILLIAM PALEY (1743–1805): English clergyman and philosopher who taught at Cambridge University and whose writings were widely read and used as textbooks. In addition to Natural Theology, *he wrote* A View of the Evidences of Christianity *and* The Principles of Moral and Political Philosophy. *Courtesy of the Library of Congress.*

century French philosopher Henri Bergson in his book *Creative Evolution* argues precisely that.

The design argument reached its height of popularity in the eighteenth century. Its most famous proponent was William Paley, whose book *Natural Theology* devoted a great deal of attention to the design argument. Even Kant, who attacked most of the arguments for God's existence, thought the design argument was the best of the traditional arguments, although he pointed out that it did not lead to the God of traditional religious belief. At most, the design argument points toward an architect, a designer of the world, not necessarily the God of traditional Jewish and Christian belief. Nor does it inevitably point to a God of unlimited power and might, or to the conception of God as a necessary being. The argument supports the view of God as a being of great, but perhaps limited, power, of intelligence but not of omniscience. Although a limited God may not be the traditional God of Jewish and Christian faith, this view of God does offer a solution to the problem of evil. There is evil in the world because God is incapable of preventing it. The American philosopher William James found the notion of a limited God attractive precisely because it provided a rational response to the problem of evil. A similar view of God is supported by a movement known as *process theology*. According to this view, God is not identified as the principle of being but rather as the principle of value. God is good but not necessarily all-powerful. We are called on to carry on God's work of bringing about as much goodness in the world as possible. By so doing, we share in God's nature and in the process of extending goodness in the world. Such a view of God, though perhaps popular to modern sensibilities, was most decidedly not the concept of God Thomas was supporting.

Since the fifth argument has enjoyed continuing support from the time Thomas stated it in the thirteenth century, we will conclude this chapter on the cosmological arguments with a selection from William Paley's classic formulation of the argument.

William Paley: Natural Theology

Chapter I. State of the Argument.

In crossing a heath, suppose I pitched my foot against a *stone,* and were asked how the stone came to be there; I might possibly answer, that, for anything I knew to the contrary, it had lain there forever nor would it perhaps be very easy to show the absurdity of this answer. But suppose I had found a *watch* upon the ground, and it should be inquired how the watch happened to be in that place; I should hardly think of the answer which I had before given, that, for anything I knew, the watch might have always been there. Yet why should not this answer serve for the watch as well as for the stone? Why is it not as admissible in the second case, as in the first? For this reason, and for no other, viz. that, when we come to inspect the watch, we perceive (what we could not discover in the stone) that its several parts are framed and put together for a purpose, e.g. that they are so formed and adjusted as to produce motion, and that motion so regulated as to point out the hour of the day; that if the different parts had been differently shaped from what they are, of a different size from what they are, or placed after any other manner, or in any other order, than that in which they are placed, either no motion at all would have been carried on in the machine, or none which would have answered the use that is now served by it. To reckon up a few of the plainest of these parts, and of their offices, all tending to one result: —We see a cylindrical box containing a coiled elastic spring, which, by its endeavor to relax itself, turns round the box. We next observe a flexible chain (artificially wrought for the sake of flexure) communicating the action of the spring from the box to the fusee. We then find a series of wheels, the teeth of which catch in, and apply to each other, conducting the motion from the fusee to the balance, and from the balance to the pointer; and at the same time, by the size and shape of those wheels, so regulating that motion, as to terminate in causing an index;

From William Paley, *Natural Theology.* The drawings are by James Paxton from an American edition of the work in 1864.

by an equable and measured progression, to pass over a given space in a given time. We take notice that the wheels are made of brass in order to keep them from rust; the springs of steel, no other metal being so elastic; that over the face of the watch there is placed a glass, a material employed in no other part of the work; but in the room of which, if there has been any other than a transparent substance, the hour could not be seen without opening the case. This mechanism being observed (it requires indeed an examination of the instrument, and perhaps some previous knowledge of the subject to perceive and understand it; but being once, as we have said, observed and understood,) the inference, we think, is inevitable; that the watch must have had a maker; that there must have existed, at sometime, and at some place or other, an artificer or artificers, who formed it for the purpose which we find it actually to answer; who comprehended its construction, and designed its use.

I. Nor would it, I apprehend, weaken the conclusion, that we had never seen a watch made: that we had never known an artist capable of making one; that we were altogether incapable of executing such a piece of workmanship ourselves or of understanding in what manner it was performed; all this being no more than what is true of some exquisite remains of ancient art, of some lost arts, and, to the generality of mankind, of the more curious productions of modern manufacture. Does one man in a million know how oval frames are turned? Ignorance of this kind exalts our opinion of the unseen and unknown artist's skill, if he be unseen and unknown, but raises no doubt in our minds of the existence and agency of such an artist, at some former time, and in some place or other. Nor can I perceive that it varies at all the inference, whether the question arise concerning human agent, or concerning an agent of a different species, or an agent possessing, in some respects, a different nature.

II. Neither, secondly, would it invalidate our conclusion, that the watch sometimes went wrong, or that it seldom went exactly right. The purpose of the machinery, the design and the designer, might be evident, and in the case supposed would be evident, in whatever way we accounted for the irregularity of the movement, or whether we could account for it or not. It is not necessary that a machine be perfect, in order to show with what design it was made: still less necessary, where the only question is, whether it were made with any design at all.

III. Nor thirdly, would it bring any uncertainty into the argument, if there were a few parts of the watch, concerning which we could not discover or had not yet discovered, in what manner they conduced to the general effect; or even some parts, concerning which we could not ascertain whether they conduced to that effect in any manner whatever. For, as to the first branch of the case; if by the loss, or disorder, or decay of the parts in question, the movement of the watch were found in fact to be stopped or disturbed, or retarded, no doubt would remain in our minds as to the utility or intention of these parts, although we should be unable to investigate the manner according to which, or the connection by which, the ultimate effect depended upon their action or assistance; and the more complex is the machine, the more likely is this obscurity to arise. Then as to the second thing supposed, namely, that there were parts which might be spared, without prejudice to the movement of the watch, and that we had proved this by experiment—these superfluous parts, even if we were completely assured that they were such, would not vacate the reasoning which we had instituted concerning other parts. The indication of contrivance remained, with respect to them, nearly as it was before.

IV. Nor, fourthly, would any man in his senses think the existence of the watch, with its various machinery, accounted for, by being told that it was one out of possible combinations of material forms; that whatever he had found in the place where he found the watch, must have contained some internal configuration or other; and that this configuration might be the structure now exhibited, viz. of the works of a watch, as well as a different structure.

V. Nor, fifthly, would it yield his inquiry more satisfaction to be answered, that there existed in things a principle of order, which had disposed the parts of the watch into their present form and situation. He never knew a watch made by the principle of order; nor can he even form to himself an idea of what is meant by a principle of order distinct from the intelligence of the watchmaker.

VI. Sixthly, he would be surprised to hear that the mechanism of the watch was no proof of contrivance, only a motive to induce the mind to think so.

VII. And not less surprised to be informed that the watch in his hand was nothing more than the result of the laws of *metallic* nature. It is a perversion of language to assign any law as the efficient, operative cause of anything. A law presupposes an agent; for it is only the mode according to which an agent proceeds: it implies a power; for it is the order, according to which that power acts. Without this agent, without this power, which are both distinct from itself, the *law* does nothing; is nothing. The expression, "the law of metallic nature," may sound strange and harsh to a philosophic ear; but it seems quite as justifiable as some others which are more familiar to him, such as "the law of vegetable nature," "the law of animal nature," or indeed as "the law of nature" in general, when assigned as the cause of phenomena, in exclusion of agency and power; or when it is substituted into the place of these.

VIII. Neither lastly would our observer be driven out of his conclusion, or from his confidence in its truth, by being told that he knew nothing at all about the matter. He knows enough for his argument. He knows the utility of the end: he knows the subserviency and adaptation of the means to the end. These points being known, his ignorance of other points, his doubts concerning of the points, affect not the certainty of his reasoning. The consciousness of knowing little need not beget a distrust of that which he does know.

Before going on to Paley's application of the argument to a specific example of design, we should review the case he has presented for the argument. The argument itself is an argument from analogy. We could indicate the analogous relationship as follows:

Watch   :   Watchmaker

World   :   ?

Paley's answer is that the analogue to watchmaker is God. To support this analogous relationship Paley assembled an amazing catalog of examples of design, everything from the intricacies of a woodpecker's tongue to planetary motion. During the nineteenth century, much study of nature was defended on the grounds that it provided additional evidence of design, and it was not until much later that the study of nature was justifiable on its own ground.

Paley was aware of arguments against his position, and he offered answers without restating the objections. We can infer the objections from his answers as follows:

Objection 1.   *How do you know God made the world? You have never seen a world made.* Paley's answer is that when I look at a watch, the very intricateness of the mechanism would convince us that there was a watchmaker, even if we had never seen a watch made. The same thing goes for the world.

Objection 2.   *There is also evidence of lack of design in the world. A well-designed world would not contain cancer, starvation, crop failure, and the hundreds of other deficiencies that produce human suffering. Does that not argue against a designer?* Paley's answer is that just as it would not weaken our inference from watch to watchmaker if the watch does not appear to work perfectly, we can also infer that the world was the result of creative intelligence even though it contains some disorder.

Objection 3.   *You do not know enough about the world to know if it exhibits design or not.* I do not have to know all the parts of the watch to see evidence of design; similarly, it does not destroy the analogy to admit that there are parts of nature we do not understand.

Objection 4.   *The world could have come into being as the result of the random or chance operation of impersonal forces, just as the Greek philosophers thought. That explanation is just as good as the one that sees the world as being the product of a designer.* Paley's answer is that just as it is more reasonable to infer that the watch is the product of intelligent design rather than that its intricacy was only one of many possible combinations, so it also is more reasonable to think of the world as due to design rather than chance.

Objection 5.   *Nature itself may contain a principle of order which produces the apparent design we see.* When we go back to the analogy, we see that we would not account for the watch by saying that it contained some principle of order that arranged its part into an intricate mechanism. Just as we would not accept this explanation as reasonable when applied to the watch, so we should not accept it when applied to the world.

Objection 6.   *It is not the order of the world but rather an inclination of your mind that results in your assumption of design in the world.* Such an objection would seem foolish when used against the watch analogy. It is no less inadequate when used against the argument for God's existence based on design.

Objection 7.   *What you think is the result of design is really the product of the laws of nature.* How convincing would it be to assume that the watch came into existence as a result of the laws of metallic nature? Hardly convincing at all. The same is true of an appeal to the laws of nature as the source of nature's design.

Objection 8.   *Only scientists are really in a position to know the cause of the world. You are too ignorant of natural processes to argue for the existence of God on the basis of the alleged design found in the world.* One does not have to be an expert on watchmaking to reason from watch to watchmaker. Similarly, even the scientific layman knows enough to argue from the design apparent in the world to God as its source.

At this point Paley turns to another objection. We might state it as follows: *If you discovered in the watch a mechanism for producing other watches, that would destroy the analogy. Nature exhibits precisely such a mechanism. Therefore, it is nature itself, not God, that is the source of the apparent design in the world.* Paley pointed out that evidence of such a mechanism in a watch would be but another evidence of the intelligence of the watchmaker, not an argument against the existence of the watchmaker. So it is with God and the world. It is this line of argument that Paley would probably have pursued against the theory of evolution, had he known about it. Charles Darwin's book *On the Origin of Species by Means of Natural Selection* appeared in 1859. Paley published his Natural Theology in 1802, the full title of which was *Natural Theology: or, Evidences of the Existence and Attributes of the Deity Collected from the Appearances of Nature.* The following discussion shows how Paley might have responded to the theory of evolution had he been aware of it.

===

Chapter II. State of the Argument Continued.

Suppose, in the next place, that the person who found the watch, should, after sometime, discover, that, in addition to all the properties which he had hitherto observed in it, it possessed the unexpected property of producing, in the course of its movement, another watch like itself, (the thing is conceivable;) that it contained within it a mechanism, a system of parts, a mould for instance, or a complex adjustment of lathes, files, and other tools, evidently and separately calculated for this purpose; let us inquire, what effect ought such a discovery to have upon his former conclusion.

I. The first effect would be to increase his admiration of the contrivance, and his conviction of the consummate skill of the contriver. Whether he regarded the object of the contrivance, the distinct apparatus, the intricate, yet in many parts intelligible mechanism, by which it was carried on, he would perceive, in this new observation, nothing but an additional reason for doing what he had already done,—for referring the construction of the watch to design, and to supreme art. If that construction *without* this property or, which is the same thing, before this property had been noticed, proved intention and art to have been employed about it, still more strong would the proof appear, when he came to the knowledge of this farther property, the crown and perfection of all the rest.

II. He would reflect, that though the watch before him were, *in some sense,* the maker of the watch which was fabricated in the course of its movements, yet it was in a very different sense from that in which a carpenter, for instance, is the maker of a chair; the author of its contrivance, the cause of the relation of its parts to their use. With respect to these, the first watch was no cause at all to the second: in no such sense as this was it the author of the constitution and order, either of the parts which the new watch contained, or of the parts by the aid and instrumentality of which it was produced. We might possibly say, but with great latitude of expression, that a stream of water ground corn; but no latitude of expression would allow us to say, no stretch of conjecture could lead us to think, that the stream of water built the mill, though it were too ancient for us, to know who the builder was. What the stream of water does in the affair, is neither more nor less than this; by the application of an unintelligent impulse to a mechanism previously arranged, arranged independently of it, and arranged by intelligence, an effect is produced, viz. the corn is ground. But the effect results from the arrangement. The force of the stream cannot be said to be the cause or author of the effect, still less of the arrangement. Understanding and plan in the formation of the mill were not the less necessary, for any share which the water has in grinding the corn; yet is this share the same as that which the watch would have contributed to the production of the new watch, upon the supposition assumed in the last section. Therefore,

III. Though it be now no longer probable, that the individual watch which our observer had found was made immediately by the hand of an artificer, yet doth not this alteration in any-wise affect the inference, that an artificer had been originally employed and concerned in the production. The argument from design remains as it was. Marks of design and contrivance are no more accounted for now than they were before. In the same thing, we may ask for the cause of different properties. We may ask for the cause of the color of a body, of its hardness, of its heat; and these causes may be all different. We are now asking for the cause of that subserviency to a use, that relation to an end, which we have remarked in the watch before us. No answer is given to this question by telling us that a preceding watch produced it. There cannot be design without a designer; contrivance, without a contriver; order, without choice; arrangement, without anything capable of arranging; subserviency and relation to a purpose, without that which could intend a purpose; means suitable to an end, and executing their office in accomplishing that end, without the end ever having been contemplated, or the means accommodated to it. Arrangement, disposition of parts, subserviency of means to an end, relation of instruments to a use, imply the presence of intelligence and mind. No one, therefore, can rationally believe, that the insensible, inanimate watch, from which the watch before us issued, was the proper cause of the mechanism we so much admire in it;—would be truly said to have

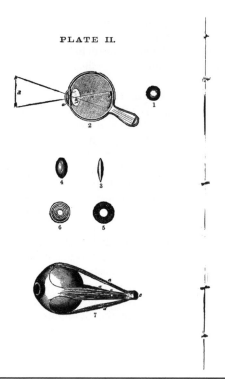

PLATE II.

CHAPTER III.

PLATE II. — THE EYE.

FIG. 1. The *crystalline lens of a fish*; it is proportionably larger than in other animals, and perfectly spherical.

FIG. 2. A section of the human eye. It is formed of various *coats*, or membranes, containing pellucid humours of different degrees of density, and calculated for collecting the rays of light into a focus, upon the nerve situated at the bottom of the eye-ball. The external membrane, called *sclerotic*, is strong and firm; and is the support of the spherical figure of the eye: it is deficient in the centre, but that part is supplied by the *cornea*, which is transparent and projects like the segment of a small globe from one of larger size. The interior of the sclerotic is lined by the *choroid*, which is covered by a dark mucous secretion, termed *pigmentum nigrum*, intended to absorb the superfluous rays of light. The *choroid* is represented in the plate by the black line. The third and inner membrane, which is marked by the white line, is the *retina*, the expanded optic nerve.

Within these coats of the eye, are the *humours*. *a*, the *aqueous* humour, a thin fluid like water; *b*, the *crystalline lens*, of a dense texture; *c*, the *vitreous* humour, a very delicate gelatinous substance, named from its resemblance to melted glass. Thus the crystalline is more dense than the vitreous, and the vitreous more dense than the aqueous humour: they are all perfectly transparent, and together make a compound lens, which refracts the rays of light issuing from an object, *d*, and delineates its figure *e*, in the focus upon the retina, inverted.

FIG. 3. The *lens of the telescope.*

FIG. 4. The crystalline *lens*, or, as it has been called, the crystalline humour, of the eye.

FIG. 5, 6. A plan of the circular and radiated fibres which the *iris* is supposed to possess; the former contracts, the latter dilates the pupil, or aperture formed by the inner margin of the iris.

FIG. 7. *a, a, a, a*, the four *straight* muscles, arising from the bottom of the orbit, where they surround, *c*, the optic nerve; and are inserted by broad, thin tendons at the fore part of the globe of the eye into the tunica sclerotica.

311

James Paxton supplied notes, plates and illustrations, two of which are reprinted here from the American edition of Natural Theology *of 1864.*

constructed the instrument, disposed its parts, assigned their office, determined their order, action, and mutual dependency, combined their several motions into one result, and that also a result connected with the utilities of other beings. All these properties, therefore, are as much unaccounted for as they were before.

IV. Nor is anything gained by running the difficulty farther back, *i.e.* by supposing the watch before us to have been produced from another watch, that from a former, and so on indefinitely. Our going back ever so far brings us no nearer to the least degree of satisfaction upon the subject. Contrivance is still unaccounted for. We still want a contriver. A designing mind is neither supplied by this supposition, nor dispensed with. If the difficulty were diminished the farther we went back, by going back indefinitely we might exhaust it. And this is the only case to which this sort of reasoning applies. Where there is a tendency, or, as we increase the number of terms, a continual approach towards a limit, *there,* by supposing the number of terms to be what is called infinite, we may conceive the limit to be attained; but where there is no such tendency, or approach, nothing is effected by lengthening the series. There is no difference, as to the point in question, (whatever there may be as to many points,) between one series and another; between a series which is finite, and a series which is infinite. A chain, composed of an infi-

PLATE I.

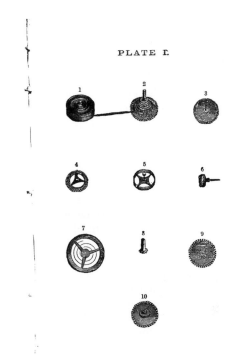

CHAPTER 1.

PLATE I. — THE WATCH.

FIG. 1. The *box*, or *barrel*, containing the main spring, which is the first power; and the *chain*, which communicates the power to—

FIG. 2. The *fusee* and *great* wheel. The fusee is tapered at the top to correct the irregular recoil of the spring. The great wheel turns—

FIG. 3. The *centre* wheel and pinion, which makes one revolution in an hour, carries the minute hand, and turns—

FIG. 4. The *third* wheel and pinion, which turns the contrite wheel.

FIG. 5. The *contrite* wheel, which makes one revolution in a minute, and turns the balance or escape wheel.

FIG. 6. The *balance* wheel, which acts upon the pallats of the verge, and escapes or drops from one pallat to another alternately, thereby keeping the balance in constant vibration.

FIG. 7. The *balance verge* and *balance* or *pendulum spring*, which regulates the whole machine.

FIG. 8. The *cannon pinion*, affixed to the centre wheel arbour, on which the minute hand is placed.

FIG. 9. The *minute* wheel.

FIG. 10. The *hour* wheel. The two last mentioned wheels are turned by the cannon pinion, and having a greater number of teeth, move much slower than the cannon pinion, and mark the hour by the hand on the dial.

The above is a description of the several wheels alluded to by Paley. Their relative situation, and combined movement, may be seen by the simple inspection of a watch.

306

nite number of links, can no more support itself, than a chain composed of a finite number of links. And of this we are assured, (though we never *can* have tried the experiment,) because, by increasing the number of links, from ten, for instance, to a hundred, from a hundred to a thousand, &c. we make not the smallest approach, we observe not the smallest tendency, towards self-support. There is no difference in this respect (yet there may be a great difference in several respects) between a chain of a greater or less length, between one chain and another, between one that is finite and one that is infinite. This very much resembles the case before us. The machine which we are inspecting demonstrates, by its construction, contrivance and design. Contrivance must have had a contriver; design, a designer; whether the machine immediately proceeded from another machine or not. That circumstance alters not the case. That other machine may, in like manner, have proceeded from a former machine: nor does that alter the case; contrivance must have had a contriver. That former one from one preceding it: no alteration still; a contriver is still necessary. No tendency is perceived, no approach towards a diminution of this necessity. It is the same with any and every succession of these machines; a succession of ten, of a hundred, of a thousand; with one series as with another; a series which is finite, as with a series which is infinite.

In whatever other respects they may differ, in this they do not. In all, equally, contrivance and design are unaccounted for.

The question is not simply, How came the first watch into existence? which question, it may be pretended, is done away by supposing the series of watches thus produced from one another to have been infinite, and consequently to have had no such *first,* for which it was necessary to provide a cause. This, perhaps, would have been nearly the state of the question, if nothing had been before us but an unorganized, unmechanized substance, without mark or indication of contrivance. It might be difficult to show that such substance could not have existed from eternity, either in succession (if it were possible, which I think it is not, for unorganized bodies to spring from one another), or by individual perpetuity. But that is not the question now. To suppose it to be so, is to suppose that it made no difference whether we had found a watch or a stone. As it is, the metaphysics of that question have no place; for, in the watch which we are examining, are seen contrivance, design; an end, a purpose; means for the end, adaptation to the purpose. And the question which irresistibly presses upon our thoughts, is, whence this contrivance and design? The thing required is the intending mind, the adapting hand, the intelligence by which that hand was directed. This question, this demand, is not shaken off, by increasing the number or succession of substances, destitute of these properties; nor the more, by increasing that number to infinity. If it be said, that, upon the supposition of one watch being produced from another in the course of that other's movements, and by means of the mechanism within it, we have a cause for the watch in my hand, viz. the watch from which it proceeded: I deny, that for the design, the contrivance, the suitableness of means to an end the adaptation of instruments to a use, (all which we discover in a watch,) we have any cause whatever. It is in vain, therefore, to assign a series of such causes, or to allege that a series may be carried back to infinity; for I do not admit that we have yet any cause at all of the phenomena, still less any series of causes either finite or infinite. Here is contrivance, but no contriver: proofs of design, but no designer.

V. Our observer would farther also reflect, that the maker of the watch before him, was, in truth and reality, the maker of every watch produced from it; there being no difference (except that the latter manifests a more exquisite skill) between the making of another watch with his own hands, by the mediation of files, lathes, chisels, &c. and the disposing, fixing, and inserting of these instruments, or of others equivalent to them, in the body of the watch already made, in such a manner as to form a new watch in the course of the movements which he had given to the old one. It is only working by one set of tools instead of another.

The conclusion which the *first* examination of the watch, of its works, construction, and movement, suggested, was, that it must have had, for the cause and author of that construction, an artificer, who understood its mechanism, and designed its use. This conclusion is invincible. A *second* examination presents us with a new discovery. The watch is found, in the course of its movement, to produce another watch, similar to itself: and not only so, but we perceive in it a system or organization, separately calculated for that purpose. What effect would this discovery have or ought it to have, upon our former inference? What, as hath already been said, but to increase, beyond measure, our admiration of the skill which had been employed in the formation of such a machine! Or shall it, instead of this, all at once turn us round to an opposite conclusion, viz. that no art or skill whatever has been concerned in the business, although all other evidences of art and skill remain as they were, and this last and supreme piece of art be now added to the rest? Can this be maintained without absurdity? Yet this is atheism.

Is the design argument completely convincing? Obviously not. Otherwise there would be no atheists. Even believers in God would probably agree that the design argument is inconclusive: It gives some but not absolute evidence of God's existence. If the design argument were completely convincing, if there were no plausible counterarguments to it, then we would not *believe* in God but would *know* that there was a God. This state of affairs, however, would fundamentally change our relationship to God, a relationship based on faith commitments.

Questions for Discussion

1. State in your own words the feature of an argument for God's existence that makes it a *cosmological* argument.

2. Thomas' arguments from change and causality are based on the notion of *contingency.* Explain how this notion is vital to the success of the arguments.

3. Does the theory of evolution undercut the argument from design? Why or why not?

4. Does the argument from design lead to the same conception of God as does the ontological argument? Give reasons for your answer.

5. Of the arguments for God's existence we have surveyed, which do you find most convincing? Least convincing?

CHAPTER 28

The Problem of Evil

All the arguments *for* belief in God have to confront a major argument *against* belief in God: the problem of evil. The problem can be stated in many ways, but perhaps the clearest was the form in which Epicurus stated it: "Is God willing to prevent evil, but not able? Then he is impotent. Is he able but not willing? Then he is malevolent. Is he both able and willing? Whence then is evil?"

Put in its simplest form, the problem of evil comes down to this: Take your pick, either believe in a God of limited power who cannot prevent evil, or believe in a God of unlimited power who chooses to allow evil. There is a third option: You can *avoid* the problem of evil by denying that there is a problem. Some Eastern religions, such as Hinduism, think that evil is *maya,* or illusion. Hindus believe that, like the physical world itself, evil is not real but only a passing illusion from which salvation frees us when we reach nirvana, the state of eternal blessedness. In a similar way atheists also deny the problem of evil; evil is just a part of the world, and there is no God to make it a problem. A person who believes there is no God could say, "We live in a world that has features about it that cause human suffering and pain. I do not like this state of affairs and would change it if I could, but since I cannot, I must learn to endure the things about human existence that cause distress." This was the view accepted by some ancient philosophers and defended by certain existential philosophers, such as Albert Camus and Jean-Paul Sartre.

To summarize, evil becomes a philosophical problem because it seems difficult to believe that there is a God of unlimited power and that such a God loves us when there is so much evil in the world. If God has unlimited power and goodness, then why does God not eliminate evil from the world? This is the problem of evil at its barest formulation.

To consider possible answers to this question, first look at the nature of evil itself. Evil is that which causes pain, destruction, and human suffering. Much of the evil present in the world results from human beings doing terrible things to each other: war; use of famine as a political weapon; neglect of diseases which have known cures; inattention to poverty, ignorance, and injustice; failure to improve the welfare of the unfortunate; and resistance to changes in the social order that would redirect human productive capacities into making the world better and eliminate the production of weapons and instruments of destruction. The list could go on and on, for as you review the catalog of human evils, ask yourself just how much better the world could be if everyone acted according to even minimal standards of human decency. Then ask yourself to estimate what percentage of evil in the world is due to human beings. Fifty percent? Sixty percent? Perhaps an even higher percentage?

The Free Will Defense

Calculations such as these are important to the free will defense, a major tactic used by those who defend both the power and love of God. According to this line of argument, in order for human beings to be truly free to do good, they must also be free to do evil. We can therefore explain much of the evil in the world as due to the exercise of this free will. If human beings were not free, if we were robot-like automatons, then we could be programmed to do only the right thing, thereby eliminating much of the evil in the world. The free will defense comes up against a problem: the existence of natural evil. Natural evil is that evil not due to human action but to the operation and functioning of the world. Even if all people in the world did all in their power to eliminate pain and suffering, there would still be earthquakes that cause death and suffering, floods that devastate, droughts that ravage, volcanos, typhoons, tornadoes, and other natural disasters that destroy and ruin. Then there is disease: the numbing and racking pain of cancer, the heartbreak of ailments for which there is no known cure, the death of children from maladies that snuff out their young lives, the debilitating diseases of the aged, epidemics, and plagues. Again, the list could go on. These instances of evil are not due to human freedom but to the way the world is. Why does a God of love and might allow these things to happen?

A Limited God?

As was mentioned earlier, one possible way out of the problem of evil is to believe in a deity who is limited in power and therefore unable to eliminate evil completely. Like the formulation of the problem of evil itself, the limited-God solution was also chosen by some ancient philosophers, such as Plato, in the nineteenth century by John Stuart Mill and William James, and in our own time by those theologians who defend process theology, which conceives of God as the savior of the world rather than its creator. Process theologians envision God as a moral force in the world exerting persuasive love rather than compulsive power in the affairs of human beings. In a similar way of dealing with the problem of evil, some ancient religions held a dualistic view which accounted for evil as due to the activities of an evil god against whom a good god was battling. Zoroastrianism in ancient Persia and Manichaeism in the third century C.E. held dualistic views in which two deities, one good and one evil, compete for human loyalty, with the outcome being very much in doubt. Dualism explains evil in the world as a result of the activity of the evil deity because the good deity is unable to prevent it. Neither Christianity nor Judaism is dualistic, for neither faith sees the demonic powers as coequal with God, which is what a true dualism demands.

The problem of evil becomes most intense when one believes in the traditional God of Judaism and Christianity—a God of unlimited power and love—and in the reality of evil. How to explain that an all-powerful, benevolent, loving God nevertheless tolerates evil is the problem to be dealt with in a *theodicy,* the defense of God's goodness in spite of the presence of evil.

In the reading that follows, the noted philosopher of religion, John Hick, takes a phrase from the poet John Keats which refers to the present world as a "vale of soul-making." Hick points out that the view of the divine-human relationship supposed by some is not that of a loving parent but that of a zookeeper. "They think of God's relation to the earth on the model of a human being building a cage for a pet animal to dwell in. If he is humane he will naturally make his pet's quarters as pleasant and healthful as he can." Instead of this, Hick argues for a view of human life as developmental; the world is the kind of place where adversity can bring about moral fortitude and pain can bring about spiritual maturity. "The picture with which we are working," Hick says, "is thus developmental and teleological. Man is in the process of becoming the perfected being whom God is seeking to create. However, this is not taking place—it is important to add—by a natural and inevitable evolution, but through a hazardous adventure in individual freedom." Rather than think of God as keeper of pet animals in a cage, it is better to think of God's relationship to human beings as analogous to that of a loving parent. Hick adds that "to most parents it seems more important to try to foster quality and strength of character in their children than to fill their lives at all times with the utmost possible degree of pleasure. If, then, there is any true analogy between God's purpose for his human creatures, and the purpose of loving and wise parents for their children, we have to recognize that the presence of pleasure and the absence of pain cannot be the supreme and overriding end for which the world exists. Rather, this world must be a place of soul-making."

John Hick: The Vale of Soul-Making Theodicy

In the light of modern anthropological knowledge some form of two-stage conception of the creation of man has become an almost unavoidable Christian tenet. At the very least we must acknowledge as two distinguishable stages the fashioning of *homo sapiens* as a product of the long evolutionary process, and his sudden or gradual spiritualization as a child of God. But we may well extend the first stage to include the development of man as a rational and responsible person capable of personal relationship with the personal Infinite who has created him. This first stage of the creative process was, to our anthropomorphic imaginations, easy for divine omnipotence. By an exercise of creative power God caused the physical universe to exist, and in the course of countless ages to bring forth within it organic life, and finally to produce out of organic life personal life; and when man had thus emerged out of the evolution of the forms of organic life, a creature had been made who has the possibility of existing in conscious fellowship with God. But the second stage of the creative process is of a different kind altogether. It cannot be performed by omnipotent power as such. For personal life is essentially free and self-directing. It cannot be perfected by divine *fiat,* but only through the uncompelled responses and willing co-operation of human individuals in their actions and reactions in the world in which God has placed them. Men may eventually become the perfected persons whom the New Testament calls 'children of God,' but they cannot be created ready-made as this.

The value-judgement that is implicitly being invoked here is that one who has attained to goodness by meeting and eventually mastering temptations, and thus by rightly making responsible choices in concrete situations, is good in a richer and more valuable sense than would be one created *ab initio* in a state either of innocence or of virtue. In the former case, which is that of the actual moral achievements of mankind, the individual's goodness has within it the strength of temptations overcome, a stability based upon an accumulation of right choices, and a positive and responsible character that comes from the investment of costly personal effort. I suggest, then, that it is an ethically reasonable judgement, even though in the nature of the case not one that is capable of demonstrative proof, that human goodness slowly built up through personal histories of moral effort has a value in the eyes of the Creator which justifies even the long travail of the soul-making process.

The picture with which we are working is thus developmental and teleological. Man is in process of becoming the perfected being whom God is seeking to create. However, this is not taking place—it is important to add—by a natural and inevitable evolution, but through a hazardous adventure in individual freedom. Because this is a pilgrimage within the life of each individual, rather than a racial evolution, the progressive fulfilment of God's purpose does not entail any corresponding progressive improvement in the moral state of the world. There is no doubt a development in man's ethical situation from generation to generation through the building of individual choices into public institutions, but this involves an accumulation of evil as well as of good.[1] It is thus probable that human life was lived on much the same moral plane two thousand years ago or four thousand years ago as it is today. But nevertheless during this period uncounted millions of souls have been through the experience of earthly life, and God's purpose has gradually moved towards its fulfilment within each one of them, rather than within a human aggregate composed of different units in different generations.

If, then, God's aim in making the world is 'the bringing of many sons to glory,'[2] that aim will naturally determine the kind of world that He has created. Antitheistic writers almost invariably assume a conception of the divine purpose which is contrary to the Christian conception. They assume that the purpose of a loving God must be to create a hedonistic paradise; and therefore to the extent that the world is other than this, it proves to them that God is either not loving enough or not powerful enough to create such a world. They think of God's relation to the earth on the model of a human being building a cage for a pet animal to dwell in. If he is humane he will naturally make his pet's quarters as pleasant and healthful as he can. Any respect in which the cage falls short of the veterinarian's ideal, and contains possibilities of accident or disease, is evidence of either limited benevolence or limited means, or both. Those who use the problem of evil as an argument against belief in God almost invariably think of the world in this kind of way. David Hume, for example, speaks of an architect who is trying to plan a house that is to be as comfortable and convenient as possible. If we find that 'the windows, doors, fires, passages, stairs, and the whole economy of the building were the source of noise, confusion, fatigue, darkness, and the extremes of heat and cold' we should have no hesitation in blaming the architect. It would be in vain for him to prove that if this or that defect were corrected greater ills would result: 'still you would assert in general, that, if the architect had had skill and good intentions, he might have formed such a plan of the whole, and might have adjusted the parts in such a manner, as would have remedied all or most of these inconveniences.'[3]

But if we are right in supposing that God's purpose for man is to lead him from human *Bios,* or the biological life of man, to that quality of *Zoe,* or the personal life of eternal worth, which we see in Christ, then the question that we have to ask is not, Is this the kind of world that an all-powerful and infinitely loving being would create as an environment for his human pets? or, Is the architecture of the world the most pleasant and convenient possible? The question that we have to ask is rather, Is this the kind of world that God might make as an environment in which moral beings may be fashioned, through their own free insights and responses, into 'children of God'?

---

[1]This fact is symbolized in early Christian literature both by the figure of the Antichrist, who continually opposes God's purposes in history, and by the expectation of cataclysmic calamity and strife in the last days before the end of the present world order.
[2]Hebrews ii, 10.
[3]*Dialogues Concerning Natural Religion,* pt. xi. Kemp-Smith's ed. (Oxford: Clarendon Press, 1935), p. 251.

Such critics as Hume are confusing what heaven ought to be, as an environment for perfected finite beings, with what this world ought to be, as an environment for beings who are in process of becoming perfected. For if our general conception of God's purpose is correct the world is not intended to be a paradise, but rather the scene of a history in which human personality may be formed towards the pattern of Christ. Men are not to be thought of on the analogy of animal pets, whose life is to be made as agreeable as possible, but rather on the analogy of human children, who are to grow to adulthood in an environment whose primary and overriding purpose is not immediate pleasure but the realizing of the most valuable potentialities of human personality.

Needless to say, this characterization of God as the heavenly Father is not a merely random illustration but an analogy that lies at the heart of the Christian faith. Jesus treated the likeness between the attitude of God to man, and the attitude of human parents at their best towards their children, as providing the most adequate way for us to think about God. And so it is altogether relevant to a Christian understanding of this world to ask, How does the best parental love express itself in its influence upon the environment in which children are to grow up? I think it is clear that a parent who loves his children, and wants them to become the best human beings that they are capable of becoming, does not treat pleasure as the sole and supreme value. Certainly we seek pleasure for our children, and take great delight in obtaining it for them; but we do not desire for them unalloyed pleasure at the expense of their growth in such even greater values as moral integrity, unselfishness, compassion, courage, humour, reverence for the truth, and perhaps above all the capacity for love. We do not act on the premise that pleasure is the supreme end of life; and if the development of these other values sometimes clashes with the provision of pleasure, then we are willing to have our children miss a certain amount of this, rather than fail to come to possess and to be possessed by the finer and more precious qualities that are possible to the human personality. A child brought up on the principle that the only or the supreme value is pleasure would not be likely to become an ethically mature adult or an attractive or happy personality. And to most parents it seems more important to try to foster quality and strength of character in their children than to fill their lives at all times with the utmost possible degree of pleasure. If, then, there is any true analogy between God's purpose for his human creatures, and the purpose of loving and wise parents for their children, we have to recognize that the presence of pleasure and the absence of pain cannot be the supreme and overriding end for which the world exists. Rather, this world must be a place of soul-making. And its value is to be judged, not primarily by the quantity of pleasure and pain occurring in it at any particular moment, but by its fitness for its primary purpose, the purpose of soul-making.[4]

---

[4]The phrase 'the vale of Soul-making' was coined by the poet John Keats in a letter written to his brother and sister in April 1819. He says, 'The common cognomen of this world among the misguided and superstitious is "a vale of tears" from which we are to be redeemed by a certain arbitrary interposition of God and taken to Heaven—What a little circumscribed straightened notion! Call the world if you Please "The vale of Soul-making".' In this letter he sketches a teleological theodicy. 'Do you not see,' he asks, 'how necessary a World of Pains and troubles is to school an Intelligence and make it a Soul?' (*The Letters of John Keats*, ed. by M. B. Forman. London: Oxford University Press, 4th ed., 1952, pp. 334–5.)

In all this we have been speaking about the nature of the world considered simply as the God-given environment of man's life. For it is mainly in this connection that the world has been regarded in Irenaean and in Protestant thought.[5] But such a way of thinking involves a danger of anthropocentrism from which the Augustinian and Catholic tradition has generally been protected by its sense of the relative insignificance of man within the totality of the created universe. Man was dwarfed within the medieval world-view by the innumerable hosts of angels and archangels above him—unfallen rational natures which rejoice in the immediate presence of God, reflecting His glory in the untarnished mirror of their worship. However, this higher creation has in our modern world lost its hold upon the imagination. Its place has been taken, as the minimizer of men, by the immensities of outer space and by the material universe's unlimited complexity transcending our present knowledge. As the spiritual environment envisaged by Western man has shrunk, his physical horizons have correspondingly expanded. Where the human creature was formerly seen as an insignificant appendage to the angelic world, he is now seen as an equally insignificant organic excrescence, enjoying a fleeting moment of consciousness on the surface of one of the planets of a minor star. Thus the truth that was symbolized for former ages by the existence of the angelic hosts is today impressed upon us by the vastness of the physical universe, countering the egoism of our species by making us feel that this immense prodigality of existence can hardly all exist for the sake of man— though, on the other hand, the very realization that it is not all for the sake of man may itself be salutary and beneficial to man!

However, instead of opposing man and nature as rival objects of God's interest, we should perhaps rather stress man's solidarity as an embodied being with the whole natural order in which he is embedded. For man is organic to the world; all his acts and thoughts and imaginations are conditioned by space and time; and in abstraction from nature he would cease to be human. We may, then, say that the beauties and sublimities and powers, the microscopic intricacies and macroscopic vastnesses, the wonders and the terrors of the natural world and of the life that pulses through it, are willed and valued by their Maker in a creative act that embraces man together with nature. By means of matter and living flesh God both builds a path and weaves a veil between Himself and the creature made in His image. Nature thus has permanent significance; for God has set man in a creaturely environment, and the final fulfilment of our nature in relation to God will accordingly take the form of an embodied life within 'a new heaven and a new earth'.[6] And as in the present age man moves slowly towards that fulfillment through the pilgrimage of his earthly life, so also 'the whole creation' is 'groaning in travail', waiting for the time when it will be 'set free from its bondage to decay'.[7]

---

[5]Thus Irenaeus said that 'the creation is suited to [the wants of] man; for man was not made for its sake, but creation for the sake of man' (*A.H.* v. xxix. I), and Calvin said that 'because we know that the universe was established especially for the sake of mankind, we ought to look for this purpose in his governance also'. (*Inst.* I. xvi. 6.)
[6]Revelation xxi, 1.
[7]Romans viii, 21–22.

And yet however fully we thus acknowledge the permanent significance and value of the natural order, we must still insist upon man's special character as a personal creature made in the image of God; and our theodicy must still center upon the soul-making process that we believe to be taking place within human life.

This, then, is the starting-point from which we propose to try to relate the realities of sin and suffering to the perfect love of an omnipotent Creator. And as will become increasingly apparent, a theodicy that starts in this way must be eschatological in its ultimate bearings. That is to say, instead of looking to the past for its clue to the mystery of evil it looks to the future, and indeed to that ultimate future to which only faith can look. Given the conception of a divine intention working in and through human time towards a fulfilment that lies in its completeness beyond human time, our theodicy must find the meaning of evil in the part that it is made to play in the eventual outworking of that purpose; and must find the justification of the whole process in the magnitude of the good to which it leads. The good that outshines all ill is not a paradise long since lost but a kingdom which is yet to come in its full glory and permanence.

From this point of view we must speak about moral evil; about pain, including that of the lower animals; about the higher and more distinctively human forms of suffering; and about the relation between all this and the will of God as it has been revealed in Jesus Christ.

Questions for Discussion

1. In his analysis, Hick distinguishes between merely physical life *(Bios)* and spiritual life *(Zoe)*, using the two Greek words to identify each. Do you think this distinction is defensible? Explain.

2. Hick's theodicy addresses moral evil as an ingredient in soul making. Is his theodicy as effective in explaining natural evil? Why or why not?

3. Human free will is at the center of the "Vale of Soul-Making" theodicy. Implicit in the theodicy is the assumption that only a certain kind of world is compatible with morally free beings. What might some of the characteristics of such a world be?

4. Do you find the "Vale of Soul-Making" approach persuasive? Give reasons for your answer.

5. Hick says that his view, "instead of opposing man and nature," stresses "man's solidarity as an embodied being with the whole natural order." Explain what you think this means.

Suggestions for Further Reading

Alder, Mortimer J. *How to Think About God.* New York: Macmillan, 1980. A discussion in nontechnical language of arguments for God.

Gale, Richard M. *On the Nature and Existence of God.* Cambridge: Cambridge University Press, 1992. Offers an analysis of the work of analytic philosophers supporting theism.

Haught, John F. *God After Darwin: A Theology of Evolution.* Boulder, CO: Westview Press, 2000. Argues that Darwin's explanation for the origins of life are not per se hostile to religion.

Morris, Thomas V. *God and the Philosophers: The Reconciliation of Faith and Reason.* New York: Oxford University Press, 1994. Twenty philosophers give accounts of their own personal journeys to religious belief.

Polkinghorne, John. *Belief in God in an Age of Science.* New Haven: Yale University Press, 1998. Reflections on the compatibility of religion and science by an internationally known physicist and theologian.

Stewart, David. *Exploring the Philosophy of Religion.* 5th ed. Upper Saddle River, NJ: Prentice Hall, 2001. A discussion of topics in philosophy of religion by one of the authors of this text.

PART 7

Philosophy of Art (Esthetics)

CHAPTER 29

Introduction to the Philosophy of Art

Throughout the book we have been saying that philosophy is a critical and reflective activity aimed at a wide variety of subject matter areas outside of philosophy. Thus, we have invited you to look at philosophy as a series of "philosophies of": philosophy of religion, philosophy of science, and so on. In this same sense, we shall look at esthetics (sometimes spelled *aesthetics)* in this chapter as the philosophy of art. Esthetics is concerned with all the philosophical questions surrounding art. First there are important normative questions: What is art? What is the essence of artistic creativity and appreciation? Is art primarily a source of pleasure, or does it provide a kind of religious or metaphysical knowledge? Does art help in articulating the aspirations of a particular social group, thus serving as a means of social unification and cohesion? Is there any one thing which all the arts have in common?

Consider a number of works of art: an opera, a painting, a Greek temple, an abstract bronze sculpture, a poem, a piece of modern dance, a play, and a novel. What do all these have in common? If we try to be specific, our description will not apply to everything on the list. Some, but not all, for example, are objects of visual and perceptual delight (not the novel, for example). Some are representational, but what about the temple, or the abstract sculpture? If we look for more general features (significant form, expression of implicit meaning), our account is apt to be too vague. But if there is nothing they share in common, how can we possibly come up with an adequate definition, and without a definition, how can we construct a general theory of art?

The difficulty of defining art is similar to the problem we encountered in the previous section of defining religion. Just as we found it difficult to discover one single activity or belief common to all religions, it is similarly difficult to find one sort of creation or a single activity that is common to all forms of art. One approach, as we saw in our discussion of religion, would be to group various kinds of artistic activities by their family resemblances and speak of families of art objects or activities. While an interesting activity in itself, it is not one that we shall occupy ourselves with in this section. Instead, we shall focus on other philosophical issues that arise from the activity of artists.

The Problem of Artistic Expression

There is a host of philosophical problems arising out of confusions and misunderstandings concerning the vocabulary of art. Artists produce art and their audiences enjoy it, often without the need for a great deal of intellectual thought or talk. But other people like to think and talk about art, in addition to producing and enjoying it—people such as art critics, art instructors, art historians, and sometimes artists themselves. The problem these people face is that a special vocabulary for talking about the arts has never emerged, and we are forced to borrow words from other areas of discourse and transpose them into art in order to talk about it. What often happens in that case is that these words and concepts carry connotations into the discussion of art that really belong to a totally different kind of activity.

Take, for example, the so-called problem of expression. It seems very natural to say that art expresses the artist's emotions or feelings. But as soon as we put it in these terms we may be tempted to think of artistic expression in the way we think of other sorts of expression, and this may lead to trouble. Suppose in repairing my front porch I hammer my thumb instead of the nail. I will certainly express myself by uttering some appropriate remark. But is this what we think artistic expression is like? There are similar problems associated with other concepts used in art criticism: symbolism (which we shall look at later in this chapter), the artist's intention, imagination, and so on.

Difficult metaphysical problems also occur in esthetics. What, for example, is a work of art? Is it a physical object? What about a piece of music? Is that a physical object? There is the sheet music, and there are the sound waves produced from a particular performance or recording of that piece of music, but are these what you mean by *music?* What if we burn the sheet music, and cancel the performance; have we destroyed the music? If not, does it follow that music exists, as one philosopher said, "in one's head"? Or is it somehow a combination of mental and physical components? If so, how are they joined together (recall a similar difficulty in the mind-body problem, in Part 3).

Finally, there are epistemological problems associated with esthetics. Do we have reliable knowledge concerning art? Are judgments about works of art objective, scientific judgments, or are they purely personal and subjective? At first you may think this is rather easy to answer; after all, art is whatever you think it is. Beauty is in the eye of the beholder. Or at least that is the view of a good many people. If this expresses a view you hold, you would not be alone, for perhaps the most widely held view about the nature of art is that there are no *objective* standards to judge one work of art from another, and that each person is the best judge of what art is. If you think that there are no objective standards by which to judge a work of art, you would hold the view that art is entirely subjective; art is whatever pleases you.

The interesting thing about a subjectivist view of art is that it cannot be refuted. You can insist from now to doomsday that there is nothing in art itself in terms of which we can judge it objectively, and no one will be able to refute you, simply because your subjectivist position rules out any possible objective evidence. Someone could expose you to a wide range of art objects and ask you to rank them in terms of their degrees of interest to you. Then together you could probe beneath your own preferences to see if you could make explicit the standards in terms of which you made your rankings. But if you still insist that art cannot be judged by any objective standards, any attempt to dissuade you will fail, and you will have to move on to another issue.

What can be said in favor of an objectivist view of art, the view that there are objective standards of *some kind* in terms of which art can be judged? After all, people do make judgments about art and decide that some works of art are better than others. Museum directors and acquisitions committees have to decide which paintings to purchase for their permanent collections. Music directors have to determine whether a new symphony is worthy of being performed. Art critics make judgments about the artistic merit of various kinds of art work and attempt to give reasons for their judgments. And this presupposes standards of some sort. Any time we are put in a position of offering reasons for our conclusions, we are in the process of moving away from a purely subjectivist view to a more objectivist position. Of course, we can still argue over different *standards,* but appealing to standards does mark a step away from "I choose it because I like it." We could say, if we are committed to a thoroughgoing subjectivism, that museum directors, acquisitions committees, art critics, and so on, are really doing nothing but (notice that troublesome phrase again) foisting off on a gullible public their own subjective reactions to art. But at least the art critics believe that they are responding to something in the art work itself when they judge it, and this is a belief we should examine.

≡ The Role of Esthetic Experience

The foregoing are some of the kinds of questions which arise when we look at esthetics as the philosophy of art. In this sense esthetics will be concerned with a number of separate, individual questions, which may *not* therefore produce any coherent, all-embracing theory of the underlying nature or essence of art. But there is another tradition in esthetics which tries to do just that—give us a general theory of art. Historically (roughly since the eighteenth century) esthetics has been more narrowly defined as the investigation of the nature of our esthetic *experience,* whether of art works or of objects of natural beauty, such as the Rocky Mountains, a sunset, or a lake. Is there any distinguishing feature of all such esthetic experiences, something which they all have but is not shared by any other kind of experience? Philosophers in the eighteenth century thought they had an answer. What distinguishes esthetic experience from every other kind of experience is something variously described as *detachment, disinterestedness,* and *distance.* And this theory of esthetic experience was very widely held by estheticians until quite recently, when it has come under sharp attack.

What do these expressions mean—*detachment, disinterestedness,* and *distance?* They all sound rather negative. Let us consider an example. Suppose a person is looking at a tree. Let us say that it is an old, well-formed oak tree standing on a hilltop. Is this person's experience an esthetic experience? Remember that philosophy is primarily a reflective rather than a dogmatic enterprise. That means that you can answer this question as well as anyone, simply by philosophically reflecting on it. What would you say? To help you, suppose we fill in the context a little more. Suppose that it is winter and the person, whose home is heated with a wood-burning stove, is wondering, while looking at the tree, whether it will produce enough firewood to last through the winter. Or imagine that the tree stands next to the person's house and that the tree has a large dead branch which stretches out over the roof of the house, and our observer is concerned mainly about whether the dead branch might fall on the house in a bad windstorm. Finally, suppose this person has the day off and has stopped to look at the tree on a walk through the fields.

Which of these would you call an esthetic experience? Surely the last, but why? Putting it negatively, it is because the individual was not looking at the tree for its utilitarian value as firewood, or as a possible threat. Putting it more positively, it was because the viewer was looking at the tree for its own sake and for the pleasure one gets simply by looking at it. This is the distinction that words like *detachment* and *disinterestedness* try to capture. In the last example, the observer was *detached* from the usual everyday, practical attitude and was not an *interested* party, *interested* in what could be done with the tree (displaying the kind of disinterestedness which a judge ought to have in a court case), and we might say that the observer has established a certain *distance* or perspective from the usual utilitarian attitude toward the world. Implied here is a certain view of human psychology: that our ordinary view of the world is self-interested, pragmatic, and utilitarian; that we generally look at things from the standpoint of how they will help or hurt us; and that the esthetic attitude is the exception to this rule, the relatively rarer moments when we relax our strong survival mechanism and experience objects simply for the joy of experiencing them.

When we ask what art is or what esthetic experience is, we expect these phenomena to be examined in and of themselves. And we expect resulting theories to tell us what *they* are and not what *something else* is to which they might be related in some way. It is like the student who wrote on the final exam, "The question reminds me of another, even more interesting question which I would like to answer." Historically many theories of art have been extrinsic, defining art in terms of its function in aiding other, nonart activities—that art is a form of communication, or self-expression, a way of representing the world, a source of relaxation or stimulation, and so on. And the complaint against all such theories is that they fail to define what art is in its own right—that they are *not intrinsic* definitions.

Those theories which look to the intrinsic, internal character of art works are called *formalist,* since they pay attention only to the arrangement, pattern, or *form* of elements (line, color, shape, and so on) *within* the art work. Extrinsic theories stress the representational and expressive *content* which the art work *refers* to, and so the debate between intrinsic and extrinsic theories is often expressed as the battle over form and content.

On the one hand, the theory of the esthetic attitude, in its emphasis on the distance and detachment from the rest of the world, seems to stress the *intrinsic* character of art for art's sake. On the other hand, however, esthetic distance and detachment can be seen as the detachment and distance which a symbol has from what it symbolizes, and in *this* sense art stands apart from life, not in the sense that it is unrelated to life but in the sense that it is *about* life. A history book on the Civil War is not, of course, the same as the Civil War itself. There is a clear and sharp distinction between the two; one is a bloody war and the other is a book. But the two are clearly related insofar as the book is a book *about* the Civil War. The same is generally true of anything which has human meaning or significance; there are always two things in the meaning relation, the symbol and the thing symbolized, and they are related to one another in the sense that the first is about, or refers to, the second.

To recapitulate, the modern theory of esthetic experience is a further analysis and reflection on what has become our ordinary intuitions. But these common sense intuitions may be so deeply ingrained and internalized within us, so much a part of our normal outlook, assumed and taken for granted, that it is difficult for us to see them. How can we see what appears most obvious to us? Perhaps only by way of a contrast. Without a contrast, our own way of seeing things will always seem "normal" and obviously "right," perhaps the *only* way to see things, and therefore invisible to us. With that in mind, let us consider for a moment a contrasting point of view.

Most big city art museums have rooms devoted to African art and pre-Columbian American Indian art. Many people collect, buy and sell these objects as art works, and beautifully illustrated art books have been written on them. But consider for a moment where these objects came from and how they were originally used by the people who made them. Many of the ceramic pieces from Mexico and Central America are grave goods made to accompany the dead into an afterlife. Much the same is true in ancient China and Egypt. Everything we

Ancient Chinese Han Dynasty (206 B.C.E.–220 C.E.) miniature (16 × 25 inch) terra cotta horse-drawn carriage placed in the tomb of a deceased official for use in the afterlife. Photo courtesy of H. Gene Blocker.

need in this life is made available to the dead for their use in an afterlife, except that they are now in the form of miniature ceramic or wooden replicas or effigies —small figurines of musicians, guards, servants and horses, for example. The only people to ever see these objects were the people who made them, the family members who purchased them, and the priest who cast whatever magical spells are required to make them come to life and perform in the "land of the dead" (that is, make these little ceramic and wooden figurines play music or serve food). As recently as forty or fifty years ago West Africa farmers could not begin their annual planting until the high priests had initiated a ceremonial dance in the fields by masked performers reenacting the original farming techniques given the people by their gods. The first Europeans who saw them in the late eighteenth and early nineteenth century saw them as false religious idols and accordingly destroyed as many of them as they could. Only later, beginning around 1904, did European artists, including Picasso, begin thinking of these same objects as works of fine art, and even started imitating them in their own art. Today art museums display these same wooden masks, art books describe them and galleries in Europe and North America sell them as works of art.

But what *are* these wooden and ceramic objects, really? Are they works of art? Were they made by artists? Were they meant to be esthetically appreciated?

Even though we today look at these objects as works of "fine art," the people who originally made and used them did not; at least this was not their primary purpose. These objects were not used "esthetically," but for ceremonial purposes; they did not have to be enjoyable to look at, only sufficiently representational (of a musician, for example) to perform its ritual function (to play music beyond the grave, to call forth the agricultural gods, or chase away the evil spirits). The people who made them were not expressing their own individual feelings, attitudes and beliefs, but conforming to the traditional pattern required by the religious traditions of that particular society. The objects certainly were not made to be admired, as is obvious in the case of the grave goods. Neither were African masks made to be looked at continuously, since they were stored away out of sight most of the time and are only brought out once a year to be seen during the planting ceremony.

These examples provide an idea, by way of contrast, of what is meant by the esthetic attitude toward works of "fine art" made by "artists." These are objects made for the main purpose of being viewed esthetically, that is, to be enjoyed just for the pleasure and satisfaction of looking at and listening to them. The esthetic experience of works of art, in other words, is non-utilitarian, where "utilitarian" means making and using something for some non-esthetic reason. You don't make a sandwich just look at it but to eat. If someone has made a burglar alarm, we don't set it off just to hear how it sounds—in fact, we hope it won't go off.

In contrast, why do you listen to music? You probably do not listen to music with any expectation of personal gain beyond the pleasure of the experience itself, as opposed, for example, to listening to an accounting class lecture (from which you expect something—a good grade on the next test, leading to a good grade in the class, leading to a degree, and a job, a house in the "burbs" with a BMW in the garage, perhaps). But then you go home and listen to music only for its own sake. The people who make "works of art" are not just skilled craftspersons. We think of them as "artists" who have something important to say or express. Artists who just say the same things over and over again, or those who just say what other artists have already been saying for a long time are not considered as good as artists who have something new to say and new ways of saying it.

What are they "saying" and "telling" us? A moment's reflection shows how hard the answer is to put in words. Somehow the people we think of as artists, or at least as great artists, are expressing or saying something that cannot be said in some more ordinary way through the ordinary use of language. The musicians we love are expressing how things feel to them and how things in general seem to be. They are relating a kind of mood or a point of view. What is this overall mood or point of view? To find out you just have to listen to the music. The artist has expressed this unique perspective in and only in music. The meaning or message is there for anyone who bothers to listen from an esthetic point of view. It is all there in the music; just listen.

But now going back to the contrast with pre-Columbian American Indian ceramic grave goods and the masks used earlier in West African planting cere-

A Gelede mask from the Yoruba, one of the largest ethnic groups in Nigeria and Benin, used to attract and lead evil spirits out of a village. Photo courtesy of H. Gene Blocker.

monies, we can see that people have not always looked at things in this "esthetic," "fine art" kind of way. As natural as the esthetic attitude may seem to us, it is not universal, not a permanent part of human nature. It appears at a point in the history of certain cultures and may just as easily disappear later and be replaced by another way of looking at things. Being able to recognize that these views are subjective shows that contexts do indeed shift and change over time and from culture to culture.

These ideas of esthetic enjoyment, fine art and artist arose in what we call the modern period—roughly from the end of the seventeenth century through the middle of the twentieth century. The period before that we can conveniently refer to as "premodern," followed by "the modern," and the period we are now in, often referred to as the "postmodern" period.

If, as we said earlier, philosophy is a reflection on our ordinary, common sense intuitions, then we can easily formulate from our analysis above the main points about the modern conception of esthetic experience:

1. Esthetic experience is nonutilitarian.
2. Esthetic experience is detached from ordinary self-interested pursuits (it is disinterested).

3. Works of art are made to be viewed esthetically and just to be enjoyed for no other purpose.
4. Everyone can appreciate art just by adopting the esthetic point of view (it is universal in all human beings).
5. Artists see things in a unique way and creatively find innovative ways of communicating that to us.
6. Artists, or at least the great artists, show us how to look at the world, how to understand ourselves, who we are, and what our world is like.
7. Works of art (or at least great works of art) express these unusual ideas of artists.
8. Great works of art must be innovative, be creative, and express new ideas in new ways.
9. The history of art is the history of great innovations by great artists (the first one to do this, the first one to do that, etc.).
10. Art is not hard to understand. It just requires our adopting the esthetic point of view.

In the chapters that follow we will focus on an important issue in contemporary esthetics, namely the question of whether art should be censored because it is offensive or causes violence, especially towards women. This is an especially interesting subject because of the very different ways art works have traditionally depicted the female body. In much archaic art from around the world, nude female figures are thought to represent or symbolize principles of fertility—of crops, animals, as well as the human population, and were probably used in religious practices to magically ensure this highly desired fertility. In Classical Greek and Renaissance European art the nude figure is considered part of "high humanistic art," representing, or symbolizing the essence of human nature—whereby the human body represents or symbolizes the divine, godlike quality of human beings at their most noble and sublime. But from Roman times there has also been a more popular art depicting the nude human body in ways which were obviously meant to stimulate sexual arousal or to make fun of sexuality—a kind of visual "dirty joke."

Consider for a moment the vast range of uses of pictures of nude women we find today—a painting by Rubens in the city art museum, a pin-up in the garage mechanic's office, a centerfold in *Playboy,* an African or pre-Columbian Central American Indian fertility figure in the anthropology museum, a sex manual, an illustration for a biology or medical textbook, and finally an advertisement for a hard-core pornographic movie or video.

Debate on this question shows the growing split between traditional modernist estheticians and more contemporary theorists. Traditional modernist estheticians tend to defend art against all forms of censorship on the grounds that properly understood, art ("real art," the Rubens, not the mechanic's pinup) is too detached from real life to have much immediate impact on it, while some contemporary theorists reject the boundaries separating art and life, high art and popular culture, and tend to regard art simply as part of the social, economic, and political real world in which racism, sexism, and violence flourish.

In the following chapter, the contemporary American esthetician, H. Gene Blocker, shows the relation of the traditional esthetic attitude to the detachment of art from life, except symbolically. Next, the art historian Kenneth Clark argues that the idea that art can create a predetermined emotional or behavioral effect, such as erotic stimulation or a demeaning attitude toward women, is a confusion of the *esthetic* enjoyment of art proper with various nonesthetic notions. Finally, a contemporary literary theorist, Jennifer Jeffers, argues that art is far too deeply embedded in the context of real life to be detached or disengaged from everyday social reality, which constantly spawns racist and sexist attitudes and behavior.

Questions for Discussion

1. Can you give examples from our own time of objects that were originally made for utilitarian purposes but are now considered to be works of art?

2. The point was made in the discussion that the esthetic attitude may be particular to specific cultures at specific times. Do you think that everyone even in our own time and in our own culture has this attitude? Explain.

3. You and a friend go to an exhibit of local artisans. Your friend says, "These are crafts, not art." What considerations would you bring to bear on the discussion of whether you were looking at crafts or fine art?

4. Some of the modern art sections of museum present ordinary objects as fine art. What considerations do you think led the museum to agree to this designation?

5. This is difficult to express, but what do you think artists are trying to *say?* Are they expressing emotions? Some deeper truth? Some new way of looking at the world?

CHAPTER 30

The Value of Art

In the eighteenth and nineteenth centuries, esthetic theories spoke of art in terms of its distance from the world of ordinary experience. The view that art is unrelated to the world, except insofar as it provides a perspective from which to view the world, was the prevailing theory about art until the modern period described in the previous chapter. The way this point was made was to refer to the experience of a work of art as a special kind of experience different from, say, the experience of eating a good meal or solving a mathematical problem. Esthetic theories principally dealt with the issue of how works of art affect us differently than do other objects within our experience such as the utilitarian objects mentioned in the previous chapter.

The term used to describe the unique features of experiencing a work of art was *the esthetic attitude,* and esthetic theories looked for the unique features of this attitude as contrasted with, for example, the moral and religious points of view. An important aspect of the esthetic attitude, according to these theories, was the removal of the art work from any practical interest such as whether the work inflamed passion, incited to riot, or even had an economic value on the art market. Art was viewed as intrinsically important, art for its own sake, and the quarrel among art theorists was over how art accomplished its unique role. On the one hand were those who argued that art's principal role was to express emotion. Other theorists argued that whereas emotion was important in art, the real issue was whether, and how, art *communicates* emotion.

Closely related to the theory that the role of art is to communicate emotion is the view that art is just another vehicle for conveying *meaning.* Just as words are symbolic vehicles for expressing meaning—*chair* refers to the construction on which we sit, *bed* refers to the object on which we sleep, *house* refers to the structure in which we live—so art works are symbolic expressions that refer to things in the real world. And this theoretical approach gets even more complex. There can be multiple meanings in a work of art. *Moby Dick* is not just a tale about a large albino whale; Melville's story has multiple, deeper meanings. The questions that estheticians ponder are not only what these meanings are but how a work of art conveys meaning, as in John Ciardi's famous essay, "How Does a Poem Mean?"

This quarrel was engaged in also by artists, who are cautious about attempts to assign meanings to their works. When someone asked Picasso if his painting of a red bull's head represented the rise of fascism in Europe, Picasso is said to have replied, "No, it represents the head of a red bull." Robert Frost similarly denied repeatedly that the last lines of his poem "Stopping by Woods on a Snowy Evening" were about death. It is, he would always say, about a man stopping his carriage to view a field newly filled with snow. Artists frequently deny that there is any deeper meaning beyond the surface content of their works, or that their works have any meaning at all. But if artworks have no meaning, or if they do not convey complex emotions, what point do they have? No point, say still other art critics. The role of art is not to communicate, not to mean anything, not even to stir emotions, but just to be. Art in this view is just another object in the world that elicits certain kinds of responses from the viewer or reader or listener, depending on what kind of art it is. Instead of theories about the meaning of works of art, or the proper ways to interpret art, what we should be doing is simply enjoying art. In the words of art critic Susan Sontag, ". . . in place of a hermeneutics we need an erotics of art."

These are some of the issues that H. Gene Blocker, a contemporary esthetician, explores in the following reading dealing with the esthetic attitude. He contrasts the eighteenth-century view that art has distance and detachment from the "real" world with the postmodern claim that all art is political. Along the way he also deals with the question of whether art is an elitist undertaking or whether the category "art" should include what is commonly referred to as popular culture. Beavis and Butthead as cultural and artistic icons? Maybe this is a bit hard to take, but some contemporary art theorists would argue that, like it or not, the distinction between "high" and "low" art has disappeared, and the real issue is not what is art and what is not but who is in control.

H. Gene Blocker: The Esthetic Attitude

To begin with, what exactly is meant by the esthetic attitude around which so much Western esthetics since the eighteenth century has been established? The word "esthetics," as a noun and in the plural form (with a final "s"), refers to a philosophical investigation of art and natural beauty, that is, a branch of philosophy which is concerned with art and questions of beauty. But, as an adjective and in the singular {without the final "s"), it refers to a kind of experience that people have, the so-called "esthetic experience," or "esthetic attitude." *Esthetics* and *esthetic attitude* are related in the sense that defining esthetic experience was the main task of esthetics in the eighteenth and nineteenth centuries and continues to be an important task of esthetics today, despite the argument of some contemporary philosophers, such as George Dickie, that there is no such thing as esthetic experience. Today the subject-matter of esthetics has greatly expanded to include many areas of interest besides the experience of the audience e.g., artistic creativity, the social and political aspects of the art world, and so on. Nonetheless, the quality and character of the viewer's enjoyment of art and objects of natural beauty (that is, esthetic experience) continues to occupy the attentions of estheticians.

The main assumption underlying this investigation is that a person may be interested in an object for different reasons and that this level and type of interest will determine the viewer's point of view or "attitude," which in turn will determine, or at least influence, what and how the viewer sees it. Suppose that during the night someone's house burns to the ground. Different people will be concerned with this incident in different ways which will be reflected in the way they experience and describe that event. The owner of the house is obviously concerned by the loss of personal property. The owner's parents living in another town are mainly concerned about the family's safety. The neighbors, if they do not know the family very well, will be primarily interested in the danger to their own adjacent homes. The police are primarily interested in keeping traffic flowing smoothly and safely along the road in front of the burning house, maintaining easy access for the fire trucks (and later to prevent looting). Firefighters are absorbed in the purely practical matter of getting the fire put out, while the fire safety inspector is concerned with how the fire started. The insurance agent wants to know the extent of damage and also whether it is the result of arson. Finally, passersby will mainly be curious and excited by a vicarious sense of danger and adventure, while the newspaper reporter will see the fire simply as a newsworthy local event. We can easily imagine how these different orientations will result in very different perceptions and descriptions of the fire.

Assuming that this psychological theory about attitudes and perspectives is sound, we can go on to try to group the various attitudes into broader types and to ask more generally, what is the *moral* point of view or the *religious* point of view, or, finally, the *esthetic* point of view? In this last case, we are asking whether there is any distinctive or essential feature which uniquely defines the experience which people have in the enjoyment of art works and objects of natural beauty which qualifies that experience to be called esthetic, and if so what that feature is. Or, to put the point differently, under what conditions is a man looking at a tree or a woman or a mountain an esthetic, as opposed to some other kind of experience? The answer which has been offered, though in widely different forms, over the past two hundred years, is that an esthetic experience is characterized by the "three D's"—disinterestedness, detachment and emotional distance. In more ordinary terms, the experience is esthetic if the person views the object for no ulterior, practical or immediately selfish or utilitarian motive. A viewer looks at it, we say, for its own sake, or simply for the joy of looking at it. Because of the primarily practical concern with a house burning, the esthetic point of view toward the fire in our example above might seem callous. But it could occur. That is, one of the bystanders, seeing there is nothing more to be done, may simply be fascinated by the sight of this huge flame, leaping up into the night sky—beautiful and terrifying (though of no personal danger to the bystander).

To say that an esthetic experience is not enjoyed for what it subsequently leads to is not to say that there are no good reasons for wanting to have that experience. The reason we treasure esthetic experiences is precisely for their intrinsic value, for the value they have in and of themselves—not for later experiences they may lead to. We get up early in the morning in order to get to work on time; we want to get to work on time in order to keep our job; we want to keep our job so we will continue receiving a regular weekly paycheck; we want this paycheck in order to buy a new car; we want the new car . . . and so on. These are all "extrinsically" valuable experiences or activities—valuable not for their own sakes but for the sake of something else. But what if *every* experience and activity had only extrinsic value —then we would always be doing everything for the sake of something else. In the end, we might wonder, what is it all for? In the end, isn't there something which we want for its own sake—perhaps to be successful, powerful, loved, needed, or accepted? These are intrinsically valuable activities and experiences, those for the sake of which we do everything else—get up in the morning, go to work, save our money, buy the car, and so on. In this sense, esthetic experiences are one of the most important sorts of intrinsically valuable experiences available to human beings.

Looked at in this way, an esthetic experience is a rather *unusual* kind of experience. Most of our looking at the world is practically oriented, as a result of which we do not usually *look* at things at all; we merely *see* them, as the English esthetician, Roger Fry, once said. For most practical purposes I do not need to see more of an object than is necessary to correctly classify that object. I see at a glance that it is a taxi which I need to take me to town. But if you were to ask me later what make of car it was, or to describe its design, or trim, I would surely be unable to answer. I was not visually exploring every aspect of the car, but only that tiny fraction which sufficed to tell me that it was in fact a taxi—the fact that it is a car, rather than a van or a truck, its characteristic yellow color, the "taxi" decal on the top is probably all I need to know that it is a taxi and therefore all I really noticed. But in an esthetic experience all those potentially visible aspects of an object which are usually ignored become available for visual inspection and enjoyment. But then we do not just see the thing; we *look* at it. "Seeing" is sometimes called a "success verb"; you either see it or you don't. It is all or nothing, and all at once. But in looking at something which we enjoy looking at, we take our time, savoring each detail, going back over certain parts again and again, and perhaps returning time after time for another look at this same object.

This attitude is most prominently displayed in the art museum, the music hall, and the theater, places which have been explicitly designed to encourage the adoption of the esthetic attitude and to help in the training of members of the audience in the proper attitude to adopt in the presence of works of art, that is, to behave as mere spectators who have come to look and to listen, but not to comment on or interact with the art object. The lighting, the arrangement of the seats, the picture frame, the stage all help us to focus on the art object and to blot out, except marginally or peripherally, other distracting, nonesthetic elements (such as the people in front of you, the changing of the scene sets, the falling and rising of the curtain, and so on).

The immediate consequence of the impersonal and nonutilitarian posture of the esthetic attitude is to isolate the object of this esthetic attention from its mundane, physical surroundings, transforming it into a self-contained whole, unconnected with the rest of the world, except symbolically. This is what the twentieth-century French philosopher, Jean-Paul Sartre, calls the "unrealizing" function of esthetic experience and what is often referred to as the "willing suspension of disbelief." In order to experience the novel, painting or play esthetically, one must realize that the events represented in these art works are fictional, that is, that they are not contiguous with ordinary space-time physical reality. The unrealizing function of esthetic experience is closely related to its disinterestedness. To say esthetic perception is not concerned with practical consequences is just to say that in esthetic experience we do not perceive the object as a real object with real consequences for us. It is the function of the arena, the stage, the picture frame, and the pedestal to transform and elevate the object from its ordinary space-time. This also ensures the adoption of the esthetic attitude on the part of the audience, who are trained to interact with and participate in the esthetic "fiction" or "semblance," but only in esthetically appropriate ways, whether as merely spectators, passively contemplating the esthetic object, or more actively participating but within carefully defined esthetic boundaries, separating fiction from reality.

One may weep for the hero's mortal wounds, but one must not call the doctor; one may hiss and boo the villain, but one must not rush onto the stage to disarm him. (In the film *The Piano* there is a scene of the performance of a British Christmas pantomime, including a typical shadow play in which a man appears to attack a woman with an axe. The British are shocked when the indigenous Maoris in the audience rush onto the stage to stop the "axe murder." The British had been socialized into adopting the esthetic attitude in certain appropriate settings, while the native Maoris had no such esthetic distancing traditions in their traditional society.)

As a result of the attitude of detachment and disinterestedness, the esthetic attitude is generally more reflective or contemplative in orientation, and as a result of *that,* the object of esthetic attention is generally understood symbolically to refer to meanings and significant content of a quite general though undefined sort. When I look at a tree from a practical point of view, to see how much firewood it will yield, I see that object simply as an instance of the category "tree." It is just a particular instance of a tree. But when I disengage myself from such practical concerns and look at the tree for its own sake, then my attention may be drawn to the general symbolic significance of the tree as the link, for example, between heaven and earth, or the monumentality, quiet dignity, strength, and stability of the tree, or its protective aspect. It is no longer simply a member of the category "tree," but an object which seems to partake of quite general and far-ranging meaning and significance.

Only by the "unrealizing" act of psychic distance, in which beliefs are temporarily suspended, can one object come to represent something which it is not, especially where the object is concrete and what it represents is something quite general, such as rebirth and renewal, or the dialectical tension between creative and destructive forces. The paradox of the esthetic attitude is that one is simultaneously aware of both the symbol and of what it symbolizes. The mystery of artistic representation and impersonation is the simultaneous belief and disbelief in their identity and distinction. Those lines on paper become a generalized human face, but only if I know full well that they are not a face but only lines drawn on paper. The actor becomes Hamlet only if I know he is an actor playing the part of Hamlet.

Though removed from everyday life, the emotional interest in an object at this symbolic level can be intense, especially since it involves an ordering of experience which is quite impossible in the chaos and confusion of everyday life.

This symbolic meaning also transcends the concerns of a particular regional or ethnic group. Although we no longer worship Dionysus, we can still enjoy the plays of Sophocles and Euripides which were once a part of that worship. We continue to appreciate the tragedy because our esthetic attitude has detached it from its religious context and transformed it into a potent, cross-cultural symbol which it was not for its original audience. Once the esthetic dimension has emerged as an independent entity, it becomes possible to deliberately, self-consciously create symbolic meaning in art. Once we see that from within the gaze of the esthetic attitude ordinary physical objects from everyday life take on symbolic meaning, it becomes possible to isolate, select, reorganize, and manipulate such symbolic content in deliberately constructed patterns which possess far greater esthetic intensity than objects of natural beauty which are less tightly organized and unified.

The distancing effect of the traditional esthetic attitude has a direct bearing on the current controversy whether art should be censored because it leads to violence, especially towards women. Today many women object to the treatment of women in works of art. There are at least two problems here. First, is the pornographic portrayal of women in a way which seems likely to incite violence toward women. Of course, if what we said above about the esthetic attitude is correct, representations of women viewed esthetically cannot have this immediate, overt effect. The second problem is perhaps more serious; it concerns what women have come to *represent* or *symbolize* in art. Many art works represent women as symbols of fertility, emotion, intuition, nurturing, passivity, weakness. Of course, one reason women have become symbols of such generalized meaning is that, even outside art, many people in the past thought that women were actually like that—that they really were more emotional, caring, weaker, more passive, and so on. As a result, artists have found it convenient to use representations of women to symbolize these ideas.

It is also true that by representing women in this light, artists themselves have *contributed* to these stereotypes of women. And so today, when the facts about women no longer support these stereotypes, women nonetheless continue to symbolize such ideas, and this encourages many people in our society to continue to think of women in the old clichéd ways. The objection to such stereotyped representations of women is not only that they are false and demeaning, but that they indirectly influence behavior towards women—stereotypes influence attitudes which, in turn, influence behavior.

Does looking at a painting of a female nude cause sexual desire or arousal? Does hearing a story of a wolf eating a little girl's grandmother shock or traumatize us? If not, why not? Esthetic attitude theorists say no, and the reason is that the esthetic attitude of esthetic experience distances us from any such immediately practical outcomes. The "unrealizing" aspect, as Sartre put it, of the esthetic attitude makes it more contemplative and reflective and therefore the art work has a more symbolic relation to reality, rather than a direct, practical relationship to reality.

Of course, we have to admit that in all representational art there is a reference to the real world—the point of view created in the art work sheds light on the real world which it is in some sense "about." In this sense art can challenge, create, alter, modify perspectives, attitudes, points of view about things in general. The artist often utilizes the symbolic meaning already associated in society with the female body; but by placing this representation of the woman within the

Yoruba effigy bowl. For over ten thousand years the female body has been used to represent or symbolize fertility. Compare the use of the female body in this African carving with the nude in European painting and also with pornographic and erotic pictures. Photo courtesy of H.Gene Blocker.

created, fictionalized context of a particular work of art, the artist also creates a perspective or point of view through which the audience is invited to view the female subject, not only in this art work, but *in general*. And this generalized attitude or perspective might lead to action, but only in the indirect way attitudes influence action, creating at most a tendency to act in certain ways. But even so, the effect on the audience of the attitude created by the art work is generally only partial and temporary, competing as it is with many other appealing, attractive perspectives.

We must not exaggerate the power of artists; at most they may succeed in drawing the viewer temporarily into the artist's point of view, sharing the artist's attitude toward women, for example, but generally only for a little while. When the movie is over and we walk outside the mood is generally gone (though it may have a more subtle effect on our general attitude, or general way of looking at things). Sometimes the artist would *like* to change people's attitudes and behavior but is usually frustrated precisely because the effect of the art work is only temporary—it generally lasts only so long as the audience is viewing the work. Afterwards most people slip right back into their customary attitudes.

Most people are also capable of entertaining a number of different alien points of view—trying them on for size, as it were, without permanently adopting them. I can hear the vegetarian, or the religious fundamentalist, or the "new age" point of view, for example. I understand these perspectives; I can imagine what it would be like to live within and see the world from those points of view, but I don't have to *adopt* them. That is, most of us can entertain but finally *resist* many different perspectives. This is one of the ways we learn about other people and other cultures, by seeing how other people see the world.

The modernist tradition of the esthetic attitude trains and develops that flexibility to enjoy temporarily trying on different perspectives without having to adopt any one of them. Those who support censorship, on the other hand, argue that we are not capable of this flexibility and sophistication—that some works of art cause an immediate reaction (seeing the film I go out and "act out" the beating, the rape), or less extremely, that we are not able to resist being drawn permanently into points of view that we do not choose for ourselves but which are insidiously forced upon us by our exposure to art (making us racists, sexists, xenophobic, and so on).

Part of the postmodern support of censorship springs from a rejection of any distinction between fine art and popular culture. Whereas modernist estheticians agree that we are less able to resist the influence of *popular* culture than we are able to resist the influence of fine art, postmodernist estheticians deny there is any meaningful distinction in this regard and argue that we are *equally* vulnerable to *all* art forms. Of course, there are some very general social conditions which do indeed cause us to adopt those attitudes which are most prevalent in the particular society in which we happen to have been raised. From parents, teachers, radio, TV, and what we might call in very general terms "popular culture," there is indeed a very strong influence on us from which most of us can never escape or resist, or indeed are even aware of. By the time we enter the first grade we have been acculturated ("brain-washed") into the mores of our particular society. But that is not due to art, at least not what modernist estheticians mean by art. According to the modernist esthetic tradition, art makes us reflect on our society, makes us conscious of these background mores and traditions and often calls them into question. In the modernist tradition we are trained to be aware of the point of view through which a particular artist deliberately sets out to portray a certain situation, and so we are perfectly aware of the difference, for example, between Thomas Hardy's pessimistic attitude toward the world and that of the average person. For this reason modernism insists that we are not "brainwashed" by Hardy's perspective, but merely see it for what it is—one person's point of view which we allow ourselves to entertain temporarily while enjoying the novel, but then set aside when we have finished the book.

Postmodern theorists discount the distinction between "fine art" and "popular culture." What we call art is just a somewhat more elitist form of general culture and is therefore equally influential in the formation of cultural values. The postmodernist also denies that artists are as aware and in control of their product as they may think (and as modernist art critics and estheticians have generally given them credit for). Historically, we think of Tolstoy as deliberately setting out to create a point of view from which he intends we should view the world—the world according to Tolstoy. But really, say the postmodernists, Tolstoy is no more in charge, or acting alone, than the person who produces comic books, Saturday morning cartoons, TV advertising. Nor are we any more aware of the intentions of the fine artist than we are aware of the intentions of the sophisticated advertiser or politician. The idea of the artist's deliberate intention which we are fully aware of is simply an illusion, say the postmodernists. Neither, by the same token, are we any more able to distance ourselves esthetically from the point of view of a work of fine art than we are to TV ads or sitcoms. In every case, say the postmodernists, it is the whole structure of society which determines values, attitudes, and the idea that individuals can consciously detach themselves, much less disagree or resist, is simply an illusion.

It comes down to who is in control. The modernist position emphasizes the control of the individual artist to deliberately create a work which is meant to draw the viewer temporarily into the artist's point of view, as well as the control of the viewing audience to try on different perspectives, knowing they are alien perspectives, much as we might try on different hats, before finally buying one (or perhaps not buying any of them). The postmodernist position emphasizes a kind of all-encompassing social climate of thought-control in which we are subconsciously manipulated, not by unscrupulous individual artists who know what they're doing, but by more amorphous social forces, institutions—by "society." In some ways this difference may be due more to changes in art and society than to different interpretations of the same art and society. TV channel-surfing is a more widespread activity today than reading a "serious" novel. Perhaps the modernist esthetic attitude was appropriate for reading a novel, but not for channel-surfing.

Questions for Discussion

1. What does Blocker mean by the "esthetic attitude"? Are there really experiences which are "esthetic" in nature? If so, give some examples from your own experience in which you first look at an object in a nonesthetic way and then in an esthetic way.

2. How much "in control" are we to accept or reject the point of view portrayed in movies, pictures, music, and television? Do you think there is any difference in this regard between "fine art" and popular culture (our being more in control in the case of fine art than in the case of popular culture)?

3. What influence do you think art has on life? Do you agree with Blocker's claim that the esthetic attitude distances art from life, except "symbolically"?

4. Can art change the way we look at the world? Can you think of examples from history or from your own experience? Would Harriet Beecher Stowe's *Uncle Tom's Cabin* be an example (or would Blocker argue this was not an example of "high" art)?

CHAPTER 31

Art as Ideal

Imagine a ninth grade class of students on an outing. It is perfectly appropriate for their teacher to take them to the Museum of Art where they will see, among other things, famous paintings of nude women. Yet the teacher wouldn't dare take the class to an adult book store where they could see even more pictures of naked women. Why is this? What is the difference between these pictures of unclothed women? At first, we might say that the difference is that the first is *art,* while the second is *erotic* and *pornographic.* But this just shows that the word *art* has flattering, praiseworthy connotations, whereas words like *pornographic* have shameful, dirty, immoral connotations. But it does not tell us *why* some pictures of naked women are given the high-minded, praise worthy label of art while others are given the shameful label of *pornography.*

The difference lies partly in the way (or style) in which the female figures have been done and partly in the use to which they are put. The first is something one could tell just from looking at the pictures themselves, apart from anything else. The second could only be detected by knowing something about the background reasons for which and the context in which the pictures were made. And, of course, these two tend to go together. Advertisers use pictures to get people to buy certain products; war propagandists use pictures to get people willingly to sacrifice for the war effort, and to accomplish these ends certain subjects must be selected, and more important, they must be portrayed in a certain way—an ad portraying attractive young people enjoying themselves using the product, and so on. Erotic pictures are used to arouse and stimulate sexual desire and pornographic pictures to ridicule, humiliate, and facilitate fantasies of power over women—all are rendered in a style designed to accomplish such ends. In the art of the classical nude, on the other hand, the unclothed female body is *not* used to instigate any direct action, like going out to buy the product, have sex, or beat someone up, but rather to depict an ideal conception of beauty, perfection, spiritual harmony, and the highest humanistic ideals. Of course, the *proper* use of such pictures does not prevent someone from misusing them in *other* ways—an adolescent boy may find magazine advertisements of women modeling underwear or illustrations from an anatomy textbook or even nude paintings in the Museum of Art erotically stimulating. But this is a clear misuse of such pictures and contrary to the style in which they were done. And just as those who advertise women's underwear and those who publish anatomy textbooks would strenuously object to demands from antipornography groups to ban such illustrations because some people have abused their intended use, so artists and museum curators strongly object to the censorship of nude paintings on similar grounds.

Recently, women's groups have challenged the distinction between the esthetic use and style of the artistic nude, on the one hand, and the erotic and pornographic use and style of naked women on the other. While these lines of demarcation may have held true in the past, they argue, they no longer hold today. Today's art, they claim, has broken down the boundaries which once existed between art and pornography. Today's art, they say, is meant to shock, stimulate, hurt, shake us up; and what used to be called pornographic and erotic is now simply part of mainstream late twentieth century art. And even in the "good old days" when high art was separated from trash, they ask, why was it that only *women's* bodies were shown nude and not *men's*? Of course, there are male nudes in art, especially in ancient Greek art, but it is true that the great majority of nude figures in modern European art are female. Does this art really represent "spiritual and humanistic ideals," or isn't it simply a more subtle form of men enjoying looking at women? And, even though of a more refined, genteel sort, doesn't this still demean and humiliate women, putting them in the role of objects to be stared at, rather than autonomous human beings in their own right?

In his classic study of the nude, Sir Kenneth Clark offers the best defense possible of the traditional notion of the nude as the highest subject matter of art. Of course, he insists, we must acknowledge that there are subtle erotic overtones in most nude art, but he argues that this is not a "call to action," and moreover, that it is balanced by the search for a kind of perfection we do not find in everyday life, for formal beauty of line and contour, and the attempt to embody abstract spiritual values in physical, human form.

Kenneth Clark: The Naked and the Nude

The English language, with its elaborate generosity, distinguishes between the naked and the nude. To be naked is to be deprived of our clothes, and the word im-

From Kenneth Clark, "The Naked and the Nude" in *The Nude: A Study in Ideal Form*. Princeton University Press, 1953. Used by permission of the National Gallery of Art, Washington, D.C.

plies some of the embarrassment most of us feel in that condition. The word "nude," on the other hand, carries, in educated usage, no uncomfortable overtone. The vague image it projects into the mind is not of a huddled and defenseless body, but of a balanced, prosperous, and confident body: the body re-formed. In fact, the word was forced into our vocabulary by critics of the early eighteenth century to persuade the artless islanders that, in countries where painting and sculpture were practiced and valued as they should be, the naked human body was the central object of art.

For this belief there is a quantity of evidence. In the greatest age of painting, the nude inspired the greatest works: and even when it ceased to be a compulsive subject it held its position as an academic exercise and a demonstration of mastery. . . . It may have suffered some curious transformations, but it remains our chief link with the classic disciplines. When we wish to prove to the Philistine that our great revolutionaries are really respectable artists in the tradition of European painting, we point to their drawings of the nude. . . . . .

These comparisons suggest a short answer to the question, "What is the nude?" It is an art form invented by the Greeks in the fifth century, just as opera is an art form invented in seventeenth-century Italy. The conclusion is certainly too abrupt, but it has the merit of emphasizing that the nude is not the subject of art, but a form of art.

It is widely supposed that the naked human body is in itself an object upon which the eye dwells with pleasure and which we are glad to see depicted. But anyone who has frequented art schools and seen the shapeless, pitiful model that the students are industriously drawing will know this is an illusion. The body is not one of those subjects which can be made into art by direct transcriptions—like a tiger or a snowy landscape. Often in looking at the natural and animal world we joyfully identify ourselves with what we see and from this happy union create a work of art. This is the process students of aesthetics call empathy, and it is at the opposite pole of creative activity to the state of mind that has produced the nude. A mass of naked figures does not move us to empathy, but to disillusion and dismay. We do not wish to imitate; we wish to perfect. We become, in the physical sphere, like Diogenes with his lantern looking for an honest man, and, like him, we may never be rewarded. Photographers of the nude are presumably engaged in this search, with every advantage; and having found a model who pleases them, they are free to pose and light her in conformity with their notions of beauty; finally, they can tone down and accentuate by retouching. But in spite of all their taste and skill, the result is hardly ever satisfactory to those whose eyes have grown accustomed to the harmonious simplifications of antiquity. We are immediately disturbed by wrinkles, pouches, and other small imperfections, which, in the classical scheme, are eliminated. By long habit we do not judge it as a living organism, but as a design; and we discover that the transitions are inconclusive, the outline is faltering. We are bothered because the various parts of the body cannot be perceived as simple units and have no clear relationship to one another. In almost every detail the body is not the shape that art had led us to believe it should be. Yet we can look with pleasure at photographs of trees and animals, where the canon of perfection is less strict. Consciously or unconsciously, photographers have usually recognized that in a photograph of the nude their real object is not to reproduce the naked body, but to imitate some artist's view of what the naked body should be. . . .

So that although the naked body is no more than the point of departure for a work of art, it is a pretext of great importance. In the history of art, the subjects that men have chosen as nuclei, so to say, of their sense of order have often been in themselves unimportant. For hundreds of years, and over an area stretching from Ireland to China, the most vital expression of order was an imaginary animal biting its own tail. In the Middle Ages drapery took on a life of its own, the same life that had inhabited the twisting animal, and became the vital pattern of Romanesque art. In neither case had the subject any independent existence. But the human body, as a nucleus, is rich in associations, and when it is turned into art these associations are not entirely lost. For this reason it seldom achieves the concentrated aesthetic shock of animal ornament, but it can be made expressive of a far wider and more civilizing experience. It is ourselves and arouses memories of all the things we wish to do with ourselves; and first of all we wish to perpetuate ourselves.

This is an aspect of the subject so obvious that I need hardly dwell on it; and yet some wise men have tried to close their eyes to it. "If the nude," says Professor [Samuel] Alexander, "is so treated that it raises in the spectator ideas or desires appropriate to the material subject, it is false art, and bad morals." This high-minded theory is contrary to experience. In the mixture of memories and sensa-

Three Female Nudes Dancing, *by*
Pablo Picasso. Photo courtesy of
Prentice Hall, Inc.

tions aroused by Rubens' *Andromeda* or Renoir's *Bather* are many that are "appropriate to the material subject." And since these words of a famous philosopher are often quoted, it is necessary to labor the obvious and say that no nude, however abstract, should fail to arouse in the spectator some vestige of erotic feeling, even though it be only the faintest shadow—and if it does not do so, it is bad art and false morals. The desire to grasp and be united with another human body is so fundamental a part of our nature that our judgment of what is known as "pure form" is inevitably influenced by it; and one of the difficulties of the nude as a subject for art is that these instincts cannot lie hidden, as they do, for example, in our enjoyment of a piece of pottery, thereby gaining the force of sublimation, but are dragged into the foreground, where they risk upsetting the unity of responses from which a work of art derives its independent life. Even so, the amount of erotic content a work of art can hold in solution is very high. The temple sculptures of tenth-century India are an undisguised exaltation of physical desire; yet they are great works of art because their eroticism is part of their whole philosophy.

Apart from biological needs there are other branches of human experiences of which the naked body provides a vivid reminder—harmony, energy, ecstasy, humility, pathos; and when we see the beautiful results of such embodiments, it must seem as if the nude as a means of expression is of universal and eternal value. But this we know historically to be untrue. It has been limited both in place and in time. There are naked figures in the paintings of the Far East, but only by an extension of the term can they be called nudes. In Japanese prints they are part of *ukioye,* the passing show of life, which includes, without comment, certain intimate scenes usually allowed to pass unrecorded. The idea of offering the body for its own sake, as a serious subject of contemplation, simply did not occur to the Chinese or Japanese mind, and to this day raises a slight barrier of misunderstanding. In the Gothic North the position was fundamentally very similar. It is true that German painters in the Renaissance, finding that the naked body was a respected subject in Italy, adapted it to their needs, and evolved a remarkable convention of their own. But Dürer's struggles show how artificial this creation was. His instinctive responses were curiosity and horror, and he had to draw a great many circles and other diagrams before he could brace himself to turn the unfortunate body into the nude.

Only in countries touching on the Mediterranean has the nude been at home, and even there its meaning was often forgotten. . . .

As I have said, in our Diogenes search for physical beauty our instinctive desire is not to imitate but to perfect. This is part of our Greek inheritance, and it was formulated by Aristotle with his usual deceptive simplicity. "Art," he says, "completes what nature cannot bring to a finish. The artist gives us knowledge of nature's unrealized ends." A great many assumptions underlie this statement, the chief of which is that everything has an ideal form of which the phenomena of experience are more or less corrupted replicas. This beautiful fancy has teased the minds of philosophers and writers on aesthetics for over two thousand years, and although we need not plunge into a sea of speculation, we cannot discuss the nude without considering its practical application, because every time we criticize a figure, saying that a neck is too long, hips are too wide or breasts too small, we are admitting, in quite concrete terms, the existence of ideal beauty. Critical opinion has varied between two interpretations of the ideal, one unsatisfactory because it is too prosaic, the other because it is too mystical. The former begins with the belief that although no individual body is satisfactory as a whole, the artist can choose the perfect parts from a number of figures and then combine them into a perfect whole. Such, we are told by Pliny, was the procedure of Zeuxis when he constructed his *Aphrodite* out of the five beautiful maidens of Kroton. ... Naturally the theory was a popular one with artists: but it satisfied neither logic nor experience. Logically, it simply transfers the problem from the whole to the parts, and we are left asking by what ideal pattern Zeuxis accepted or rejected the arms, necks, bosoms, and so forth of his five maidens. And even admitting that we do find certain individual limbs or features that, for some mysterious reason, seem to us perfectly beautiful, experience shows us that we cannot often recombine them. They are right in their setting, organically, and to abstract them is to deprive them of that rhythmic vitality on which their beauty depends.

To meet this difficulty the classic theorists of art invented what they called "the middle form." They based this notion on Aristotle's definition of nature, and in the stately language of Sir Joshua Reynolds' *Discourses* it seems to carry some conviction. But what does it amount to, translated into plain speech? Simply that the ideal is composed of the average and the habitual. It is an inspiring proposition, and we are not surprised that Blake was provoked into replying, "All Forms are Perfect in the Poet's Mind but these are not Abstracted or compounded from Nature, but are from the Imagination." Of course he is right. Beauty is precious

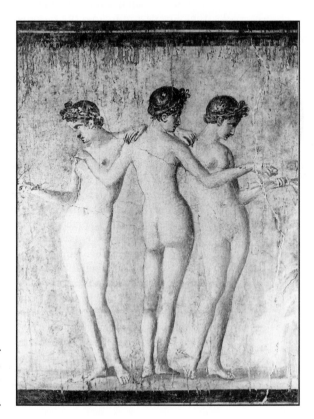

The Three Graces,
Roman Painting, Pompeii.
Courtesy of The Bettmann Archive.

and rare, and if it were like a mechanical toy, made up of parts of average size that could be put together at will, we should not value it as we do. But we must admit that Blake's interjection is more a believer's cry of triumph than an argument, and we must ask what meaning can be attached to it. Perhaps the question is best answered in Crocean terms. The ideal is like a myth, in which the finished form can be understood only as the end of a long process of accretion. In the beginning, no doubt, there is the coincidence of widely diffused desires and the personal tastes of a few individuals endowed with the gift of simplifying their visual experiences into easily comprehensible shapes. Once this fusion has taken place, the resulting image, while still in a plastic state, may be enriched or refined upon by succeeding generations. Or, to change the metaphor, it is like a receptacle into which more and more experience can be poured. Then, at a certain point, it is full. It sets. And, partly because it seems to be completely satisfying, partly because the mythopoeic faculty has declined, it is accepted as true. What both Reynolds and Blake meant by ideal beauty was really the diffused memory of that peculiar physical type developed in Greece between the years 480 and 440 B.C., which in varying degrees of intensity and consciousness furnished the mind of Western man with a pattern of perfection from the Renaissance until the present century.

Once more we have returned to Greece, and it is now time to consider some peculiarities of the Greek mind that may have contributed to the formation of this indestructible image.

The most distinctive is the Greek passion for mathematics. In every branch of Hellenic thought we encounter a belief in measurable proportion that, in the last analysis, amounts to a mystical religion, and as early as Pythagoras it had been given the visible form of geometry. All art is founded on faith, and inevitably the Greek faith in harmonious numbers found expression in their painting and sculpture, but precisely how we do not know. The so-called canon of Polykleitos is not recorded, and the rules of proportion that have come down to us through Pliny and other ancient writers are of the most elementary kind. Probably the Greek sculptors were familiar with a system as subtle and elaborate as that of their architects, but we have scarcely any indication as to what it was. There is, however, one short and obscure statement in Vitruvius that, whatever it meant in antiquity, had a decisive influence on the Renaissance. At the beginning of the third book, in which he sets out to give the rules for sacred edifices, he suddenly announced that these buildings should have the proportions of a man. He gives some indication of correct human proportions and then throws in a statement that man's body is a model of proportion because with arms or legs extended it fits into those "perfect" geometrical forms, the square and the circle. It is impossible to exaggerate what this simple-looking proposition meant to the men of the Renaissance. To them it was far more than a convenient rule: it was the foundation of a whole philosophy. Taken together with the musical scale of Pythagoras, it seemed to offer exactly that link between sensation and order, between an organic and a geometric basis of beauty, which was (and perhaps remains) the philosopher's stone of aesthetics. Hence the many diagrams of figures standing in squares or circles that illustrate the treatises on architecture or aesthetics from the fifteenth to the seventeenth century. . . .

Francis Bacon, as we all know, said, "There is no excellent beauty that hath not some strangeness in the proportion. A man cannot tell whether Apelles or Albert Dürer were the more trifler; where of the one would make a personage by

Art Versus Pornography

In 1972, sixteen years after he had written his book on the nude, Sir Kenneth Clark was called to speak before a British government investigative panel on pornography to differentiate as best he could the art of the nude from pornography. As we see from this excerpt, Clark bases his defense of nude art on the modern esthetic distinction between fine art as essentially nonutilitarian from other utilitarian uses of pictures. Even if we agree with Clark, we might still favor the ban on pornography. That is, we might agree with Clark that nude art is not pornography and should therefore not be censored, but still insist that because pornography is socially dangerous it should be banned or at least severely restricted. Those who support pornography, not as art but as pornography, do so in the name of free speech and freedom of the press. Nonetheless, Clark's argument is important since, assuming we decided to ban or restrict pornography, we would need to know exactly what pornography is, and especially how it differs from other superficially similar forms of fine art.

To my mind art exists in the realm of contemplation, and is bound by some sort of imaginative transposition. The moment art becomes an incentive to action it loses its true character. This is my objection to painting with a communist programme, and it would also apply to pornography. In a picture like Correggio's *Danäe* the sexual feelings have been transformed, and although we undoubtedly enjoy it all the more because of its sensuality, we are still in the realm of contemplation. The pornographic well-paintings in Pompeii are documentaries and have nothing to do with art. There are one or two doubtful cases—a small picture of copulation by Géricault and a Rodin bronze of the same subject. Although each of these is a true work of art, I personally feel that the subject comes between me and complete aesthetic enjoyment. It is like too strong a flavor added to a dish. There remains the extraordinary example of Rembrandt's etching of a couple on a bed, where I do not find the subject at all disturbing because it is seen entirely in human terms and is not intended to promote action. But it is, I believe, unique, and only Rembrandt could have done it.

[Source: *Pornography: The Longford Report.* London: Coronet, 1972, pp. 99-100.]

geometrical proportions: the other by taking the best part out of divers faces to make one excellent." This very intelligent observation is unfair to Dürer; and suggests that Bacon, like the rest of us, had not read his book on human proportions, only looked at the plates. For, after 1597, Dürer abandoned the idea of imposing a geometrical scheme on the body, and set about deducing ideal measurements from nature, with a result, as may be imagined, somewhat different from his analyses of the antique; and in his introduction he forcefully denies the claim that he is providing a standard of absolute perfection. "There lives no man upon earth," he says, "who can give a final judgment upon what the most beautiful shape of a man may be; God only knows that . . . 'Good' and 'better' in respect of beauty are not easy to discern, for it would be quite possible to make two different figures, neither conforming with the other; one stouter, the other thinner, and yet we might scarce be able to judge which of the two excelled in beauty."

So the most indefatigable and masterly constructor of ideal proportions abandoned them halfway through his career; and his work, from the *Nemesis* onward, is a proof that the idea of the nude does not depend on analyzable proportions alone. And yet when we look at the splendidly schematized bodies of Greek sculpture, we cannot resist the conviction that some system did exist. Almost every artist or writer on art who has thought seriously about the nude has concluded that it must have some basis of construction that can be stated in terms of measurement: and I myself, when trying to explain that a photograph did not satisfy me, said that I missed the sense of simple units clearly related to one another. Although the artist cannot construct a beautiful nude by mathematical rules, any more than the musician can compose a beautiful fugue, he cannot ignore them. They must be lodged somewhere at the back of his mind or in the movements of his fingers. Ultimately he is as dependent on them as an architect.

Dipendenza: that is the word used by Michelangelo, supreme as a draftsman of the nude and as an architect, to express his sense of the relationship between these two forms of order. And in the pages that follow I often make use of architectural analogies. Like a building, the nude represents a balance between an ideal scheme and functional necessities. The figure artist cannot forget the components of the human body, any more than the architect can fail to support his roof or forget his doors and windows. But the variations of shape and disposition are surprisingly wide. . . .

So our surmise that the discovery of the nude as a form of art is connected with idealism and faith in measurable proportions seems to be true, but it is only half the truth. What other peculiarities of the Greek mind are involved? One obvious answer is their belief that the body was something to be proud of, and should be kept in perfect trim.

We need not suppose that many Greeks looked like the *Hermes* of Praxiteles, but we can be sure that in fifth-century Attica a majority of the young men had the nimble, well-balanced bodies depicted on the early red-figure.

The Greeks attached great importance to their nakedness. Thucydides, in recording the stages by which they distinguished themselves from the barbarians, gives prominence to the date at which it became the rule in the Olympic games, and we know from vase paintings that the competitors at the Panathenaic festival had been naked ever since the early sixth century. Although the presence or absence of a loincloth does not greatly affect questions of form, and in this study I shall include figures that are lightly draped, psychologically the Greek cult of nakedness is of great importance. It implies the conquest of an inhibition that oppresses all but the most backward people; it is like a denial of original sin. This is not, as is sometimes supposed, simply a part of paganism: for the Romans were shocked by the nakedness of Greek athletes, and Ennius attacked it as a sign of decadence. Needless to say, he was wide of the mark, for even the most determined nudists of all were the Spartans, who scandalized even the Athenians by allowing women to compete, lightly clad, in their games. He and subsequent moralists considered the matter in purely physical terms; but, in fact, Greek confidence in the body can be understood only in relation to their philosophy. It expresses above all their sense of human wholeness. Nothing that related to the whole man could be isolated or evaded; and this serious awareness of how much was implied in physical beauty saved them from the two evils of sensuality and aestheticism.

At the same party where Kritobalos brags about his beauty Xenophon describes the youth Autolykos, victor of the Pankration, in whose honor the feast was given. "Noting the scene," he says, "the first idea to strike the mind is that beauty has about it something regal; and the more so if it chance to be combined (as now in the person of Autolykos) with modesty and self-respect. Even as when a splendid object blazes forth at night, the eyes of men are riveted, so now the beauty of Autolykos drew on him the gaze of all; nor was there one of those onlookers but was stirred to his soul's depth by him who sat there. Some fell into unwonted silence, while the gestures of the rest were equally significant."

This feeling, that the spirit and body are one, which is the most familiar of all Greek characteristics, manifests itself in their gift of giving to abstract ideas a sensuous, tangible, and, for the most part, human form. Their logic is conducted in the form of dialogues between real men. Their gods take visible shape, and on their appearance are usually mistaken for half-familiar human beings—a maidservant, a shepherd; or a distant cousin. Woods, rivers, even echoes are shown in painting as bodily presences, solid as the living protagonists, and often more prominent. Here we reach what I take to be the central point of our subject: "Greek statues," said Blake, in his *Descriptive Catalogue,* "are all of them representations of spiritual existences, of gods immortal, to the mortal, perishing organ of sight; and yet they are embodied and organized in solid marble." The bodies were there, the belief in the gods was there, the love of rational proportion was there. It was the unifying grasp of the Greek imagination that brought them together. And the nude gains its enduring value from the fact that it reconciles several contrary states. It takes the most sensual and immediately interesting object, the human body, and puts it out of reach of time and desire; it takes the most purely rational concept of which mankind is capable, mathematical order, and makes it a delight to the senses; and it takes the vague fears of the unknown and sweetens them by showing that the gods are like men and may be worshipped for their life-giving beauty rather than their death-dealing powers.

To recognize how completely the value of these spiritual existences depends on their nudity, we have only to think of them as they appear, fully clothed, in the Middle Ages or early Renaissance. They have lost all their meaning. . . . The academic nudes of the nineteenth century are lifeless because they no longer embodied real human needs and experiences. They were among the hundreds of devalued symbols that encumbered the art and architecture of the utilitarian century.

The nude had flourished most exuberantly during the first hundred years of the classical Renaissance, when the new appetite for antique imagery overlapped the medieval habits of symbolism and personification. It seems then that there was no concept, however sublime, that could not be expressed by the naked body, and no object of use, however trivial, that would not be the better for having been given human shape. . . .

Such an insatiable appetite for the nude is unlikely to recur. It arose from a fusion of beliefs, traditions, and impulses very remote from our age of essence and specialization. Yet even in the new self-governing kingdom of the aesthetic sensation the nude is enthroned. The intensive application of great artists has made it into a sort of pattern for all formal constructions, and it is still a means of affirming the belief in ultimate perfection. "For soule is forme; and doth the bodie make," wrote Spenser in his *Hymne in Honour of Beautie,* echoing the words of the Florentine Neoplatonists, and although in life the evidence for the doctrine is inconclusive, it is perfectly applicable to art. The nude remains the most complete example of the transmutation of matter into form.

Nor are we likely once more to cut ourselves off from the body, as in the ascetic experiment of medieval Christianity. We may no longer worship it, but we have come to terms with it. We are reconciled to the fact that it is our lifelong companion, and since art is concerned with sensory images the scale and rhythm of the body is not easily ignored. Our continuous effort, made in defiance of the pull of gravity, to keep ourselves balanced upright on our legs affects every judgment on design, even our conception of which angle shall be called "right." The rhythm of our breathing and the beat of our hearts are part of the experience by which we measure a work of art. The relation of head to body determines the standard by which we assess all other proportions in nature. The disposition of areas in the torso is related to our most vivid experiences, so that, abstract shapes, the square and the circle, seem to us male and female; and the old endeavor of magical mathematics to square the circle is like the symbol of physical union. The starfish diagrams of Renaissance theorists may be ridiculous, but the Vitruvian principle rules our spirits, and it is no accident that the formalized body of the "perfect man" became the supreme symbol of European belief. Before the *Crucifixion* of Michelangelo we remember that the nude is, after all, the most serious of all subjects in art; and that it was not an advocate of paganism who wrote, "The Word was made flesh, and dwelt among us . . . full of grace and truth."

Questions for Discussion

1. Although he plays it down, what role does Clark give eroticism in "high art" nude painting?

2. Why does Clark prefer Italian to German nude painting?

3. According to Clark, what does the female nude represent in European art?

4. What, according to Clark, is the difference between "the nude" and "the naked"?

5. How would you use the distinctions Clark makes to counteract charges that an exhibition featuring nudes is pornographic?

CHAPTER 32

Esthetics and Ideology

In different ways Clark and Blocker have tried to defend the modernist theory of the elevated stature of "high" art, detached from the hurly-burly and often emotionally overheated practical reality of everyday life, through the distancing effect of the "esthetic attitude" in "esthetic experience." According to this tradition, art, or at least "high" art, when correctly, that is, "esthetically," enjoyed, does not and cannot lead to overt, violent racist or sexist behavior. Of course, there are pornographic movies, politically propagandistic paintings and plays, erotically stimulating pictures, but these are not works of "fine art"—they are not examples of "high" art. In the reading which follows, the contemporary literary theorist, Jennifer Jeffers, challenges this modernist tradition and introduces a postmodern reading, or interpretation of the role of the female nude in Western culture.

Jeffers argues that from the beginning of the modernist tradition, even in the "high art" tradition of European painting which Clark discusses, women are portrayed as men like to see them, or more accurately, stare, gape or "gaze" at them. From Rubens to the latest *Sports Illustrated* annual swimsuit edition, the female nude (or near nude) is portrayed as an object of male consumption—whether as coy, fertile, titillating, or more overtly as a "sex kitten," naughtily eager to give men sexual pleasure. Because these images are so pervasive in our culture, Jeffers argues, this is not only how *men* like women to be and look, but how many *women* think they ought to look and act. From endless visual advertisements portraying flawless, healthy, unusually beautiful young women smoking cigarettes, drinking beer or soft drinks, we all grow up in this society to think this is how women should look and act. So pervasive is this standardized model of female beauty and social role that we are seldom even aware of it. Whether as men or women, we unconsciously and completely accept the image.

In an interesting and ironic way, some contemporary female artists attempt to make us more aware of this socially constructed image by parodying, lampooning and making fun of this male image of women. Of course, very few real women can fit this idealized model, but this just provides an opportunity for people to make money advertising the latest diet, exercise equipment, and even surgical corrections, adding or subtracting where appropriate—not just to be physically fit or healthy, but to look the way men expect women to look. What is perhaps most troubling and controversial in Jeffers' discussion is the way in which she traces this social, predominantly male, construction of the image of the female body to the modern Renaissance "high art" tradition which Kenneth Clark portrays as an idealistic quest for perfection, particularly as this "high art" tradition evolves in the late nineteenth and early twentieth centuries into our middle-class mass media culture.

Blocker called attention to the vicious cycle of widespread sexist attitudes toward women leading to the artistic use of the female nude as an artistic *symbol* of all that is nurturing, fertile, weak, passive, and so on, which in turn further perpetuates such gender stereotypes, which, coming now full circle, encourages their further use as artistic symbols, and so on and on and on. The problem remains how to break this vicious cycle—whether through artistic lampooning of the stereotype, gender education, the steady erosion of the stereotype through more appropriate female role models, or through censorship of sexist, erotic, and pornographic art.

Jennifer Jeffers: "The Politics of Representation: The Role of the Gaze in Pornography"

The Politics of Representation

The primary purpose of this article is to chart the coordinates of a dominate ideological perspective on the map of Western culture and society. The dominate ideological perspective I shall call, borrowing from contemporary French philosophy, the gaze. The gaze is motivated by a desire to control and attain the object of its desire. Practically speaking, the gaze is the code, a chain of signifiers or an image or group of images, that perceives, mediates and manages the world from a certain vantage point. I am interested in the code of representation in Western painting and the modern photographic image. In particular, I explore the assumptions and meanings overt and covert in the way Western culture has read the female nude in art and/or the female body according to a code of representation. As the French linguist de Saussure states, "every means of expression used in society is based, in principle, on collective behavior or—what amounts to the same thing—convention." From art to media and advertisements to pornographic images of women, the culturally constructed gaze determines how we "see" these images through our inherited "convention"—which can be and often is for the female in our society quite different from actual experience. The gaze, therefore, is a powerful instrument in its ability to discount experience in favor of an accepted ideology. Indeed, the gaze is more than a system or manner of viewing representations of people; the gaze is an entire ideology that governs our behavior: attitude, thinking and, from a larger societal view, our economy and institutions.

I. The Nude, the Naked and the Gaze

In *The Nude: A Study of Ideal Form,* Kenneth Clark is careful to separate the cultured artistic, painterly female nude from the non-cultured, potentially obscene naked woman represented in painting. In his study, Clark privileges the nudes by Rubens and Raphael, for instance, because they represent an "unself-conscious piety as the sheaves of corn and piled-up pumpkins that decorate a village church at harvest festival." In terms of iconic meaning the female form embodies nature as goodness, represents bounty and fecundity and in her posture a passive availability that assures the male gaze access to, ability to "penetrate," her "secrets." While Rubens' *Three Graces* is prized by Clark, Dürer's *Women's Bath* provokes his wrath as the only good points of Durer's vision are those taken from past masters: "Gothic curiosity and horror . . . . The figure on the left is almost Michelangelesque, the woman combing her hair in the center is taken from a Venus Andyomene . . . . The fat monster on the right confirms his feeling of the obscenity of the whole situation and must have been observed from nature . . . ." Hence, for Clark, there is a difference between the female nude in art and the naked woman drawn from nature. Aesthetically speaking, we may even agree with Clark that the Rubens is more "pleasant" to behold than the Dürer—but in that agreement we would only be displaying the acculturated attitude that I wish to expose in this article.

In the history of Western art the female nude has a privileged position as an icon for patriarchal society. The female represented by the male artist is not only beauty idealized, she is also beauty defined, controlled, contained and possessed. An object of the male perspective, both painter and viewer, the female nude becomes a constructed figure produced and consumed by a genderized gaze. This gaze is not strictly confined to art but becomes an entire mode of perception for our culture; the male gaze, historically speaking, is that which perceives. We have a cultural myth which states that this perception is constituted by the rational or the logical, is acculturated and has the ability to act upon the world in a meaningful manner. Whereas the female perspective reflects, quite literally as a mirror reflects, the male gaze; the female is constituted by irrationality or that which is not governed by logic, nature and is passive in that the world acts upon it and is given its very existence as object to be perceived. The myth of the West states that "Woman" is constituted by the irrational, uncontrolled and unkempt forces, including sexuality, that keep "Man" from establishing a rational and coherent hold on the world. As Clark emphasizes, the female nude is to be contrasted from a naked woman. If the female, by nature, embodies that which is uncontrollable and potentially transgressive, then art, the very embodiment of Western culture, will "clean her up," will re-present the female in art so that all that is transgressive is ordered, rational and beautiful.

The boundary between the female nude in so-called high art and the naked woman in, perhaps, a less elevated art, is essential to understanding what constitutes art, even erotic art, and what comprises the obscene. In contemplative or high art the sexuality is latent. According to Clark, with overt sexuality sublimated, the (male) artist uses that rechanneled energy for a "higher" purpose—to create an image or icon to represent, to stand in for, that original impulse of sexuality for the purpose of aesthetic contemplation. The success of the artist's sublimation is measured in the viewer's reaction to the painting. If the viewer becomes sexually aroused by Rubens' *Three Graces,* then Rubens did not successfully sublimate his feeling and did not successfully produce a painting worthy of contemplation. In general, according to Clark, should the viewer become aroused by the content of the painting (nymphs bathing, for example) then that painting has crossed the boundary from high art to "low" art. This boundary, of course, is a construction produced by the male gaze. What is ironic is that the boundary exists as a ruse for titillation; art historians, curators and artists themselves derive pleasure from playing on, around and just across the boundary of the obscene, a boundary that is endlessly reconstituted.

Art depends on the boundary between art and obscenity; likewise, pornography depends on maintaining the same distinction. Those interested in art are usually put off by obscenity, whereas those looking for pornography are put off by art. This basic differentiation is illustrated by an apt recounting of a story from a French author by the early twentieth-century Freudian, Hanns Sachs:

> He tells that one evening strolling along the streets of Paris he noticed a row of slot machines which for a small coin showed pictures of women in full or partial undress. He observed the leering interest with which men of all kind and description, well dressed and shabby, boys and old men, enjoyed the peep show. He remarked that they all avoided one of these machines, and wondering what uninteresting pictures it might show, he put his penny in the slot. To his great astonishment the generally shunned picture turned out to be the Venus of Medici. Now he begins to ponder: Why does nobody get excited about her? She is decidedly feminine and not less naked than the others which hold such strong fascination for everybody. Finally he finds a satisfactory answer: They fight shy of her because she is beautiful.

The Venus of Medici is "beautiful" because she has been placed into a high art context, she is presented as an autonomous body and she is an ideal representation of woman consisting of paint pigment on a flat surface. The women in

Courtesy of the Bettmann Archive.

the pictures that were of interest to the Parisian men are representations of "real" women captured, most likely, in poses that suggest the photographer's intrusion into their intimate moments. The photographs crossover the boundary from the nudity of the Venus of Medici to the nakedness of woman. These photographs constituted, it would seem, turn of the century pornography. The contemporary definition of pornography is interesting because it, too, keeps art and life separate: "obscene writings, drawings, photographs, or the like, especially those having little or no artistic merit" *(Random House Dictionary, Unabridged)*. The etymology of the word pornography goes back to Greece: "pórne" meant harlot and "-graphos" as a suffix was a combining form meaning drawn or written. In ancient Greece, females were kept as sexual slaves, and so, the drawing, etching and writing about these women is the etymological origin of the word: representations of harlots or sex slaves. Little has changed in three millennia. While we may be able to grasp the fundamental distinction between that which constitutes nudity in high art and comprises nakedness in "low" art, the problematic area—the boundary—is defining that which constitutes the obscene. The dictionary offers three different definitions: one, "offensive to morality or decency; indecent; depraved;" two, "causing uncontrolled sexual desire;" three, "abominable; disgusting; repulsive." To be sure, the raging issues in the contemporary debate concerning pornography center around the naming of the indecent, policing sexual desire and drawing the line between sex and violence. These issues I will discuss in section three, **Pornography and the Invisible.**

Returning to the female nude in art, the male gaze goes through a transition in the latter half of the nineteenth century and early twentieth century. While there are many social, political and economic factors that render this change, I would like to point out two in direct reference to our discussion concerning the female nude and the gaze. First, at the turn of the twentieth century artists began painting the female nude from fetishized perspectives; male artists began focusing on the breasts, buttocks, barely concealed genitals, torso, nape of the neck, the body draped as if dead, headless or in compromising positions. Art critic Carol Duncan in *The Aesthetics of Power* finds the new middle-class male artists' depictions of women disturbing: "What distinguishes these pictures and others in this period from most previous nudes is the compulsion with which women are reduced to objects of pure flesh, and the lengths to which the artist goes in denying their humanity." An example of the draping female nude which Duncan finds especially "brutal" is *Reclining Nude* by Kees Van Dongen. In the Dongen is the disturbing, if not perverse, attitude of the new reigning "high" art: "The erotic imaginations of modern male artists . . . re-enact in hundreds of particular variations a remarkably limited set of fantasies . . . the male confronts the female nude as an adversary whose independent existence as a physical or spiritual being must be assimilated to male needs, converted to abstractions, enfeebled or destroyed." The results were that the early Moderns painted their female nudes from incommodious, contorted, and fetishized perspectives which resulted in female bodies represented in pieces and fragments. What is significant concerning the new "high" art representation of the female nude at the turn of the century and in relation to pornography is that this new attitude coincides with the mass produced photographic image. The concurrence produces the second alteration in the perception and rendering of the female form. What occurs is that the respectable, high art images of the female nude are transferred to the photographer's studio where this "limited set of fantasies" is played out in front of the camera lens. From an economic point of view, photographic images are relatively inexpensive, can be mass produced and, therefore, widely available: witness the Parisian men from Sachs story. Pornography was fully realized with the advent of moving pictures; now the male gaze had less imaginative work to do in order to satisfy its fantasy; unfortunately for women, "real life" females were required to "stage" the male gaze fantasy.

II. Desire and the Gaze

What it means to be an object of a male gaze must be understood in the larger context of our contemporary culture and society because the gaze permeates all aspects of our late Capitalist lives. First of all, when we look at something that we like, or at something that we wish to have, we look at the object with desire. Desire initially creates the gaze. Capitalism seizes our desire and translates it into a means of exchange and commodity. Through this commodification of desire, Capitalism gains control, "deterritorializes" desire by subverting traditional codes and then "reterritorializes" desire by directing our desire toward the equivalent standard of exchange and commodity. Contemporary philosophers and psychoanalysts have pointed to the Freudian construction of the Oedipal triangle (mommy, daddy, me) as a primary means of channeling desire in order to control the consumer masses in the Capitalist society; all desire is concentrated, spent and bound in the configuration of the nuclear family. The problem with the Oedipal triangle and psychoanalysis is that they preserve and sustain the Platonic notion of desire as lack. In the *Symposium* Socrates asks Agathon: "Then isn't it probable or isn't it certain that everything longs for what it lacks, and that nothing longs for what it doesn't lack?" Agathon and the entire Western tradition of philosophers and psychoanalysts agree with Socrates. It is the nineteenth century philosopher, Friedrich Nietzsche, who calls into question the Platonic notion of desire as a negative attribute. Borrowing from Nietzsche, contemporary philosophers have constructed desire along the lines of production or activity and not through the pursuit of an object or through the lack of an object. The epistemological, moral and political stakes are quite high in this game of desire, as Capitalist society, playing on desire as lack, has thoroughly circumscribed our lives and infiltrated our desires, not only at the level of commodity and exchange, but also at the level of our bodies, our ideas, our actions, our knowledge, science and technology and, of course, our fantasies. We are manipulated, we recognize that fact, and yet we want more.

In late twentieth-century culture, we recognize that the gaze is construction for our manipulation, yet we "buy into" that construction through our support of the media, commodification and our manifest desire for what Capitalists sell us. What is interesting, if not ironic, about the construction of the gaze in the past and especially in contemporary times is that the object of the gaze, or those who are being manipulated by the image that sells the object, refuse to, or simply cannot, understand themselves as manipulated. In other words, women try to imitate the images that the gaze constructs in the media, advertisements and other forms of commodification; in this way, women support and affirm their own manipulation. Men, too, are manipulated by the culture that affirms a certain way of looking and a certain ideology; though few would question its origin or its practice.

Indeed, what emerges from this manipulation is an ideology that constitutes the female through *representation* based on a constructed male ideology which, if anything, consciously departs from the experience of being female. The most obvious result of this construction is the domination, the sheer power, of one half of the population to manage and moderate the other half of the population through a controlling iconic image. Because the ordered image is attractive to men, and because women believe in the ideal that is projected for them, women strive to attain in reality this constructed image. Our culture of the 1990s sustains and perpetuates this ideology, despite the feminist movement and the fact that increasing numbers of women hold positions of power in the market place. These aspects do not change the fact that women are haunted by an *image* of an ideal; no one in late-Capitalist society is immune to the constant barrage of television, magazine and film images that assail us. The struggle to achieve an image is manifest in our obsession to alter our bodies evidenced, especially for young women, in eating disorders, the preoccupation with exercise, not for health reasons but appearance alteration, and cosmetic surgery. Everyday we, both male and female, are bombarded by ubiquitous advertisements which produce a feeling of inadequacy in terms of our bodies, our lifestyle, our bank accounts and our own self-image. No one in our society is immune to the desire to look/be like someone else or change enough of who/what we are to feel "okay." Interestingly, those ideals produced by a traditional high art male gaze have infiltrated late Capitalism's metaphors to sell you a new image and/or a new body: exercise equipment promises "The Image You Want," diet supplements promise "a sculptured physique," and liposuction hands you the chisel with "Facial & Body sculpturing." Capitalism creates the ideal, the desire, then it *sells* you the means to attain it. As long as Capitalism can generate a feeling of lack in consumers, perpetuating a desire for the "object" that they lack, the system will continue to manipulate, probably with increased efficiency, society.

A clue to this seemingly mysterious gaze of manipulation is found in the way that our culture and society is structured. The contemporary philosopher, Michel Foucault, theorizes that a "binary division," emerges as an institution gains authority in a society: "Generally speaking, all the authorities exercising individual control function according to a double mode; that of binary division and branding (mad/sane; dangerous/harmless; normal/abnormal)" *(Discipline and Punish)*. Another contemporary philosopher, Gilles Deleuze, comments on this division and extends Foucault's thought, "the great dualities" stem from the binary nature of our society and create unbridgeable differences "between different classes, or the governing and the governed, or the public and the private" *(Foucault)*. With the gaze this binary is evident: the one who sees and the one who is seen. Yet, what is not evident in this binary configuration is that which is *not* seen. In terms of the representation of nude and naked women what is seen are bodies, what is not seen is the condition or set of conditions that puts the female into the place of object. The role of the gaze, one who sees and one who is seen, is to protect the ideology that renders the female invisible as a person and visible as an object.

III. Pornography and the Invisible

The gaze that constructs images of women in art is the same gaze that constructs images of women in pornography. From seemingly innocuous representations of women prized by Kenneth Clark, to the early Moderns' aggressive perversion of the female body, to late twentieth-century abstract paintings of women such as De Kooning's *Woman I,* the female body is a represented object of the male gaze. Art of the early Moderns is often referred to as "erotic art" and the work of the late twentieth-century painters, like that of De Kooning's, slips out of the category of representation into the category of "abstraction." Yet, what is clear is that the female form is being presented in new, literally form-altering ways; where the female form was once idealized now the female form is truncated, contorted, fetishized and "abstracted" into inhuman or subhuman shapes. The desire that constructs the gaze of the fragmented woman, or the contorted orgasmic or dying woman, desires submission on the part of the object—on the part of the female. The code of submission makes visible the body or body part in a manner that discounts the actual person in the representation: the body is for sale, anyone with an attractive body part will do. Representing the fragmented female body has become the forte of Capitalism, the product is sold on the basis of the expectation of the gaze. The consumer knows the game: if I buy this product I will gain the object I lack, which is not the object for sale, but the body that is selling the product. A recent advertisement for moisture cream presents in a dramatic black and white photograph of a fragmented woman: one breast fading into the shadow, one hand, the nape of the neck and lips.

As we discovered in section one, the boundary between art and pornography is demarcated by the ambiguous, in terms of application, definition of the obscene. Yet, the definitions of obscenity are not ambiguous: "depraved," that which "causes uncontrolled sexual desire," and "abominable, disgusting, repulsive." Perhaps pornographers would say that it is the second definition of the obscene to which their products cater: "uncontrolled sexual desire." Indeed, "good" pornography on the part of the gaze would be that which does not lead the person to "contemplation," as in art, but to excitation at both a mental and physical level. But the obscene in pornography, especially since the 1960s, is no longer confined to erotic titillation geared to the sexually naive but basically "nice guy." This depiction of the "nice guy" who reads and views pornography is also a myth; the "nice guy" who reads *Playboy* or *Penthouse* is being manipulated by Capitalist "pornocrats," though the "nice guy" will be the last to admit it. Pornography, the writing or representation of "harlots," is a seven billion dollar a year industry in the United States. Its economic power and political sanctification are legion. This power has opened new doors on to the gaze's "desire"; now for one's pleasure there is: sadism, torture, rape, gang rape, child molestation and so-called "snuff" films where women experience most of the above then are actually killed—all for the gaze's viewing pleasure.

Those who are invisible are the women (and now children) whose body and body parts are used for the staging of the gaze's pleasure. While we may be quick to point out that the pornography that would qualify as "depraved" and "abominable, disgusting and repulsive" is "hardcore" and relatively few partake of it, the gaze that constructs hardcore porn constructs also the so-called "soft" porn, and, in turn, the ideology and political power that sustains this gaze maintains the objectification of women at all levels of society. The success of the mainstream pornographic magazine industry is built upon the respectable, even acculturated, male gaze "contemplating" the (fragmented) female form; suddenly Hugh Heffner and Kenneth Clark seem to be "talking" the same language. From *Making Violence Sexy* Andrea Dworkin and Catharine MacKinnon explain *Playboy's* marketing strategy:

> The format of *Playboy* was developed to protect the magazine from prosecution under obscenity law. Writing from recognized writers was published to meet a standard of worth that would get the magazine First Amendment protection. The First Amendment was then used by *Playboy* to protect its sexual exploitation of women. *Playboy* sells women.
>
> The use of women as objects in *Playboy* is part of how *Playboy* helps to create second-class status for women. Women in *Playboy* are dehumanized by being used as sexual objects and commodities, their bodies fetishized and sold. The term "bunny" is used to characterize the

woman as less than human—little animals that want sex all the time, animals that are kept in hutches.

The women in *Playboy* are presented in postures of submission and sexual servility. Constant access to the throat, the anus, and the vagina is the purpose of the ways in which the women are posed. . . .

Underlying all of *Playboy*'s pictorials is the basic theme of all pornography: that all women are whores by nature, born wanting to be sexually accessible to all men at all times. *Playboy* particularly centers on sexual display as what women naturally do to demonstrate this nature.

The male gaze constructs an ideal sexual partner in terms of physical form, desire, submission and, perhaps most uncannily, in terms of the female always already "knowing" what it is the male desires sexually. This latter aspect is uncanny because it seems dubious that, biologically speaking, being female a woman will "intuitively know" that which is erotically and sexually pleasing for a male body. The woman who knows a man's erotic desire and who is always available is the ideal woman in every man's fantasy. It is exactly this mythical creation of the ideal woman that dominates pornography; the male gaze constructs the "sex kitten" image for the consumption of an entire culture. The seemingly sophisticated magazine *Playboy,* for example, has succeeded in projecting this male fantasy for generations, presenting a false "norm" for women, all women, to live up to as a test of femininity—which has absolutely nothing to do with being female.

Women in magazines, in porn films and in shaving cream television commercials are visible from the male gaze perspective. Despite the extraordinary number of images of women in art, media and communication, women are invisible as subjective equal members in society and will continue to be mere objects as long as the ideology that sustains the male gaze controls our desire. Yet, we resist seeing ourselves, both female and male, as somehow manipulated by representations and a constructed gaze. Women, no less than men, resent the coming to terms with the underlying social constructs that this ideology divulges about the nature of our desire:

Now I think that all of the incredibly upset and passionate and disturbed and angry responses to pornography when feminists address the issues have to do with the fact that we are finally getting down to the raw nerves, which is: what this sexual system is; how male sexuality does in fact colonize us, set our limits, how in fact we are defined by this male sexuality. And we don't like it. We resent it and very often the way we express that resentment is by expressing resentment towards those who make us aware of it. But it also raises terrifying questions—about the nature of our own sexuality, about the ways in which we are complicit in our own degradation. None of this is pleasant. All of it is terrible, and yet without facing this, what are we to do? We have to face it.

"Interview with Andrea Dworkin"
Feminist Review, No. 11, 1982

From the high art ideal of the female nude to the fetishized female body in late twentieth-century Capitalism, the gaze has and continues to "colonize" our sexuality, limit our choices and make invisible the conditions that perpetuate and sustain the gaze's power. The politics of representation constructs an ideology that governs, not only the way we see, but also what we see and even if we see certain aspects and people that the gaze wishes to render invisible.

Questions For Discussion

1. What does Jeffers mean by "the gaze?" Do you agree with her analysis? Why or why not?

2. Contrary to Clark, Jeffers argues that the boundary separating the female nude of high art and the obscene picture of a naked woman is ironically a ruse for titillation. What are Jeffers' reasons for holding this position? How sound do you find this argument?

3. What is the difference, according to Jeffers, between the "high art" nudes of the late nineteenth and early twentieth centuries and those of an earlier period? How does this affect the "high art," "low art" boundary?

4. In what sense, if any, are women said to be "invisible"? Do you agree with this claim? Why or why not?

Suggestions for Further Reading

Beardsley, Monroe C. *Aesthetics: Problems in the Philosophy of Criticism.* Indianapolis: Hackett, 1981. The best introduction to esthetics by a well-known defender of traditional esthetics against recent criticisms.

Blocker, H. Gene, and Jennifer Jeffers, eds. *Contextualizing Aesthetics: From Plato to Lyotard.* Belmont, CA: Wadsworth, 1999. A reader with lengthy introductions that covers the history of esthetics from ancient to contemporary times. One of the co-editors is an author of this book.

Danto, Arthur. *The Transfiguration of the Commonplace.* Cambridge, MA: Harvard University Press, 1981. A modern classic by a leading esthetician defending the definability of art as understood by the "art world."

Dickie, George. *An Introduction to Aesthetics.* New York: Oxford University Press, 1997. The latest introductory book by America's leading esthetician defending Dickie's analytic revision and reformulation of traditional esthetics.

Social and Political Philosophy

PART 8

CHAPTER 33

Social and Political Philosophy

Introduction to Social Philosophy

Social philosophy is that branch of philosophy which is concerned with social relationships among people, particularly those relations which exist in the nation or state. Parallel with other areas of philosophy, the social philosopher does not try to determine empirically what kinds of societies actually exist and how they in fact differ from one another. This is the task of the social scientist. The social philosopher is rather concerned with normative questions surrounding the nature of the state and its justification, as well as evaluative questions concerning the ideal kind of social arrangements within the state and in particular the proper relationship between the government and its citizens. Let us look at a representative sampling of such questions.

First, is there any good reason why we ought to have a state at all? What would be wrong with people doing as they please and cooperating when and if they wish? Assuming, however, that we ought to have a state, what kind should it be: a monarchy, a military dictatorship, a democracy, or what? If we decide on democracy, should there be a division of powers between different branches (executive, legislative, judicial) and if so, what relationships should there be between the various branches of government? Then, too, how much and what sort of power should the state have over the individual? Should the state adopt a minimal role, a kind of night watchman, organizing the military in time of war, a police force for domestic problems, perhaps building a major system of roads, for example, but no more? Or should the state enter fully into the life of the society, directing education, establishing national goals, running the economy, directly or indirectly, channeling individuals into employment most needed by the society at a particular time, and so on?

A second way of looking at those questions would be from the viewpoint of the individuals who make up a state. Does the ordinary citizen have any duty or responsibility to obey the authority of the state, and if so, why, and to what extent? Assuming the citizens have an obligation in general to obey duly established laws of the state, are they obliged to obey any and all laws? Is civil disobedience or rebellion ever justified? And if so, how, and on what grounds? How much freedom from governmental restraint should the individual have, and on what basis? Where, if at all, should we place limits on the rights of people to lead their own lives as they see fit?

In the process of answering these questions, the social philosopher also, as we will see below, tries to clarify persistently ambiguous terms of political language: equality, freedom, human rights, punishment, to mention some of the most troubling. When we speak of equality do we mean that everyone should have the same share of society's goods, such as land and money, or only that they should have an equal opportunity to compete for those goods? What do we mean when we say that everyone should be "free"? Do we mean that everyone should be free to do as he or she pleases, or that people should be free to get their fair share of what most people consider valuable, such as income, medical care, a good job, an adequate retirement program, and so on? Assuming we can answer the question of society's right to punish those who break the law, what exactly do we mean by *punishment?* Avenging the wrong the criminal has done? Preventing the lawbreaker from further mischief? Discouraging others from breaking the law? Rehabilitating the criminal? Or what? The different goals of punishment often oppose and contradict one another and lead to radically different and opposed social policies.

There is perhaps no area of human activity other than politics where the influence of philosophers is more evident. The philosophies of John Locke, Rousseau, Voltaire, even such ancient thinkers as Plato and Aristotle, had a profound influence on the development of the governmental institutions of the United States. The Constitution of the United States, the Declaration of Independence, and the Bill of Rights borrow heavily from the social philosophy of John Locke. John Stuart Mill, along with his father James Mill and their friend Jeremy Bentham, exerted enormous influence on the social reforms enacted by the British Parliament in the nineteenth century. Other thinkers such as Thomas Hobbes and Adam Smith also influenced the development of the constitutional monarchy in Great Britain and the emergence of capitalism, at least in part. Any historical or political reality as complex as capitalistic economies cannot be attributed to a single cause or even a few causes. Nonetheless, the change from feudalism to capitalism was aided by the shift in thinking that was led by philosophers.

A complete comparison of social philosophies is a topic so broad that we must settle on a more limited task. We will look at a single question: the relation between the individual and the society as a whole. Should the individual's rights be limited for the good of society, or should society's welfare be subordinated to the good of the individual (does the part exist for the sake of the whole, or the other way around)? To illustrate the tension between the individual and the society, consider the debate between champions of economic justice and supporters of political liberty.

Equality and Human Rights

The most obvious and dramatic arena for the debate about the relationship of the individual and the state was the cold war debate between the democracies of the West led by the USA and the Eastern Communist-bloc countries led by the USSR. The cold war is now over, but the end of the cold war is by no means the end of the debate between the underlying ideals of the libertarian capitalist right and the egalitarian socialist left, for the essentials of that debate continue to take place where they have always taken place, though in a quieter and less dramatic form—*within* each of the countries of the East and West and indeed in every country in every part of the world today. This is and remains the central and single most important social and political debate of our times. It is not, any longer, simply the cold war debate between East and West as to which form of government is better: the free-market democracies of the West or the controlled economies of the East; that seems to have been decisively answered now in favor of the free-market democracies. Today the debate is rather how to combine and balance in one social system individual liberties with a more equal distribution of social goods that require governmental regulation of the marketplace. The debate has also expanded to include the question of the proper relationship between individual countries and multi-national bodies which claim the right to regulate the practices of these countries.

At first it might appear that the Western democracies and the Communist-bloc countries had radically and irreconcilably different notions of freedom, rights, equality, and justice which could never be combined into one system. In theory, at least, the Western democracies arose from an eighteenth-century libertarian notion of the freedom of individuals to pursue their goals largely free from governmental restraint, while the socialist countries arose from the nineteenth-century Marxist ideal of an equal distribution of all social goods. The libertarian model advocates what is sometimes called "negative" freedom (or negative rights), that is, freedom *from* governmental restraint (or the right to be free from governmental restraint). These are the freedoms (and rights) guaranteed in the Bill of Rights. The socialist model, on the other hand, advocates freedom (and rights) in what is often called a "positive' sense, that is, the freedom (and right) *to have* adequate housing, health care, a job, education, retirement income, paid vacations, and so on.

The first view of the state's role sees freedom (and the guarantee of rights) as the removal of societal restrictions on the individual; the other sees freedom (and the securing of rights) as a kind of societal structure that paternalistically encourages and nourishes the full development of the individual's potential into a complete social human being. Obviously, these two views may conflict. You may not *want* to do those things that society considers good for you and your full social development. By the same token, if you are allowed to do pretty much as you please, you may not develop your full potential as a human being, and so you may *not* be free to create and enjoy art, for example, just as the child who is free to quit piano lessons will not be free (that is, not be able) later in life to play the piano. And these two conceptions of freedom (and rights) have obvious political ramifications.

According to the libertarian model, everyone is said to be equal in the sense that everyone has a right to equal opportunity. Imagine a foot race. If everyone starts at the same time and from the same place and if no one is allowed to take a short cut or is artifically handicapped in some way, then we say that everyone has an equal chance. This is what is meant by equality of opportunity. But, of course, they can't all win, and that is what is meant by the inequality of outcome, that is, of the result. You are free to compete for a place in the best university or professional school, for a job, for election to public office, or fame as a rock star, but you are *not* guaranteed you will get what you are competing for. As a result, equality of opportunity is compatible with great inequality of outcome in terms of wealth, power, and other social goods. Of course, many inequalities of opportunity remain in all libertarian societies due to discrimination and nepotism, but even if all inequalities of opportunity could be removed, there would still be winners and losers, the haves and the have nots. Because of the possibilities of being a winner, the traditional libertarian model encourages greater initiative. The socialist ideal, on the other hand, favors a more equal distribution of society's goods to everyone. This is why the socialist ideal is often referred to as *egalitarianism,* meaning equality. According to the socialist or egalitarian ideal, everyone will earn more or less the same, a physician and a bus driver, everyone will have more or less the same quality of housing and education, the government leader and the street sweeper. This is what is meant by equality of outcome. In such a system, the security of a guaranteed comfortable life is offset by the lack of initiative in getting ahead.

If everyone is free in the traditional libertarian sense, then because of inequalities among people in intelligence, ability, and so on, and more important, because of the freedom of the rich and powerful to pass their wealth on to their children (whether of superior ability or not), the result is that although all are free to do what they would like, most people do not have the means of actually achieving this. In nineteenth-century England, for example, a Welsh coal miner was "free" to own a wealthy house, send his children to the private schools from where they could enter the most prestigious and lucrative jobs in science, industry and government, but was at the same time utterly incapable of doing so. He was free in the sense that there were no explicit restrictions against his owning land or capital, but at the same time he was incapable of carrying out this desire

*The Parthenon, which dominates the acropolis in Athens, was built in the fifth century B.C.E.
and was the symbol of Athenian glory when the Greeks gave us the first example of democratic
government. The word democracy derives from two Greek works that mean "rule of the people."
Photo by David Stewart.*

for severe lack of funds, and of acquiring the funds for lack of adequate education, and so on. But how is he to achieve these things or at least an equal chance of obtaining them? Only by possessing the proper education and training. But who is to pay for this? Certainly the Welsh coal miner could not. The funds must come from those who have more money, the wealthy. But why should they voluntarily agree to help him? They are not in any way restricting his rights. "You are free, my good man," they will tell him, "to go out and earn your way just as we did a hundred years ago. Take an extra job, save, send your children to a good school, gradually work your way up; there's nothing stopping you but your own lack of initiative." But, if not by voluntary agreement, then how are we to get the money from these wealthy people except by forcing them to relinquish it against their will (either through taxation or direct expropriation)? If we do this, are we not violating their traditional rights to get and keep wealth, and to pass it on to their children?

It looks as though we can only achieve the egalitarian goal at the expense of liberatarian principles. The major political debate in all democracies today continues to be how to combine these two apparently irreconcilable goals.

But notice—if the egalitarian freedom, or right, cannot be achieved by the poor miner, or voluntarily by the wealthy owner of the mines, then it will never be achieved except by government interference. Left to itself, the free market-place will always result in a division of haves and have-nots. So in order to achieve the egalitarian human rights, we have to alter our conception of the role of government—away from the ideal of minimal government simply pro-tecting the rights of the individual to get on with his or her own life, and to-ward the ideal of government as providing minimal guarantees to all of its citizens on a more equitable basis. And this is the connection between differ-ent concepts of freedom and differences in the relation of the individual to the society as a whole. The traditional libertarian freedoms demand a minimal watchdog government to keep others from interfering in the freedom of each individual to get on with life as each sees fit. The ideal of egalitarian freedom demands just the opposite, a strong centralized government entering into every phase of life—from wages, to education, to health care—to insure that everyone has a decent life.

What Is Justice?

But what *is* fair and just? Libertarians look at their ideal and say that it is a fair and just distribution of the social goods (money, housing, education, jobs, and so on) because of the equality of opportunity and the individual liberties in their system. If you and I are salespersons for the same company, working on the same commission basis, then if you earned more last month than I did because you are smarter, more aggressive, more hard-working, or for any other honest and legal reasons, then you *deserve* to earn more than I did and it is perfectly fair and just that you should. "Equal pay for equal . . ." what? The libertarians say equal pay for *equal ability* or *productivity*. The socialist, egalitarian ideal, on the other hand, regards this sort of result of the libertarian system as terribly *un*just, while they regard their own system as far more just since everything there is more evenly divided, and everyone is free to enjoy equally the wealth and other bene-fits which their society has to offer. "Equal pay for equal human need and equal worth as a human being." Is it fair and just, the egalitarian asks, for one person to have more than another just because of the accidents of heredity which ge-netically favor some fortunate individuals with superior intelligence, good looks, and a dynamic personality? And is it fair that some should have more because their wealthy and powerful parents were able to give them a head start in life through private schools, private lessons, travel opportunities, books and intelli-gent discussion at home, and so on? And, by the same token, is it fair or just, the egalitarian continues, that a person born with few of either genetic or environ-mental advantages should suffer through life as a result? In fact, the egalitarian asks, can we really separate equality of opportunity from equality of outcome? Do the children of poor parents really have the same chance of success as the children of wealthy parents?

The Contemporary Reality

Unrestricted libertarianism is largely a thing of the past, just as the socialist ideal is just that, an ideal. In the relatively pure libertarianism of the nineteenth century, individuals were almost completely free to dispose of whatever money they earned legally and almost completely free to run their business in the most efficient means possible consistent with free market realities. If children were willing to do the work for less than anyone else, then the factory owners were free to employ them. Since they owned the factory and the land on which it sat, they were also free to run the factory in the most economical way possible, including dumping toxic materials into the streams or into the air or maintaining an uncomfortable and unhealthy work environment if this would help cut costs and boost profits. Today, by contrast, those same factory owners must obey dozens of regulations concerning taxes, social security benefits, waste disposal, all of which greatly reduce their personal freedom to dispose of their own property. Similarly, the idealistic egalitarian vision wherein all share equally in all social goods is a fading ideal. Today, by contrast, individuals in some socialist countries are encouraged to work hard by being allowed to keep a larger share of social goods, resulting each year in greater and greater income differentials in these countries.

Nonetheless, the debate between libertarian and egalitarian ideals continues because the two are hard to reconcile and there is no complete consensus as to which should be given greater priority. Much as we might like to have a measure of both, they seem to pull in opposite directions, and so, like oil and water, are extremely hard to mix. If we want to more evenly distribute the nation's wealth in order to achieve more equal educational and health benefits for all, how is that to be achieved? In particular, who is going to pay for it? And how is that money to be obtained? It can only come from the more wealthy members of society, including wealthy corporations, and they are certainly not going to give it up voluntarily. It must be taken from them by force of law, that is, through an accelerated income tax scheme, and inheritance tax, and other measures actually practiced in most of the Western democracies today. And how can you prevent wealthier and better educated families from giving their children a head start on the children of poorer and less educated families except by forcing children of more advantaged families to attend the same schools, busing them, if necessary, to different school districts, or restricting the money their parents can spend on their curricular and extracurricular education? But then you are necessarily diminishing their individual freedom and right to keep whatever they fairly earn and to pass that on to their children when they die, and, while alive, to raise their family and help their children as they see fit. Only in a relatively more centralized, planned state in which individual liberties are somewhat diminished can social welfare programs be implemented. By the same token, individual liberties and free enterprise incentives can never take place in socialist countries unless and until the state relaxes its control of the economy and allows a more uneven distribution of wealth.

The problem we face, whether libertarian-leaning or egalitarian-leaning, is how to reconcile these opposed conceptions of social justice. The intense debates in the United States today over employment quotas, affirmative-action programs, welfare rights, the rights of the homeless, the constitutionality of supporting schools through local community property taxes, and countless other questions of a just distribution of social goods all turn on the more fundamental issue of the conflict between the freedom of individuals to dispose of what they have fairly earned as they wish, and the right of everyone to a more equal share of social goods. Those on the political right (generally the haves) claim that the egalitarian system is unfair or unjust to them because it violates their basic freedom and right to dispose of what they have fairly earned through their own natural talents and efforts, forcing them, in effect, to work like slaves against their will for other people whom they don't know or care about. Those on the political left (generally the have-nots) claim that the libertarian ideal is unfair because it forces them to live in abject poverty, through no fault of their own, as the rich inevitably get richer and the poor, poorer in the free-market capitalist system.

Which system is really more fair or just? Our intuitions seem to pull us in both directions, and so are not very helpful. If you ask your friends what they think, you will probably get a variety of opinions ranging from the libertarian to the egalitarian ideal. We are morally and politically torn between the two. The great challenge is their reconciliation.

Because of its economic implications, the libertarian-egalitarian debate outlined above is probably the most politically intense aspect of the larger question of the relationship of the individual and the state. In its most extreme form, the question comes down to this: does the individual exist to serve the state, or does the state exist to serve the individual?

Questions for Discussion

1. Although the social and political issues change, the underlying debate remains the same. What recent news reports show the ongoing debate between the ideals of greater individual liberty and greater governmental control?

2. What is your own view in this debate between the libertarian ideal and the egalitarian goal? What reasons can you give to support your position?

3. This question anticipates some of the subsequent discussion, but what issues can you identify as being part of the debate both within democracies and among nations?

4. What are some of the attempts within our own national life of reconciling the ideals of libertarianism and egalitarianism?

5. The debate between libertarianism and egalitarianism always seems to be tilted toward one of the poles of this duality. At the current moment, which tendency seems to be dominant in national life? Give examples to illustrate your answer.

CHAPTER 34

The Libertarian View of the State

John Locke (1632–1704) is an important social philosopher, whose views directly and greatly influenced the Declaration of Independence of the United States, the Bill of Rights, and the Constitution. Much of Jefferson's language in the Declaration of Independence was taken directly from Locke, especially the important sentence concerning "life, liberty, and the pursuit of happiness" (although Jefferson deliberately substituted *happiness* for Locke's term *property*). As Jefferson wrote later, it was not his intention in drafting the Declaration of Independence to invent new views, but to make clear the general position of philosophers such as Locke, Hume, and Rousseau to the general populace.

These philosophers, along with Hobbes, are known as the social contract theorists, and they expressed a major change in political thought about the nature of the state. The aim of these seventeenth- and eighteenth-century social philosophers was to determine the justification for the state's authority over its citizens. What right does one group have to enact laws which others are forced to obey? And, turning the question around, what obligation does the individual have to obey those laws? In short, why should we obey the law? It is not a question of empirically discovering what power governments actually do have, or the psychological motives which citizens have (fear, conformity, and such) for following social rules, but rather the normative question: What, if anything, gives governments the legitimate right to make and enforce laws, and what moral obligation or duty, if any, do we have to obey those laws?

This is an important question, for its answer will also tell us what a good (that is, legitimate, rightful) government is like, and how it differs from illegitimate governments which have no right to command loyalty or obedience. And this will in turn tell us what types of governments we are obligated to support and what

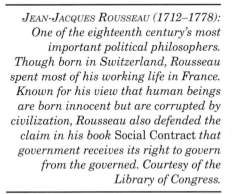

JEAN-JACQUES ROUSSEAU (1712–1778):
One of the eighteenth century's most
important political philosophers.
Though born in Switzerland, Rousseau
spent most of his working life in France.
Known for his view that human beings
are born innocent but are corrupted by
civilization, Rousseau also defended the
claim in his book Social Contract *that*
government receives its right to govern
from the governed. Courtesy of the
Library of Congress.

types we have a right and even a duty to oppose and rebel against. Again, Jefferson used Locke's arguments to show that the Americans were justified in rebelling against England.

The Social Contract

Locke's plan, like that of the other social contractarians, is to imagine what life was like before people joined together into social states with governing bodies, and then to consider what reasons people might have for joining together into a stable society. Since it is assumed that any attempt to band together will be fruitless unless all come to some mutual agreement, the original founders of the society will, in effect, sign a mutual pact, bond, or contract, and this social contract will, once we have reconstructed it, tell us precisely what the reciprocal duties and obligations are of the governing body and the ordinary citizens.

Locke accordingly distinguishes between living in a "state of nature" (prior to social organization) and in governed societies. This, of course, presupposes a great deal. It presupposes both that there *was* a state of nature which existed prior to any social organization, which has been challenged by more recent social contractarians, and it also presupposes that the rational basis of all government is permanently fixed once and for all time by the original contract.

Jefferson: Declaration of Independence

We hold these truths to be self-evident, that all men are created equal, that they are endowed by their Creator with certain unalienable Rights, that among these are Life, Liberty and the pursuit of Happiness.—That to secure these rights, Governments are instituted among Men, deriving their just powers from the consent of the governed,—That whenever any Form of Government becomes destructive of these ends, it is the Right of the People to alter or to abolish it, and to institute new Government, laying its foundation on such principles and organizing its powers in such form, as to them shall seem most likely to effect their Safety and Happiness.

Locke: Concerning Civil Government

Men being . . . by nature all free, equal, and independent, no one can be put out of this estate, and subjected to the political power of another, without his own consent, which is done by agreeing with other men to join and unite into a community for their comfortable, safe, and peaceable living one amongst another, in a secure enjoyment of their properties, and a greater security against any that are not of it, . . . it being only with an intention in everyone the better to preserve himself, his liberty and property. . . . Whensoever, therefore, the legislative shall transgress this fundamental rule of society, and . . . endeavor to grasp . . . an absolute power over the lives, liberties, and estates of the people, by this breach of trust they forfeit the power the people had put into their hands . . . and it devolves to the people, who have a right to resume their original liberty, and by the establishment of the new legislative . . . provide for their own safety and security, which is the end for which they are in society.

In the state of nature there are no restrictions imposed on anyone to do someone else's bidding, and in that sense people in a state of nature are completely free. The only restraint upon human behavior in this primitive stage is that imposed by reason itself. That is, Locke is suggesting that a rational person, one who followed the dictates of reason rather than be led by emotions, would not needlessly harm others. Locke also believes that in the state of nature, humans are more or less equal in mental and physical strength and have a natural right to protect themselves and to punish anyone who violates their freedom and security (again within reason).

Locke himself recognizes that his critics would question whether there ever was such a historical state of affairs. Contemporary social contractarians, such as John Rawls, do not interpret the social contract doctrine to be a claim that such a condition existed in actual history, but only that it is a useful imaginative device to get clear in our own minds just what the reasons are which justify the authority of government over the governed. If we hypothetically suppose that we had no government whatsoever, and try to imagine what that would be like, we may discover the reasons which make governments and laws desirable and acceptable to people. These are not the actual motives which produced ancient governments, but they may well be good reasons for justifying the existence of governments today. Nonetheless, Locke himself seems to believe that there really was a state of nature.

The Proper Role of Government

Although Locke's description of the state of nature is not as grim as that of other social contractarians such as Hobbes (who described life in the state of nature as "solitary, poor, nasty, brutish and short"), it is nonetheless clearly full of problems. Although people are naturally free in a state of nature, they are unlikely to enjoy this freedom because of the greed and irrationality of some self-centered individuals. In this respect Locke and other social contractarians are more pessimistic about human nature and the possibility of changing it. If people were or could become more loving, social, or rational, there simply would be no need for governmental control. But because of our selfishness, greed, and irrationality, we need government to protect us from ourselves. So, Locke argues, when people realize the situation fully, they freely choose jointly to impose restrictions on themselves and to limit their freedom, but only in order to secure a greater measure of freedom and happiness and well-being than they could achieve on their own. Two rights or freedoms we must give up upon entering the ordered society are the right to protect ourselves from injury, and the right to punish those who wrong us. Now we must turn the latter task over to the police and the courts.

Suppose you had to choose between being totally free of all governmental regulations, in a state of anarchy where all others were equally free to do what they pleased, and living in a society where there were rules which protected your rights while at the same time limiting your freedom to take from other people. Which would you choose? Perhaps the closest real-life parallel to the state of na-

The Constitution of the United States was the first founding document of a modern state to exemplify Locke's ideal of a society brought into being by a social contract. Courtesy of The Bettmann Archive.

ture is a country at the end of a devastating war, in chaos, with looting, rape, and pillage. Few, if given the choice, would choose the latter. In that sense, we may say that there are good reasons for having governments, whether people actually choose them for these reasons or not.

The consequences which follow from Locke's views are now obvious. Government exists only by the consent of the people governed. There is no other legitimate reason at all. It follows that although people agreeing to the social contract could choose a monarchy or oligarchy, it is much more likely that they would select a democratic form of government, in which they not only choose the form of government but have a say in the formation of laws, rulers, and so on. The social contract position, in other words, presents a good argument for selecting democracy as the best form of government.

It also follows that governments which do not serve to protect the interests of the governed and which do not operate with their consent are *not* legitimate, and can thereby be ignored or overthrown. It was this basis for revolution that was appealed to by Jefferson when he wrote the Declaration of Independence. And if

JOHN LOCKE (1632–1704): Founder of political liberalism and British empiricism. Locke formulated a metaphysics underlying the natural science of Boyle and Newton. He is author of An Essay Concerning Human Understanding *and* Two Treatises on Government. *Courtesy of the Library of Congress.*

there has ever been a government formed with something like a social contract document, the United States would seem to qualify for this distinction.

John Locke: The State and the State of Nature

Of the State of Nature

To understand political power aright, and derive it from its original, we must consider what state all men are naturally in, and that is a state of perfect freedom to order their actions and dispose of their possessions and persons as they think fit, within the bounds of the law of nature, without asking leave, or depending upon the will of any other man.

A state also of equality, wherein all the power and jurisdiction is reciprocal, no one having more than another; there being nothing more evident than that creatures of the same species and rank, promiscuously born to all the same advan-

From John Locke, *The Second Treatise of Government,* selections from Chapters 2, 5, 8, 9, and 19.

tages of nature, and the use of the same faculties, should also be equal one amongst another without subordination or subjection, unless the Lord and Master of them all should by any manifest declaration of His will set one above another, and confer on him by an evident and clear appointment an undoubted right to dominion and sovereignty.

And that all men be restrained from invading others' rights, and from doing hurt to one another, and the law of nature be observed, which willeth the peace and preservation of all mankind, the execution of the law of nature is in that state put into every man's hand, whereby everyone has a right to punish the transgressors of that law to such a degree as may hinder its violation. For the law of nature would, as all other laws that concern men in this world, be in vain if there were nobody that, in the state of nature, had a power to execute that law, and thereby preserve the innocent and restrain offenders. And if anyone in the state of nature may punish another for any evil he has done, everyone may do so. For in that state of perfect equality, where naturally there is no superiority or jurisdiction of one over another, what any may do in prosecution of that law, everyone must needs have a right to do.

Of Property

God, who hath given the world to men in common, hath also given them reason to make use of it to the best advantage of life and convenience. The earth and all that is therein is given to men for the support and comfort of their being. And though all the fruits it naturally produces, and beasts it feeds, belong to mankind in common, as they are produced by the spontaneous hand of nature; and nobody has originally a private dominion exclusive of the rest of mankind in any of them as they are thus in their natural state; yet being given for the use of men, there must of necessity be a means to appropriate them some way or other before they can be of any use or at all beneficial to any particular man. The fruit or venison which nourishes the wild Indian, who knows no enclosure, and is still a tenant in common, must be his, and so his, i.e., a part of him, that another can no longer have any right to it, before it can do any good for the support of his life.

Though the earth and all inferior creatures be common to all men, yet every man has a property in his own person; this nobody has any right to but himself. The labor of his body and the work of his hands we may say are properly his. Whatsoever, then, he removes out of the state that nature hath provided and left it in, he hath mixed his labor with, and joined to it something that is his own, and thereby makes it his property.

Thus the grass my horse has bit, the turfs my servant has cut, and the ore I have dug in any place where I have a right to them in common with others, become my property without the assignation or consent of anybody. The labor that was mine removing them out of that common state they were in, hath fixed my property in them.

Of the Beginning of Political Societies

Men being, as has been said, by nature all free, equal, and independent, no one can be put out of this estate, and subjected to the political power of another, without his own consent, which is done by agreeing with other men to join and unite into a community for their comfortable, safe, and peaceable living one amongst another, in a secure enjoyment of their properties, and a greater security against any that are not of it. This any number of men may do, because it injures not the freedom of the rest; they are left as they were in the liberty of the state of nature. When any number of men have so consented to make one community or government, they are thereby presently incorporated, and make one body politic, wherein the majority have a right to act and conclude the rest.

For when any number of men have, by the consent of every individual, made a community, they have thereby made that community one body, with a power to act as one body, which is only by the will and determination of the majority. For that which acts any community being only the consent of the individuals of it, and it being one body must move one way, it is necessary the body should move that way whither the greater force carries it, which is the consent of the majority; or else it is impossible it should act or continue one body, one community which the consent of every individual that united into it agreed that it should; and so everyone is bound by that consent to be concluded by the majority. And therefore we see that in assemblies empowered to act by positive laws, where no number is set by that positive law which empowers them, the act of the majority passes for the act of the whole, and of course determines, as having by the law of nature and reason the power of the whole.

And thus every man, by consenting with others to make one body politic under one government, puts himself under an obligation to every one of that society, to submit to the determination of the majority, and to be concluded by it; or else this original compact, whereby he with others incorporates into one society, would signify nothing, and be no compact, if he be left free and under no other ties than he was in before in the state of nature. For what appearance would there be of any compact? What new engagement if he were no farther tied by any decrees of the society, than he himself thought fit, and did actually consent to? This would be still as great a liberty as he himself had before his compact, or anyone else in the state of nature hath, who may submit himself and consent to any acts of it if he thinks fit.

For if the consent of the majority shall not in reason be received as the act of the whole and conclude every individual, nothing but the consent of every individual can make anything to be the act of the whole, which considering the infirmities of health and avocations of business, which in a number, though much less than that of a commonwealth, will necessarily keep many away from the public assembly, and the variety of opinions, and contrariety of interest, which unavoidably happen in all collections of men, 'tis next to impossible ever to be had. And therefore if the coming into society be upon such terms it will be only like Cato's coming into the theater, *tantum ut exiret*. Such a constitution as this would make the mighty leviathan of a shorter duration than the feeblest creatures, and not let it outlast the day it was born in; which cannot be supposed till we can think that rational creatures should desire and constitute societies only to be dissolved. For where the majority cannot conclude the rest, there they cannot act as one body, and consequently will be immediately dissolved again.

Whosoever therefore out of a state of nature unite into a community must be understood to give up all the power necessary to the ends for which they unite into society, to the majority of the community, unless they expressly agreed in any number greater than the majority. And this is done by barely agreeing to unite into one political society, which is all the compact that is, or needs be, between the individuals that enter into or make up a commonwealth. And thus that which begins and actually constitutes any political society is nothing but the consent of any number of freemen capable of a majority to unite and incorporate into such a society. And this is that, and that only, which did or could give beginning to any lawful government in the world.

Every man being, as has been shown, naturally free, and nothing being able to put him into subjection to any earthly power but only his own consent, it is to be considered what shall be understood to be sufficient declaration of a man's consent to make him subject to the laws of any government. There is a common distinction of an express and a tacit consent, which will concern our present case. Nobody doubts but an express consent of any man entering into any society makes him a perfect member of that society, a subject of that government. The difficulty is, what ought to be looked upon as a tacit consent, and how far it binds, i.e., how far anyone shall be looked on to have consented, and thereby submitted to any government, where he has made no expressions of it at all. And to this I say that every man that hath any possession or enjoyment of any part of the dominions of any government doth thereby give his tacit consent, and is as far forth obliged to obedience to the laws of that government during such enjoyment as anyone under it; whether this his possession be of land to him and his heirs for ever, or a lodging only for a week; or whether it be barely traveling freely on the highway; and in effect it reaches as far as the very being of anyone within the territories of that government.

Of the Ends of Political Society and Government

If man in the state of nature be so free, as has been said, if he be absolute lord of his own person and possessions, equal to the greatest, and subject to nobody, why will he part with his freedom, this empire, and subject himself to the dominion and control of any other power? To which, it is obvious to answer, that though in the state of nature he hath such a right, yet the enjoyment of it is very uncertain, and constantly exposed to the invasions of others. For all being kings as much as he, every man his equal, and the greater part no strict observers of equity and justice, the enjoyment of the property he has in this state is very unsafe, very unsecure. This makes him willing to quit this condition, which, however free is full of fears and continual dangers; and it is not without reason that he seeks out and is willing to join in society with others, who are already united, or have a mind to unite, for the mutual preservation of their lives, liberties, and estates, which I call by the general name, property,

The great and chief end, therefore, of men's uniting into commonwealths, and putting themselves under government, is the preservation of their property; to which in the state of nature there are many things wanting.

First, there wants an established, settled, known law, received and allowed by common consent to be the standard of right and wrong, and the common measure to decide all controversies between them. For though the law of nature be plain and intelligible to all rational creatures; yet men, being biased by their interest, as well as ignorant for want of study of it, are not apt to allow of it as a law binding to them in the application of it to their particular cases.

Secondly, in the state of nature there wants a known and indifferent judge, with authority to determine all differences according to the established law. For everyone in that state, being both judge and executioner of the law of nature, men being partial to themselves, passion and revenge is very apt to carry them too far, and with too much heat in their own cases, as well as negligence and unconcernedness, to make them too remiss in other men's.

Thirdly, in the state of nature there often wants power to back and support the sentence when right, and to give it due execution. They who by any injustice offend, will seldom fail, where they are able by force to make good their injustice; such resistance many times makes the punishment dangerous, and frequently destructive to those who attempt it.

Thus mankind, notwithstanding all the privileges of the state of nature, being but in an ill condition, while they remain in it, are quickly driven into society. Hence it comes to pass that we seldom find any number of men live any time together in this state. The inconveniences that they are therein exposed to by the irregular and uncertain exercise of the power every man has of punishing the transgressions of others, make them take sanctuary under the established laws of government, and therein seek the preservation of their property. It is this makes them so willingly give up everyone his single power of punishing, to be exercised by such alone, as shall be appointed to it amongst them; and by such rules as the community, or those authorized by them to that purpose, shall agree on. And in this we have the original right and rise of both the legislative and executive power, as well as of the governments and societies themselves. For in the state of nature, to omit the liberty he has of innocent delights, man has two powers.

The first is to do whatsoever he thinks fit for the preservation of himself, and others within the permission of the law of nature, by which law, common to them all, he and all the rest of mankind are of one community, make up one society, distinct from all other creatures. And were it not for the corruption and viciousness of degenerate men there would be no need of any, other no necessity that men should separate from this great and natural community; and associate into lesser combinations.

The other power a man has in the state of nature is the power to punish the crimes committed against that law. Both these he gives up when he joins in a private, if I may so call it, or particular political society, and incorporates into any commonwealth separate from the rest of mankind.

But though men when they enter into society give up the equality, liberty and executive power they had in the state of nature into the hands of the society, to be so far disposed of by the legislative as the good of the society shall require; yet it being only with an intention in everyone the better to preserve himself, his liberty and property (for no rational creature can be supposed to change his condition with an intention to be worse), the power of the society, or legislative constituted by them, can never be supposed to extend farther than the common good, but is obliged to secure everyone's property by providing against those three defects above-mentioned that made the state of nature so unsafe and uneasy.

Of the Dissolution of Government

He that will with any clearness speak of the dissolution of government ought, in the first place, to distinguish between the dissolution of the society and the dissolution of the government. That which makes the community, and brings men out of the loose state of nature into one politic society, is the agreement which everyone has with the rest to incorporate and act as one body, and so be one distinct commonwealth. The usual and almost only way whereby this union is dissolved, is the inroad of foreign force making a conquest upon them.

Besides this overturning from without, governments are dissolved from within.

First, when the legislative is altered, civil society being a state of peace amongst those who are of it, from whom the state of war is excluded by the umpirage which they have provided in their legislative for the ending all differences that may arise amongst any of them, it is in their legislative that the members of a commonwealth are united and combined together in one coherent living body. This is the soul that gives form, life, and unity to the commonwealth. From hence the several members have their mutual influence, sympathy, and connection. And, therefore, when the legislative is broken or dissolved, dissolution and death follow. For the essence and union of the society consisting in having one will, the legislative, when once established by the majority, has the declaring and, as it were, keeping of that will. The constitution of the legislative is the first and fundamental act of the society, whereby provision is made for the continuation of their union, under the direction of persons and bonds of laws made by persons authorized thereunto by the consent and appointment of the people, without which no one man or number of men amongst them can have authority of making laws that shall be binding to the rest. When any one or more shall take upon them to make laws, whom the people have not appointed so to do, they make laws without authority, which the people are not therefore bound to obey; by which means they come again to be out of subjection, and may constitute to themselves a new legislative, as they think best, being in full liberty to resist the force of those who without authority would impose anything upon them. Everyone is at the disposure of his own will when those who had by the delegation of the society the declaring of the public will, are excluded from it, and others usurp the place who have no such authority or delegation.

In these and the like cases, when the government is dissolved, the people are at liberty to provide for themselves by erecting a new legislative, differing from the other, by the change of persons, or form, or both, as they shall find it most for their safety and good. For the society can never, by the fault of another, lose the native and original right it has to preserve itself; which can only be done by a settled legislative, and a fair and impartial execution of the laws made by it. But the state of mankind is not so miserable that they are not capable of using this remedy, till it be too late to look for any. To tell people they may provide for themselves by erecting a new legislative, when by oppression, artifice, or being delivered over to a foreign power, their old one is gone, is only to tell them they may expect relief when it is too late, and the evil is past cure. This is in effect no more than to bid them first be slaves, and then to take care of their liberty; and when their chains are on tell them they may act like free men. This, if barely so, is rather mockery than relief; and men can never be secure from tyranny if there be no means to escape it till they are perfectly under it. And therefore it is that they have not only a right to get out of it, but to prevent it.

Whensoever, therefore, the legislative shall transgress this fundamental rule of society, and either by ambition, fear, folly, or corruption, endeavor to grasp themselves or put into the hands of any other an absolute power over the lives, liberties, and the estates of the people, by this breach of trust they forfeit the power the people had put into their hands, for quite contrary ends, and it devolves to the people, who have a right to resume their original, and by the establishment of the new legislative (such as they shall think fit) provide for their own safety and security, which is the end for which they are in society.

Questions for Discussion

1. What does Locke mean by the "state of nature?" Do you think such a state of affairs ever existed? If not, is it a useless concept for social philosophy?

2. What right does government have, according to Locke, to restrict my freedom in any way? Do you agree? Why or why not?

3. How does Locke explain one's right to own property? Do you find his account convincing? Give reasons for your answer.

4. When, according to Locke, are people justified in rejecting and rebelling against the authority of the state? What grounds does Locke suggest for this justification? What is your assessment of Locke's position?

5. If Locke were alive today and lived in your country, what political party would he join?

CHAPTER 35

The Individual and the State

John Stuart Mill's essay *On Liberty* is one of the founding documents of political liberalism. As the term implies, nineteenth-century liberalism viewed the liberty of the individual as paramount. The threat faced by citizens, then as now, was the encroachment of government on personal liberty. Whether the liberty involved was political, economic, or religious, the history of governments had been to restrain individual freedom for the sake of a greater good, often using draconian means of enforcing government's edicts. Today the term is, with an ironic twist, applied mainly to those points of view that favor an expanded role of government in bringing about greater social and economic justice.

The remaining readings in this section will explore this notion of liberalism by looking at two issues: the relation of the individual to the state, and the status of minority groups within the larger community. The two issues are related in that both deal with how much power the government should exert over the lives of its citizens.

John Stuart Mill (1806–1873) was the great spokesperson for the maximum freedom for the individual. Mill was an English philosopher identified with the social movement known as *utilitarianism*, an ethical view that originated with the writings of Jeremy Bentham. With Bentham, Mill rejects the notion of inherent natural rights and argues on utilitarian grounds for the social utility of individual freedom as a justification for a government that acts to protect and not to abridge those freedoms.

The selection that follows is from Mill's classic work *On Liberty,* which remains a classic in Western political philosophy. In the essay Mill argues that it is socially useful for individuals to be free to do as they please as long as they do not harm others. He also argues that the state should not intervene paternalistically even to prevent people from harming themselves either physically or morally. In this treatise Mill traces the history of various attempts to limit the political

---

Will the Real Liberal Please Stand Up?

Liberalism begins with a defense of the freedom of the individual from undue governmental interference. Its most fundamental tenet is that there are limits on what a government can ask of an individual. The debate centers on what can be asked of the individual and, on its flip side, what restraints should be placed on majority rule.

Nothing is more contentious than resolving the disagreement about what should be done when promoting the interests of one individual or group involves abridging the freedom of others. Consider "hate speech." Do free speech rights include verbally abusing those who differ from us? And what about economic issues? People may have free speech but be homeless and destitute, so what about their right to a decent living? One can be fully endowed with the right to religion, free speech, the right to vote, but what does all this mean to a street person, for whom having a right to hold elective office means little.

There are two different philosophical responses to this. Some argue that in addition to the rights listed above, we also should also have the right to adequate social and economic goods. They argue that society as a whole will benefit and the welfare of everyone will be enhanced if we adopt policies that provide a more equitable distribution of social and economic goods. But these views clash with those who put a primary value on the right to own and privately dispose of one's own property, since they believe a more equal distribution of social and economic good can be achieved only by taking away from those who have more to give to those who have less.

Who are the real liberals—those who argue for maximum individual freedom from government intervention in their lives (nineteenth-century liberalism) or those who think government should work for a more equitable distribution of society's economic and social benefits (twentieth-century liberalism)? Since liberals have long been pulled in both directions, two forms of liberalism have emerged today: "libertarian liberals," who emphasize property rights, and "egalitarian liberals," who emphasize the right of every individual to equal respect and dignity.

---

power of the ruling elite from the Magna Carta, which limited the power of the king, to the view that political power resides in the people themselves. He argues that the one remaining threat to liberty is the possibility that majority rule could impose a tyranny over nonconforming individuals. This can be avoided, he argues, by limiting majority rule to those cases where an individual's behavior actually harms others.

As you read Mill ask yourself whether you would go as far as he does in reject-ing laws that paternalistically protect you. Do you favor seat belt laws, for in-stance? Would you favor laws outlawing all smoking? Would you support laws that enable the use of drugs within one's home? Should the government protect us from ourselves? You might also wonder what exactly is meant by "harm to others." What about someone who is brain dead and has no hope of recovering from a coma because she had a motorcycle accident and was not wearing a helmet. Her be-havior caused psychological harm to her parents, siblings, and her own children—not to mention the enormous medical expenses, much of which must be borne by ordinary taxpayers. Can the same sort of argument be made regarding harm to others caused by smoking? In addition to the dangers of second-hand smoke, should we include the costs of health care for smokers, the loss of productivity caused by the habit, and the psychological loss to friends and family when a loved one is dying from a smoking-related disease?

Although Mill's essay dates from the nineteenth century, the issues he raises are still very much with us, and the ongoing debate about the proper role of gov-ernment in regulating the lives of its citizens will likely continue.

John Stuart Mill: On Liberty

The object of this Essay is to assert one very simple principle, as entitled to gov-ern absolutely the dealings of society with the individual in the way of compulsion and control, whether the means used be physical force in the form of legal penal-ties, or the moral coercion of public opinion. That principle is, that the sole end for which mankind are warranted, individually or collectively, in interfering with the liberty of action of any of their number, is self-protection. That the only purpose for which power can be rightfully exercised over any member of a civilized com-munity, against his will, is to prevent harm to others. His own good, either phys-ical or moral, is not a sufficient warranty. He cannot rightfully be compelled to do or forbear because it will be better for him to do so, because it will make him hap-pier, because, in the opinions of others, to do so would be wise, or even right. These are good reasons for remonstrating with him, or reasoning with him, or persuad-ing him, or entreating him, but not for compelling him, or visiting him with any evil in case he do otherwise. To justify that, the conduct from which it is desired to deter him, must be calculated to produce evil to someone else. The only part of the conduct of anyone, for which he is amenable to society, is that which concerns others. In the part which merely concerns himself, his independence is, of right, absolute. Over himself, over his own body and mind, the individual is sovereign.

It is, perhaps, hardly necessary to say that this doctrine is meant to apply only to human beings in the maturity of their faculties. We are not speaking of chil-dren, or of young persons below the age which the law may fix as that of manhood

From John Stuart Mill, *On Liberty,* selections from chapters 1, 2, and 5.

or womanhood. Those who are still in a state to require being taken care of by others, must be protected against their own actions as well as against external injury.

It is proper to state that I forgo any advantage which could be derived to my argument from the idea of abstract right, as a thing independent of utility. I regard utility as the ultimate appeal on all ethical questions; but it must be utility in the largest sense, grounded on the permanent interests of man as a progressive being. Those interests, I contend, authorize the subjection of individual spontaneity to external control, only in respect to those actions of each, which concern the interest of other people. If anyone does an act hurtful to others, there is a *prima facie* case for punishing him, by law, or, where legal penalties are not safely applicable, by general disapprobation. There are also many positive acts for the benefit of others, which he may rightfully be compelled to perform; such as, to give evidence in a court of justice; to bear his fair share in the common defence, or in any other joint work necessary to the interest of the society of which he enjoys the protection; and to perform certain acts of individual beneficence, such as saving a fellow creature's life, or interposing to protect the defenceless against ill usage, things which whenever it is obviously a man's duty to do, he may rightfully be made responsible to society for not doing. A person may cause evil to others not only by his actions but by his inaction, and in either case he is justly accountable to them for the injury. The latter case, it is true, requires a much more cautious exercise of compulsion than the former. To make anyone answerable for doing evil to others, is the rule; to make him answerable for not preventing evil, is, comparatively speaking, the exception. Yet there are many cases clear enough and grave enough to justify that exception. In all things which regard the external relations of the individual, he is *de jure* amenable to those whose interests are concerned, and if need be, to society as their protector. There are often good reasons for not holding him to the responsibility; but these reasons must arise from the special expediencies of the case: either because it is a kind of case in which he is on the whole likely to act better, when left to his own discretion, than when controlled in any way in which society have it in their power to control him; or because the attempt to exercise control would produce other evils, greater than those which it would prevent. When such reasons as these preclude the enforcement of responsibility, the conscience of the agent himself should step into the vacant judgment seat, and protect those interests of others which have no external protection; judging himself all the more rigidly, because the case does not admit of his being made accountable to the judgment of his fellow creatures.

But there is a sphere of action in which society, as distinguished from the individual, has, if any, only an indirect interest; comprehending all that portion of a person's life and conduct which affects only himself, or if it also affects others, only with their free, voluntary, and undeceived consent and participation. When I say only himself, I mean directly, and in the first instance: for whatever affects himself, may affect others *through* himself; and the objection which may be grounded on this contingency, will receive consideration in the sequel. This, then, is the appropriate region of human liberty. It comprises, first, the inward domain of consciousness; demanding liberty of conscience, in the most comprehensive sense; liberty of thought and feeling; absolute freedom of opinion and sentiment on all subjects, practical or speculative, scientific, moral, or theological. The liberty of expressing and publishing opinions may seem to fall under a different principle, since it belongs to that part of the conduct of an individual which concerns other people; but, being almost of as much importance as the liberty of thought itself, and resting in great part on the same reasons, is practically inseparable from it. Secondly, the principle requires liberty of tastes and pursuits; of framing the plan of our life to suit our own character; of doing as we like, subject to such consequences as may follow: without impediment from our fellow creatures, so long as what we do does not harm them, even though they should think our conduct foolish, perverse, or wrong. Thirdly, from this liberty of each individual, follows the liberty, within the same limits, of combination among individuals; freedom to unite, for any purpose not involving harm to others: the persons combining being supposed to be of full age, and not forced or deceived.

No society in which these liberties are not, on the whole, respected, is free, whatever may be its form of government; and none is completely free in which they do not exist absolute and unqualified. The only freedom which deserves the name, is that of pursuing our own good in our own way, so long as we do not attempt to deprive others of theirs, or impede their efforts to obtain it. Each is the proper guardian of his own health, whether bodily, or mental and spiritual. Mankind are greater gainers by suffering each other to live as seems good to themselves, than by compelling each to live as seems good to the rest. . . .

Apart from the peculiar tents of individual thinkers, there is also in the world at large an increasing inclination to stretch unduly the powers of society over the individual, both by the force of opinion and even by that of legislation: and as the tendency of all changes taking place in the world is to strengthen society, and diminish the power of the individual, this encroachment is not one of the evils which tend spontaneously to disappear, but, on the contrary, to grow more and more formidable. The disposition of mankind, whether as rulers or as fellow citizens, to impose their own opinions and inclinations as a rule of conduct on others, is so energetically supported by some of the best and by some of the worst feeling incident to human nature, that it is hardly ever kept under restraint by anything but want of power; and as the power is not declining, but growing, unless a strong barrier of moral conviction can be raised against the mischief, we must expect, in the present circumstances of the world, to see it increase. . . .

The time, it is to be hoped, is gone by, when any defense would be necessary of the "liberty of the press" as one of the securities against corrupt or tyrannical government. No argument, we may suppose, can now be needed, against permitting a legislature or an executive, not identified in interest with the people, to prescribe opinions to them, and determine what doctrines or what arguments they shall be allowed to hear. This aspect of the question, besides, has been so often and so triumphantly enforced by preceding writers, that it needs not be specially insisted on in this place. . . .

In politics, again, it is almost a commonplace, that a party of order or stability, and a party of progress or reform, are both necessary elements of a healthy state of political life; until the one or the other shall have so enlarged its mental grasp as to be a party equally of order and of progress, knowing and distinguishing what is fit to be preserved from what ought to be swept away. Each of these modes of thinking derives its utility from the deficiencies of the other; but it is in a great measure the opposition of the other that keeps each within the limits of reason and sanity. Unless opinions favourable to democracy and to aristocracy, to property and to equality, to co-operation and to competition, to luxury and to abstinence, to sociality and individuality, to liberty and discipline, and all the other standing antagonisms of practical life, are expressed with equal freedom, and enforced and defended with equal talent and energy, there is no chance of both elements obtaining their due; one scale is sure to go up, and the other down. Truth, in the great practical concerns of life, is so much a question of the reconciling and combining of opposites, that very few have minds sufficiently capacious and impartial to make the adjustment with an approach to correctness, and it has to be made by the rough process of a struggle between combatants fighting under hostile banners. On any of the great open questions just enumerated, if either of the two opinions has a better claim than the other, not merely to be tolerated, but to be encouraged and countenanced, it is the one which happens at the particular time and place to be in a minority . . .

We have now recognized the necessity to the mental well-being of mankind (on which all their other well-being depends) of freedom of opinion, and freedom of the expression of opinion, on four distinct grounds: which we will now briefly recapitulate.

First, if any opinion is compelled to silence, that opinion may, for aught we can certainly know, be true. To deny this is to assume our own infallibility.

Secondly, though the silenced opinion be an error, it may, and very commonly does, contain a portion of truth; and since the general or prevailing opinion on any subject is rarely or never the whole truth, it is only by the collision of adverse opinions that the remainder of the truth has any chance of being supplied.

Thirdly, even if the received opinion be not only true, but the whole truth; unless it is suffered to be, and actually is, vigorously and earnestly contested, it will, by most of those who receive it, be held in the manner of a prejudice, with little comprehension or feeling of its rational grounds. And not only this, but, fourthly, the meaning of the doctrine itself will be in danger of being lost, or enfeebled, and deprived of its vital effect on the character and conduct: the dogma becoming a mere formal profession, inefficacious for good, but cumbering the ground, and preventing the growth of any real and heartfelt conviction, from reason or personal experience . . . .

A further question is, whether the State, while it permits, should nevertheless indirectly discourage conduct which it deems contrary to the best interests of the agent; whether, for example, it should take measures to render the means of drunkenness more costly, or add to the difficulty of procuring them, by limiting the number of the places of sale. On this as on most other practical questions, many distinctions require to be made. To tax stimulants for the sole purpose of making them more difficult to be obtained, is a measure differing only in degree from their entire prohibition; and would be justifiable only if that were justifiable. Every increase of cost is a prohibition, to those whose means do not come up to the augmented price; and to those who do, it is a penalty laid on them for gratifying a particular taste. Their choice of pleasures, and their mode of expending their income, after satisfying their legal and moral obligations to the State and to individuals, are their own concern, and must rest with their own judgment. These considerations may seem at first sight to condemn the selection of stimulants as special subjects of taxation for purposes of revenue. But it must be remembered that taxation for fiscal purposes is absolutely inevitable; that in most countries it is necessary that a considerable part of that taxation should be indirect; that the State, therefore, cannot help imposing penalties, which to some persons may be prohibitory, on the use of some articles of consumption. It is hence the duty of the State to consider, in the imposition of taxes, what commodities the consumers can best spare; and *a fortiori* to select in preference those of which it deems the use, beyond a very moderate quantity, to be positively injurious. Taxation, therefore, of stimulants, up to the point which produces the largest amount of revenue (supposing that the State needs all the revenue which it yields) is not only admissible, but to be approved of.

The question of making the sale of these commodities a more or less exclusive privilege, must be answered differently, according to the purposes to which the restriction is intended to be subservient. All places of public resort require the restraint of a police, and places of this kind peculiarly, because offences against society are especially apt to originate there. It is, therefore, fit to confine the power of selling these commodities (at least for consumption on the spot) to persons of known or vouched-for respectability of conduct; to make such regulations respecting hours of opening and closing as may he requisite for public surveillance, and to withdraw the licence if breaches of the peace repeatedly take place through the connivance or incapacity of the keeper of the house, or if it becomes a rendezvous for concocting and preparing offences against the law. Any further restriction I do not conceive to be, in principle, justifiable. . . .

I have reserved for the last place a large class of questions respecting the limits of government interference, which, though closely connected with the subject of this essay, do not, in strictness, belong to it. These are cases in which the reasons against interference do not turn upon the principle of liberty; the question is not about restraining the actions of individuals, but about helping them: it is asked whether the government should do, or cause to be done, something for their benefit, instead of leaving it to be done by themselves, individually, or in voluntary combination.

The objections to government interference, when it is not such as to involve infringement of liberty, may be of three kinds.

The first is, when the thing to be done is likely to be better done by individuals than by the government. Speaking generally, there is no one so fit to conduct any business, or to determine how or by whom it shall be conducted, as those who are personally interested in it. This principle condemns the interferences, once so common, of the legislature, or the officers of government, with the ordinary processes of industry . . . .

In many cases, though individuals may not do the particular thing so well, on the average, as the officers of government, it is nevertheless desirable that it should be done by them, rather than by the government, as a means to their own mental education, a mode of strengthening their active faculties, exercising their judgment, and giving them a familiar knowledge of the subjects with which they are thus left to deal. This is a principal, though not the sole, recommendation of jury trial (in cases not political); of free and popular local and municipal institutions; of the conduct of industrial and philanthropic enterprises by voluntary associations. These are not questions of liberty, and are connected with that subject only by remote tendencies; but they are questions of development . . . as parts of national education; as being, in truth, the peculiar training of a citizen, the practical part of the political education of a free people, taking them out of the narrow circle of personal and family selfishness, and accustoming them to the comprehension of joint interests, the management of joint concerns, habituating them to act from public or semi-public motives, and guide their conduct by aims which unite instead of isolating them from one another. Without these habits and powers, a free constitution can neither be worked nor preserved, as is exemplified by the too often transitory nature of political freedom in countries where it does not rest upon a sufficient basis of local liberties. The management of purely local business by the localities, and of the great enterprises of industry by the union of those who voluntarily supply the pecuniary means, is further recommended by all the advantages which have been set forth in this essay as belonging to individuality of development, and diversity of modes of action. Government operations tend to be everywhere alike. With individuals and voluntary associations, on the contrary, there are varied experiments, and endless diversity of experience. What the State can usefully do, is to make itself a central depository, and active circulator and diffuser, of the experience resulting from many trials. Its business is to enable each experimentalist to benefit by the experiments of others, instead of tolerating no experiments but its own.

The third, and most cogent reason for restricting the interference of government, is the great evil of adding unnecessarily to its power. Every function superadded to those already exercised by the government, causes its influence over hopes and fears to be more widely diffused, and converts, more and more, the active and ambitious part of the public into hangers-on of the government, or of some party which aims at becoming the government. If the roads, the railways, the banks, the insurance offices, the great joint-stock companies, the universities, and the public charities, were all of them branches of the government; if, in addition, the municipal corporations and local boards, with all that now devolves on them, became departments of the central administration; if the employees of all these different enterprises were appointed and paid by the government, and looked to the government for every rise in life; not all the freedom of the press and popular constitution of the legislature would make this or any other country free otherwise than in name. And the evil would be greater, the more efficiently and scientifically the administrative machinery was constructed, the more skilful the arrangements for obtaining the best qualified hands and heads with which to work it. . . .

If every part of the business of society which required organized concert, or large and comprehensive views, were in the hands of the government, and if government offices were universally filled by the ablest men, all the enlarged culture and practiced intelligence in the country, except the purely speculative, would be concentrated in a numerous bureaucracy, to whom alone the rest of the community would look for all things: the multitude for direction and dictation in all they had to do; the able and aspiring for personal advancement. To be admitted into the ranks of this bureaucracy, and when admitted, to rise therein, would be the sole objects of ambition. Under this regime, not only is the outside public ill-qualified, for want of practical experience, to criticize or check the mode of operation of the bureaucracy, but even if the accidents of despotic or the natural working of popular institutions occasionally raise to the summit a ruler or rulers of reforming inclinations, no reform can be effected which is contrary to the interest of the bureaucracy. . . .

A government cannot have too much of the kind of activity which does not impede, but aids and stimulates, individual exertion and development. The mischief begins when, instead of calling forth the activity and powers of individuals and bodies, it substitutes its own activity for theirs; when, instead of informing, advising, and, upon occasion, denouncing, it makes them work in fetters, or bids them stand aside and does their work instead of them. The worth of a State, in the long run, is the worth of the individuals composing it; and a State which postpones the interests of *their* mental expansion and elevation, to a little more of administrative skill, or of that semblance of it which practice gives, in the details of business; a State which dwarfs its men, in order that they may be more docile instruments in its hands even for beneficial purposes, will find that with small men no great thing can really be accomplished; and that the perfection of machinery to which it has sacrificed everything, will in the end avail it nothing, for want of the vital power which, in order that the machine might work more smoothly, it has preferred to banish.

Questions for Discussion

1. Pick an item from today's newspaper that reports a dispute between groups or between a group and the government. Which side of the issue do you think Mill would defend?

2. We previously encountered Mill in the section of this book on ethics. Do you think his political and social philosophy is consistent with his ethical views? Give reasons for your answer.

3. Discuss the evolution of the term "liberal." How would you account for this change?

4. Mill wrote in the nineteenth century. Would he have expressed any of his views differently were he writing in the twenty-first century? Explain.

5. An American president declared that "the age of big government is over." In many democracies around the world, the role of government is being reduced. How would you account for this in light of Mill's *Essay?*

CHAPTER 36

Individual Happiness and Social Responsibility

Before leaving the issue of the rights of the individual and the limits of government, it is important to look at a question about human nature itself. An area of tension in Western liberal thought focuses on the extent to which the individual can be conceived as and identified as an atomic entity independent of the community in which the individual is embedded. Some versions of liberalism start with fully formed individuals having values and rights and then use this concept as a basis for constructing a social order. Others argue that this is distorted thinking, since individuals really exist only as persons with values and rights within an already existing community.

There are two old traditions in Western thought on this issue. The ancient Greek philosophers viewed human beings as unavoidably social creatures who required a social framework in which to realize their full humanness. A person who withdraws from society to seek only private goods was perceived to be an anomaly, an aberration. From the Greek term for "one's own" (*idios*) came the word "idiot" to describe such a person. Aristotle in both his writings on ethics and politics argues that the individual can achieve full potential only through cultivating the proper human relationships. Home, family, friends, and finally the civic unit (for Greeks, the *polis*, or city-state) provide the context in which one develops the full human potential. In the following article the contemporary American philosopher Mark Holowchak argues that we have gone too far toward liberal individualism, and that a shift is urgently needed back toward the ancient Greek model of communitarianism.

Holowchak makes the case that by our very nature we human beings are so constructed that true happiness requires an integration, not only of all aspects of one's personality, but "an integration within a social and political unit." As he points out, this view is diametrically opposed to the currently popular view, which he refers to as liberalism, or liberal morality, according to which human beings are completely autonomous and self-contained individuals. According to contemporary liberal morality, any social coercion of individuals is warranted only insofar as it promotes still greater individual freedom. So long as my desires do not conflict with yours then each of us should be left alone to pursue our individual wants.

Holowchak traces this extreme individualism of liberal morality to modern thinkers, especially the empiricist philosophers, Hobbes, Hume, and Mill, who stressed the priority of emotions over reason in morality—"X is good" means "I like it," or "it gives me pleasure." There is no rational or objective way to determine what is really right or wrong, according to this empiricist liberalism, and since different people and different societies like, want and desire different things, there is no objective right or wrong. All is relative to subjective likes and dislikes.

But Holowchak claims this is a terribly mistaken reading of human nature. According to Holowchak, people are social creatures. Development of true independence and autonomy can only occur, he argues, within a social setting. To develop your full potential as an individual you must be able to function comfortably within a social order. In the end liberal morality contradicts itself and therefore makes no sense. Happiness can only be found in the integration within social and political institutions.

This means a return to the more balanced view of the ancient Greeks, in which we not only demand our individual rights but also assume our duties and responsibilities towards others, where we not only seek to satisfy our personal wants and desires, but also strive for a reasoned social ideal which binds people together for the common good, however difficult that may be to achieve in actual practice.

M. Andrew Holowchak: Happiness and Justice in "Liberal" Society: Autonomy as Political Integration

I. Happiness as Integration

The topic, "happiness," has traditionally been and continues to be the focal point of and most seductive issue in philosophical discussions in ethics. While many, such as Aristotle and Mill, take it to be the end of all human activity, almost all (if not all) philosophers acknowledge that it is a valuable, if not essential, component of a good life.

The notion that happiness is, in some sense, a type of integration is nothing new. This is unquestionably mainstream in philosophical accounts of happiness as well as most nonphilosophical accounts. In early Greek culture, for instance, the very walls at the famous sanctuary of Apollo at Delphi contained the words, "Know yourself" (*gnothi seauton*) and "Nothing in excess" (*meden agan*), which suggest that good living, for the Greeks, was a matter of self-integration as well as integration with one's environment. In *Republic*, Plato takes himself, through Socrates, to have answered the challenge of Thrasymachus (that justice and happiness are nothing but the advantage of the stronger) in Book I by an argument in Book IV that is designed to show that justice and happiness are a harmony of the soul. In our own day, Bertrand Russell says that happiness is, in part, rationality and rationality is a type of "internal harmony."[1] He elaborates:

> [T]he greatest happiness comes with the most complete possession of one's faculties. It is in the moments when the mind is most active and the fewest things are forgotten that the most intense joys are experienced. This indeed is one of the best touchstones of happiness.[2]

That happiness involves some sort of personal integration—that is, getting to know oneself or attaining a sort of inner harmony between the discordant parts of one's mental apparatus—is noncontroversial. What is relatively controversial, however, is the thesis that a necessary condition for happiness is integration within a social and political unit. To show this, I must first make a case against what I take to be the received view of morality today: liberalism. For it is through the miscarriage of liberal morality that we can best see why personal integration cannot occur without a political body.

II. Liberalism

The received view of happiness today is liberalism. At the political level, liberalism states that individuals are fundamental units of political analysis and, thereby, prior to their communities and institutions. Liberalism asserts that people are autonomous and self-contained individuals, whose rights precede those of any collection of individuals or those of any institution. According to this view, any coercion by institutions is warranted only when it advances individuals' liberty.

As moral policy, liberal philosophy asserts that as long as my values, based on my desires or wants, do not conflict with yours, then I ought to be free to do what I want (while you ought to be free to do the same)—what is sometimes called the "principle of maximum liberty." My desires are what enable me to be an individual; and freely acting upon them, in concert with or without reason, is the purest expression of both my autonomy and my happiness. In other words, openly following my desires in my own unique way is what makes me an individual.

Liberalism has its roots in the empiricist philosophers such as Bacon, Hobbes, Locke, and Hume—each of whom tied moral assertions to will, appetites, desires, and/or affections. When empiricists turned to morality, most found little warrant

---

[1]1996, pp. 85–87 (New York: Liveright Publishing Company).
[2]Ibid, p. 87.

for any account underpinned by reason.[3] For instance, Hume, in *An Enquiry Concerning the Principles of Morals*, argues that the rules of morality are not derived from reason. They are left to our passions. He states: "And as reasoning is not the source, whence either disputant derives his tenets; it is vain to expect, that any logic, which speaks not to the affections, will ever engage him to embrace sounder principles."[4] Morality is for Hume merely a matter of descriptive psychology. The various manifestations of liberal morality today—descriptivism, naturalism, emotivism, and postmodernism—in reducing morality to wanting or desiring, have by fiat degraded morality to one form or another of hedonism.

There is perhaps no more celebrated expression of liberal thinking than Mill's *On Liberty*. Here Mill states that the principle of maximal liberty is a principle of individuation. Mill says, "If a person possesses any tolerable amount of common sense and experience, his own mode of laying out his existence is the best, not because it is the best in itself, but because it is his own mode."[5] Individuality allows humans to express themselves fully—that is, to give full vent to their desires. Thus it leads to progress and happiness:

> It is desirable, in short, that in things which do not primarily concern others, individuality should assert itself. Where not the person's own character but the traditions or customs of other people are the rule of conduct, there is wanting one of the principle ingredients of human happiness and the chief ingredient of individual and social progress.[6]

Through individual expression, people find happiness, and society is the ultimate benefactor.[7]

It is not difficult to see why liberalism has taken root so firmly today, both morally and politically. The notions that (1) we as individuals are prior to and more fundamental than our communities while (2) we are different from other persons seem intuitively sensible. Concerning the first, institutions comprise individuals and, of these, only individual people are living, breathing things. How can an institution have rights or any properties whatsoever that are independent of its inhabitants at a given time? Second, what is more obvious than the inherent differences among people? Liberalism, through pivoting on individuals, captures both of these intuitions.

III. The Case Against Liberalism

In spite of its lure, liberalism is wrong. It is wrong, first and foremost, because individuals are not privileged in political analysis. People are social creatures. We

---

[3]Locke being an exception.

[4]Hume 1998, p. 3 (*An Essay Concerning the Principles of Morals*, Oxford University Press).

[5]1985, p. 132–133 (*On Liberty*, New York: Penguin Books).

[6]Ibid, p. 120. It is interesting that Mill links happiness with progess here.

[7]For Mill, the many benefit indirectly, because only in a free society is genius allowed to flourish and, when genius flourishes, society flourishes. This is the main argument in chapter three of *On Liberty* and it shows that his intentions are anything but straightforwardly egalitarian.

live in societies, not because of need, but because we overwhelmingly prefer to live in societies. This is no smug, *a priori* claim about the essence of human beings, but instead a guarded and correct observation about how people do in fact actually live. Even the earliest expositor of liberal thinking, John Locke, in *The Second Treatise of Government*, concedes that humans are naturally disposed toward communal living, though he calls such state-of-nature societies "prepolitical" insofar as they lack a common superior to handle disputes.[8]

Liberals insist, through due regard for freedom of individuals, that we are essentially autonomous and wanting individuals, and only incidentally social creatures. In a recent attack on liberal morality, Bob Brecher writes concerning liberals' failure to embed individuals in a society and their vacuous notion of "autonomy":

> Just as the alleged incorrigibility of what we want serves finally to undermine moral justification, so its allegedly value-free conception of harm in the end obscures and even makes paradoxical the liberal insistence that interference with individual autonomy is justified only 'to prevent harm to others'. For in failing to see individuals as embedded within the society and various sub-groups in which they live, it cannot deal adequately with those harms that are morality-dependent, harms which cannot be recognized from a value-neutral vantage-point.[9]

One may sensibly object, nonetheless, that choosing a political existence, through the numerous rules and regulations of any society, puts constraints on our autonomy and capacity for individuation. In choosing a political existence, however, we do not sacrifice individuality, but rather we optimize the occasions for realizing it. There are countless opportunities for creative, human expression within any given society—except, perhaps, the most oppressive ones. Diversity of people means diversity of wants, and the latter means numerous and different opportunities for originality and human happiness. That these *seem to be* offset by other instances where we cannot get what we want is no sufficient rejoinder. Social institutions, especially those that are democratically diverse, offer us many more opportunities for happiness than they take away.

In short, the social or political nature of human beings—the fact that true autonomy of individuals only occurs within a nonoppressive social setting—shows that individuals are not prior to communities, but coextensive with them. It is not the "individual *qua* individual," but the "individual *qua* social being" or the "social individual" that is the fundamental unit of political analysis. Liberals, then, irresponsibly hide behind the buzzword, "autonomy," while they fail to realize that there can be no coherent notion of the word in an asocial context. Consequently, the liberal notion of happiness as freedom for self-expression/and self-determination lacks content and, therefore, is empty.

---

[8]Our preference for political life is merely rationally chosen regard for security of interests (chapter 19).

[9]1998, p. 155 (*Getting What You Want: A Critique of Liberal Morality*, New York: Routledge).

The most pernicious and vapid form of liberalism today is postmodernism. Postmodernism thrives in certain fashionable philosophical sects, in the sociological literature, and in most "democratic" societies. This view is difficult to put into words. There are as many different formulations as there are advocates, and even advocates often admit to this confusion.[10] Whatever their differences, postmodernists, to a person, all agree that philosophy has come to a turning point, where it must be either discontinued or, at least, radically transformed. Strictly speaking, postmodernists reject any meaningful, traditional notion of rationality and offer, instead, a happy anti-authoritarianism which takes as its basis freedom and desire as embedded within the ever-changing conventions and constructions of society. It rails against any meaningful sense of philosophy as it has been traditionally done and offers nothing substantive in its place. Brecher has this to say concerning postmodernist confusion:

> Postmodernism is the outcome of the destructive dialectic between the twin peaks of empiricism and liberalism: their squeamishness about reason and their misconceivedly atomized—because deracinated—conception of the individual.[11]

A postmodernist morality, then, is liberalism taken to its chaotic extreme. Individuals as irrational beings follow the various currents of antagonistic impulses that swirl about helter-skelter within themselves and their vacillating society. With postmodernism, there is absolutely no room for any sensible conception of morality. Thus we are compelled to return to the larger notion of ethics—that is, the notion of living a good life—where "good" can only be construed as a going with the flow of one's impulses.

If I am correct in insisting that liberalism is the received view today, then we have moved away from the provinciality of morality and its emphasis on rightness or wrongness of actions, back to full-fledged ethics. With liberalism as moral policy, however, we have not done so from any richer or more complete notion of human agency and culpability. We have done so merely because the notion of a right or wrong action makes no sense when basing morality *exclusively* upon desires. We have fallen back upon the self-service morality of egoistic hedonism and there is no longer room for reason to intercede, except in an instrumental fashion.[12]

A final criticism of liberalism is that it bases morality and political theory on what is most bestial and least praiseworthy in humans: human selfishness. In criticizing the "egalitarian" political institutions of recent times, Gandhi had this to say:

---

[10]Baynes et al. 1989, p. 3 (*After Philosophy: End or Transformation?* Cambridge, MA: The MIT Press).

[11]Brecher 1998, p. 4.

[12]That is, devising strategies that enable one to overcome obstacles in order to pursue one's desires. Compare Freud's ego and id.

Socialism and Communism of the West are based on certain conceptions which are fundamentally different from ours. One such conception is their belief in the essential selfishness of human nature. I do not subscribe to it, for I know that the essential difference between man and brute is that the former can respond to the call of spirit in him and can rise superior to the passions that he owns in common with the brute and therefore superior to selfishness and violence which belong to brute nature and not to the immortal spirit of man.[13]

As Gandhi fully knew, no political institution, based on individuals as egoistic wanting entities, is capable of thriving.

What I have aimed to show previously is not that the liberal moral and political platforms are inherently putrefied and debased, but that the moral-political pendulum, from ultra-conservatism, has swung too far to *ultra*-liberalism. In embracing autonomy as its highest good, liberalism has gone too far, so much so that it is without meaning—at least, if it is the case, as observation strongly suggests, that humans are inherently social creatures.

If this argument is compelling, there can be no conception of individuals' happiness that divorces these individuals from their social context. Therefore, for an adequate notion of happiness, we must look within the various social and political institutions in which people live. It is in these institutions that we achieve our fullest autonomy and the most diverse and fulfilling means of human expression. It is through integrating ourselves in these institutions that we find happiness. Thus, to be happy, one must be politically integrated—that is, rationally responsive not only to one's own desires and wants, but also to those of others in one's community and the needs of the community itself.

IV. Political Integration and Social Responsibility

Modern times do require an escape from the provinciality of liberal moral and political theory to an expanded notion of what it means to be happy. Here, I suggest, we can learn something from the ancient Greeks in our attempt to reevaluate what it means to live a good life today.

Overall, Greeks regarded happiness (*eudaimonia*, literally, "being blessed with a good god within") as the development of a certain type of virtuous character. "Ethics," Aristotle himself tells us, comes from the Greek words, (*ethos*, short 'e') and (*éthos*, long 'e')—the former meaning roughly "habit," the latter, "character." Living the right kind of life, then, mostly comprises developing a stable, moral character through a proper mode of habituation from childhood as well as the cultivation of our rational faculty at the appropriate age.[14]

For the Greeks, then, living a good life was much more than egoistic pleasure seeking or having a moral perspective. Happiness was a way of life and the Greek way of life, especially during the time of Plato and Aristotle, was essentially political (centered on the *polis* or city-state) in nature. Individuals served

---

[13]1996, p. 133 (Mahatma Gandhi: *Selected Political Writings*, Indianapolis: Hackett).
[14]Aristotle's *Nicomachean Ethics* X.9 (1179b5–19).

under and considered themselves subordinate to the *polis*.[15] After all, the good of the *polis* depended crucially on a sense of duty to it and a just division of labor to ensure that all citizens could be as happy as possible—in other words, that no citizens would be outstandingly happy at the expense of others who might suffer inordinately.[16]

What ensured this sense of duty and willingness to cooperate for the "good of the whole"? Classical Greeks bought into a sense of communitarianism. For Socrates, Plato states, it is plain mindfulness, first, that the polis is more divine than its inhabitants and, second, that it gives to its citizens much more than they can ever hope to give in return.[17] For Plato, it is an external sense of justice. Justice, he says, is something to be valued for its own sake as much as for the sake of its beneficial consequences.[18] For Aristotle, it is *filia*—here, to be understood not so much as "friendship" but rather as communal ties of genuine affection within a *polis* (for utility, pleasure, or goodness).[19]

Classical Greek notions of communitarianism were certainly sociological reflections of their times. Clearly there were stark defects in Greek political thought and moral theory, most of which reflected their societal ills. The most striking defect was their incurably elitist and aristocratic slant. Regard for the rights and autonomy of all individuals in a community, with the possible exception of Epicureans, was something foreign to Classical Greek thinking. But my aim here is philosophical, not sociological. Autonomy, which is part of the very fabric of democratic societies today, does seem to have as much right to be regarded as a virtue as does any other traditional virtue.

If we judge by the works of ancient Greek moral and political thinkers, the Greek view of life and justice, in spite of its failings, was certainly more robust than is ours. There is little sense of rightness or justice with today's liberal morality and policy, and these merely protect individuals' rights to pursue their own ends through the gratification of their own impulses. Morality and constitutions, based chiefly on gratification of impulses, have no true foundation and cannot endure. Today we delight in disagreement, not for the sake of serving as a springboard for consensus or truth in the future, but as an end itself. We tolerate differences of opinion, however absurd and unfounded, with bubbling enthusiasm. Our wisdom consists of a kind of "perplexed" poise with a touch of buoyant grace in the face of adversity.

Toleration of divergent opinion is, of course, a very good thing—especially in matters unsettled by rational dispute—but it is not and ought not to be an end in itself. As humans, we want answers to the questions we ask. It may be that

[15]E.g., one of the underlying themes of Plato's *Crito.*
[16]Plato's *Republic,* IV (420b–421c).
[17]*Crito* p. 50c–51.
[18]*Republic,* II.358a
[19]Though it is listed as just one of the many political virtues in Book II (1108a27–28), *filia* was so crucial for Aristotle's notion of community that he devotes two of his ten books of the *Nicomachean Ethics,* Books VIII and IX, to it.

many of these questions do not presently admit of answers. Others may never admit of answers. Still, level-headed dispute will serve provisionally, at least, to help us differentiate sensible from senseless questions.

With a focus on cultivating and maintaining excellence of character and evaluating the justness of an act by the goodness of the person committing that act, Greek ethics and politics placed a premium on responsibility and justice, in spite of the fact that there was no sense of "individual" in Greek political thought as there is modern-day democracies. "Individual" took meaning only insofar as people took part in their community and developed communal ties. Today, regardless of ethical perspective, we call *actions* just or unjust, not the agents performing them, as did the Greeks. This change of perspective is significant for culpability. We do not want to blame ourselves when what we do goes wrong, if we can blame the action itself.

The received moral view today leaves no place for responsibility squarely on the shoulders of an agent. After all, liberal morality is a matter of autonomous agents fulfilling personal desires. Reason in not judgmental of but instrumental for wants. Communities are meant only to serve individuals. Duty to others, to community, and to anything other than self is ignored. Constitutions undergirded by liberal policy are thus decadent.

The picture that I draw, many will say, is grossly exaggerated. If we could travel back to ancient Greece, we would see as much (perhaps even more) lust, greed, indulgence, and selfishness as we do in modern "democratic" societies. I do not challenge this objection at all, for this is not chiefly what is at issue here. My aim, as I mention above, is philosophical and not sociological. What is at issue here are the philosophic visions of their time and ours.

The great men of ancient Greece had a broader and grander philosophic vision than our politicians and philosophers, both men and women, have today. Theirs was a *rational* ideal of binding people together for the common good. Our predominant ideal today is individuation with scant regard for reason. We would do well to remember what Aristotle often said: We are, by nature, political animals.[20] Our good is thus to be had principally in political institutions. Autonomy, if is it expressed as an asocial ideal or even if it is just expressed indifferently to institutionalization, is an unhappy and ephemeral ideal. We need to be reminded that, as communities are founded to serve individuals, they only work well when individuals work together for the good of their communities.

V. Concluding Remarks

In summary, the received moral and political view, liberalism, is disappointing not in its recognition of autonomy as an important value, but in its insistence that autonomy is our one or, at least, chief value. Moreover, liberalism refuses to acknowledge that true autonomy is to be found only within political institutions —especially those that are democratically diverse. Last, liberalism elevates as a

---

[20]*Nicomachean Ethics,* 1162a16–19 & 1169b16–22, *Eudemian Ethics,* 1242a19–28, and *Politics,* 1253a7–18 & 1278b15–30.

fixed natural disposition what is perhaps least worthy of promotion, human self-ishness, and wholly neglects human self*less*ness of spirit, which has an equally good claim to be considered as a human tendency. Realizing this, liberalism as a guide to happiness can do no other than disappoint. In a word, the liberal view of happiness, at any level, is a matter of *dis*integration, not integration.

Nonetheless, if my account of happiness as both personal and political integration is correct, it explains why true happiness is so slippery. Just like the acquisition of any skill, procuring happiness takes planning, focus, discipline, and persistence. Only those persons who devote themselves to a lifetime of personal discovery and growth *and* who place themselves within and at the service of both their community and others can find the equanimity and can achieve the stability of character that is distinctive of all happy people.

Questions for Discussion

1. What are the positive values of liberal morality? How are they sometimes distorted when taken in isolation?

2. Give some additional examples of how extreme liberalism produces unwanted side effects in our culture.

3. Connect up the discussion of classical liberalism from the previous chapter with the discussion in this chapter of contemporary forms of liberalism.

4. What is the connection between empiricism and liberalism? How does this relate to ethical subjectivism and relativism?

5. Is it possible in a society as racially, religiously, and ethnically diverse as the United States to rationally strive for a social ideal of the common good to which we are all committed?

CHAPTER 37

Minority Group Rights

The range of issues with which philosophy is concerned is vast, but none is older than the topic of the organization of human society. One of the evidences of this interest is Aristotle's treatise entitled *Politics,* from the Greek word for the city-state. In his view, the ideal human community was the *polis* or city, and the ideal size for the polis was a unit large enough to have economic viability yet small enough for a person to traverse in a day. From the existence of many, separate Greek city states arose confederations of states sharing common cultural and religious identities. Yet even in a region where citizens of these cities all spoke the same language and shared in the same religious traditions, conflicts arose that reflected different ideas of social order and cultural identity. *The Peloponnesian War by* Thucydides details the sad story of conflict among peoples who had many things in common—history, language, religion—yet still went to war with each other.

In the article that follows, the authors give a brief history of the rise of nationalism and the nation-state. They then point out that in the aftermath of the disappearance of the large empires of the nineteenth and twentieth centuries and the end of the Cold War with the accompanying breakup of the Soviet Union, we have to face anew what we mean by "nation" and national identity. This question is made all the more acute by the fact that around the world one finds groups who identify themselves as a "nation" yet who live within the national borders of a country or across the borders of several countries. These people may share a common history, language, and culture and find themselves unable, or unwilling, to assimilate themselves into the culture of the country in which they live. This sense of ethnic identity and cultural affinity can erupt into forms of nationalism calling for separateness and often producing bloody conflicts. At the same time, supra-natural entities, such as the United Nations, seem to be gaining authority and power to intervene in the internal affairs of sovereign nation-states, often on behalf of their ethnic minorities.

From the time of the Enlightenment beginning in the seventeenth and eighteenth centuries the voices of philosophers such as Voltaire and Rousseau in France, Hobbes and Locke in Great Britain, called for the ideal of universal rights and political liberty. This ideal was embedded in the founding documents of the United States in the ringing sentences of Jefferson's Declaration of Independence, which spoke of the unalienable rights to life, liberty, and the pursuit of happiness. As these ideals were worked out in practice, rights were not extended universally—not to Africans brought to the shores of the New World, not to the indigenous peoples of North America, not even fully to European females. Within countries where human rights were honored, at least in theory, groups were denied those same rights either because of their racial identity or their cultural difference.

Today with the emergence of many smaller countries resulting from the dissolution of the former Soviet Union and the breakdown of Yugoslavia, with independence movements for various peoples developing in Southeast Asia, Africa, and even within Europe, we see new calls for the recognition of nationhood that are inconsistent with existing national borders. Within culturally diverse countries, such as the United States, there is less talk about the "melting pot" concept of cultural assimilation and more attention given to the ideal of diversity as something of a lumpy stew in which each ethical and cultural identity is preserved. What does "multiculturalism" mean in this context? Ethnic integration or the development of an entirely new culture, a new national identity? In the state of California, no racial majority exists; will it be possible to identify a "California culture"? Will a new identity be forged that is neither European, Hispanic, African-American, or Asian? How will democratic ideals be honored in a multicultural society so that the identity of minorities is honored while the will of the majority, where such exists, is allowed to hold sway?

These are not easy questions, but they are important ones. The world faces a new reality, one no longer fixated on the Cold War with the standoff between two superpowers that pushed all ethnic and cultural rivalries to the background. Today the calls for recognition and sometimes even independence of cultural and ethnic groups force us to look again at the notions of nationhood and ethnic identity. In the article that follows, two philosophers provide guidance through this thicket of difficult issues.

Elizabeth Smith and H. Gene Blocker: Minority Groups and the State

In the days since the collapse of the Berlin Wall we have seen unparalleled changes in international political alignments. The relative stability of the Cold

Reprinted with permission of the authors from *Applied Social and Political Philosophy*, Elizabeth Smith and H. Gene Blocker, eds. Upper Saddle River, NJ: Prentice Hall, 1993.

War era has ended and given rise to a period of transition so swift and wide-spread that cartographers are unable to redraw maps quickly enough to reflect the ongoing changes. . . .

What is occurring is primarily a political reordering which shifts attention away from the super powers and relations among them as the primary focus of importance, to concentrations of groupings of people both larger and smaller than the traditional nation-state. On the one hand, there is a growing consensus that we ought to have geopolitical cooperation and exercise of power at the multi-national world level, perhaps through the United Nations, and, on the other hand, at the opposite end of the spectrum, a growing resurgence of demands for autonomy and "self-determination" by a proliferating number of smaller, ethnic and other minorities. Developments at these two seemingly opposite levels are nonetheless intimately related to one another in the sense that there is increasing concern about minorities being persecuted by the nation-states within which they currently exist. The sovereignty of Iraq might be abridged in favor of Kurdish rights; the sovereignty of Serbia is being challenged in favor of the rights of Bosnians and Croats. Ethnic and racial groups within South Africa, Kuwait, and Israel also demand protection and a measure of self-determination.

Clearly the most obvious reason for this shift of attention and concentration of power is the end of the Cold War. So long as the United States and its allies were locked in a nuclear standoff with the Soviet Union and its allies, no larger world political power could have much impact on these issues. At the same time, so long as the superpowers were deadlocked, there was no alternative but to respect the sovereignty of the superpower nation-states and their nation-state allies and client states, with the result that individual nation-states were free to suppress ancient claims of their ethnic minorities to self determination. Apart from the inability of each superpower to interfere in the internal affairs of the other (and their allies and client states), there was also the presumption that in the noble language of the Enlightenment, ethnic, racial and religious group solidarity had come to be seen as a politically irrelevant consideration.

Before the eighteenth century, people were accustomed to identify themselves as members of rather small groups, and then extended their community to larger groups such as Croatians, Lithuanians, Kurds, Protestants, Arabs, Jews, black or white. Identification with ethnic and religious groups led to much petty but bloody conflict among people. But once it was claimed, in the Enlightenment declarations about the universal and inalienable rights of man, that we are all primarily human beings, sharing equally with every other human being a common and proud "one world" humanity, it was hoped that all the petty, narrow-minded factionalism of the past would gradually fade away. We now see that presumption to have been an illusion, an overly optimistic dream which has now faded. This is a bitter disappointment to political liberals and those influenced by the Enlightenment ideal that all humanity has one common nature.

Historically, "nationalism" was defined in terms of universal human rights in a way which made it seem that ethnic, tribal, racial, and linguistic identities were unimportant. In France and in America at the end of the eighteenth century, the foundations of government, legitimizing modern nation-states, was discussed in enlightened terms of the rights which every human being possesses simply by virtue of being a human being—irrespective of whether that human being is a man or a woman, black or white, slave or free, Croatian or Serbian, Protestant or

Roman Catholic, Christian or Jew, Yoruba or Ibo. Nonetheless, the subtext presupposed that the ideal nation-state was in fact an ethnically and culturally identical people forming themselves into a nation-state. The failure to recognize this subtext has had very serious consequences which are only now being realized.

Nationalism can be understood more broadly to mean the subjective perception of a group of people that they are united, or joined together in any one of several nonlegal, nonpolitical senses of group identity—on the basis of language, ethnicity, religion, race, culture, history or some combination of these. As such it is not a political or legal grouping but one which is primarily perceptual and in that sense "mythological." In this sense, "national" self-identity need not be based on biological or historical fact. . . . Another aspect of this subjective, "mythological," perceptual aspect of nationalism is the implication that how one sees oneself depends to a large extent on how *others* see us. So long as European Jews in early nineteenth century Germany (during the Napoleanic regime) who took German names, sincerely converted to Christianity, and culturally assimilated in every way to German culture were still perceived as Jews, to that extent the "reformed" assimilationists were forced to see *themselves* as Jews first and Germans second, if at all. And to the extent that black Americans are perceived by white Americans as a separate community, they tend to perceive themselves as blacks first.

But here we must distinguish between the biological, anthropological *phenomenon* of nationalism and the emergence of the *concept* of "nationalism" as a key term in political discussions. The first is as old as human kind; the second as recent as the late eighteenth century. As Aristotle points out, "man is a social animal." But this means more than the fact that human beings want and need to live together in social communities. It also means that human beings tend to identify themselves with the particular cultural group of which they are members and to regard people of other cultural groups as alien, "others." For example, the word which many Native American and traditional African groups use to refer to themselves simply means "the people." This is the biological and anthropological root of the phenomenon of ethnic nationality. . . .

On the other hand, as a term used in historical, political and sociological contexts, the *concept* of "nationalism" in its earliest phase is linked with eighteenth century Enlightenment ideas of the universal rights of man and with democracy as a superior form of government of "the people," by "the people" and for "the people." This idea developed first in Europe where, historically, groups which had shared for hundreds of years some cultural, linguistic sense of identity were already living, more or less, in contiguous geographical areas which were already recognized, more or less, as autonomous or semi-autonomous regions. An important preliminary stage on the road to the modern nation-state was the development of a centralized monarchy in Britain and France at the end of the Middle Ages which succeeded in wresting control from competing princes to consolidate a centralized national government.

The paradigm case was that of France where a culturally defined people living in a contiguous geographical area which had long been centrally governed by a monarch demanded in the eighteenth century that they should rule themselves. Other cases fall progressively away from this paradigm. German, and less obviously so, Italian speaking peoples, for example, like the French, sought a political unity to coincide with their cultural and linguistic sense of identity. But *unlike* the French this involved more than simply changing the form of government by revolutionary means. It also required constituting a new regional, political unit—creating out of many smaller principalities a modern Germany and a modern Italy—a political unity which already existed in the case of France. Later this idea was expanded still further to include people who perceived themselves as united in some nonpolitical sense but who were not politically organized within geographical borders, or who had no recent history, however checkered, of political independence—European Jews, Black Americans, Slavs, Kurds, Armenians. . . .

To some extent, therefore, the "nation" creates the "state" in the sense that an ethnic nationality demands to be a state. But to some extent it is also true that the "state" creates the "nation." Obviously the larger the population and the geographical area involved, the more differences there will be among "the people" thus joined together. They may all speak the same language but have somewhat different customs, or religious beliefs, and historical and economic histories. "Nation-building" will then be a matter of creating a greater sense of solidarity among all the people living within the state, to create of the state a "nation." Nonetheless, despite such flexibility in defining "group membership," historically there have been some groups which are excluded from full membership—Gypsies, Jews, freed African slaves, conquered indigenous groups, such as American Indians. And these groups are excluded despite the universalist language of the eighteenth century "declaration of the rights of man" which might seem to include *everyone*. When Martin Luther King, in his "I have a dream" speech, said that "America had defaulted on the promissory note that all men would be granted the unalienable rights of life, liberty, and the pursuit of happiness," he was harking back, as Lincoln had done earlier in his Gettysburg address, not to the Constitution, but to Jefferson's Declaration of Independence. . . .

The key question which was not fully or consciously addressed then or now is precisely who belongs to the "nation." Who are "the people"? It is like membership in a club. Certain people belong and share equally rights and responsibilities of membership. Others may be invited to join, but still others are excluded and do not share in the rights, privileges and responsibilities of full membership. Because of the universalist language of the eighteenth century in which these rights were discussed, along with the failure to consider explicitly the "nationalist" requirements for "membership," confusions persist, including the false expectation that everyone living within the geographical boundaries is automatically included in "we the people," when in fact some are included and some are excluded.

We should not be surprised, therefore, that this hidden subtext begins to surface today in the rise of ethnic tensions in Eastern Europe and the countries of the former Soviet Union. So long as some political communities, such as the United States, Canada and Australia, seemed to be thriving as "melting pots" harmonizing a rich palette of races, religions and ethnic groups, and so long as the Soviet Union succeeded in blocking and strangling ethnic demands by its imposition of a socialist ideal which transcended and superseded all ethnic and religious rivalries, the dream of "the melting pot" seemed for many decades a reality. Now we seriously question that dream. What does or should provide the basis for inclusion into a political community? Should the Serbs bond with the Croats in one nation or become two? Can the Hindus and Muslims live together as one country? Can the blacks, Hispanics, Koreans and whites "all get along" in Los Angeles?

Western Europeans were understandably pleased to hear their Eastern European neighbors embracing the rationalist/universalist language of the universal rights of man in defending their declarations of independence from Communist totalitarianism, but these same Westerners were soon disappointed to find the actual implementation of those "rights" quickly degenerating into the bloody conflict known as "ethnic cleansing." Like America and France in the eighteenth century, Germany and Italy in the nineteenth century, so today, the Hungarians, Rumanians, Lithuanians, Armenians, Croats, Serbs express their demand for ethnic autonomy and self-determination in the universalist language of the universal rights of man. We are only surprised because we are only now, more than 200 years later, beginning to realize the deep ambiguity and conceptual confusions surrounding the Enlightenment ideal of the rights of man. . . .

Nationalism, then, in its most general sense is the perception which a group of people has of itself as possessing some sort of nonpolitical identity—ethnic, historical, linguistic, cultural, religious, racial—who demand "self-determination" in the sense of a supposed right to construct a political state which coincides with the nation (or at least some measure of autonomy within a larger state composed of other "nationalities"). American Indians, for example, did not originally have a concept of themselves as an "Indian nation" but as bands which had varying relationships with other bands, forming tribal groups which in turn entered into relationships with each other. In a similar way, Africans did not perceive themselves as a single group until they saw that Europeans so regarded them, and began to join together in a united front against the white European invaders. In the early nineteenth century many European ethnic minorities enthusiastically embraced the new conception of nationalism and made it part of the rhetoric of their demands for autonomy and self-determination. It was not until the twentieth century (when, unfortunately, it was too late for many of them) that African and Native American groups began to express their demands for autonomy and self determination in the European language of "nationalism."

Colonialism was at once a kind of nationalism (expansionist, militarist type) and at the same time it created artificial states without a sense of nationhood. States of Africa carved up by European colonial powers at the end of the nineteenth century joined together different ethnic, tribal groups into colonial states and divided other ethnic, tribal groups into different colonial states. For example, Nigeria is composed of dozens of different ethnic groups, some of whose tribal members (e.g., Yoruba) live beyond the borders of Nigeria in neighboring French-speaking Benin Republic. What identity these people have (first simply as "Africans" and then as "Nigerians") came largely from the white European colonial rulers. Only with the arrival of the Europeans did the Africans begin to see and think of themselves as "Africans"—not just as racially distinct but also as culturally distinct and, from the European colonial point of view, generally inferior to white European culture. From the European point of view, the aim of colonialism was in part an expression of nationalism, as the "white man's burden" to bring civilization to "primitive," mostly nonwhite peoples. And it was only through the European colonial powers that African peoples later came to think of themselves as Nigerians, Ghanaians, and so on. African "nationalism" was primarily the desire of people who now saw themselves as "African" for freedom from an alien colonial, European power. It was only the historical accident that they had been divided into various "countries" that this nationalist sense had to be directed to freeing each country, one by one, from various European colonial powers—French, English, Portuguese, German, Belgium, Spanish and Italian. Nationalism in Africa now expresses itself most often in the armed struggle for ethnic, tribal supremacy, or at least, autonomy.

There is no single solution to such a range of complex problems. Certainly we need to respect the right of groups to self-determination. If, as seems to be the case, group identification is so important to so many individuals' sense of self and self esteem and value, then group rights would seem to follow from our more familiar notion of individual rights. Group rights would appear to be an extension of the individual's right to full self development. In other words, we must add to individual rights the notion of group rights, allowing the deeply felt desire of many "nationalities" to achieve a measure of autonomy and self-determination. This could take various forms, short of but including the ideal of each nationality becoming an independent nation-state, for example, regional autonomy, multiple language usage, respect for different religions and religious customs and holidays, perhaps even fixed group representation, or, as in Lebanon, rotation of government offices attached to specific ethnic nationalities. Sovereignty is thereby severely restricted since states cannot be allowed to oppress rights of groups living therein. If this is to be seen as a positive rather than negative development, a case needs to be made for defending international law and order even where it opposes national sovereign at the nation-state level, whether in Iraq, Somalia, or the former Yugoslavia.

In other cases, however, in West Africa, for example, and other regions of the world which have only a recent history of political organization at the nation-state level, we need to encourage nation-building and multinational cooperation, speeding the evolution *away from* ethnic nationalism at the tribal level, experimenting with various forms of multinational unification around *political* principles rather than ethnic, racial, linguistic, religious and other (ancient) cultural forms of identity. Without organization at the nation-state level, it is hard to imagine a collection of ethnic minorities having sufficient technological, industrial, communications facilities and infrastructure to be able to participate effectively, as an equal, in the modern world. After several "false starts" toward democratic modernization during the colonial and neo-colonial periods, the end of the Cold War marks the beginning of an optimistic sense throughout West Africa of a "second chance" at democracy which will *accelerate* the movement toward the formation of viable nation-states in that region.

Regions of the world where we could more easily imagine a move away from the nation-state as the preferred political grouping are those in which nation-states have evolved to the point of effective regional cooperation, such as seems to be happening in Europe, and is perhaps beginning to take place in North America and the Americas more generally. Even so, nation-states will probably continue to be important for some time to come, though in a somewhat diminished capacity. In some cases this will involve greater access of all minorities to assimilation to full citizenship in the larger nation-state (invitation to full membership). But in other cases it means a greater tolerance for diversity of different ethnic nationalities within a single nation-state. This last alternative implies a synthesis of "integration" and "separation"—integrating all individuals of all ethnic nationalities into the *political* and *economic* life of the nation-state, but also encouraging a degree of *cultural* and *ethnic* diversity (of language, custom, religion, music, taste, etc.). In the United States, for example, this might involve Hispanics speaking Spanish, listening to Hispanic radio, watching Hispanic TV programs and films, studying Hispanic history and culture, and so on; African Americans learning more about African and African American history and culture, and so on, with members of all ethnic groups participating fully in the middle-class "American dream" economically and professionally.

Another goal of "multiculturalism" is to embrace African, Chinese, Native American, etc. cultural contributions—not just for African Americans, Chinese Americans, Native Americans, respectively, but for *all* (and particularly for white) Americans. This is the sense of multicultural education which would emphasize nation-building, ethnic integration rather than ethnic separation, encouraging the idea, for example, that jazz is not a "black music" but an American music; "California Zen" is not a Chinese or Japanese religion but now an American religion; Mexican-American, Chinese-American food is American cuisine; and that American Indian traditions should become traditions for all Americans. African and Native American history, for example, would be taught to white students as well as African and Native American students. This would be a difficult and distant goal since these efforts will antagonize those who *do not* identify with these traditions, and who see integration of diverse cultures as the loss of their own cultural identity. Whichever way we go, how can we work to respect the rights not only of individuals but of groups when they may conflict with each other?

Similar problems of balancing integration and separation occur whenever and wherever minority groups living among a majority people were not "invited" to live there as citizens enjoying full rights of citizenship. American Indians and the Hispanics of the southwest did not "invite" Europeans to live within their geographical boundaries, nor did Europeans "invite," until much later, American Indians to become citizens of the United States. Chinese were invited to the United States (and to many other countries as well) initially only on work permits; not to become citizens. Other immigrants in similar circumstances were Asian Indians in Africa, Chinese in Malaysia, Koreans in Japan, Turkish workers in Germany, or Palestinian workers in Kuwait. In the past, groups suffering religious and other forms of persecution, such as Jews and Gypsies, were allowed to live in restricted areas, "ghettos," within certain countries, e.g., Germany, as an invited minority, but were not allowed the rights of full citizenship. The problem occurs with the passage of time—does the fourth generation descendant of Korean, Indian, Chinese, Palestinian workers, Jew, Gypsy, etc. operate under the same contractual agreement which their forefathers consented to fifty, a hundred or two hundred years ago? At what point does it become unrealistic to regard these minorities as "aliens" who are expected eventually to return "home"? If they have been allowed to stay, there would appear to be an implied consent that they can eventually become citizens. And if so, then they must be allowed full rights of citizenship. If this is not the intention, host countries should regularly and periodically update worker permits (and where the workers are no longer needed, discontinue the worker permit, thereby requiring the individuals to return to their home countries). Then it would be clear that they are not citizens, but temporary guest workers, remaining at the pleasure of the host country for renewable five-year contract periods, for example, as long as they are needed. It does not seem fair after four or five generations (during which time nothing was said or done about their immigration status) either to insist that they go "home" or to be allowed to remain without the rights of full citizenship.

But if the minority group has been granted full citizenship rights, it seems only reasonable to allow them the choice of whether and to what extent to assimilate into the cultural life of the majority community. To grant them citizenship but not allow them to culturally assimilate is, in effect, a contradiction, since to actually enjoy many of the rights of citizenship individuals must be able to interact as equals with the mainstream, majority culture. . . .

One might wonder how it can be fair to demand that the majority *allow* the minority to culturally assimilate but *not require* the minority to assimilate culturally to the majority even if the minority don't want to. The answer is that "success" in the nation-state, as defined by the majority culture, depends on success *within* the majority culture which can only be accomplished by assimilation *into* the majority culture. Preventing minorities from assimilating works to the great disadvantage of members of the minority culture who *want* to be "successful" by the standards of the majority culture, whereas it is hard to see how the refusal of a minority to fully assimilate culturally could greatly affect the "success" of members of the mainstream majority culture in an adverse way. Some may object that members of the majority culture *prefer* to be culturally "pure" and that, however questionable or abhorrent we may find their reasons, they have the *right* to require cultural assimilation by outsiders as the only way to remain as culturally "pure" as they can. But this "harm" of "offensiveness" must be weighed against the more obvious and overt harm to the alienated minority. If a member of a minority wants to be "successful" by the standards of the mainstream majority culture, then they must be allowed full access (equal opportunity) to do so. On the other hand, if a member of a minority (or indeed any individual) rejects the majority standards of "success," they should be free to do as they please so long as they do not "harm" others.

We have considered a number of solutions to the problem of reconciling ethnic identity with multi-ethnic cooperation. What determines what is the best solution in a particular situation? Primarily, it should be based on the "will of the people"—both as individuals and as members of groups with which individuals identify. If the individuals and groups which have been "invited" to become citizens want to assimilate, they must be allowed to do so by removing all barriers of discrimination, negative stereotypes, and so on. If individuals and groups insist on self-determination and political autonomy, this must be supported, either with full autonomy as independent nation-states or with some measure of regional autonomy. If individuals and groups want political integration and cultural separation this too must be allowed and facilitated.

In the past, one of the strongest arguments *against* group rights, especially the right of an ethnic minority to secede from the larger nation-state, has been the practical necessity of forming a viable nation-state with a wide enough range of natural resources to be relatively self-sufficient militarily and economically. But that argument seems to carry less weight today as we move toward multinational political and economic associations. Why can't Nunavut, the new self governing Native American territory in northern Canada, function as a politically autonomous entity within an American (including North, Central and South American) military and economic multinational cooperative association? Certainly, there is little resistance today to the break-up of Eastern European nation-states into a multitude of tiny nationalistic states under the larger Pan-European umbrella. Perhaps in the future the greatest incentive for ethnic minorities to remain within a larger nation-state will simply be the convenience and economic efficiency of a single monetary unit, unified educational and professional standards, a common highway system, a common language, etc. But even that incentive may erode over time, especially in the new European union and even today in the informal US-Canadian-Mexican PanAmerican association which could function in many ways as a single nation (exchangeability of money, porous borders, similar educational and professional standards, an interconnected highway system, mutual access to radio and television transmission, and so on).

Questions for Discussion

1. Can you make a utilitarian argument for the importance of guarding minority rights? What do you think should be the limits of majority rule regarding minority groups?

2. To what do you attribute the call for separate nation status for certain groups (as in Europe, for example) even among nations that are prosperous and at peace?

3. What are some of the forces that bind people together into a nation? What are some of the forces that drive them apart?

4. What challenges will face a political unit when it has no majority population, when everybody is a "minority"?

5. To what extent do you see a "new world order" emerging that may eventually replace the nation-state as the sovereign entity? What do you see as the advantages and the dangers of such a trend?

Suggestions for Further Reading

Beitz, Charles R. *Political Equality*. Princeton: Princeton University Press, 1989. Discusses theory and application of the principles of political equality in contemporary democracy.

Berlin, Isaiah. *Four Essays on Liberty*. Oxford: Oxford University Press, 1969. A classic work analyzing different notions of political freedom.

Nielsen, Kai. *Equality and Liberty*. Totowa, NJ: Rowman and Allenhead, 1985. A defense of radical socialist egalitanarism.

Nozick, Robert. *Anarchy, State and Utopia*. New York: Basic Books, 1977. A clear defense of radical libertarianism.

Rawls, John. *A Theory of Justice*. Cambridge, MA: Harvard University Press, 1970. One of the most widely read and discussed philosophy books by a contemporary philosopher that develops a compromise between egalitarianism and libertarianism.

Rawls, John. *The Law of Peoples*. Cambridge: Harvard University Press, 1999. Rawls applies his theory of justice as fairness to issues in democratic liberalism.

Eastern Thought

PART 9

CHAPTER 38

Philosophy East and West

"East is east and west is west, and never the twain shall meet." So wrote Rudyard Kipling after many years of service in the British colonial government in India. Certainly the culture of the East (primarily India, China, and Japan, which are by no means identical with one another) is very different from that of the West (primarily Europe and North America), but that does not mean each culture is incapable of understanding certain features of the other. It does not mean the two cannot be compared. However different Eastern and Western cultures are, precise points of similarity and difference can be constructively brought out in a comparative study.

As the world becomes "smaller" year by year, it is increasingly important to develop an understanding of culture centers around the globe which are very different from our own. One way to compare cultures is to compare and contrast the different religions, art forms, educational systems, family practices, governmental institutions—assuming that all cultures have *some* form of religion, art, government, education, and so on. But what about philosophy? Does every culture have a philosophy, however different it may be from the philosophies of other cultures? It all depends on what we mean by the term *philosophy*. As we saw in Part 1, there is in ordinary English an everyday sense of the word *philosophy* in which we say that every person has his or her own "philosophy" (his or her "philosophy of life," as we say). The same could be said of whole societies or cultures. Insofar as each society or culture has its own idea of itself, its own conception of what is important in life, and its own notions of what the world is like in general terms, there is a sense in which each society or culture can be said to have its own "philosophy" (or world view). This is one of the things sociologists and anthropologists study when they examine different societies and cultures—what was (or is) the "philosophy" of the Native Americans, or what was their "philosophy of life" (world view) and how did (or does) that differ from, say, the ancient Egyptians' "philosophy," or "philosophy of life" (world view)?

Multiple Meanings of Philosophy

This discussion of whether to apply the term *philosophy* to Eastern modes of thought brings us back to some of the same issues we explored in the beginning of this book. As we saw in Part 1, the word *philosophy* is also used in a more technical sense to indicate a particular methodology—a specialized way of investigating and organizing ideas—one which is critical, logical, analytical, systematic, and so on. And in *that* sense, *not* everyone is a philosopher or has a philosophy. In this second sense European philosophy arose at a particular point in Greek history. Greeks before Thales did not have philosophy in this second sense. And if the Greeks before Thales had no philosophy or philosophers, it is possible that other societies and cultures had no philosophy or philosophers. Of course, just as philosophy arose in European culture at a particular time and place, so it is possible that philosophy arose at various points in time in other, non-European cultures. In this second sense of *philosophy,* it may turn out that some cultures have philosophy and some do not, and we cannot dogmatically assert before examining the facts either that *all* cultures must have philosophy or that *none* do except European cultures. We must patiently and empirically look at each culture to see whether it does or does not have a philosophy, and, of course, if it does, then we will naturally want to study it either alongside European philosophy or perhaps by incorporating all the different regional philosophies into a more comprehensive "world philosophy."

But notice that at this point we may be accused of "ethnocentrism" or "Eurocentrism"—the bias in favor of one's own culture as naturally superior to all others. Just as *philosophy* is "normative," as we saw in Part 1, so the word philosophy is also normative, that is, value-laden. To say that a culture did not develop a philosophy sounds belittling or demeaning and to say that they had a philosophy sounds like a compliment. As each region of our planet tries to define itself in as positive a manner as possible, each becomes highly sensitive to pejorative or belittling assessments of its own culture—especially those made by outsiders.

And here is a second point we should notice regarding "ethnocentrism" and "Eurocentrism": The question whether there is any non-European philosophy is generally a question raised by European philosophers about some other, non-European group, and whenever group A attempts to describe group B, there is always a possibility of cultural bias. Whose conception or definition of philosophy are we using when we ask whether the thought systems of other cultures count as "philosophy"? Well, of course, our own—not because we feel that this is the best of many conceptions or definitions of the word *philosophy,* but simply because that is all we've got! Up to now *philosophy* is a word which arose within, and whose meaning was determined by Western, European thought. For better or worse, no matter how "fair-minded" we may try to be, any description of another culture's thought systems must be comparative in nature, comparing its thought systems to our own.

This is also true more generally. All cross-cultural descriptions are comparative —inevitably, culture A must use A's words and concepts to describe culture B. (What else have they got?) Even when we ask about Chinese religion, *religion* is an English word which we are trying to impose on an alien culture. Perhaps they don't have a word in their own language which translates exactly as our word *religion*. Similarly, in the case of "African art" or "American Indian art," the very question "What kind of art did Native American Indian cultures have?" presupposes something which may well be false, namely, that Native Americans not only made things which we see as fitting our concept (in English) of "art," but that they, too, had a similar concept—that is, a word reasonably accurately translated as art— a word which they understood to mean something very much like what we understand the word *art* to mean.

One reason it may well be a mistake to think that other cultures have concepts like "art" and "religion" is that these concepts in English and other European languages presuppose a division of society and culture into distinct functional regions—in which art is more or less separated from religion, which is more or less separated from agricultural, military, political, and scientific concerns—as in our culture. In many world cultures no such separation ever took place, and in cultures where what *we* call artistic activities are mixed together with what *we* call religious, agricultural, military, and political activities, concepts like our concepts of art and religion simply don't arise. In such cultures it makes no sense (even if you speak their language and they yours) to ask "What is your religion, what is your art?" They may make wooden statues for ancestor spirits to temporarily "occupy," and to which they make offerings of food and drink, and of which they ask (that is, "pray") for help for a successful harvest, battle, or marriage; but they have no sense of which part of this complex is their "art," which part is "religion," which part is "agriculture," and so on. These questions will make no sense to them, though they will, of course, make sense to us. *We* are the ones interested in *their* "art" and "religion."

So, even in the case of "art" and "religion," where it is widely believed that *all* cultures and societies have some art and some religion, the possibility of bias and misunderstanding arising from cross-cultural comparison presents a serious problem—not only for the scientific investigations of the anthropologist and sociologist, but also for those wishing to adequately take account of the cultural sensitivities of the groups we are describing.

Western and Non-Western Thought Systems

Suppose now we take the word *philosophy* as defined in our second sense (where philosophy is understood as a critical, reflective, rational, and systematic approach to questions of very general interest) and apply that definition to different thought systems around the world. Are any of these non-Western thought systems "philosophy" in this sense, and if so, which ones? But even if we accept this second sense of philosophy as the most appropriate for our purposes, it will not be easy to apply our new standard to different thought systems, for we must still decide what exactly we *mean* by words such as *critical* and *rational,* and *how* critical and rational a thought system must be to count as philosophy.

For this reason, opinion is divided among philosophers whether there is any non-Western philosophy, and if there is, how many distinct kinds of philosophy there are. Many philosophers hold that there are three great original centers of philosophy in the world—Greek (or Western), Indian, and Chinese. All three arose at approximately the same time (roughly 600 B.C.E.), though, so far as we know, quite independently of one another. All three arose as critical reflections on their own cultural traditions. Cultures which are *not* philosophical are those which tend to accept their own mythological world view simply on the authority of tradition. "We believe this because it is our ancient belief; our people have always believed this." Philosophy, by contrast, arises precisely at that point in the history of a culture when, for various reasons, that traditional outlook is called into question. "We have always been taught to see the world in this way, but how can we be sure that this is really correct?" At this point individual philosophers come forward with the boldness and audacity, and we might even say the conceit, to begin at the beginning, asking fundamental questions, confident they can come up with the right answers! No longer do we say, "This is how our people see the world," but rather, "Anaximander asserts this theory; Thales held another view; Aristotle disagreed with both and developed a radically different position," and so on. Far from a traditional uniformity of opinion, the onset of philosophy is generally marked by a proliferation of many different, competing views, whose proponents engage in endless debates, arguing for their favorite doctrines and against all the others. But why should we believe any of these philosophers with their radically different ideas? Certainly not from any traditional authority, but only from the weight of rational evidence which they adduce. In this sense early Greek, Indian, and Chinese thinkers tried to *prove* their individual theories by carefully defining their terms, drawing distinctions, and by constructing arguments for their positions and counterarguments against the positions of their opponents.

Nonetheless, logic and analysis are *not* as developed among early Indian and Chinese thinkers as it was among the Greeks, especially beginning with Plato and Aristotle, and by stressing the *degree* of logical and analytical development, some philosophers conclude that Indian and Chinese thought systems are *not* sufficiently philosophical to be considered philosophy, but are more properly called "religion" or "mythology," and so conclude that the *only* philosophy in the world is Western philosophy. Still other philosophers, though a much smaller group, would extend considerably the list of cultures which have produced philosophy to include African philosophy, American Indian philosophy, and so on.

Probably most philosophers would agree that Western philosophy sets the standard for philosophy and that of all the world's cultures, besides Western culture, the ones which come closest to that philosophical standard are those of India and China. Since both Indian and Chinese thought systems are generally classified as "Eastern," there is at least a prima facie case for an "Eastern philosophy."

However we finally decide the question of whether Eastern thought is "philosophy" or not, it is certainly very interesting in its own right and might be usefully compared on similar issues with Western philosophy. Such a comparison can be very useful, for example, in showing alternative ways of looking at things which philosophers may have failed to notice by working within only one system of thought. Every system of thought has built into it fundamental assumptions which are typically not examined but which are more or less taken for granted. To become aware of these assumptions it is often useful and even necessary to compare them with something different but similar from another thought system.

═══ Thought Systems and Action

To discuss the differences in thought systems in East and West without discussing the effects such differences have on behavior would be to ignore an important part of the topic. Even without being ethnocentric, it is easy to assume that everyone in the world holds that certain points of view are obvious. For example, it is a common assumption that all cultures of the world value individual liberty and personal freedom. It is not so much a matter of claiming that these views are the best so much as assuming that they are obvious to everyone. When, therefore, a culture seems to be restrictive of individual liberty a common Western response is to label such societies as repressive and callous toward personal freedom. Examples of such cultural variations are not hard to find. Many nations in Southeast Asia are racing away from their colonial past toward fully developed economies that promise more material comforts for all. And they are succeeding at it too, with annual economic growth rates of 8 to 9 percent. In many of these countries there is not a free press, and it is simply not part of the cultural orientation which tends away from individual and personal considerations toward collective and group welfare. A further examination of the religious traditions of these countries, as well as the overarching thought systems that have dominated their history, reveals that primary emphasis is not placed on the single individual but upon the family, the well-ordered society, and the good of the whole.

In contrast Western societies, especially those that have been principally affected by the writings of Jean-Jacques Rousseau, John Locke, Thomas Hobbes, and civil libertarians stemming from the Anglo-American philosophical tradition, stress the primacy of the individual over the collective. Instead of subordinating the rights of the individual for the good of society, the Western ideal is to protect the rights of individuals even if it means that certain societal goals are more difficult to achieve. Thus, full freedom of expression, of the press, of democratic debate, and of representative government is grounded in the philosophical tradition of the West.

As Eastern societies embrace many of the technological innovations of the West, and contribute to the improvement and marketing of such innovations, the question they continually face is to what extent the philosophical traditions of the West inevitably accompany Western technology. In several countries there are re-vivalist movements that renounce the incursion of Western values along with Western technologies and urge the return to a purer, more fundamental set of val-ues. Such fundamentalist movements, whether they be labeled religious or philo-sophical, are continuing to have a major impact on the political life of several countries both in the Near East and in Southeast Asia. In such thought systems we find concerns expressed for some of the same issues that occur in Western thought: What is human nature? What principles should we choose by which to live? Is there a significance to life beyond our everyday experiences? What stan-dards should a country adopt in order to provide for a well-ordered society?

Part 9 will focus on two of these issues. The first deals with the issue of human nature. Chinese thinkers, especially Confucius, have dealt with this topic exten-sively, and we will examine this topic in the writings of three major Confucian-ists: Mencius, Xun Zi, and Dong Zhongshu. A second issue that the final chapter in Part 9 will address is the issue of freedom and nature and will deal with this in two senses. The first points to the issue of the significance of individual, human decisions in the vast cosmic scope of things. The second will address to what extent the individual can even be said to act freely. Closely allied to this will be the issue of how the individual is affected by nature.

Questions for Discussion

1. Based on your knowledge of what the term "philosophy" means, do you think it should be used to refer to non-Western thought systems? Why or why not?

2. What are some of the safeguards we can adopt to keep our discussion of the thought systems of other cultures from becoming ethnocentric?

3. One of the ongoing debates in Asian countries is whether they can adopt Western technology without also having to accept Western attitudes that accompany that technology. What is your response to this issue?

4. What are some of the reasons it is important to study the thought systems of other cultures?

CHAPTER 39

Eastern Thought: Theories of Human Nature

Like Western philosophers, Eastern philosophers, especially Chinese philosophers, have been interested in human nature. Of course, people are different from one another—each person is different from all others and the people of one part of the world often seem very different from the people in other parts of the world. But philosophers wonder how much of this difference is due to conditioning, socialization, environment, and education, and how much, if any, are we born with? Are there any respects in which *all* human beings are fundamentally alike at birth? How much of the way we are is due to "nature" and how much to "nurture"? How much of a person's success or failure in life is due to inherited, genetic factors and how much to the influence of family, education, socialization? This is the central question of human nature.

Human Nature and Nurture

At first we might think this question could be settled empirically—just look and see whether human beings from different countries, social backgrounds, and historical periods are all alike in some ways, and if so, in what ways, exactly. A little reflection will reveal that this is not nearly as easy as it first appears. As a matter of fact, people are very *dis*similar, but it is hard to tell whether this is due to the fact that there *is* no human nature or simply due to the effects of education and socialization on a fundamentally similar human nature. Aristotle said that human beings were by nature rational. But if we look to see for ourselves, we see that most people behave irrationally much of the time. Does this mean that Aristotle was wrong? Or does it simply mean that although human beings are born with the capacity to think and behave rationally, this disposition is frequently offset by other factors—their emotions, their "animal instincts," lack of training and discipline of their rational capacity?

How can we tell which of these hypotheses is true? Perhaps we could examine young children of two or three years of age. However, even they have probably been influenced in some ways by their culture. Some tests indicate that very young boys respond to identical situations very differently from young girls, boys being more aggressive, girls more submissive. But does this prove that boys are naturally more aggressive and girls more submissive? Many feminists would say, no; all this shows, they say, is that even by the age of two or three, boys have already been acculturated to behave more aggressively and girls more passively. Similarly, when Freudians claim that human beings are by nature selfish and aggressive, and followers of Erich Fromm say that people are by nature more loving and social, there is clear counterevidence against *both* theories. Against Freud's view is the evidence of many loving, social people; against Fromm's position is the fact that there exist many selfish, aggressive individuals.

Claims about human nature are therefore *normative* and not entirely empirical. When Aristotle says human beings are rational by nature, he means that people are more truly human when they display their rationality and that they abandon their human nature when they behave irrationally. This normative claim implies that human beings *ought* to behave rationally, not that they actually do. Part of this normative claim is that in general it is good to follow one's nature. If you are a chipmunk, you ought to follow your chipmunk nature—be the best you can be as a chipmunk. But if you happen to be a human being, you should follow your human nature—be the most you can be as a human being; fulfill your human potential. But that will only make sense if our human nature is something good and positive—being rational, loving, and so on, and not something evil and negative—being aggressive, selfish, greedy, and so on. Most, though not all, human nature theorists therefore attribute some *positive* capacity to human nature and claim that people are inherently rational, loving, and so on. After all, what is the use of a theory which claims human nature is fundamentally evil? (As we will see shortly, such theories *can* be used to support intrusive and repressive governmental measures to *control* our inherently wicked tendencies.) Otherwise, most human nature theorists would like to encourage all of us to follow our basic nature. In general, it is good to follow one's nature, and if that nature is said to be something positive, like being rational or loving, then it is socially constructive and educationally sound to encourage young people to follow their basic human nature.

Ought Implies Can

To say that someone *ought* to do something implies that they *can* do it. In this sense, "ought" implies "can." Thus, claims about human nature are also claims about capacities, potentialities, and not simply empirical generalizations about actual behavior. Again, when Aristotle says human nature is rational, he means that this is what human beings are capable of, in ways which other life forms are not, that thinking and behaving rationally is a uniquely human potential. But human beings have many capacities, the potential to be and do many different things. If human nature theories are claiming no more than the fact that people are *capable* of this or that, the claim is far too weak, for people are capable of anything: murder, altruism, hard work, laziness, creativity, conformism. But if that is all that is being claimed, it is tantamount to *denying* that there is a human nature. Claims about human nature must assert more than a mere capacity or potentiality; they must claim that there is a *tendency* of people to be or act a certain way along with the normative injunction that, since it is generally good to follow one's nature, this is how people therefore *ought* to behave. All other things being equal, and in the absence of defeating conditions, the claim now is that people will generally tend to be rational, loving, or whatever and, knowing that this is our true nature, we ought to follow our nature as much as possible.

Strong and Weak Claims

Claiming that all people do in fact actually exhibit all the time what is claimed to be their "human nature" is much too strong a claim (since it is too easily falsified). On the other hand, merely claiming that all people have this capacity or potentiality is far too weak a claim (since this is too easy to prove; i.e., it is not falsifiable). What needs to be shown is that there is a tendency to behave one way over others, and that is how people will in fact behave in the absence of defeating conditions. All theories of human nature must therefore have an "escape clause" by which to explain counter examples. If people are by nature rational, why do they so often behave so irrationally? If people are by nature loving, why do they so often act so selfishly? Human nature theories are claiming that this is how people would behave were it not for certain defeating conditions. What are some of these "defeating conditions?" Perhaps their emotions overwhelm their fundamentally rational nature. Or we could say that their physical, animal instincts (of aggression, sex, fear, food, power) clash with an underlying loving human nature. Finally, we could be saying that a basically aggressive and selfish human nature is offset and curbed by socialization and education and a system of rewards and punishments.

Three Confucian Theories of Human Nature

In the reading for this chapter we will look at three Confucian theories of human nature. Confucianism is the most important philosophy of China. It traces back to the man Confucius in the sixth century B.C.E. Actually this name, Confucius, is a Latinized version of Kong Zi, where Kong is the family name and Zi (*or* Tzu) is a title, like "master," a title attached to all the ancient Chinese philosophers—Mo Zi, Lao Zi, Hanfei Zi, and so on. Confucius himself did not have a theory of

Scene from the Life of Confucius, by Chinese Ming Dynasty "1368–1644". Confucious is 42 years old, retires from office and pursues his studies with a large band of disciples.

human nature but said only that at birth all people are "close" to one another while through education they became "far" apart. This suggests that Confucius thought there *was* a human nature, but he never said what it was. All people are born alike, he said, but he never said *how* they were alike at birth, that is, whether they were good, evil, rational, loving, or whatever.

The two main followers of Confucius, Mencius (another Latinized version of Meng Zi, "Master Meng") and Xun Zi did speculate on what human nature was but came up with opposite conclusions. Mencius held that human nature was basically good, whereas Xun Zi said human nature was basically evil. Later, another Confucianist, Dong Zhongshu, developed a more sophisticated theory of the conflict within each person between the individual's human nature and instinctual feelings as a kind of compromise between Mencius and Xun Zi.

According to Mencius, all human beings have the "beginnings" of goodness within them. That is, all people are born with the potential and tendency to be kind-hearted and virtuous, though Mencius also said that this potential can either be nourished and developed so that the individual becomes a good person or else neglected, thwarted, and perverted so that the individual becomes a bad person. Mencius is not saying, then, that children are moral beings from birth. He realizes that they must be trained, taught, and learn by practice and experience. He also agrees that children who are neglected or mistreated will usually turn out badly. Nonetheless, his theory holds that in either case there is an innate tendency or disposition to be good. In the right environment an acorn will grow into an oak tree; that is its nature to do so. If the acorn is robbed of water, sunlight, and proper soil it will be stunted and shriveled. In Mencius' most famous example, he asks what is the immediate and spontaneous response of any person upon seeing a child about to fall into a well. Mencius does not want us to imagine someone thinking this over for five or ten minutes, but right now, at this very moment, you suddenly glimpse a child on the verge of falling into a well. What would you feel? What would you do? Mencius says everyone naturally and spontaneously wants to rush to save the child. This does not mean that everyone is a morally good person but only that everyone is born with the "beginning" of the Confucian virtue of "ren," or "human heartedness."

Mencius on Human Nature

In Mencius' debate with Kao Zi, Kao Zi argues in effect that there *is* no human nature, that there is no greater tendency for people to be good than to be evil or indifferent. In other words, Kao Zi argued that human beings are infinitely pliable or malleable and can be made to become anything whatever, and there is no greater disposition or tendency to become one thing rather than another. Kao Zi's analogy is with the flow of water. Water, Kao Zi argues, can be made to flow east, west, south, or north. All you have to do is dig a channel from a lake in an eastwardly direction to get the water to flow east. But if someone blocks that channel and digs another southward, then the water will just as easily flow toward the south. The water itself, Kao Zi insists, has no built-in tendency to flow in any given direction, and in that sense, by analogy, human beings have no inherent nature. In the "nature-nurture" debate, it is all nurture, according to Kao Zi. Mencius' reply is that although water can be made to flow with equal ease north, south, east or west, it nonetheless does tend to flow downwards, and that indeed the only reason it can be made to flow westward, for example, is that it naturally flows down. In other words, to make the water flow to the west, you must dig the westward channel deeper than the other channels. The water will always flow down; if the lowest level is the westward channel, then and only then will the water flow westward.

Of course, we can also force the water to flow upwards, as when we splash water, but this can only happen if we constantly work at it. As soon as we relax, even for a moment, and leave matters alone, the water naturally flows downward once more. What Mencius is saying, by analogy, is that while it is certainly true and important that we can shape and mold human behavior through education, we can only do this successfully where we work with an existing tendency of human nature. Only by modifying an already existing human nature can we modify human behavior. Every human society has rules for regulating human sexuality, for example, but how easily could we enforce upon everyone in the society total lifelong abstinence? Or imagine trying to institute sexual codes among creatures who had absolutely no sexual drives. Only if there is already a sex drive can we hope to regulate, modify, shape, channel, and thereby alter human behavior. Just as we can splash water upwards, so we can attempt to stifle human nature. But the question is, how easy is it? Which is easier, restricting a teenager's food intake to one cup of watery soup a day or to two meals a day of low-fat balanced nutrition? Both are difficult, but if the first is *more* difficult, doesn't this show that it is going against the grain of our inherent nature?

Xun Zi on Human Nature

Xun Zi argues against Mencius that human nature is essentially evil, by which he means selfish and aggressively antisocial. It is only through education, training, discipline and the threat of punishment, Xun Zi argues, that people become socially cooperative. Somewhat like Hobbes' social contract theory, Xun Zi speculates that originally people were free to follow their own selfish bent without fear of recrimination or punishment. But when they realized that they were as often the victims of aggressive abuse as its perpetrators, that they were getting stolen from as often as they were taking what they liked from others, they willingly accepted the authority of a ruler capable of maintaining order and punishing transgressions.

Like Hobbes, Xun Zi argues from his view that human nature is essentially evil to the need for a strong central governmental authority to control human behavior by education and a system of rewards and punishments. What do you suppose would happen, Xun Zi asks, if this governmental authority were removed? Can anyone doubt that chaos would result as the strong rode rough shod over the weak with no law enforcement to prevent and punish them?

One major difference between Mencius' and Xun Zi's theories of human nature is that Mencius, like Aristotle, defines human nature as that which is uniquely and distinctively human, whereas Xun Zi defines human nature as that which all people possess, even if that is also shared by the lower animals. If we define human nature as Xun Zi does (as what all people have in common), then we will point to the tendencies people do actually have to be greedy, selfish, and aggressive, but if we define human nature as Mencius does (as that which is unique to people) then we tend to discount greedy behavior, since that is shared by lower animals, and to emphasize instead the capacity of human beings to develop virtuous behavior, to become moral creatures, loving and caring for one another, concerned with the other's welfare. The reason Mencius, like Socrates, would rather die than act immorally is that to act immorally is to destroy the most precious thing in the world—one's humanity.

Dong Zhongshu on Human Nature

Dong Zhongshu finds a middle ground between the views of Mencius and Xun Zi. He agrees with Mencius that in a sense human nature contains the "seeds" of goodness, but he disagrees with Mencius that this is enough to say that human beings are by nature good. The "seed" of goodness is not actually good any more than a tomato seed is a tomato. In order to become good that "seed" must be nurtured, cultivated, thus agreeing more with Xun Zi's emphasis on the necessary role of government to educate and train people to become good citizens. Another analogy Dong uses is the capacity of the eye to see. The ability of the eye to see is obviously a dispositional property. Dong asks an interesting question: Can a person see when asleep? Well, in one sense we would have to say no. People who are asleep are unable to see something in front of their eyes. But in another sense sleeping persons *can* see. All we have to do is wake them up! Can you speak Swedish? Again, the answer is yes (in a sense) and no (in a different sense). Most of us cannot here and now carry on a conversation in Swedish; and in that sense we can't speak Swedish. But if you were offered a billion dollars to learn Swedish in the next five years, you probably could—and in that sense you can (learn to) speak Swedish.

Dong Zhongshu also develops a theory, somewhat like Plato's, that human nature must compete with a person's innate tendencies to greed and selfishness. Like Plato, Dong has a model of human psychology in which opposing forces are in constant conflict with one another. There is an innate part of us which wants to be socially cooperative, giving, and caring; but there is another innate part of us which wants it all for ourselves.

Of course, one could ask, if both these tendencies are innate, then aren't they both parts of human nature? And here the answer probably has to do with what we said earlier about human nature being a "normative" concept. Like Mencius, Dong would like to say that human nature is the higher and better part of human beings, that morally good part which human beings alone are capable of. The instinctive, emotional, physical part which we all have but which we also share with the lower animals is just as innate, but doesn't have the "normative" quality of the morally good potential of human nature. Dong Zhongshu says that when Mencius claims that people are good he is comparing them with the lower animals. Compared to animals people at least have the capacity for moral goodness. But that is not what we *ought* to be comparing people to, Dong Zhongshu continues; we should be comparing people to the moral ideal we demand of people. More like Xun Zi, Dong Zhongshu argues that we should hold people up to a higher standard, in terms of which we don't want to say that people are *good* but that they are *not* good. Compared with animals people are good; compared with the philosophical sage, they are not good.

In one way the difference between Dong Zhongshu and Mencius is a matter of degree. Mencius does not say that people are born as morally good individuals. He insists that this requires cultivation and training. He calls the innate goodness the "beginnings" of goodness. Nonetheless, he differs from Dong Zhongshu in seeing more good in people than does Dong Zhongshu. For Mencius the "beginnings" of goodness are really good, though on a small scale which must be further encouraged and developed; for Dong Zhongshu the "seeds" of goodness are not themselves good at all but only have the potential to become so. Both the tomato seed and the ripe tomato have the potential to become tomato juice, for example. But while Mencius wants to claim that the tomato actually has within it some of the qualities of tomato juice, Dong insists that the tomato seed isn't at all like tomato juice.

The Role of Government

The main difference between Mencius and Dong Zhongshu is in their view of the role of government in fostering moral goodness. Mencius would have government take a far less intrusive role, merely encouraging, cultivating the beginnings of moral goodness which already exist. Dong Zhongshu, like Xun Zi, on the contrary, believes that government must mold and shape human beings who have the capacity for goodness but cannot become good without the intervention of the state. For Mencius government leaders *encourage* people to be moral by setting a good example for all to follow. For Dong Zhongshu government leaders *force* people to be moral by establishing a system of rewards and punishments.

A similar "nature/nurture" debate goes on today concerning the capacity of human beings to learn language. Of course, people are capable of learning a language, but how much of this is innate and how much is taught? Do parents teach children to speak or do children just pick it up? Mencius' theory is like those who say today that children are not taught to speak a language but just pick it up in

Mencius, originally Mengzi or Men-Tse, c. 371-c.289. Phil. & Sage, born in Shantung, China. He found a school modelled on that of Confucious and travelled China for some 20 years searching for a ruler to implement Confucian moral and political ideals. The search was unsuccessful, but his conversations with other rulers, disciples and others are recorded in a book of sayings (Book of Mengzi). His ethical system was based on the belief that human beings are innately and instinctively good. 3rd century B.C. line drawing.

a favorable environment. Dong's view comes out if we ask whether American students will learn Swedish by just picking it up or only by hard study and rigorous practice? For Dong becoming a morally good person is like an American learning Swedish—it can be done but only with a great deal of training, practice, and discipline.

Mencius: The Book of Mencius

2A:6. Mencius said, "All men have the mind which cannot bear [to see the suffering of] others. The ancient kings had this mind and therefore they had a government that could not bear to see the suffering of the people. When a government that cannot bear to see the suffering of the people is conducted from a mind that cannot bear to see the suffering of others, the government of the empire will be as easy as making something go round in the palm.

"When I say that all men have the mind which cannot bear to see the suffering of others, my meaning may be illustrated thus: Now, when men suddenly see a child about to fall into a well, they all have a feeling of alarm and distress, not to gain friendship with the child's parents, nor to seek the praise of their neighbors and friends, not because they dislike the reputation [of lack of humanity if they did not rescue the child]. From such a case, we see that a man without the feeling of commiseration is not a man, a man without the feeling of shame and dislike is not a man; a man without the feeling of deference and compliance is not a man; and a man without the feeling of right and wrong is not a man. The feeling of commiseration is the beginning of humanity; the feeling of shame and dislike is the beginning of righteousness; the feeling of deference and compliance is the beginning of propriety; and the feeling of right and wrong is the beginning of wisdom. Men have these Four Beginnings just as they have their four limbs. Having these Four Beginnings, but saying that they cannot develop them is to destroy themselves. When they say that their ruler cannot develop them, they are destroying their ruler. If anyone with these Four Beginnings in him knows how to give them the fullest extension and development, the result will be like fire beginning to burn or a spring beginning to shoot forth. When they are fully developed, they will be sufficient to protect all people within the four seas (the world). If they are not developed, they will not be sufficient even to serve one's parents."

6A:2. Kao Tzu said, "Man's nature is like whirling water. If a breach in the pool is made to the east it will flow to the east. If a breach is made to the west it will flow to the west. Man's nature is indifferent to good and evil, just as water is indifferent to east and west." Mencius said "Water, indeed, is indifferent to the east and west,

From Wing-Tsit Chan, translator, "The Book of Mencius" in *A Source Book in Chinese Philosophy.* Copyright © 1963 by Princeton University Press; renewed 1991. Reprinted by permission of Princeton University Press.

but is it indifferent to high and low? Man's nature is naturally good just as water naturally flows downward. There is no man without this good nature; neither is there water that does not flow downward. Now you can strike water and cause it to splash upward over your forehead, and by damming and leading it, you can force it uphill. Is this the nature of water? It is the forced circumstance that makes it do so. Man can be made to do evil, for his nature can be treated in the same way."

6A:6. Kung-tu Tzu said, "Kao Tzu said that man's nature is neither good nor evil. Some say that man's nature may be made good or evil, therefore when King Wen and King Wu were in power the people loved virtue, and when Kings Yu and Li were in power people loved violence. Some say that some men's nature is good and some men's nature is evil. . . . Now you say that human nature is good. Then are those people wrong?"

Mencius said, "If you let people follow their feelings (original nature), they will be able to do good. This is what is meant by saying that human nature is good. If man does evil it is not the fault of his natural endowment. The feeling of commiseration is found in all men; the feeling of shame and dislike is found in all men; the feeling of respect and reverence is found in all men and the feeling of right and wrong is found in all men. The feeling of commiseration is what we call humanity *(ren);* the feeling of shame and dislike is what we call righteousness *(yi)*; the feeling of respect and reverence is what we call propriety *(li)* and the feeling of right and wrong is what we call wisdom *(zhi).* Humanity, righteousness, propriety and wisdom are not drilled into us from outside. We originally have them with us. Only we do not think [to find them]. Therefore it is said, 'Seek and you will find it, neglect and you will lose it.' "

6A:7. Mencius said, "In good years most of the young people behave well. In bad years most of them abandon themselves to evil. This is not due to any difference in the natural capacity endowed by Heaven. The abandonment is due to the fact that the mind is allowed to fall into evil. Take for instance the growing of wheat. You sow the seeds and cover them with soil. The land is the same and the time of sowing is also the same. In time they all grow up luxuriantly. When the time of harvest comes, they are all ripe. Although there may be a difference between the different stalks of wheat, it is due to differences in the soil, as rich or poor, to the unequal nourishment obtained from the rain and the dew, and to differences in human effort. Therefore all things of the same kind are similar to one another. Why should there be any doubt about men? The sage and I are the same in kind. Therefore Lung Tzu said, 'If a man makes shoes without knowing the size of people's feet, I know that he will at least not make them to be like baskets.' Shoes are alike because people's feet are alike. There is a common taste for flavor in our mouths. I-yi was the first to know our common taste for food. Suppose one man's taste for flavor is different from that of others, as dogs and horses differ from us in belonging to different species; then why should the world follow I-ya in regard to flavor? Since in the matter of flavor the whole world regards I-ya as the standard, it shows that our tastes for flavor are alike. The same is true of our ears. Since in the matter of sounds the whole world regards Shih-k'uang as the standard, it shows that our ears are alike. The same is true of our eyes. With regard to Tzu-tu, none in the world did not know that he was handsome. Any one who did not recognize his handsomeness must have no eyes. Therefore I say there is a common taste for flavor in our mouths, a common sense for sound in our ears, and a common sense for beauty in our eyes. Can it be that in our minds alone we are not alike? What is it that we have in common in our minds? It is the sense of principle and righteousness (*yi-li,* moral principles). The sage is the first to possess what is common in our minds. Therefore moral principles please our minds as beef and mutton and pork please our mouths?"

6A:8. Mencius said, "The trees of the Niu Mountain were once beautiful. But can the mountain be regarded any longer as beautiful since, being in the borders of a big state, the trees have been hewed down with axes and hatchets? Still with interest given them by the days and nights and the nourishment provided them by the rains and the dew, they were not without buds and sprouts springing forth. But then the cattle and the sheep pastured upon them once and again; that is why the mountain looks so bald. When people see that it is so bald, they think that there was never any timber on the mountain. Is this the true nature of the mountain? Is there not [also] a heart of humanity and righteousness originally existing in man? The way in which he loses his originally good mind is like the way in which the trees are hewed down with axes and hatchets. As trees are cut down day after day, can a mountain retain its beauty? To be sure, the days and nights do the healing, and there is the nourishing air of the calm morning which keeps him normal in his likes and dislikes. But the effect is slight, and is disturbed and destroyed by what he does during the day. When there is repeated disturbance, the restorative influence of the night will not be sufficient to preserve (the proper goodness of the mind). When the influence of the night is not sufficient to preserve it, man becomes not much different from the beast. People see that he acts like an animal, and think that he never had the original endowment (for goodness). But is that his true character? Therefore with proper nourishment and care, everything grows, whereas without proper nourishment and care, everything decays. Confucius said 'Hold it fast and you preserve it. Let it go and you lose it. It comes in and goes out at no definite time and without anyone's knowing its direction.' He was talking about the human mind. . . ."

6A:10. Mencius said, "I like fish and I also like bear's paw. If I cannot have both of them I shall give up the fish and choose the bear's paw; I like life and I also like righteousness. If I cannot have both of them, I shall give up life and choose righteousness. I love life, but there is something I love more than life, and therefore I will not do anything improper to have it. I also hate death, but there is something I hate more than death, and therefore there are occasions when I will not avoid danger. If there is nothing that man loves more than life, then why should he not employ every means to preserve it? And if there is nothing that man hates more than death, then why does he not do anything to avoid danger? There are cases when a man does not take the course even if by taking it he can preserve his life, and he does not do anything even if by doing it he can avoid danger. Therefore there is something men love more than life and there is something men hate more than death. It is not only the worthies alone who have this moral sense. All men have it, but only the worthies have been able to preserve it."

6A:15. Kung-tu Tzu asked, "We are all human beings. Why is it that some men become great and others become small?" Mencius said, "Those who follow the greater qualities in their nature become great men and those who follow the smaller qualities in their nature become small men." "But we are all human beings. Why is it that some follow their greater qualities and others follow their smaller qualities?" Mencius replied, "When our senses of sight and hearing are used without thought and are thereby obscured by material things, the material things act on the material senses and lead them astray. That is all. The function of the mind is to think. If we think, we will get them (the principles of things). If we do not think, we will not get them. This is what Heaven has given to us. If we first build up the nobler part of our nature, then the inferior part cannot overcome it. It is simply this that makes a man great."

2A:2. ". . . Always be doing something without expectation. Let the mind not forget its objective, but let there be no artificial effort to help it grow. Do not be like the man of Sung. There was a man of Sung who was sorry that his corn was not growing, and so he pulled it up [taller]. Having been tired out he went home and said to his people, 'I am all tired. I have helped the corn to grow.' When his son ran to look at it, the corn had already withered."

Xun Zi: The Nature of Man is Evil

The nature of man is evil; his goodness is the result of his activity. Now, man's inborn nature is to seek for gain. If this tendency is followed, strife and rapacity result and deference and compliance disappear. By inborn nature one is envious and hates others. If these tendencies are followed, injury and destruction result and loyalty and faithfulness disappear. By inborn nature one possesses the desires of ear and eye and likes sound and beauty. If these tendencies are followed, lewdness and licentiousness result, and the pattern and order of propriety and righteousness disappear. Therefore to follow man's nature and his feelings will inevitably result in strife and rapacity, combine with rebellion and disorder, and end in violence. Therefore there must be the civilizing influence of teachers and laws and the guidance of propriety and righteousness, and then it will result in deference and compliance, combine with pattern and order, and end in discipline. From this point of view, it is clear that the nature of man is evil and that his goodness is the result of activity.

Crooked wood must be heated and bent before it becomes straight. Blunt metal must be ground and whetted before it becomes sharp. Now the nature of man is evil. It must depend on teachers and laws to become correct and achieve propriety and righteousness and then it becomes disciplined. Without teachers and laws, man is unbalanced, off the track, and incorrect. Without propriety and righteousness, there will be rebellion, disorder, and chaos. The sage-kings of antiquity, knowing that the nature of man is evil, and that it is unbalanced, off the track, incorrect, rebellious, disorderly, and undisciplined, created the rules of propriety and righteousness and instituted laws and systems in order to correct man's feelings, transform them, and direct them so that they all may become disciplined and conform with the Way (Tao). Now people who are influenced by teachers and laws, accumulate literature and knowledge, and follow propriety

Xun Zi, from "Hsun Tzu" in Wing-Tsit Chan, translator. *A Source Book in Chinese Philosophy*. Princeton: Princeton University Press, 1969; renewed 1991. Used by permission of Princeton University Press.

and righteousness are superior men, whereas those who give rein to their feelings, enjoy indulgence, and violate propriety and righteousness are inferior men. From this point of view, it is clear that the nature of man is evil and that his goodness is the result of his activity.

Mencius said, "Man learns because his nature is good." This is not true. He did not know the nature of man and did not understand the distinction between man's nature and his effort. Man's nature is the product of Nature; it cannot be learned and cannot be worked for. Propriety and righteousness are produced by the sage. They can be learned by man and can be accomplished through work. What is in man but cannot be learned or worked for is his nature. What is in him and can be learned or accomplished through work is what can be achieved through activity. This is the difference between human nature and human activity. Now by nature man's eye can see and his ear can hear. But the clarity of vision is not outside his eye and the distinctness of hearing is not outside his ear. It is clear that clear vision and distinct hearing cannot be learned. Mencius said, "The nature of man is good; it [becomes evil] because man destroys his original nature." This is a mistake. By nature man departs from his primitive character and capacity as soon as he is born, and he is bound to destroy it. From this point of view, it is clear that man's nature is evil.

By the original goodness of human nature is meant that man does not depart from his primitive character but makes it beautiful, and does not depart from his original capacity but utilizes it, so that beauty being [inherent] in his primitive character and goodness being [inherent] in his will are like clear vision being inherent in the eye and distinct hearing being inherent in the ear. Hence we say that the eye is clear and the ear is sharp. Now by nature man desires repletion when hungry, desires warmth when cold, and desires rest when tired. This is man's natural feeling. But now when a man is hungry and sees some elders before him, he does not eat ahead of them but yields to them. When he is tired, he dares not seek rest because he wants to take over the work [of elders]. The son yielding to or taking over the work of his father, and the younger brother yielding to or taking over the work of his older brother—these two lines of action are contrary to original nature and violate natural feeling. Nevertheless, the way of filial piety is the pattern and order of propriety and righteousness. If one follows his natural feeling, he will have no deference or compliance. Deference and compliance are opposed to his natural feelings. From this point of view, it is clear that man's nature is evil and that his goodness is the result of his activity.

Someone may ask, "If man's nature is evil, whence come propriety and righteousness?" I answer that all propriety and righteousness are results of the activity of sages and not originally produced from man's nature. The potter pounds the clay and makes the vessel. This being the case, the vessel is the product of the artisan's activity and not the original product of man's nature. The artisan hews a piece of wood and makes a vessel. This being the case, the vessel is the product of the artisan's activity and not the original product of man's nature. The sages gathered together their ideas and thoughts and became familiar with activity, facts, and principles, and thus produced propriety and righteousness and instituted laws and systems. This being the case, propriety and righteousness, and laws and systems are the products of the activity of the sages and not the original products of man's nature.

As to the eye desiring color, the ear desiring sound, the mouth desiring flavor, the heart desiring gain, and the body desiring pleasure and ease—all these are products of man's original nature and feelings. They are natural reactions to stimuli and do not require any work to be produced. But if the reaction is not naturally produced by the stimulus but requires work before it can be produced, then it is the result of activity. Here lies the evidence of the difference between what is produced by man's nature and what is produced by his effort. Therefore the sages transformed man's nature and aroused him to activity. As activity was aroused, propriety and righteousness were produced, and as propriety and righteousness were produced, laws and systems were instituted. This being the case, propriety, righteousness, laws, and systems are all products of the sages. In his nature, the sage is common with and not different from ordinary people. It is in his effort that he is different from and superior to them.

It is the original nature and feelings of man to love profit and seek gain. Suppose some brothers are to divide their property. If they follow their natural feelings, they will love profit and seek gain, and thus will do violence to each other and grab the property. But if they are transformed by the civilizing influence of the pattern and order of propriety and righteousness, they will even yield to outsiders. Therefore, brothers will quarrel if they follow their original nature and feeling but, if they are transformed by righteousness and propriety, they will yield to outsiders.

People desire to be good because their nature is evil. If one has little, he wants abundance. If he is ugly, he wants good looks. If his circumstances are narrow, he wants them to be broad. If poor, he wants to be rich. And if he is in a low position, he wants a high position. If he does not have it himself, he will seek it outside. If he is rich, he does not desire more wealth, and if he is in a high position, he does not desire more power. If he has it himself, he will not seek it outside. From this point of view, it is clear that people desire to be good because their nature is evil.

Now by nature a man does not originally possess propriety and righteousness; hence he makes strong effort to learn and seeks to have them. By nature he does not know propriety and righteousness; hence he thinks and deliberates and seeks to know them. Therefore, by what is inborn alone, man will not have or know propriety and righteousness. There will be disorder if man is without propriety and righteousness. There will be violence if he does not know propriety and righteousness. Consequently by what is inborn alone, disorder and violence are within man himself. From this point of view, it is clear that the nature of man is evil and that his goodness is the result of his activity.

Mencius said, "The nature of man is good." I say that this is not true. By goodness at any time in any place is meant true principles and peaceful order, and by evil is meant imbalance, violence, and disorder. This is the distinction between good and evil. Now do we honestly regard man's nature as characterized by true principles and peaceful order? If so, why are sages necessary and why are propriety and righteousness necessary? What possible improvement can sages make on true principles and peaceful order?

Now this is not the case. Man's nature is evil. Therefore the sages of antiquity, knowing that man's nature is evil, that it is unbalanced and incorrect; and that it is violent, disorderly, and undisciplined, established the authority of rulers to govern the people, set forth clearly propriety and righteousness to transform them, instituted laws and governmental measures to rule them, and make punishment severe to restrain them, so that all will result in good order and be in accord with goodness. Such is the government of sage-kings and the transforming influence of propriety and righteousness.

But suppose we try to remove the authority of the ruler, do away with the transforming influence of propriety and righteousness, discard the rule of laws and governmental measure, do away with the restraint of punishment, and stand and see how people of the world deal with one another. In this situation, the strong would injure the weak and rob them, and the many would do violence to the few and shout them down. The whole world would be in violence and disorder and all would perish in an instant. From this point of view, it is clear that man's nature is evil and that his goodness is the result of his activity. . . .

Shall we consider humanity, righteousness, laws, and correct principles as basically impossible to be known or practiced? If so, even Yu could not have known or practiced them. Shall we consider every man in the street to be without the faculty to know them or the capacity to practice them? If so, at home he would not be able to know the righteous relation between father and son and outside he would not be able to know the correct relations between rule and minister. But this is not the case. Every man in the street is capable of knowing the righteous relation between father and son at home and the correct relations between ruler and minister outside. It is clear, then, that the faculty to know them and the capacity to practice them are found in every man in the street. Now, if every man's faculty to know and capacity to practice are applied to the fact that humanity and righteousness can be known and practiced, it is clear that he can become Yu. If in his practices and studies day after day for a long time, he concentrates his mind, has unity of purpose, thinks thoroughly and discriminately, and accumulates goodness without stop, he can then be as wise as the gods, and form a trinity with Heaven and Earth. Thus the sage is a man who has reached this state through accumulated effort.

Some one may say, "The sage can reach that state through accumulated effort but not everyone can do so. Why?" I answer that he can, but he does not do it. An inferior man can become a superior man, but he does not want to. A superior man can become an inferior man, but he does not want to. It is not that they cannot become each other. They do not do so because they do not want to. . . .

Dong Zhongshu: Man's Nature is Neither Good Nor Evil

In his real character man has both humanity *(jen)* and greed. The material forces responsible for both humanity and greed are found in his person. What is called the person is received from Heaven *(T'ien,* Nature). Heaven has its dual operation of yin and yang (passive and active cosmic forces), and the person also has his dual nature of humanity and greed. There are cases when Heaven restricts

Dong Zhongshu, "Luxuriant Gems of the 'Spring and Autumn Annals'," from Wing-Tsit Chan, translator. *A Source Book in Chinese Philosophy.* Princeton: Princeton University Press, 1969; renewed 1991. Reprinted by permission of Princeton University Press.

the operation of yin and yang, and there are cases when the person weakens his feelings and desires. [The way of man] and the Way of Heaven are the same. . . .

Therefore man's nature may be compared to the rice stalks and goodness to rice. Rice comes out of the rice stalk but not all the stalk becomes rice. Similarly, goodness comes out of nature but not all nature becomes good. Both goodness and rice are results of human activity in continuing and completing the creative work of Heaven, which is outside of Heaven's own operation, and are not inherent in what Heaven has produced, which is within its operation. The activity of Heaven extends to a certain point and then stops. What stops within the operation of Heaven is called human nature endowed by Heaven, and what stops outside the operation of Heaven is called human activity. Man's activity lies outside of his nature, and yet it is inevitable that [through training] his nature will become virtuous. . . .

Man's nature may be compared to the eyes. In sleep they are shut and there is darkness. They must await the awakening before they can see. Before the awakening it may be said that they possess the basic substance (quality) to see, but it cannot be said that they see. Now the nature of all people possesses this basic substance but it is not yet awakened; it is like people in sleep waiting to be awakened. It has to be trained before it becomes good. Before it is awakened, it may be said to possess the basic substance to become good but it cannot be said that it is already good. It is the same as the case of the eyes being shut and becoming awakened. If we leisurely examine this matter with a calm mind, the truth becomes evident. Man's nature being in sleep, as it were, and before awakening is the state created by Heaven (Nature). . . . Both nature and feelings are the same in a state of sleep. Feelings are [part of] nature. If we say that nature is already good, what can we say about feelings [which are sources of evil]?

The nature of man is like a silk cocoon or an egg. An egg has to be hatched to become a chicken, and a silk cocoon has to be unravelled to make silk. It is the true character of Heaven that nature needs to be trained before becoming good. Since Heaven has produced the nature of man which has the basic substance for good but which is unable to be good [by itself], therefore it sets up the king to make it good. This is the will of Heaven. The people receive from Heaven a nature which cannot be good [by itself], and they turn to the king to receive the training which completes their nature. It is the duty of the king to obey the will of Heaven and to complete the nature of the people . . .

Now to claim on the basis of the true character of the basic substance of man that man's nature is already good [at birth] is to lose sight of the will of Heaven and to forgo the duty of the king. If the nature of all people were already good, then what duty is there for the king to fulfill when he receives the mandate from Heaven?. . . Now the nature of all people depends on training, which is external, before it becomes good. Therefore goodness has to do with training and not with nature. If it had to do with nature, it would be much involved and lack refinement, and everyone would become perfect by himself and there would be no such people as worthies and sages. . . .

Someone says, "Since nature contains the beginning of goodness and since the mind possesses the basic substance of goodness, how can nature not be regarded as good?"

I reply, "You are wrong. The silk cocoon contains [potential] silk but it is not yet silk, and the egg contains the [potential] chicken but it is not yet a chicken. If we follow these analogies, what doubt can there be? Heaven has produced mankind in accordance with its great principle, and those who talk about nature should not differ from each other. But there are some who say that nature is good and others who say that nature is not good. Then what is meant by goodness differs with their various ideas. There is the beginning of goodness in human nature. Let us activate it and love our parents. And since man is better than animals, this may be called good—this is what Mencius meant by goodness. . . . Practice loyalty and faithfulness and love all people universally. And be earnest and deep and love propriety. One may then be called good—this is what the Sage meant by goodness.

Therefore Confucius said, "A good man is not mine to see. If I could see a man of constant virtue, I would be content." From this we know that what the Sage called goodness is not easy to match. It is not simply because we are better than animals that we may be called good. If merely activating the beginning and being better than animals may be called goodness, why is it not evident [from the beginning]? That being better than animals is not sufficient to be called goodness is the same as being wiser than plants is not sufficient to be called wisdom. The nature of people is better than that of animals but may not be regarded as good. The term knowledge (wisdom) is derived from the word sageliness. What the Sage ordered is accepted by the world as correct. To correct the course of day and night depends on the polar star, and to correct suspicions and doubts depends on the Sage. From the point of view of the Sage, the generation without a king and people without training cannot be equal to goodness. Such is the difficulty to match goodness. It is too much to say that the nature of all people can be equal to it. If evaluated in comparison with the nature of animals, the nature of man is of course good. But if evaluated in comparison with the goodness according to the way of man [as it should be], man's nature falls short. It is all right to say that human nature is better than that of animals, but it is not all right to say that their nature is what the Sage calls goodness. My evaluation of life and nature differs from that of Mencius. Mencius evaluated on the lower level the behavior of animals and therefore said that man's nature is good [at birth]. I evaluate on the higher level what the Sage considers to be goodness, and therefore say that man's nature is not good to start with. Goodness is higher than human nature, and the Sage is higher than goodness."

Questions for Discussion

1. Do you think the writings of Mencius, Dong Zhongshu, and Xun Zi are religious or philosophical? Why is it so difficult to classify them?

2. Do you think human beings can ever be completely "natural?" Why or why not?

3. What arguments are given in the readings to support the view that human beings are inherently evil and must be trained to become virtuous? Do you find these arguments compelling?

4. What arguments can you assemble to support your view, whether you think that nature is more important than nurture in human development or vice versa?

5. As you read Mencius, did you find any common ground with Aristotle's view of moral development? Explain.

CHAPTER 40

Eastern Thought: The Individual and the Collective

In the preceding chapter we discussed an Eastern view of human nature. In order to do this properly we would need to know a great deal more about how Eastern thought systems understand the role of the individual in the larger perspective of family, society, and even the larger cosmic whole.

Before we in the West can begin to understand Eastern thought, we must realize that it is not just an Oriental version of Western thought. As was mentioned in the introduction to this section, one difference between the philosophical traditions of the West and its Eastern parallels is that Eastern thought is a complete intellectual and spiritual tradition in its own right, comprising many different systems of thought from different periods and geographical areas. Nor is Eastern "philosophy" just philosophy in the fairly technical sense in which we generally use the term in the West. What we call the philosophies of the East are attempts to answer the ultimate problems of the universe and life in a way that often collapses the distinctions we draw between philosophy, religion, morality, and politics.

One need only consider a simple but important example of the relationship between moral-religious concerns and philosophical analysis in our own tradition in order to understand its parallel in Eastern thought. Suppose you ask a basically religious question: "What must I do to achieve salvation?" This is not an academic question but a practical concern of immense personal importance. Now suppose you are told, "You must believe that Jesus was God incarnate who redeems you from your sins." At this point you may get sidetracked from a religious quest into a theological, conceptual puzzle. "Wait," you say. "I thought God was a spiritual, immaterial being. So how can God become flesh? And even if God could, was this materialization *part* of God or *all* of God, or what? And even if this did occur, how does this help me now, two thousand years later? How does it work?" This is not a religious dilemma but an intellectual problem concerning conceptual puzzles of a metaphysical nature about identity and causality. Nonetheless you may find yourself unable to return to your religious question until you can get this conceptual problem behind you.

Now the philosopher comes along, in the form of a theologian, to help you dispose of this puzzle. In a sense the theologian says, Jesus and God are different, and in a sense they are one and the same. How so? Just as the same substance can have different properties without itself changing in any essential way, so the spiritual nature of God can take on material form without undergoing substantial change. God the Father and God the Son are different manifestations of the same underlying substance. Thus, a philosophical solution has been used to solve a philosophical problem arising out of a religious concern. And this is precisely how theologians of the twelfth and thirteenth centuries used Aristotle's analysis from centuries earlier to straighten out various conceptual difficulties in Christian belief. A similar interplay between religion and philosophy occurs in Eastern thought.

Part of the difficulty facing a Western observer is the sheer variety and intricacy of Eastern thought. Over a span of some five thousand years there have been hundreds of religious, philosophical, moral, scientific, logical, mathematical, historical, and literary theories in the many countries we lump together as the "East" (well over half the world's population). It at first appears impossible, perhaps even pretentious, to attempt to summarize such a rich intellectual tradition in a few pages. However, there is an approach to this rich variety of religious and intellectual systems that at least allows for a summary of certain basic tenets of Eastern thought. Western intellectuals have interpreted later Hinduism, Buddhism (especially the later Chinese and Japanese schools), and Taoism in terms of what Aldous Huxley called the "Perennial Philosophy." The first premise of this Perennial Philosophy of the East is that human beings are not alienated from but essentially identical with the objective reality of the world. The second premise is that this reality is not alienated from but identical with the highest spiritual, religious forces. When we discover the innermost secrets of reality we have discovered ourselves; when we truly come to terms with ourselves we thereby come to terms with the ultimate spiritual reality of the universe. God, nature, humans—all are one. In the classical formula of the *Upanishads,* "Tat tuam asi," "You are that."

In this context, anxiety over power and alienation disappears. If nature is not an alien object standing apart and separate from a person, then there is nothing to get out of the world. The illusion of getting and grabbing is as silly as a pound of sugar trying to borrow a cup of sugar from itself. It simply cannot be done. The anxiety of continually trying to get ahead is also based on confusion. Who is getting ahead? A personal ego pitting itself against the whole world. In Eastern thought the real self is inseparable from the world's reality, and getting ahead is like a racehorse trying to beat itself.

Historical Backgrounds

The Perennial Philosophy of which Huxley spoke began with late Hinduism in India, from which Buddhism evolved and which later passed into China where it blended with Chinese Taoism and Confucianism, and then moved on to Japan. The one theme which unites the great traditions of Hinduism and Buddhism is the underlying assumption of *karma* and *reincarnation*. Most Eastern thought assumes that the individual ego is born over and over again into different bodies, sometimes as human beings and sometimes as lower animals, depending on the moral and intellectual quality achieved in one's previous life. Morality thus extends beyond this life; whether a person becomes a human being or a mouse in the next life depends on how the individual lives this life. This principle of moral consequences is known as *karma*. It is interesting to note that Plato held a similar view, but by and large this position was not accepted widely in the Western tradition. This is nowhere more apparent than in the different attitudes toward life after death. In the West, where we place such value on the personal identity of the psychological ego (the "I"), most people desire that ego to continue beyond death. In the East the problem is not how to attain life after death but how to get rid of it. To the Easterner, life after death is undesirable. The central religious problem for the East is how to end the continuous wheel of rebirth *(samsara)*. This is what the Eastern religious devotee means by the question, "What must I do to achieve eternal salvation?" Basically, most Eastern answers have come in the form of establishing an attitude of mind *(vidya)* which breaks the karma chain linking life and death *(samsara)*. This release of the ego *(moksa)* occurs when the self discovers its true identity, not as an individual, separate ego, but as "that"—the whole of reality. In the Eastern view, that thing which is born and reborn again and again is not me. I am *that*. Persons are never separate objects and cannot continue to be separate for the reason that there are no separate, individual objects anywhere in the world. Unhappiness is caused by a false view of the independent existence of the self and the world, and salvation comes from a correct view of their identity.

These basic Eastern beliefs nonetheless raise several serious *philosophical* problems. In what sense are there no objects, no multiplicity, no divisions? Does this mean that you and I, for example, are one and the same? Are you responsible for my bills? Is there no difference between a classroom full of chairs and an empty classroom? This begins to sound strange, confusing, and disquieting. And if these things are illusions, what *is* really there? Nothing? That is scary. Am I *that*? How so? As we will see, there is no way to avoid these problems short of keeping our mouths shut and our pens still, for the problems arise out of the way we normally talk and think about things in everyday life. As Immanuel Kant noted, our everyday forms of thought lead to contradictions whenever we try to think about ultimate reality. And as the twentieth-century Western philosopher Ludwig Wittgenstein said, the very words we use lead us into philosophical puzzles. But this is even worse in a religious context because as we saw before, these conceptual puzzles sidetrack the mind and inhibit spiritual progress toward what is at heart a simple and important realization. So while solving this sort of philosophical problem is not really a religious matter, we can see how important it became in the minds of Eastern religious thinkers in clearing the path toward religious release.

Hinduism

Hinduism, an extremely rich, many-faceted religion, stretches far back into the earliest recorded religious experiences. The earliest text is the *Rig Veda* (2000-1500 B.C.E.), a collection of ceremonial hymns to various gods who, historically and evolutionarily, belong to the same family of gods as Odin, Zeus, and Venus, worshipped by the ancient Greeks and pre-Christian northern Europeans. The hymns appear to have accompanied sacrifices which, as in ancient Greece, were the chief religious function. The gods, Agni, god of fire; Varuna, god of the sea and air; Indra, god of the thunderbolts, plus gods of sun, moon, and so on, demanded sacrifices and hymns of praise.

In sharp contrast, the *Upanishads* appeared about a thousand years later. In this work the gods requiring endless sacrifices have been replaced by two central concepts, Atman and Brahman, and the claim that they are identical. Atman is the true self while Brahman is the underlying nature of the universe. The point of the *Upanishads* is that salvation is to be achieved through the realization that Atman is Brahman, "Thou art that." However, in the *Upanishads* the old order of nature gods and sacrifices is not entirely repudiated but simply reinterpreted in a new light and reabsorbed in an ongoing, developing Hinduism. In this respect Hinduism is very conservative and has rarely rejected old thoughts and beliefs in favor of new ones. Contemporary Hindu religious beliefs include Brahmanism (the identity of Atman and Brahman); sacrificial worship of specific theistic gods such as Brahma, the creator (not to be confused with Brahman); Shiva, the destroyer; Vishnu, the preserver; and many other lesser gods.

A good example of this synthesizing of apparently diverse elements is Hinduism's second most important scripture, the *Bhagavad Gita,* or "Song of God" (second century, B.C.E.). This is only a small part of a long epic poem, the *Mahabharata,* in which Krishna, a manifestation of the ancient god Vishnu, appears to persuade a dubious nobleman, Arjuna, to take up arms and fight the opposing

*Krishna is the earthly incarnation of Vishnu,
the preserver and supporter of the universe.*

army, which is actually made up of his own relatives and countrymen. Though never contradicting the Upanishadic position, the *Bhagavad Gita* presents belief in a personal savior God. Although Krishna presents many arguments for Arjuna to consider, his main case is that Arjuna should put his faith and trust in Krishna. This view, known as *bhakti theism,* is nonetheless presented as perfectly compatible with the old doctrine of the *Upanishads* that, since there is no real difference between slayer and slain, one should not worry too much, from the standpoint of eternity, about the necessity of killing or being killed.

The second major element of the *Bhagavad Gita* is an ethical position that brings about an important compromise between the Upanishadic position that all goal-directed action has bad karma implications and the ordinary human sense of responsibility to act in certain situations. If we try to avoid all purposeful, goal-directed activity, how could we ever get anything done, working at our jobs, raising a family, serving the community, and so on? Basically Krishna's position turns on a valuable distinction between a naive action attached to illusory goals and a knowing action fully aware that there is really nothing to be achieved and no one to achieve it but doing it anyway. Viewed in this latter way, one need not retreat from an active life but should enter into life as into a game or a dance where there is nothing to be achieved but the game or dance itself. It is difficult to overemphasize how opposed this is to the Western bias toward teleological, that is, goal-directed, purposeful action. Without this modification, the older Upanishad theory is suitable only for a priestly class devoted entirely to meditation *(upanishad* originally meant "to sit"). The attempt to synthesize the *Bhagavad Gita* with the *Upanishads* and the *Rig Veda* eventually culminated in Vedanta ("the end of the Vedas") in which the central doctrines of all three works are preserved in a form which has lasted virtually unchanged until the present day. This is the Hindu's theology and is largely the work of the great ninth-century scholar, Sánkara.

In the *Upanishads* Brahman is identified with the world and Atman with the self, and the two are said to be eternally one and the same. This belief raises several conceptual and philosophical problems. First of all, it is contrary to our everyday experiences since it appears as though there are many different, changing things in the world and many different, changing impressions going on inside a person's mind. Sánkara, the great Vedanta scholar (circa 800 C.E.), held that reality is one and there is no duality anywhere. But this suggests a kind of duality of reality and appearance. To discount the apparent multiplicity of things in the world as we experience it, one must contrast the real with the illusory, a position which ends up admitting two things—appearance and reality. It does no good to say that individual things do not exist; they are stubbornly there and must be accounted for somehow. Sánkara maintained that these things can be said neither to exist nor not to exist, a statement similar to Plato's famous phrase that things in the physical world "roll about between being and nonbeing." But like quicksand, this just gets us deeper and deeper into the philosophical debate.

We can call things "appearances" or "illusions" *(Maya)* if we like, but this raises the question as to how appearances are related to reality. From a religious standpoint, metaphysical issues can actually get in the way of religious concerns. The basic metaphysical solution to the relation of appearance and reality is to treat appearances as properties of an underlying substance. In order to answer conceptual puzzles arising out of what were originally religious questions, Hindu scholars were led into a kind of scholarly metaphysical philosophy not unlike the great Western tradition of Plato, Spinoza, and Hegel (though this is admittedly a Western way of putting it).

The ever-changing, multifarious world of sensations is, from the metaphysical standpoint, simply a modification of the basic underlying reality, Brahman, in the same way that clay figures are modifications of a basic clay substance. According to the Hindus, underlying all our hopes, desires, plans, daydreams, thoughts, impressions, and so on is an unseen substance, Atman. Thus, there are two basic entities in the world, Brahman and Atman, related to everything else as substance is to mode or quality. Moreover, these two things are ultimately somehow one and the same thing!

≣ Taoism

The Confucian tradition we examined earlier stresses the need for human culture to mold and perfect human nature in order to create a morally just and correct social order of morally motivated human beings. The Taoist tradition stresses the importance of the natural oneness of human beings with the whole of nature. Which is more important, human beings or nature, that is, the ways in which people are *different* from the rest of the natural world or the ways in which people are a *part* of nature? Which is more valuable, the artificial culture human beings create in art, religion, law, and literature, or the natural order? The Confucians stressed the first, the Taoists the second. When Chinese intellectuals considered moral and political development, they looked to Confucianism. When they wondered about the broader question of the place of human beings in the larger universe, they turned to Taoism. While Confucianism was generally the official doctrine of the state, Taoism was the choice of poets and scholars in the privacy of their homes during their personal reflections.

The Taoists remind us of Western Romantics who hold that human good or well-being does not come from engaging in those activities which *differentiate* human beings from the rest of the world (in art, law, and so on), but in rejecting human artificiality in favor of a return to one's original, natural self and a sense of oneself as *part* of and a rather *small* part of, the entire natural world. "Nature first," as our modern-day ecologists are fond of saying. The Taoist morality is not, like the Confucian morality, to cultivate our peculiarly human virtues of *ren, li,* and the like, but to be natural, unpretentious, modest, and yielding to the forces of nature rather than trying to overcome them through human technological manipulation. Because Taoism emphasizes our oneness with the rest of nature, Taoists, like the Buddhists, also emphasized the inadequacy of human concepts to describe a fundamentally nonhuman universe. We call an object large, but it is also small relative to other objects. Words like *difficult* and *easy, good* and *evil, high* and *low, being* and *nonbeing* are clearly relative terms, relative to one another; to the perspective of the speaker and to the context. None of these concepts is absolute; each is defined in terms of the other. Although they are opposites, each is necessary to the other, there is no good without evil; no hot without cold; no reality without illusion; no being without nonbeing, and so on.

In this sense Taoism holds the view that reality is one and indivisible, identical with the self; known not through words, concepts, and logic but by direct experience. Little is known of the origins of Taoism, but sometime before the Han dynasty (206 B.C.E.–220 C.E.) there appeared a collection of eighty-one religious

Lao Tzu (ca. 604–531 B.C.) Chinese philosopher and founder of Taoism. Line drawing.

verses known as the *Tao Te Ching* and attributed to Lao Tzu. Taoism has a down-to-earth flavor in keeping with the practical orientation of Chinese thinkers who have always been suspicious of otherworldly speculation.

Taoist simplicity is not simple-mindedness; it reflects a sophisticated conception of human freedom based on naturalness, which has had a marked effect both on Confucianism and later Chinese and Japanese schools of Buddhism. The Taoist view of freedom is in direct contrast with the Western conception and deserves special attention. In the West freedom is seen in opposition to causal determinism. According to determinism everything has a cause, and this is understood to mean that nothing is free. Thus, a free act is defined as one which is uncaused, at least by factors outside the agent's control. As long as I can determine all my acts, I am free. The problem is that the springs of action, the ultimate motivation, do not seem to be in my control, and this suggests that I am not free. I am free to choose a medical career and, having decided on that, I am free to choose what university to attend, and so on. But why do I want to become a physician? Because I want to help suffering humanity? But why do I want that? Did I choose that? Is that something I have control over; or is it something outside my control, something I was born with or had instilled in me by the time I was able to think about it? As we trace the causal chain of actions back in time, we inevitably reach a point where the desire or motivation is simply given, not chosen. Looked at in this way, freedom is merely an illusion; there is the appearance of freedom in the short run, but in the final analysis we are not free. It is this conception of freedom which creates anxiety over trying to control everything.

The Taoist approach is quite different. They say that the anxiety to control is precisely what is not free or spontaneous, but awkward and fumbling. You are most free when you are not tightly controlling every syllable you utter but letting it flow. Similarly in playing a sport. As soon as you become self-conscious and try to control each move, you become awkward and inept. The freest and most spontaneous exercise is when you have the confidence in your inner workings to just let go and do it. The springs of action are in you and a part of you, often the product of practice and training. But they are not subject to conscious control. Nor do they need to be. There is a place for conscious control when special problems arise within the activity, but the activity as a whole cannot be consciously controlled. For the Taoist, this does not mean that we are determined but that we are free. It does imply loosening the sharp distinction we cling to between me and the rest of the world. The springs of action go far back beyond my own existence, perhaps into the dim recesses of our evolutionary past. Perhaps the reason I want to help others and to be rich and respected is traceable to a survival instinct which I share with the entire animal kingdom. In that case my confidence in myself is a confidence in the bond I share with the rest of the world. After all, I did not create myself. When rational thought first appears it is to articulate feelings and instincts which precede it and over which it has no final control. The Taoist message, then, is to trust in your own nature and its origins in the nature of the universe. Just let it be. The Taoist theory of action, known as wu-wei (no-action), is similar in some respects to the theory just discussed in the *Bhagavad Gita*. Of course, people must act; we cannot avoid acting. But, according to the Taoists, we should not impose our human designs on nature but act naturally, spontaneously following and conforming to Nature, without trying to contradict or second-guess Nature.

The word *Tao* means "way." Like the ancient Greek Stoics before them, Taoists want to live life in accordance with the way things are. Nature is the great teacher. We must learn not to live our lives in opposition to nature but in cooperation with nature. At a time when we in the West are seeing the destructive effects of our lifestyles on our natural environment, we can perhaps open up to the wisdom of the Taoists, which counsels us to seek the path that will bring our lives into harmony with both nature and our own inner being.

Despite fundamental differences between Indian Buddhism and Chinese Taoism, Buddhism was successfully introduced into China by means of a Taoist interpretation. When Indian Buddhist monks attempted to introduce Buddhism in China, they found that Chinese intellectuals could not at first grasp the foreign ideas of *karma, moksa,* and *nirvana,* along with all the intricate Indian logic and metaphysical speculation which were so alien to Chinese traditions. As a result, these early Buddhists resorted to *ko yi,* that is, deliberately explaining Buddhism in terms of Taoist terminology with which Chinese intellectuals were already familiar. The result was a new form of Chinese Buddhism, a blend of Indian and Chinese traditions, which we know today as Zen Buddhism. (Actually *zen* is a Japanese word for the Chinese *Ch'an Na,* or simply *Ch'an,* which, in turn, is a Chinese word for the Indian term *dhyana,* meaning "meditation.")

The readings that follow are brief selections from the *Bhagavad Gita* and the *Tao Te Ching,* the most famous Taoist text. In these you can see the metaphysical issues that in many respects are so like those raised in Western philosophy, and in many other ways, so different.

The Path of Yoga

Sanjaya reported:
Krishna's words to Arjuna, whose mind was heavy with grief
    and whose eyes were filled with tears of pity, were:

Your sorrow, Arjuna, is unmanly and disgraceful.
It stands in the way of heavenly fulfilment.

Don't be a coward, Arjuna.
It doesn't become you at all.
Shake off your weakness and rise!

Arjuna replied:
How can I fight Bhishma and Drona,
fitter objects for my veneration?

Why, it would be preferable to live as a beggar
than kill these great nobles.
Their murder will stain with blood all my joys and feelings
even while I live, even in this world.

Who can say which is better, Krishna,
we defeating them or they defeating us?
Dhritarashtra's *sons* are our enemies.
Killing them would bring us life-long misery.

From *The Bhagavad Gita,* Translated by P. Lal. Calcutta: Writers Workshop, 1971. Used by permission.

Paralyzed by pity, full of doubts,
I ask for your grace.
I am your worshipper. Put me on the right path.
Show me what is good for me.

I know of nothing that can remove this sense-killing sorrow,
neither tyranny over the gods, nor kingship of the earth.

Sanjaya continued:
These were Arjuna's words to Krishna.
He added, *I will not fight,*
and lapsed into silence.

To Arjuna, sad in the middle of the battlefield,
Krishna, as if smiling said:

You mourn those, Arjuna,
who do not deserve mourning.
The learned mourn neither the living nor the dead.
(Your words only sound wise.)

Do not think that I did not exist,
that you do not exist,
that all these kings do not exist.
And it is not that we shall cease to exist in the future.

To the embodied Atman boyhood, maturity and old age
continue imperceptibly.
And just that happens with the acquisition of a new body.
This does not confuse the steady soul.

Heat, cold, pain, pleasure—
these spring from sensual contact, Arjuna.
They begin, and they end.
They exist for the time being.
You have to learn to put up with them.

The man whom these cannot distract,
the man who is steady in pain and pleasure,
is the man who achieves serenity.

The untrue never is;
the True never isn't.
The knowers of truth know this.

And the Self that pervades all things is imperishable.
Nothing corrupts this imperishable Self.
How utterly strange that bodies are said to be destroyed
when the immutable, illimitable and indestructible Self lives on!
Therefore, rise, Arjuna, and fight!

Who sees the Self as slayer;
and who sees it as slain, know nothing about the Self.
This, Arjuna, does not slay.
It is not slain.

This is without birth, without death,
It does not become existent after previous nonexistence;
nor does it cease existence after previous existence.
This is birthless, changeless, and eternal.
It does not die when the flesh dies.

And if a man thinks of it as imperishable, changeless, and birthless,
how can he possibly kill, or make another kill?

As a person throws away last year's clothes
and puts on a new dress,
the embodied Self throws away this lifetime's body
and enters another that is new.

Weapons do not harm this Self;
fire does not burn it,
water does not wet it,
wind does not dry it.

This cannot be cut, kindled, wetted, dried;
immobile, immovable, immutable, all-pervasive,
this is eternal.

This is unmanifest, unknowable; and unchangeable.
Now you have this wisdom, Arjuna,
now you should not grieve.

Even if it were constantly to be born,
and constantly to die, you should not grieve.

For death is sure of that which is born,
and of that which is dead, birth is certain.
Why do you grieve then, over the inevitable?

All beings are unmanifest in the beginning,
manifest in the middle, and again unmanifest at the end.
Is this a cause for grief?

Some imagine the Self as extraordinary;
others say it is a miracle,
others have heard it described as a mystery.
Still others have heard of it but remain unconvinced.

I repeat: This embodied Self, Arjuna, is imperishable,
You have no reason to grieve for any creature.

Think of your natural duty, and do not hesitate, for there is nothing
greater to a warrior than a just war.

Lucky are soldiers who strive in a just war;
for them it is an easy entry into heaven.

But if you persist in being a coward,
your dignity and your duty are lost;
and you expose yourself to shame.

The world will connect your name with infamy,
and they who once praised you shall think of you as a coward.

Your enemies will hurl insults at you.
Arjuna, what could be more demeaning?

Die, and you go to heaven.
Live, and the world is yours.
Arise, Arjuna, and fight!

Equate pain and pleasure, profit and loss,
victory and defeat.
And fight!
There is no blame this way.

The truths of the path of knowledge I have told you.
Listen now to the truths of action.
These two together can break the fetters of karma.

There is no waste of half-done work in this,
no inconsistent results;
an iota of this removes a world of fear.

In this there is only single-minded consistency;
while the efforts of confused people
are many-branching and full of contradiction.

There is no constancy in the man
who runs after pleasure and power,
whose reason is robbed by the fool's flattery,
and, abiding by the rules of the Vedas,
proclaims that there is nothing else.
The honeyed rituals of the Vedas, promising enjoyment and power,
are certain to lead him into fresh births.

The Vedas deal with three qualities.
Know them, detach yourself from them,
keep your poise,
detach yourself from selfishness,
and be firm in your Self.

The Vedas are a useless pond to a person aware of his Self;
a pond when water has flooded the land.

Your duty is to work, not to reap the fruits of work.
Do not go for the rewards of what you do,
but neither be fond of laziness.

Steady in Yoga, do whatever you must do;
give up attachment, be indifferent to failure and success.
The stability is Yoga.

Selfish work is inferior
to the work of a balanced, uncoveting mind; shelter
yourself in this mental stability, Arjuna.
Harassed are the runners after action's fruits.

With this mental poise,
you shall release yourself from evil and good deeds.
Devote yourself to this Yoga
it is the secret of success in work.

The steadfast in wisdom, the steadfast of mind,
giving up the fruits of action,
achieve the perfect state.

When your mind is no longer obscured by desire,
repose shall come to you concerning what is heard
and what is yet to be heard.

When your mind, so long whirled in conflicting thought,
achieves poise, and steadies itself in the Self;
you shall have realised Yoga.

Arjuna asked:
Who is the man of poise, Krishna?
Who is steady in devotion?
How does he speak, rest, walk?

Krishna answered:
He has shed all desire;
he is content in the Self by the Self.

He is steady. He endures sorrow.
He does not chase pleasure.
Affection, anger and fear do not touch him.

He is not selfish.
He does not rejoice in prosperity.
He is not saddened by want.

He can recall his senses from their objects
as the tortoise pulls in its head.

Objects scatter away from the good but lazy man,
but desire remains.
In the perfect state, however, desire also goes.

Yes, this is true, for the violent senses
rock the reason of the wisest man.

But the steadfast man thinks of me,
and commands his desires.
His mind is stable, because his desires are subdued.

Meditation on objects breeds attachment;
from attachment springs covetousness
and covetousness breeds anger.

Anger leads to confusion,
and confusion kills the power of memory;
with the destruction of the memory choice is rendered impossible
and when moral choice fails, man is doomed.

But a person who is established in firmness,
free from pleasure and repugnance,
traversing experience with his senses restrained—
such a person finds tranquillity.

When tranquillity comes, sorrow goes;
a person whose wisdom is tranquil is closest to Realization.

The wavering person possesses no knowledge,
and indeed no incentive to contemplate.
There is no tranquillity for a person who will not contemplate;
and there is no bliss without tranquillity.

The mind is the ape of the wayward senses;
they destroy discrimination,
as a storm destroys boats on a lake.

Only that man can be described as steady
whose feelings are detached from their objects.

The night of all beings
is the daylight of the restrained man;
and when dawn comes to all,
night has come for the perceiving sage.

The ocean, deep and silent, absorbs a thousand waters.
The saint absorbs a thousand desires,
ending in bliss, which is not for the passionate.

Undistracted, passionless, egoless,
he finds bliss.

Bliss is to be in Brahman, Arjuna,
to suffer no more delusion.
In bliss is eternal unity with Brahman,
though life itself is snuffed out.

The Yoga of Action

Arjuna asked:
If, as you say, Krishna, knowledge excels action,
why do you urge me to this terrible war?

You bewilder me with confusing speech;
tell me that one truth by which I may find you.

Krishna replied:
At the time of a person's birth, Arjuna,
two methods are offered:
for the contemplative the Yoga of knowledge,
for the active the Yoga of action.

No one reaches the state of rest through inaction;
and abandonment of work does not lead to perfection.
For look, not a moment gives rest, not a moment is without work;
the senses, products of Nature, compel all to work.

He is a fool and a scoundrel who abstaining from action,
nevertheless sits and dreams up sensual visions.

But he excels, who commands his senses by his mind,
and continues exertion in the Yoga of work.

Work is superior to inaction,
inaction will not keep even the body together.
Therefore, Arjuna, work, but work selflessly.

All deeds are traps, except ritual deeds.
Hence the need for selfless action.

Lao Tzu: The Tao Te Ching

1. The Tao that can be told of is not the eternal Tao;
   The name that can be named is not the eternal name.
   The Nameless is the origin of Heaven and Earth;
   The Named is the mother of all things.

   Therefore let there always be non-being so we may see their subtlety,
   And let there always be being so we may see their outcome.
   The two are the same,
   But after they are produced, they have different names.

From Wing-Tsit Chan, translator, *The Way of Lao Tzu* (Tao Te Ching), The Library of Liberal Art. Used by permission of Prentice Hall.

They both may be called deep and profound.
Deeper and more profound,
The door of all subtleties!

2. When the people of the world all know beauty as beauty,
     There arises the recognition of ugliness.
    When they all know the good as good,
     There arises the recognition of evil.
    Therefore:
       Being and non-being produce each other;
       Difficult and easy complete each other;
       Long and short contrast each other;
       High and low distinguish each other;
       Sound and voice harmonize with each other;
       Front and back follow each other.

    Therefore the sage manages affairs without action *(wu-wei)*
    And spreads doctrines without words.
    All things arise, and he does not turn away from them.
    He produces them, but does not take possession of them.
    He acts, but does not rely on his own ability.
    He accomplishes his task, but does not claim credit for it.
    It is precisely because he does not claim credit that his
    accomplishment remains with him.

4. Tao is empty (like a bowl),
     It may be used but its capacity is never exhausted.
    It is bottomless, perhaps the ancestor of all things.
    It blunts its sharpness,
    It unties its tangles.
    It softens its light.
    It becomes one with the dusty world.
    Deep and still, it appears to exist forever.
    I do not know whose son it is.
    It seems to have existed before the Lord.

5. Heaven and Earth are not humane *(ren)*.
     They regard all things as straw dogs.
    The sage is not humane.
     He regards all people as straw dogs.
    How Heaven and Earth are like a bellows!
    While vacuous, it is never exhausted.
    When active it produces even more.
    Much talk will of course come to a dead end.
    It is better to keep to the center.

14. We look at it and do not see it;
          Its name is The Invisible.
     We listen to it and do not hear it;
          Its name is The Inaudible.
     We touch it and do not find it;
          Its name is The Subtle (formless).

     These three cannot be further inquired into,
     And hence merge into one.
     Going up high it is not bright; and coming down low, it is not dark.
     Infinite and boundless, it cannot be given any name;
     It reverts to nothingness.
     This is called shape without shape,
     Form without objects.
     It is The Vague and Elusive.
     Meet it and you will not see its head.
     Follow it and you will not see its back.
     Hold on to the Tao of old in order to master the things of the present.
     From this one may know the primeval beginning (of the universe).
     This is called the bond of Tao.

18. When the great Tao declined,
          The doctrines of humanity and righteousness arose.
     When knowledge and wisdom appeared,
          There emerged great hypocrisy.
     When the six family relationships are not in harmony,
          There will be the advocacy of filial piety and deep love to children.
     When a country is in disorder;
          There will be praise of loyal ministers.

19. Abandon sageliness and discard wisdom;
          Then the people will benefit a hundredfold.
     Abandon humanity and discard righteousness;
          Then the people will return to filial piety and deep love.
     Abandon skill and discard profit;
          Then there will be no thieves or robbers.
     However, these three things are ornament and not adequate.
     Therefore let people hold on to these:
          Manifest plainness,
          Embrace simplicity,
          Reduce selfishness,
          Have few desires.

56. He who knows does not speak.
          He who speaks does not know.

Close the mouth.
Shut the doors.
Blunt the sharpness.
Untie the tangles.
Soften the light.
Become one with the dusty world.
This is called profound identification.
Therefore it is impossible either to be intimate and close to him or to
    be distant and indifferent to him.
It is impossible either to benefit him or to harm him,
It is impossible either to honor him or to disgrace him.
For this reason he is honored by the world.

63. Act without action.
Do without ado.
Taste without tasting.
Whether it is big or small, many or few, repay hatred with virtue.
Prepare for the difficult while it is still easy.
Deal with the big while it is still small.
Difficult undertakings have always started with what is easy,
And great undertakings have always started with what is small.
Therefore the sage never strives for the great,
And thereby the great is achieved.
He who makes rash promises surely lacks faith.
He who takes things too easily will surely encounter much difficulty.
For this reason even the sage regards things as difficult,
And therefore he encounters no difficulty.

Questions for Discussion

1. As you read through the selections from *The Bhagavad Gita* and the *Tao Te-Ching,* do you find any teachings similar to those of Western religious and philosophical traditions? Explain.

2. *The Bhagavad Gita* proposes a metaphysical view that reduces the significance of individual choice and, by extension, makes the individual much less important than the collective. Explain how this occurs.

3. Contrast the Taoist view of freedom with Western views of freedom.

4. How do the doctrines of karma and reincarnation influence Hindu attitudes toward conduct?

5. Now that you have had an opportunity to examine some examples of different Indian and Chinese thought systems, do you think there is any

common thread through them all which could be called "Eastern philosophy"? If so, what is it? If not, why do you think so many people have *thought* there was?

Suggestions for Further Reading

Chan, Wing-tsit. *A Source Book in Chinese Philosophy.* Princeton: Princeton University Press, 1963. The best translations of the major works of Chinese philosophy.

Fung, Yu-lan. *A History of Chinese Philosophy,* trans. Derk Bodde. Two vols. Princeton: Princeton University Press, 1983. The first and still most influential attempt to explain Chinese thought to a Western audience as "philosophy."

Fung, Yu-lan. *A Short History of Chinese Philosophy.* New York: Macmillan, 1966. A shorter, more accessible version of Fung's two-volume *History.* Written in English by Fung.

Hanson, Chad. *A Daoist Theory of Chinese Thought.* Oxford: Oxford University Press, 1992. A major new interpretation of Chinese philosophy from a Taoist (Daoist) rather than Confucian perspective.

Radhakrishnan, Sarvepalli. *Indian Philosophy.* Two vols. Oxford: Oxford University Press, 1994. Influential attempt by India's best-known philosopher to introduce Indian thought to a Western audience.

Radhakrishnan, Sarvepalli and Charles A. Moore, eds. *A Sourcebook in Indian Philosophy.* Princeton: Princeton University Press, 1989. The best translation of original sources of Indian philosophy.

Glossary of Terms

Absurdist: The view that the world is intrinsically unreasonable and meaningless, often expressed in works of fiction, especially prominent in the 1950s. Absurdists frequently define absurdity as the separation or alienation of thought from reality.

Act utilitarianism: A theory offered by utilitarians who insist that when contemplating each act we should choose to do that which will produce the greatest good or happiness.

Agnosticism: The view that it is impossible to attain certain kinds of knowledge. In religion it is used to refer to the view that we cannot know either that God does or does not exist.

Analects (Lun Yu): The collected sayings of Confucius.

Analogical language: A way of speaking about an object by comparing it to something else. To say that an animal is intelligent is to say that the animal's behavior is like the behavior (in this case intelligence) that belongs properly only to humans. The analogy is as follows: Intelligence:man::__:animal. Analogical language has been defended by some philosophers as the only way we can speak of God.

Analytic: A statement is analytic if its truth or falsity can be determined by analysis of the terms in the statement alone. Statements that are analytically true are said to be true by definition, or logically true.

A posteriori: Refers to knowledge that is derived from the senses.

A priori: Refers to knowledge that is derived solely from reason independently of the senses. The truth of *a priori* knowledge is claimed to be both necessary and universal.

Argument: A series of statements that are related in such a way that some of the statements, called premises, are said to provide proof for another statement, referred to as the conclusion.

Arjuna: The Pandava prince to whom Lord Krishna reveals the various paths to spiritual liberation in the *Bhagavad Gita.*

Atheism: The assertion that God does not exist.

Atman: Hindu term for the ultimate Self; which is held to be identical with Brahman, the ultimate reality.

Atomism: Metaphysical view originated by the ancient Greek philosophers Democritus and Leucippus which held that all reality is ultimately composed of small bits of stuff called atoms. Atoms are not further divisible; the term *atom* means uncuttable. The theory was popularized by the writings of the Greek philosopher Epicurus.

Autonomy: The term literally means "self-legislated." For Kant, autonomy was a key notion for morality, since an act can have moral significance only if it is willed freely and without compulsion by a rational being.

Axiomatic: Something basic or fundamental; in a system such as geometry, axioms are the statements from which other parts of the system of thought are derived.

Bhagavad Gita: Literally, "Song of the Lord," a long devotional poem, constituting part of the *Mahabharata,* in which Krishna teaches the secret of nonattached action.

Brahman: Literally, "that which makes great," the Vedic and Hindu term for the ultimate reality.

Buddha: An enlightened being; also used to refer to the historical Buddha, Siddhartha Gautama.

Buddhism: A way of thought and practice that emphasizes moral practice, meditation, and enlightenment. Founded by Siddhartha Guatama, the Buddha, in India, sixth century B.C.E.

Capitalism: An economic system in which the means of production are privately owned and government does not interfere with the "free market forces" of "supply and demand."

Categorical imperative: For Kant, the unconditional moral law that can be expressed as the rule that we should act on that principle that we could make a universal law. If we cannot universalize our principle without contradiction, the action resulting from the principle is immoral.

Ch'an: Chinese form of Mahayana Buddhism emphasizing meditative insight; known in Japan and the West as Zen.

Cogito ergo sum: "I think, therefore I am." A principle taken by René Descartes to be self-evident and irrefutable.

Coherence theory: The theory that truth consists in the coherence or interdependence of beliefs within a system of thought, rather than the correspondence of those beliefs with an external reality.

Confucianism: Chinese tradition based on the teachings of Confucius and his followers, particularly Mencius and Xun Zi.

Copernican revolution: The views of the Polish astronomer Nicolaus Copernicus, who showed that the sun, not the earth, is the stationary body around which the planets move (thereby reversing the prevailing views concerning the relationship of the sun and earth). Kant referred to his views as a (second) Copernican revolution because they reversed the prevailing views in epistemology by emphasizing the *active* role of the mind in generating knowledge, in contrast to the mind's passive role in the empirical philosophies of Locke and Hume.

Correspondence theory: The theory that truth consists in the correspondence or matching of a belief or statement to the real world. The statement "The cat is on the mat" is true, according to this theory of truth, if and only if the cat is indeed on the mat.

Cosmological: Derived from the Greek word meaning order and used to refer to the natural world as an ordered system. Applied to a type of argument for the existence of God, it refers to that kind of reasoning which proceeds from the apparent order and regularity of the world to God as the best explanation for this order.

Deduction: An argument whose conclusion is claimed to follow necessarily from the premises of the argument.

Deontological: Derived from the Greek word for "ought" and referring to any ethical system which makes the morality of an action depend on one's acting out of a sense of duty. Kant's ethical system is deontological.

Dependent origination: The Buddhist teaching that existence is of the nature of process and totally interconnected.

Detachment: In esthetics, detachment is the defining characteristic of esthetic experience. The proper way to view works of art or natural beauty, according to this view, is to disengage from our usual utilitarian, practical orientation to the world and begin looking at things simply for the sake of looking at them.

Dharma: The way or law of truth, virtue, and righteousness.

Dharmas: In Buddhism, the ultimate constituents of existence.

Dialectic: The process of critically examining a theory to see if it contains unacceptable consequences, in which case it is refined and corrected, subjected to the same test, further refined and amended, and so on.

Dilemma: The problem that occurs when a theory or belief leads to one of two unacceptable consequences.

Disinterestedness: One of several closely related proposed criteria for defining esthetic experience. According to this characterization, an esthetic experience differs from other types of experiences in that it is not motivated by a desire for personal gain.

Distance: One of several closely related attempts to define the differentiating characteristic of esthetic experience. According to this view, esthetic experience differs from other kinds of experience in terms of the psychological space or distance we establish between ourselves and the object we are viewing.

Distributive justice: The most fair way to divide the total amount of social goods among all the citizens.

Dogmatism: A term used by Immanuel Kant to refer to philosophical views, and especially metaphysical theories, offering a priori principles that are not rationally grounded.

Dualism: An explanation offered in terms of two equal but opposed realities or principles. Good and evil, mind and matter, are dualisms.

Egalitarian: Political doctrine that no one has a right to a greater share of social goods than another, that individuals do not deserve the results of superior innate talents and abilities.

Egoism: The ethical theory that holds that self-interest is the rule of conduct. Psychological egoism is the claim that people in fact only act out of self-interest. Ethical egoism is the view that people *ought* to act out of self-interest, not that they necessarily do so act.

Empiricism: The view that all human knowledge is derived from the senses.

Emptiness (sunyata): The Mahayana teaching that separate and permanent existence is devoid of reality.

Enlightenment: In Mahayana Buddhism, the direct seeing of the truth that liberates.

Epistemology: The philosophical discipline that inquires into the nature, origins, and limits of human knowledge; theory of knowledge.

Esse est percipi: "To be is to be perceived." A Latin phrase used by George Berkeley to express his view that reality is mind-dependent.

Esthetic experience: According to many philosophers of art since the eighteenth century, esthetic experience is a fundamental type of human experience, and the main task of a philosophy of art, according to these estheticians, is to correctly define the nature of the experience of art works and objects of natural beauty.

Esthetics: Philosophy of art; the philosophical inquiry into the nature of art and beauty. Sometimes spelled *aesthetics*.

Ethical absolutism: The view that there are absolutes in ethics, that is, moral standards that are independent of the personal preferences of individuals. *See* Objectivism.

Ethical relativism: The view that there are no objective moral standards, and that the principles for conduct are relative to individuals or societies.

Ethics: The philosophical investigation of the principles governing human actions in terms of their goodness, badness, rightness, and wrongness.

Ethnocentrism: The willingness to judge the actions and principles of other societies by the standards of one's own society.

Existentialism: A philosophical movement that takes the central question of philosophy to be that of the meaning of human existence. Although it has roots in the thought of such nineteenth-century philosophers as Søren Kierkegaard and Friedrich Nietzsche, existentialism emerged as a distinctive philosophical movement in Europe after World War II and is associated with the work of such thinkers as Jean-Paul Sartre and Gabriel Marcel in France and Martin Heidegger in Germany.

Expressionism: The theory of art which holds that art is primarily the expression of human emotions and feeling. Expressionism thus defines art in terms of its relationship to the human *experience* of art, both in creating and in enjoying it.

Extrinsic criteria: In esthetics, judging an art work by standards external to and therefore presumably irrelevant to art itself; such as moral considerations, educational interest, or economic attractiveness. In general, extrinsic criteria are criteria external to that which is being judged by them.

Filial piety (xiao):   The love that exists naturally within a family; one of the grounds of respect and virtue in Confucianism.

Form: *See* Idea.

Formalism: In esthetics, the theory that only intrinsic factors within the art work are relevant for viewing, interpreting, or criticizing the work. These factors usually include the relationship, pattern, or form existing among the parts of the art work, such as line, color, shape, and so forth.

Hedonism: Derived from the Greek word for pleasure, hedonism is the ethical philosophy that holds the view that pleasure is the goal of life. Most philosophical hedonists have held, however, that intellectual pleasures are superior to sensual pleasures.

Hermeneutics: A theory of interpretation. Originally the term was used to refer to rules for interpreting written texts, especially sacred ones. In more recent years the term has been expanded to refer to the principles of understanding other human activities as well, including art and the artifacts of a culture.

Hypothetical imperative: Kant's term for a command that is conditional; a command of the if–then form would be a hypothetical imperative.

Idea: Derived from the Greek word for "form," the term *idea* was used by Plato not to refer to something mental but to those eternal realities that exist apart from our knowing them.

Idealism: The metaphysical view that explains reality as comprising minds and ideas; according to idealists, all reality is mind-dependent. Often postulated as an absolute mind, as in Hegel's idealism; or God, as in Berkeley's idealism. *See Esse est percipi.*

Imitation: In esthetics, the view that art is essentially the attempt to provide either an idealized copy or replica of objects in the external world.

Induction: Both a method of learning about the world by examining empirical reality and a kind of argument demonstrating such knowledge, in which the premises strengthen but do not completely demonstrate the truth of the conclusion. *See* Deduction.

Innate ideas: An idea, according to Plato and others, with which a person is born, such as the idea of God, and various mathematical, logical, and moral ideas.

Intrinsic criteria: In esthetics, standards for appreciating, interpreting, and criticizing a work of art which arise solely within the art work itself; such as the interrelationships among the parts of the art work. In general, criteria that are derived from that which is to be judged by them.

Jen: *see* Ren.

Karma: Action, including the results of action that inevitably accrue to the agent, producing bondage.

Krishna: The God who teaches Arjuna the path to liberation in the *Bhagavad Gita*.

Li: Confucian virtue of propriety.

Liberal: Political doctrine that individuals should be free from governmental restraint, especially in matters which do not harm others: freedom of speech, conscience, association, religion. Liberalism differs from libertarianism primarily in the libertarian emphasis on the right of an individual to accumulate an unequal share of wealth through native talent and ability, which the liberal opposes as a harm to others.

Libertarian: Political doctrine that each individual should be maximally free from governmental restraint, especially as regards the freedom of the individual to accumulate and dispose of an unequal share of social goods through superior intelligence, or other talents and abilities.

Logical positivism: The view that philosophy has no method independent of that of science and that philosophy's only task is logical analysis. According to the principle of verifiability, which was defended by logical positivists as a way of distinguishing meaningful statements from nonsense, a statement is meaningful if and only if it is analytic or can be verified empirically.

Materialism: The view that all reality is matter. Anything that is real is to be explained in terms of matter and the motion of matter.

Maya: The appearances of things, concealing the deeper reality.

Metaethics: A philosophical investigation of the terms and principles used in an ethical system, as opposed to an attempt to deal with an actual ethical problem. An example of metaethical analysis is the attempt to analyze how the term *right* functions in discourse or in an ethical theory.

Metaphysics: The philosophical inquiry into the nature of ultimate reality. In contemporary usage, the term includes the analysis of fundamental philosophical principles.

Middle Way: Name given to Buddhism because it lies in the middle between indulgence and asceticism, between being and nonbeing, and between determinism and indeterminism.

Modus ponens: The traditional name, from the Latin meaning "the affirming mode," for the basic argument form:

$$P \rightarrow Q$$
$$\underline{P}$$
$$\therefore Q$$

Modus tollens: The traditional name, from the Latin meaning "the denying mode," for the basic argument form:

$$P \rightarrow Q$$
$$\underline{-Q}$$
$$\therefore -P$$

Moksa: Liberation from all constraints, including the cycle of birth and death.

Monism: A metaphysical theory that explains reality in terms of a single substance or principle. Both materialism and idealism are monistic views.

Mysticism: The view that the ultimate reality can be directly experienced even though it cannot be known objectively.

Natural theology: That which can be known about God purely by the power of human reason unaided by revelation. Natural theology claims to be able to provide proofs of God's existence either completely *a priori,* and therefore independent of the senses, or *a posteriori,* that is, based on certain facts about nature.

Necessary conditions: Necessary conditions for something are those factors without which that thing cannot exist, as breathing is a necessary condition for human life.

Nirvana: (In Pali, *nibbana.*) Elimination of all forms and conditions of suffering.

Nonattachment: Nonattachment to the fruits of action as the key to fulfilling one's duties without accumulating karmic bondage according to the *Bhagavad Gita.*

Normative: That function of philosophy concerned with establishing standards for distinguishing the correct from the incorrect, whether in ways of reasoning, believing, esthetic judgments, or acting.

Objectivism: In ethics, the view that ethical assertions can be true or false and that there are objective principles of ethics independent of personal preferences.

Ontological: Derived from the Greek word for *being,* the term relates to the question of the being of anything. The ontological argument is an argument for God's existence based solely on an analysis of the concept of the being of God. Ontology is the metaphysical inquiry into the nature of being in general.

Pantheism: A philosophical view which identifies God with the visible universe; derived from two Greek words, *theos* ("God") and *pan* ("all").

Phenomenology: A twentieth-century movement that insisted upon immediate experience, undistorted by previous theories and assumptions as the only proper point of departure for philosophy. Phenomenologists believed that anything of which we can be conscious is a legitimate field for philosophical inquiry.

Pluralism: The view that an acceptable theory can be based on more than one ultimate principle, as opposed to monistic theories, which insist on only one major principle. *See* Monism.

Premise: A reason offered in an argument in support of a conclusion. *See* Argument.

Rationalism: The view that appeals to reason, not the senses, as the source of knowledge. In its most extreme form, rationalism insists that *all* knowledge is derived from reason.

Ren: Main Confucian virtue, the principle of humanity, what makes a person human, usually understood as the ability to think of other people as one thinks of oneself, that is, with the respect and consideration due a fellow human being.

Representation: In esthetics, the reference that something in an art work has to an object existing outside the art work, which arises not by imitating or copying that object, but by standing for it as a symbol stands for what it symbolizes.

Rig Veda: Oldest of the Vedas, the sacred texts that form the foundation of Hinduism, compiled between the twelfth and tenth centuries B.C.E.

Right: In social/political philosophy, used as a noun, the basis of a legitimate claim which one person has or can make on another, whether that claim is based on innate, universal human characteristics ("unalienable rights"), morality, or social legislation.

Samsara: In Indian thoughs the continuous wheel of birth and death of ordinary, unenlightened human life.

Sovereignty: The supreme and independent government power and authority as possessed and claimed by a state or community, usually a nation-state.

Tabula rasa: Latin for "blank tablet"; a phrase used by John Locke to refer to the human mind before it has received information from the senses. Locke thought that the mind is like a blank slate until the senses impress upon it information about the external world.

Tao: The way or path of enlightenment, used in both Taoism and Confucianism.

Taoism: Chinese tradition based on following the natural way (Tao) as taught by Lao Tzu and Chuang Tzu.

Teleological: Relating to purposes or goals. The term is derived from the Greek word *telos,* which means "end" or "purpose."

Tien: Usually translated "heaven"; in Confucianism, the ultimate source and moral paradigm of all things.

Upanishads: Concluding portion of the Vedas containing sacred knowledge of reality.

Utilitarianism: The ethical theory associated with the work of Jeremy Bentham, James Mill, and John Stuart Mill in the nineteenth century. Utilitarians hold that actions are moral if they aim at the general good, or the greatest good for the greatest number of people.

Utility principle: The principle of utilitarianism that says that we ought to do what will produce the greatest good for the greatest number of people. Sometimes it is referred to as "the greatest happiness principle."

Validity: A feature of arguments in which the relation between premises and conclusion is such that if the premises are true, the conclusion could not be false.

Vedanta: Hindu philosophical tradition rooted in the Upanishads; concerned with understanding the relation between Brahman and the world.

Verification principle: A principle suggested by A. J. Ayer by means of which it is possible to distinguish meaningful statements from nonsense. According to the verification principle, a statement is meaningful if and only if it is analytic or can in principle be verified empirically.

Vidya: In Eastern thought, the direct, unmediated insight into the true nature of ultimate reality as the key to liberation according to Hinduism and Buddhism.

Yi: Confucian virtue of moral righteousness, the moral capacity to recognize what is right and to do it *because* it is right.

Zen: A form of Mahayana Buddhism that flourished in Japan, emphasizing direct meditative insight.

 Index

B

E

M

L

Q–R